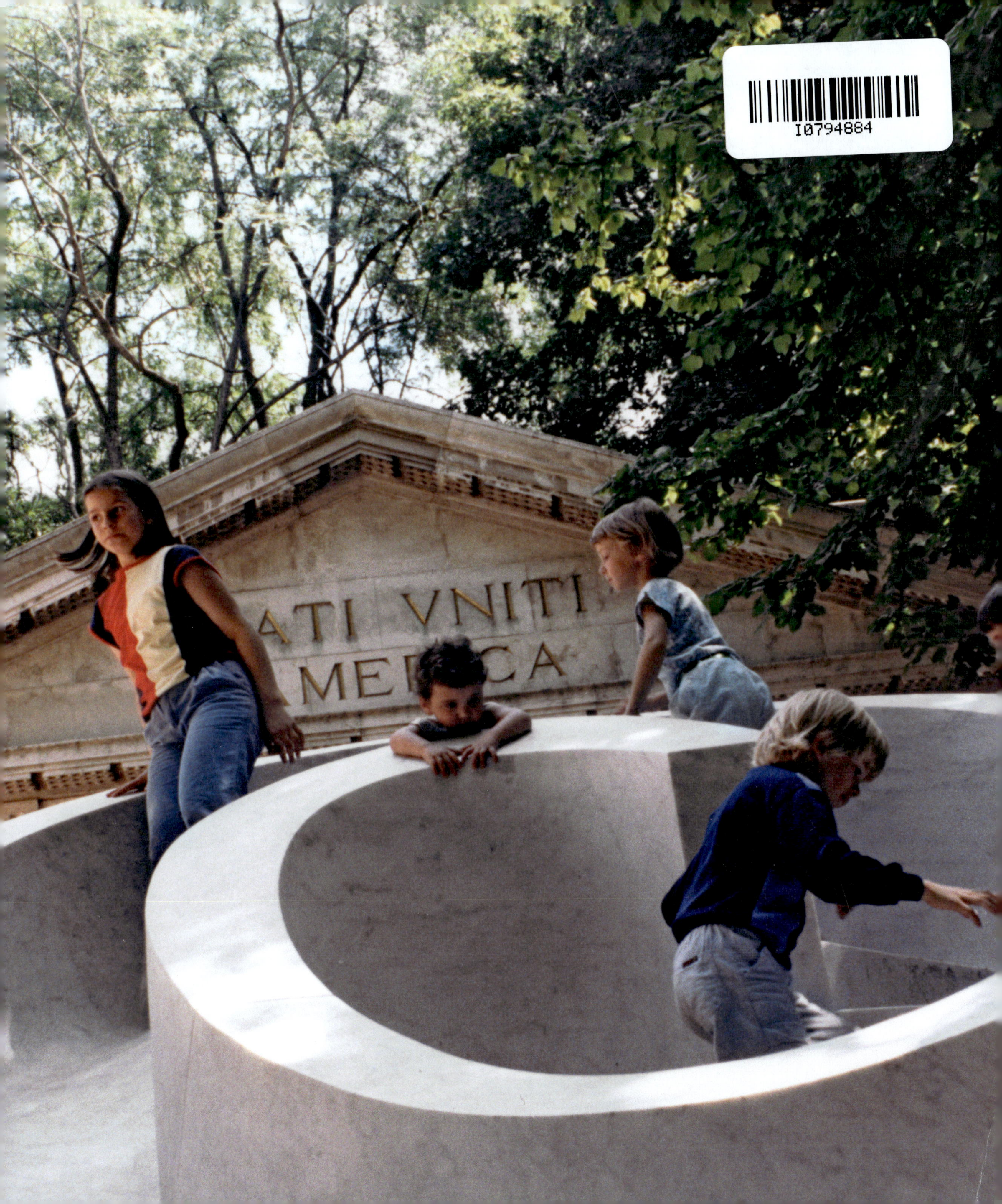
ATI VNITI

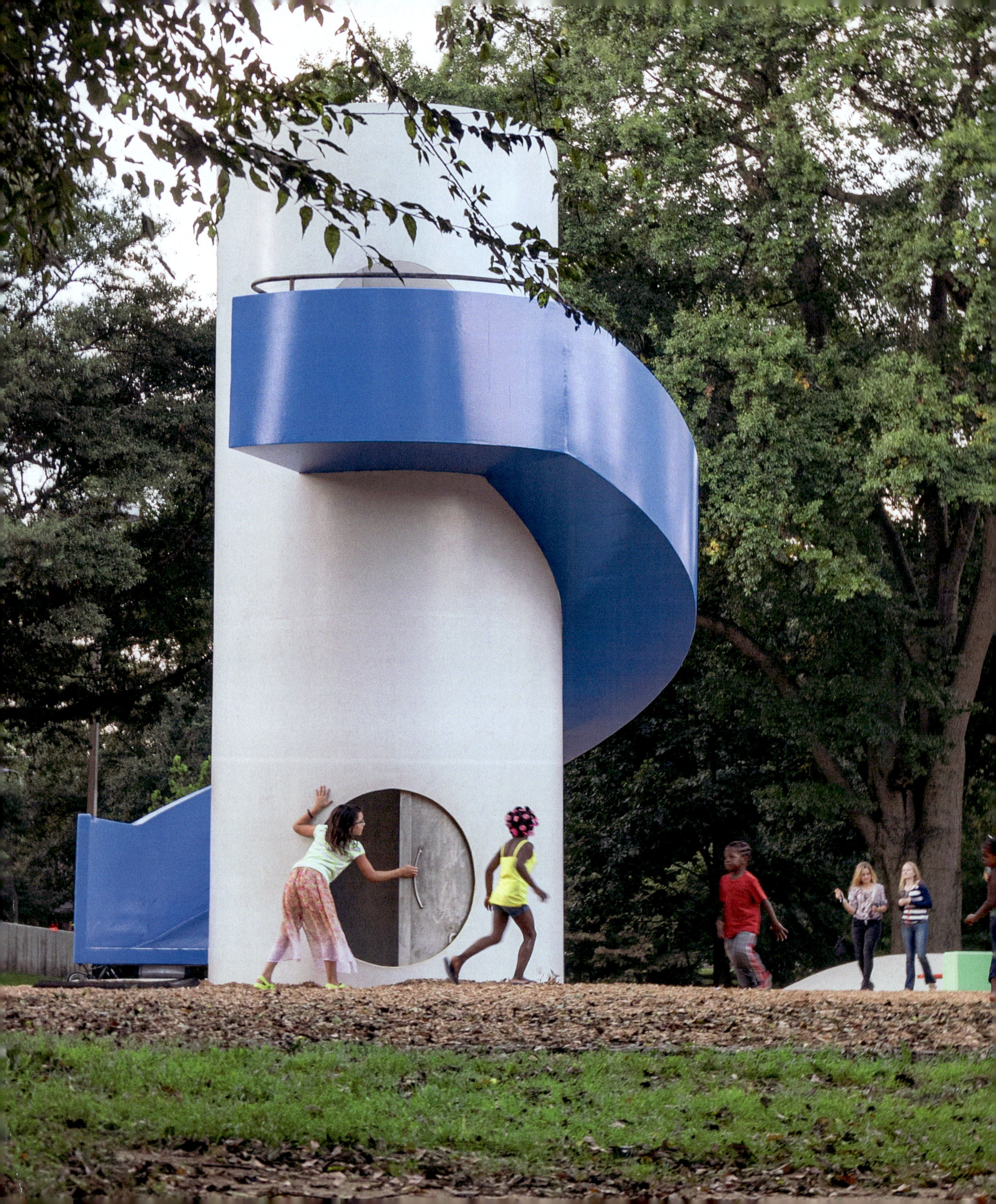

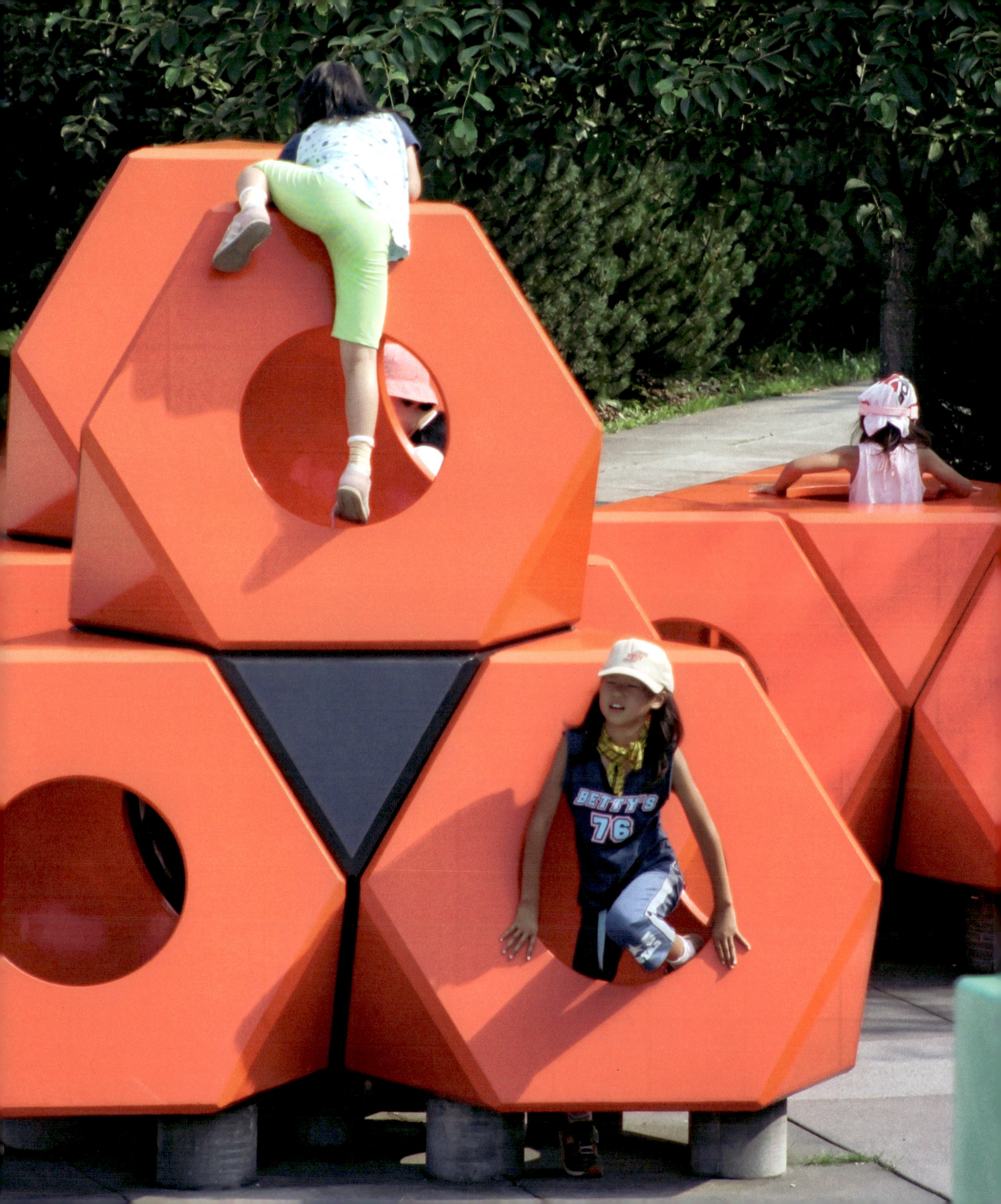
BETTY'S
76

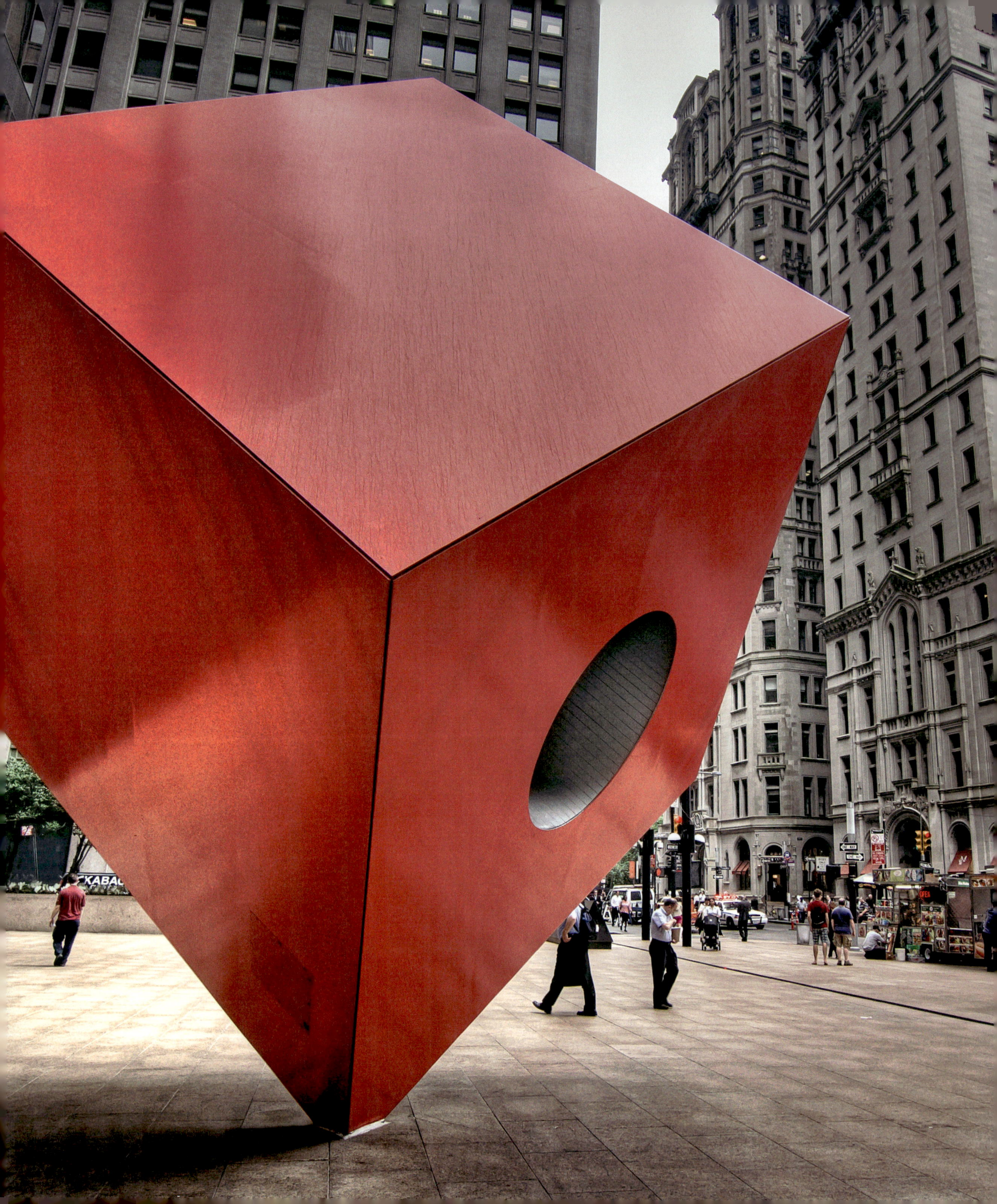

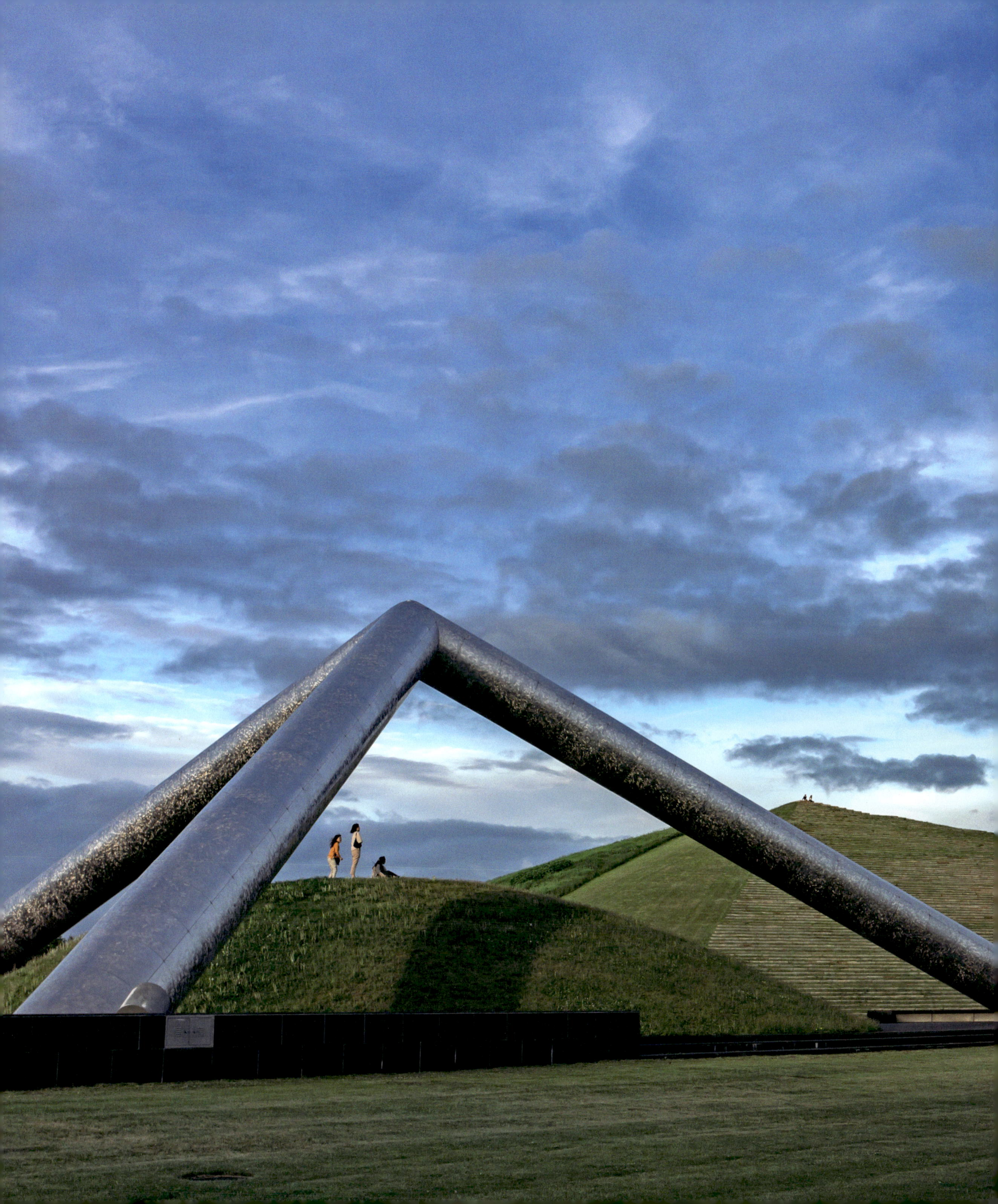

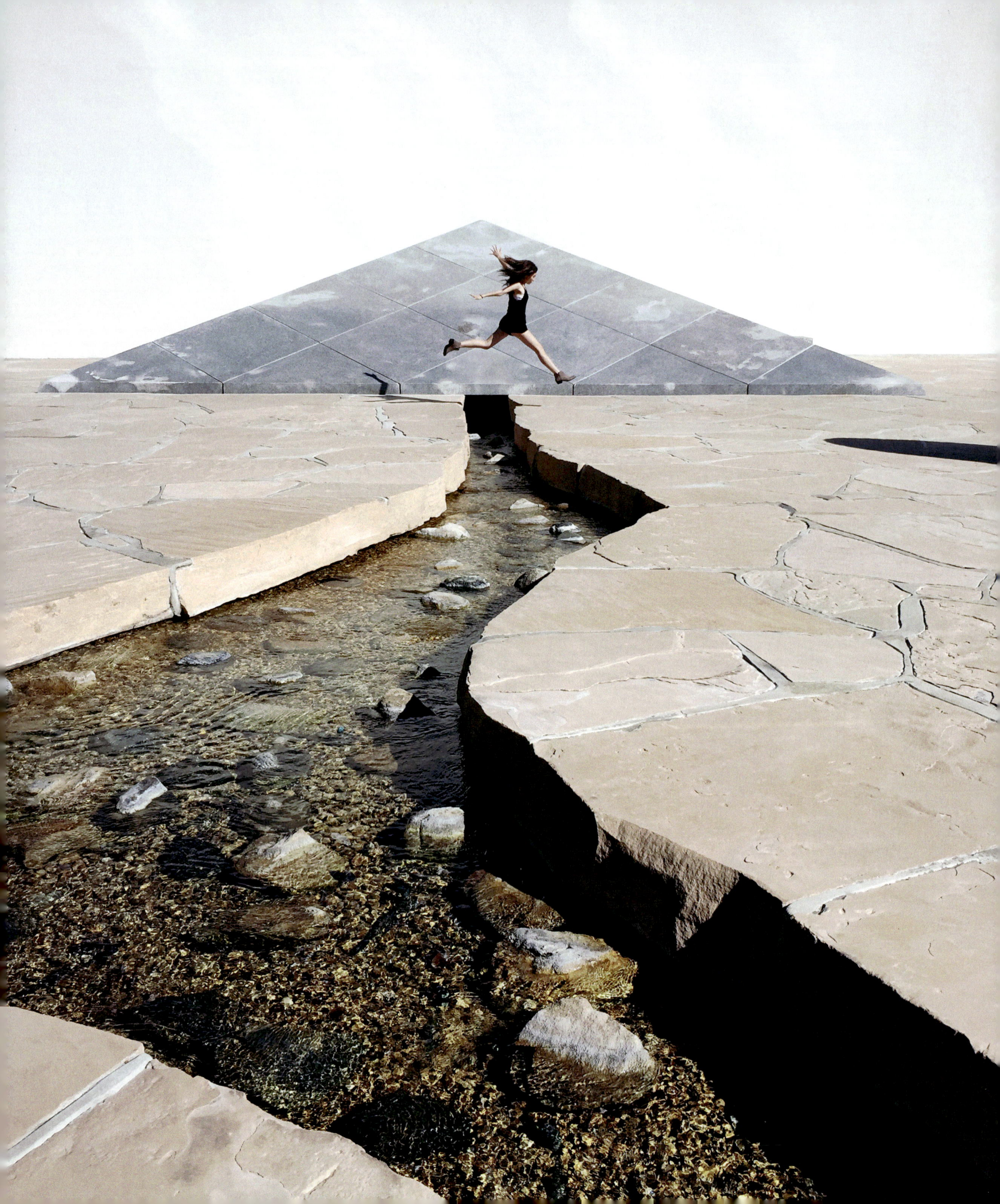

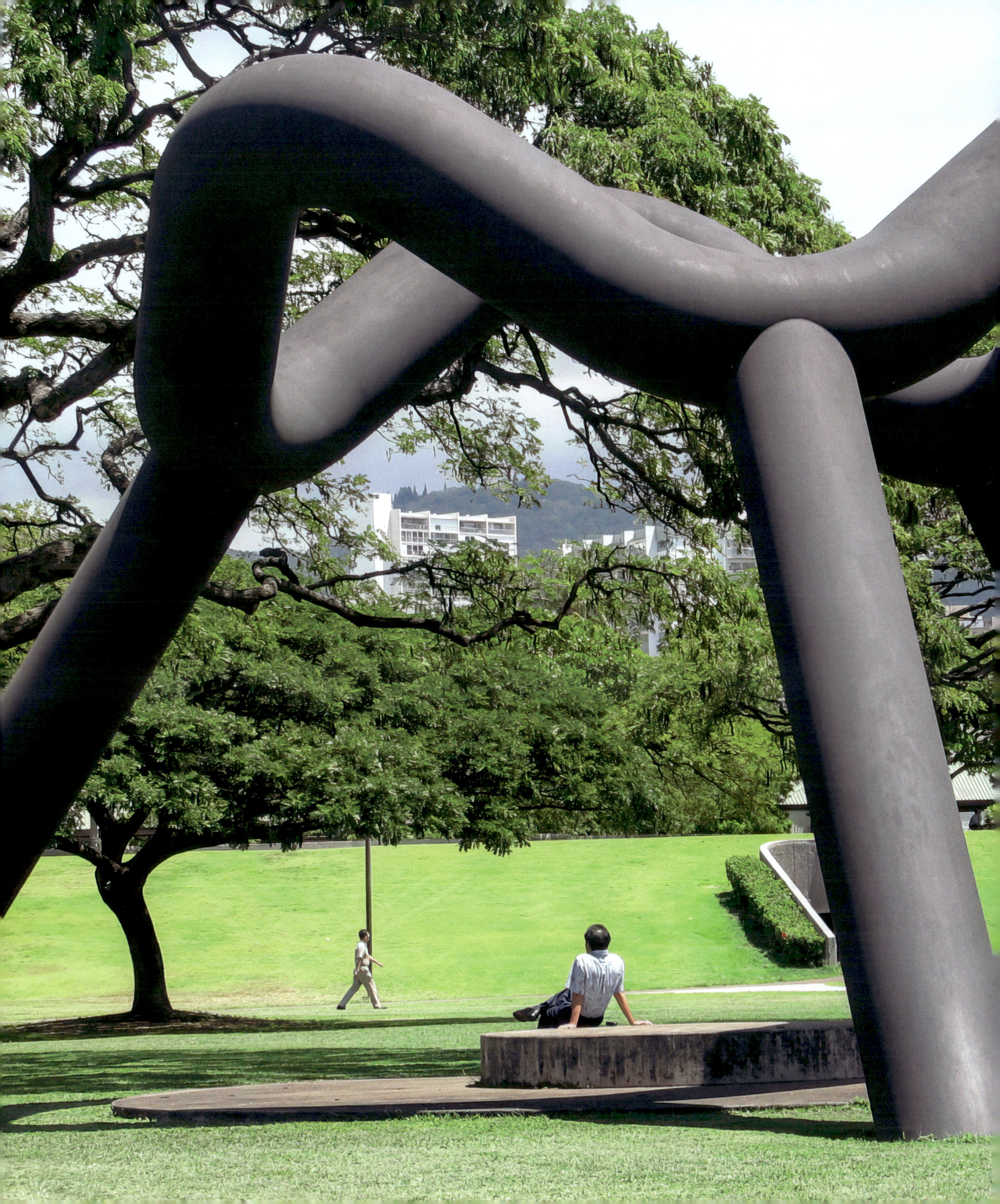

ISAMU

NOGUCHI

PRESTEL
Munich · London · New York

FOREWORD

The visionary work of Isamu Noguchi (1904–1988) is at last emerging from the shadows. Although his work has been presented in exhibitions across the world for almost 100 years, it has not received the full critical appreciation it deserves. The varied approach and inclusive ideas of this innovative artist resulted in an output of powerful sculptural expressions in a multitude of fields: between the 1920s and the 1980s, Noguchi created autonomous objects, political memorials, light sculptures, stage sets, playgrounds, gardens and more. His interdisciplinary and global approach alongside the variety of materials and forms he employed posed a challenge to the dominant art world in the twentieth century. A true artistic polymath, he was famous and overlooked at the same time, highly praised and often misunderstood. More recently, however, art lovers, scholars and artists alike are rediscovering his magnificent oeuvre and re-evaluating its critical impact and relevance. Whereas Noguchi's *Akari* light sculptures and his iconic *Coffee Table* have been celebrated since the 1950s, his body of work as a whole, with its conversion and transformation of cultural traditions and its exploration of the relationship between the planet and the individual, is particularly pertinent today.

Noguchi was born in 1904 in Los Angeles, the son of a Japanese poet, Yonejirō Noguchi, and an American writer, Léonie Gilmour. Not given a name until he was two years old, he was confronted early on with questions of identity, belonging and discrimination, and these would accompany him through the next eight decades of his life. Having spent part of his childhood in Japan – where he encountered traditional woodworking techniques – at the age of thirteen Noguchi travelled alone, under the name Sam Gilmour, to the United States to attend a school in Indiana. While a pre-medical student in the early 1920s, Noguchi underwent training with the Italian sculptor Onorio Ruotolo in New York's Lower East Side, and he later assisted the Romanian sculptor Constantin Brâncuși in Paris. Through his connections with a number of artists in New York in the 1930s, Noguchi developed a social and political consciousness that strongly informed many of his works. His experiences of living in an internmentcamp for Japanese Americans for six months in 1942 following the attack on Pearl Harbor influenced the fragile and fragmented 'interlocking sculptures' that followed. Echoes of the red-brown Arizona desert landscape of the Poston Internment Camp would continue to appear in his work for the rest of his career.

Noguchi's dedication to the qualities and possibilities of materials as well as his experiences of travelling, living and working in different parts of the world, from the US and Japan to Europe, Mexico, India and China, are reflected in his humanist and civic approach to sculpture making. This major survey celebrates Noguchi as a global citizen who pushed the boundaries of sculpture by embracing social, environmental and spiritual consciousness.

In 1986, towards the end of his life, Noguchi was invited to represent the US at the Venice Biennale, a project that involved both pride and disappointment: his far-sighted interdisciplinary approach and his confidence in the *Akari* as light sculptures were poorly understood. Twelve years after his death, in 2001, the *Akari* were the starting point for a survey exhibition of his work organised by the Vitra Design Museum in Weil am Rhein, Germany, which was presented at nine venues across seven countries.

The world has changed dramatically in the years since, as has the wider perspective on Noguchi's work. The Barbican, London, the Museum Ludwig, Cologne, and the Zentrum Paul Klee, Bern, in collaboration with the LaM – Lille Métropole Musée d'art moderne, d'art contemporain et d'art brut, are excited and proud to present the first touring exhibition of Noguchi's work in Europe in twenty years, and the first to present a detailed overview. The incredible range of Noguchi's work and its cultural, social and political foundations have only just begun to be discovered by a broad public. It is a pleasure to be able to offer an extensive, in-depth experience of the artist's oeuvre, which, situated as it is always between countries, cultures, disciplines and techniques, remains fresh and relevant today.

The exhibition and this book are the result of a wonderful collaboration between our three institutions and their respective teams, particularly the dedicated curators, Florence Ostende, Rita Kersting and Fabienne Eggelhöfer. Their perspectives on Noguchi not only provide the backbone of the exhibition but are presented in their essay contributions to this catalogue. Another of the highlights of this publication, beautifully designed by Tino Graß, is the roundtable discussion with artist Danh Vo and curators Katy Siegel and Karen L. Ishizuka, chaired by curator Devika Singh.

Isamu Noguchi would have not been possible without the substantial support of The Isamu Noguchi Foundation and Garden Museum, New York, and especially its senior curator, Dakin Hart, whose essay here offers a glimpse of his extensive knowledge and distinctive insights on Noguchi. The Noguchi Foundation, with its rich holdings, carefully prepared and graciously loaned more than 140 works for the exhibition. In addition, the Foundation generously shared resources and expertise. Curator Matthew Kirsch provided the support for the Chronology developed by Catherine Howe, and along with assistant curator Kate Wiener offered crucial assistance on both the catalogue and the exhibition: the online Isamu Noguchi Archive formed the core of our research and allowed the exploration of correspondence, early exhibition brochures and countless images and manuscripts when travelling was not possible due to the Covid-19 pandemic. We express our deep gratitude to the entire Noguchi Foundation team for this fruitful partnership, in particular to its director Brett Littman, deputy director Jennifer Lorch, registrar and collections manager Larry Giacoletti and archivist Janine Biunno.

The pandemic meant that loans of works from several international museums and collections could not go ahead. We are therefore especially grateful to the museums and collections that, against all odds, supplied important works and enabled this retrospective to be realised. The Whitney Museum of American Art, New York, has been the biggest institutional supporter of Noguchi through the years, organising retrospectives of his work in 1968 and 2004, among other offerings, and has extended this affiliation here by generously lending his *Humpty Dumpty* (1946) as well as *The Queen* (1931). The Museum of Modern Art, New York, which included the artist in several exhibitions from early in his career, especially those organised in Europe in the 1950s by its International Council, kindly lent *Mitosis*. Another important museum that cooperated with Noguchi during his lifetime is the Walker Art Center in Minneapolis, which has generously contributed *Cronos* (1947). We are extremely grateful to The Fralin Museum of Art, University of Virginia, and Kröller-Müller Museum, Otterlo, for their generous loans. We extend many thanks to the directors, curators and registrars who made these important loans and their preparation possible under difficult circumstances. We also express our gratitude to Alexandra Snyder May, granddaughter of R. Buckminster Fuller. A lifelong friend and artistic partner of Noguchi, Fuller's 1929 experimental portrait by the artist is a valuable contribution to the exhibition, as are the ceramic works *Marriage (Senbei Buton) (Worn Out Futon)* (1952) from the collection of Lucy Lamphere and *Cage Vase Kago (Basket)* (1952) from a private collection in New York.

Barbican, Museum Ludwig and Zentrum Paul Klee would particularly like to thank the Terra Foundation for American Art for its generous support of all four iterations of this exhibition. We are grateful for their commitment to fostering cross-cultural dialogues on American art and could not have realised this ambitious project without their support.

Noguchi represented his country on many occasions but, like many other American citizens of Japanese descent, was also discriminated against by the US government during the Second World War. Noguchi was Japanese American, but he was also a truly global artist who explored different cultural traditions both alone and with partners, creatives and professionals all over the world. We hope visitors and readers will come away inspired by Noguchi's imaginative and risk-taking approach to sculpture as a living environment.

Jane Alison
Head of Visual Arts
Barbican

Yilmaz Dziewior
Director
Museum Ludwig

Nina Zimmer
Director
Kunstmuseum Bern –
Zentrum Paul Klee

Isamu Noguchi at work on *Study of Abraham Lincoln* in Newark, New Jersey, 1922

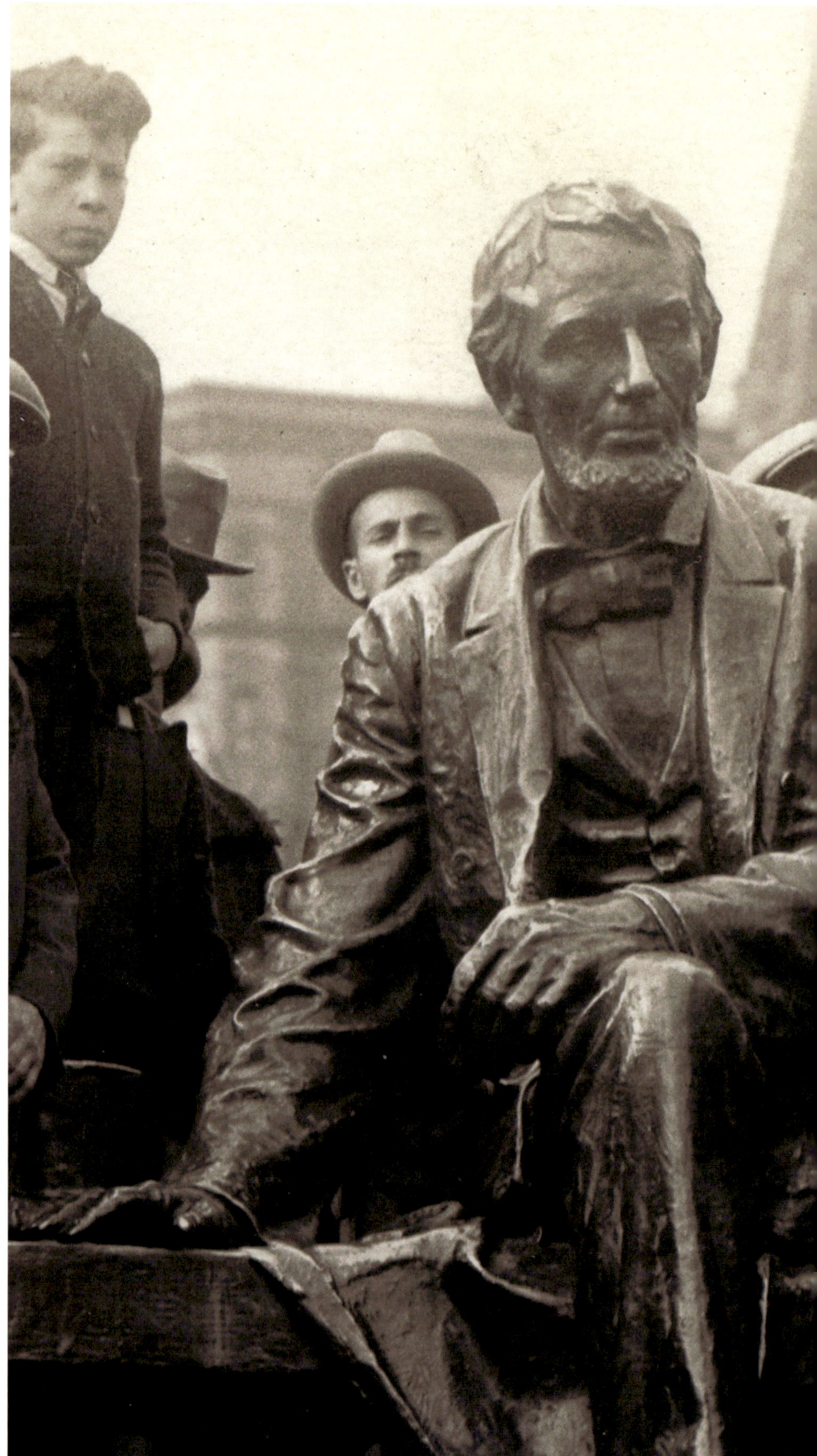

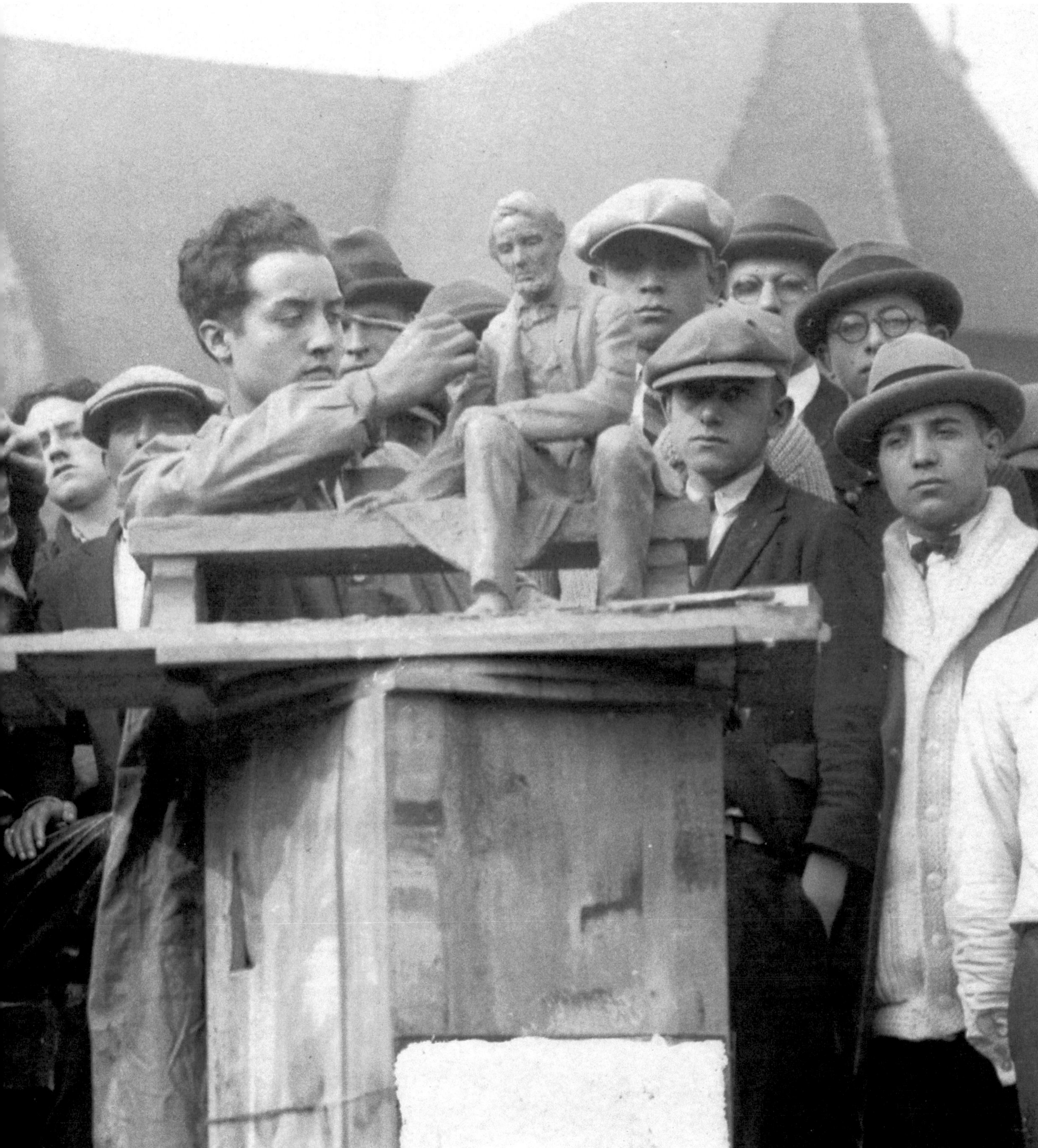

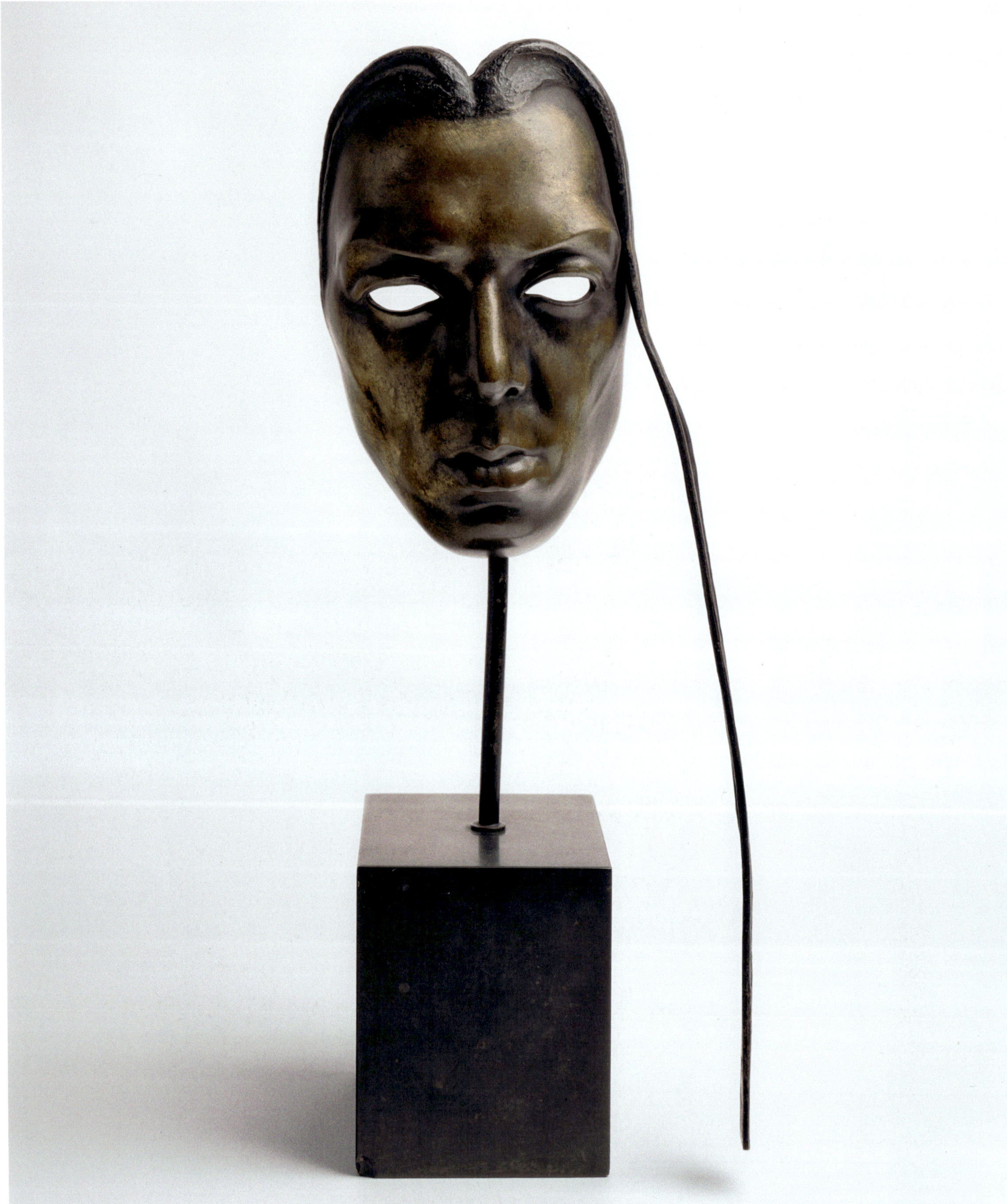

Michio Itō, 1926
Bronze
46.4 × 18.1 × 12.1 cm

Michio Itō in *Pizzicati*, 1929

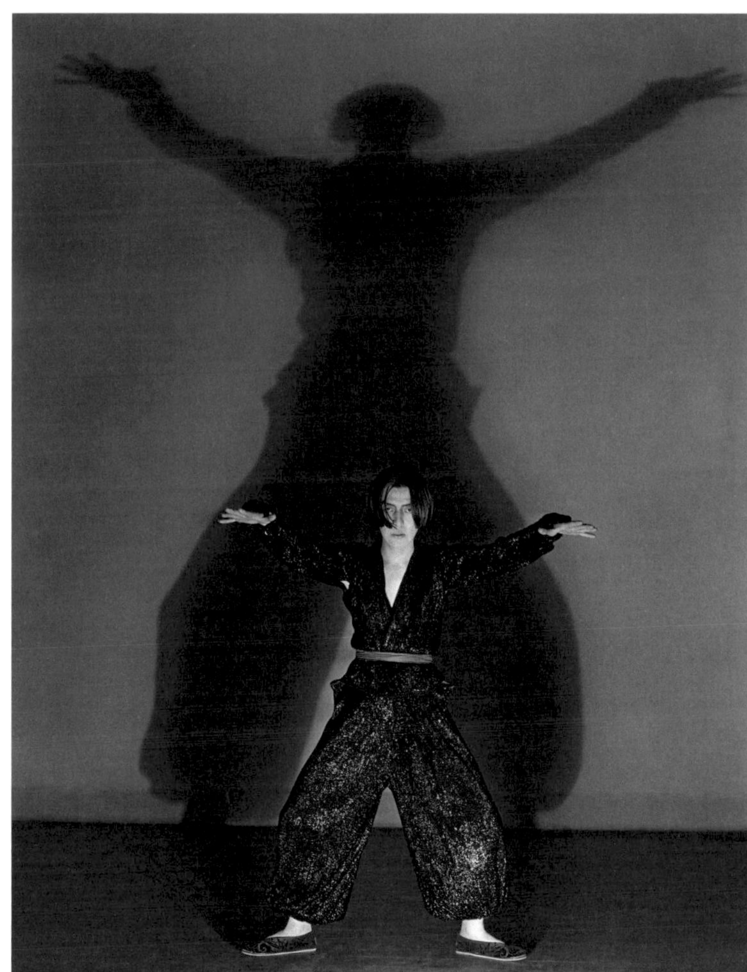

Abstraction in Almost Discontinuous Tension (Tensegrity), 1928
Brass and wire
59.1 × 119.4 × 44.5 cm

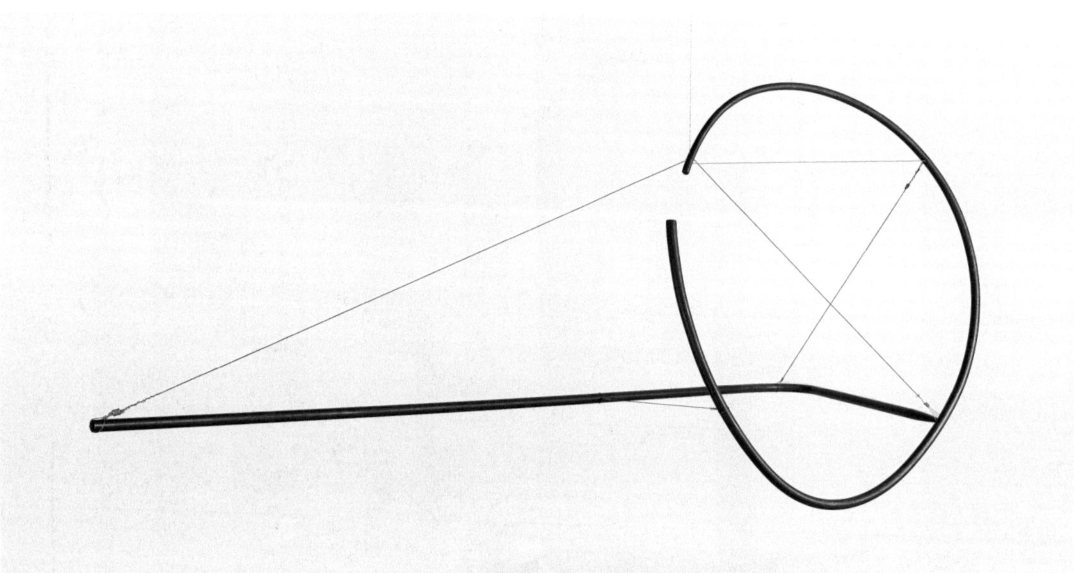

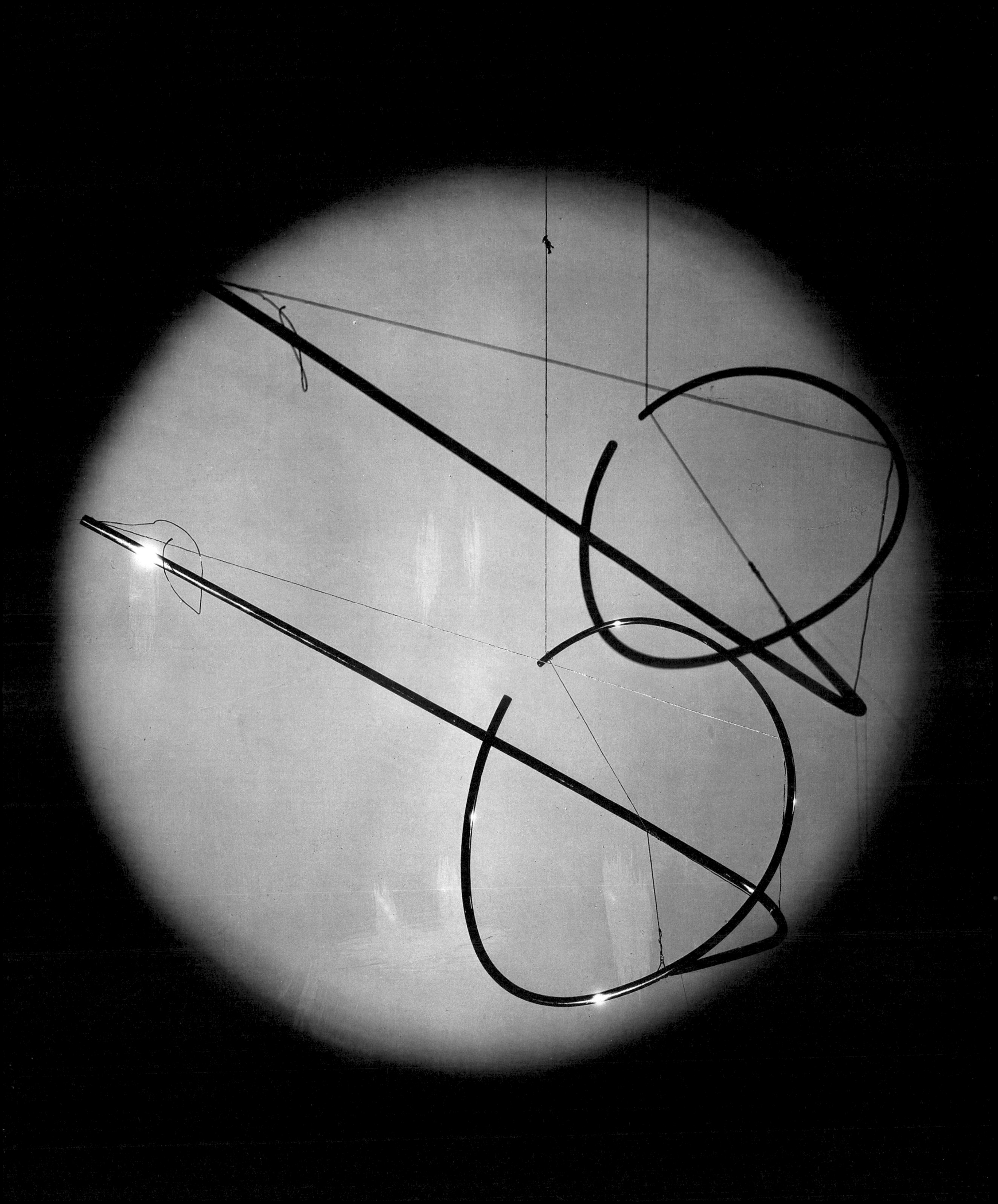

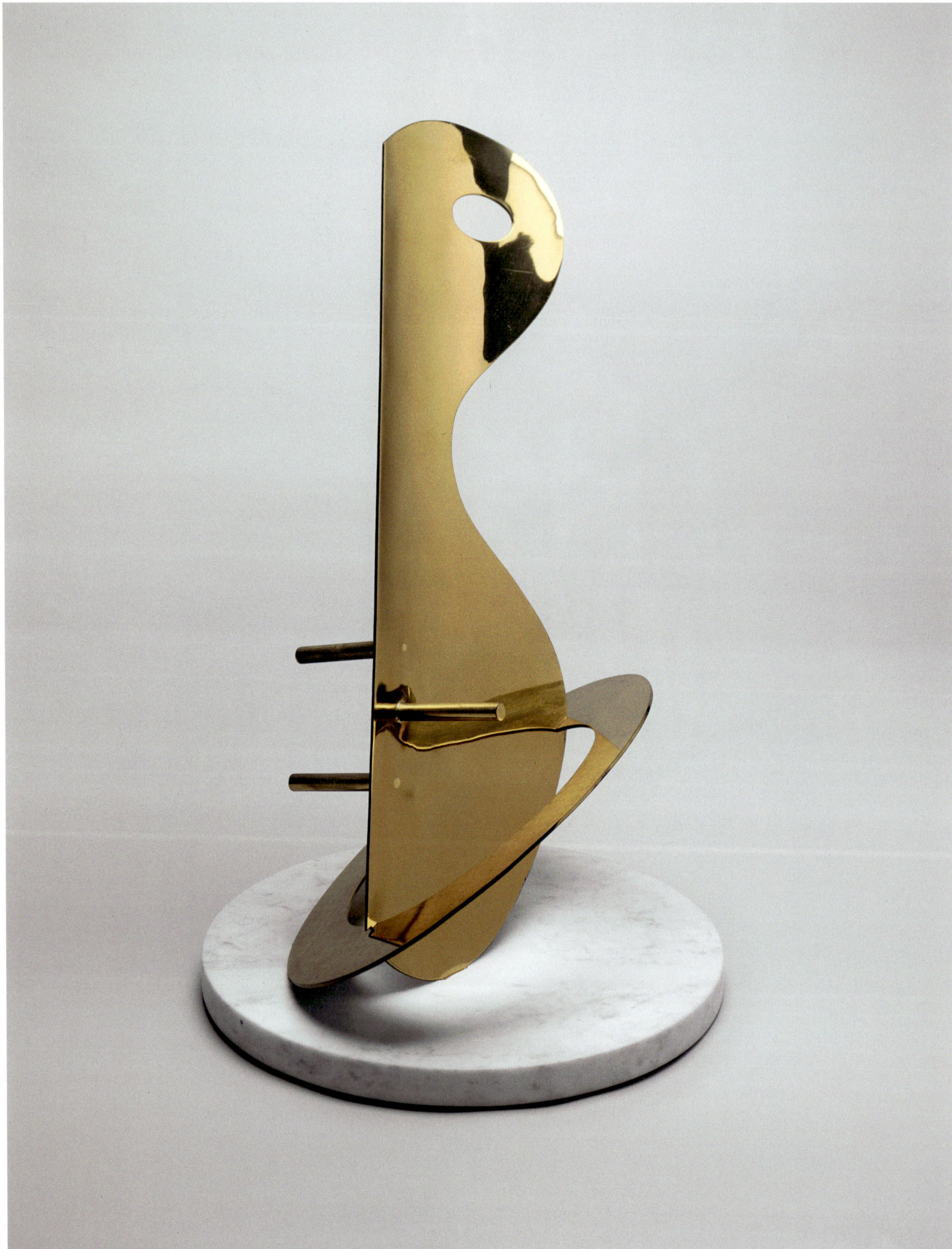

Leda, 1928
Aluminium bronze and brass
59.4 × 30.2 × 32.1 cm

With the work I was doing in sheet metals (ship-brass), I was interested in getting a certain plasticity of form, like something alive – and I wanted it to imply a certain imminent motion. Joints, if possible, were never fixed (no welding) but grooved, held by gravity or tension.

1967

Red Seed, 1928
Wood and aluminium
36.8 × 34.3 × 27.3 cm

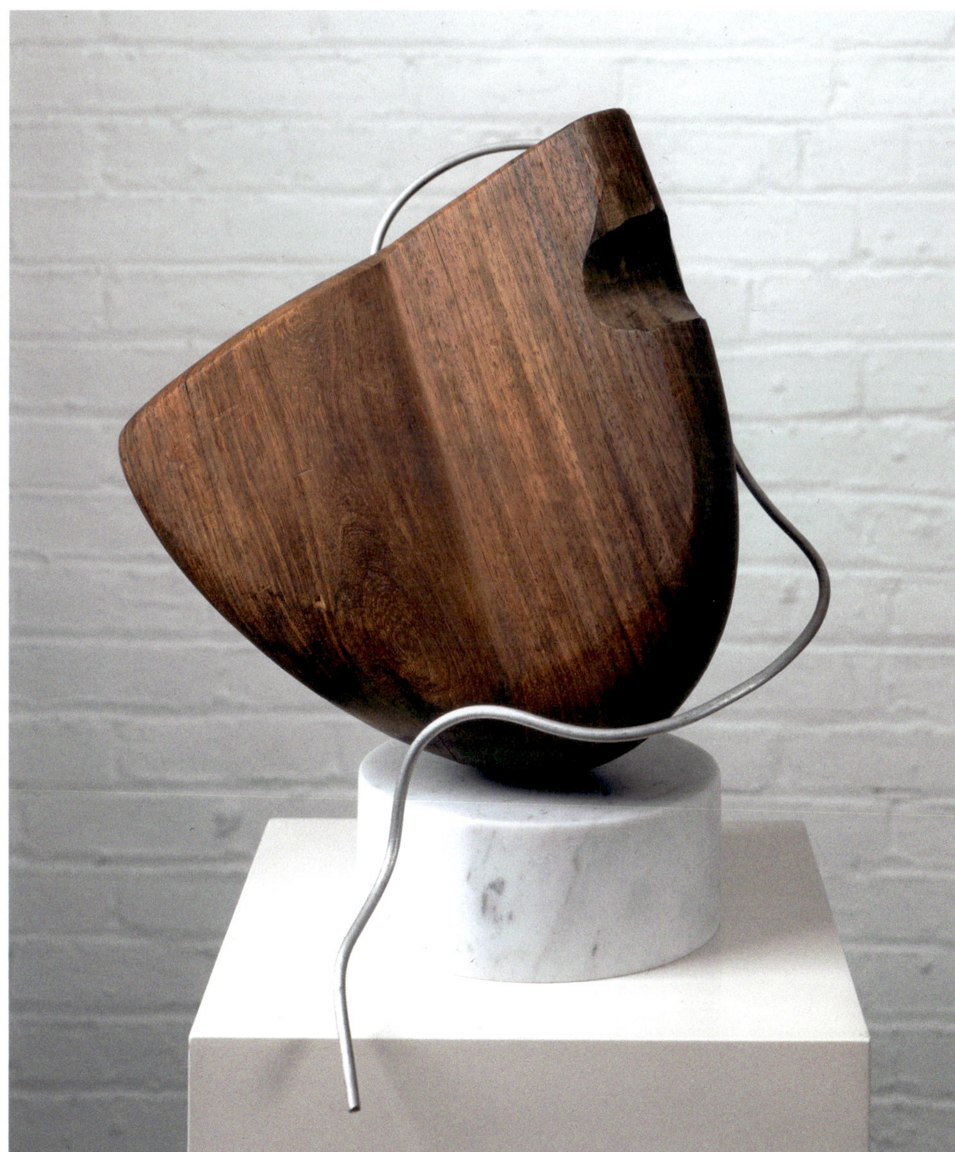

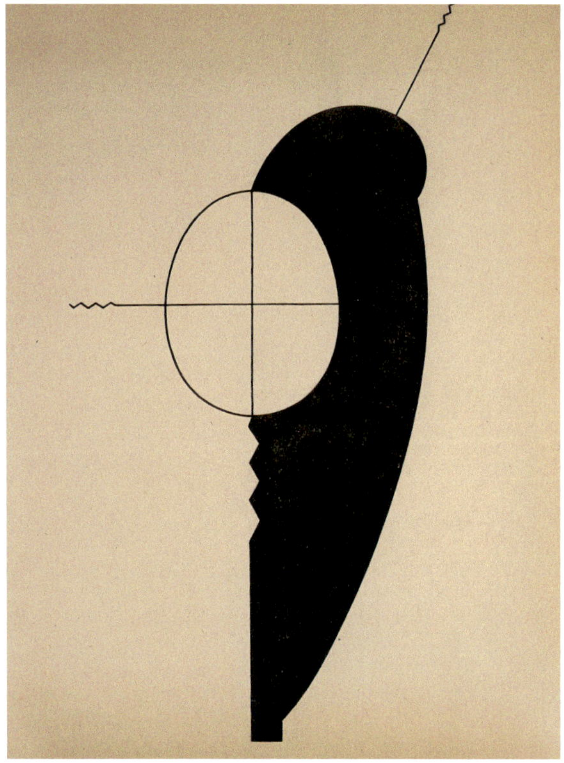
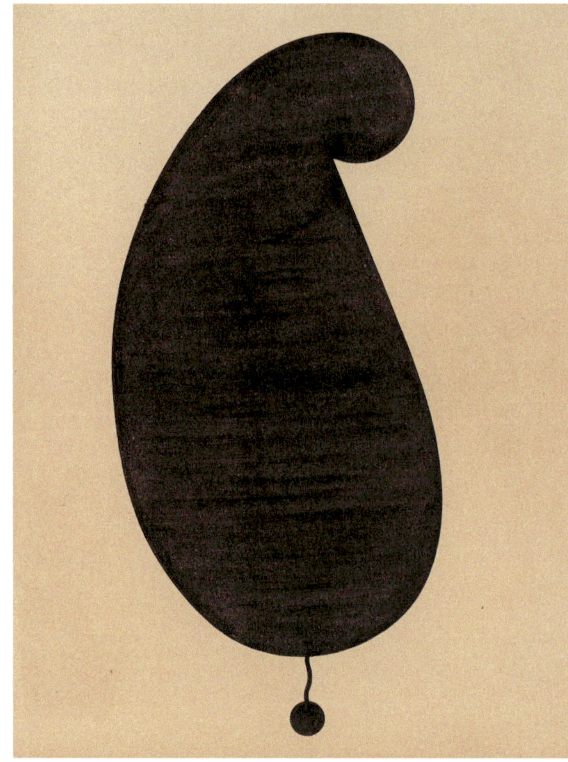
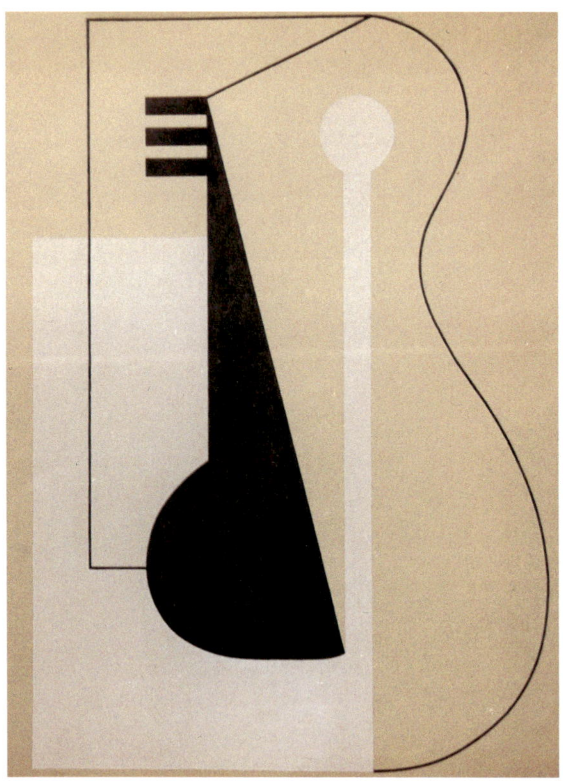
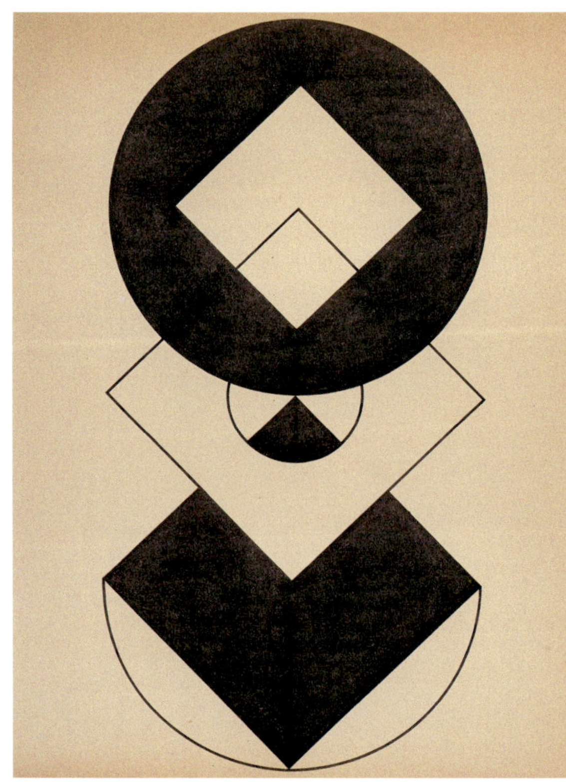

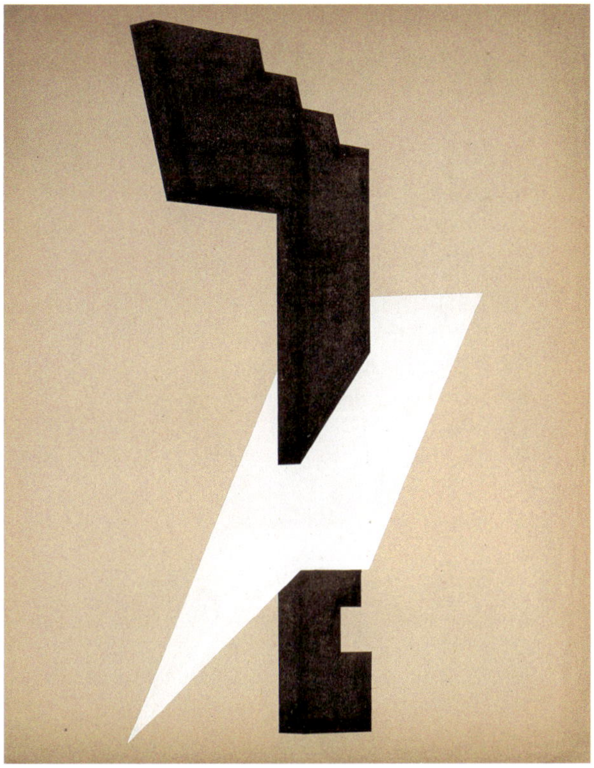

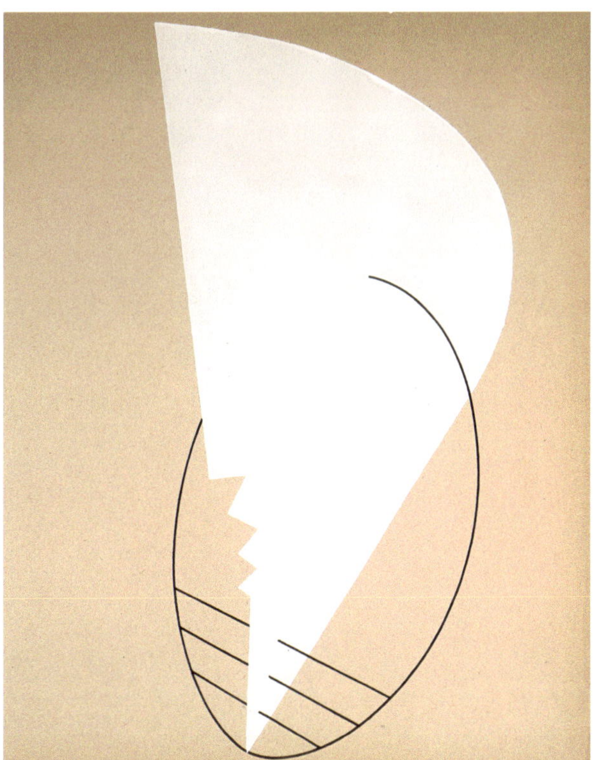

Six *Paris Abstractions*, 1928
Gouache on paper
Each: 65.4 × 50.2 cm

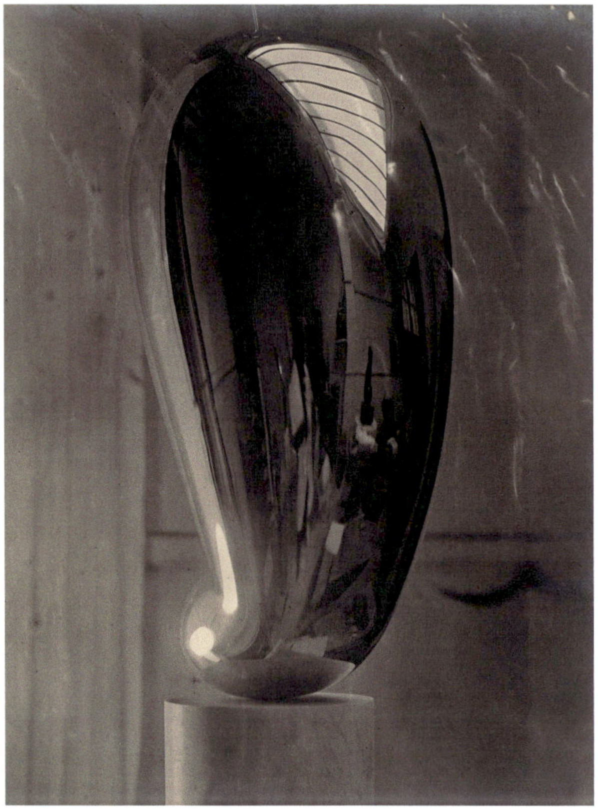

Globular, 1928
Brass
50.8 × 23.2 × 29.2 cm

The exhibition of Brâncuși that year [1926] on the beautiful top floor of the Brummer Gallery completely crystallized my uncertainties. I was transfixed by his vision.

1967

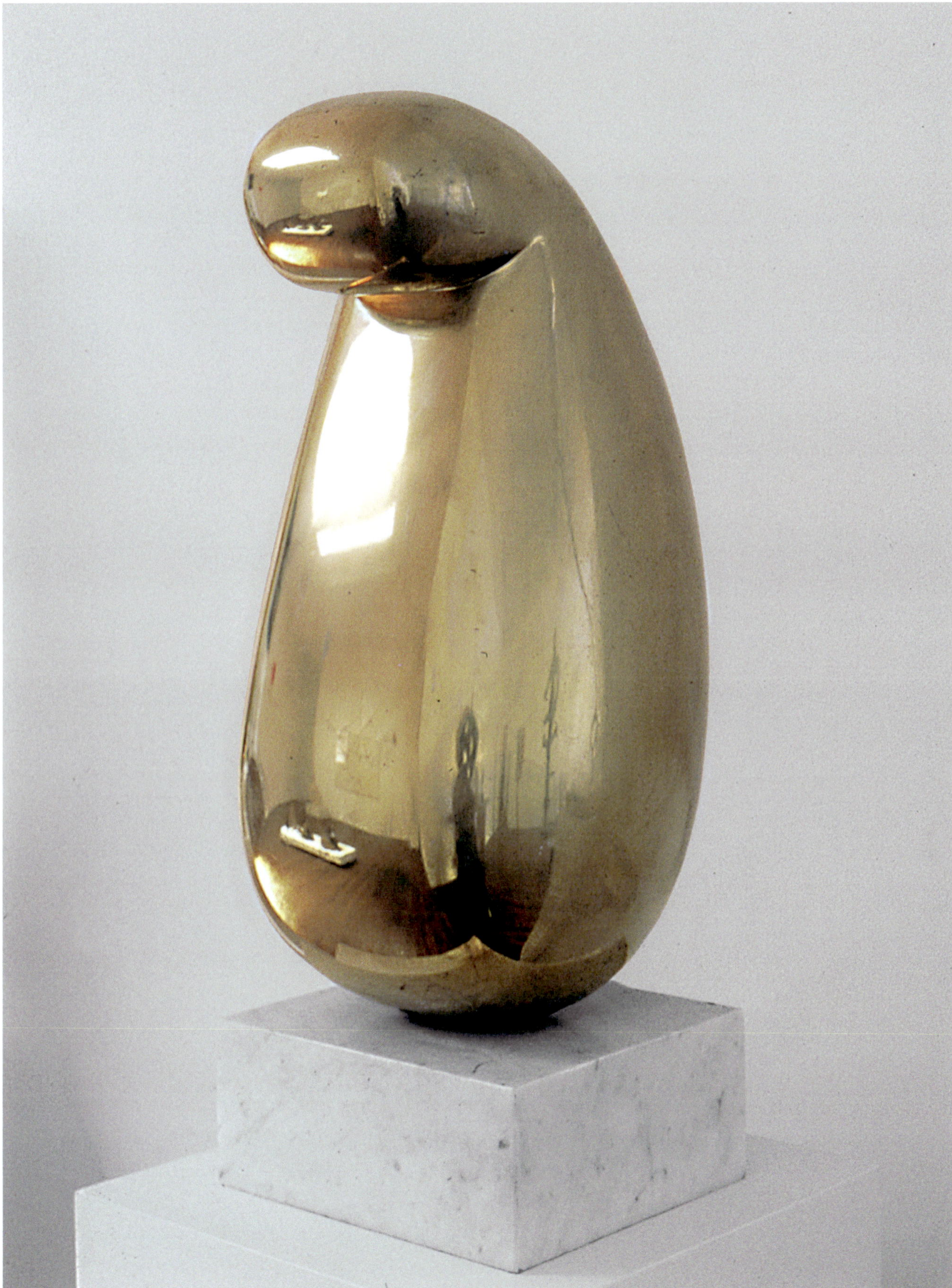

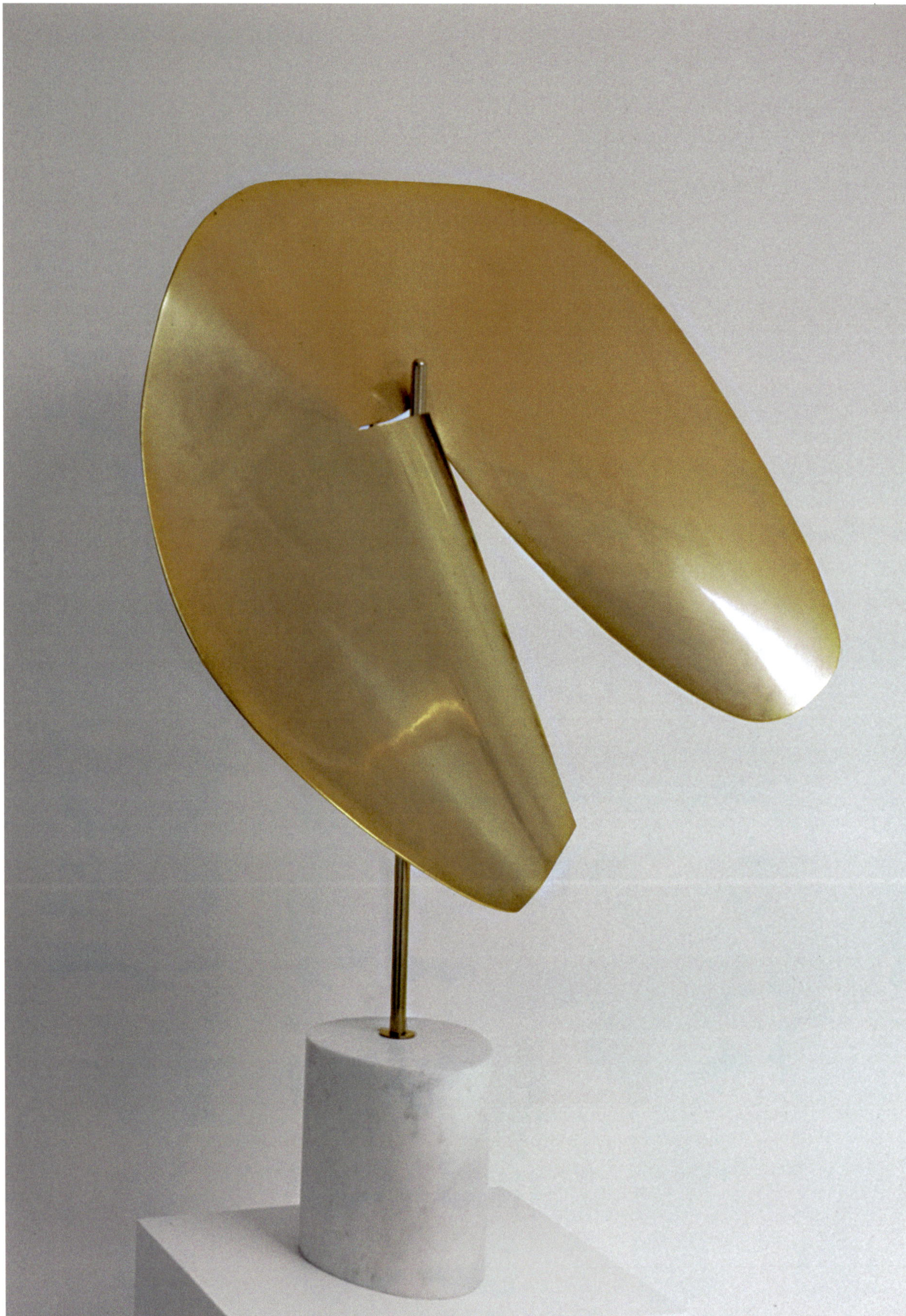

Positional Shape, 1928
Brass, gold plated
67 × 53 × 30.5 cm

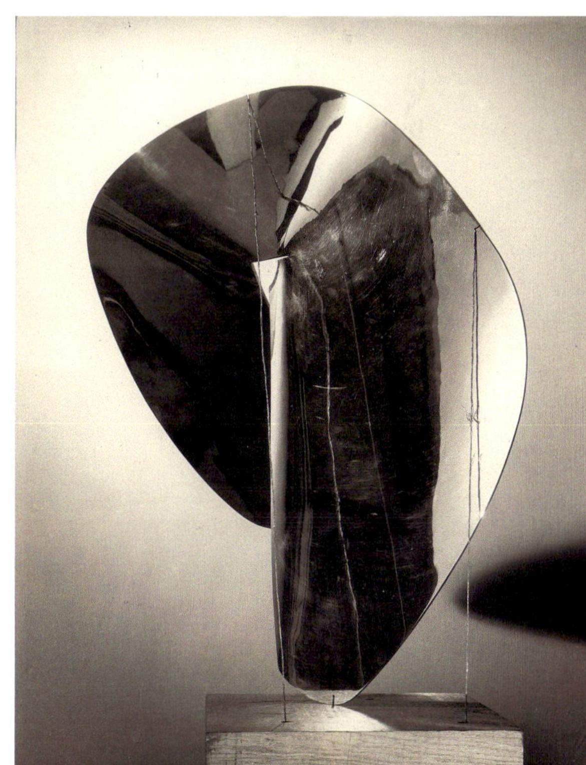

Noguchi in his studio in Gentilly, France, c. 1928

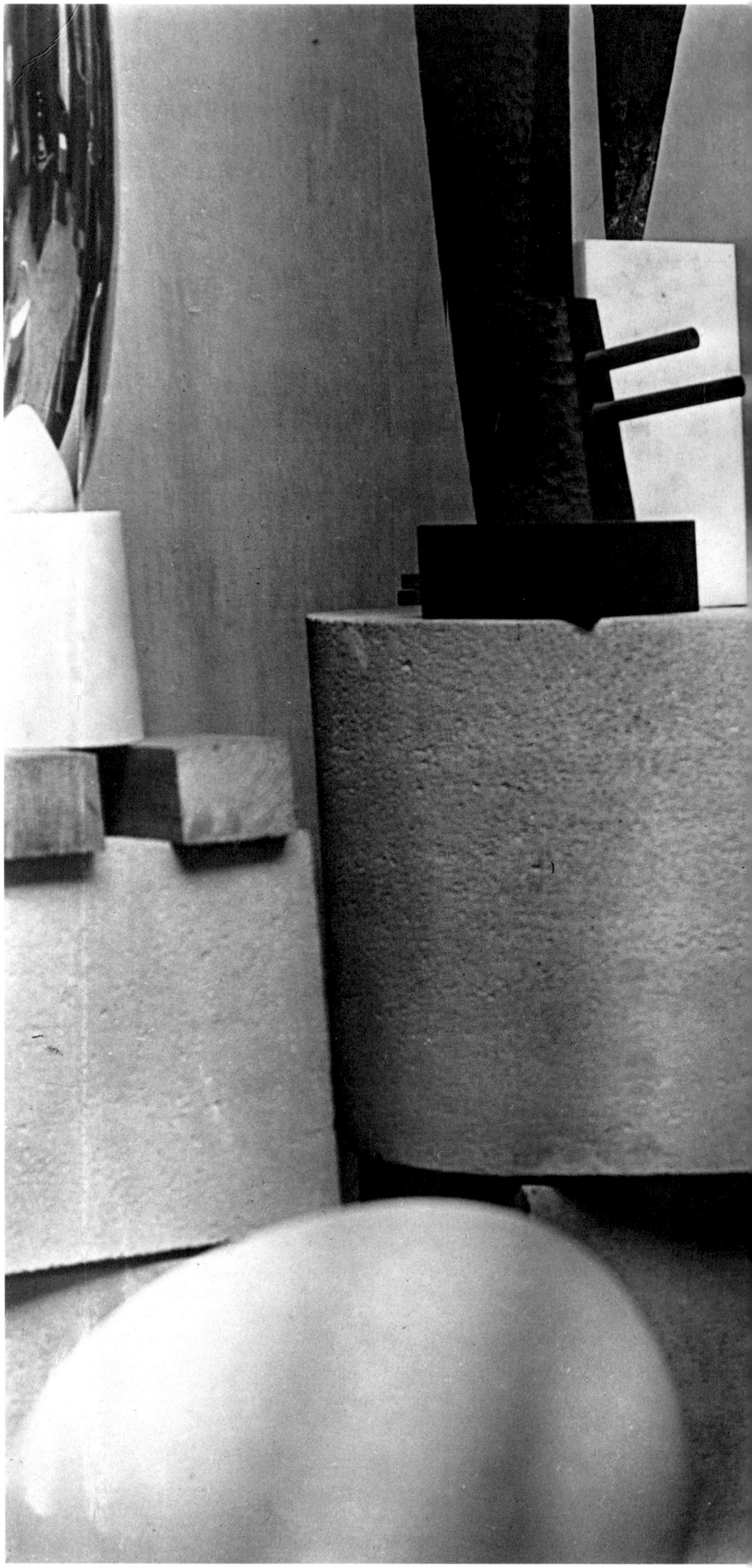

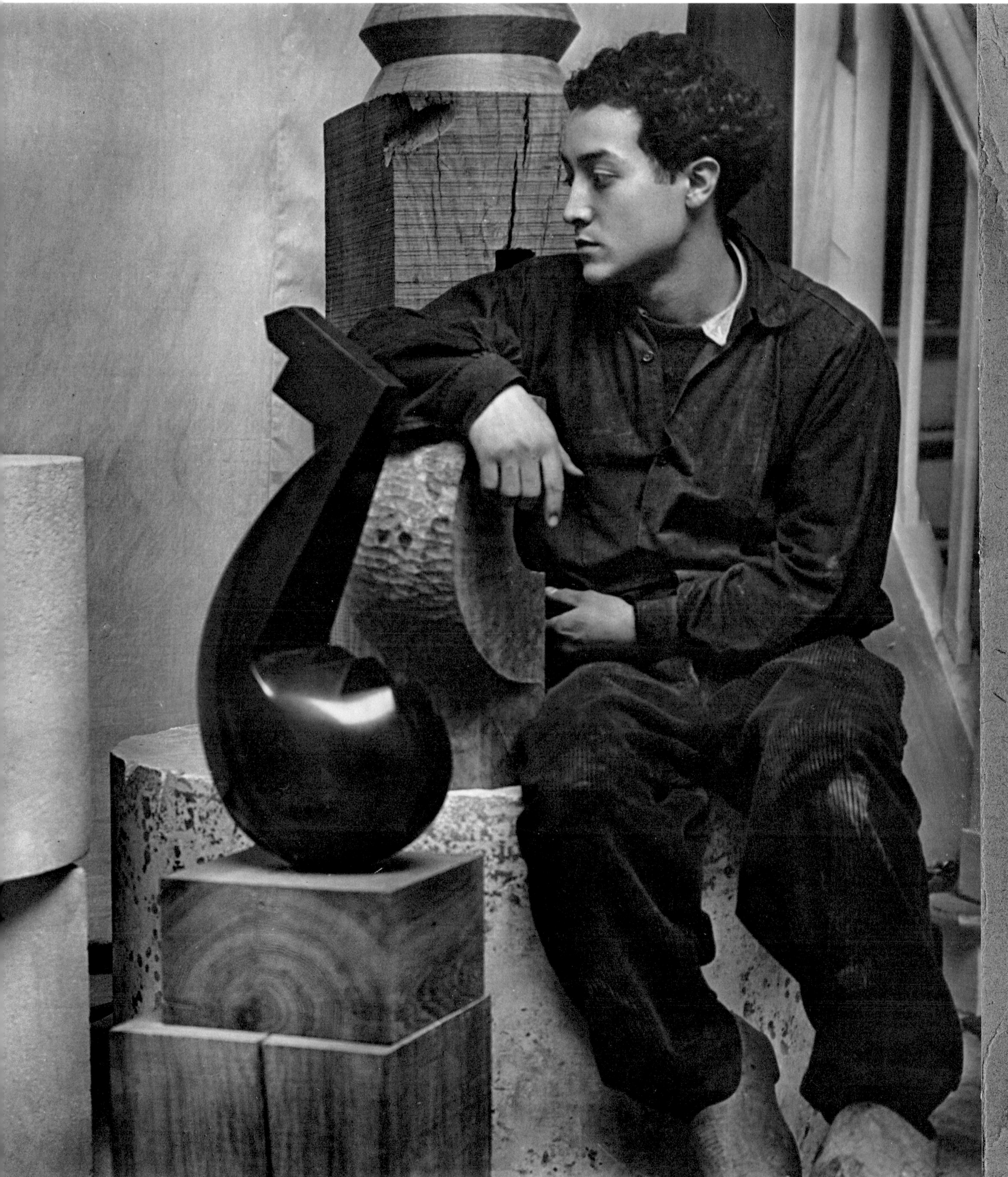

NOGUCHI IN EUROPE: INFLUENCES AND RECEPTION

Rita Kersting and Nana Tazuke-Steiniger

As a citizen of the world, Isamu Noguchi was at home everywhere (and nowhere), but above all in the United States and Japan. Yet the artist also lived on and off in Europe, mostly in France and Italy, where he had studios for a time. He explored landscapes with prehistoric cultural sites, such as Lascaux, Stonehenge and Avebury, where he was captivated by the notion of 'stones as art', as well as Roman arenas, Baroque squares and museums. The material marble led the sculptor to the Greek roots of the European continent but also transported him back into his own childhood, during which his mother told him of the legends of the Greeks – a foundation for many of his sculptures, from *Leda* (1928, p. 20) to *Orpheus* (1958, p. 202), and for his decades-long collaboration with the choreographer Martha Graham.

'As usual, Paris was the place I returned to start again', Noguchi wrote towards the end of his life.[1] After the artist had earned his first money sculpting portrait heads, he proceeded to Paris, where he worked for six months as an assistant in the studio of Constantin Brâncuși and became acquainted with the dedicated artisanal processing of both wood and, in particular, stone. The young sculptor was shaped by Brâncuși's all-pervasive professional sobriety and his precision in handling tools and surfaces, as well as his interest in myths and his bond with nature, which were rooted in his Romanian homeland.[2] Noguchi was also deeply influenced by the abstracted physicality in the master's works, which he absorbed and translated in part into erotically shaped

1 Isamu Noguchi, '1949', manuscript, c. 1983, p. 1, The Noguchi Museum Archives, MS_WRI_008_001.

2 See for example Noguchi's text on the occasion of what would have been Brâncuși's 100th birthday: 'Erinnerungen an Brancusi' [Recollections of Brancusi], in *Constantin Brâncuși*, exh. cat., Wilhelm Lehmbruck Museum, Duisburg (Duisburg: Wilhelm-Lehmbruck-Museum der Stadt Duisburg, 1976), pp. 19–24; for the English-language version see 'Recollections of Brancusi', 20 February 1976, The Noguchi Museum Archives, MS_COR_431_001.

landscape sculptures or into biomorphic figures composed of pieced-together fragments and which were hence transportable. His lifelong interest in environments also had its origin in his apprenticeship with Brâncuși, whose later commission for a meditation temple in Maheshwar, India, as well as his famous First World War monument in Târgu Jiu, Romania (1938, comprising *The Table of Silence*, *The Gate of the Kiss* and the *Endless Column*), opened new interconnections between scultpure and landscape, the human body and philosophy.

In 1927–28 Noguchi met numerous immigrants who belonged to the Parisian art scene across Cubism, Surrealism and Dada: Morris Kantor, Ossip Zadkine and André Kertész, as well as Americans such as Alexander Calder, Man Ray, Marion Greenwood, Alzira Boehm and Stuart Davis, many of them highly politicised, not least by André Breton and the recently founded Communist Party of France. During this period his friends also included Tsuguharu Foujita and Arno Breker, the latter of whom produced a portrait of Noguchi that is now in Düsseldorf.[3] Whereas Foujita and Breker later indulged in fascist propaganda, in the 1930s Calder, Greenwood, Davis and Noguchi championed anti-fascist and communist causes as part of the American Artists' Congress and the Artists' Union in New York, among other organisations.[4]

3 The portrait sculpture has been in the offices of the Bädergesellschaft Düsseldorf, the municipal swimming pool headquarters, since 1986.

4 Isamu Noguchi, 'What's the Matter with Sculpture', *Art Front*, 16 (September–October 1936), pp. 13–14, The Noguchi Museum Archives, MS_WRI_004_001.

Apart from a break between 1934 and 1948, during which many of his acquaintances went into exile in New York, Noguchi travelled to Paris every year until 1960. The city twice constituted the point of departure for trips that lasted several months and spanned continents. After a few years spent in Japan, in 1958 he returned to Paris with stones he had found there for a prominent commission: the design of the gardens for the UNESCO Headquarters by Marcel Breuer (p. 297). In the middle of Paris, not far from the Eiffel Tower, Noguchi created a garden measuring 1,700 square metres whose plants, stones, pond and fountains incorporated elements of traditional Japanese gardens and in part reinterpreted them in a brutalist manner. The *Jardin de la Paix*, or *Garden of Peace*, was received solely as a Japanese garden; there was little mention in the reviews of the fact that Noguchi, as an artist producing work in the context of Surrealism in Paris and New York, had developed his very own sculptural language over the course of the preceding thirty years.[5] It is already apparent here that Noguchi's interdisciplinary creative work, with his profound interest in the renewal and expansion of different traditions of autonomous and applied art, constituted too great a challenge for its productive reception in Europe. Despite multiple exhibitions at the Galerie and Fondation Maeght between 1947 and 1982 – among them the famous Exposition Internationale du Surréalisme, titled *Le Surréalisme en 1947*, which was curated by André Breton, Marcel Duchamp and Frederick Kiesler and included Noguchi's complex model for a *Contoured Playground* (1941, pp. 88–89) – he did not make a mark in France. Noguchi was and continues to be known first and foremost as a designer. The Centre Pompidou, which holds the world's most important collection of works by Brâncuși and even has a reconstruction of his studio, possesses nothing more than a few *Akari* objects by Noguchi. The Musée d'Art Moderne de la Ville de Paris does not have a single work by him.

5 'A Japanese garden … offers a place for meditation. It was designed by Isamu Noguchi, an American garden designer and sculptor (with Japanese father and American mother), according to the traditional manner renewed by the talent of the sculptor.' 'Le Jardin de la Paix', *Le Courrier*, special issue *La Maison de l'Unesco*, 11 (November 1958), p. 32, The Noguchi Museum Archives, B_CLI_0264_1958.

The reputation of the *UNESCO Gardens*, however, reached the planners of the new Israel Museum in Jerusalem, who commissioned Noguchi to design its 2-hectare Billy Rose Art Garden. The enormous garden environment, its contours carved from the hillside on which it stands, was inaugurated in 1965 along with the museum building by Al Mansfeld and Dora Gad and the Shrine of the Book by Kiesler, who was a friend of Noguchi's and took a similar pleasure in experimentation, drawing on a wide range of influences from all over the world. For the first time, Noguchi designed not only the surface but the land, the landscape itself, with its hills, valleys and terraces.[6]

When Noguchi said that Paris was the place where many things started, this also holds true for this large-scale work in Israel. By 'start' he may have also had his single mother Léonie Gilmour in mind, who fostered his artistic talent and whose extraordinary independence had a major influence on him. As one of America's outstanding students, in 1893 she used her scholarship to study for a year at the Sorbonne in Paris. This meant taking a decision against graduating from an American college, as to do both was not financially possible. Without a university degree, but with a French acute accent in her name, Léonie henceforth led a life that was extremely autonomous for the period.[7]

The first institutional presentation of a work by Noguchi in Europe took place in 1938 at the Jeu de Paume in Paris, where the first of numerous touring exhibitions was shown that were organised as national presentations of American art, among others by the Museum of Modern Art (MoMA), New York. The exhibition bore the title *Trois siècles d'art aux États-Unis* (Three Centuries of American Art) and was curated by A. Conger Goodyear, the president of MoMA, who incorporated Noguchi's terracotta portrait of his uncle Takagi (1931, pp. 42–43) into the show – a dated choice for Paris in view of Noguchi's abstract and increasingly political works in the 1930s.[8] Many prominent displays of Noguchi's works in Europe, for instance at the World's Fair in Brussels in 1958, documenta II in Kassel in 1959 and, at the end of his life, the American Pavilion at the Venice Biennale in 1986, were the result of such exports motivated by cultural policy. Noguchi was one of a number of artists selected for these exhibitions not by the respective European institution but by American cultural officials. With Noguchi, Ben Shahn, Jackson Pollock, Helen Frankenthaler and many others, the United States presented itself in Europe as a new leading cultural nation after the war: tolerance, openness and diversity were the democratic values that the works sent across the Atlantic were meant to embody – by selected artists whose names already promised diversity. While the progressiveness of the art was intended to support the integration of the West within a new world order, the representatives of Congress at home in Washington criticised the political sentiments of many of the artists assigned to this mission, especially during the McCarthy era.[9]

Noguchi was one of 35 American artists chosen by Porter McCray, director of the MoMA International Program, for documenta II in 1959, held in the West German city of Kassel, near the border with the German Democratic Republic.[10] With *Night Land* (1947, p. 298), *The Self* (1956, p. 298) and *Bird C* (or *Mu*; 1950) Noguchi presented three sculptures inspired by Surrealism. *Night Land* was installed outside, in front of the Orangerie building alongside sculptures by Henry Moore and Ossip Zadkine, and reflected, among other things, the traumatic time Noguchi spent in an internment camp during the Second World War as part of the US government's years-long incarceration of more than 100,000 people of Japanese descent, of which the European

6 Within this landscape he erected walls as abstract geometric shapes, influenced by his visits to eighteenth-century astronomical observatories in Delhi and Jaipur, India. See Matt Kirsch, *The Jantar Mantars of Northern India: Noguchi as Photographer*, exh. brochure, The Noguchi Museum, New York (New York: The Isamu Noguchi Foundation and Garden Museum, 2015), and Devika Singh, 'Multiple Perspectives: Isamu Noguchi and the Jantar Mantar', in *Clear Black Smoke: Mohammed Qasim Ashfaq*, exh. cat. (London: Hannah Barry Gallery, 2017), pp. 32–37.

7 Lisa Yin Zhang, 'The Incomplete Chronicle of Léonie Gilmour', 2020, www.noguchi.org /isamu-noguchi/digital-features/the-incomplete-chronicle-of-leonie-gilmour, accessed 1 February 2021

8 *Trois siècles d'art aux États-Unis*, exh. cat., Jeu de Paume, Paris (Paris: Éditions des Musées Nationaux, 1938), p. 50, https://assets.moma.org/documents/moma_catalogue_3597_300061928.pdf, accessed 1 February 2021. One year later, in 1939, Noguchi designed a table for Goodyear's new house that anticipated the 'interlocking sculptures' of the 1940s.

9 Sigrid Ruby, *Have We an American Art? Präsentation und Rezeption amerikanischer Malerei im Westdeutschland und Westeuropa der Nachkriegszeit* (Weimar: VDG, 1999), p. 88.

10 Noguchi was one of seventeen American artists whose names documenta curator Arnold Bode and his team sent in advance to Porter McCray (a list based on exhibitions previously organised in Europe by MoMA), who then, according to the documenta catalogue, sent a total of 35 artists to Kassel.

public was not fully aware at the time. In a lecture to academy students in Venice in 1970, Noguchi mentioned this experience, which took place in 1942 shortly after the attack on Pearl Harbor, and questioned why only those of Japanese descent, and not German or Italian, were detained in the US.[11] In general, little notice was taken of Noguchi's contribution to documenta, it being thrust aside in every respect by the spectacular 'super formats' created by American Abstract Expressionist painters.[12]

Five years later, at documenta III (1964), Noguchi presented *Lessons of Musokokushi* (1962, p. 301), a five-part floor arrangement composed of bronze 'stones' – a reference to Musō Kokushi, the honorofic name of the fourteenth-century Zen monk and master gardener Musō Soseki – that the sculptor produced at, of all places, the American Academy in Rome. This sculpturally complex work between statuary art and sculpture, naturally and specifically fashioned form, object and landscape, Japanese tradition and scatter piece posed too great a challenge for the reception of the exhibition, which included 280 artists. *Lessons of Musokokushi* was not mentioned in a single review of documenta III.[13] It is all the more interesting that ten years later, the director of the Kunsthalle Düsseldorf, Jürgen Harten, asked the artist for precisely this work for an exhibition he was planning for 1974.

By that point, Noguchi had shown his work in three solo exhibitions in European galleries. The first of these was when Claude Bernard presented the artist in Paris in 1964; Bernard had already sold *The Self* to the Tate in London in 1960 and published a catalogue in which Noguchi's body of work was described in its full breadth for the first time in Europe. In 1968 Noguchi transferred to the Gimpel Fils and Gimpel & Hanover galleries in London and Zurich, where he had solo shows in 1968 and 1972. The artist did not make it easy for his gallerist Peter Gimpel, as in 1968 he did not want to sell anything for tax reasons and then promptly raised his prices.[14] However, thanks to these galleries, and by dint of his presentations at the World's Fair in Brussels and documenta II, Noguchi's work, including powerful 'interlocking sculptures' and, in the broadest sense, surrealistic sculptures, found entry into private collections such as those of Walter Bechtler in Zollikon, Michel and Susi Meyer in Kilchberg and Bo Boustedt in Gothenburg, as well as the Tate (1960), the Kröller-Müller Museum in Otterlo (1966) and the Lehmbruck Museum in Duisburg (1970). One of the few longer reviews of Noguchi's work, written by Jean-Christophe Ammann, who at the time was one of Harald Szeemann's assistants at the Kunsthalle Bern, appeared in *Art International* in 1969. With reference to the exhibition at Gimpel & Hanover in Zurich in 1968, he wrote: 'Noguchi is an important artist who is difficult to gauge by Western standards. He recognised and sculpturally exploited key developments in twentieth-century art early on, subsequently distanced himself from them, became "reactionary", in order to then again take a position in the vanguard.'[15] Ammann describes Noguchi's point of departure as the purity of form, the form as symbol, with an intense emotional colouring that is generated by means of narrative counterpoints, lacerations, notches, openings, contacts and hanging. 'With sculptures like these,' Ammann wrote, 'Noguchi stands at the centre of that movement that objectivises emotional situations in a highly fascinating way (e.g. Reiner Ruthenbeck). Constantin Brâncuși … and Alberto Giacometti … substantially influenced the artist. An influence that continues to be palpable to this day without coming across as a limitation.'[16] The explicit search here for criteria

11 'International University of Art lecture with Noguchi transcript', 11 October 1970, p. 6, The Noguchi Museum Archives, MS_WRI_030_005.

12 Albert Schulze Vellinghausen in the *Frankfurter Allgemeine Zeitung*, 25 July 1959, quoted in Ruby, *Have We an American Art?*, p. 413. Ruby also gives an account of the ideological conflicts that took place beforehand as well as the struggle for visibility and metres of wall space.

13 The work was not even illustrated in the extensive photographic reconstruction of documenta III published by the documenta archive. Harald Kimpel and Karin Stengel, *documenta 3 1964*, Schriftenreihe des documenta-Archiv 12 (Bremen: Edition Temmen, 2005).

14 Correspondence in the archive between Noguchi and Peter Gimpel provides insight into the problems with respect to restrictions imposed on the artist and his expectations of the gallery. Letter from Isamu Noguchi to Peter Gimpel, 25 January 1972, The Noguchi Museum Archives, MS_GAL_014_003.

15 Jean-Christophe Ammann, 'Schweizer Brief', *Art International*, vol. 13, no. 2 (20 February 1969), p. 53.

16 Ibid.

with which to assess Noguchi's work, the author's distancing and his subsequent fitting description of the pieces, and ultimately his inadequate categorisation of them in direct proximity with the young German artist Ruthenbeck as well as alongside Brâncuși and Giacometti, is representative of the general uncertainty with which Noguchi's oeuvre was met.

The exhibition in which Harten invited Noguchi to participate would be held at the Kunsthalle in Düsseldorf, the West German city where many foreign artists in the 1960s and '70s began their international careers. The Kunsthalle, the Kunstverein, Galerie Schmela and, especially, Galerie Konrad Fischer were considered springboards. But Noguchi, born in 1904, was twenty years older than conceptual artists such as Sol LeWitt, Carl Andre or Robert Morris, who, as white Americans, encountered familiar structures in the Rhineland with respect to their academic training and artistic concerns. Unlike Noguchi, for whom the Second World War, in the middle of his life, brought various setbacks and interruptions, the Land, Conceptual and Minimal artists, as part of a progressive movement, were more self-evidently connected with the current European art scene and its gallerists, critics, collectors and curators.[17] To put it more bluntly, one could say that Noguchi was too old, too solitary artistically – despite his collaborations – too isolated in his own mercurial immersion in highly diverse areas. This was aggravated by the fact that the European scene was heavily discriminatory. And Noguchi was seen as a Japanese artist: the exhibition Harten was planning would be titled *Japan: Tradition und Gegenwart* (Japan: Tradition and the Present) and would present Japanese artists from three generations. Puzzled, after receiving the invitation Noguchi wrote to his gallery in Zurich about the Kunsthalle 'wanting to show Japanese artists (although I do not see how I qualify as such)'.[18] Yet rather than decline to participate in 'the exhibition of Japanese (which I am not)', Noguchi asked his gallerist Peter Gimpel to send – in addition to *Lessons of Musokokushi*, which Harten had requested – two works that were likely to bring the show's approach into question: *Victim* (1962) and *From Stone Mountain* (probably the sawn up and reassembled *Young Mountain* of 1970).[19] In the end, instead of sending *Victim* and *Mountain*, the gallery supplied two more decorative marble sculptures, *Floor Frame* (1970, pp. 224–25) and *Downward Pulling* (1972), which reflect less critically on (the view of) Japanese identity and tradition.

Added to his misleading categorisation as Japanese, non-Western and formalist was an admiration of Noguchi's artisanal perfection, which in the years around 1970 must have acted as a virtual deterrent to the progressive, non-inclusive European art scene and catapulted Noguchi out of the prevailing discourse. In 1968, on the occasion of Noguchi's retrospective at New York's Whitney Museum of American Art, critics had already extolled his work's virtuosity, subtlety and overpowering beauty and in part excoriated it, in the same breath, as old-fashioned. 'But in the end one is depressed … to find that so much esthetic refinement, so much intrinsic craft should generate so little power', wrote Hilton Kramer in the *New York Times* – criticism that surely spread rapidly within the European art scene as well, which at the time was closely intertwined with New York's.[20]

In a letter in 1968, Rudi Oxenaar, director of the Kröller-Müller Museum in Otterlo, Netherlands, who had acquired two sculptures for the collection, presented Noguchi with the prospect of a retrospective, a plan that fizzled out.[21]

17 The curator Kasper König, a central figure for the flow of information on contemporary art and who at the time commuted between the United States and Europe, was familiar with Noguchi and his work from, among others, the Galerie Cordier & Ekstrom, where König earned money assisting in the setting up of installations. In the 1960s, Noguchi was not one of the – primarily Conceptual – artists whom König recommended to his European colleagues. In 1984 he then invited the artist to take part in the large-scale exhibition *Westkunst* in Cologne (in which he did not participate, however). Letter from Maja Oeri to Isamu Noguchi, 13 August 1980, The Noguchi Museum Archives, MS_COR_141_010.

18 Letter from Isamu Noguchi to Anne Rotzler, 30 November 1973, The Noguchi Museum Archives, MS_GAL_020_029.

19 Letter from Isamu Noguchi to Peter Gimpel, 30 November 1973, The Noguchi Museum Archives, MS_EXH_128_005.

20 Hilton Kramer, 'Isamu Noguchi: A Selective Anthology', *New York Times*, 21 April 1968.

21 Letter from R.W.D. Oxenaar to Isamu Noguchi, 7 June 1968, The Noguchi Museum Archives, MS_GAL_096_008.

The artist's projects in Europe remained few and far between but included the magnificent installation of the bright red *Octetra* on the Piazza del Duomo in the medieval Italian town of Spoleto (p. 303), for which he was invited along with R. Buckminster Fuller – again as a politico-cultural US import, this time by Priscilla Morgan, co-organiser of the international Festival di Spoleto and an intimate friend of the artist. Noguchi developed a vividly painted red concrete sculpture that he placed in cheerful and delicate relationship with the Romanesque cathedral. With their round openings, the four tetrahedron-like modules corresponded with the rosettes on the cathedral's impressive west facade. The holes in the surfaces of these elements invited people to engage in play – and with this surprisingly fitting contemporary element, the centuries-old square acquired an additional function. The object resembles the theatre and dance props that Noguchi designed to establish a connection between human and sculptural bodies. Here the stage is the city's central square, into whose everyday life Noguchi inscribes his sculpture.

Noguchi wanted to make this desire to transfer sculpture into the reality of life palpable in a new and particularly distinct way on the occasion of his most important appearance in Europe, the exhibition in the American Pavilion at the Venice Biennale in 1986. The curator of the pavilion, Henry Geldzahler, invited the 82-year-old Noguchi to represent the United States in Venice precisely 'because [his work] was not well known in Europe. Because his calm and meditative sculpture is the antidote of the image that Europeans have of American culture as aggressive and uncouth – the land of Reagan and Rambo.'[22] Noguchi, who had always suffered under his uncertain situatedness, was proud – though also sceptical – of the nomination and seized the prominent opportunity to clarify his broad concept of sculpture. Besides current stone sculptures, including a slide made out of Carrara marble (*Slide Mantra*, 1986, pp. 252–53), models for playgrounds and a metal helix structure, he exhibited *Akari* objects – sculptures not made out of stone or metal but out of paper and which are illuminated not from the outside but from within. In the accompanying publication, Geldzahler, who owed his renown as a curator to his early collaboration with Pop artists, highlights the political orientation of Noguchi's early oeuvre, his continuous reinvention of traditions, but neglects to describe his contemporary importance and the selection of works for the pavilion in view of an art scene that was again behaving more conservatively, especially in the 1980s. Geldzahler does not elaborate on the helix sculpture as the backbone of Noguchi's presentation between art and life or address the radical nature of the *Akari*. Thus he also failed to relate an understanding of the exhibition to the public, the press or the biennale's jury that would clarify its objective and its power. Noguchi's hope of being awarded the Golden Lion was disappointed, and there was scarcely a single review in Europe that received Noguchi's work in a friendly and productive way: a review in *Kunstforum International* maintained that 'the presentation of several more recent works by the now 82-year-old Isamu Noguchi (of Japanese descent) … was incapable of tearing open any new perspectives.'[23] In view of the overall display, *Die Zeit* made the following assessment: 'Because one did not want to see America (two grey battleships anchored before San Marco did not exactly multiply the number of friends of America) win an award, one also ignored Isamu Noguchi, that is to say the life's work (surely not ideally presented in Venice) of a prominent sculptor who does not stand for American imperialism but for the positive tradition of

22 Mary Anne Staniszewski, 'Art, Inc.: Behind the Biennale', *Manhattan, Inc.* (July 1986), p. 126.

23 Harry Zellweger, 'Biennale Reflexions', *Kunstforum International*, vol. 85 (1986), p. 136. For a comprehensive examination of Noguchi's participation in the biennale, see Glenn Adamson, 'Representing America: Isamu Noguchi at the 1986 Venice Biennale', May 2019, www.noguchi.org/isamu-noguchi/digital-features/representing-america-isamu-noguchi-at-the-1986-venice-biennale.

the multi-ethnic nation.'[24] Numerous reviews were negative: 'Restrained interventions in the stone … oversized paper lamps … slightly obtrusive designer simplicity', wrote the German weekly *Der Spiegel*.[25] *The Times* polemicised: Noguchi's '*What is Sculpture?* … seems really to pose the question: How little can you get away with and still be called sculpture? … one mostly has the impression of having wandered unawares into a Conran lighting showroom.'[26] Thirty years earlier, *The Times* had been one of the English newspapers to sharply criticise Noguchi when he designed the costumes and stage set for a Royal Shakespeare Company production of *King Lear* in 1955, describing them as 'ridiculous'.[27] John Gielgud, who played Lear in the play, had valued Noguchi's designs for Martha Graham, which lent freedom to the script and the actors, and in response to the stagnant Shakespearean tradition extended an invitation to the initially sceptical Noguchi as an outsider to British theatre.[28] The scathing criticism of the radically new interpretation – including the script – was then publicly attributed precisely to this outsider: 'Courtiers are dressed like space-men', 'Lear looks like a Gruyere cheese', 'the most distracting settings and costumes imaginable', wrote the press.[29] Gielgud even agreed with the negative criticism, referring to the production as a catastrophic failure and claiming that Noguchi's costumes had impeded the play and stood in the way of its success.[30] What is characteristic is that a major share of the criticism was directed towards Noguchi's work and that no mention was made of the underlying decisions made by the Royal Shakespeare Company regarding stage direction.

Evidently, Noguchi and his art did not sufficiently fit into the categories, strongly determined by the art market, that were fundamental to success in the confined and discriminatory European art scene following the Second World War. The first European retrospective tour of Noguchi's work, which took place from 2001 to 2003, twelve years after his death, finally presented a wide range of works from his oeuvre. Yet *Isamu Noguchi: Sculptural Design* still took a somewhat narrow view by placing weight on the design facets of Noguchi's practice and its relationship with Japan. This can also be seen in the catalogue, which emphasised the applied aspects of the artist's work, a focus supposedly evidenced by his text 'Sculpture as Invention', which he had written in the 1950s and which was now published in the catalogue. In this personal summary of his work Noguchi describes his wish, 'perhaps because of my somewhat alien situation, to bring sculpture into a more direct involvement with the common experience of living'.[31] He outlines his deep fascination with conceptual and technical innovation and explains how his diverse activities in numerous fields are united by the aim of puncturing the conventional idea of sculpture – all leading ultimately to the creation of the *Akari*:

> What I did was to bring an ancient art to our modern art by integrating it with electricity (as I had done with lunars). I coined for them the name AKARI, which in Japanese means light (as illumination), just as our word light does. It also suggests lightness as opposed to weight … I believe akari to be a true development of an old tradition. The qualities that have been sought are those that were inherent to it, not as something oriental but as something we need. The superficial shapes or functions may be imitated but not these qualities.[32]

24 Petra Kipphoff, 'Halbierte Löwen im Luna-Park: Kunst im Gedränge der Nationen', *Die Zeit*, 4 July 1986, www.zeit.de/1986/28/halbierte-loewen-im-luna-park/komplettansicht, accessed 17 February 2021.

25 Jürgen Hohmeyer, 'Durch die Wunderkammer', *Der Spiegel*, 30 June 1986, www.spiegel.de/spiegel/print/d-13520259.html, accessed 1 February 2021.

26 Russell John Taylor, 'Slipping So Easily into the Surreal', *The Times*, 1 June 1986.

27 'Palace Theatre: *King Lear*', *The Times*, 27 July 1955.

28 Letter from George Devine to Isamu Noguchi, 29 October 1954, The Noguchi Museum Archives, MS_PROJ_025_004.

29 *Northern Daily Echo* and the *Daily Sketch* (for 'courtiers' and 'Gruyere', respectively), quoted in Paula Wilkinson, 'Gruyere Cheese & Space Fiction – "King Lear", 1955', www.shakespeare.org.uk/explore-shakespeare/blogs/gruyere-cheese-space-fiction-king-lear-1955, 4 December 2013; 'Palace Theatre: *King Lear*' ('distracting settings').

30 Michiko Kakutani, 'Lear, Shakespeare's "Impossible" Role, Animates a New Play', *New York Times*, 1 November 1981, www.nytimes.com/1981/11/01/theater/lear-shakespeare-s-impossible-role-animates-a-new-play.html, accessed 1 February 2021; Michael Billington, 'Walking a Tightrope to Great Acting', *The Guardian*, 23 May 2000, www.theguardian.com/film/2000/may/23/1, accessed 1 February 2021.

31 Isamu Noguchi, 'Sculpture as Invention', in *Isamu Noguchi: Sculptural Design*, exh. cat., Vitra Design Museum, Weil (Weil am Rhein: Vitra Design Museum, 2001), p. 155.

32 Ibid., pp. 155–56.

To convey the complex qualities of the *Akari* beyond their appearance as lamps was one of the tasks of experimental theatre director Robert Wilson, who was commissioned by the curators to choreograph the presentation. The show's orientation towards the applied arts was further reflected in the choice of venues: the exhibition was to be shown not at the Kunstmuseum Basel but at the Vitra Design Museum in Weil; not at the Centre Pompidou but at the Maison de la Culture du Japon in Paris; not at the Museum Ludwig but at the Museum für Angewandte Kunst in Cologne; as well as at the Design Museum in London, founded by Sir Terence Conran.[33] Perhaps most successful was the presentation at the Museo Reina Sofía in Madrid, where Noguchi's oeuvre was embedded in a different, new and more complex setting, here in the context of a prominent art collection that included overtly political works such as Pablo Picasso's seminal anti-war painting *Guernica* (1937). Now, twenty years on, for this European retrospective in London, Cologne, Bern and Lille, the six-decade career of Isamu Noguchi is presented to its full extent: daringly interdisciplinary and wide-ranging but always potent and powerfully coherent. Refracted through the prism of identity, politics, social engagement, history and utopia, the tremendous scope and contemporary relevance of his work can now hopefully be experienced.

33 In the catalogue, the Museum für Angewandte Kunst in Cologne is named as the venue, but it cancelled at short notice. Shortly before that, in 1999, the Museum Ludwig in Cologne presented Noguchi in the exhibition *Kunstwelten im Dialog: Von Gauguin bis zur globalen Gegenwart* (Art Worlds in Dialogue: From Gauguin to the Global Present); his works were also displayed, likewise in a global context, in 2016 at the Haus der Kunst, Munich, in *Postwar: Art between the Pacific and the Atlantic, 1945–1965*, in this case with a focus on the period after the Second World War and the atomic bomb.

Rita Kersting, Deputy Director, and Nana Tazuke-Steiniger, Research Fellow, Museum Ludwig, Cologne

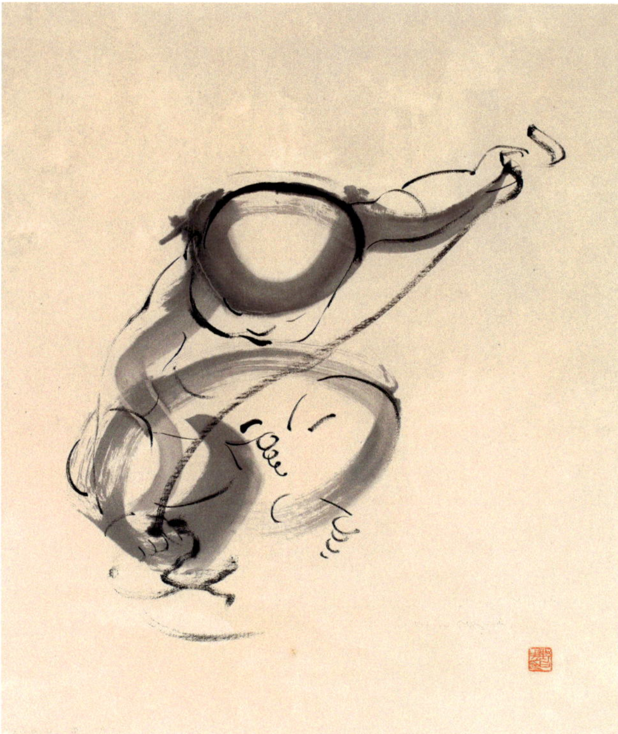

Peking Brush Drawing (Baby with String), 1930
Ink on paper
88.9 × 75.9 cm

Peking Brush Drawing, 1930
Ink on paper
89.2 × 146.1 cm

Peking Brush Drawing, 1930
Ink on paper
221 × 121.9 cm

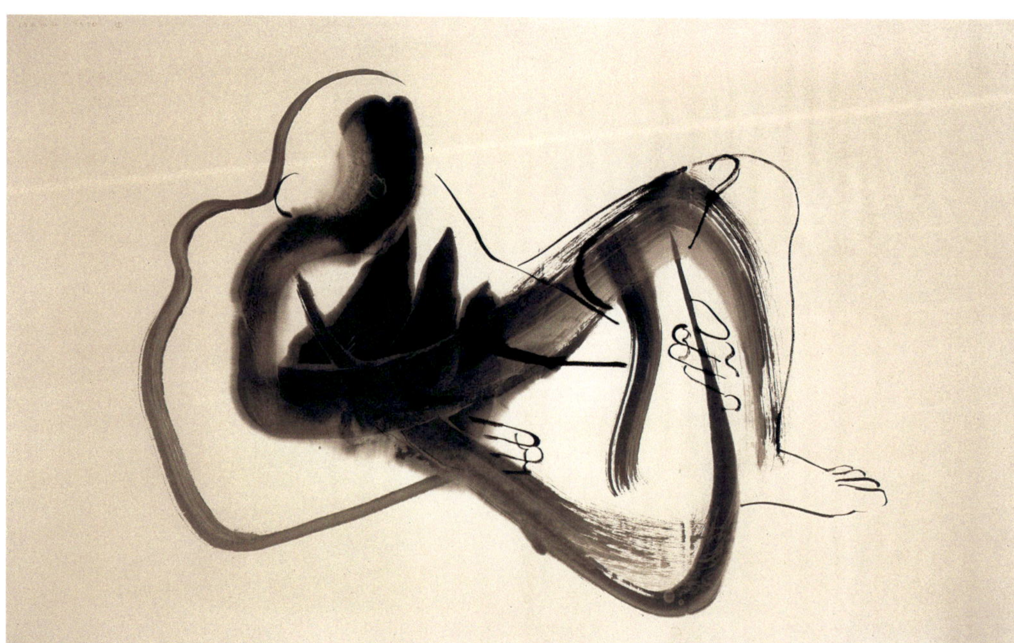

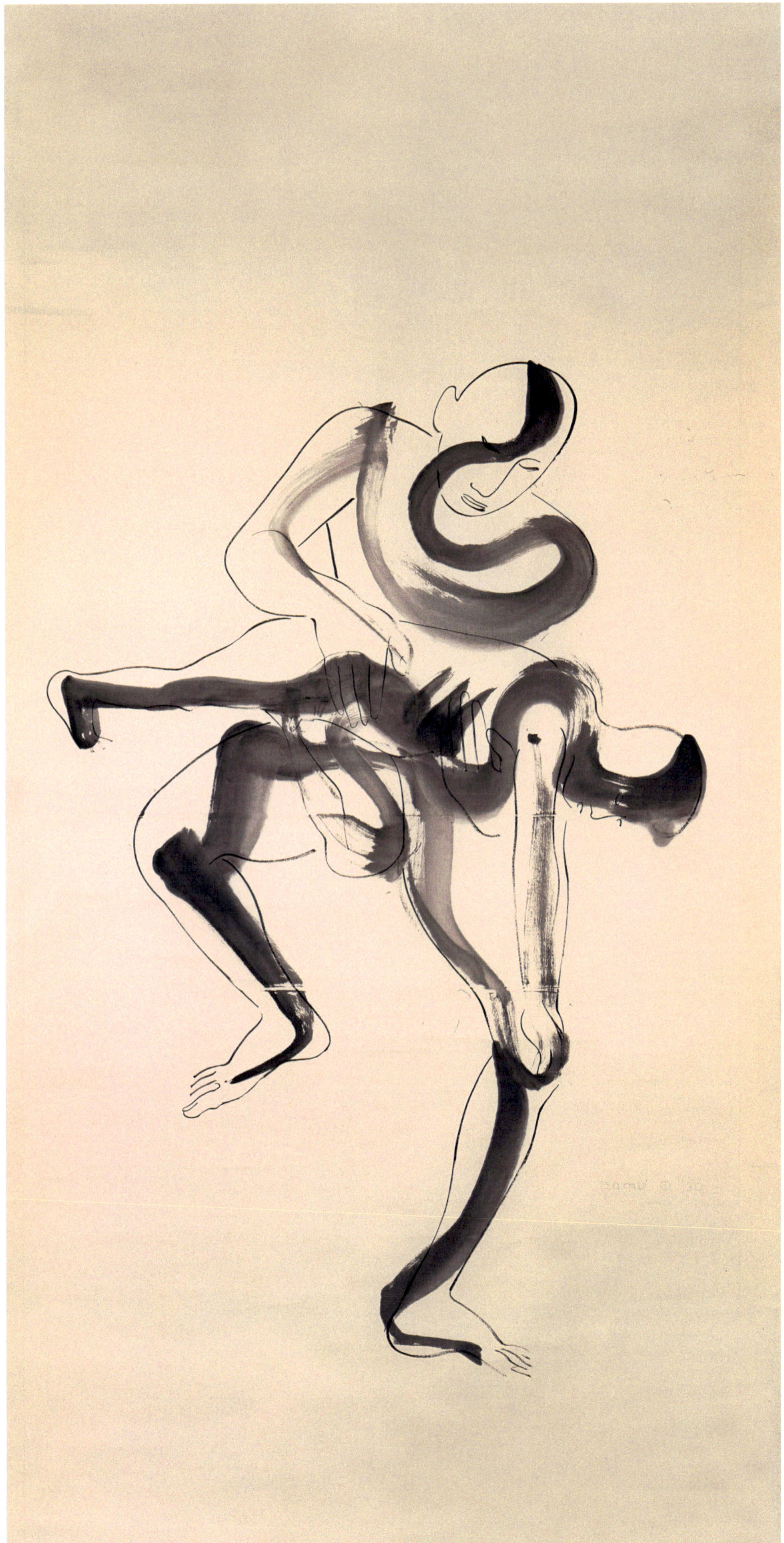

Chinese Girl (Girl Reclining on Elbow), 1930
Dental plaster
25.7 × 48.6 × 28.9 cm

The Queen, 1931
Terracotta
111.4 × 42.9 × 39.4 cm

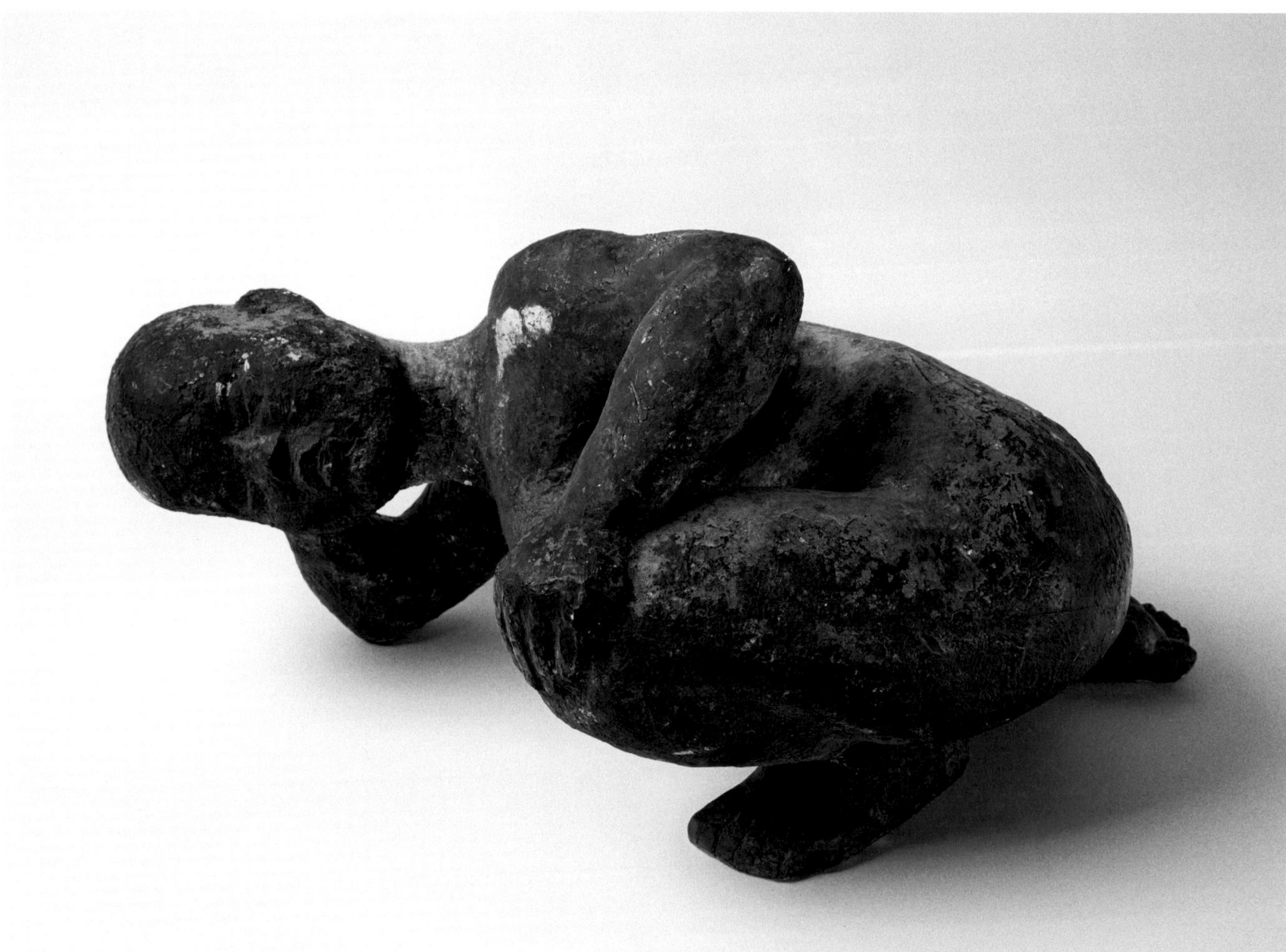

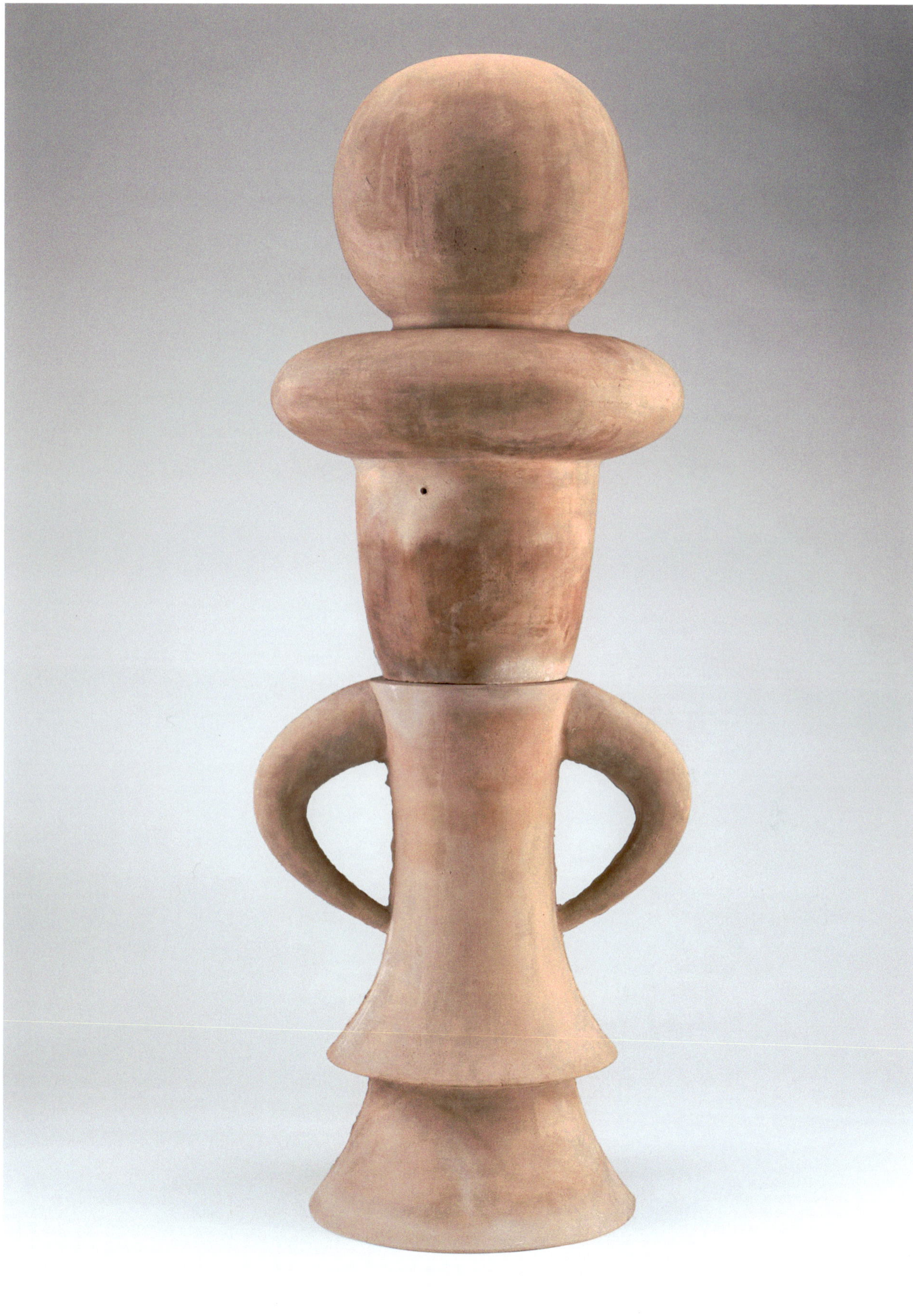

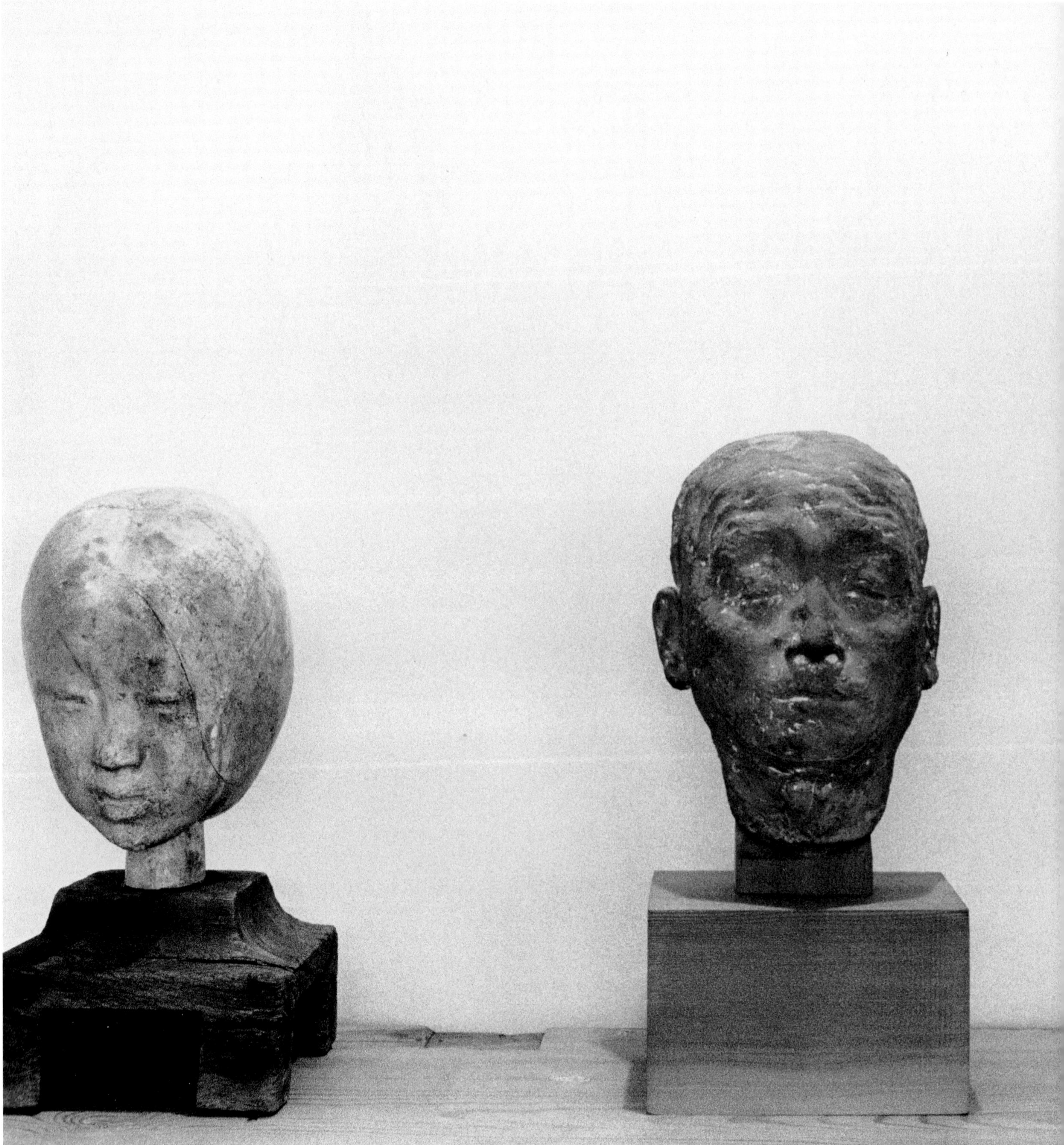

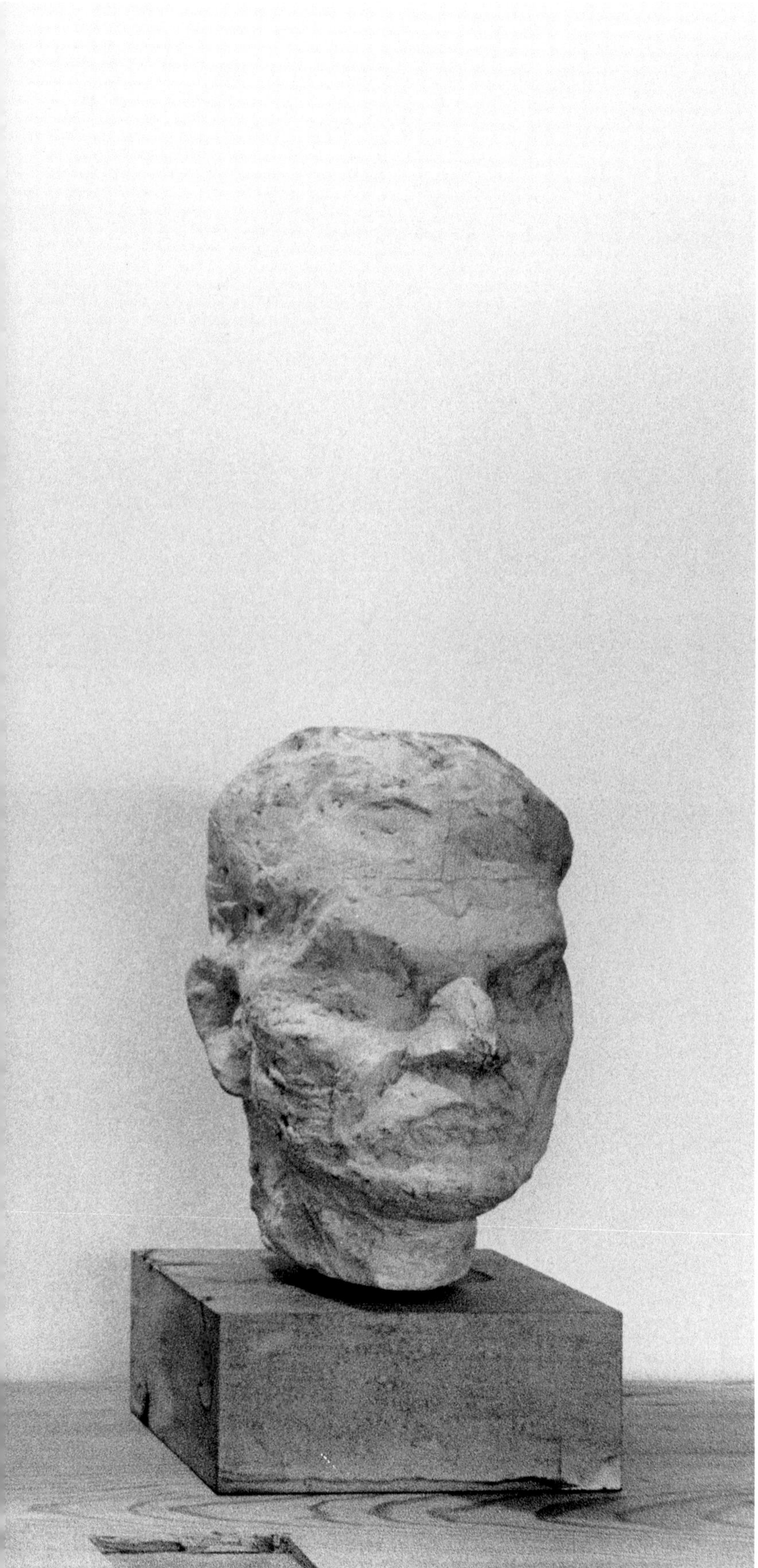

Left to right:
Tsuneko-san (Head of a Japanese Girl), 1931
Plaster of Paris
29.5 × 19.4 × 23.5 cm

Uncle Takagi (Portrait of My Uncle), 1931
Terracotta
31.4 × 22.2 × 21.6 cm

José Clemente Orozco, 1931
Terracotta
30.8 × 20.3 × 26 cm

Suzanne Ziegler, 1932
Wood
41.6 × 22.2 × 27.9 cm

Tsuneko-san (Head of a Japanese Girl),
1931 (cast c. 1933)
Bronze
29.2 × 18.1 × 22.2 cm

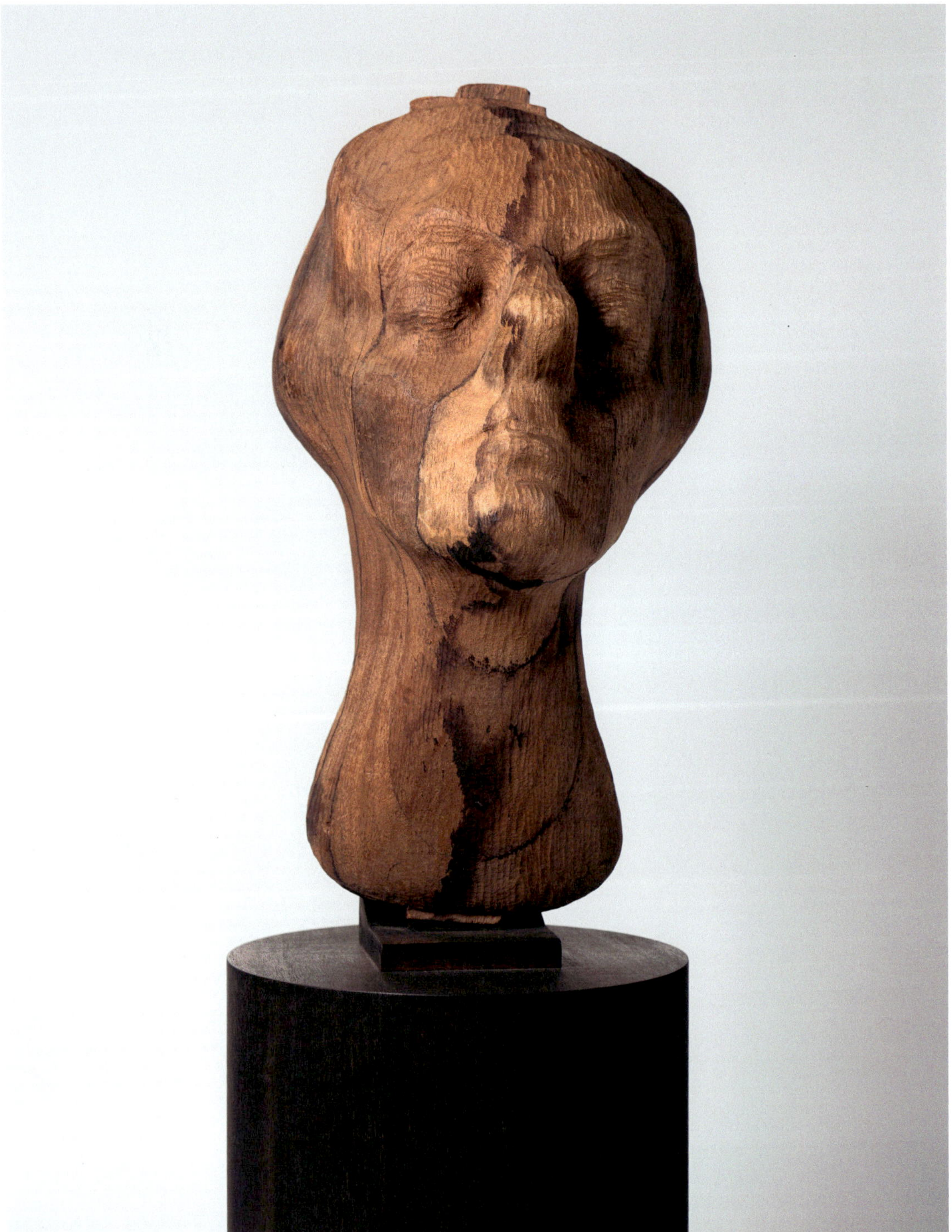

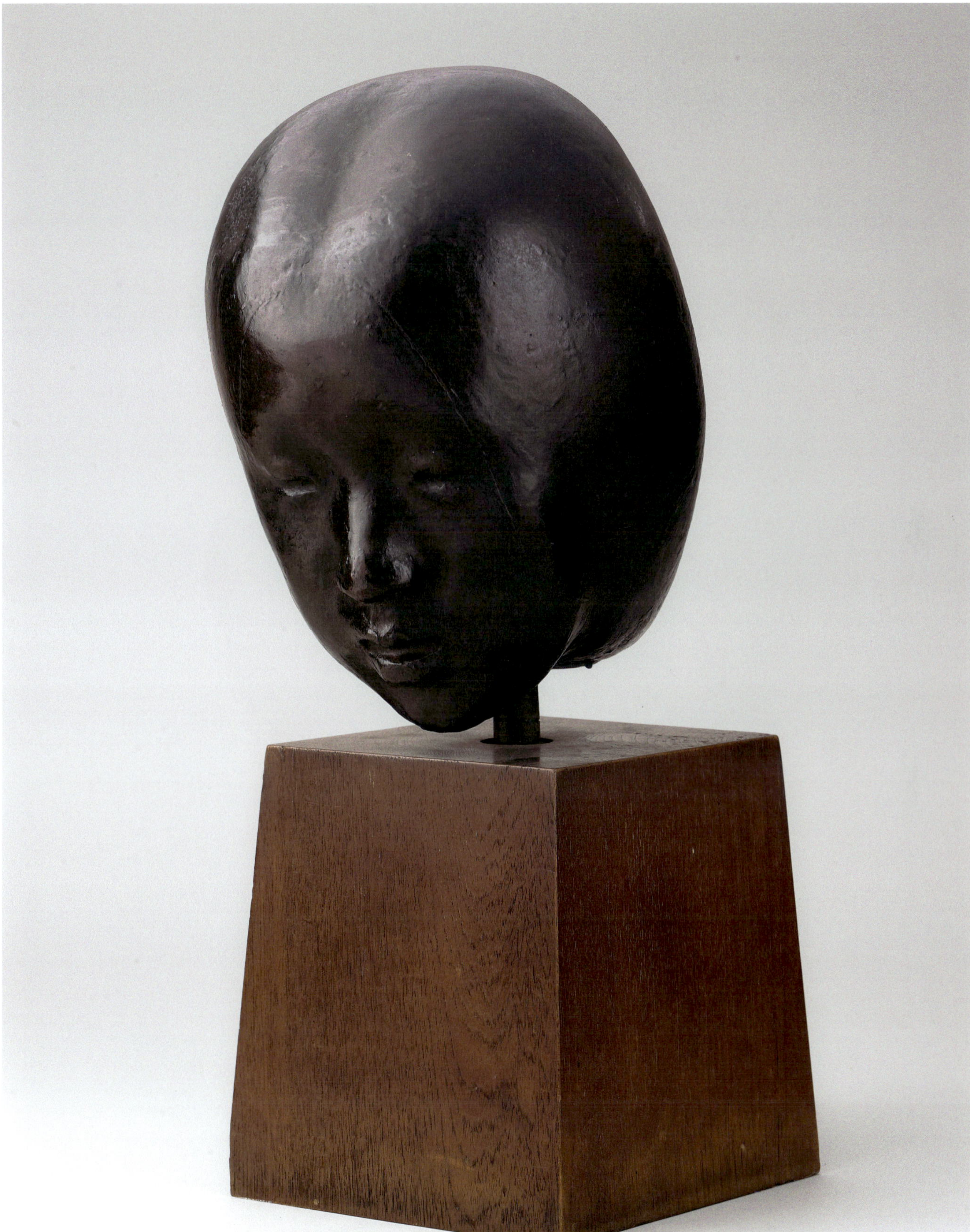

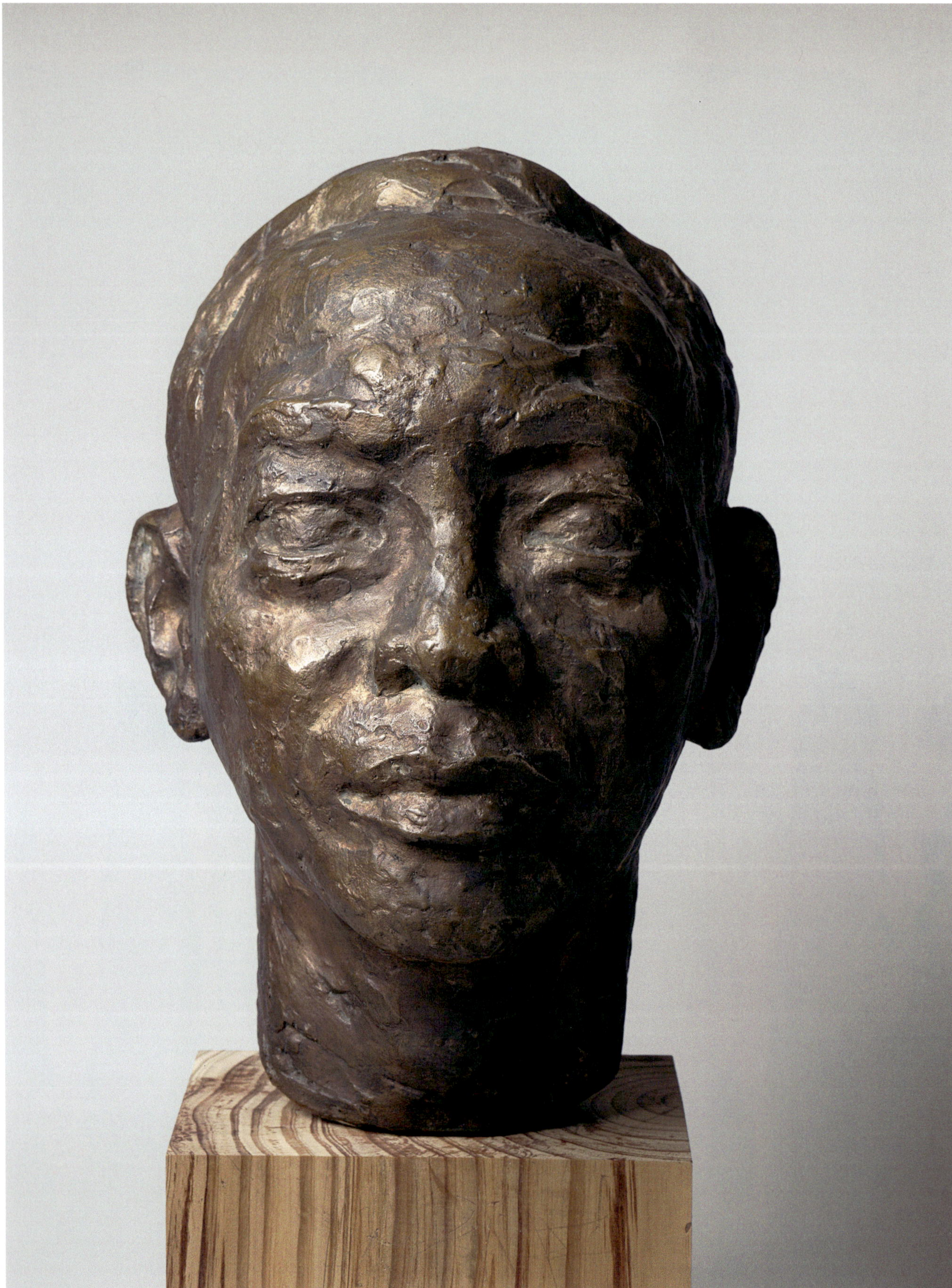

Sukarno, 1950
Bronze with brown patina
35.9 × 25.4 × 27.3 cm

Tara Pandit, c. 1947
Bronze
31.4 × 19.7 × 21.9 cm

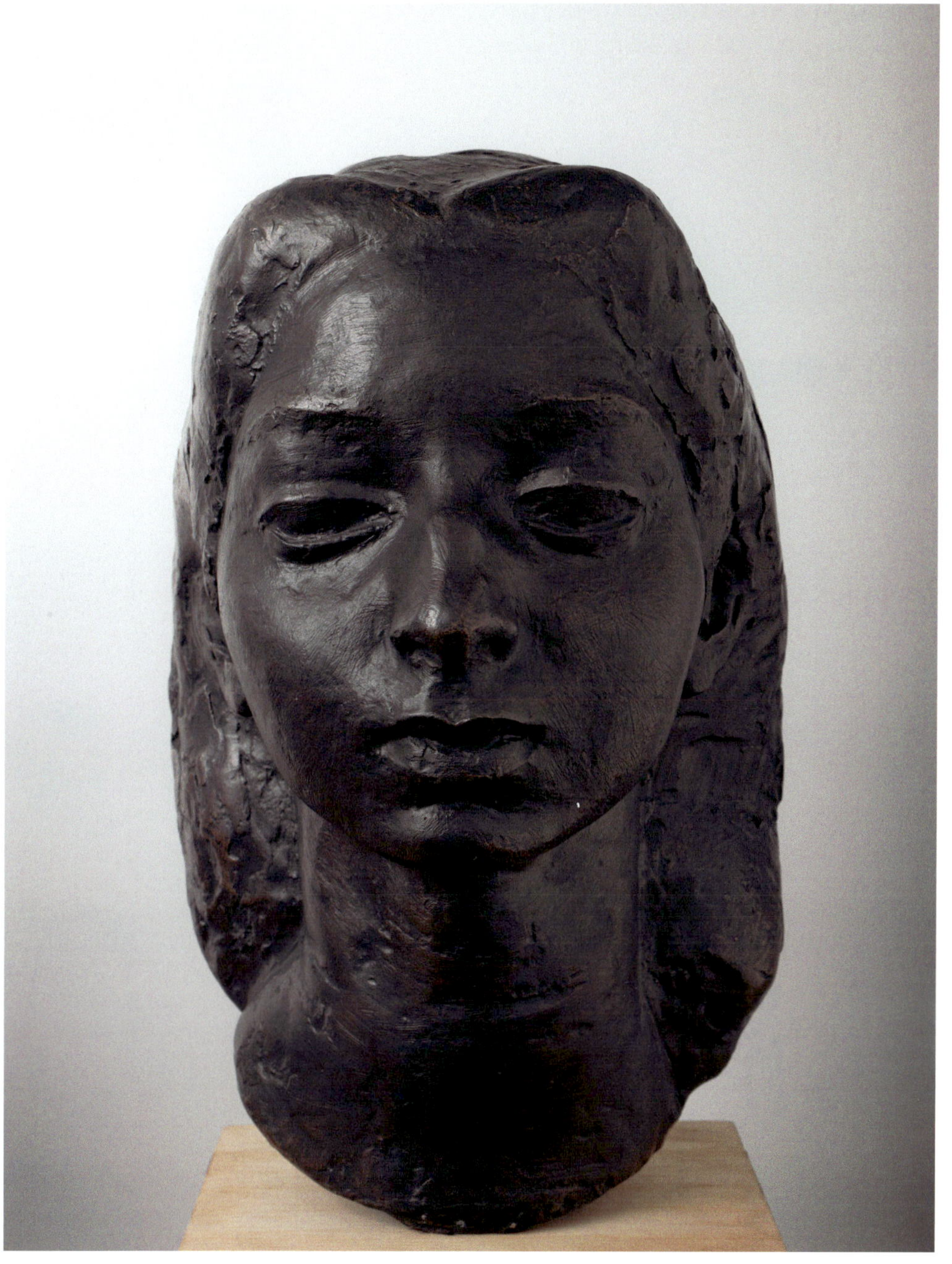

Exhibition view of *Fifteen Heads by Isamu Noguchi*, Marie Sterner Gallery, New York, 1–14 February 1930

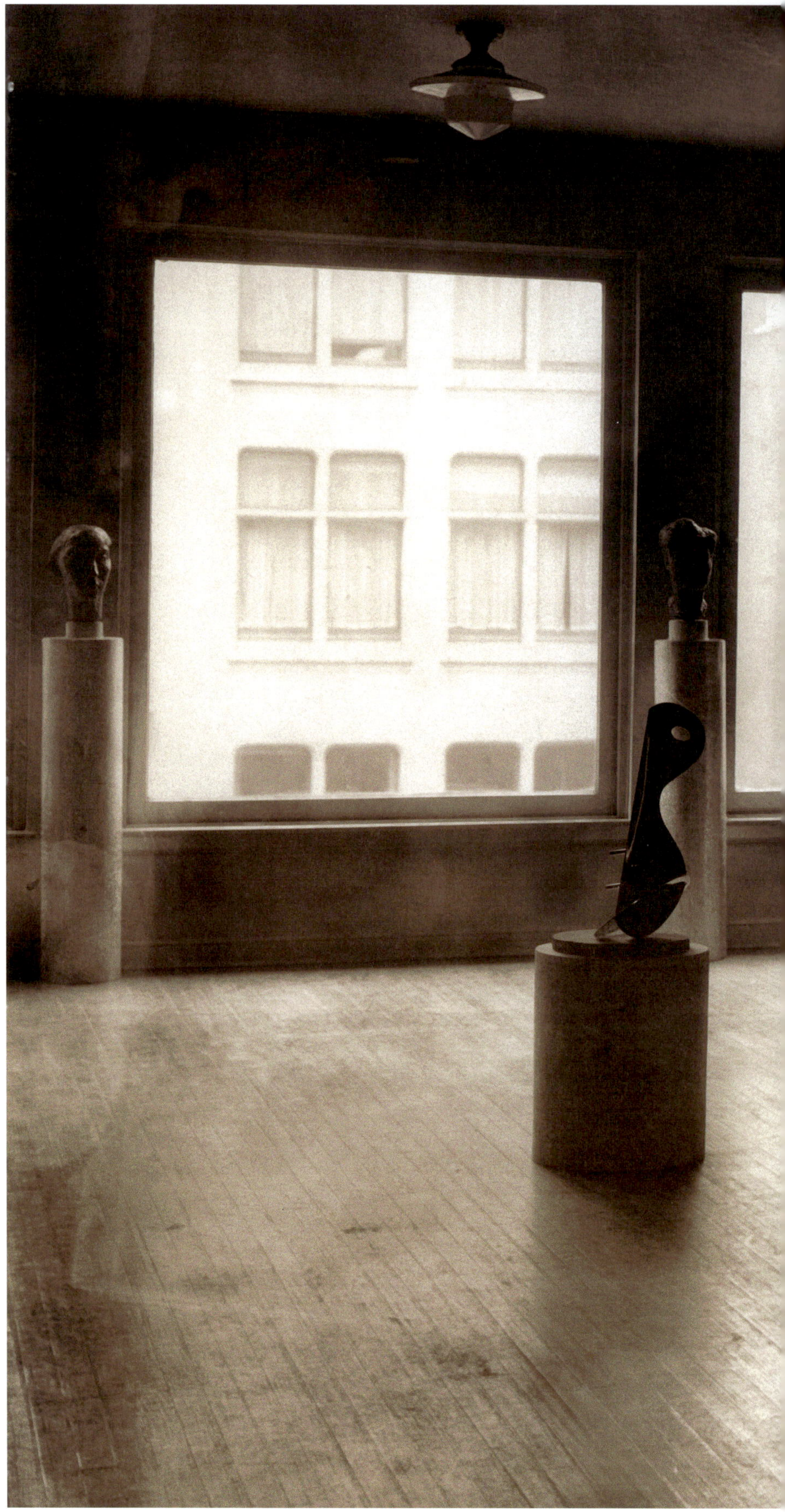

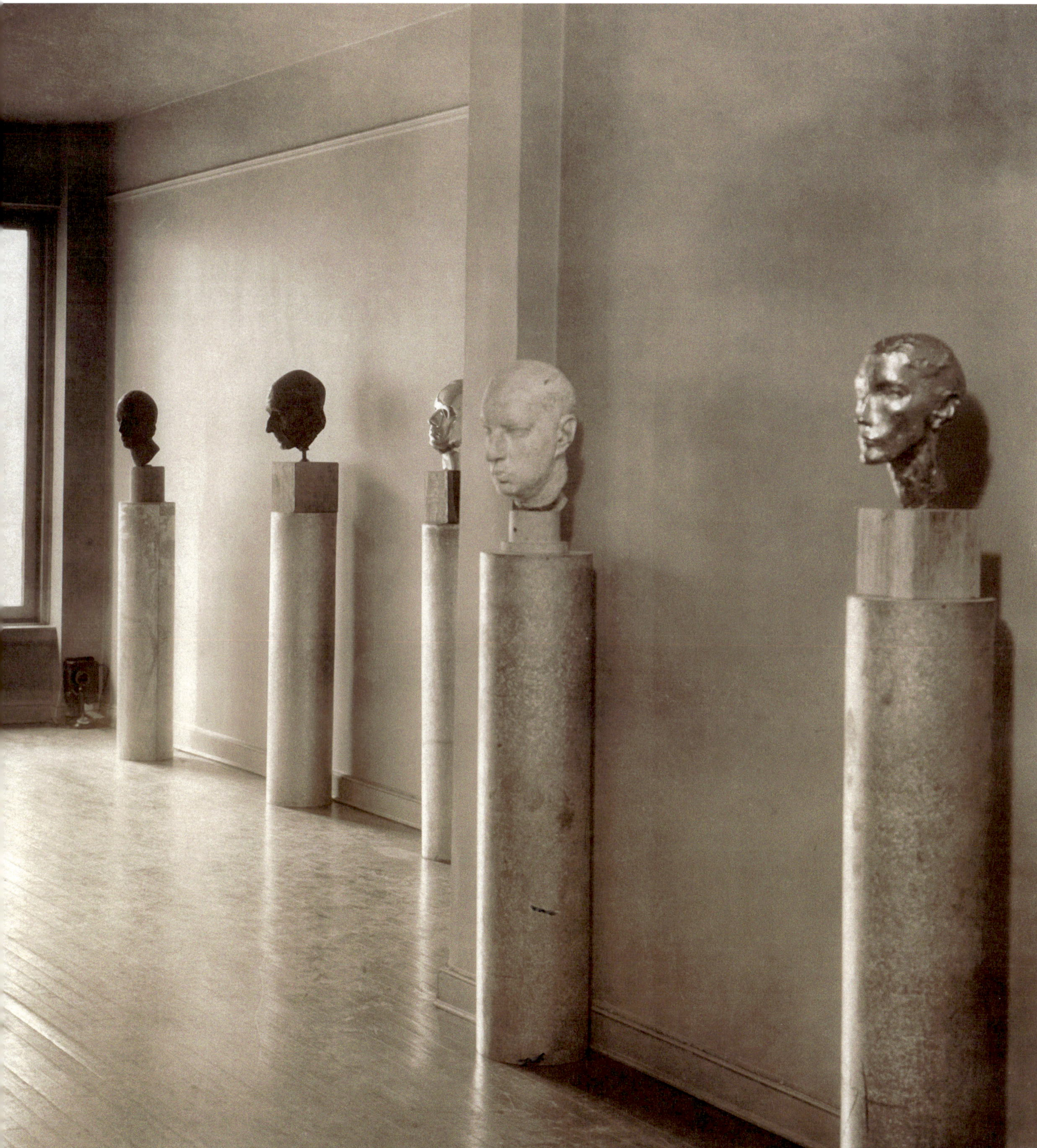

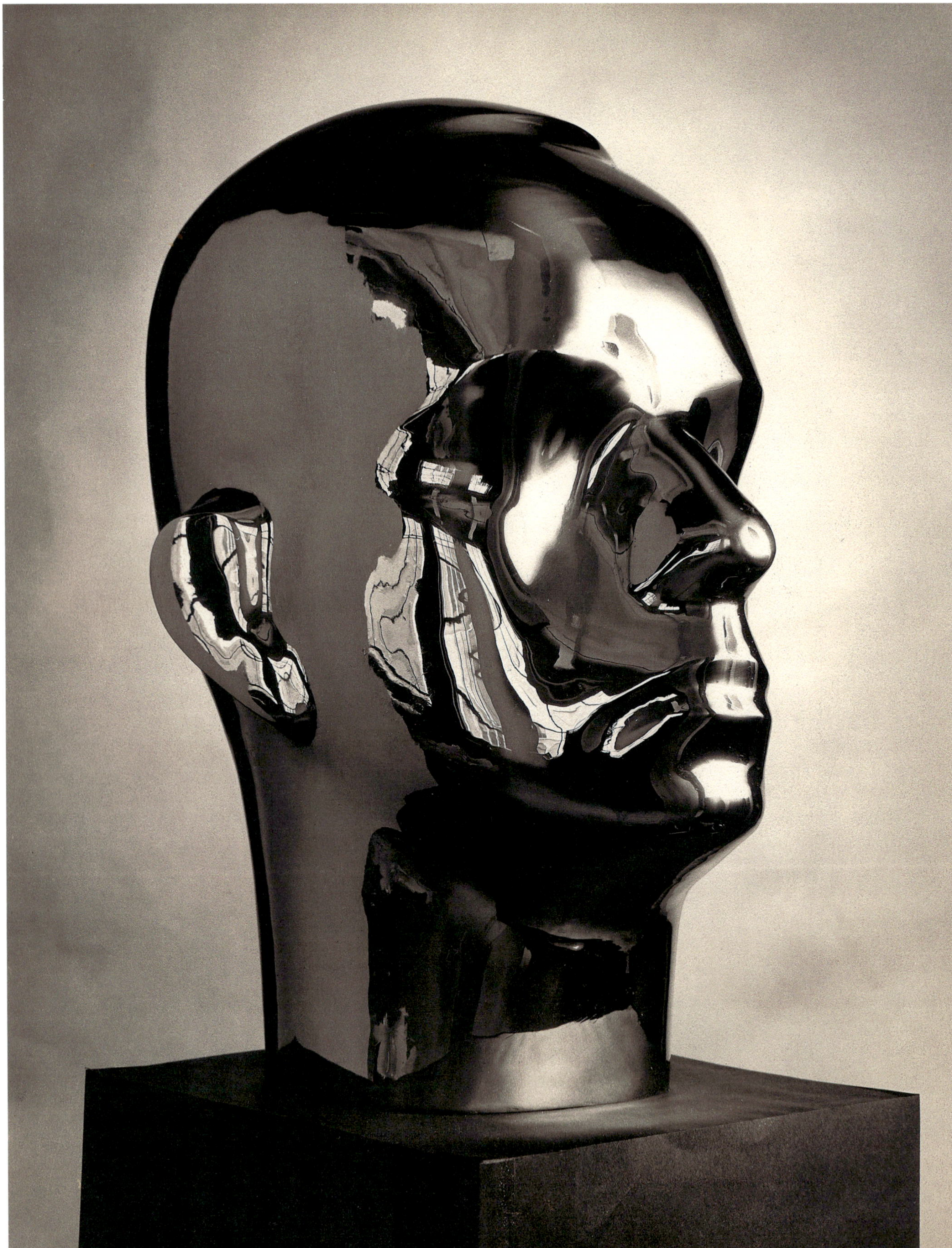

R. Buckminster Fuller, 1929
Bronze, chrome plated
33.7 × 20 × 25.4 cm

R. Buckminster Fuller at Black Mountain College, North Carolina, 1949

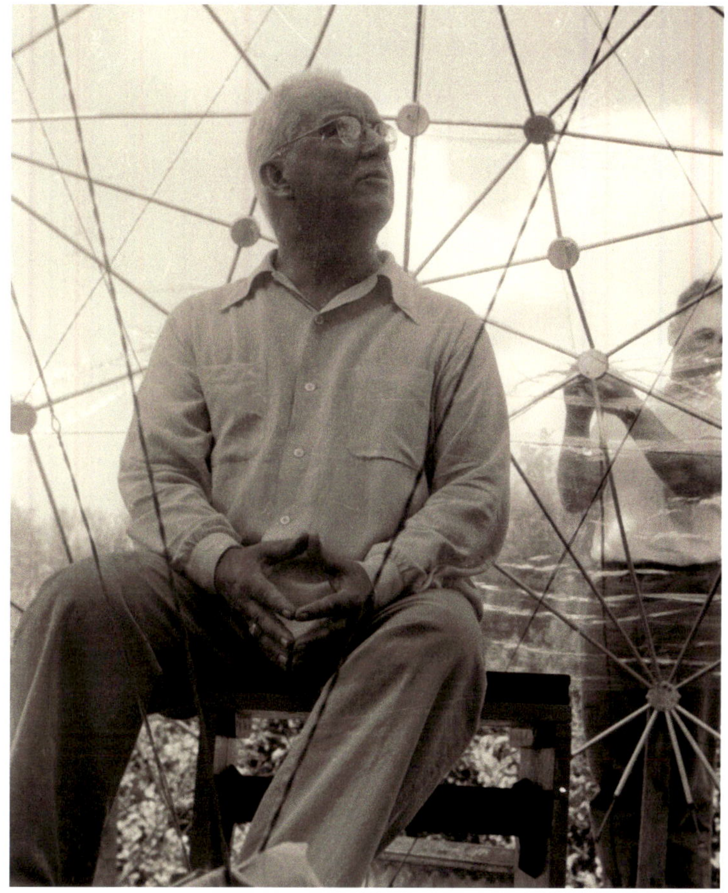

He was also a great influence on me, because he represented America and the new technology of space and structures. He was, you might say a messiah – a man who dreamed and who tried to teach people about the world as he saw it; the structural world and his idea of the future which he thought could come from proper application of engineering.

1986

R. Buckminster Fuller and Isamu Noguchi
Model for the Dymaxion Car, 1932–33
Painted plaster
7.9 × 26.7 × 8.3 cm

R. Buckminster Fuller and Isamu Noguchi
Models for the Dymaxion Car, 1932–33
Plaster
Dimensions unknown

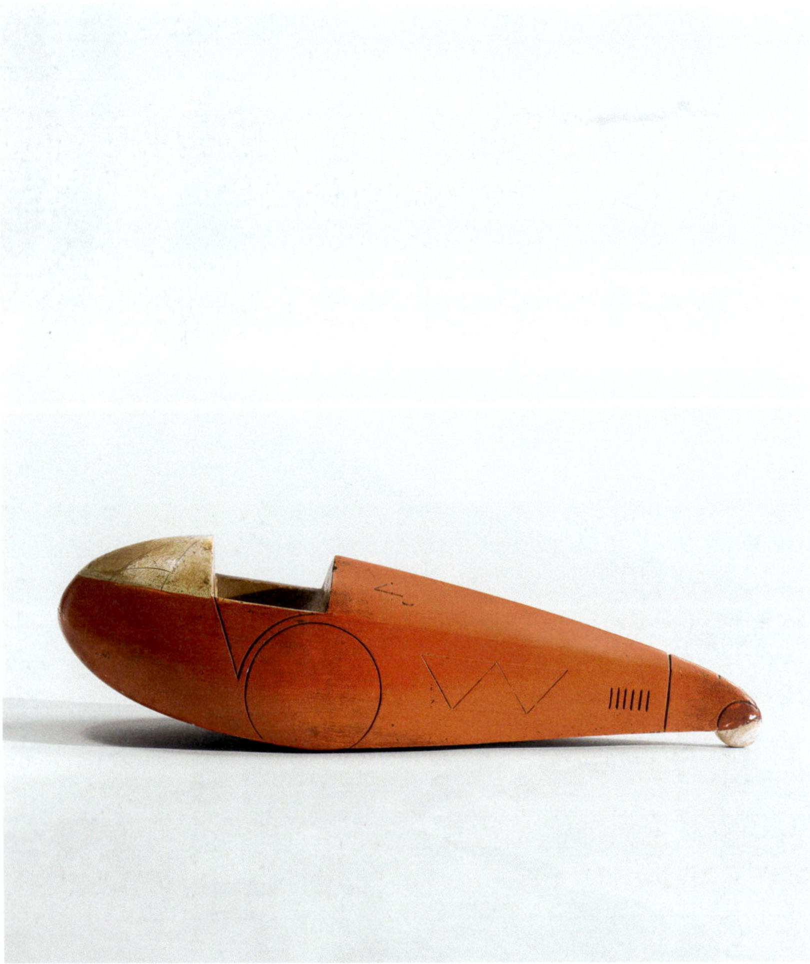

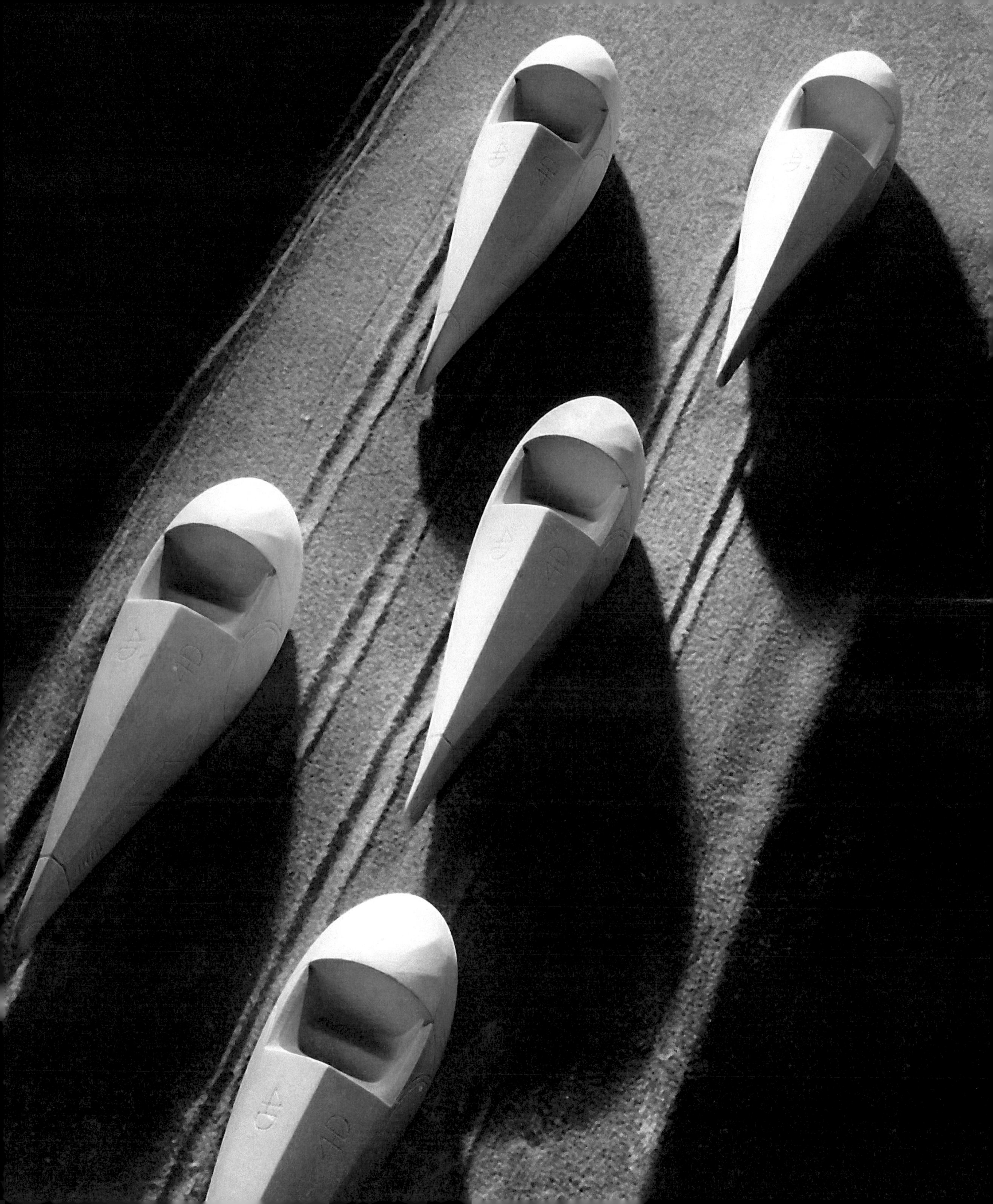

WORLD CONSCIOUSNESS: ISAMU NOGUCHI AND R. BUCKMINSTER FULLER

Florence Ostende

Isamu Noguchi's kaleidoscopic career across sculpture, architecture, dance and design spanned six decades of the twentieth century, running parallel with the development of the turbojet engine, quantum mechanics, nuclear power, radiocarbon dating, artificial hearts, modern rocketry and DNA sequencing. Noguchi thought of sculpture as invention, which he considered a characteristically American attitude: 'every American is an inventor, in a sense. After all, that's how America was made, by invention – a screwdriver, a gear, or what-have-you … We Americans admire people like Alexander Graham Bell. They are the real artists of America.'[1] His belief in the utopian value of technological progress was profoundly influenced by his encounter with architect and inventor R. Buckminster Fuller in 1929; he later said of him: 'Believing in man's essential rationality, Bucky remains the supreme optimist – there is a way out … He is a true believer, a prophet of our times.'[2]

In a telegram to Noguchi written in 1940, Fuller inscribed four words that summarised the scope of their intellectual dialogue: 'TRIANGLE INTELLIGENCE FAITH LOVE'.[3] This enigmatic slogan composed of conflicting but attracting

1 Isamu Noguchi, 'Artists in Their Own Words: Isamu Noguchi by Paul Cummings' (1979), in *Isamu Noguchi: Essays and Conversations*, ed. Diane Apostolos-Cappadona and Bruce Altshuler (New York: Harry N. Abrams, 1987), p. 138. See also Isamu Noguchi, 'Sculpture as Invention', after 1951, The Noguchi Museum Archives, MS_WRI_017_001.

2 Isamu Noguchi, 'Buckminster Fuller: A Reminiscence of Four Decades', *Architectural Forum*, no. 136 (January–February 1972), p. 59, reprinted in *Isamu Noguchi: Essays and Conversations*, p. 119.

3 R. Buckminster Fuller, telegram to Isamu Noguchi, 15 April 1930, The Noguchi Museum Archives, MS_COR_254_006.

polarities mirrored the dialectic creativity that shaped their five-decade friendship.[4] The coexistence of rationality, intuition, pragmatism, play and spirituality was instrumental to their shared purpose to serve humanity. Noguchi conceived of sculpture as an ecosystem of dynamic forces affecting each other, as in nature's own structure: 'What I'm really interested in is continuity. I believe it's called entropy, this dissolution, this participation of the awareness of the continuity of things which is an appreciation of nature, the flow. I come from some place,I disappear into some place.'[5] Fuller believed that Noguchi could materialise such flow because he was able to embrace nature's unpredictable irregularities. Noguchi interpreted this dynamic notion of dialectics in the arrangement of eighteen Aji granite stones in *Practice Rocks in Placement* (1982–83): 'Impersonal parts that became a whole, like beads that make a necklace. It is synergy, as Bucky claimed, that makes a whole which is more than its parts.'[6]

4 Isamu Noguchi, 'Lecture at International University of Art', 9 October 1970, p. 8, Noguchi Archive, MS_WRI_028_006. See also Valerie J. Fletcher, *Isamu Noguchi: Master Sculptor* (London: Scala, 2004), p. 45.

5 Transcript of 'A Conversation with Isamu Noguchi' by Nancy E. Miller, 8 July 1977, p. 5, The Noguchi Museum Archives, MS_WRI_046_001.

6 Isamu Noguchi, *The Isamu Noguchi Garden Museum* (New York: Harry N. Abrams, 1987), p. 38.

However, a few months before Fuller's death in 1983, Noguchi wrote a letter to his friend addressing the estrangement the pair now felt from one another:

> I am sorry to hear from Priscilla, that you feel our friendship betrayed by my rather despairing attitude toward the quality of life that science has brought and your importance to me in this awareness … Industry is their tool not ours and art becomes more and more subject to their economy … Perhaps I fail in optimism – I do not fail in my deep regard for our long friendship and unbound gratitude for all you have taught me.[7]

7 Isamu Noguchi, letter to R. Buckminster Fuller, 19 April 1983, The Noguchi Museum Archives, MS_COR_246_025.

What could have caused this disillusionment felt by Noguchi, an artist who shared Fuller's belief in the power of creation and invention as a vital, regenerative force in civilisation? This essay explores the intellectual foundations and historical contingency that provoked moments of rupture and synergy between the two polymaths' shared ambition to improve the way people live and humanity's relationship to the planet Earth. 'I know where every foreseeably available second should go', Fuller told his friend in the wake of his 85th birthday: 'towards advancing the chances of all humanity becoming physically successful and metaphysically gratified'. Acknowledging the critical role of friends and relatives in supporting his life's purpose, the author of *Critical Path* concluded: 'I love you. Bucky.'[8]

8 R. Buckminster Fuller, letter to Isamu Noguchi, 7 November 1980, The Noguchi Museum Archives, MS_COR_246_006.

Hope for the Future

Fuller's remarkably dense study of Noguchi published in the magazine *The Palette* in 1960 conflated the artist's life with mankind's great technical and scientific achievements: 'Isamu Noguchi and the airplane were both born in the United States of America in the first decade of the twentieth century.'[9] He recalled their first encounter as occurring in 'the year Henry Ford made chrome nickel steel commercially available for the first time in history'.[10] In 1929, Noguchi made a bronze bust of his new friend, which he plated with a layer of shiny chrome (p. 50), a new material used in automobile manufacturing and commercial design. His portrait in chrome represented Fuller's ideals, which the sculptor defined as the 'American dream of material progress',[11] a future characterised by technological optimism and invention. In 1933 Noguchi

9 R. Buckminster Fuller, 'Isamu Noguchi', *The Palette: The Magazine of the Connecticut Arts Association* (Winter 1960), p. 2, The Noguchi Museum Archives, B_CLI_0673_1960.

10 Ibid., p. 21. Although Fuller writes, 'I met Isamu Noguchi on his return to America in 1928', their first encounter is known to have taken place in 1929.

11 Noguchi, 'Buckminster Fuller: A Reminiscence', p. 119.

pursued his interest in the figure of the inventor with the chrome-plated model *Monument to Ben Franklin* (p. 66), considering the politician's 1752 kite experiment with electricity 'an expression of America' combining 'intelligence and practicality', qualities he aspired to and likewise admired in Fuller.[12] Amid the grim landscape of the Great Depression, Fuller's sheet aluminium Dymaxion House, an idea first conceived in 1927, was a forerunner of mass-produced affordable housing and embodied the myth of American industry as promoting the most modern advances in engineering and technology. Noguchi's choice of stainless steel, a symbol of the flourishing automobile industry, for *News* (1938–40, p. 79), a commission for the Associated Press Building at 50 Rockefeller Plaza, mirrored the new technologies of speed and communication associated in the public imagination with American freedom.

12 Thomas Hine, 'A Flashy Birthday Gift to Philadelphia', *Philadelphia Inquirer*, 10 March 1982, Section B, pp. 1 and 4, quoted in Hayden Herrera, *Listening to Stone: The Art and Life of Isamu Noguchi* (London: Thames & Hudson, 2015), p. 356.

The first collaboration to emerge from the dialogue between the pair was the plaster model for Fuller's aluminium Dymaxion Car (1932–33, p. 52), a prototype vehicle that the inventor hoped would eventually be able to travel on land, sea and in the air. Its streamlined, aerodynamic curves similarly characterised Noguchi's *Miss Expanding Universe* (1932). Suspended from the ceiling, this female figure in lightweight cast aluminium seemed to soar like a plane. Inspired by Hubble's law, which describes the unfixed, expanding nature of the universe, the sculpture made direct reference in its title – which was suggested by Fuller – to the astrophysicist Arthur Eddington's recent book *The Expanding Universe*.[13] Celebrated on the cover of Fuller's architecture magazine *Shelter* in November 1932 (p. 280), the plaster cast for *Miss Expanding Universe* (p. 68) expressed the sculptor's passionate love for the dancer and choreographer Ruth Page. Their shared interest in the infinity of space and cosmic scale echoed their boundless devotion to one another. Page performed her dance *Expanding Universe* the same year in a costume Noguchi designed (p. 69), a sack dress whose jersey cloth stretched to extend the sculptural possibilities of body weight, mass and gravity. Under the spell of Albert Einstein's theory of relativity, Page wrote a short poem-statement on her dance piece in which she described her choreographical gesture as a fourth-dimensional cosmic expansion against flat Earth theory and as 'non-Euclidean-cosmic-relativity Einsteinean geometry'.[14]

13 Sir Arthur Eddington, *The Expanding Universe* (London: Cambridge University Press, 1933). The publication was preceded by a lecture given in Cambridge, Massachusetts, in September 1932. See Dakin Hart, 'Space, Choreographed: Noguchi and Ruth Page', exhibition pamphlet, The Noguchi Museum, New York (New York: The Isamu Noguchi Foundation and Garden Museum, 2013), n.p.

14 Ruth Page, statement about *Expanding Universe*, undated (Jerome Robbins Dance Division, New York Public Library for the Performing Arts), reproduced in *On Becoming an Artist: Isamu Noguchi and his Contemporaries, 1922–1960*, ed. Amy Wolf (New York: The Isamu Noguchi Foundation and Garden Museum, 2010), p. 51.

A few years later, Noguchi paid tribute to Einstein's formula of mass–energy equivalence, $E = mc^2$, in his mural *History Mexico* (1936, pp. 82–83), conveying its importance as a positive force to transform the world and redefine fundamental realities for human existence. Set amid the triumphant clenched fist of the worker and iconographic depictions of capitalism, fascism and war, this symbol of scientific knowledge and hope for the future had been drawn from a telegram from Fuller to the artist that unpacked the revolutionary equation as 'A UNIT AND A RATE OF PERFECTION'.[15] In his statement 'What's the Matter with Sculpture', written that same year, Noguchi advocated 'micro- and macro-cosmic' science as instrumental to sculpture's political and social role in combatting 'today's problems'.[16] Growing increasingly sceptical of the idea of pure abstract sculpture, which he associated with his early apprenticeship with Constantin Brâncuși in Paris, Fuller became his new mentor: 'Your ideas were an abstraction which I could accept as being part of life and useful.'[17]

15 R. Buckminster Fuller, telegram to Isamu Noguchi, Fuller MSS, Box 39, vol. 62, reproduced in Shoji Sadao, *Buckminster Fuller and Isamu Noguchi: Best of Friends* (New York/Milan: The Isamu Noguchi Foundation and Garden Museum/5 Continents Editions, 2011), p. 107.

16 Isamu Noguchi, 'What's the Matter with Sculpture', *Art Front*, 16 (September–October 1936), pp. 13–14, reprinted in *Isamu Noguchi: Essays and Conversations*, p. 18.

17 Isamu Noguchi in Michael Blackwood, dir., *Isamu Noguchi*, documentary (Michael Blackwood Productions, 1972).

Noguchi's early mentor Edward A. Rumely, an industrialist and founder of the progressive Interlaken School in Indiana, had encouraged his students to become 'artists, inventors and captains of industry'.[18] Combining Jean-Jacques Rousseau's philosophy of experience, John Dewey's pragmatism and Frederick Winslow Taylor's efficiency principles, the school's hands-on, practical training introduced Noguchi to carpentry, agriculture and industrial techniques during his short stay before the school closed unexpectedly in August 1918 for the war effort. Rumely had supported his former student's foray into industrial design, including his manufactured stove timer *Measured Time* (c. 1932) and the baby monitor *Radio Nurse* (1937, p. 85) in Bakelite – the first synthetic plastic. *Radio Nurse*, his first patent, perfectly illustrated Noguchi's dual background in traditional craft and machine efficiency.[19] His confidence in progress and the future of humanity alongside his interest in cellular structure were also present in his unrealised *Medical Building Frieze* (c. 1937), whose representation of blood transfusions and medical technology recalled his earlier premedical studies at Columbia University.

18 Deborah A. Goldberg: 'Visionary Designer and "World Citizen"', in Goldberg, *Isamu Noguchi, Patent Holder: Designing the World of Tomorrow*, exh. cat., The Noguchi Museum and Geoffrey Yeh Art Gallery, New York (New York: St John's University, 2015), p. 4.

19 Over the course of his lifetime Noguchi realised thirteen patents in the US and twenty in Japan.

Reflections

Noguchi was, in Fuller's words, 'history's first world-town, industrial philosophy artist'.[20] His machine age vocabulary, exemplified by the materiality of chrome, aluminium and stainless steel, addressed the role of science in developing the future of humanity while making visible certain physical and phenomenological qualities not yet captured by scientific discourse: 'What Noguchi saw that others did not see, was that completely reflective surfaces provided a fundamental invisible sculpture, hidden in and communicating through a succession of live reflections of images surrounding the invisible sculpture.'[21] Fuller, whose very first invention allowed seaplanes to land safely on water, compared these perceptions to a seapilot trying to land on mirror-like water: it is only when the distorted shapes of the environment are reflected in it that we can see it and attest to its existence.

20 Fuller, 'Isamu Noguchi', p. 4.

21 Ibid., p. 21.

Inspired by Fuller's redecoration of Romany Marie's tavern in Greenwich Village with silver paint, Noguchi painted his loft in silver from floor to ceiling: 'one was almost blinded by the lack of the shadows. There I made his portrait head in a chromeplated bronze, also form without shadow.'[22] The polished chrome of the Fuller bust would bounce back distorted reflections, making the precise features and contours of the face hard to read. The hazy blur of the eye sockets evoked Fuller's childhood spent perceiving large, distorted patterns as reality, having been born with crossed eyes: 'While I saw two dark areas on human faces, I did not see a human eye or a teardrop or a human hair until I was four.'[23] Though the mirrored head was directed outward on to the surrounding world, the smooth cavities of the eyes looked inward, into an invisible space only Fuller – the mind of a visionary – could see. This omnidirectional gaze onto the world and into the self materialised Einstein's metaphor for the curved structure of space: if you looked out into the universe with a sufficiently powerful telescope, you'd see the back of your own head.[24] This alternative perspective was echoed in Noguchi's self-portrait *Boy Looking through Legs (Morning Exercises)* (1933, pp. 70–71), a body arranged in an extreme arc so as to look at the world upside down. This flipped horizon is perceived through the young boy's translucid blue eyes – a signifier of the artist's Japanese American biracial heritage – eager to discover the world and where he belongs.

22 Noguchi, 'Buckminster Fuller: A Reminiscence', p. 116.

23 R. Buckminster Fuller, 'Comprehensive Design Strategy, Phase II (1967) Document 5', World Resources Inventory, Southern Illinois University, Carbondale, Illinois, available at Buckminster Fuller Institute, www.bfi.org/sites/default/files/attachments/literature_source/wdsd_phase2_doc5_chronofile.pdf, accessed 13 April 2021.

24 Paul Davies, *Space and Time in the Modern Universe* (New York: Cambridge University Press, 1977), p. 151.

One fundamental idea uniting these two portraits (and the two men's friendship) was the profound belief in the intimate porosity between interiority and exteriority, between the self and the universe. Fuller's first text on Noguchi, entitled 'Colloidals in Time' (1932), highlighted the sculptor's words on channelling the world into self-less art: 'the universe flows through the self for expression.'[25] This disbelief in art for art's sake was at the heart of the artist's wish 'to view nature through nature's eyes, and to ignore man as an object for special veneration', which called to mind Fuller's revelatory dictum: 'you do not belong to you. You belong to Universe.'[26] Both men looked to the structure of nature for primordial forms and patterns that could serve and improve humanity.

25 R. Buckminster Fuller, 'Colloidals in Time: Isamu Noguchi', *Shelter*, vol. 2, no. 5 (November 1932), p. 111.

26 Quoted in Barry M. Katz, '1927, Bucky's Annus Mirabilis', in *New Views on R. Buckminster Fuller*, ed. Hsiao-yun Chu and Roberto G. Trujillo (Stanford, CA: Stanford University Press, 2009), p. 23.

Noguchi captured Fuller's transcendental-mystical view of life in the figure *Glad Day* (1930, p. 279), which he gifted to him. Inspired by William Blake's picture of the same name, also known as *Albion Rose* (c. 1794), this portrait expressing Fuller's vitality in powerful outstretched limbs was made, according to their common friend the architect Shoji Sadao, 'probably in recognition of their shared vision of universal brotherhood, of Bucky's vision of "Universal Man" and of Blake's "idea of the Redemption of the soul and spirit from the prison of the body, and in the political sense the state of revolutionary consciousness"'.[27] Blake's philosophy of nature, imagination and freedom had a profound influence on Noguchi. A writer, editor and passionate gardener, Noguchi's mother Léonie Gilmour had written a short comparative text linking Blake's poem 'Ah! Sun-flower' and the Japanese word for a sunflower (*higuruma*, sun wheel).[28] Blake's mythology had travelled across the Atlantic via the transcendentalism of Ralph Waldo Emerson. Gilmour referred in her writing to Emerson's figure of the nonconformist and poet who speaks 'with the flower of the mind' – a prescient metaphor of the vision she nurtured for her son.[29] Coincidentally or not, Fuller's proto-feminist great-aunt Margaret Fuller was a leading figure in American transcendentalism as well as a friend and collaborator of Emerson's.

27 Sadao, *Buckminster Fuller and Isamu Noguchi*, p. 97. The author's quote refers to the British Museum's entry for *Albion Rose* (*Glad Day*).

28 Léonie Gilmour, 'Draft of "The Sunflower"', undated manuscript, The Noguchi Museum Archives, MS_FAM_050_007.

29 Léonie Gilmour quotes Emerson's essay 'The Poet' (c. 1843) in her text 'George Meredith – A Study'. See 'Leonie Gilmour notebook', manuscript, c. 1901–11, p. 6, The Noguchi Museum Archives, MS_FAM_014_001.

Searching for a New Myth

Noguchi's education across different cultures – from Jesuit Catholicism to Graeco-Roman mythology and Swedenborgian philosophy, to animistic Shinto and Buddhism[30] – played a role in his complex understanding of American identity and motivated his desire to travel the world. Fuller's vision of planetary consciousness provided Noguchi with a cosmopolitan emancipation from his binational heritage. He interpreted Noguchi's travels as an 'expansive phase' in his 'significantly universal development'[31] as somebody who embraced the world simultaneously locally, globally and cosmically. As such Noguchi was the incarnation of the 'one world-island', a notion Fuller articulated in his Dymaxion Map, in which all the world's continents are interconnected. Fuller opposed Einstein's vision of a unified cosmos, which he called 'World Two', to Newton's static and fragmented 'World One', and saw Noguchi as a pioneer who 'travelled on and on, not as a tourist, not as a dilettante escapist, not as a routine airline pilot, nor as sailor, soldier or gypsy, but as the intuitive artist precursor of World Two's normally evoluting, normally kinetic, one-town world man.'[32] He added, 'As the unpremeditated prototype artist of a one-world-town cosmos, Isamu has always been inherently at home – everywhere.'[33] However, this narrative, driven by scientific progress, did not acknowledge

30 Fletcher, *Isamu Noguchi*, p. 19.

31 Fuller, telegram to Noguchi, 15 April 1930, The Noguchi Museum Archives, MS_COR_254_006.

32 Fuller, 'Isamu Noguchi', pp. 3–4.

33 Ibid., p. 4.

the technological innovations that resulted in the devastation of the Second World War.

The Nazi–Soviet non-aggression pact of 23 August 1939 had disillusioned Noguchi in his attitude towards Marxist political ideals, and a collaborative drawing made with Arshile Gorky now conjured the growing anxiety around Hitler's invasion of Poland, which took place just a week after the pact's signing. Noguchi experienced the 1941 attack on Pearl Harbor as an 'unmitigated shock': 'With a flash I realized I was no longer the sculptor alone. I was not just American but Nisei. A Japanese American.'[34] The disenchantment that resulted from his voluntary internment in the Poston War Relocation Center in Arizona in 1942 – along with the increased violence of discrimination at a time of widespread anti-Japanese sentiment – made him question the civic role of sculpture as a form of 'social protest'.[35] *The World is a Foxhole* (1942–43, p. 102) articulated the artist's wartime existential angst: 'The war weighed heavily on my mind', he wrote, describing the sculpture as reflecting 'The thoughts of a soldier in a foxhole: a red rag atop a pole – a signal of hope and despair.'[36] This was followed by *Monument to Heroes* (1943, p. 112), a composition in the form of a fragile column with precariously positioned bones: 'The bones of the unknown – the residue of bravery, blown by winds.'[37]

34 Isamu Noguchi, *A Sculptor's World* (London: Thames & Hudson, 1967), p. 25.

35 Noguchi describes the sculpture *Death (Lynched Figure)* (1934) as originating in 'my sudden emergence into the field of social protest'. Ibid., p. 22.

36 Noguchi, *The Isamu Noguchi Garden Museum*, p. 240.

37 Ibid., p. 282.

Filmed in Noguchi's studio in 1945, avant-garde cinema pioneer Marie Menken's experimental film *Visual Variations on Noguchi* infused the artist's sculptures with a potent sense of anguish and dread, the eerie shadows and free-falling shots accompanied by the shrill sounds of bows and plectra from a composition by Lucia Dlugoszewski. Panning across the pierced, flesh-like slate of *Gregory* (1945, p. 149), inspired by the monstrous transformation of Gregor in Franz Kafka's *The Metamorphosis*, or the suspended black star of *E=MC²* (1944, p. 114), which appears as a premonition of atomic annihilation, Menken's dancing hand-held camera and fast-paced editing rendered the protruding forms as bones and knives and turned marble veins and driftwood surfaces into burnt skin. The deformed anatomies of Noguchi's 'interlocking sculptures' contrasted with the social realist style of previous works that expressed confidence in revolution and the future.

Excavating human anatomy to its very core, these biomorphic experiments were shown in major Surrealist exhibitions between 1944 and 1947. In a civilisation devastated by the atrocities of the Second World War, Noguchi contributed to a global reconfiguration of the role of the artist as searching for a new foundation for culture. His participation in *The Imagery of Chess* (1944–45), curated by Marcel Duchamp and Max Ernst at Julien Levy Gallery in New York, brought him together with a number of artists living in exile. The hostility suffered by these European émigrés resonated with Noguchi's own experiences. In 1947, his contributions to *Bloodflames* at the Hugo Gallery in New York (pp. 146–47) engaged in a dialogue with the wall-to-ceiling environment designed for the exhibition by architect and designer Frederick Kiesler. A member of Fuller's Structural Study Associates (SSA) and an advocate of non-Euclidean geometry, Kiesler conceived an immersive, theatrical set that promoted the integration of art, architecture and the viewer in a single continuum. He called this interconnection of humanity and environment 'correalism', inspired by Fuller's 'correlation', the term he used for his cosmological model of the expanding universe.[38]

38 Frederick Kiesler, 'Architecture as Biotechnique: On Correalism and Biotechnique: Definition and Test of a New Approach to Building Design', *Architecture Record* (September 1939), pp. 60–78.

Echoing Kiesler's alternative fields of vision, Noguchi developed micro and macro perspectives that exploded the scale of human perception. Based on an image of a bombed site in the African desert, the bronze-cast *This Tortured Earth* (1942–43, p. 158) was a pre-Land art view of the earth from above 'to memorialize the tragedy of war. There is injury to the earth itself. The war machine, I thought, would be excellent equipment for sculpture, to bomb it into existence.'[39] Also on display in *Bloodflames* was the sculpture *Trinity* (1945, pp. 144–45). Named after the first ever nuclear detonation, which took place in July 1945 in the New Mexico desert, the multi-angled slate figure penetrated into the heart of nuclear fission, an atom split into smaller nuclei.

39 Noguchi, *The Isamu Noguchi Garden Museum*, p. 152.

'The Blight of Industrialism'

After the death of his father in 1947 and his friend Arshile Gorky's suicide in 1948, Noguchi's disillusionment reached its peak as he questioned the social purpose of sculpture and advocated for the reintegration of the arts:

> The tragic aftermath of two wars is a moral crisis from which there is no succor for the spirit … now there is only mechanization and the concepts of power. The blight of industrialism has pushed man into a specialized corner, and more and more he is assuming the role of spectator.[40]

40 Isamu Noguchi, 'Towards a Reintegration of the Arts', *College Art Journal*, vol. 9, no. 1 (Autumn 1949), pp. 59–60, reprinted in *Isamu Noguchi: Essays and Conversations*, p. 28.

In an attempt to define the role of the artist in the atomic age and to confront the consequences of the atomic bomb, Noguchi developed a highly critical perspective on the impact of technological advances: 'If the world would wait blowing up, I wanted to find out what sculpture had once been, to what purpose, to what end, to what it might again aspire to in a world in flux.'[41]

41 Isamu Noguchi, Bollingen Notes, 1949, p. 1, The Noguchi Museum Archives, MS_BOL_022_001.

Travelling throughout Europe and Asia in 1949–50, funded by the Bollingen Foundation, he embarked on a study of the past and positioned ancient traditions as the site for innovation, turning once more to stone, which 'is always new as the latest discovery on Mars'.[42] Upon his return to Japan in 1950, his first trip there in nineteen years, Noguchi engaged with the growing scepticism regarding Japan's modernisation and expressed an increased sense of the sacred: 'What is the artist but the channel through which spirits descend – ghosts, visions, portents, the tinkling of bells.' He added: 'New concepts of the physical world and of psychology may give insights into knowledge, but the visible world, in human terms, is more than scientific truths … Art for the first time may be said to have a world consciousness.'[43]

42 Ibid., p. 3.

43 Noguchi, *A Sculptor's World*, p. 40.

While Noguchi had been less frequently in contact with Fuller during and after the war, he remained informed of his friend's development of the Dymaxion Map and geodesic domes. Evidencing his enduring loyalty to Fuller, he had intended to create a 'Dymaxion ashtray' as 'an American expression of the machine age'.[44] In 1955, a spectacular performance brought them together once again as Fuller orchestrated the airlifting of a geodesic dome by Marine Corps helicopters at the National Aircraft Show in Philadelphia. Photographs of the event taken by Noguchi captured the lightweight structure suspended in the skies like a spaceship (p. 264). As Fuller developed light paperboard domes and shelters, Noguchi achieved the ultimate in

44 Isamu Noguchi quoted by Mary Mix, 'The Sculptor and the Ashtray', unpublished, c. 1944, The Noguchi Museum Archives, MS_PROJ_059a_001. See 'The Sculptor and the Ashtray', exhibition pamphlet, The Noguchi Museum, New York (New York: The Isamu Noguchi Foundation and Garden Museum, 2020).

weightlessness – the '"less thingness" of things' – with his first prototype *Akari* light sculptures in 1951.[45] A synthesis of tradition (*washi* paper and bamboo) and modern technology (electric light and steel legs), the *Akari* embodied the interconnectedness of custom and innovation, originality and mass production. Noguchi wrote extensively on the unique flexibility and elasticity of the fibres used in *washi*, describing their qualities, chemical composition and 'tensile strength' in Fullerian terms.[46]

45 Noguchi, *A Sculptor's World*, p. 33.

46 Isamu Noguchi, drafts of 'On Washi', 13 June 1977, The Noguchi Museum Archives, MS_WRI_045_002.

In his book *Nine Chains to the Moon* (1938), Fuller had presciently used the sculptural metaphor of a paper lampshade when describing how the human brain directs signals to enable breathing and speech: 'the air chamber expands in the form of a globular Japanese lantern with spiny, spiral horizontal arches'.[47] Noguchi's interest in paper and wood as instrumental to the robust lightness of the traditional Japanese house had led him, two decades earlier, to compare Fuller's light aluminium Dymaxion House to a pagoda, with its hexagonal spine and 'central radiating interlocking umbrella-wise roofs'.[48] The delicate concentric circles and fine folded paper of the *Akari* provided a fertile ground to articulate their shared conception of two fundamental principles of nature: compression and tension. Noguchi conceived a double helix *Akari* lamp that, like the DNA structure, formed a spiral moving outward and inward at the same time: 'the paper here is in tension. The bamboo part here is in compression.' He thought of the *Akari* as a 'fluid object' in which several tetrahedra could be combined to form an 'irregular wind'.[49] Noguchi achieved a similar idea using post-tensioning in sculpture: the tension of a hidden stainless-steel cable compressing stone to achieve a balance of forces.

47 R. Buckminster Fuller, *Nine Chains to the Moon* [1938] (Mineola, NY: Dover Publications, 2020), p. 45.

48 Isamu Noguchi, 'Shelters of the Orient', *Shelter*, vol. 2, no. 5 (November 1932), p. 96.

49 Isamu Noguchi, 'Lecture at International University of Art', 7 October 1970, pp. 7, 8, 11, The Noguchi Museum Archives, MS_WRI_028_003.

It was the weightless, gravity-defying steel and glass skyscrapers of New York that inspired the works Noguchi made in 1958 in collaboration with the workshop of lighting designer Edison Price. Without any welding or fastening techniques, aluminium sheets were bent into continuous folds, like the paper of an *Akari* light or origami. They seemed to evidence a return to the artist's pre-war mindset; as he wrote:

> The new materials remake the world. We live in a tensile world of space. It is one of molecular structure and sub-atomic particles. It is the world of the airplane, the speed – my world … This would bring me in contact with that industrial apparatus which is the real America … I wanted to deny weight and substance.[50]

50 Noguchi, *A Sculptor's World*, pp. 35–36.

Suspended in the corner of his studio like a satellite in orbit, the wall sculpture *Bucky* (1943, p. 115) was a portrait of Fuller made of wooden triangles and an abstract form connected by delicate wires. From the pyramidal forms in *Monument to the Plow* (1933, p. 65), *Sculpture to be Seen from Mars* (1947, p. 159) and *California Scenario* (1980–82, p. 306) to his prismatic and hexagonal structures such as *Prismatic Table* (1957, p. 200), Noguchi's sculptural experiments and landscape projects often called to mind the geometric modelling inherent to Fuller's 'Synergetics' theory of dynamic systems, in particular triangulated structures such as the tetrahedron, which Fuller conceived as 'a minimum structural system of the Universe'.[51]

51 R. Buckminster Fuller, 'Everything I Know, Session 5', Buckminster Fuller Institute, www.bfi.org/about-fuller/resources/everything-i-know/session-5, accessed 13 April 2021.

In Orbit

The multifaceted purpose of Fuller's geodesic dome projects prompted Noguchi to apply these modular geometric patterns to playground sculptures, suggesting in 1965 that Fuller's 'large aluminum truss octet ... would make a marvelous play object' for a playground commission in Tokyo and that a geodesic sphere could function as 'a beautiful jungle gym'.[52] This eventually resulted in the playground element *Octetra* (c. 1965–66, p. 303), 'a Bucky-inspired polyhedron based on a tetrahedron that had its four corners truncated with a spherical void at its center'.[53] While Fuller and Sadao had been immersed in the vast, ambitious Tetrahedron City project (1967), a proposal for a floating city in Tokyo Bay, Noguchi's unrealised 'lunar landscape' for Expo '70 in Osaka (p. 234) included an *Octetra*, a *Tetrahedron*, a moon-like silver sphere and a projection dome, among other elements – the large scale of which reflected the idea of harmony between man-made technology and nature while also echoing Fuller's ethos of 'the transcendance [*sic*] of human values'.[54] The high-tech fountains Noguchi successfully realised for the exposition conjured the theme of 'Progress and Harmony for Mankind' promoted by its organisers; he later explored similar forms in the *Horace E. Dodge and Son Memorial Fountain* in Detroit (1972–79) as well as in proposals for a *Friendship Fountain* (1976) for the Missouri River and the geodesic dome theatre he proposed for the Martha Graham Dance Company (1976).

52 Isamu Noguchi, letter to R. Buckminster Fuller, 28 August 1965, The Noguchi Museum Archives, MS_PROJ_226_052.

53 Sadao, *Buckminster Fuller and Isamu Noguchi*, p. 184.

54 Isamu Noguchi and Pavilion Associates (Peter Floyd, John McHale, Shoji Sadao), 'U.S. Exhibit for Expo 70 at Osaka, Japan', c. 1967, The Noguchi Museum Archives, MS_COR_248_006.

Reflecting on his granite sculpture *Planet in Transit #1* (1968–72, p. 226), Noguchi described the cosmic scale of his friendship with Fuller: 'Our imagination expands as far as our expanding knowledge and beyond. We were already there in orbit, Bucky and I. New York was our city that glimmers in the distance, and we talked of time and cosmic space.'[55] With the landing of Apollo 11 on the Moon in 1969 and the widely reproduced photograph of Earth known as *The Blue Marble*, taken in 1972, space age euphoria reached its climax. The image captured the idea of the planet as a single entity of global interconnectedness. Noguchi's visits to the eighteenth-century Jantar Mantar observatory sites in Delhi and Jaipur in India between 1949 and 1960 influenced his designs for a *Sunken Garden* at Yale's Beinecke Rare Book and Manuscript Library (1960–64, pp. 218–19) and the *Garden of the Future* made for the IBM Headquarters in Armonk, New York (1964), and culminated in the spiralling marble playground sculpture *Slide Mantra* (1986, pp. 252–53). The 'awareness of outer space' represented by the study of celestial objects and astronomical instruments such as sky reflectors, found in such early observatories, was also manifest in the artist's *Sky Viewing Sculpture* (1969) at Western Washington University,[56] the *Sky Gate* (1976–77, p. 305) in Honolulu and the stainless steel tetrahedral mist fountain *Intetra* (1974–76).

55 Noguchi, *The Isamu Noguchi Garden Museum*, p. 138.

56 Noguchi, *The Isamu Noguchi Garden Museum*, p. 194.

Noguchi and Fuller's intellectual bond and mutual world consciousness continued over the following years as they visited sites together in Italy, Canada, Israel and India. But in the months leading up to Fuller's death in July 1983, Noguchi's personal correspondence with his long-time companion conveyed a growing distance between their respective attitudes to the present. In a March 1983 letter in which Noguchi expresses support for Fuller's recently published book *Grunch of Giants*, which interrogates the corporate power of the military-industrial complex, he articulates a potent sense of hopelessness and finality:

> The seizure of science by corporations brings us to this brink – the scientists from some of whom I have heard seem filled with remorse. Was there something wrong in delving into nature's secrets? Nature's own rhythm of growth and decay is replaced by an encroaching death of time.[57]

After Fuller's death, Noguchi continued to celebrate his friend's idealism, highlighting his dreams and ideas on the unlimited potential of humans and cosmic energy; he compared him to the prophetic William Blake, whose 'childlike faith' in the future was only hope for the young: 'What was so wonderful about Bucky was his constant belief in the success of the human family through science. But you all know what has happened and I myself have grown older while Bucky became always younger.'[58] These conflicting feelings must have been in Noguchi's mind as he developed his *Challenger Memorial* in 1986, commemorating the space shuttle disaster in January that year, using a spiralling column of tetrahedrons ascending into the sky.

Florence Ostende is the curator of *Isamu Noguchi* at Barbican, London

57 Isamu Noguchi, letter to R. Buckminster Fuller, 9 March 1983, The Noguchi Museum Archives, MS_COR_246_022.

58 Noguchi, 'Remembrance of R. Buckminster Fuller', c. 1983, The Noguchi Museum Archives, MS_COR_256_004.

Model for *Play Mountain*, 1933
(unrealised)
Bronze
8.6 × 64.1 × 73 cm

Model for *Monument to the Plow*, 1933
(unrealised)
Plaster
Dimensions unknown

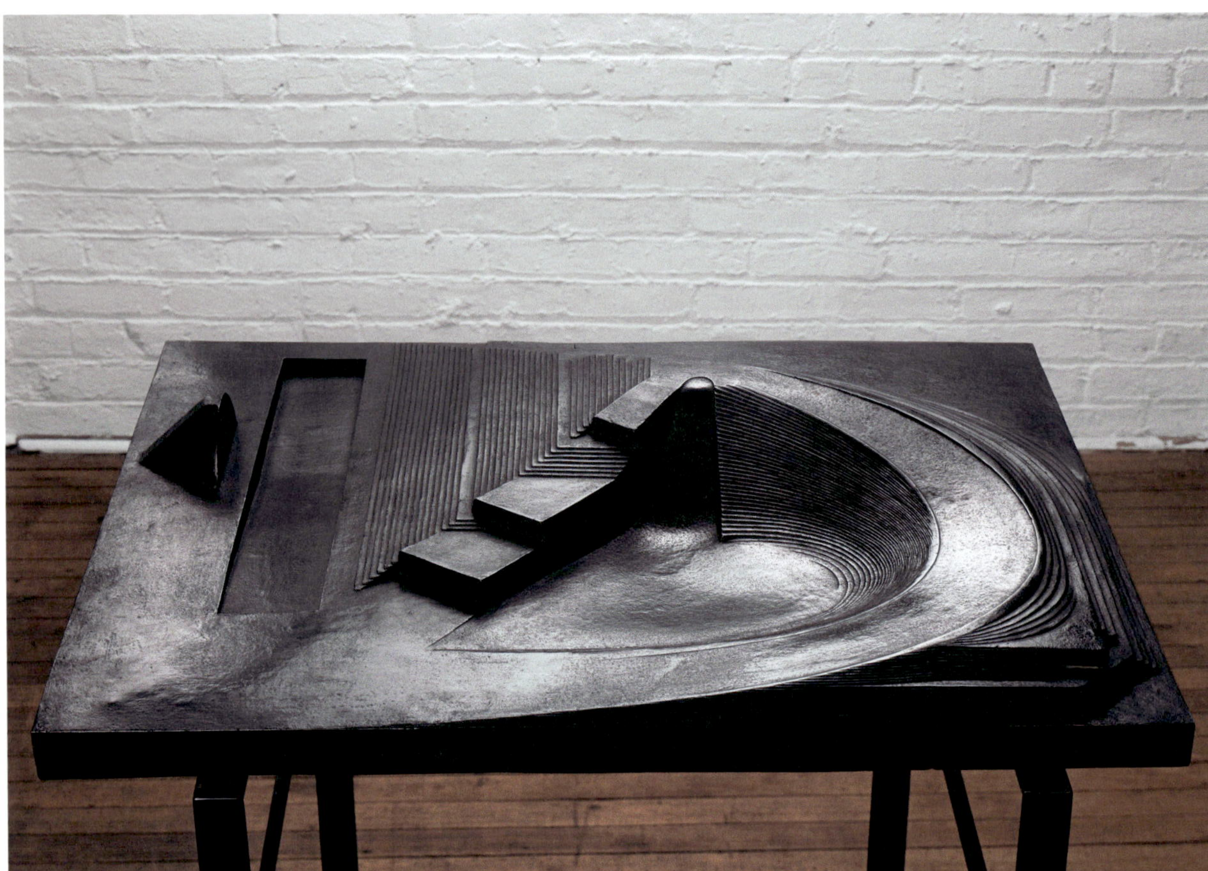

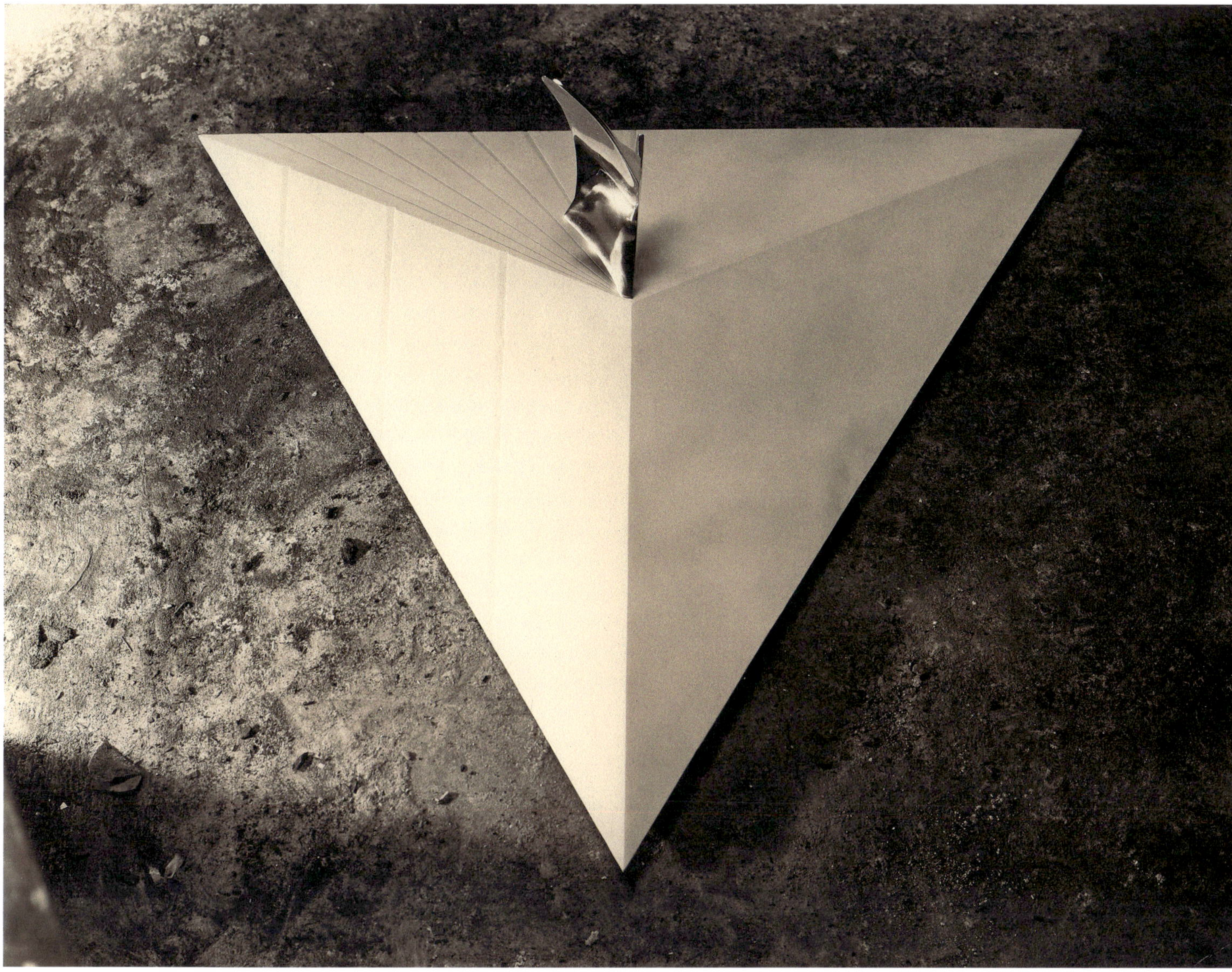

Model for *Bolt of Lightning, Memorial to Ben Franklin*, 1933–35
Bronze with chrome nickel plating and aluminium
123.2 × 59.1 × 32.4 cm

Monument to Ben Franklin, 1979–85
Stainless steel
Philadelphia
H. 31 m

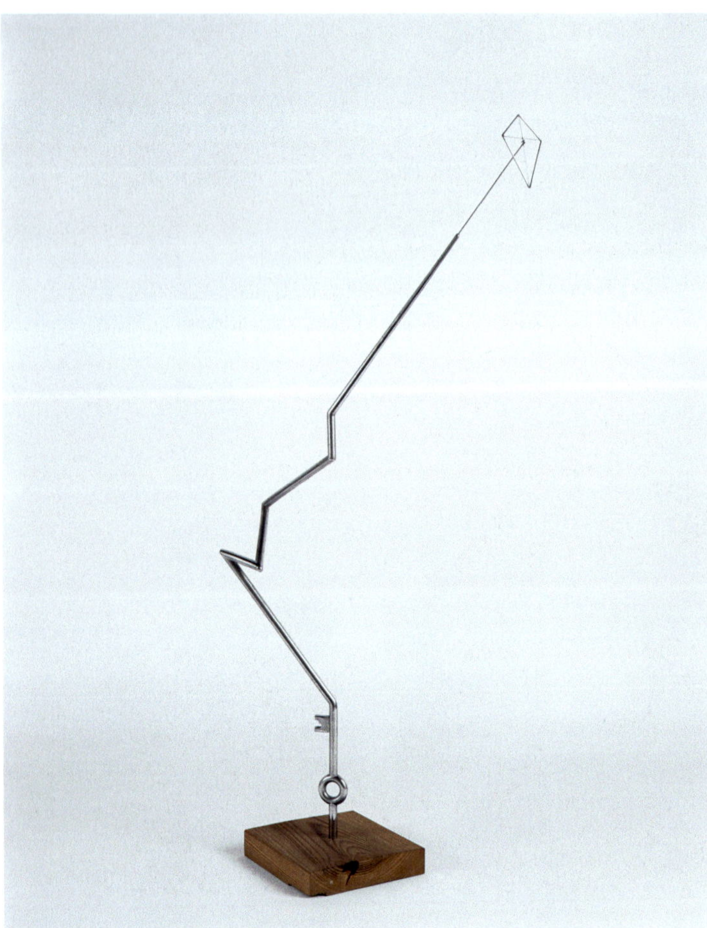

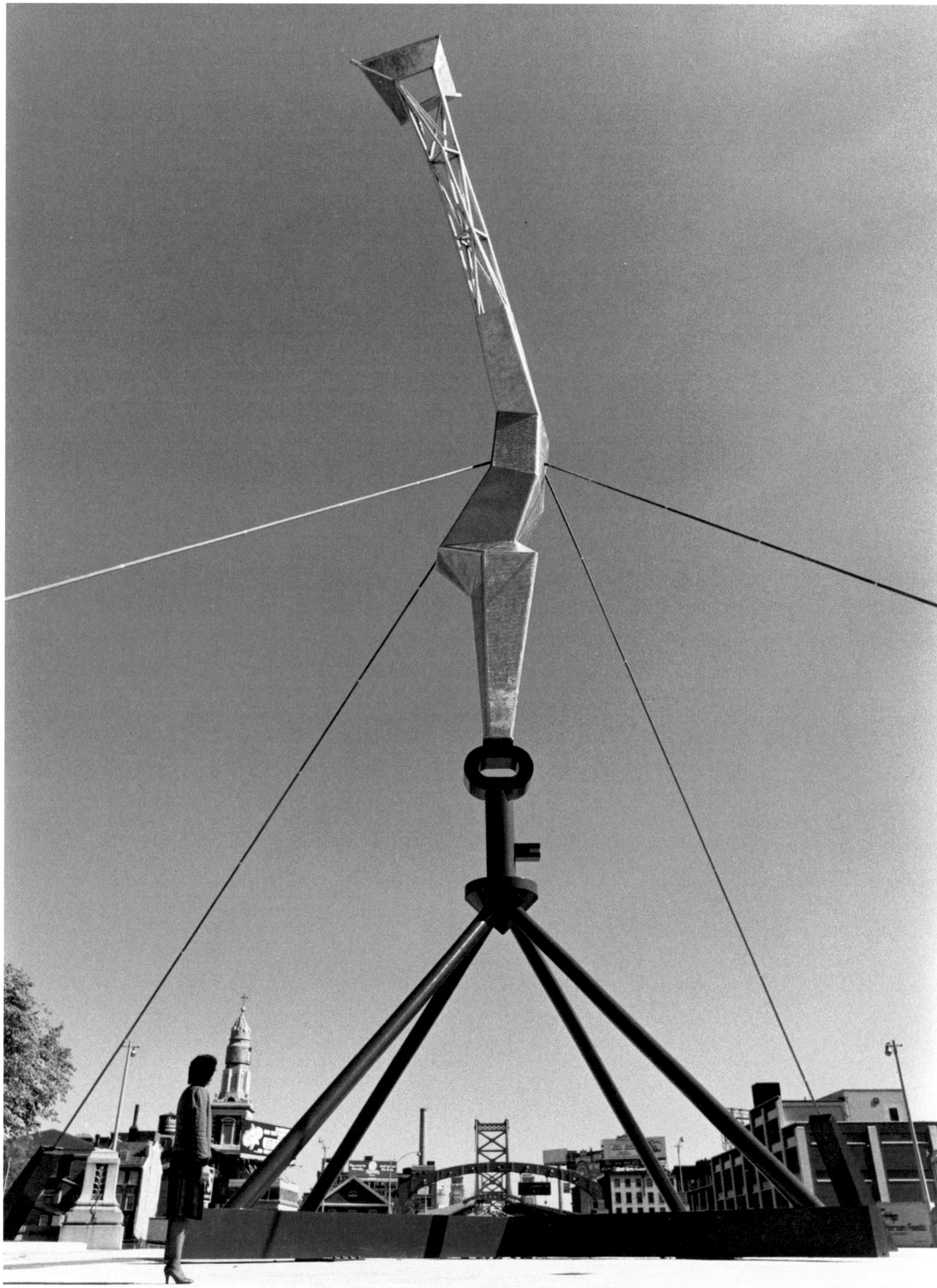

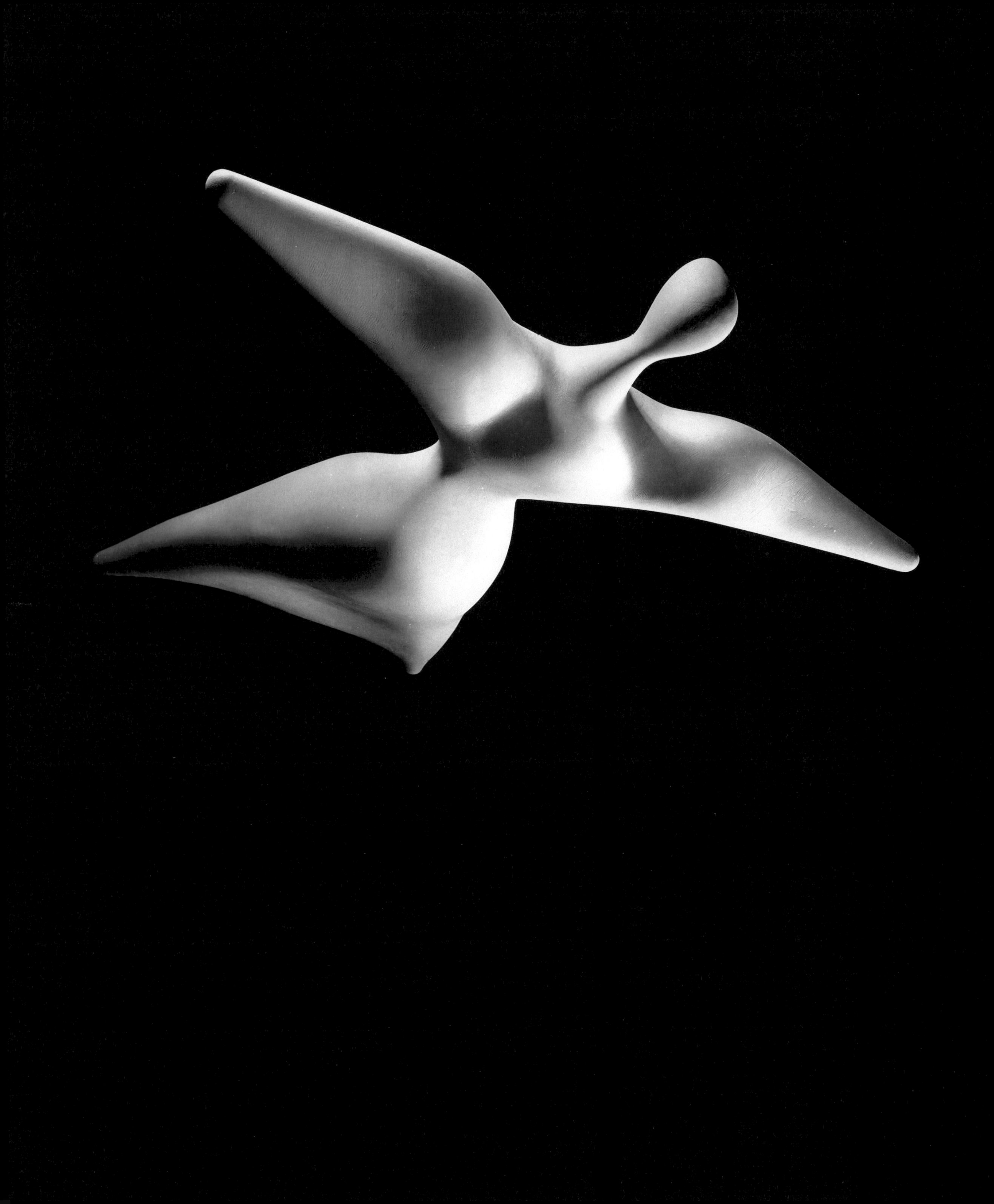

Miss Expanding Universe, 1932
Plaster
104.14 × 88.6 cm

Ruth Page in *Costume Sack* for
***Expanding Universe*, 1932**

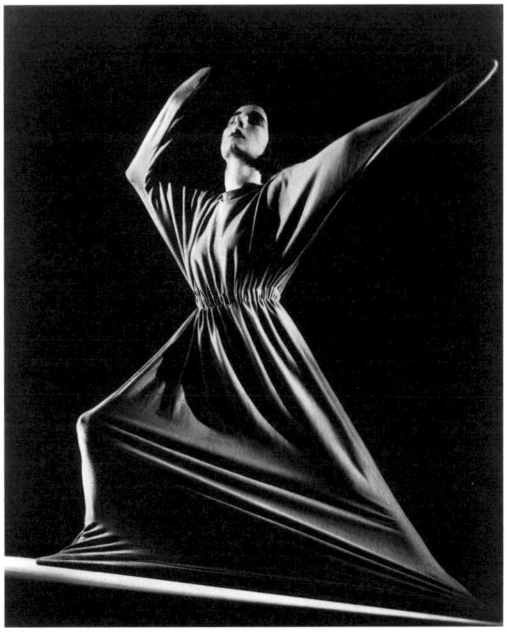

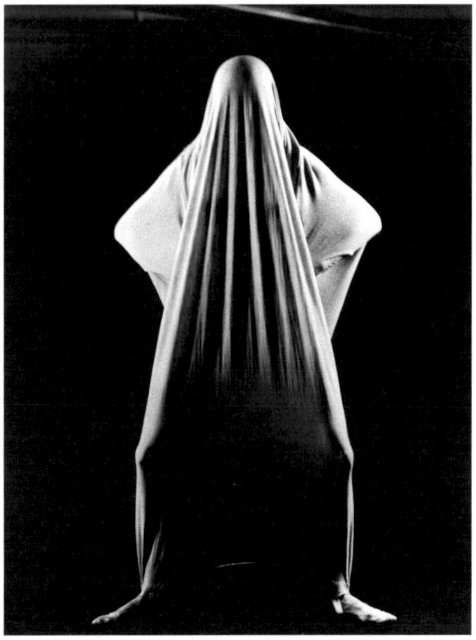

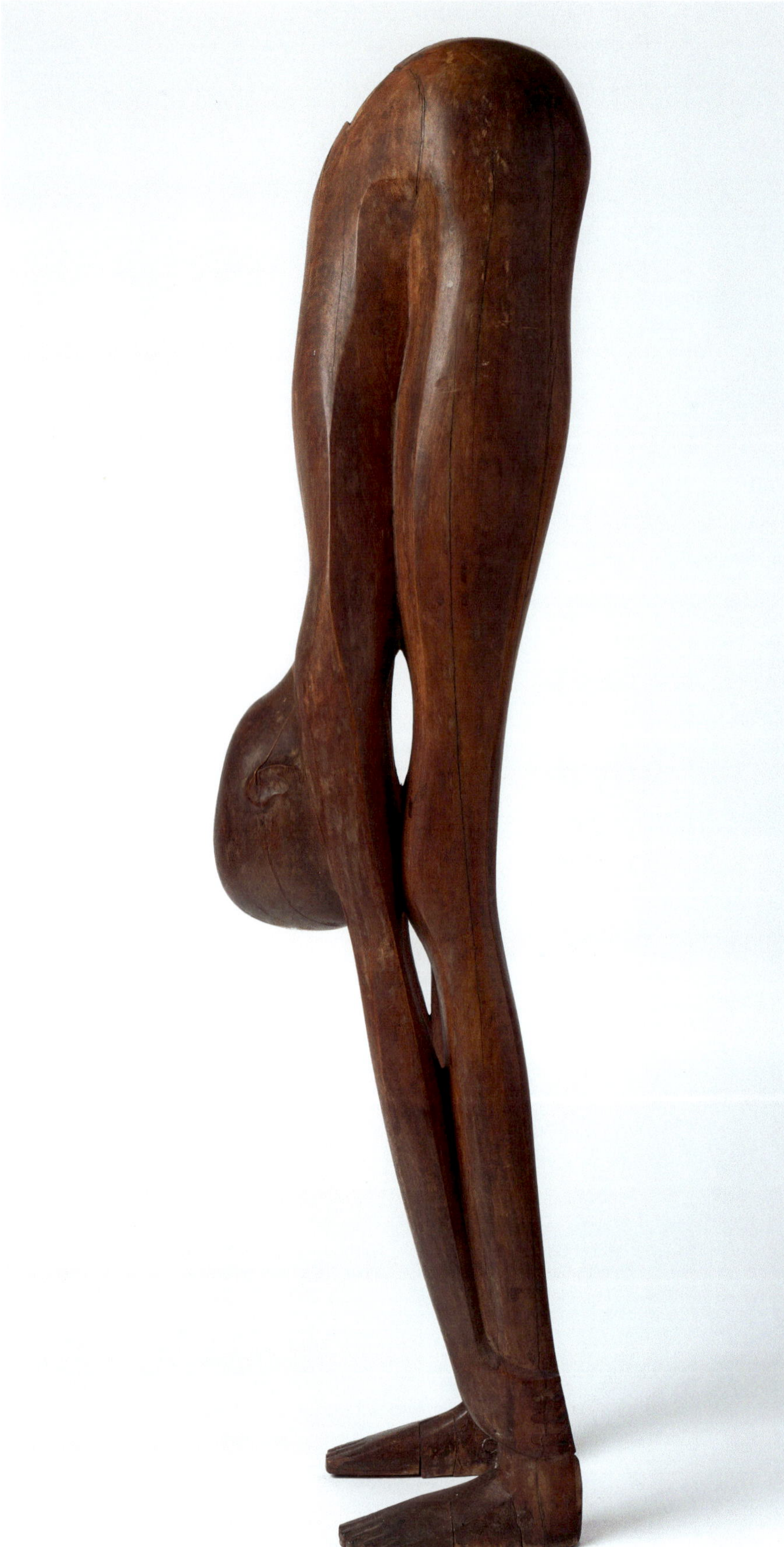

Boy Looking through Legs (Morning Exercises), 1933
Pear wood and blue beads
72.4 × 18.7 × 18.1 cm

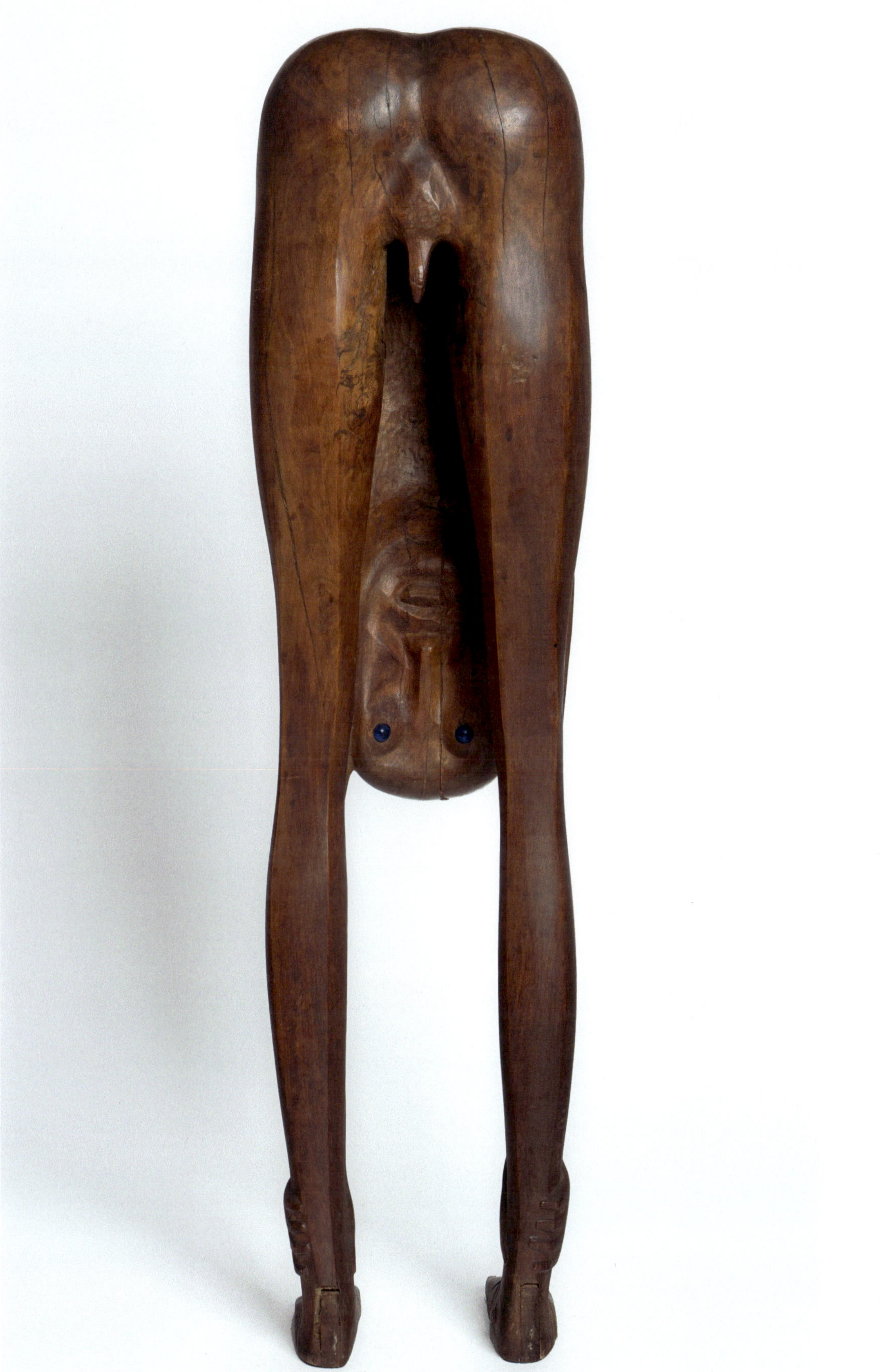

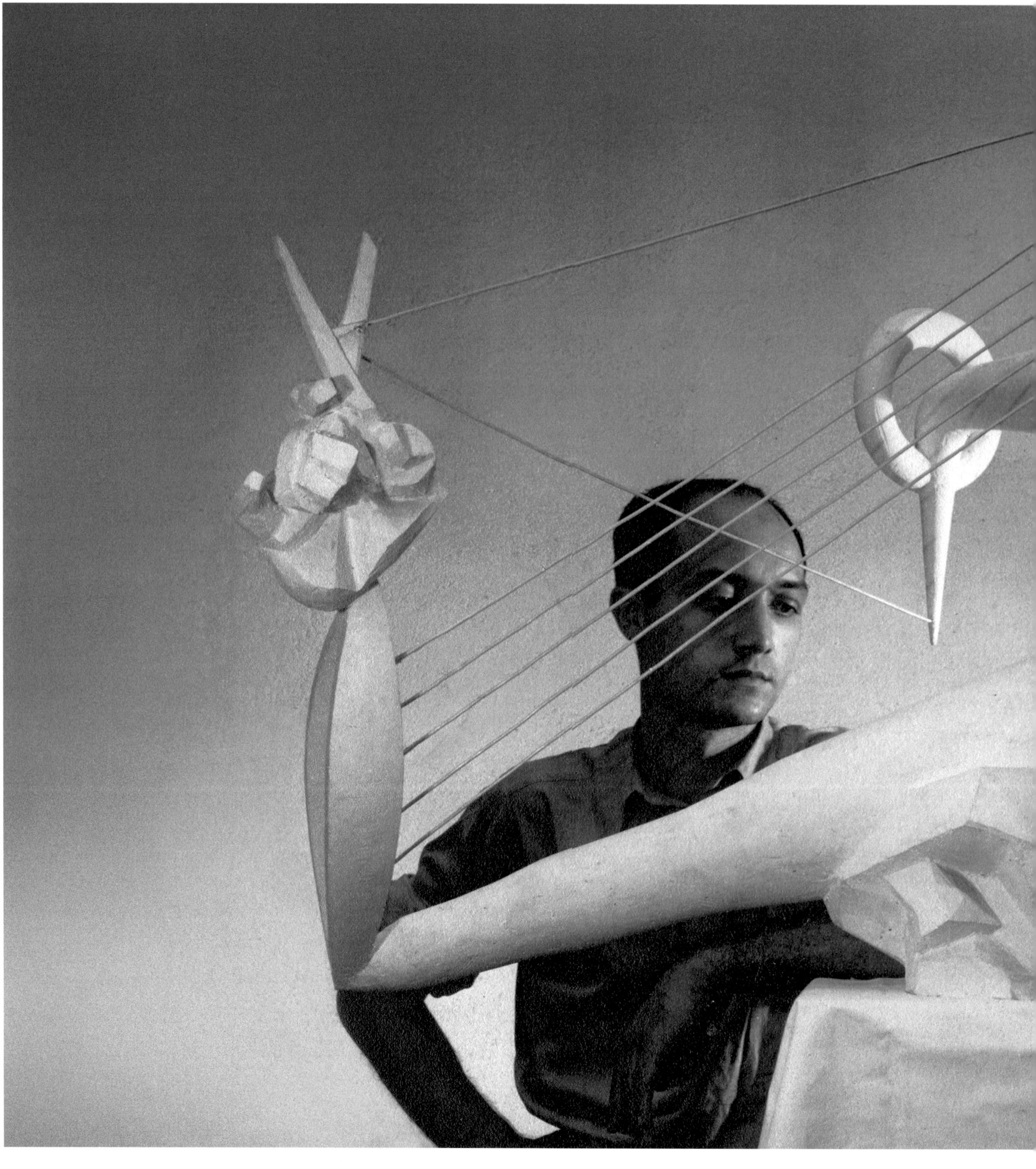

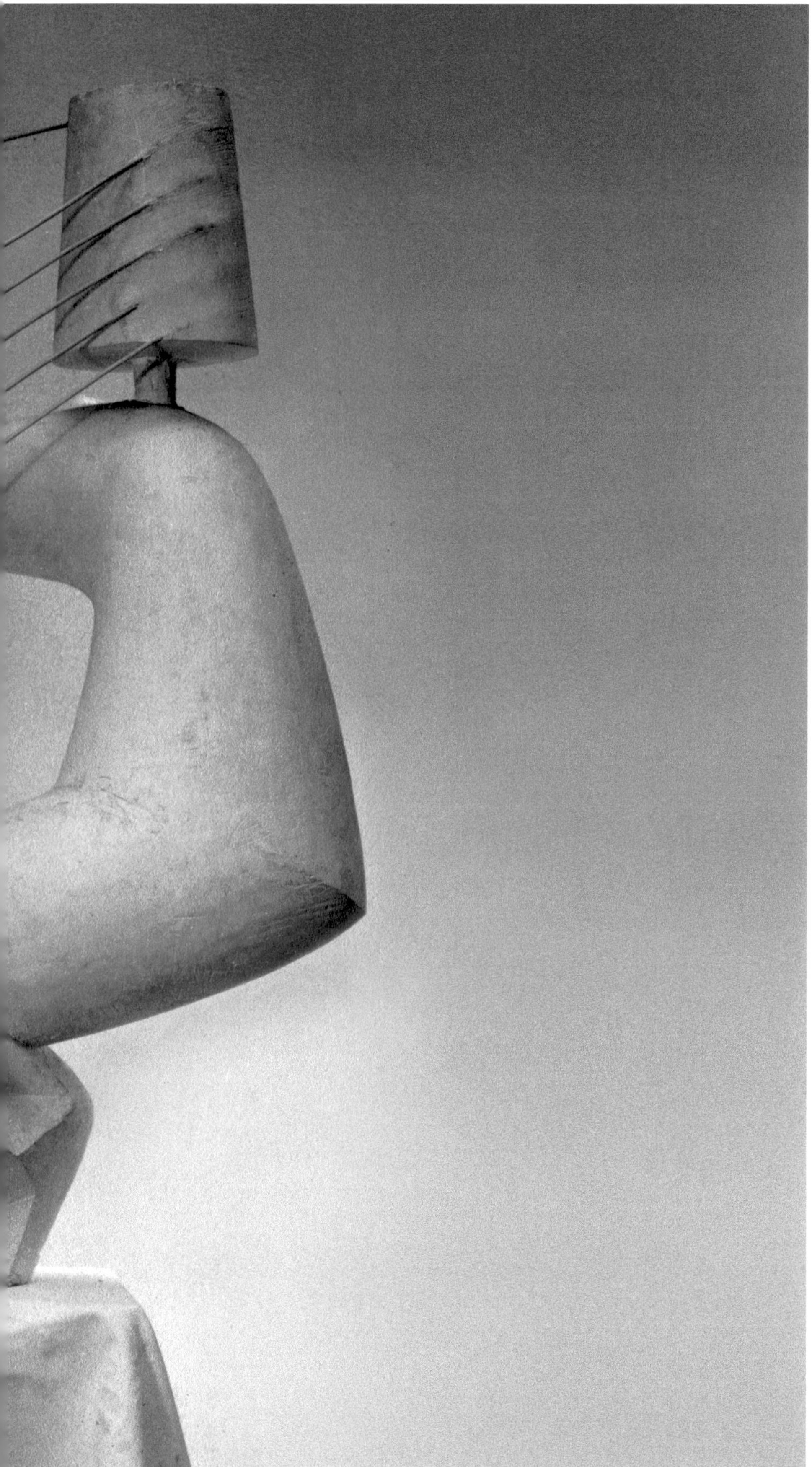

Noguchi with the plaster model for the *Carl Mackley Hosiery Workers' Memorial* (unrealised), 1933

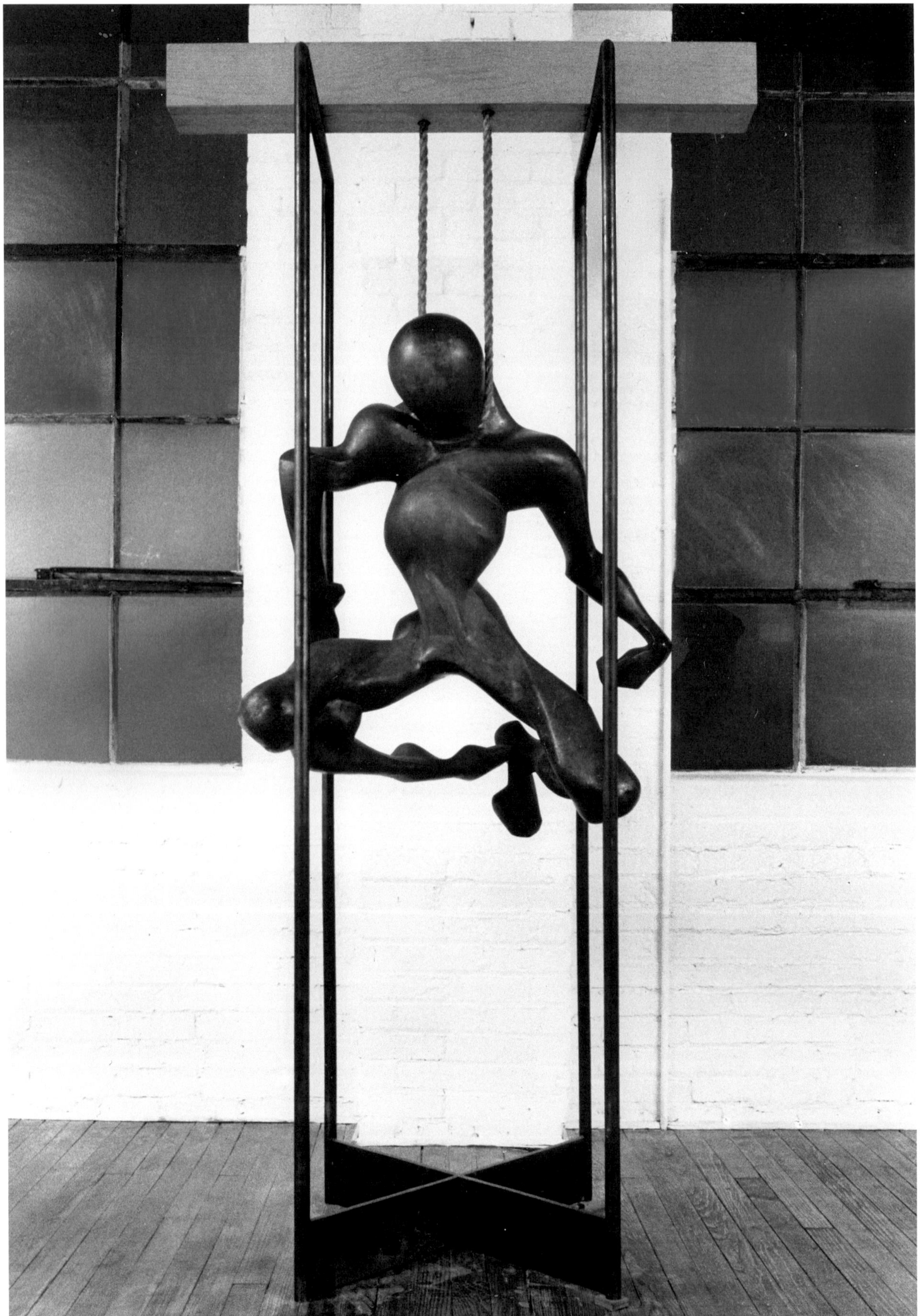

Death (Lynched Figure), 1934
Monel metal, steel, wood and rope
231.1 × 94 × 94 cm

My awareness of being an American, which came in the fall or winter of 1933, was followed in 1934 by the influence of social consciousness to the extent that when it became summer I decided to move to Woodstock, New York, to do a sculpture on the lynching of blacks.

1987

Stage set with wood element and rope for Martha Graham, *Frontier*, 1935

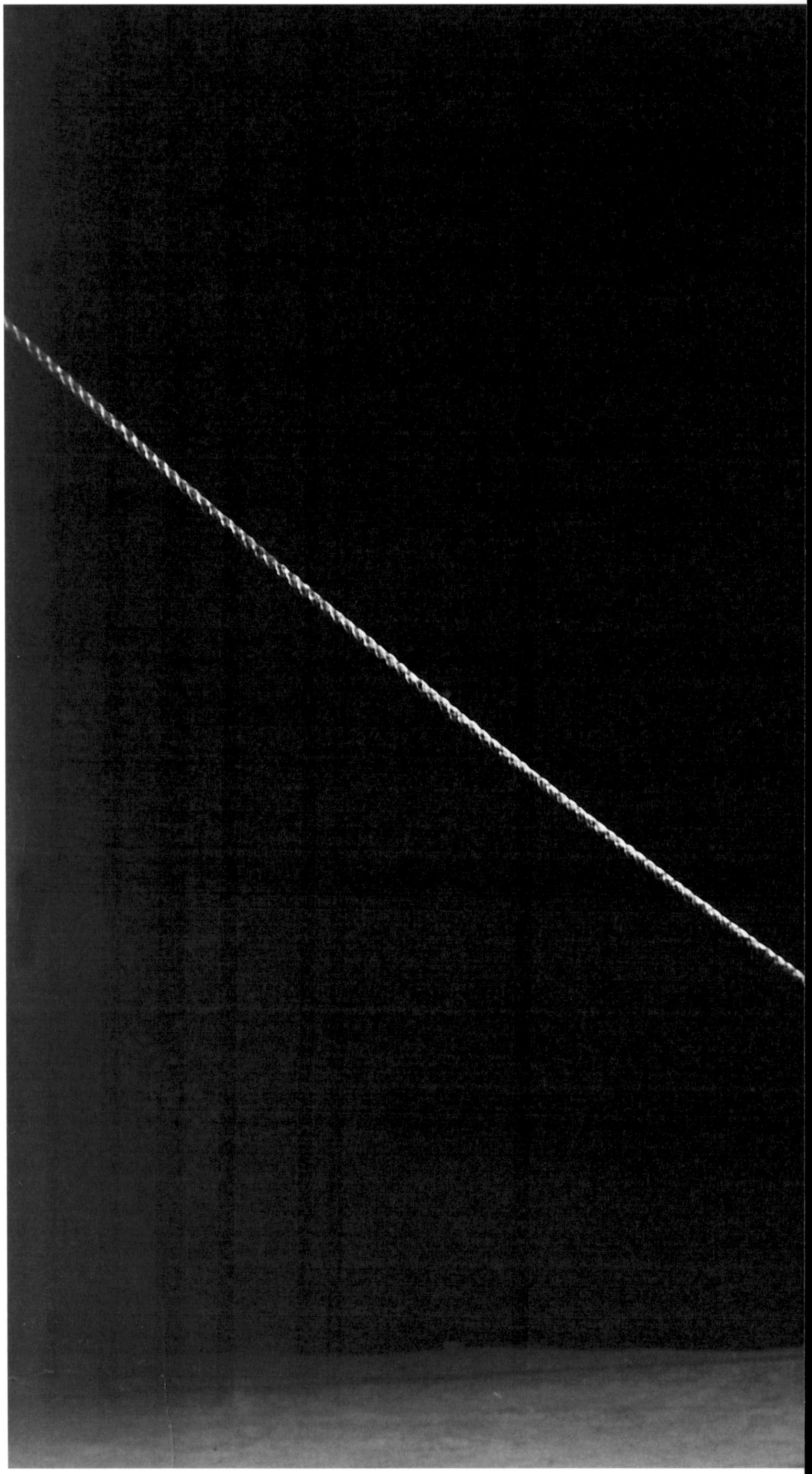

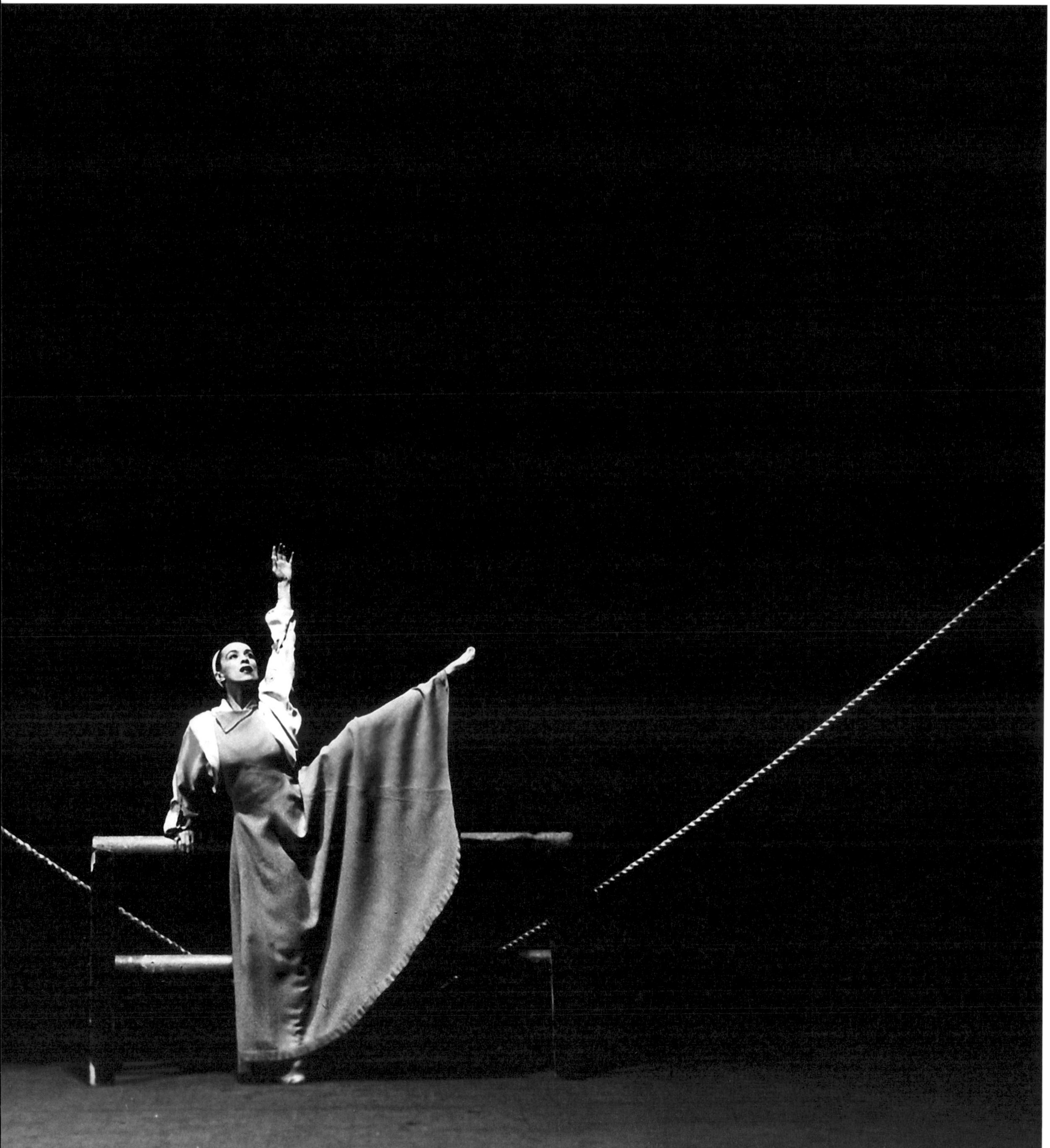

News (Associated Press Building Plaque), 1938–40
Stainless steel
609 × 518 cm

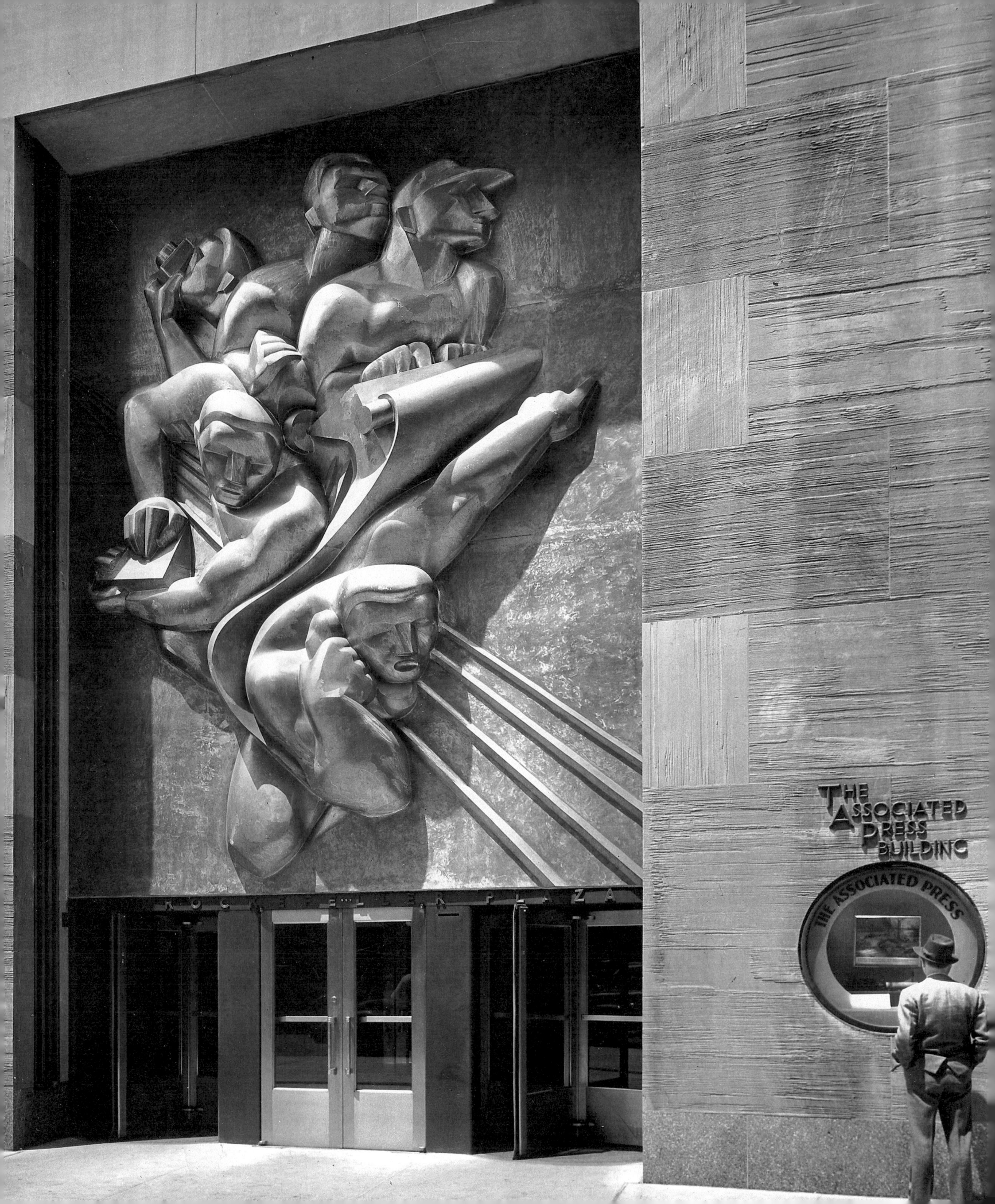
ROCKEFELLER PLAZA
THE ASSOCIATED PRESS BUILDING
THE ASSOCIATED PRESS

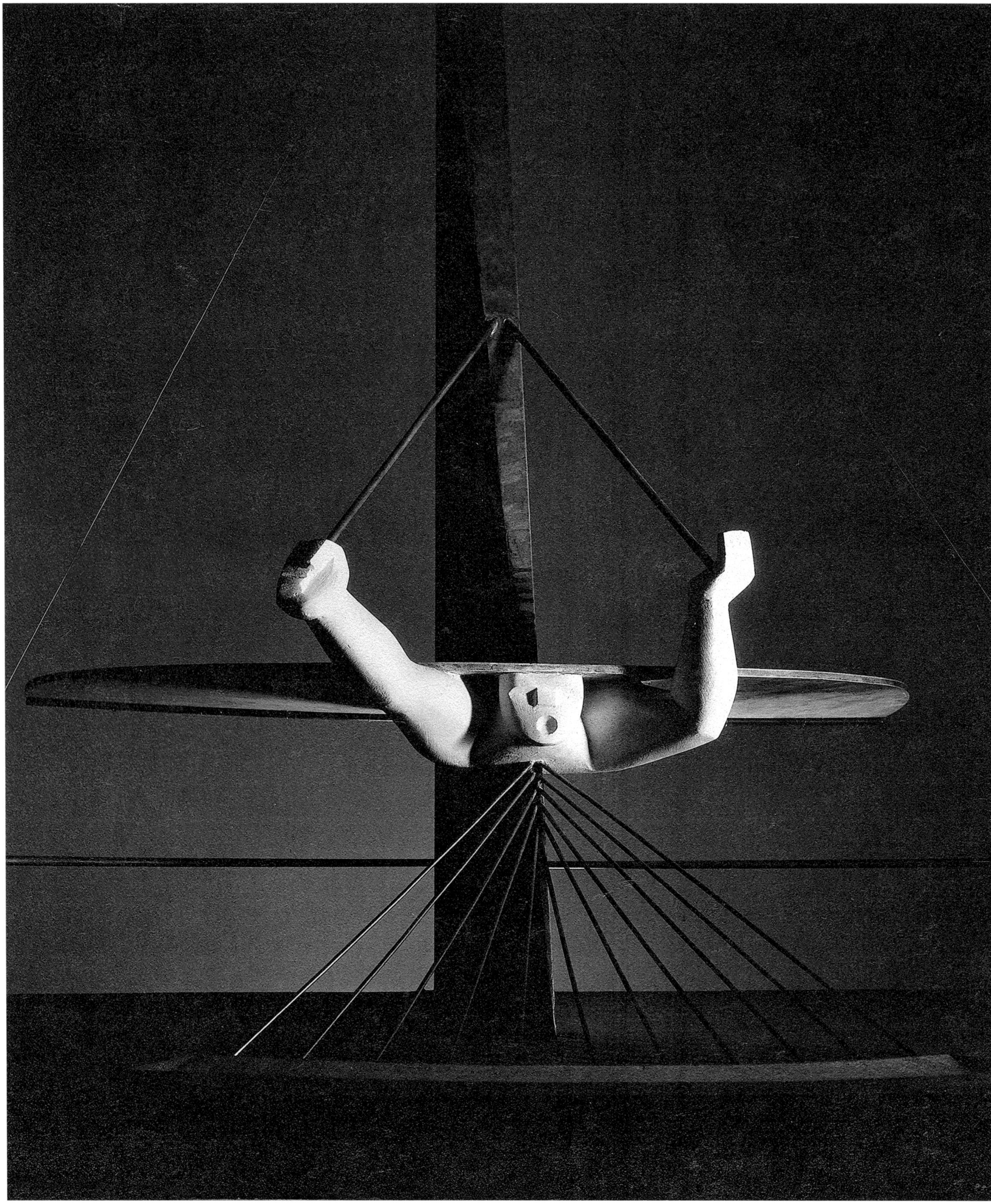

Model for a sculpture for the Pavilion of Labor at the 1939 New York World's Fair, 1938–39 (unrealised)
Plaster
15.24 × 33 × 25.4 cm

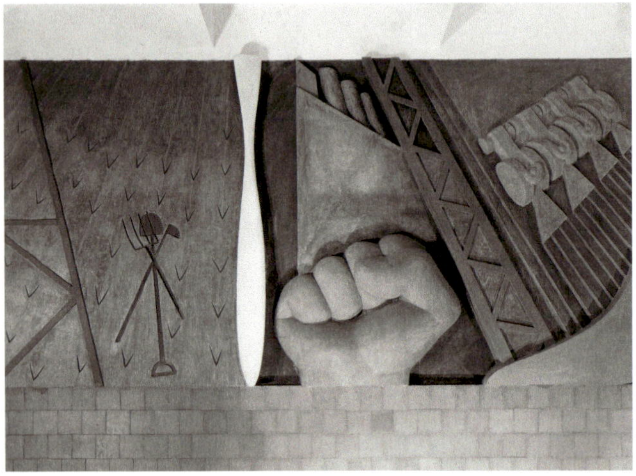

History Mexico, 1936
Cement and pigment
236.9 × 2206 × 25.01 cm

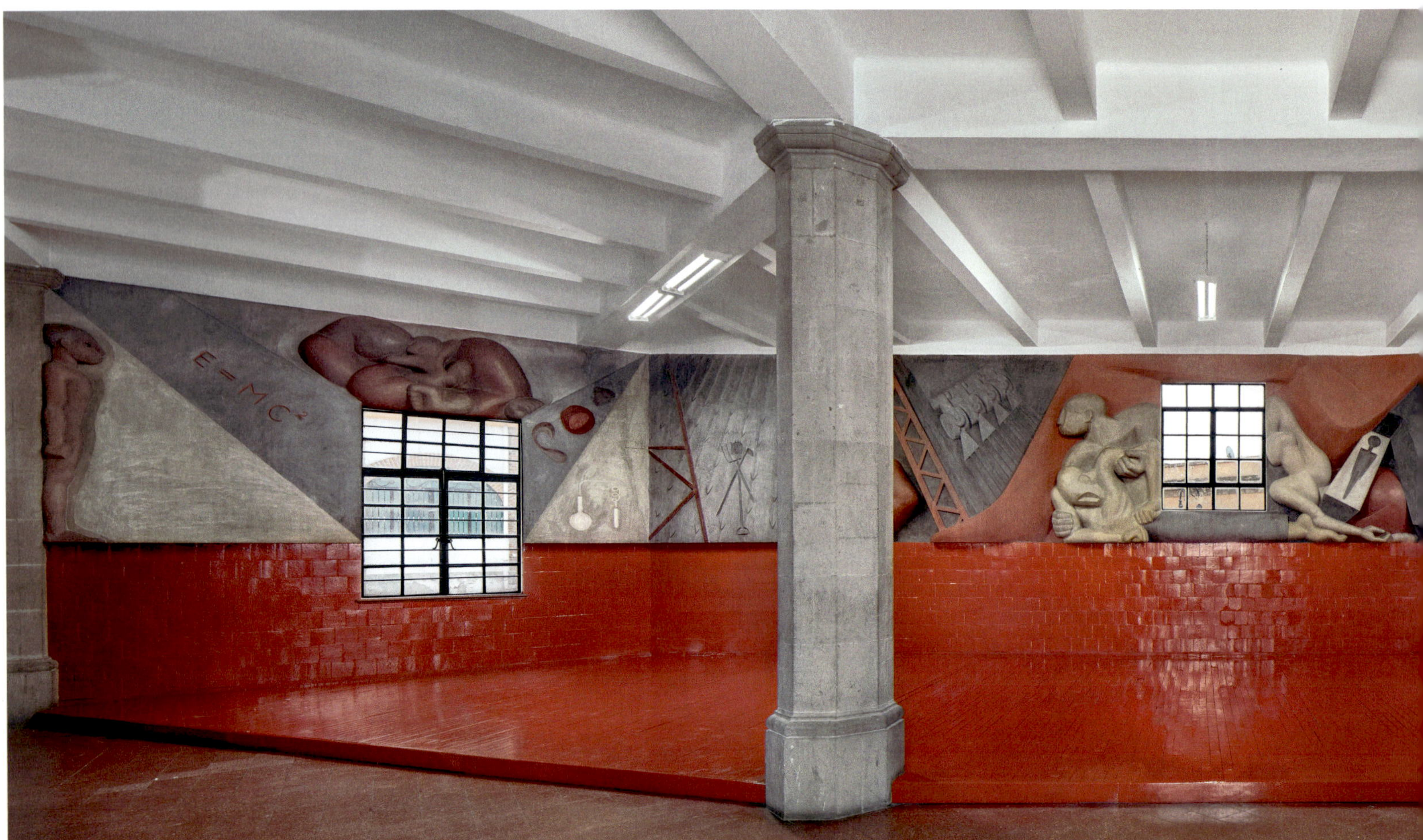

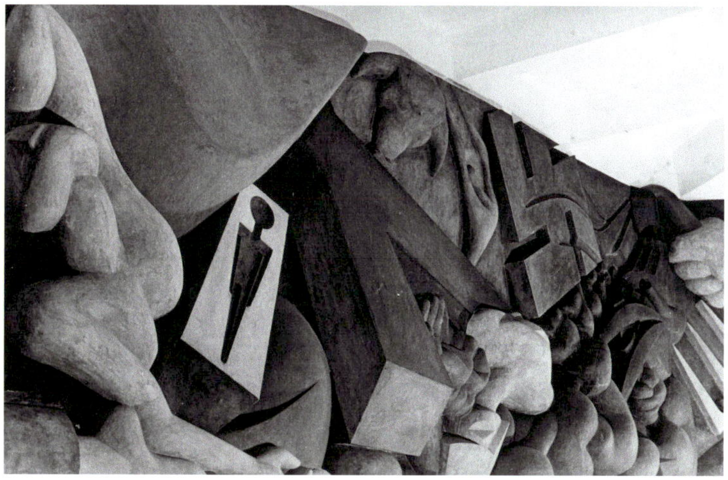

How different was Mexico! Here I suddenly no longer felt estranged as an artist; artists were useful people, a part of the community. A group of artists working in the Indian market of Abelardo Rodríguez offered me a wall to sculpt if I would agree to the same rate of pay as they were receiving for painting fresco, so much a square meter. I joyfully accepted.

This is how I made my first major work, colored cement on carved brick, two meters high and twenty-two meters long, which I called *History Mexico*. It was history as I saw it at that time, from Mexico.

It was no doubt biased by my bitter view. At one end was a fat 'capitalist' being murdered by a skeleton (shades of Posada!). There were war, crimes of the church, and 'labor' triumphant. Yet the future looked out brightly in the figure of an Indian boy, observing Einstein's equation for energy.

1967

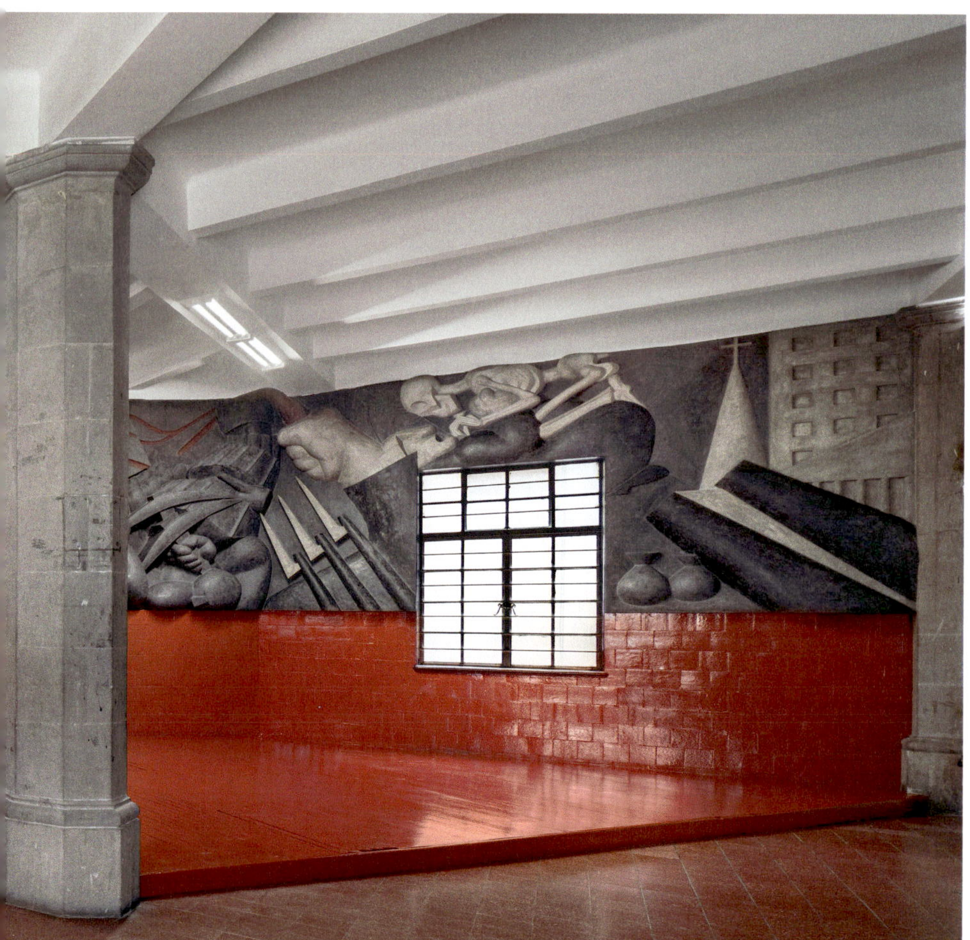

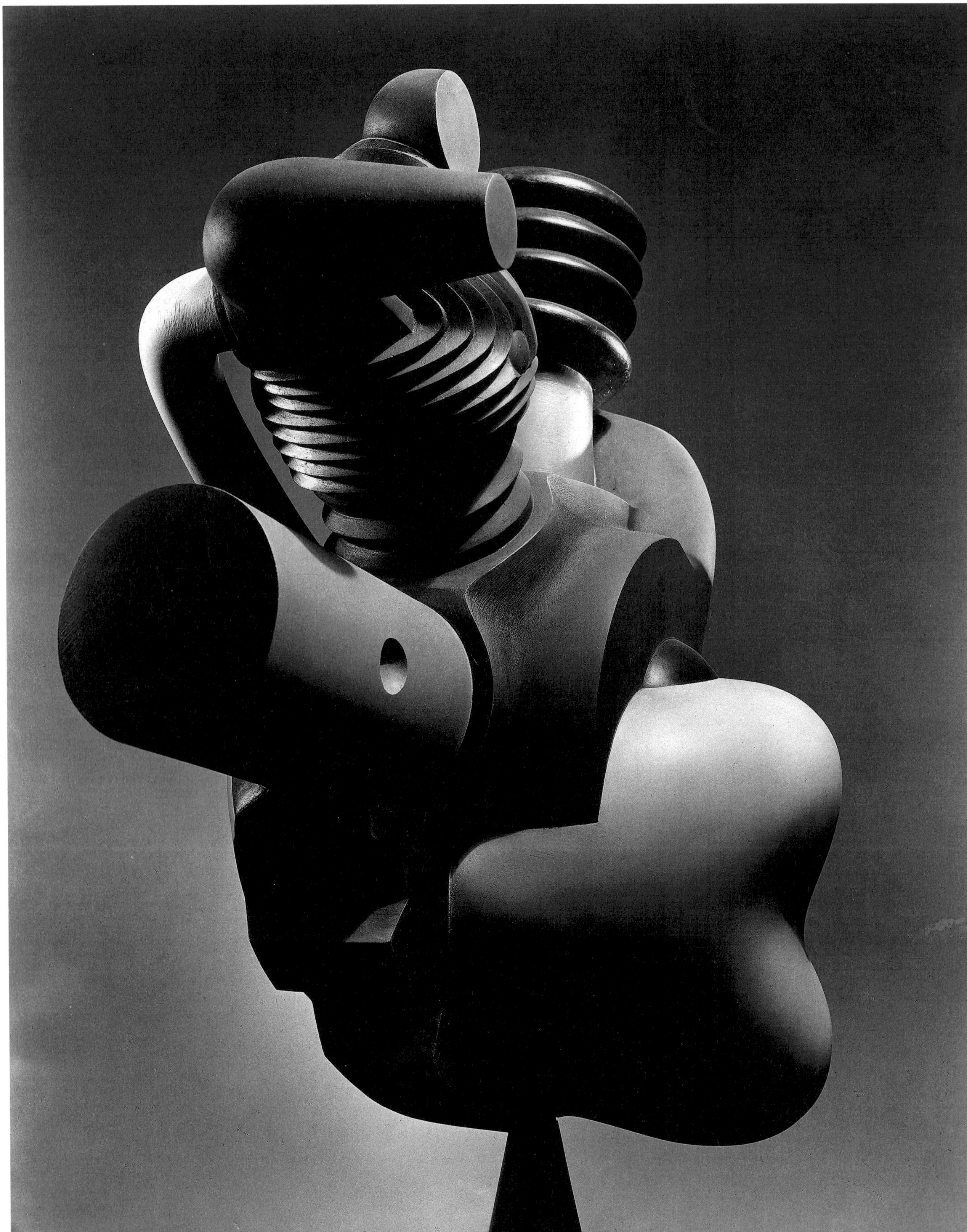

1000 Horsepower Heart, 1938
(lost)
Plaster and paint
Dimensions unknown

Radio Nurse, 1937
Guardian Ear, 1937
Manufactured by Zenith Radio Corp.
Bakelite
Radio Nurse: 21 × 17.1 × 15.9 cm
Guardian Ear: 15.9 × 10.8 × 21 cm

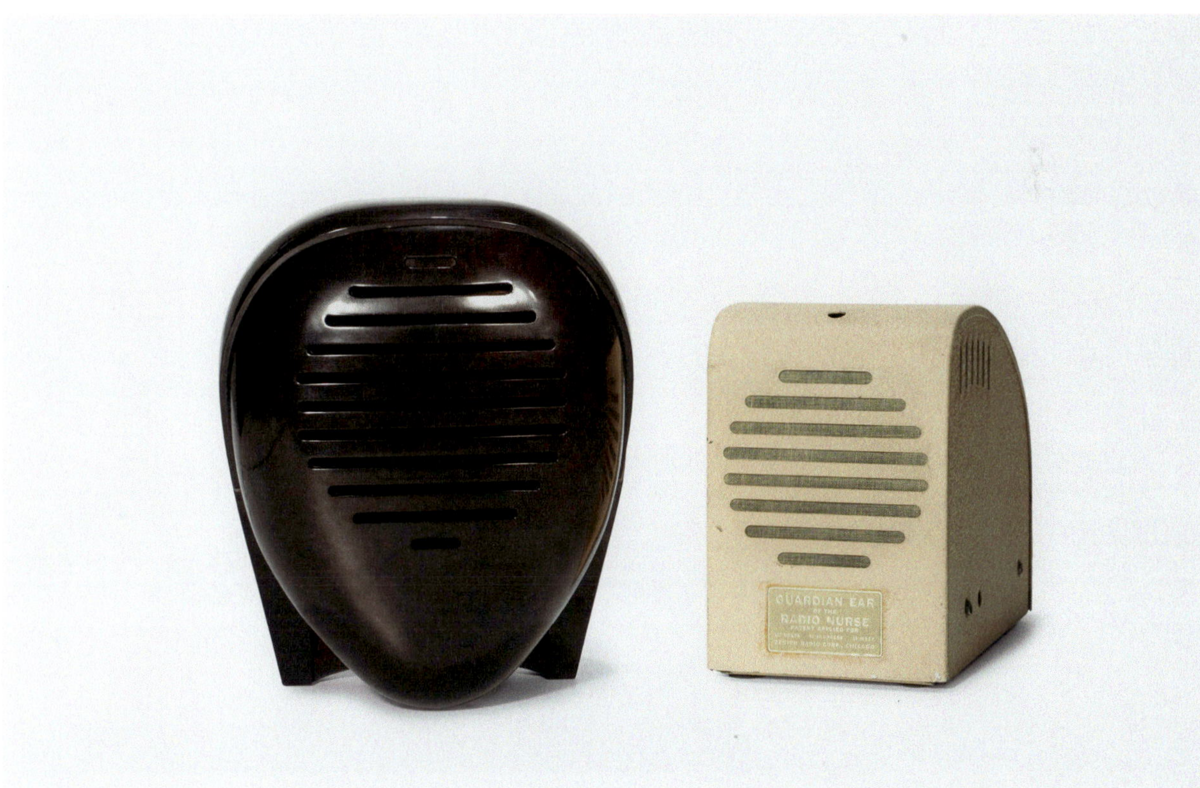

Models for playground equipment for Ala Moana Parka, Hawaii, 1940
Metal, fabric tape, wood and paint
Swings: 18.1 × 30.5 × 16.2 cm
Slide: 11.7 × 26 × 21.6 cm
Jungle Gym: 11.7 × 7.6 × 7.6 cm

I like to think of playgrounds as a primer of shapes and functions; simple, mysterious, and evocative: thus educational. The child's world would be a beginning world, fresh and clear.

1967

Models for playground equipment for Ala Moana Park, Hawaii, 1940

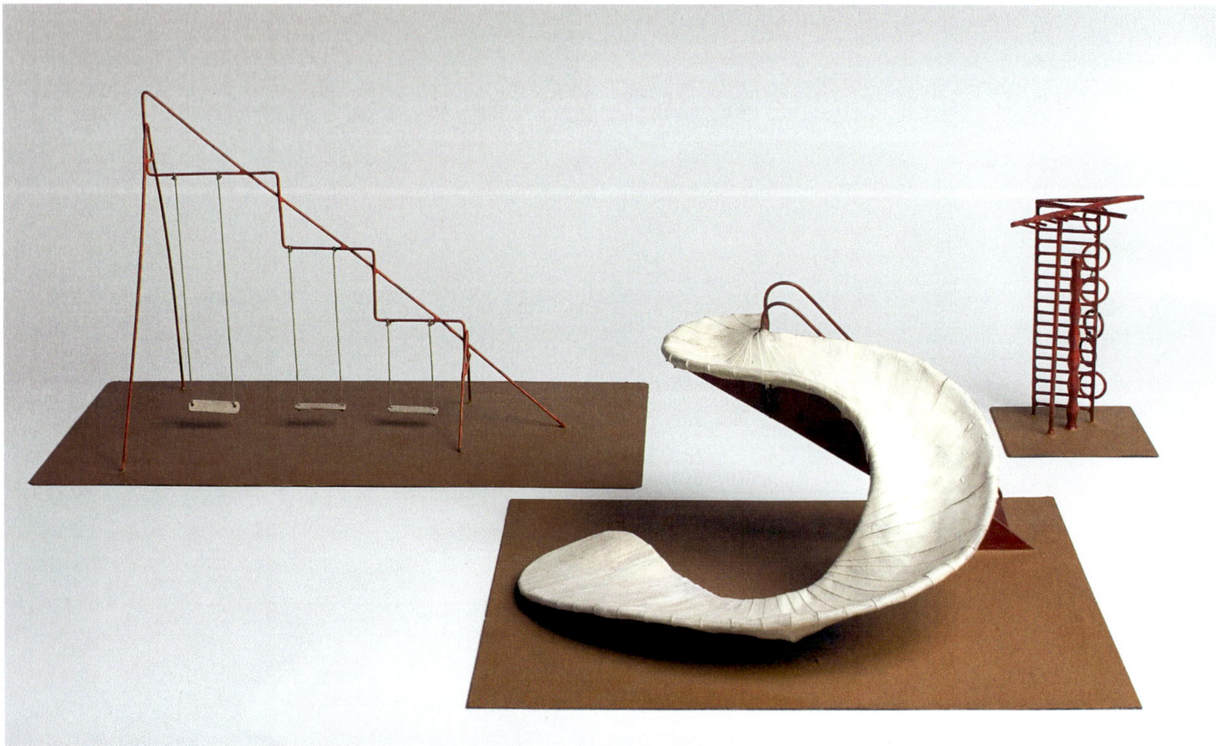

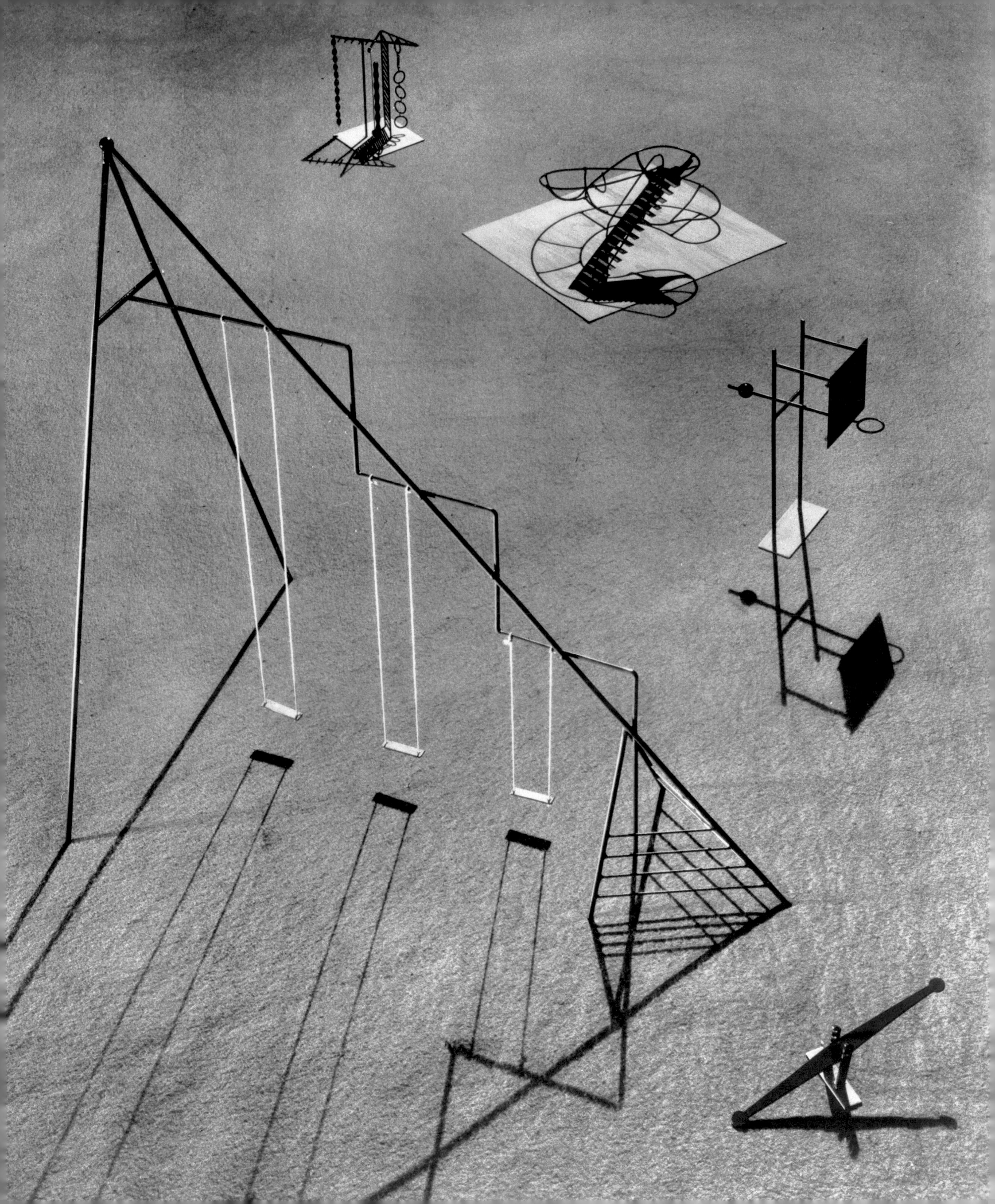

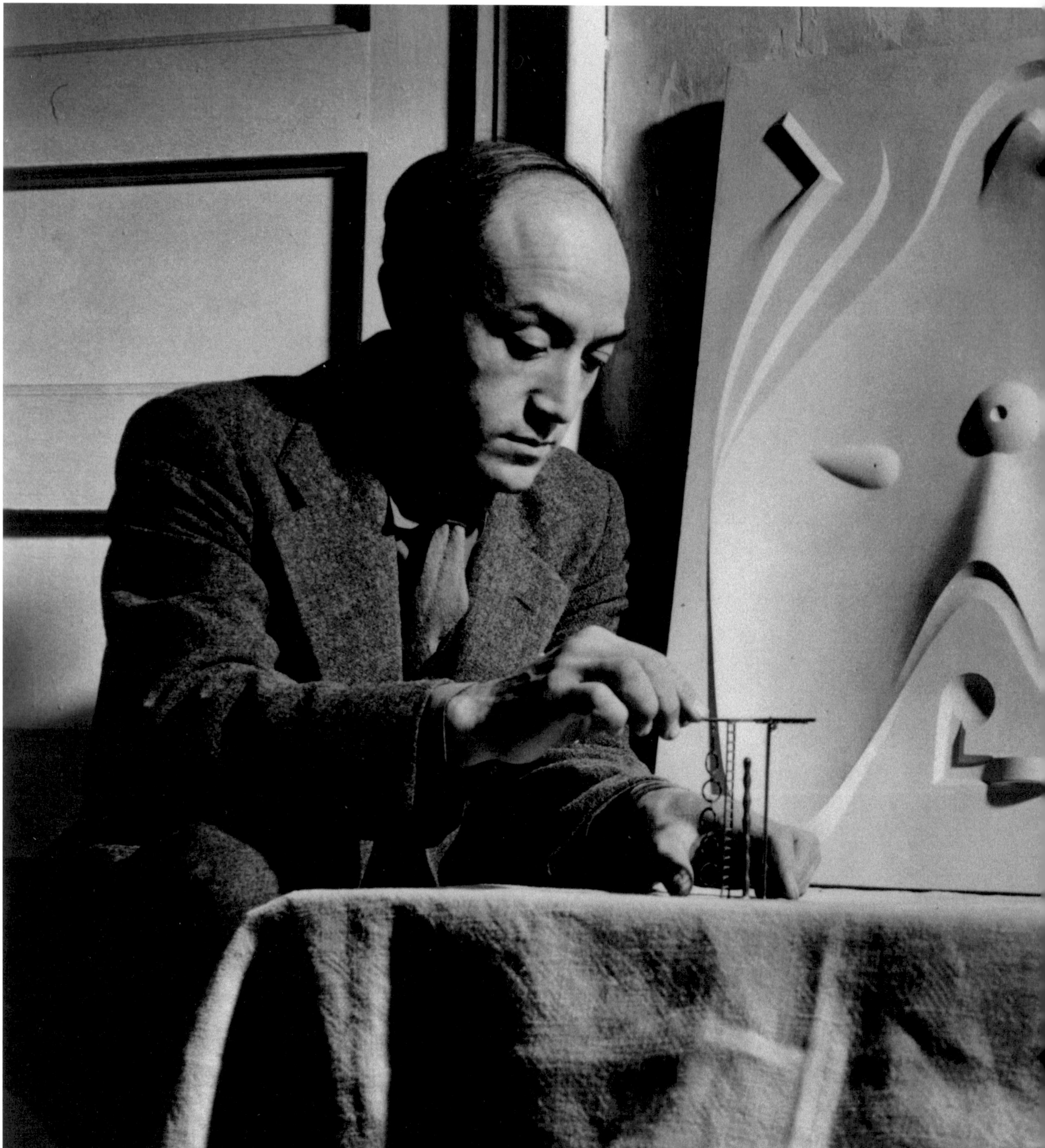

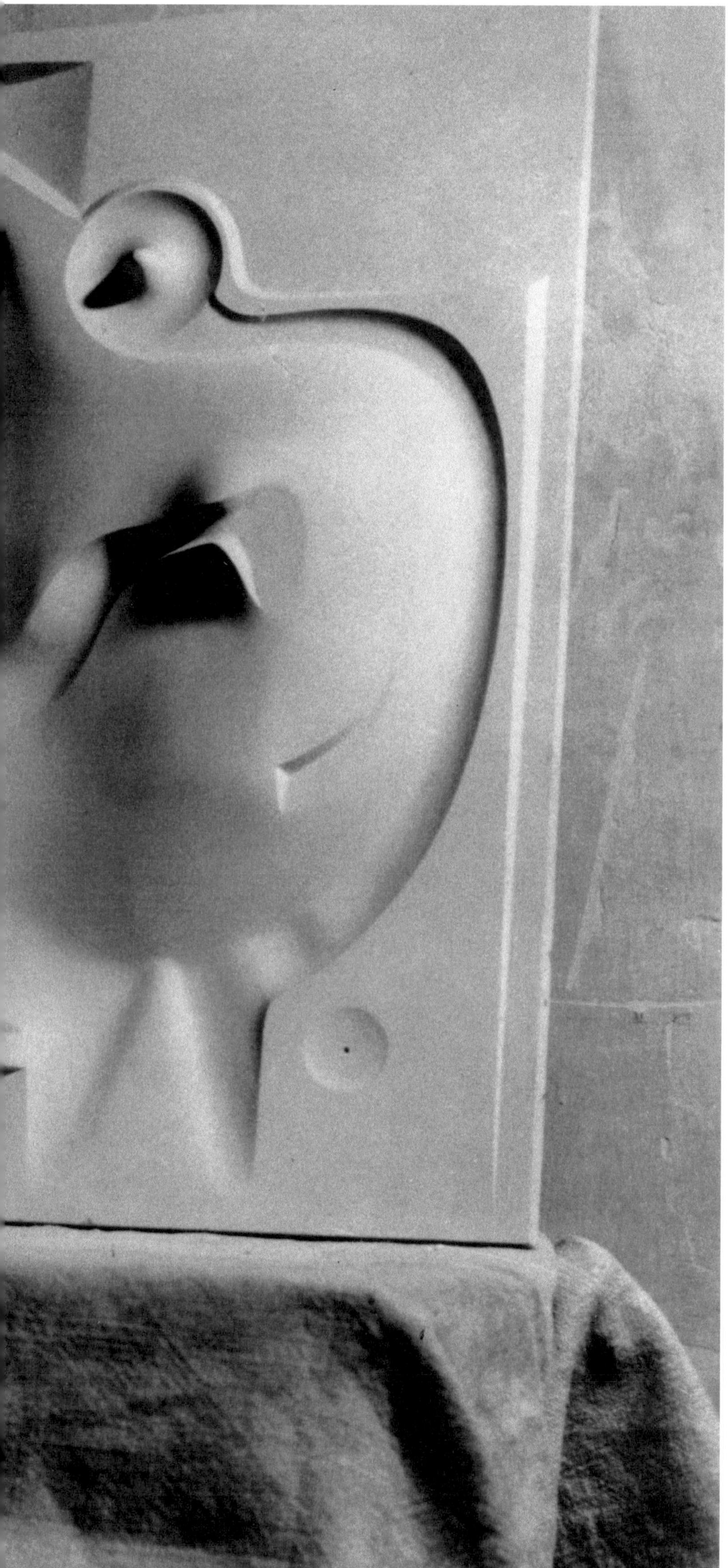

Noguchi with model for *Contoured Playground*, c. 1946

I felt obliged to answer all the dire warnings of the danger to which I would expose small children with my play equipment and so designed a *Contoured Playground*. This would be proof against any serious accidents, being made up entirely of earth modulations. Exercise was to be derived automatically in running up and down the curved surfaces. There were various areas of interest, for hiding, for sliding, for games. Water would flow in summer.

1967

SOCIAL SCULPTURE: A GLOBAL PHENOMENON

Fabienne Eggelhöfer

The pure pursuit of aesthetics and beauty was not enough for Isamu Noguchi. To his mind, art also served a social purpose in the broadest sense. He questioned any art that did not have something to do with people's lives, and hence distanced himself from the European avant-garde whose work he had seen at New York galleries. Alfred Stieglitz and Israel Ber Neumann, both of whom presented avant-garde art in their galleries, were important partners in dialogue for the young Noguchi and early supporters of his artistic aspirations. He immersed himself in modern art, yet he wanted to achieve something different, something that did not function merely as an isolated object in a gallery or museum. An exhibition of works by the Romanian sculptor Constantin Brâncuși at the Brummer Gallery, New York, in late 1926 left a particularly lasting impression on him. When, thanks to a Guggenheim scholarship, he lived in Paris for two years beginning in April 1927, he became the part-time assistant of Brâncuși, who produced abstract sculptures in a wide variety of materials. It was under this influence that Noguchi also began to create abstract sculptures, but he soon realised that it would lead to a dead end. Moreover, he felt, in his words, 'too young and inexperienced', 'too poor inside', to work abstractly.[1] During the years of the Great Depression, Noguchi felt even more strongly the need to make art that was socially and politically relevant. He thus conceived several projects for public spaces, including *Monument to the Plow*, *Play Mountain* and *Contoured Playground*, though these were not realised (pp. 64–65, 88–89). Government agencies such as the Public Works of Art Project (PWAP), a federal aid programme for public art launched in December 1933 as part of the New Deal reforms and which commissioned more than 3,700 artists to develop works of art for public buildings, did not take Noguchi's proposals into consideration. He suspected discrimination lay behind this, either because of his bicultural background –

1 'I was too poor inside to insist upon it. How [to] presume to express something from within when it was empty there? I felt myself too young and inexperienced for abstractions: I would have to live first.' Isamu Noguchi, *A Sculptor's World* (Göttingen: Steidl, 2004), p. 19.

his mother, Léonie Gilmour, was American and his father, Yonejirō Noguchi, Japanese – or because he was able to earn his keep with commissions for portrait heads and was therefore classified as a commercial artist and deemed to have sufficient income. Disappointed at being denied the chance to put his art into the service of the general public, in autumn 1935 he decided to go to Mexico City, where he was offered the opportunity to design a mural for the Abelardo L. Rodríguez market. He developed a 22-metre-long relief in coloured cement, executed in a social realist style, in which he denounced the injustices suffered in Mexico as a result of colonialism and capitalism. However, this form of social engagement did not satisfy Noguchi artistically, and he continued to ask himself how he could achieve his goal of making socially relevant art.

Noguchi regarded life and art as a perfect union and made no distinction between the so-called liberal and applied arts. His sculptures were not intended to be isolated objects but to operate in relationships with human beings as a spatial arrangement. He was open to the latest materials and techniques used in industry, yet he likewise placed value on traditional artisanship. In the following it shall be demonstrated how the exchange with others influenced Noguchi's artistic stance and how the aspirations of the schools and movements he encountered the world over corresponded with his views.

Sculpture as Form in Space

Noguchi saw sculptures not as autonomous objects but as forms that bear a relation to each other and to viewers and so constitute a space – an environment.[2] In Brâncuși's studio he had already observed how important the arrangement of individual sculptures was for the sculptor. As photographs show, Brâncuși constantly rearranged his works and created specific installations that he referred to as *groupes mobiles* (mobile groups).[3] The spatial relation of the sculptures to one another and to viewers was crucial for Brâncuși, whom Noguchi considered an artist *par excellence* and the first true 'architectural sculptor'.[4] Brâncuși worked simultaneously on ideas for sculptures in public space as well as on architectural schemes. However, it was not until 1938 that he was able to execute such a project: an installation with several large-scale sculptures in the Romanian city of Târgu Jiu, including a version of the *Endless Column*.[5] This inspired Noguchi to create *The Spirit's Flight* (1969, p. 229), a simple column made of marble nearly 2.5 metres in height. Furthermore, Brâncuși pursued his plan for a temple project, a scheme that constantly evolved but was never carried out. His interest in temples was shared by Noguchi, who was drawn to them for their value as ceremonial and ritualistic sites.

With his sculptures, Noguchi wished to develop a relationship and a channel of communication with others and hence a new relationship between sculptor and society.[6] He believed that art should not belong to individuals but have a social existence through which it can bring enjoyment to all.[7] Beginning in the 1930s he developed several projects for public parks and playgrounds, only a few of which were carried out.[8] In order to understand the role that sculpture had played in societies in the past, he applied to the Bollingen Foundation for a travel grant with the aim of writing a book on 'environments of leisure'.[9] His two-year journey commenced in May 1949. Like many of his contemporaries,

2 'A sculpture is a relationship of forms in space', Isamu Noguchi, interview with Dore Ashton, 18 September 1978, Tape #1, Side B, p. 16, The Noguchi Museum Archives, MS_WRI_047_011.

3 Friedrich Teja Bach, *Constantin Brancusi: Metamorphosen plastischer Formen* (Cologne: DuMont, 1987), pp. 109–40. A reconstruction of his studio in Paris is accessible to the public.

4 Noguchi, *A Sculptor's World*, p. 160.

5 Bach, *Constantin Brancusi*, pp. 78–96.

6 'My desire for communication on a broader level', Isamu Noguchi, 'Draft of A Visual Autobiography', c. 1959, p. 24, The Noguchi Museum Archives, MS_PUB_050_001.

7 '[A] growing reintegration of the art with society', Isamu Noguchi, '1949', c. 1983, p. 1, The Noguchi Museum Archives, MS_WRI_008_001; 'individual possession seems less significant than public enjoyment', Isamu Noguchi, 'A Proposed Study of the Environment of Leisure', c. 1949, p. 1, The Noguchi Museum Archives, MS_WRI_010_019; 'without public enjoyment the very meaning of art is in question', Isamu Noguchi, 'From an Interview with Isamu Noguchi', *The League Quarterly*, vol. 20, no. 3 (1949), p. 9.

8 For more on these projects see Ana María Torres, *Isamu Noguchi: A Study of Space* (New York: The Monacelli Press, 2000), and *Parques – Isamu Noguchi – Playscapes*, exh. cat., Museo Tamayo, Mexico City (Barcelona: RM Verlag, 2016).

9 'Subject: sculpture as it functioned in the past, in situ, as environment', Noguchi, '1949', p. 1.

Noguchi was interested in the very beginnings of art. He first visited the Lascaux cave in the Dordogne and the prehistoric dolmens and menhirs of Brittany, France.[10] His trip then took him to Italy, where he primarily studied the urban piazzas as gathering places for people and as a union of buildings, fountains and sculptures. Many years later, he made reference to the geometric composition that distinguishes many of these plazas in a design for the inner courtyard of the Beinecke Rare Book and Manuscript Library at Yale University in New Haven, Connecticut (pp. 218–19). In Greece and Egypt he visited temples, mosques and burial sites. He continued his examination of sacred sites in India, where he stayed from mid-September 1949 until early January 1950. In addition to temple complexes he visited the Jantar Mantar (literally, 'calculating instrument') observatories in Jaipur and Delhi, ensembles of buildings – or sculptures – designed according to astronomical aspects and built between 1729 and 1733. The impressions Noguchi amassed here later resonated in his designs for playgrounds for the US Pavilion at Expo '70 in Osaka (p. 234).

10 He was also especially impressed by the stone formations at Stonehenge and Avebury in Wiltshire, England, which he would visit a few years later. Ibid., p. 2.

In Santiniketan, in West Bengal, he met the artist Nandalal Bose, who had assisted the poet Rabindranath Tagore in the development of the Kala Bhavana art school.[11] Tagore had founded the school in 1919 as a reaction to the sterile, academically oriented colonial education system. Bose and Tagore drew on Mahatma Gandhi's criticism of Western capitalism and on the revaluation of village life and traditional craftsmanship in the course of Indian nation-building. They placed particular value on viewing life as a unity of human and nature, spirit and matter, as well as on the inner life of all individuals so as to create a harmonious society. A correspondence might be identified between the two artists' striving to develop a holistic system of education and the principles of the Bauhaus in Weimar, which was founded that same year.[12] Next, Noguchi travelled to Bali, where evenings filled with music, dance and theatrical performances caused him to describe the island as 'magical', a place where life merged with art.[13]

11 Noguchi describes his stay on the reverse side of a drawing portraying the sculptor Ramkinkar Baij. See 'Bollingen Drawing: "The Sculptor of Santiniketan"' (verso), c. 1949–50, The Noguchi Museum Archives, 10976. It was probably Alain Daniélou, a former teacher at the Kala Bhavana whom he also visited in India, who recommended that he travel to Santiniketan. I kindly thank Matt Kirsch, Curator of Research and Digital Content, The Noguchi Museum, for this and many other pieces of valuable information.

12 It may be no coincidence that an exhibition of Bauhaus artists took place in Calcutta in 1922 on the initiative of the Austrian art historian Stella Kramrisch, who taught at the Kala Bhavana from 1920 to 1923. See Partha Mitter, 'Teaching Art at Santiniketan and Weimar: Some Unexpected Meeting Points', in *bauhaus imaginista*, ed. Marion von Osten and Grant Watson (London: Thames & Hudson, 2019), pp. 36–41. On the exhibition in Calcutta, see Regina Bittner and Kathrin Rhomberg, eds, *The Bauhaus in Calcutta: An Encounter of the Cosmopolitan Avant-Garde*, exh. cat., Bauhaus Dessau (Ostfildern: Hatje Cantz, 2013).

13 'The magical island of Bali, the island where life and art are one', Noguchi, *A Sculptor's World*, p. 30.

The trip concluded in Japan, where Noguchi had spent his childhood as well as several months in 1931. His relationship to Japan was ambivalent, since his father, an influential poet, had at first not officially accepted him as his son. He nevertheless felt a close bond with Japanese culture. He had visited numerous temples and gardens in Kyoto in his earlier trip of 1931; during this second stay, in 1950, he focused on studying gardens. He learned that stones were believed to have a living and a dead aspect and that their selection and positioning were considered central to humans' interactions with the stone arrangements within these spaces. In March 1951 he was given the opportunity to design a garden for the first time, a commission for the newly built Reader's Digest Building in Tokyo: 'I experienced my first, almost ritual improvisation of placing them [the stones] upon the earth with an exactitude that astonished me.'[14] During his development of the *UNESCO Gardens* in Paris in the 1950s he also made reference to insights he had gained in Japan, however not with the aim of copying the Japanese tradition but to interpret it in his own way: 'To call them gardens may not be correct; they are, rather, compositions in topological space.'[15] The individual sculptures are elements of a spatial arrangement in which connections are forged among the objects and the people who traverse them.

14 Noguchi, '1949', p. 18.

15 Isamu Noguchi, 'My Sculpture' [1973], in *Isamu Noguchi: Essays and Conversations*, p. 71.

Noguchi was interested in ritual sites of all kinds where art and life could be seen to merge. He regarded the stage as one such site where rituals are performed and joyful experiences are produced. It is therefore hardly surprising that, from 1935 onwards, he designed numerous stage sets for the dancer and choreographer Martha Graham, and occasionally for Ruth Page, Erick Hawkins, Merce Cunningham and George Balanchine. Evidently proud of his contribution, he wrote:

> I may correctly claim that I am the one who brought sculpture consciousness into theater space, the interrelatedness of sculptures in space, in stage volume … And the definition of space or rather, how to define place and mood was a chief part of my effort – especially as it had mostly to do with the dance. The stage was a place of action[,] a contrived illusion, which the audience perceived as leisure, pleasure.[16]

16 Isamu Noguchi, 'Draft of Bollingen pages 138–150', p. 142, The Noguchi Museum Archives, MS_BOL_016_004.

Noguchi's achievement was in designing stage sets with which dancers could interact. In the 1920s, the Bauhaus had already generated productions that combined dance and the visual arts: alongside Oskar Schlemmer, the Swiss artist Xanti Schawinsky, who himself studied at the Bauhaus and later emigrated to the United States, had placed central importance on the modernisation of stage design. Though it is known that both Noguchi and Schawinsky regularly kept company with Marcel Duchamp in New York, a direct exchange between the two artists has not been documented. Yet there are interesting parallels between their stage designs. Schawinsky developed dynamic spatial arrangements in which dancers and stage set merged. At the invitation of Josef and Anni Albers, he began teaching painting and theatre at Black Mountain College, North Carolina, in 1936. The college was one of the most progressive in the United States and was rooted in John Dewey's theory of 'learning by doing'. In the summer, artists from New York were invited as guest teachers. Noguchi once said that he too had received enquiries on several occasions but had declined – something he later regretted – due to his general scepticism towards educational institutions.[17] When his mother had sent him, aged thirteen, to be educated at the Interlaken School in La Porte, Indiana, Noguchi had himself briefly enjoyed a progressive training influenced by Dewey's ideas. There, like at Black Mountain, students were encouraged to do crafts and to help with the gardening.[18] In 1938, Schawinsky moved to New York, where he collaborated on the exhibition *Bauhaus: 1919–1928* at the Museum of Modern Art, organised by Herbert Bayer as well as Ise and Walter Gropius. Moreover, he worked with Marcel Breuer and Walter Gropius, two further Bauhäusler, on the planning of Pennsylvania's pavilion for the 1939 World's Fair in New York, on the occasion of which Noguchi designed the *Ford Fountain* (p. 283) for the Ford Motor Company. Thereafter, Schawinsky, who was also a graphic designer, continued to engage with the issue of combining art and industrial design as well as with his aspiration for a 'total theatre'.[19]

17 See letter from Isamu Noguchi to Emma Harris, 11 May 1977, p. 142, The Noguchi Museum Archives, MS_COR_126_005.

18 Deborah A. Goldenberg, 'Isamu Noguchi: Visionary Designer and "World Citizen"', in *Isamu Noguchi, Patent Holder: Designing the World of Tomorrow*, exh. cat., The Dr M. T. Geoffrey Yeh Art Gallery, New York, in collaboration with the Isamu Noguchi Foundation and Garden Museum (New York: Geoffrey Yeh Art Gallery, 2015), p. 1.

19 For more on Schawinsky, see Raphael Gygax and Heike Munder, eds, *Xanti Schawinsky*, exh. cat., Migros Museum für Gegenwartskunst, Zurich (Zurich: JRP Ringier, 2015).

Sculptural Design

For Noguchi, there was no distinction between art for art's sake and utilitarian objects. However, he noted that he was not a 'designer', since 'all my works, tables as well as sculptures, are conceived as fundamental problems of form that would best express human and aesthetic activity involved with these objects.'[20] Concerned with solving practical formal problems as well as with the relations between humans and objects in space, he came to the conclusion that 'sculptors as well as painters should not forever be concerned with pure art or meaningful art, but should inject their knowledge of form and matter into the everyday, usable designs of industry and commerce.'[21] The notion that artists should use their skills for the design of everyday objects and create autonomous art objects that are not detached from life was one of the Bauhaus's basic principles, which were disseminated, beginning in the 1930s, by means of the emigration to the United States of numerous individuals who had formerly taught or studied there, as evidenced by the MoMA exhibition mentioned above.[22] The Russian avant-garde, whose ideas Noguchi was able to discuss with the Russian artist David Burliuk in New York, pursued similar goals.[23] Noguchi was the only American artist of his generation to radically implement these ideas.

Noguchi suspected that his readiness to design useful objects led to his not being taken seriously by art critics in the United States.[24] Although he kept company with artists of the so-called New York School, critics of the time did not associate him with it, and nor is this fact mentioned in the art historical literature to this day. It is also characteristic that his works of art, which he developed using the latest materials and techniques – such as the 'Lunars', fashioned out of magnesite and lightbulbs, or his folded sculptures made of aluminium and steel – were rejected by galleries on the grounds that they looked too commercial.[25] In his exhibitions, Noguchi consistently combined functional and non-functional objects. In 1935, for instance, he exhibited models of his unrealised objects for public space alongside sculptural works. For his presentation at the Venice Biennale in 1986 he deliberately chose his commercially distributed *Akari* lamps in order to reinforce his standpoint that 'Sculpture is more than the creation of objects of art. Sculpture is an experience that is wide and involves the total environment.'[26] Some of the pottery he produced in Japan could be used equally well as vases or as plates. In Noguchi's work, a distinction between art and design objects was as undesirable as it had been for his 'teacher' Brâncuși, who wanted to display his furniture alongside his sculptures.

In 1932 Noguchi outlined his plans to set up an industrial design company that was to be called Time Design. He sent it to Edward Rumely, who as director of the Interlaken School had been one of Noguchi's early sponsors. In the accompanying letter he also responded to Rumely's suggestion that he create a revised version of his kitchen timer *Measured Time*, which had been produced by Rumely earlier that year in Bakelite. Noguchi explained that he could not simply design a new case for the clock, since for him it was not a matter of mere aesthetics but of functionality as well.[27] His business concept for Time Design consisted in efficient, attractive and inexpensive product designs for kitchenware, lamps, furniture and components; larger projects such as aeroplanes, trains and cars; as well as 'sculptural displays' incorporating a wide range of materials, including plastic, steel, glass and terracotta. The firm was never launched, but Noguchi continued to design utilitarian objects until his death.

20 Noguchi, 'From an Interview with Isamu Noguchi', p. 8.

21 Isamu Noguchi, draft for 'What's the Matter with Sculpture', undated [1936], p. 1, The Noguchi Museum Archives, MS_WRI_004_002.

22 The following artists and architects had emigrated from Europe to the United States: Anni and Josef Albers, Walter Gropius, László Moholy-Nagy, Herbert Bayer, Ludwig Mies van der Rohe, Xanti Schawinsky, Marguerite Friedlaender, Hannes Beckmann, Lyonel Feininger and Marcel Breuer.

23 Dore Ashton, *The New York School: A Cultural Reckoning* (New York: Viking Press, 1973), p. 24. Noguchi briefly sojourned in Moscow during his trip to China in spring 1930. At that time, the avant-garde had already been forced underground in Russia owing to Stalin's dictatorship.

24 Noguchi, 'Draft of Bollingen pages 138–150', p. 140.

25 Sam Hunter, *Isamu Noguchi* (New York: Abbeville Press, 1978), p. 75; Noguchi, *A Sculptor's World*, p. 36; 'Oral History Interview with Isamu Noguchi, 1973 Nov. 7–Dec. 26' (1973), Archives of American Art, Smithsonian Institution, Washington, DC.

26 Isamu Noguchi, 'What Is Sculpture?', 8 June 1985, p. 1, The Noguchi Museum Archives, MS_WRI_069_008.

27 Letter from Isamu Noguchi to Edward Rumely, 28 October 1932, including the design for Time Design as an attachment, The Noguchi Museum Archives, MS_COR_316_005.

Noguchi's interest in industrial design was certainly also prompted by his friendship with R. Buckminster Fuller.[28] Shortly after returning from Paris, he got to know the visionary architect, who introduced him to the newest technologies and scientific theories. They shared a vision for an equitable society, to which each wanted to make their contribution. Fuller developed the Dymaxion House and Car as well as his geodesic domes, the first of which he built during a summer course at Black Mountain College in 1948. Noguchi made plaster models of the Dymaxion Car (pp. 52–53), and these were illustrated in the November 1932 issue of *Shelter* magazine, which was edited by Fuller. The cover featured an illustration of the plaster cast for Noguchi's first aluminium sculpture, *Miss Expanding Universe* (p. 280). Noguchi also published an article on traditional Japanese architecture in the same issue. He placed emphasis on the simplicity of the constructions, which were based on natural forces, and drew a comparison with Fuller's concept of Dymaxion – a portmanteau of the words 'dynamic', 'maximum' and 'ion'.[29] In 1929, Noguchi had also produced a portrait of Fuller, which he had cast in bronze and subsequently chrome-plated, a process that at the time was primarily applied in the automobile industry (p. 50).

28 On the relationship between Fuller and Noguchi, see Shoji Sadao, *Buckminster Fuller and Isamu Noguchi: Best of Friends* (New York/Milan: The Isamu Noguchi Foundation and Garden Museum/ 5 Continents Editions, 2001).

29 Isamu Noguchi, 'Shelters of the Orient', *Shelter*, vol. 2, no. 5 (November 1932), p. 96.

Synthesis of Industry and Craftsmanship

Noguchi was interested in industrial materials and techniques as well as in traditional craftsmanship. This perhaps reflected his bicultural background: he associated the United States with progress and technology, while he valued the cultivation of traditional artisanry that he observed in Japan. He made his choice of materials and tools dependent on his location. Hence in Japan he worked mainly with terracotta and stone, because, as he described it, he sought 'contact with the earth' there.[30] In New York, on the other hand, he thought it apt to work with materials such as aluminium and steel.[31] To him, it was important constantly to try out new technologies and materials so as never to be defined by them. He likewise avoided developing a specific style.[32]

When he was a child in Japan, a carpenter taught Noguchi the traditional construction method of cogged wooden beams. Years later, in 1939, he applied the technique of joined elements that hold together by means of tension and weight in his design of a table for A. Conger Goodyear. He continued to develop it in a series of sculptures in the 1940s, initially made of wood and later of slate and marble, the latter of which he was able to obtain inexpensively in New York as the material had once been popular in construction but was now increasingly being replaced by glass and steel. In 1958 he began working with sheet aluminium in the workshop of the lighting designer Edison Price. He set himself the goal of folding each work out of a single piece of aluminium – later, steel – and eliminating the use of screws or other types of fasteners. Working with industrial machinery required him to be well prepared. As in his childhood, he first produced paper models, folded according to origami techniques. His *Akari* lamps represented a further fortunate blend of traditional artisanry with modern technology. During an earlier visit to the Japanese city of Gifu, which is well known for the manufacture of paper and bamboo lanterns, he recognised the potential of this time-honoured technique when combined with electric lightbulbs. Noguchi's surely most well-known body of work developed out of this insight, with the *Akari*

30 'Why do I continuously go back to Japan, except to renew my contact with the earth?', Isamu Noguchi, 'IN Quotes', 1930–65, p. 18, The Noguchi Museum Archives, MS_WRI_048_002.

31 Noguchi, *A Sculptor's World*, p. 35.

32 'I'm suspicious of the whole business of style because … the more I change, the more I'm me, the new me of that new time. To change is to invent, to create anew. This is why I applaud change. There is an unconscious line in my work – it's unavoidable.' John Gruen, 'The Artist Speaks: Isamu Noguchi', *Art in America*, vol. 56, no. 2 (March–April 1968), p. 30.

in part continuing to finance the museum he founded to this day. Whatever technique he adopted, for Noguchi it was invariably a question of maintaining a certain 'honesty' of the material, and the resources were to be used economically, as he had earlier learned in Brâncuși's studio. (Incidentally, the economy of means was also one of the credos of the Bauhaus.)

The integration of traditional craftsmanship and modern design was one of the key goals of the Bauhaus school, just as it was at the Kala Bhavana in India. During the periods when Noguchi resided in Japan, in the 1930s and 1950s, discussions were also taking place about the extent to which the country's artisan traditions could be modernised. Whereas non-European cultures, in particular Japanese culture,[33] were examined at the Bauhaus in Weimar from 1919 to 1925 and focus was placed on the individual artisan-artist, attention was turned to industrial manufacturing by the time the school relocated to Dessau in 1926. By contrast, in India or Japan the question at hand was of how to protect the local culture from Westernization. In 1931, when Noguchi spent nearly an entire year in Japan, two movements were emerging that examined questions of design and art, industry and craftsmanship. That year, the Japanese architect Renshichirō Kawakita founded the Seikatsu Kōsei Kenkyūsho (Research Institute for Life Design). Kawakita was close friends with Japanese architects and teachers as well as with the first Japanese students at the Bauhaus in Dessau, such as Takehiko Mizutani and Michiko and Iwao Yamawaki. Both Mizutani and Kawakita saw the Bauhaus as a collective endeavour to renew art training, and in June 1931 they created an experimental Bauhaus-related exhibition for the Tokyo Academy of Arts. A year later, the Research Institute for Life Design became a private school with the name Shin Kenchiku Kōgei Gakuin (School of New Architecture and Design). The curriculum was developed through intense analysis of the Bauhaus's pedagogical approach as well as developments in Japanese modernism.[34] Although the school existed for only a few years – it had to close in 1936 under pressure from the nationalist government – it had a formative influence on numerous Japanese practitioners, including the graphic designer Yūsaku Kamekura and the fashion designer Yōko Kuwasawa, who founded their own school in Tokyo after the Second World War. Walter Gropius paid a visit there in 1954, during his only sojourn in Japan; on the same trip, he also viewed Noguchi's exhibition at the Chūō Kōron Gallery, attested to by photographs taken by Noguchi.[35]

The second movement, which also flourished in the early 1930s, was a reaction to the rapid modernisation the country was experiencing. The philosopher Sōetsu Yanagi was passionate about the country's rich cultural heritage and began to collect artisan craftwork from traditions that were in danger of disappearing. In 1936 he founded the first Japanese folk crafts museum, the Nihon Mingeikan. Convinced that beauty was to be found in simple, utilitarian everyday objects, Yanagi coined the term *mingei* – an abbreviation of *minshūteki na kōgei*, meaning 'ordinary people's crafts' – to describe folk crafts and their beauty, simplicity and functionality. As part of this concept, Yanagi believed that *mingei* objects should be able to be reproduced in quantity, inexpensively and using traditional methods, and that their authorship should remain anonymous (as opposed to being made by a 'named' craftsperson).

33 On the interactions between the Bauhaus and Japan, see Helena Čapková, 'The Bauhaus and the Tea Ceremony', *bauhaus imaginista* (online journal), www.bauhaus-imaginista.org/articles/1605/the-bauhaus-and-the-tea-ceremony, accessed 13 January 2021.

34 On this, see Helena Čapková, 'Framing Renshichirō Kawakita's Transcultural Legacy and His Pedagogy', in *bauhaus imaginista*, ed. Von Osten and Watson, pp. 56–59; Hiromitsu Umemiya, 'Naked Functionalism and the Anti-Aesthetic: The Activities of Renshichirō Kawakita in the 1930s', *bauhaus imaginista* (online journal), www.bauhaus-imaginista.org/articles/2331/naked-functionalism-and-the-anti-aesthetic, accessed 13 January 2021.

35 There are several photographs by Noguchi of Gropius at the Chūō Kōron Gallery in the Noguchi Museum Archives, for example cat. 09341.4.

We do not know to what extent Noguchi engaged with these discussions, though they would certainly have interested him. What we do know is that during renewed stays in Japan in the early 1950s, he addressed the question of the direction in which Japanese culture should develop in the post-war period. Along with his companion the artist Saburō Hasegawa, who was well acquainted with Western art, he learned more about Zen philosophy. They talked about the question of identity and how Japanese tradition could be brought forward into the here and now.[36] Noguchi wanted Japan to (re)discover its own culture.[37] He communicated his vision of a modern Japanese design that made reference to its own tradition – without, however, being nationalistic – above all to the designer Isamu Kenmochi, who worked at the Kōgei Shidōsho (Industrial Arts Research Institute) and with whom Noguchi collaborated on designs for furniture.[38] On 20 June 1950, Noguchi held a lecture at the Tokyo National Museum on modern trends in furniture design in which he pointed out that Japanese culture had made a mark on American design and that the trend in Japan towards retaining or rediscovering traditional methods could be implemented in a much purer way. He also mentioned the new schools of design in the United States and the teaching methods introduced at the Bauhaus by Gropius and László Moholy-Nagy, whom he had visited.[39]

Noguchi was a universal artist who participated in an international network. His interest in a type of design intended to touch people through its simplicity, purity of function and honesty is what connected him with all of the individuals and movements with which he came into contact over the course of his life.

Fabienne Eggelhöfer is the curator of *Isamu Noguchi* at Zentrum Paul Klee, Bern

36 Dore Ashton, *Noguchi East and West* (New York: Alfred A. Knopf, 1992), pp. 93–99; Mark Dean Johnson and Dakin Hart, eds, *The Saburo Hasegawa Reader* (Berkeley, CA: University of California Press, 2019).

37 Saburo Hasegawa, 'Days with Isamu Noguchi' [1951], in *The Saburo Hasegawa Reader*, p. 81.

38 *Design: Isamu Noguchi and Isamu Kenmochi*, exh. cat., The Isamu Noguchi Foundation and Garden Museum (New York: Five Ties Publishing, 2007), especially Bonnie Rychlak, 'Searching for the New and Authentic: Shaping the Design Production of Isamu Noguchi and Isamu Kenmochi', pp. 21–53: p. 44.

39 The lecture 'Modern Trends in Interior Furnishings' was first published in the Japanese magazine *Kōgei nyūsu* [Industrial Art News], vol. 18, no. 10 (October 1950), pp. 18–19; English translation in *Design: Isamu Noguchi and Isamu Kenmochi*, pp. 127–28.

Plan for park and recreation areas at Poston War Relocation Center, Yuma County, Arizona, 1942

N ← S

Length 1 Mile
Scale 1:100

Symbols

- Canals - Laterals
- Paths - Bridges
- Hogans Shades
- Popstands
- Dressing Rooms
- Shower Fountains
- Baseball - Softball
- Basketball
- Tennis
- Mesquite - Olive - Carob
- Palms - Date - Washingtonia
- Tamarack - Tamarisk - Willow - Cypress
- Eucalyptus - Cottonwood - Ash
- Fig - Loquat - Pomegranate - Plum
- Oleander - Jasmine
- Grape

Locations

a. Administration
b. School Area
c. Primary Play Area
d. Secondary
e. Natatorium
f. Amphitheater
g. Stage - Screen - Music
h. Dance - Gymnasium
i. Community Center
j. Theater Building
k. Cafe - Restaurant
l. Department Store
m. Market - Stores
n. Football - Track
o. Japanese Garden
p. Founders Grove
q. Church
r. Art Center
s. Settlers Grove
t. Botanical Garden
u. Zoological
v. Miniature Golf
w. Hospital
x. Hospital Garden
y. Warehouse
z. Gate

All Building Adobe

• The American Flag

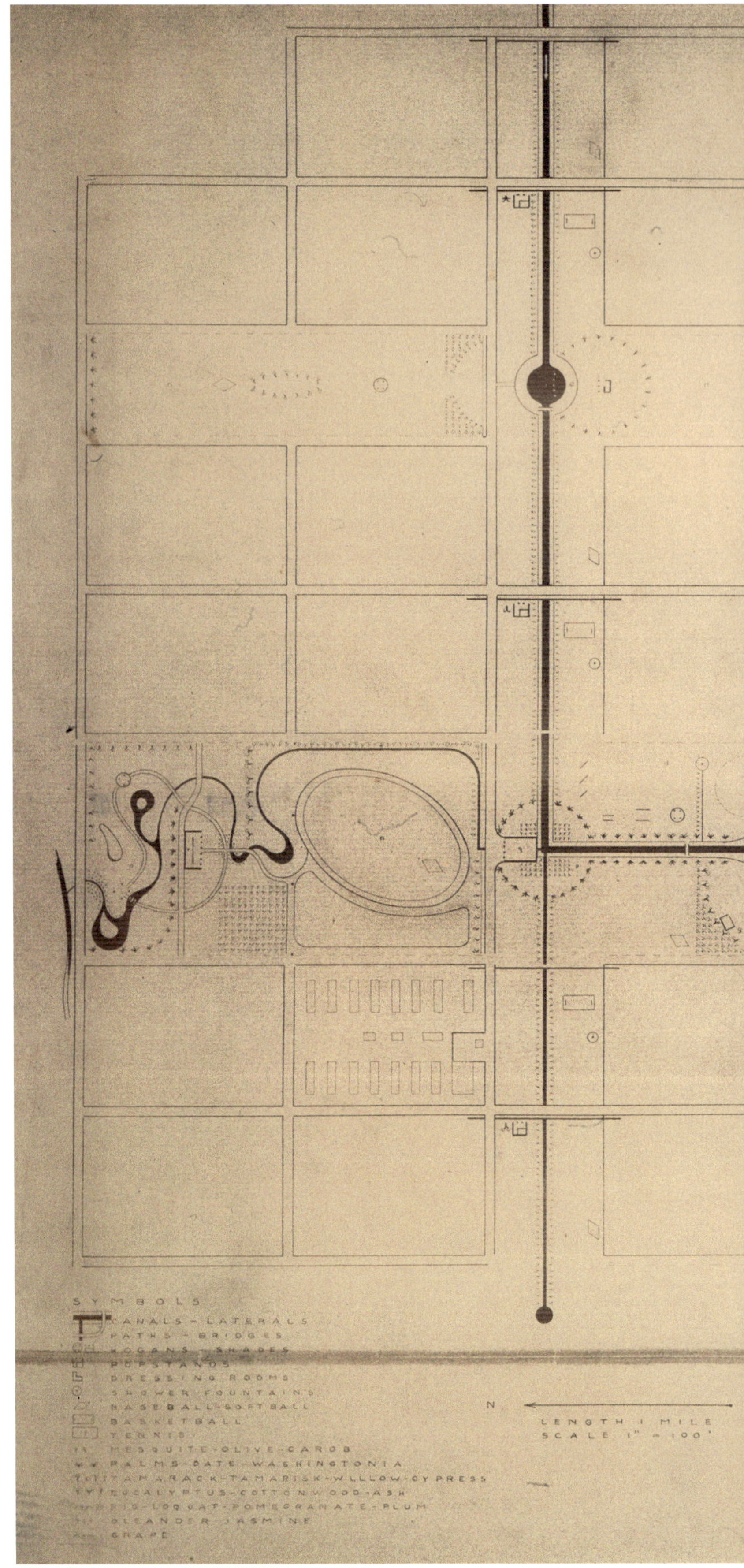

Unit II, looking southeast, Poston War Relocation Center, Yuma County, Arizona, 1942

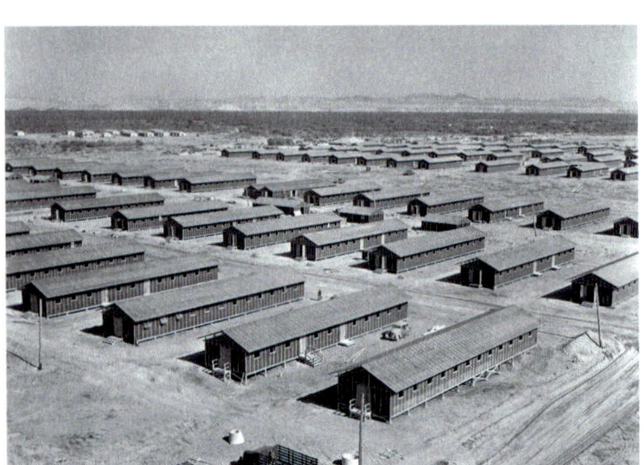

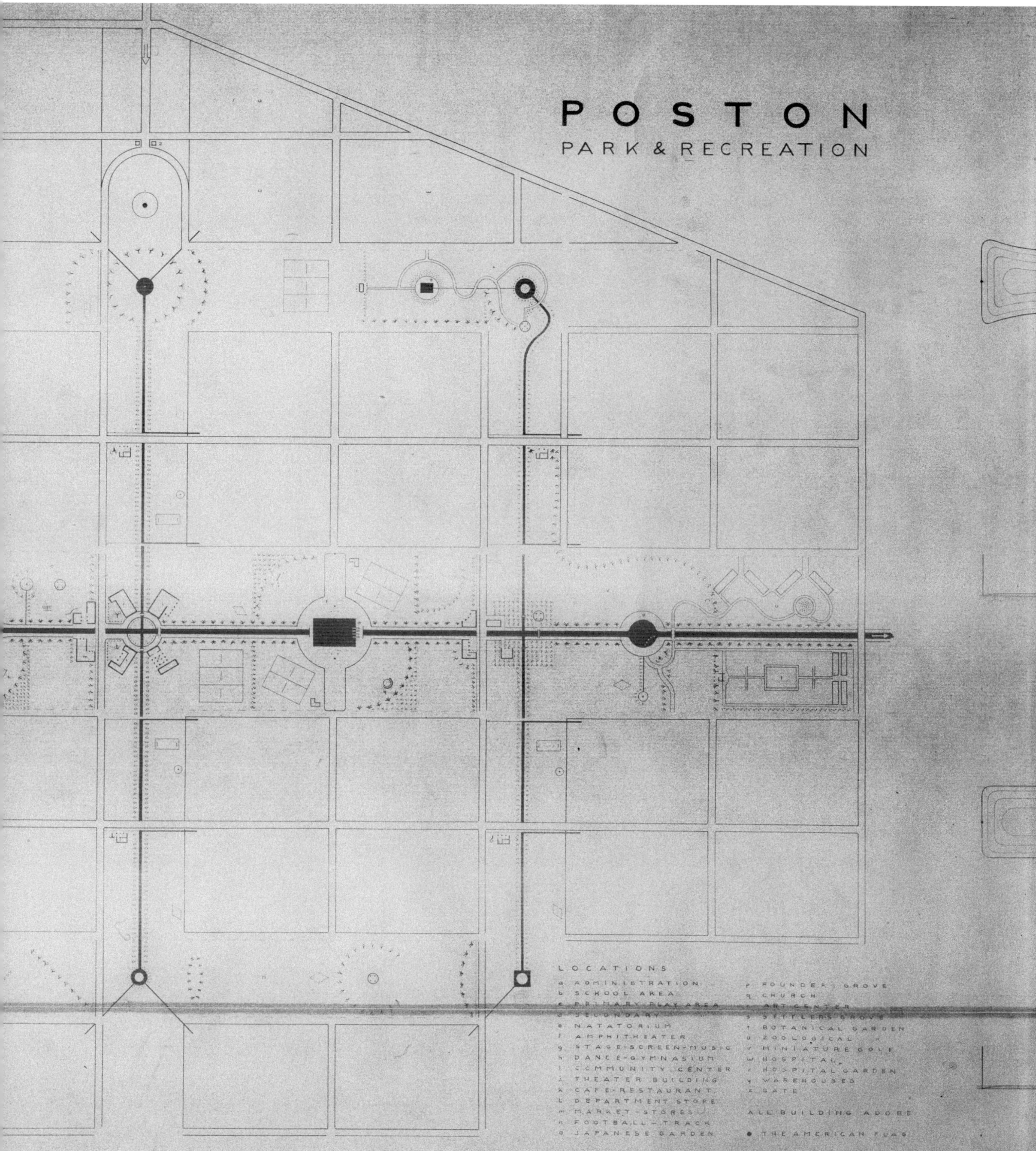
POSTON
PARK & RECREATION
LOCATIONS
a ADMINISTRATION
b SCHOOL AREA
c PRIMARY PLAY AREA
d SECONDARY
e NATATORIUM
f AMPHITHEATER
g STAGE-SCREEN-MUSIC
h DANCE-GYMNASIUM
i COMMUNITY CENTER
j THEATER BUILDING
k CAFE-RESTAURANT
l DEPARTMENT STORE
m MARKET-STORES
n FOOTBALL-TRACK
o JAPANESE GARDEN
p FOUNDERS GROVE
q CHURCH
r ART CENTER
s SETTLERS GROVE
t BOTANICAL GARDEN
u ZOOLOGICAL "
v MINIATURE GOLF
w HOSPITAL
x HOSPITAL GARDEN
y WAREHOUSES
z GATE
ALL BUILDING ADOBE
● THE AMERICAN FLAG

My Arizona, 1943
Fibreglass and Plexiglas
46.4 × 46.4 × 11.7 cm
Second state with original elements

The dust was blowing as I arrived in Poston, the new Japanese community on the floodlands of the lower Colorado River. Eye-burning dust, and the temperature seemed to stand at 120 degrees for three solid months.

1942

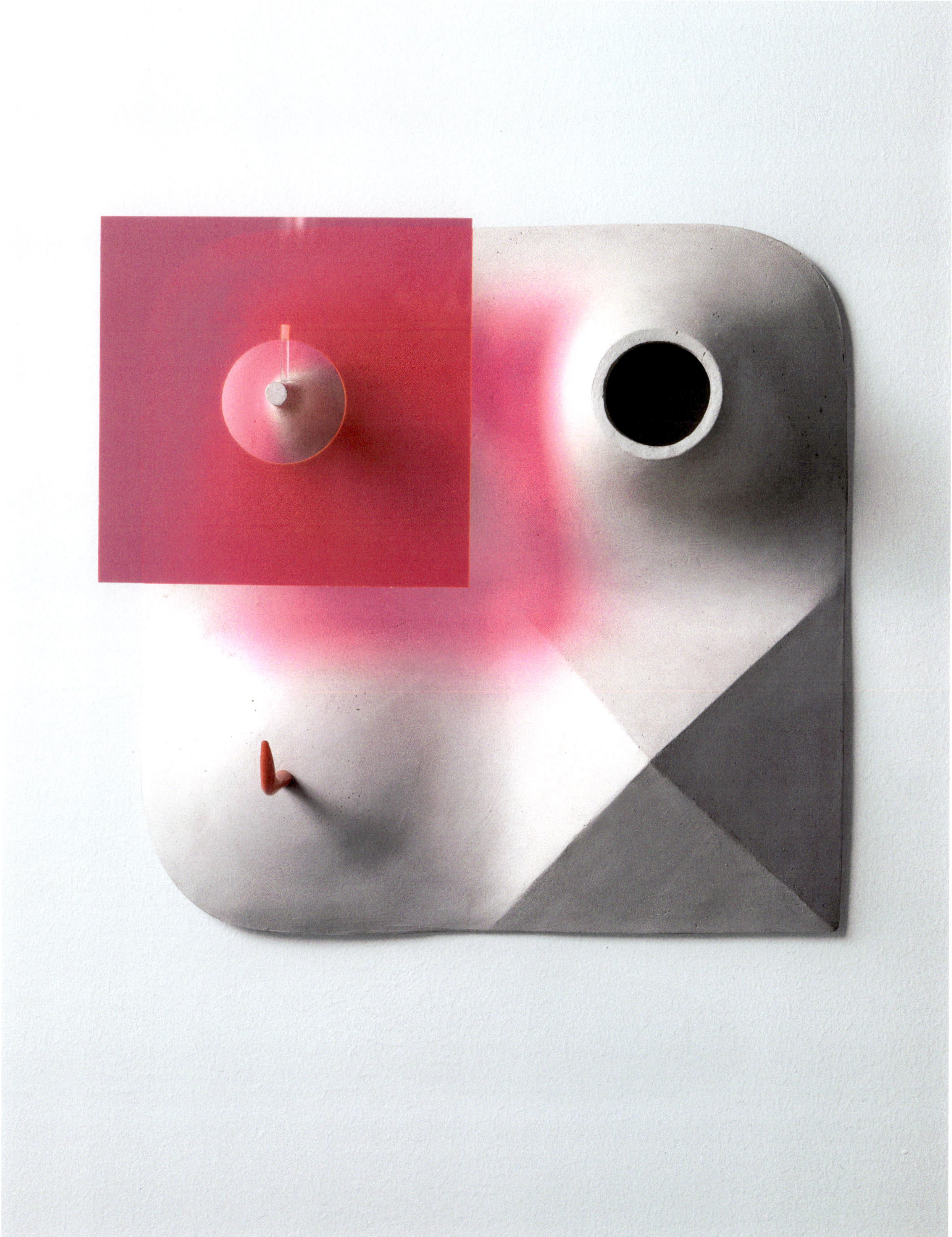

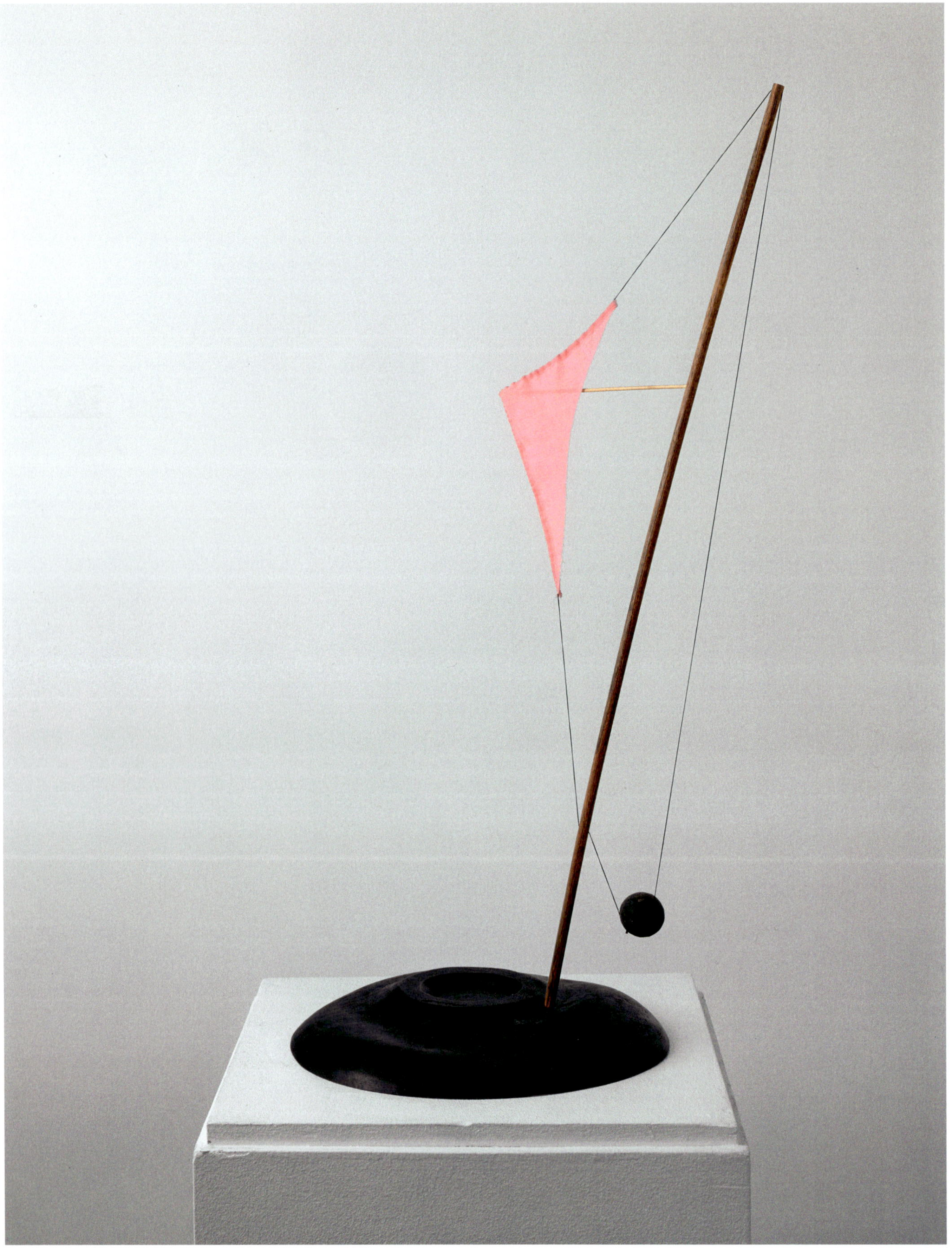

The World is a Foxhole (I am a Foxhole), 1942–43
Bronze, wood, string and fabric
81.3 × 42.5 × 34.3 cm

Yellow Landscape, 1943
(reconstructed 1995)
Magnesite, wood, string and metal fishing weight
77.5 × 82.9 × 17.1 cm

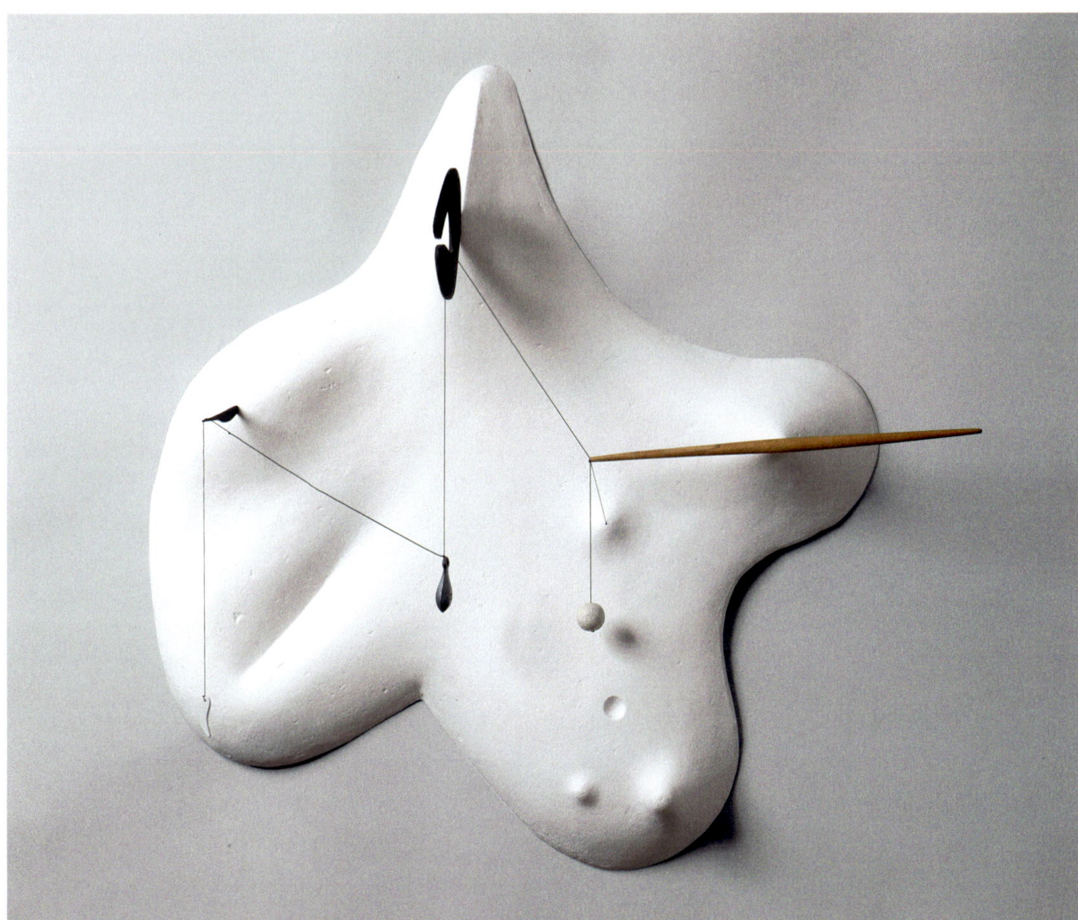

Lunar Landscape, 1944
Magnesite, cork, fishing line, acetate and electrical components
87 × 62.9 × 15.2 cm

Lunar Voyage, 1947
(for the SS *Argentina*; destroyed)
Magnesite and electrical components
Dimensions unknown

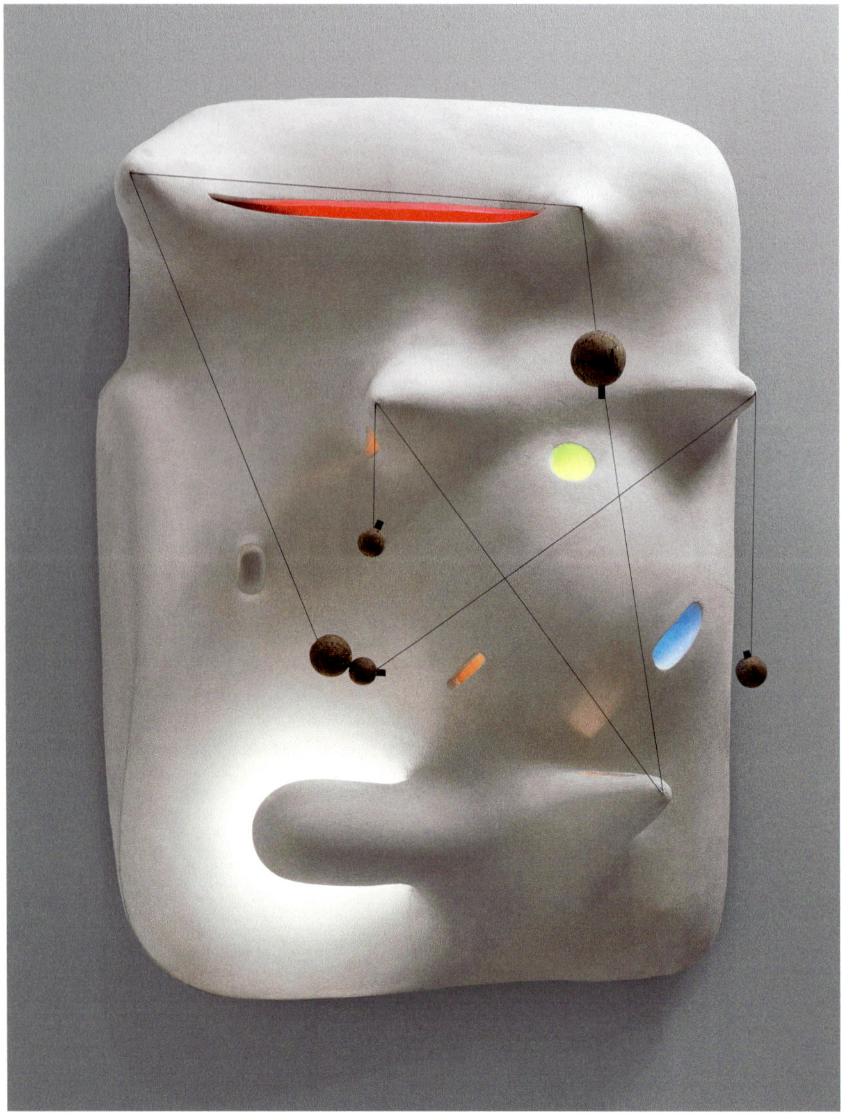

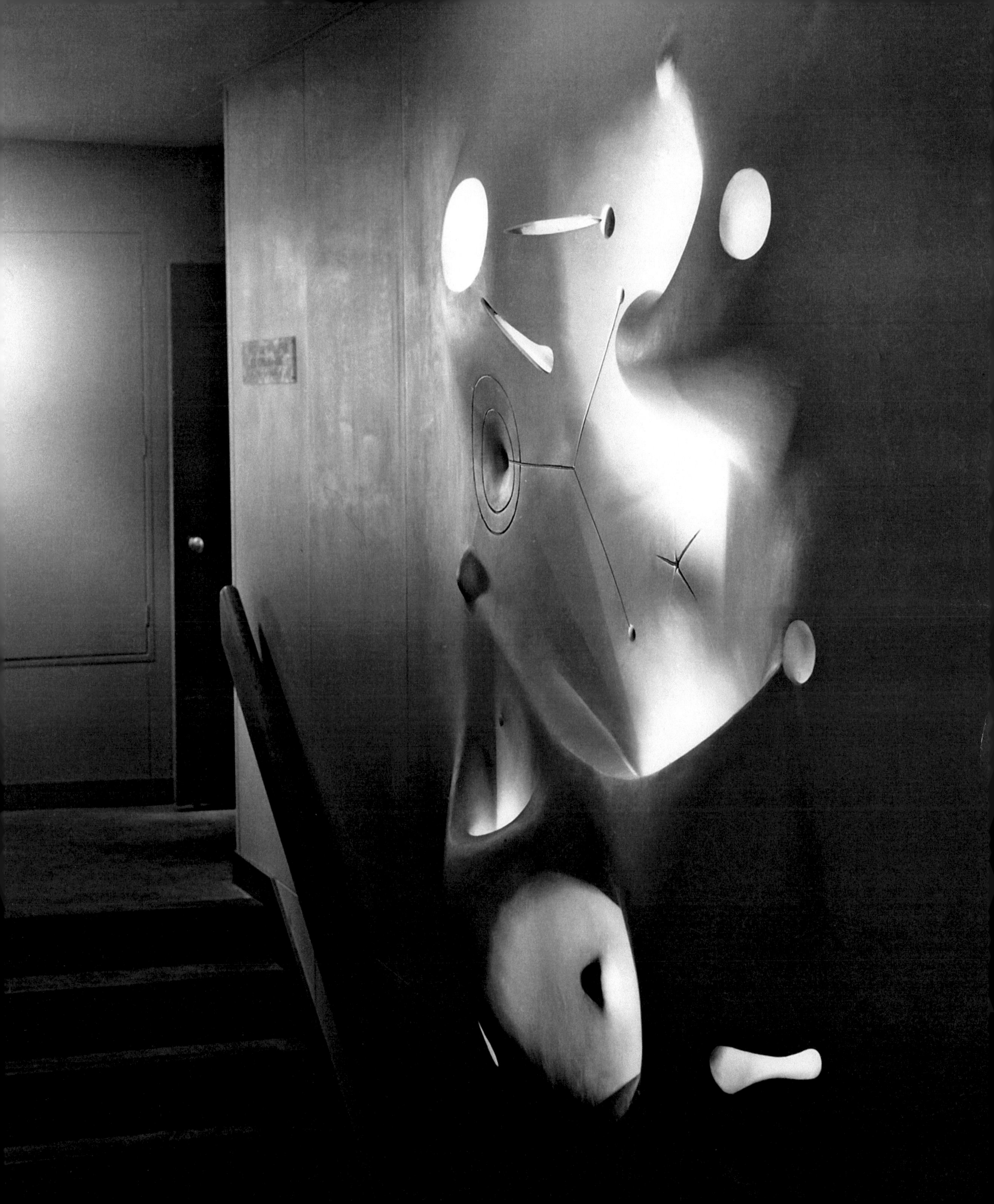

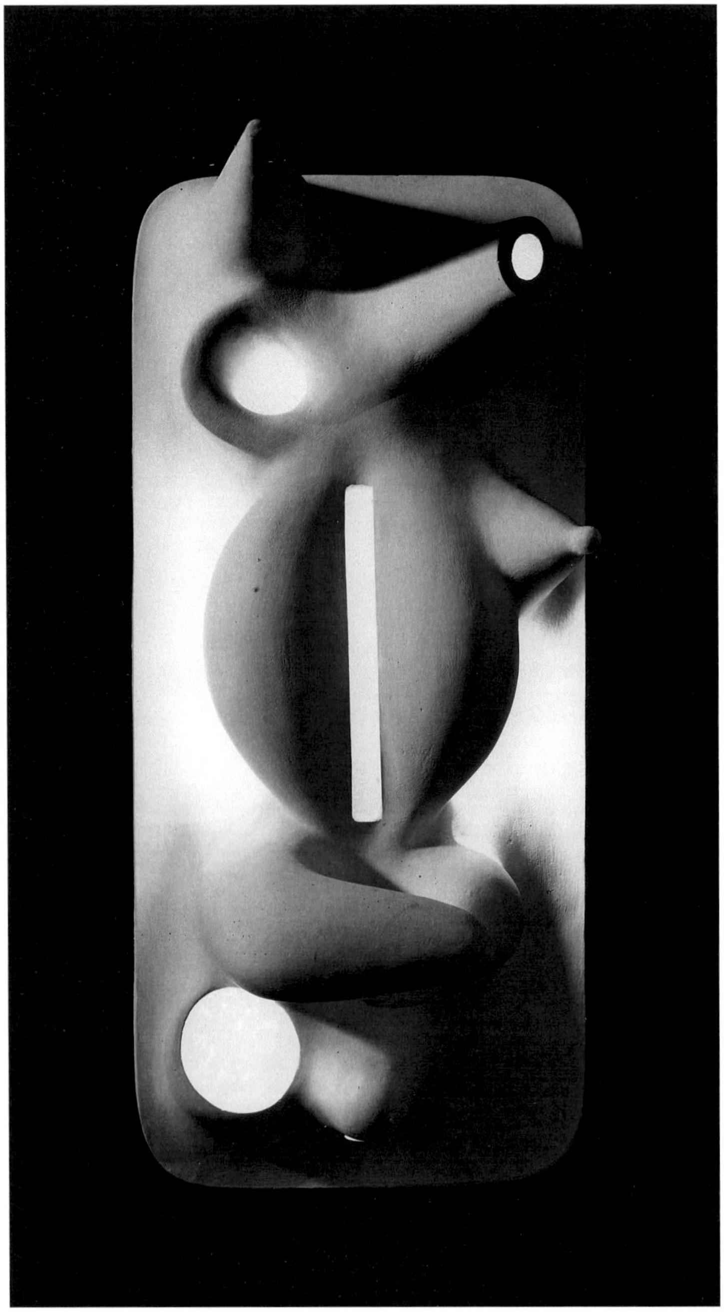

Lunar Landscape (Woman), 1944
Magnesite and electrical components
68.3 × 30.5 × 27.9 cm

Untitled, 1943–45
Plastic
49.2 × 39.7 × 29.8 cm

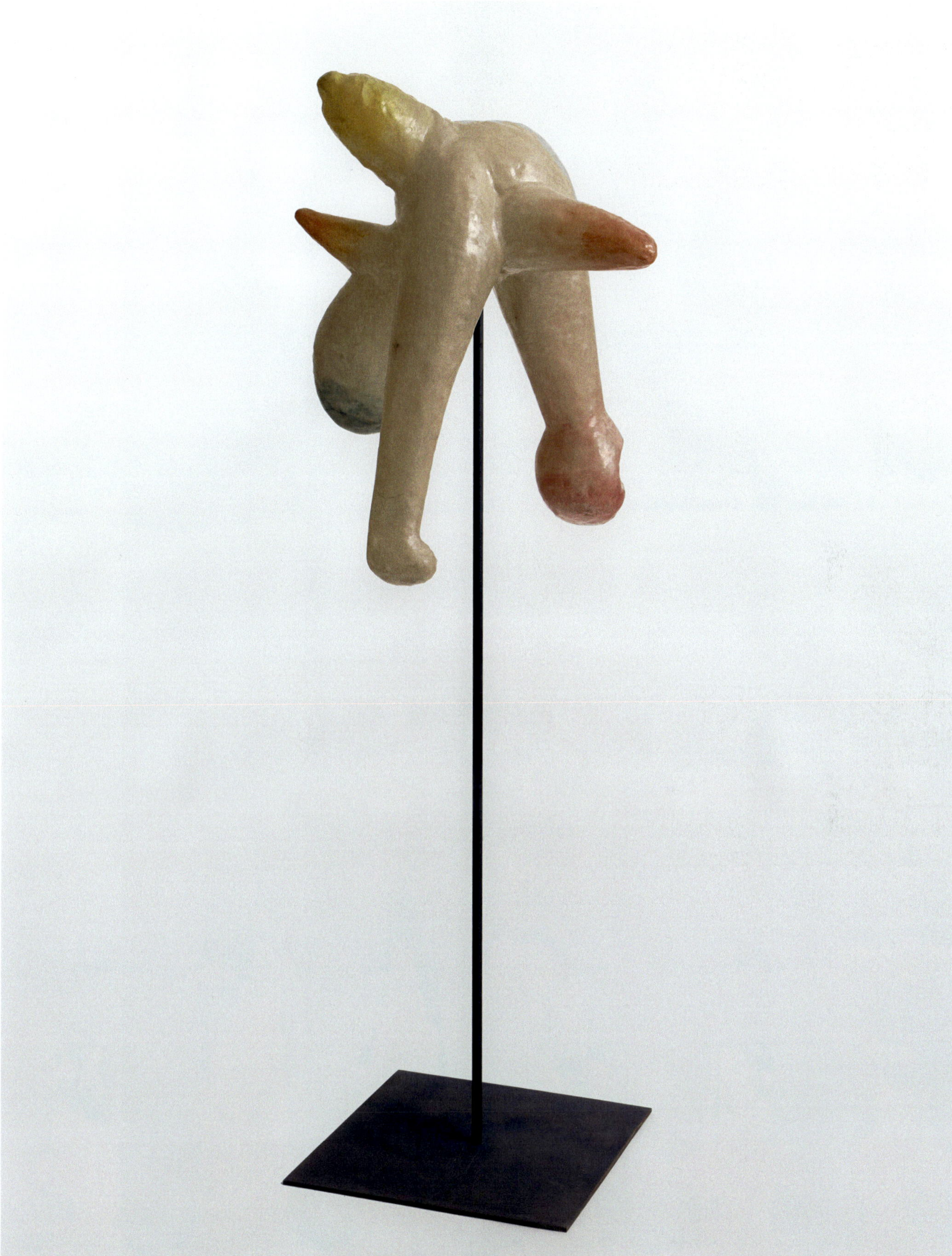

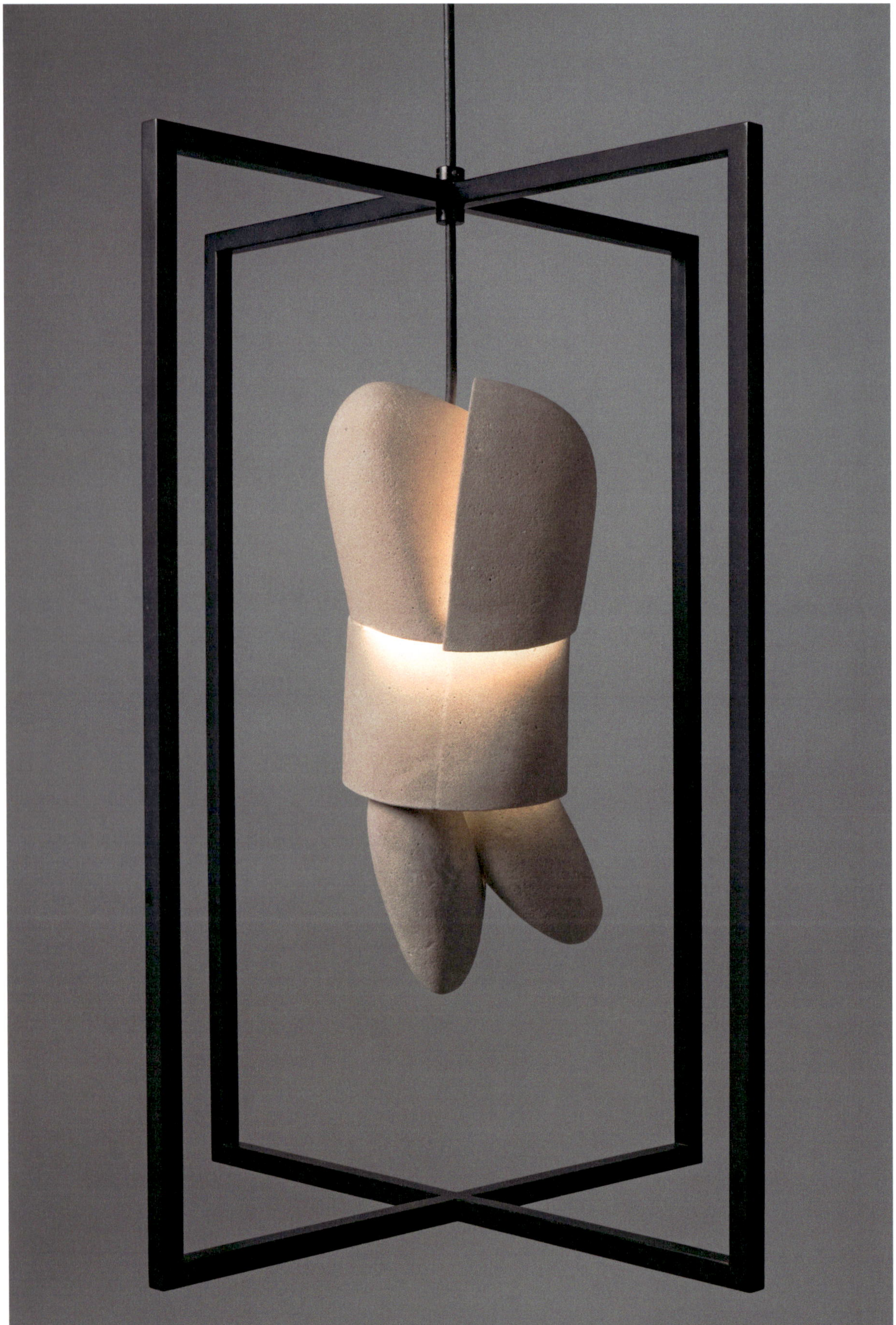

Lunar Infant, 1944
Magnesite, wood and electrical components
55.9 × 40.6 × 40.6 cm

Red Lunar Fist, 1944
Magnesite, plastic, resin and electrical components
18.1 × 21.3 × 22.2 cm

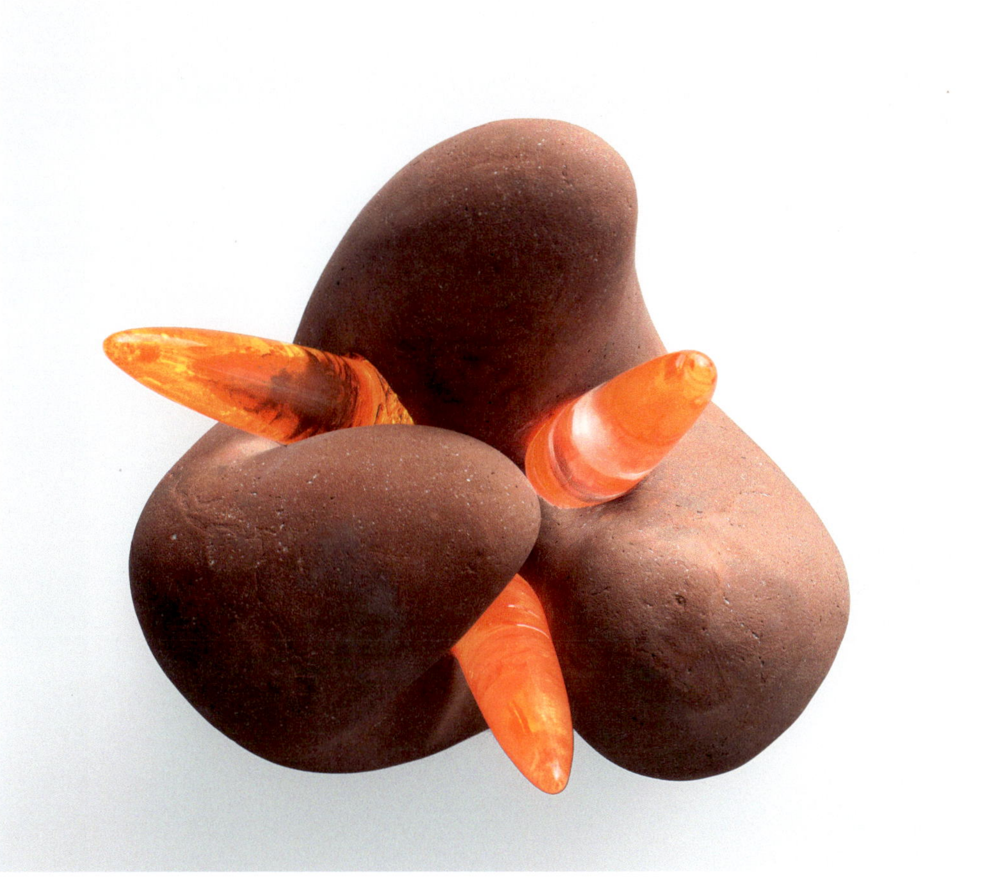

Works in Noguchi's studio on MacDougal Alley, Greenwich Village, New York, including *My Pacific, Floating Lunar, My Arizona, Structure, The World is a Foxhole, Contoured Playground, The Mountain, Musical Weathervane, The Queen, Red Lunar Fist* and others, 1940s

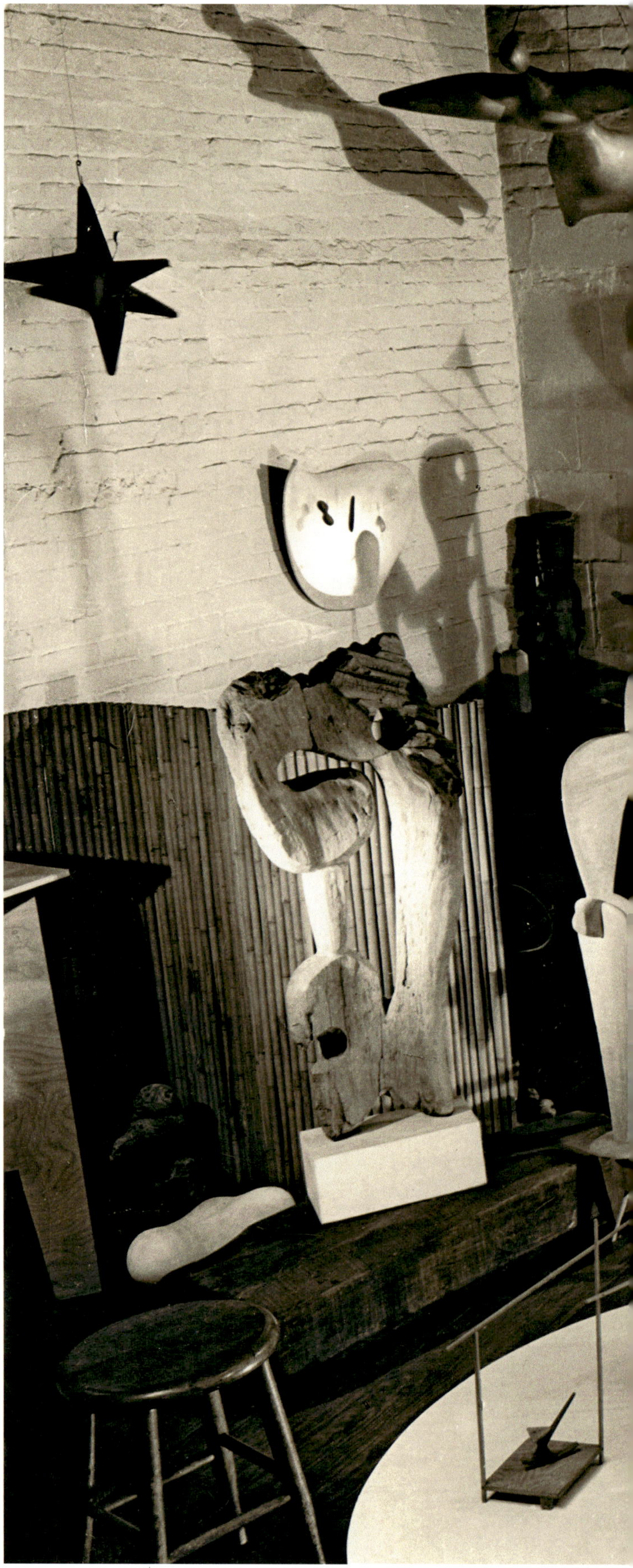

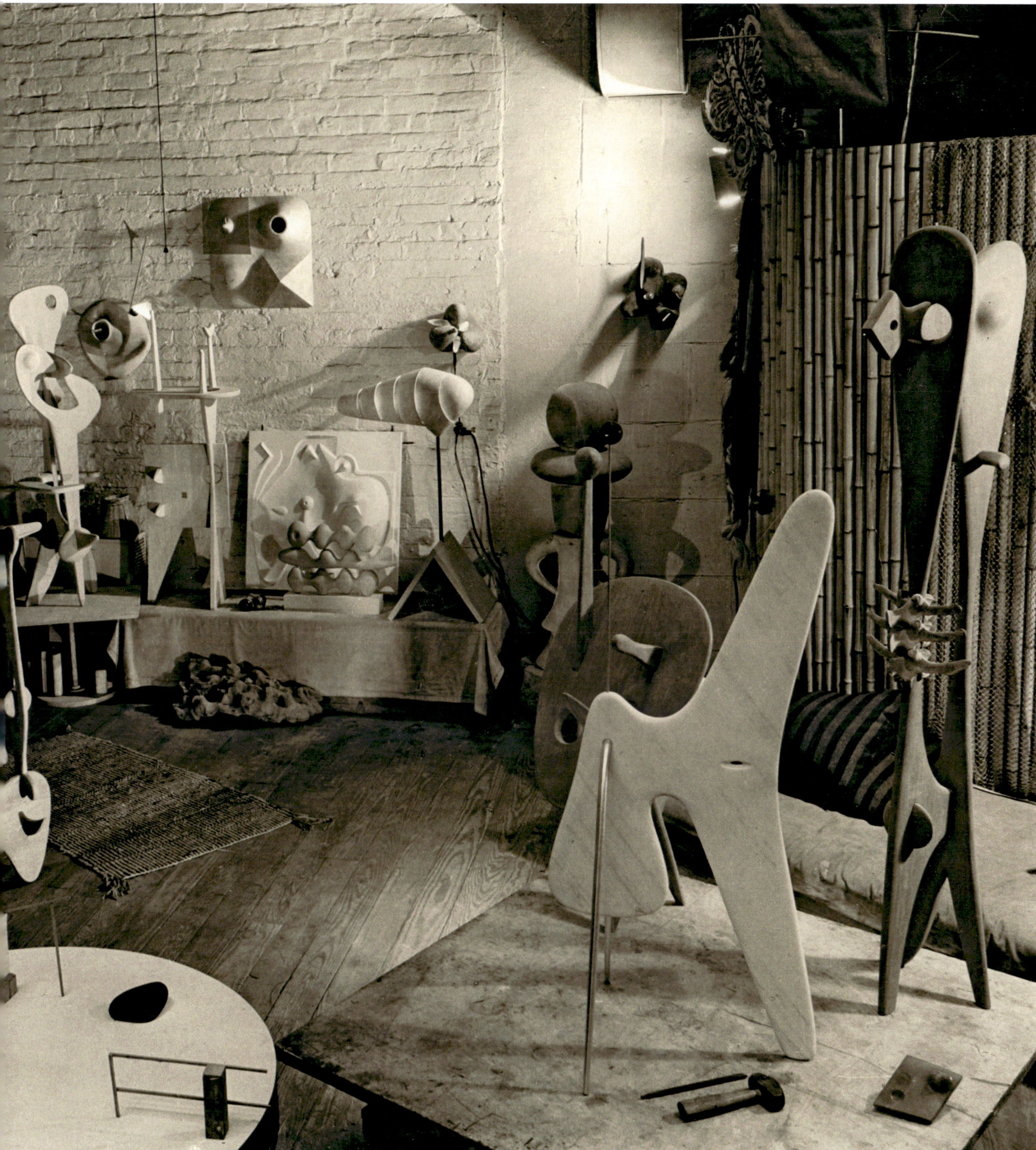

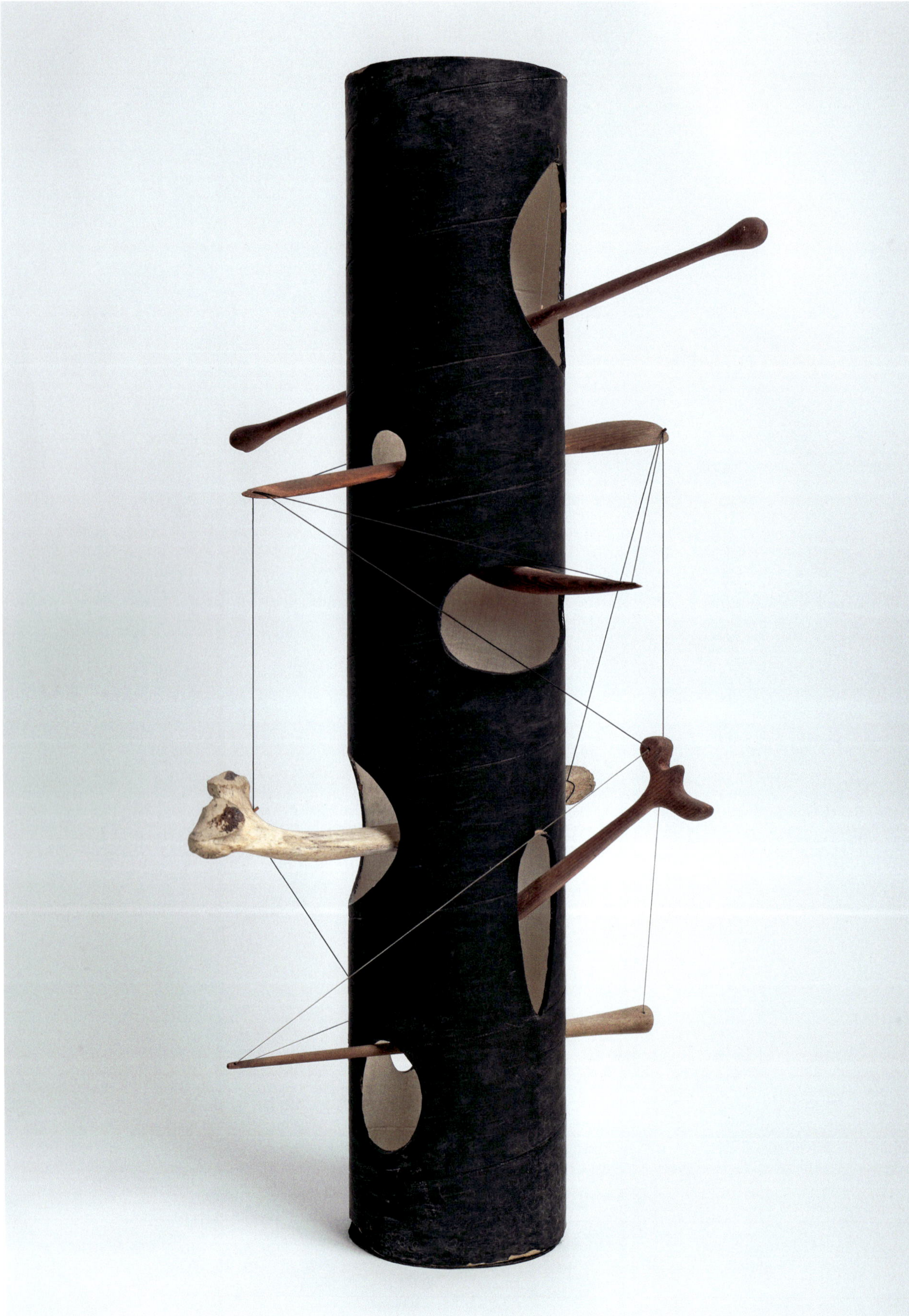

Monument to Heroes, 1943
Cardboard, wood, bones and string
71.8 × 34.6 × 24.8 cm
First of two versions

Bird's Nest (Nesting), 1947
Wood dowels, balsa wood, paper, paint and tape
42.5 × 45.7 × 33 cm

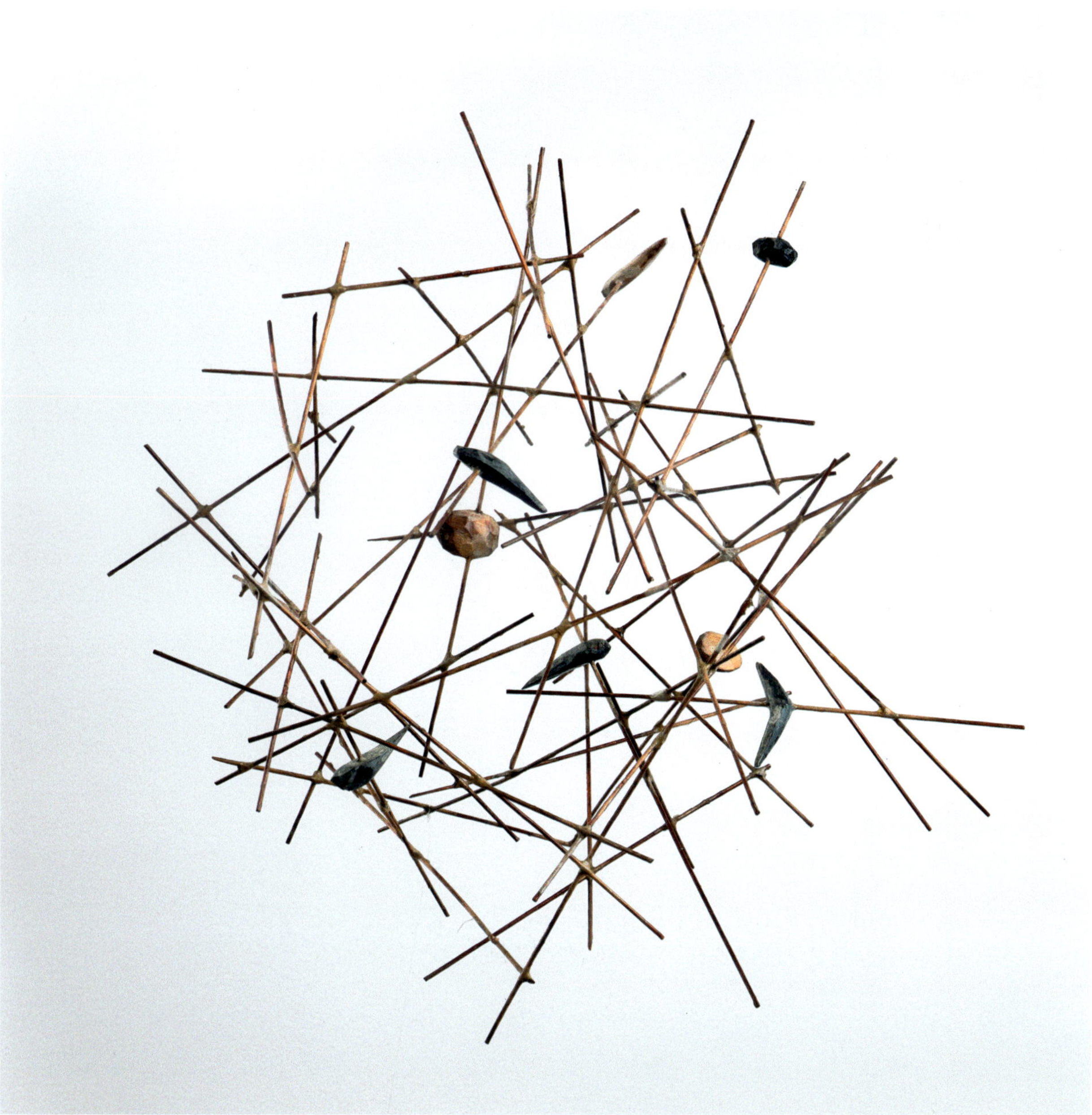

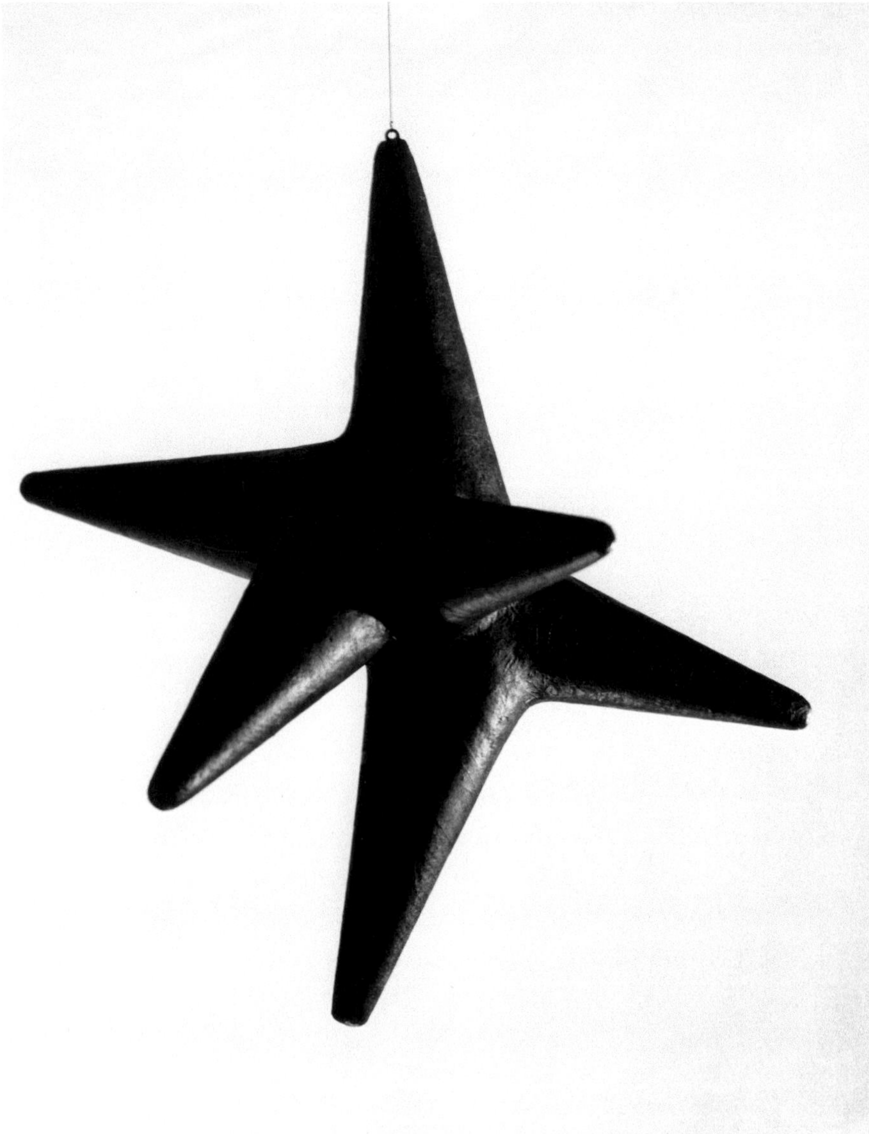

E=MC², 1944
Papier maché
34.6 × 29.8 × 25.4 cm

Bucky, 1943
Wood and wire
101.6 × 33 × 33 cm

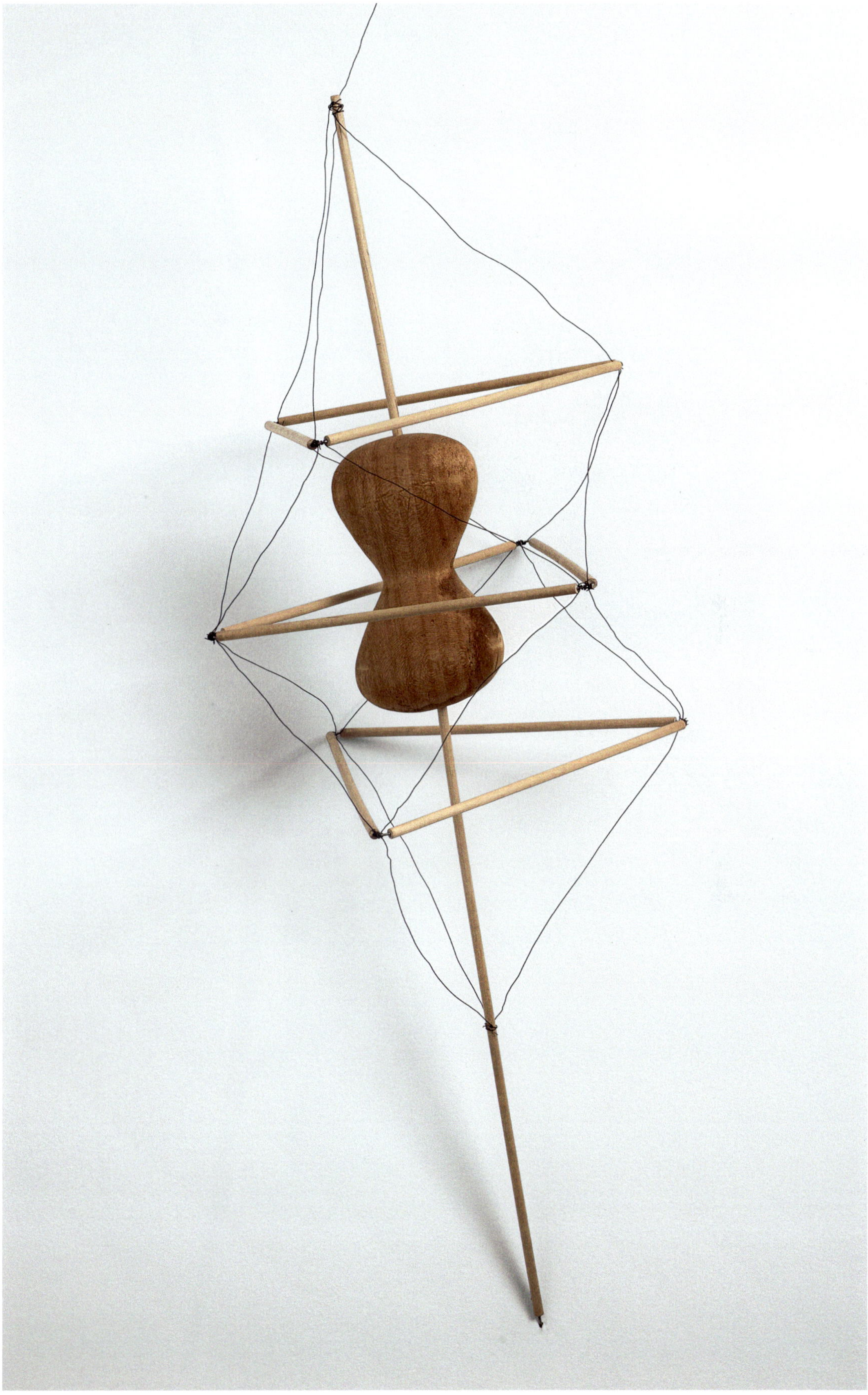

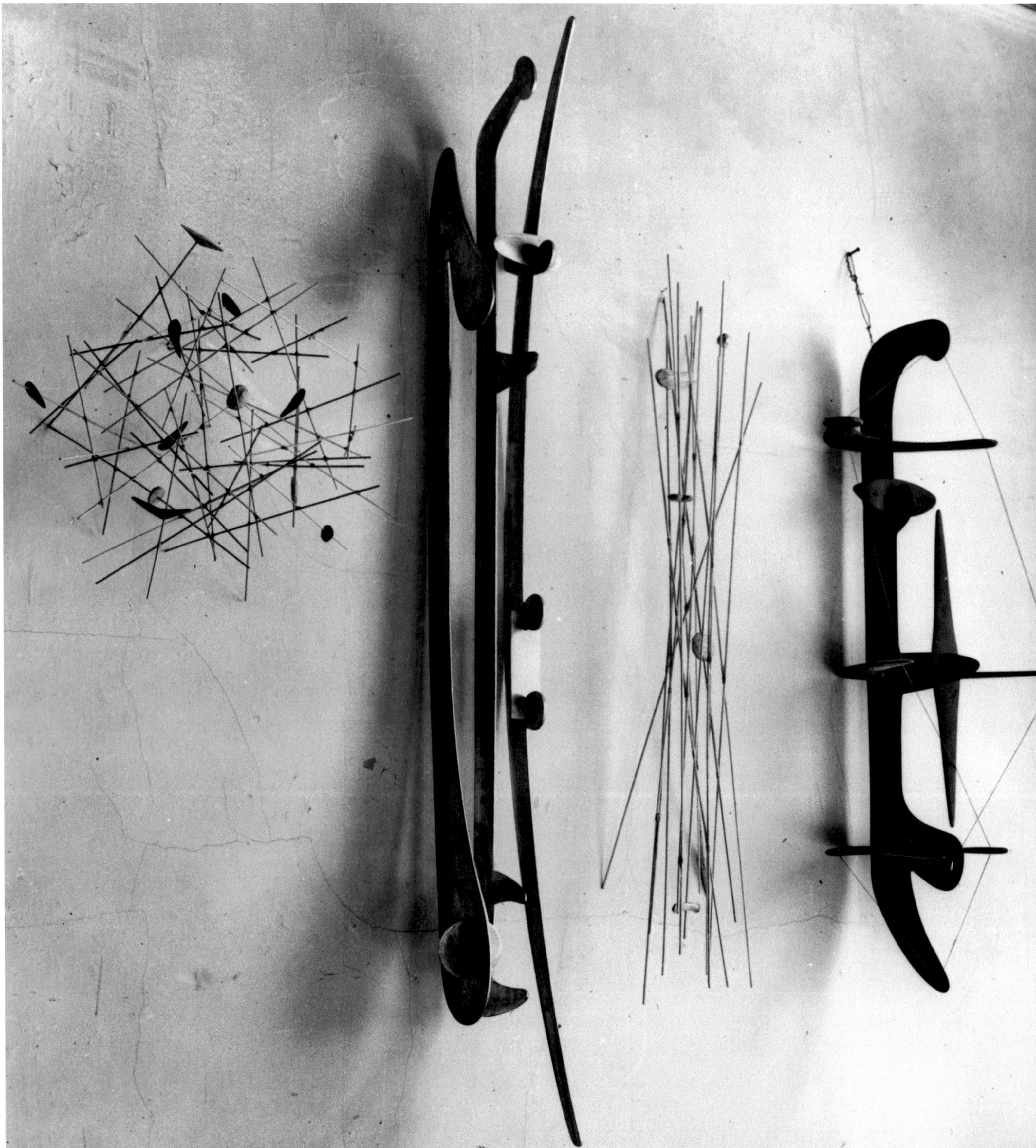

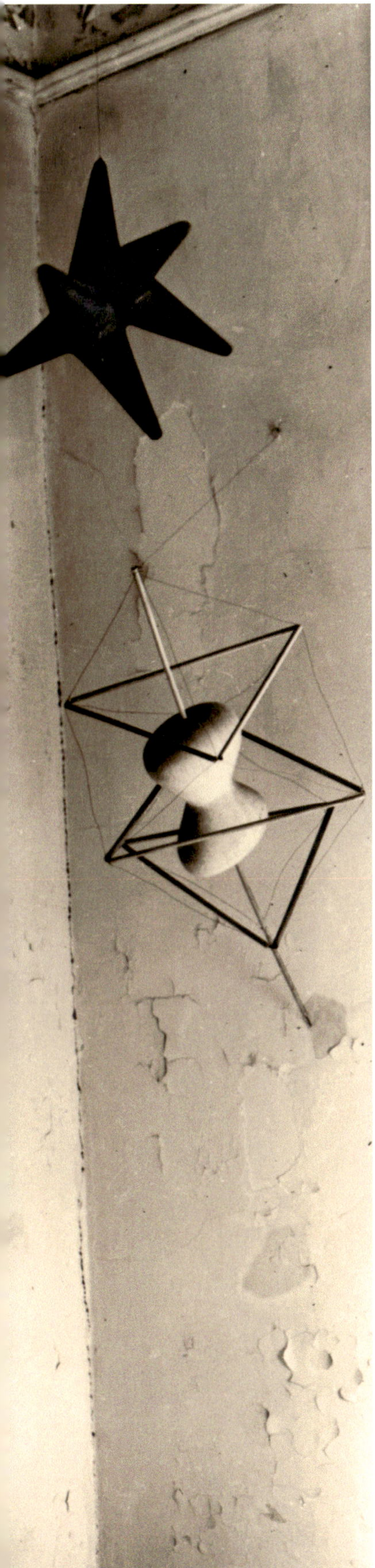

Works in Noguchi's studio on MacDougal Alley, including *Bird's Nest*, *Hanging Man*, *Composition*, *Untitled*, *Bucky* and *E=MC²*, 1947

Stage set for Martha Graham,
***Hérodiade*, 1944**

PeiJu Chien-Pott in Martha Graham,
***Hérodiade*, 2019**

Within a woman's private world, and intimate space, I was asked to place a mirror, a chair, and a clothes rack. Salome dances before her mirror. What does she see? Her bones, the potential skeleton of her body. The chair is like an extension of her vertebrae; the clothes rack, the circumscribed bones on which is hung her skin. This is the desecration of beauty, the consciousness of time.

1967

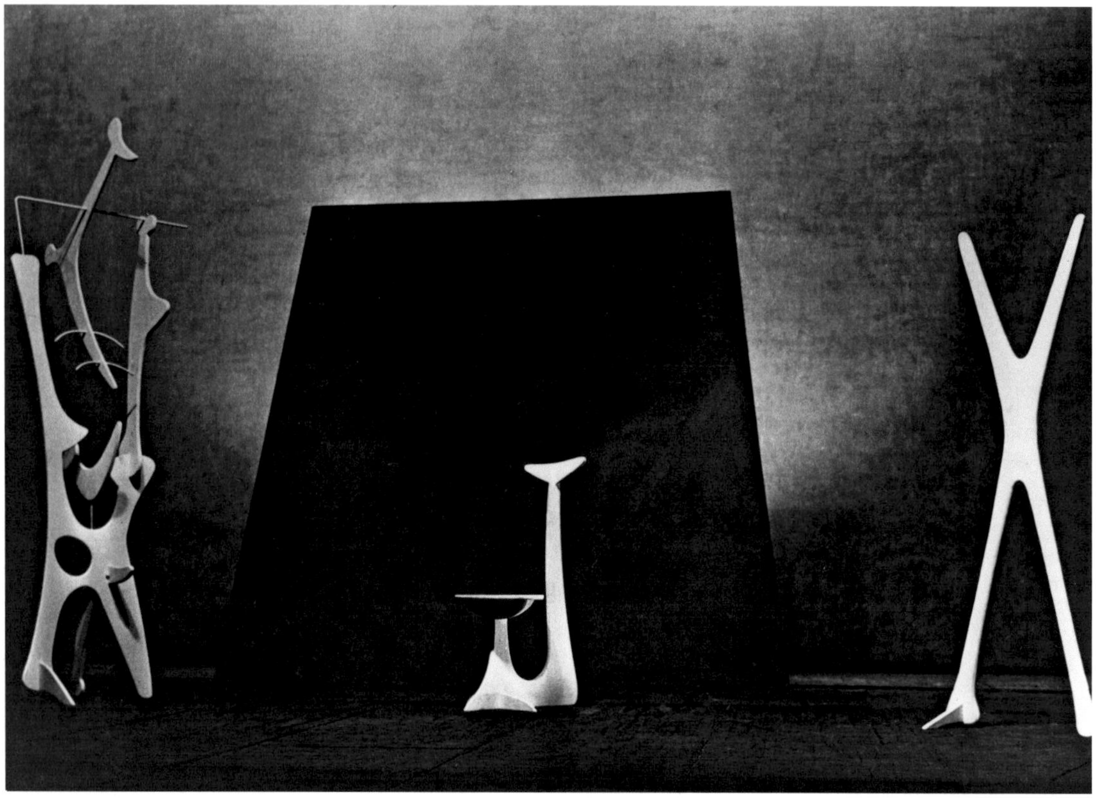

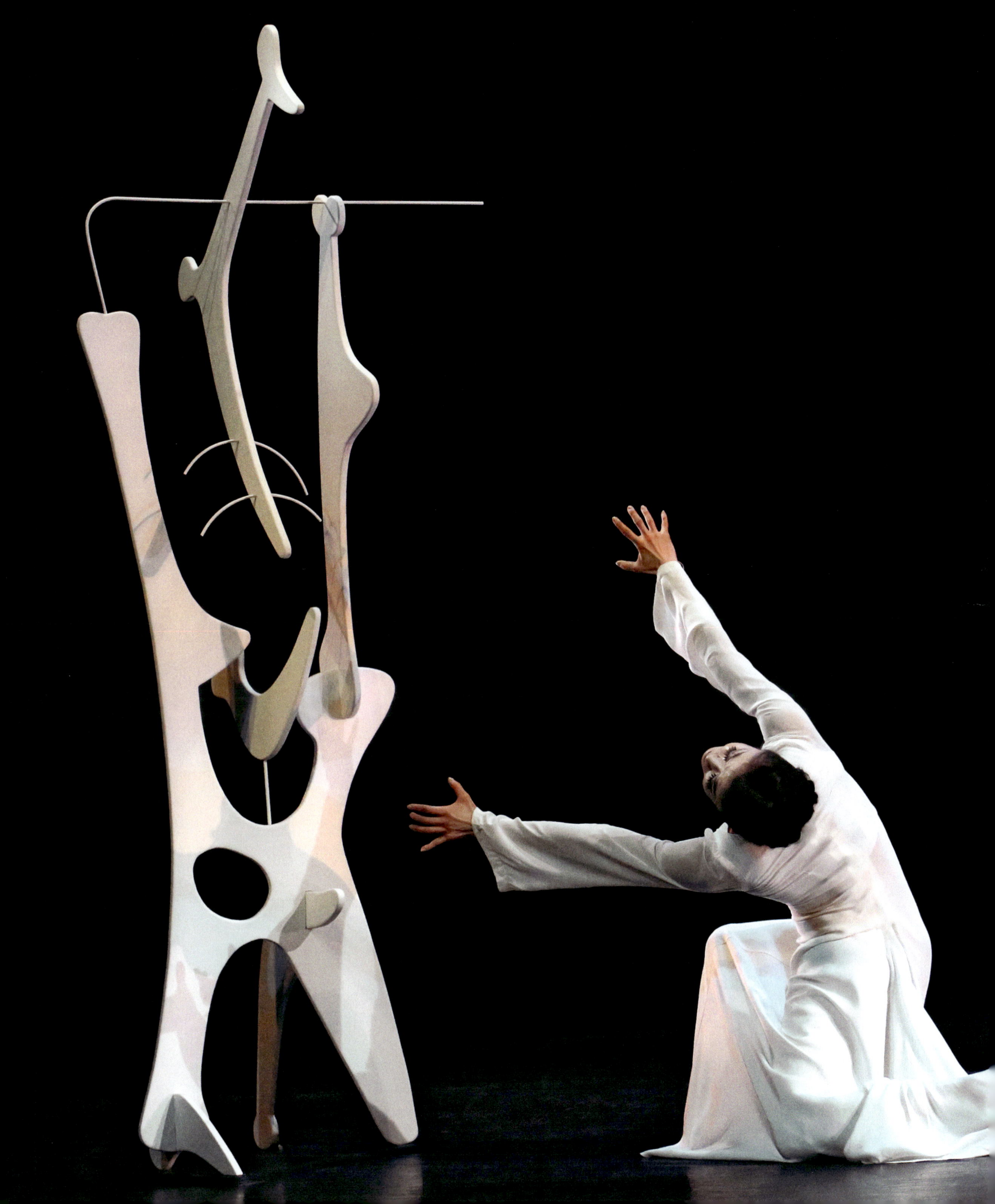

Martha Graham with *Spider Dress* for *Cave of the Heart*, 1946

Martha Graham with *Spider Dress* and *Serpent* for *Cave of the Heart*, 1946

There is a joy in seeing sculpture come to life on the stage in its own world of timeless time. Then the very air becomes charged with meaning and emotion, and form plays its integral part in the re-enactment of a ritual. Theater is a ceremonial; the performance is a rite. Sculpture in daily life should or could be like this.

1967

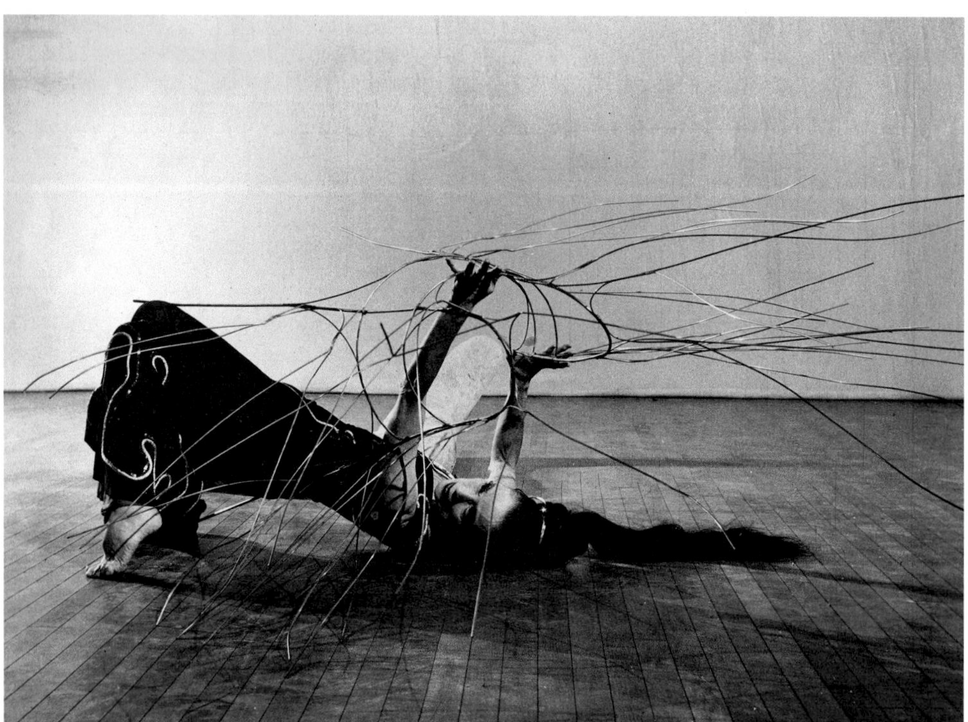

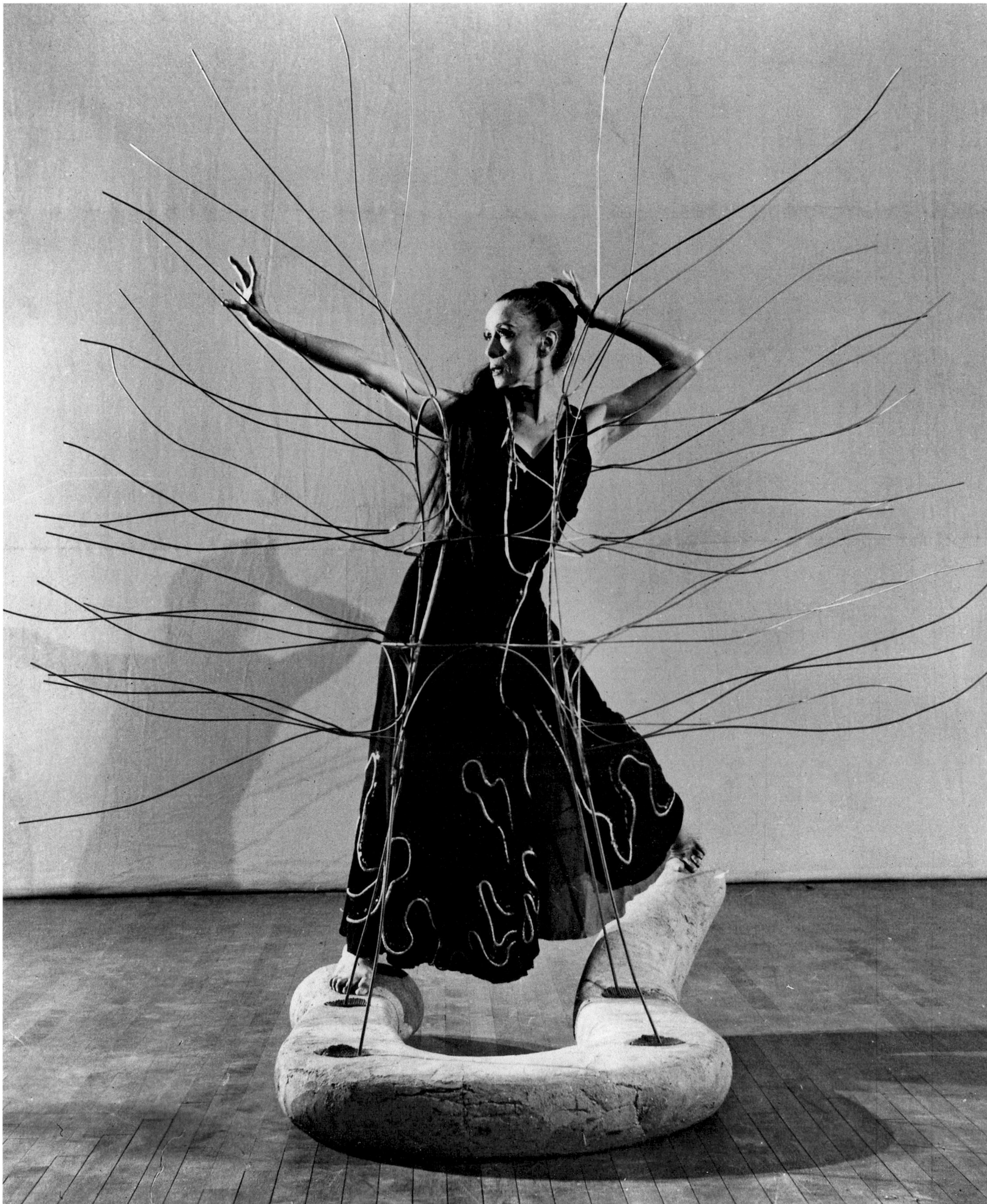

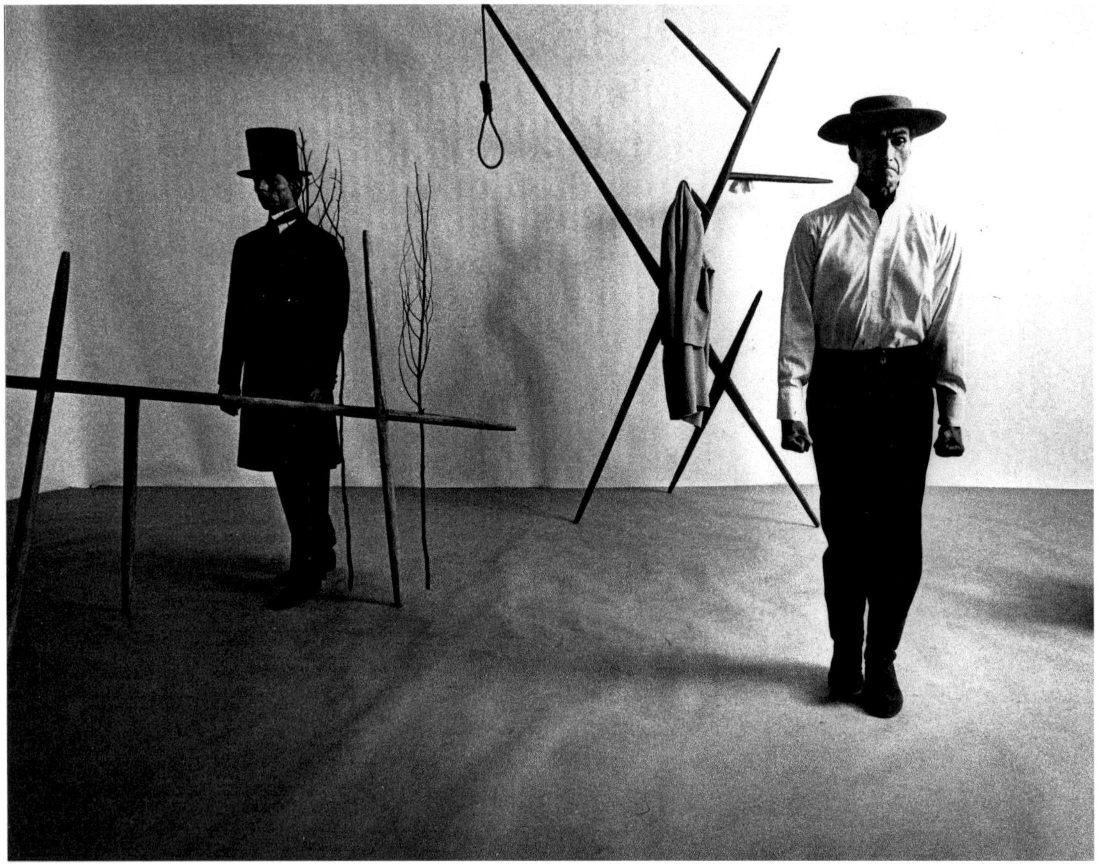

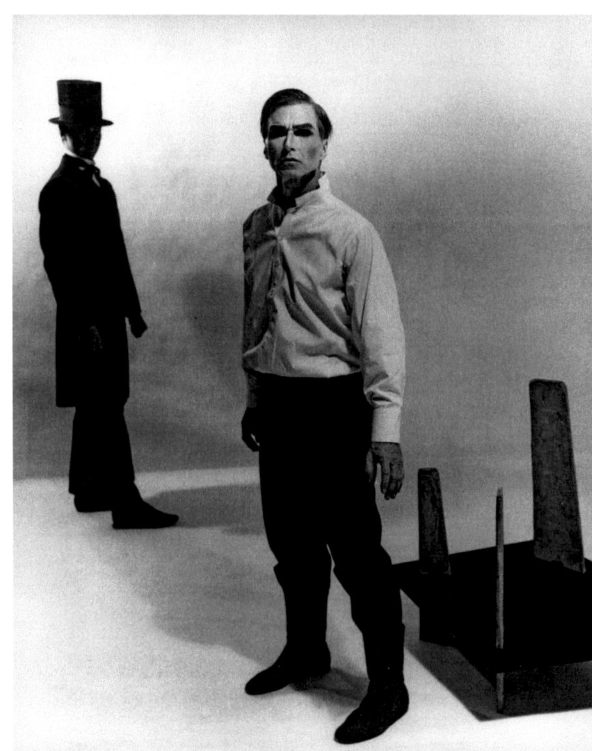

Stage set for Erick Hawkins,
***John Brown* (*God's Angry Man*), 1945**

Set elements:

***Tree with Noose*, 1945**
Wood and paint
284.5 × 195.6 × 119.4 cm

***Fence with Branches*, 1945**
Wood, paint and branches
145.1 × 203.8 × 48.3 cm

***Gravestones*, 1945**
Wood and paint
89.5 × 88.9 × 78.1 cm

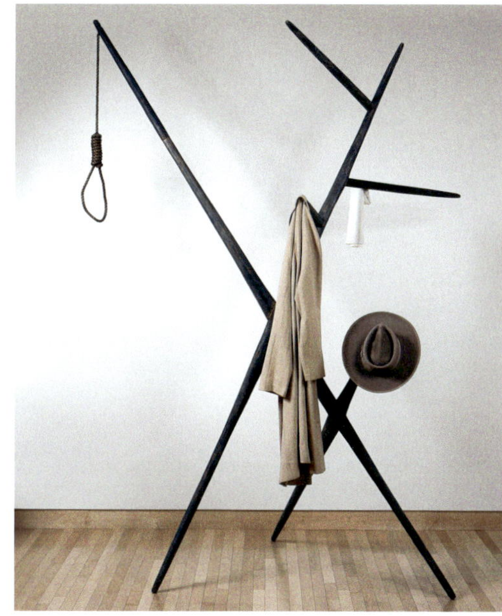

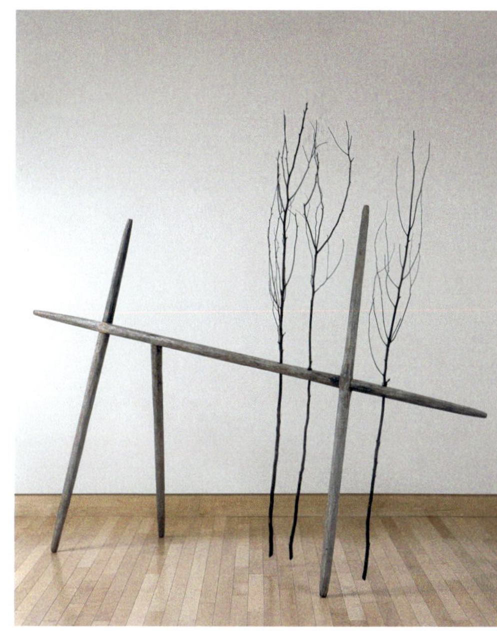

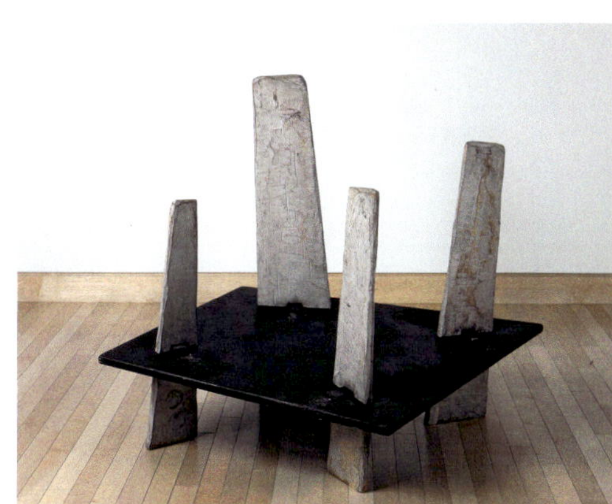

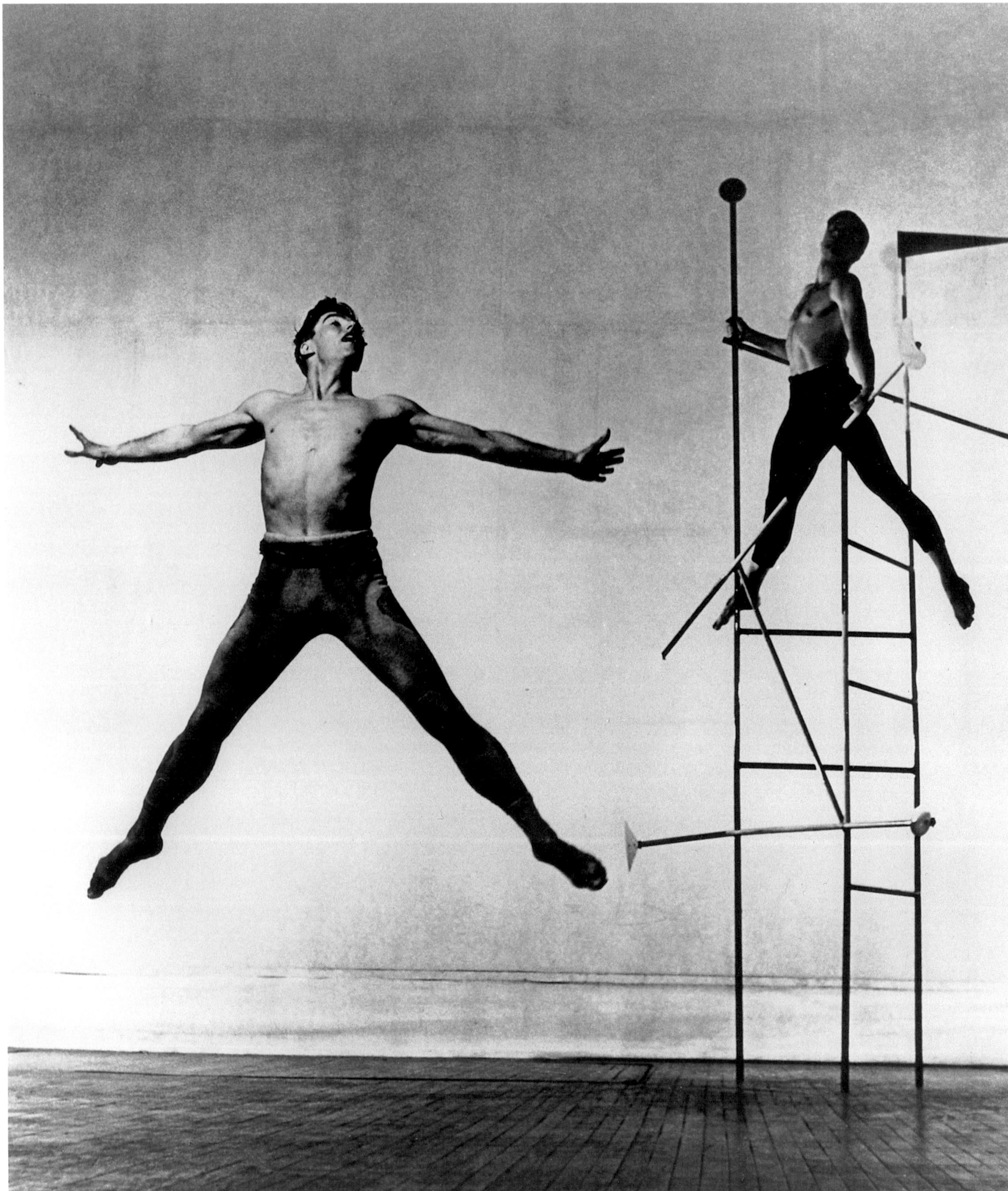

Stage set for Erick Hawkins,
***Stephen Acrobat*, 1947**

Set elements:

Jungle Gym, 1947
Steel, plastic and paint
394.3 × 224.2 × 118.4 cm

Hanging Tree, 1947
Rope, bamboo, plastic, wood and paint
213.3 × 144.8 × 19.1 cm (variable)

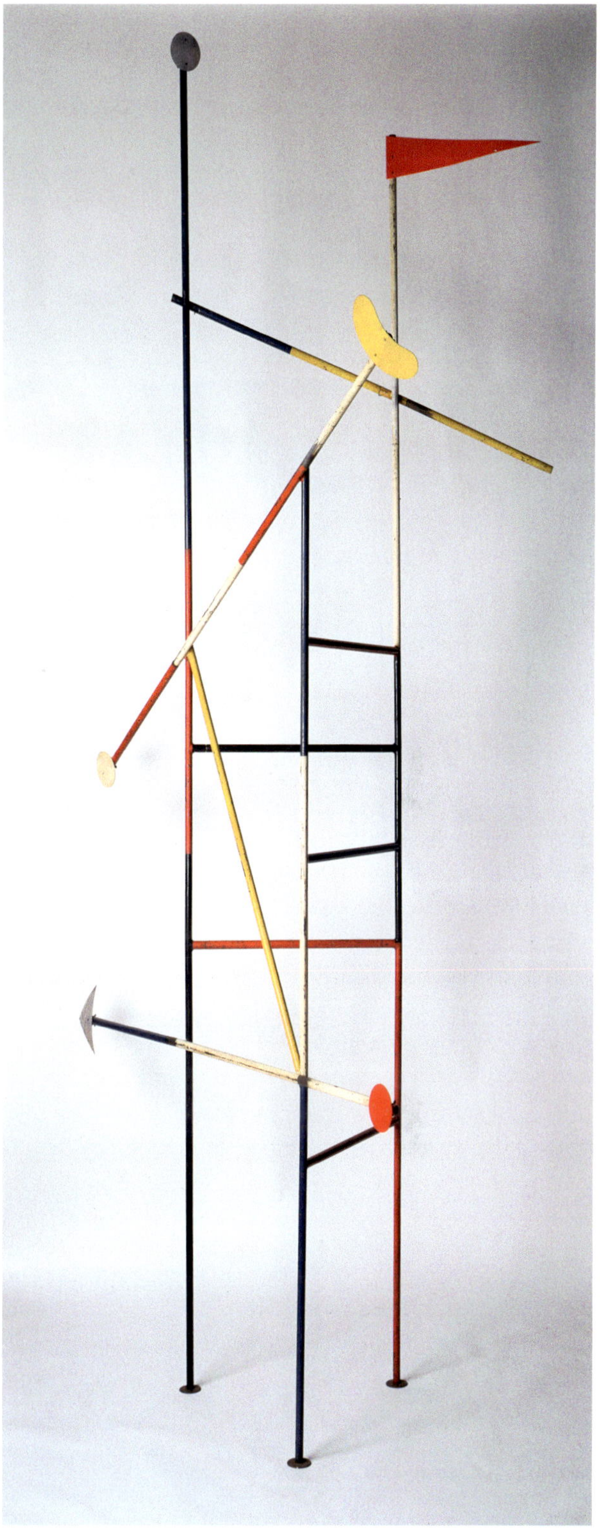

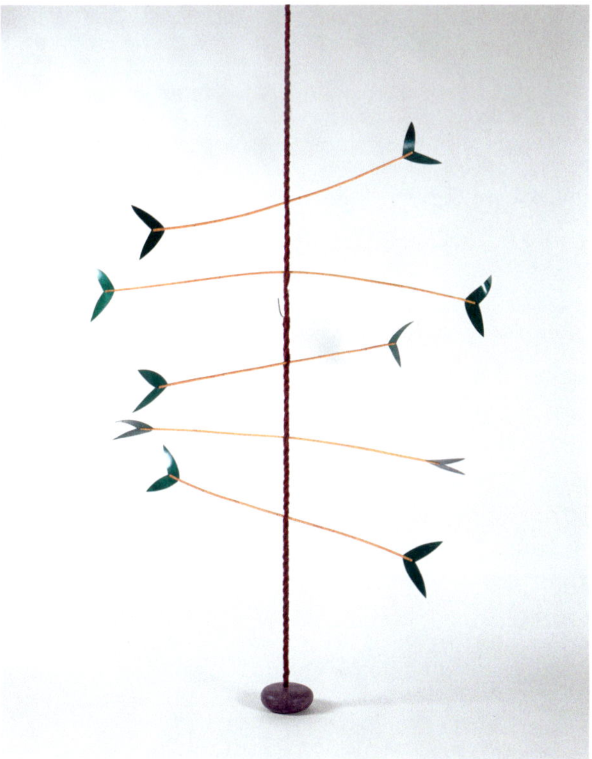

WHAT DID NOGUCHI MEAN BY 'SPACE'?

Dakin Hart

In the world and practice of sculpture, 'space' is that word that means everything and nothing. Isamu Noguchi, like many of his contemporaries, was given to waxing opaquely poetic on the subject. But unlike many of his contemporaries, his ambiguities were targeted, his seeming impenetrability well-honed, his tendency to complicate rather than explicate a matter of strategy. Noguchi was relatively unconcerned by the disadvantages of being oblique, convinced that over the long term, his perspective, as encapsulated in his work, would speak for itself. 'I always wanted to go beyond art objects,' he told the critic Dore Ashton. 'I wanted to reach what may be defined as a way of life, a space of life, or even a ghetto closed and defended from the world. Or some monadic theater, a world that exists, grows and changes from its own force.'[1]

1 Dore Ashton, *Noguchi: East and West* (Berkeley and Los Angeles, CA: University of California Press, 1992), pp. 16–17.

The best way – maybe the only way – to approach with any precision what Noguchi meant when he talked about space and its relationship with sculpture is through the lens of a kaleidoscope: by sampling the multiplicity of his understanding and allowing impressions to accrue. Noguchi was rarely better than when he was of at least three minds, and the only thing he appreciated more than a unified space-object was one achieved by composite means. This is the essence of his statement that 'To be hybrid anticipates the future',[2] which is, not incidentally, a rather Hegelian view: thesis, antithesis, synthesis. Noguchi rejected the notion of 'progress' per se, but he was a big believer in the kind of never-ending synthetic development that characterises nature's work. Human perspectives are multifaceted, and he expected art to be that way too: experiential rather than didactic, branching and connective rather than discrete and reductivist. Art was simply the technology he chose for cultivating social consciousness. All of which is a way of saying that Noguchi's conception of space – that rhetorical snark of sculptural understanding – is layered, shifting, contradictory, and ultimately achieves, from certain points of view, a satisfying, if purposefully irresolvable, wholeness.

2 Isamu Noguchi, 'I Become a Nisei', October 1942, unpublished essay for *Reader's Digest*, The Noguchi Museum Archives, MS_BIO_028_002, p. 1.

In 1949 Noguchi wrote an application for a grant to write a book about the 'environment of leisure'. In it he said he wanted to find solutions that 'define a moment of personal existence and illumine the environment of our aspirations'.[3] 'Leisure' is an odd-sounding term for what he meant, which was civic life. This he judged as necessitating the kinds of public spaces that energise and empower citizenship: above all by stimulating, and then helping to organise and contextualise, our sense of belonging. The worldwide research he conducted into spatial, architectonic, sculptural and environmental situations that contribute to what we might call humanity's faculties of civilisation were focused on social organisation and a sense of connection. Which explains why he found an abandoned miniature golf course on the Lido in Venice as compelling as Angkor Wat. In his proposal Noguchi called out temples in particu-lar, but it is clear from the context and other statements that he was using 'temple' as a shorthand for religious buildings – or, taking an even broader view, spaces in which social connection happens – which is in turn a way to evoke spiritual awareness and, taking one more step, our individual and collective search for meaning. Noguchi expected sculpture to seek nothing less than sculptural equivalents for Teotihuacan, Chartres Cathedral, the Roman Forum, Stonehenge, Tōfuku-ji and the church on a public square in New England: generative environments expressive of human aspiration.

3 Isamu Noguchi, 'A Proposed Study of the Environment of Leisure', c. 1949, p. 1, The Noguchi Museum Archives, MS_WRI_010_019.

Learning to create that sense of what makes us human was not simple. Noguchi did it in stages through an unconscious process of accumulation. His thinking developed each time he encountered a new spatial paradigm. What follows is a survey of specific works that elucidate aspects of how his thinking with regard to the many overlapping spaces in which he wanted to operate – the solar system of his understanding – gradually expanded and took shape.

Abstraction in Almost Discontinuous Tension, 1928

Noguchi's search for a communally potent sculpture began with a fairly conventional view of what art was, despite his early understanding that what he wanted to be was a social scientist. When he made *Abstraction in Almost Discontinuous Tension* (p. 18) from rolled round bar and strung wire, the idea of sculpture without mass was quite new. Pablo Picasso's cardboard and sheet metal guitars, volumetric but hollow, are the examples most often cited as the progenitors of this mode.[4] Another touchstone were the 'drawing in space' wire sculptures that his friend Alexander Calder was then making.

4 Isamu Noguchi, *Isamu Noguchi: A Sculptor's World* [1968] (Göttingen: Steidl, 2004), p. 18.

In *Abstraction in Almost Discontinuous Tension*, Noguchi tried to combine these two conceptual approaches to seeking new forms and modes of sculpture: empty volume and lines in space. He wanted to make a work whose actual form was a symbolic representation of spatial relationships. It is as much a demonstration of geometry or celestial mechanics – an orrery for the coordinate plane – as it is an artwork. But even more significant than the literal spatial departure it represents from conventional sculpture is the space of contemporary life that it occupies materially. Just as Picasso had earlier used newspaper to make his paper collages live in the moment, *Abstraction in Almost Discontinuous Tension* looks like something industrial, the product of a factory – albeit one making useless things – rather than of the studio. The story it tells is of belonging in the present – the world's present, not that of the gallery.

Miss Expanding Universe, 1932

Noguchi was more interested in the inner workings of the human cell, the atom and the solar system than in the space we think of as the natural habitat of sculpture. To an optimistic observer in the first part of the twentieth century, it seemed quite possible that we might, through the natural sciences, unlock the invisible mysteries of the forces that bind and motivate all of the mass that surrounds us. It was hard to say the same for art, despite advances such as the Surrealists' interest in dreams, the unconscious and love.

Miss Expanding Universe (p. 68) is a portrait of Noguchi's then lover, the dancer and choreographer Ruth Page, in a sack dress of his design. (She used a second, less constrictive version as a costume for her dance *Expanding Universe*, which premiered later in 1932.) The sculpture imagines her as a 'starry traveller', a spaceship (or angel) streaking through the firmament. Both the dance and the sculpture came out of a fertile three-way conversation the two carried on with Noguchi's friend the futurist R. Buckminster Fuller. Their embrace of space-time (the 'fourth dimension') was code for their openness to the idea of relativity and post-Newtonian physics. They were inspired by the publication of the English physicist Arthur Eddington's book *The Expanding Universe*, in which he explains, for a lay audience, how Edwin Hubble's observations had proved the Belgian astronomer Georges Lemaître's theory that the universe is expanding, overturning a several-thousand-year-old model of the universe as an ordered array of concentric circles. Just over a decade earlier, it was Eddington who had demonstrated through observation that gravity bends light, and that therefore Einstein's general theory of relativity was correct.

An amorphous mass of outrushing uncertainty, *Miss Expanding Universe* both occupies and represents a new understanding not just of space but of space-time: the earth-shattering awareness that there are no absolute standards in the universe.

Musical Weathervane, 1933

When Noguchi designed, modelled and hoped to mass produce a *Musical Weathervane* (p. 280), he 'was not conscious of the terms "applied design" or "industrial design"', as he wrote in his autobiography. 'My thoughts were born in despair, seeking stars in the night.'[5] Meant to be internally illuminated (with a lightbulb), at a time when electricity was still not widely available in rural America, *Musical Weathervane* was intended to bring a shining beacon to the roof of every barn in the heartland. Per its name, it was also designed to channel the wind through slits in its sides to produce 'music'.

The inspiration came from an object Noguchi encountered while living in Beijing, China, in 1930: 'small flutes made of gourds attached to pigeons', resulting in a magnificent 'whooing sound as they flew about'.[6] This was the local version of the same musical-spatial tracking system shepherds and farmers the world over have employed for centuries by putting bells on livestock. Noguchi's modest hope was to transform the environment of the American Midwest by turning the peak of every roof into the secular equivalent of a

6 Ibid.

5 Ibid., p. 21.

church steeple, lifting every homeward-bound eye and ear to the horizon. Musical Weathervane was a multimedia lodestar representing humanity's most fundamental extra-spatial concept: home.

Play Mountain, 1933

The desire to add optimistic, outward-looking centres of emotional and civic gravity to public and private space and life is a root instinct that propelled Noguchi's work from the start. At the age of 28 he proposed putting a mountain on one square block somewhere in New York City. *Play Mountain* (p. 64), as he called it, was to have taken the form of a hollow, irregularly stepped pyramid with a ramp on one side and a pond, a pool and a music shell with a stage at its base. Conceived as an all-season multipurpose site of leisure and play, it included provisions for water sliding and swimming in the summer and sledding and skating in the winter. It was roundly rejected by the then powers that be, which should not have come as a total shock since even then Noguchi thought of it, and the other earth sculptures he proposed at the time, as 'imaginary landscapes'.[7]

7 Isamu Noguchi, interview with Dore Ashton, 13 September 1978, roll 1, part 2, p. 26, The Noguchi Museum Archives, MS_WRI_047_003. The term derives from the titles of a series of five works by Noguchi's friend the experimental composer John Cage that are an aural survey of contemporary life in 1939, 1942 (two pieces), 1951 and 1952, featuring two variable-speed phono turntables, frequency recordings, muted piano and cymbal; percussion quintet; percussion sextet; twelve radios; and any 42 recordings, respectively.

Picture an artificial mountain in Midtown Manhattan, opposite the Empire State Building (1931): how it would have reoriented the urban grid and its orthogonally organised denizens. Noguchi specifically contrasted *Play Mountain* to the then dominant type of playground in the city, which he characterised as cages for birds and zoos for animals.[8] The implications of a semi-natural, non-directive playscape with the openness of nature on the general understanding of the scale and nature of city life would have been sublime.

8 Martin Friedman, *Isamu Noguchi's Imaginary Landscapes* (Minneapolis, MN: Walker Arts Center, 1978), p. 39.

Much later, speaking of *Playscapes* (1975–76, Atlanta, Georgia, p. 304), the only playground Noguchi was ever able to execute in the United States, he explained that he thought of playgrounds as 'a way of creating the world … an ideal land – on a smaller scale … I think of playgrounds as a primer of shapes and functions: simple, mysterious and evocative: thus educational.'[9] 'Imaginary landscape' is not a euphemism for a purposely unexecutable pipe dream. What Noguchi meant was an environment designed to alter our perception of our horizons by stimulating our imaginations.

9 Isamu Noguchi, *Playscapes* pamphlet, c. 1977, The Noguchi Museum Archives, MS_PROJ_046_040.

Frontier, 1935

Frontier (pp. 76–77) was Noguchi's first stage set. At first he thought of set making as an unrelated sideline, but by the time of *The Sculpture of Spaces*, the version of his much-travelled *Imaginary Landscapes* exhibition for the Whitney Museum of American Art, New York, in 1980, sets for Martha Graham occupied half of the space. He 'wished to show that … beyond objects there is always the situation, the time, the performer, and the spectator. All are in re-alignment, as Einstein might have said, in constant flux.'[10] In the black box of the theatre, every relationship between the essential participants is operative. 'Theater space', he said, is 'that area, large enough, where the imagination is free to include the performer, who may even be oneself'.[11] And if one's goal is to understand how viewer, performer, props, sets and the idea of space affect one another, there is no better site of experimentation.

10 Isamu Noguchi, *The Sculpture of Spaces*, exh. cat., Whitney Museum of American Art, New York (New York: Whitney Museum of American Art, 1980), p. 5.

11 Ibid., p. 7.

As Noguchi later reflected, 'When the time came for me to work with larger spaces, I conceived them as gardens, not as sites with objects, but as relationships to a whole. I would say this came from my knowledge of the dance theater where there is evidently a totality of experience.'[12]

12 Robert Tracy, *Spaces of the Mind: Isamu Noguchi's Dance Designs* (New York: Proscenium, 2001), p. 4.

A single rope anchored at the back of the stage that projects offstage on both sides at a 45-degree angle, the *Frontier* set threw 'the entire volume of air straight over the heads of the audience',[13] creating 'an outburst into space and at the same time an influx toward infinity'.[14] In this ideal laboratory for twisting dials, pulling levers and flipping switches, Noguchi could have had no better partner than Graham. As Noguchi explained, while he worked with the idea of landscape, she worked with 'a kind of mindscape',[15] an idea he refined in describing Graham's ballet *Dark Meadow* (1946), which he called 'a very important work about the external adventures of seeking … The work has to do with primordial time of the mind. These are spaces of mind that Martha is dealing with.'[16]

13 Noguchi, *A Sculptor's World*, p. 125.

14 Isamu Noguchi, *The Isamu Noguchi Garden Museum* (New York: Harry N. Abrams, 1987), p. 212.

15 Robert Tracy and Isamu Noguchi, 'Noguchi: Collaborating with Graham', *Ballet Review*, vol. 13, no. 4 (Winter 1986), p. 10.

16 Ibid.

In the case of *Frontier*, the specific mindscape was the myth of the indomitability of the pioneer spirit that once underlay so much of the American Dream, specifically the belief in the country's limitless potential, generated and fuelled by a national obsession with westward expansion.[17] It is a complex delusion that requires unpacking and deconstruction. As late as 1979, Noguchi was still perpetuating the myth that North America was an empty land open for the taking.

17 Also known as manifest destiny, this is the delusion that settlers in the United States had a God-given right to conquer the entirety of this continent, 'from sea to shining sea', in the words of its unofficial national anthem, 'America the Beautiful'.

> The pioneers that formed this country walked out onto a perfectly empty stage. The trouble is, things have gotten cluttered up with the debris of money-making and possessions. My function is to clean it up a bit – to make some space where there is no space, and bring back some of that frontier horizon which has been lost.[18]

18 Maryanne Conheim, 'Creating New Worlds, Still Dreaming of Playgrounds', *Philadelphia Inquirer*, 23 October 1979, p. C1.

We can hold him accountable – and we should – for remaining blind and rhetorically beholden to an ideology that elides the existence of the continent's indigenous populations. But it is important to note that Noguchi had also, by then, long since abstracted and externalised frontier-mindedness into something useful and universal, as indeed all of humanity would do in following the progress of the Space Race and the Moon landings. The notion of the horizon was particularly potent for Noguchi. It is a word he used frequently in trying to evoke the limited perspectives, such as the 'fiction of a frame or the horizon on a pedestal',[19] that he meant to escape.

19 Isamu Noguchi, 'My Sculpture', in *Isamu Noguchi*, exh. cat. (Tokyo: Minami Gallery, 1973), n.p.

Time Lock, 1944–45

There was a lot of interest in the fourth dimension among artists when the idea first emerged. The notion that mass and energy are in some sense interchangeable, and that speed affects that relationship as well as the nature of time, had an enormous effect on Noguchi. If you are looking for ways to look at and think about sculpture differently, Einsteinian physics is not a bad place to start. The reality that the seeming void of space is actually a complex invisible topography contoured by gravity suggests that the fabric of time might be folded, bent, shaped, manipulated.

> If you want to live and work in an industrialised situation, you have to use industrial materials and tools. However, I was not quite satisfied with that because I felt the limitations of such tools forced one to be a part of industry rather than free. And I felt that the old-fashioned way of doing things, for instance with stone, with your own hands, left you a greater freedom. And so I went back to stone, and I'm still working on stone … One shifts. I do, backwards and forwards. Sometimes I think I'm part of this world of today. Sometimes I feel that maybe I belong in history, or in prehistory, or that there is no such thing as time. But if you are caught in time, the immediate present time, then your choice is very limited. You can only do certain things really correctly belonging to that time. But if you want to escape from that time constraint, then the whole world – not just the most industrialised world, but the whole world – is someplace where you belong.[20]

20 John Musilli, dir., *Portrait of Isamu Noguchi*, broadcast television (New York: Camera Three Productions, 1974).

Understanding time as fluid and continuous, Noguchi treated it as a space to move around in, picking and choosing time-based connotations and combining them, as in *Time Lock* (p. 134). A capsule of cosmology, *Time Lock* is a pre-industrial object calculated to suggest an empirical grasp of an Einsteinian revelation: a model of future understanding rendered in a material, and using techniques that make it empirically comprehensible, even comforting. 'All I do', he once said, 'is provide an invasion of a different time element into the time of nature.'[21]

21 Edward M. Gomez, 'The Passing of a Purist: Isamu Noguchi, 1904–1988', *Time*, 16 January 1988, p. 37.

Garden Elements, 1958

The four-fold pamphlet for the exhibition in which *Garden Elements* was first exhibited has a hole punched in the outer panel,[22] as if to say, 'come on through.' And so do both pieces of *Garden Elements*, a pair of what seem to be altered architectural fragments: part of a roof peak, maybe, broken and tipped to one side, and the remains of a buttress, doorframe or lintel that might also have been a stele. The holes in them are deliberately ambiguous. Some appear to be the kinds of sockets that would have received the ends of beams. A round one could be that, or it might be a small window, or for ventilation.

22 *Noguchi*, Stable Gallery, New York, 29 April–30 May 1959, exhibition pamphlet, The Noguchi Museum Archives, MS_EXH_040_001.

Whether literal or metaphorical, the architectural connotations are an invitation to enter the environment of the unknowable but palpable situation in which the elements originated. This is a bit confusing, yet it is also clarifying, given that the modifier 'garden' is not structural but environmental. In the years after *Garden Elements*, Noguchi made a series of sculptures from worn-out millstones, which are often recycled in gardens for various purposes. With similar subtle changes – the addition of a hole, a little carving, reorientation – he turned them into landscapes, celestial bodies and windows on the world. 'For a garden maker, stone is the earth itself. There is no other medium which endures in all its aspects, in the constant change of ecological flow, forever in the now.'[23] Forever in the now, for Noguchi, meant forever bridging the past and the present. This all time-no time is his most important space of all. It is also the space of nature, which escapes temporal limits by ever becoming and constant renewal. 'How else than by such suggestions am

23 Noguchi, *The Sculpture of Spaces*, p. 18.

I to show our place of distance between that past and our imminent future where, as we know, rocks float in outer space, on the moon, or Mars?'[24]

24 Ibid.

Garden Elements is a folly of another order to the millstones. Though also composed of the kinds of fragments often used to situate the garden experience outside daily life, they are designed not necessarily for use in a garden but to be employed as a (free-standing rock) garden. Installed in any relationship to each other, the two elements do create a literal space. But that is not the space of principal interest to Noguchi. The piece is a prototypical example of what he meant when he said:

> Beyond architecture, the rational function and empty space, are those energy concentrations, irrational but meaningful, which constitutes the aesthetic of sculpture. Sculpture becomes for me a preoccupation with those palpable voids and pressures, the punctuations of space. If sculpture is the rock it is also the space between the rocks and between the rock and a man, and the communication and contemplation between.[25]

25 Isamu Noguchi, 'From an Interview with Isamu Noguchi', *The League Quarterly*, vol. 20, no. 3 (Spring 1949), p. 8.

Wherever you put *Garden Elements*, it is an idea of the experience of what a garden can do to motivate the mind and body to shift. 'What I want', he wrote around the same time that he first showed the work, 'is sculptures equal to myself walking.'[26]

26 Isamu Noguchi, untitled artist statement, Stable Gallery records, 1916–1999 (bulk 1953–1970), Archives of American Art, Smithsonian Institution, Washington, DC, Artist Files, 1952–1997: Box 2, Folder 21, Noguchi, Isamu, 1954–1961.

Sunken Garden for Beinecke Rare Book and Manuscript Library, 1960–64, and *Sunken Garden for Chase Manhattan Bank Plaza*, 1961–64

It is difficult to capture and convey the sheer ambition of Noguchi's overall project. It took him decades to understand how all-encompassing his 'growth outward of the idea of sculpture'[27] really was. As he put it in his autobiography, 'Beyond the reach of industrially realizable design or architecturally applied sculpture was, I felt, a larger, more fundamentally sculptural purpose for sculpture, a more direct expression of Man's relation to the earth and his environment.'[28] Nowhere is this clearer than in his public spaces, epitomised by his gardens, another term with many common meanings that he sought at once to enlist and explode. His versions, he once said, should probably more properly be called 'compositions in topological space'.[29]

27 Noguchi, *The Sculpture of Spaces*, p. 31.

28 Noguchi, *A Sculptor's World*, p. 159.

29 Noguchi, 'My Sculpture', n.p.

Or, as he explained in an essay for *Art in America* describing two unenterable stone courtyards he finished in 1964, the *Sunken Garden for Beinecke Rare Book and Manuscript Library* at Yale University, New Haven (pp. 218–19), and the *Sunken Garden for Chase Manhattan Bank Plaza* in the financial district in New York City (p. 300),

> I am not concerned here with monuments or embellishment but with gardens, by which I mean that self-contained sculpturing of space with whatever medium, be it trees, water, rocks, wire, or broken-down automobiles. The totality of the experience so controlled adds up to more than the sum of its parts. It is this larger entity that I prefer to call a garden rather than 'sculpture court,' which would imply sculpture in a space, rather than the space which has itself become a sculpture.[30]

30 Isamu Noguchi, 'New Stone Gardens', *Art in America*, vol. 52, no. 3 (June 1964), p. 84.

This reversal between an object in a space and a space that is sculpture is of course a critical distinction. Writing of the *Sunken Garden* at the Beinecke, Ashton described this extra-sensory quality as 'a feeling of extending prospects'.[31] What Noguchi meant by 'the sculpture of spaces' was an empirical manipulation of our awareness of what it feels like to be alive on this planet. 'My challenge in gardens, as in sculpture, has been to go both backwards and forward – from the traditions of nature into that larger awareness of the continuity of space and time as existed with the Mexicans, the Egyptians and all primitive people. I wanted to see the horizon again as in the beginning of things.'[32]

31 Dore Ashton, 'Art', *Arts and Architecture*, no. 6 (November 1963), p. 6.

32 Noguchi, *The Sculpture of Spaces*, p. 24.

Noguchi believed he could take perception back to a seminal place – or, to put it in mythic terms, an Edenic start – by motivating motion, literal and mental, visual and physical: by producing environments with as capacious and layered a set of spatial connotations as he could contrive. For the simple reason, as he put it as early as 1935, that he was convinced that 'Sculpture can be a vital force in our everyday life if projected into communal usefulness.'[33] In attempting to make it so – in innumerable ways and through an uncategorisable, non-hierarchical variety of means – he changed what we understand as the proper place and working space of sculpture. Describing how in Graham's hands his sculpture would come to life, he concluded, 'I don't particularly like sculpture which is not in a sense adding to experience.'[34]

33 *Isamu Noguchi*, Marie Harriman Gallery, 29 January–16 February 1935, exhibition brochure, The Noguchi Museum Archives, MS_EXH_014_001.

34 Tracy, *Spaces of the Mind*, p. 207.

The Isamu Noguchi Garden Museum (now The Noguchi Museum), 1985

Noguchi worked for more than sixty years and in eight different decades, and in every one of them he was contemporary: a fully engaged surveyor, traverser and problematiser of the environment of contemporary understanding. The museum that Noguchi left as a record of his thinking and as an index of his efforts is an institutional critique of the millennia-old relationship between sculpture and civilisation. It is the ultimate expression of his determination to explore 'sculptural space' and not settle for 'space as just a receptacle for sculpture':[35] not literal space, or metaphorical space, or conceptual space, but a dynamic intermixture of them all. By the time the Isamu Noguchi Garden Museum opened in 1985, when he was 81 years old, Noguchi had got better at articulating what he was after. In an interview with *Art News* he called the museum 'a garden museum as a metaphor for the world', created to explain 'how an artist attempted to influence its [the world's] becoming'.[36] The museum tells the story of how his intent to redefine both sides of the sculpture/space equation had formed more than fifty years earlier and was ever-present in his work: from the moment he discovered the world of Constantin Brâncuși and gave up academic sculpture, resolving to work with the universe's natural uncertainties, between common understandings and 'relative to man's motion, to time's passage, and to its constantly changing situation'.[37]

35 Noguchi, *A Sculptor's World*, p. 159.

36 Milton Esterow and Sylvia Hochfield, 'Isamu Noguchi: The Courage to Desecrate Emptiness', *Art News*, vol. 85, no. 3 (March 1986), pp. 103–9.

37 Isamu Noguchi, 'Preface', in *The Isamu Noguchi Garden Museum*, pp. 11–12.

Dakin Hart is Senior Curator at The Noguchi Museum, New York

Time Lock, 1944–45
Languedoc marble
66.7 × 52.1 × 40 cm

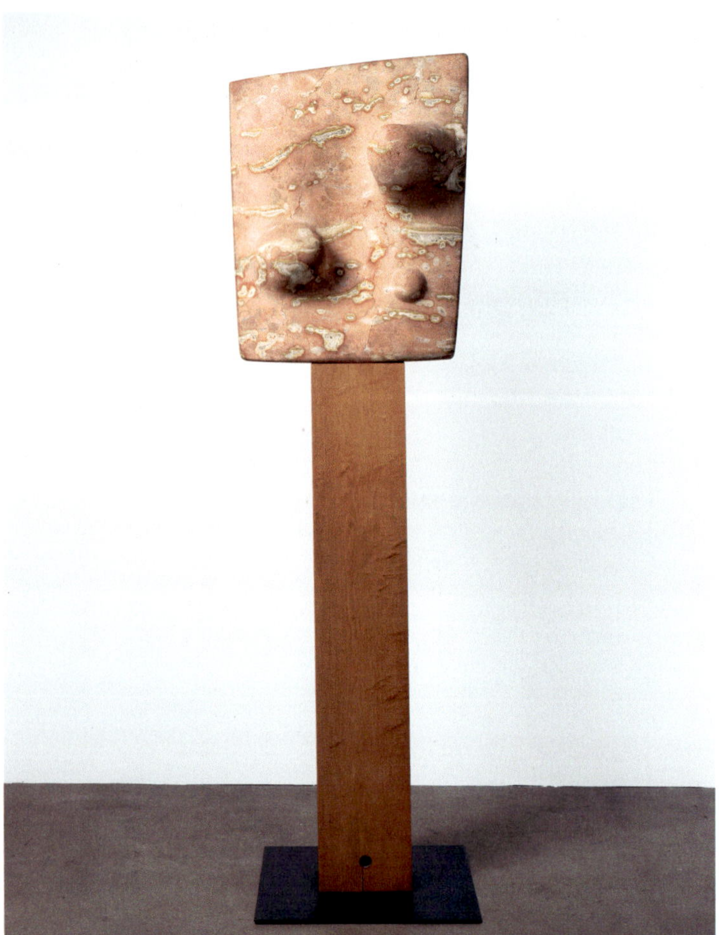

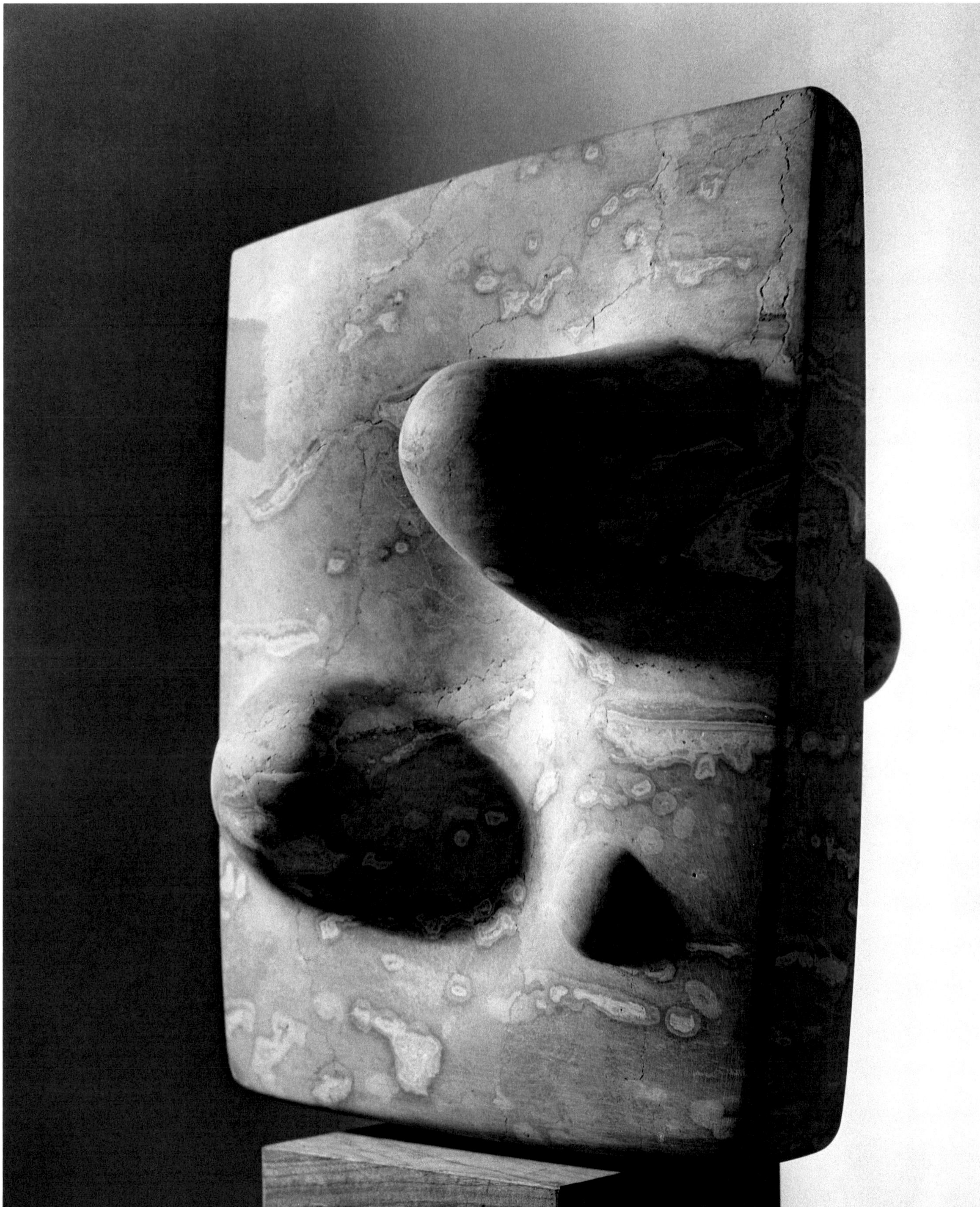

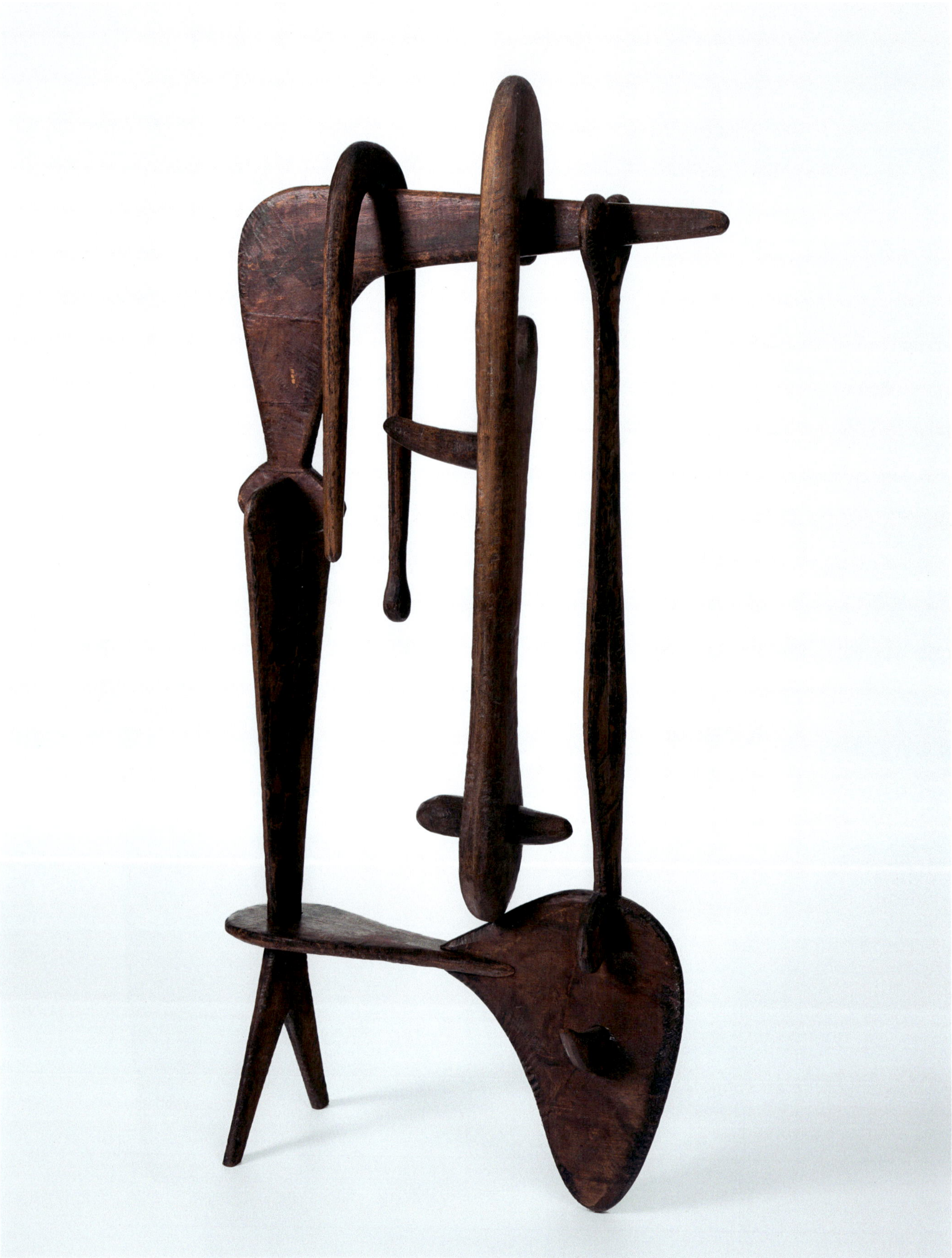

Remembrance, 1944
Mahogany
128.3 × 62.5 × 22.9 cm

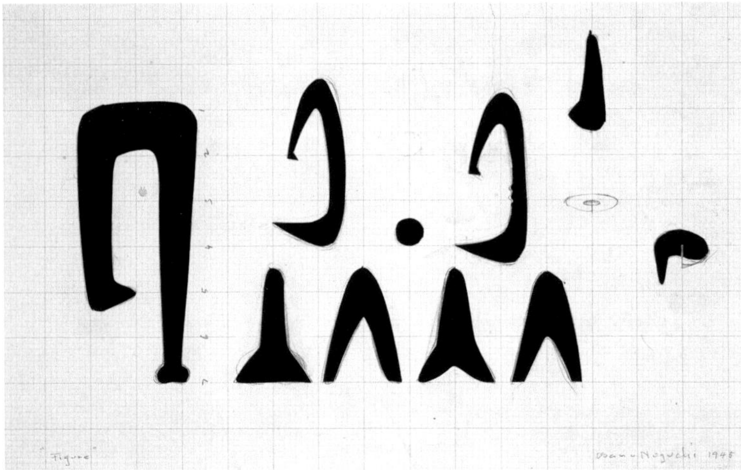

Worksheet for Figure, 1945
Pencil on graph paper
26.5 × 42.2 cm

Worksheet for Sculpture, c. 1945–47
Pencil on graph paper
64 × 76.8 cm

Noguchi assembling *Figure* in his studio on MacDougal Alley, 1944

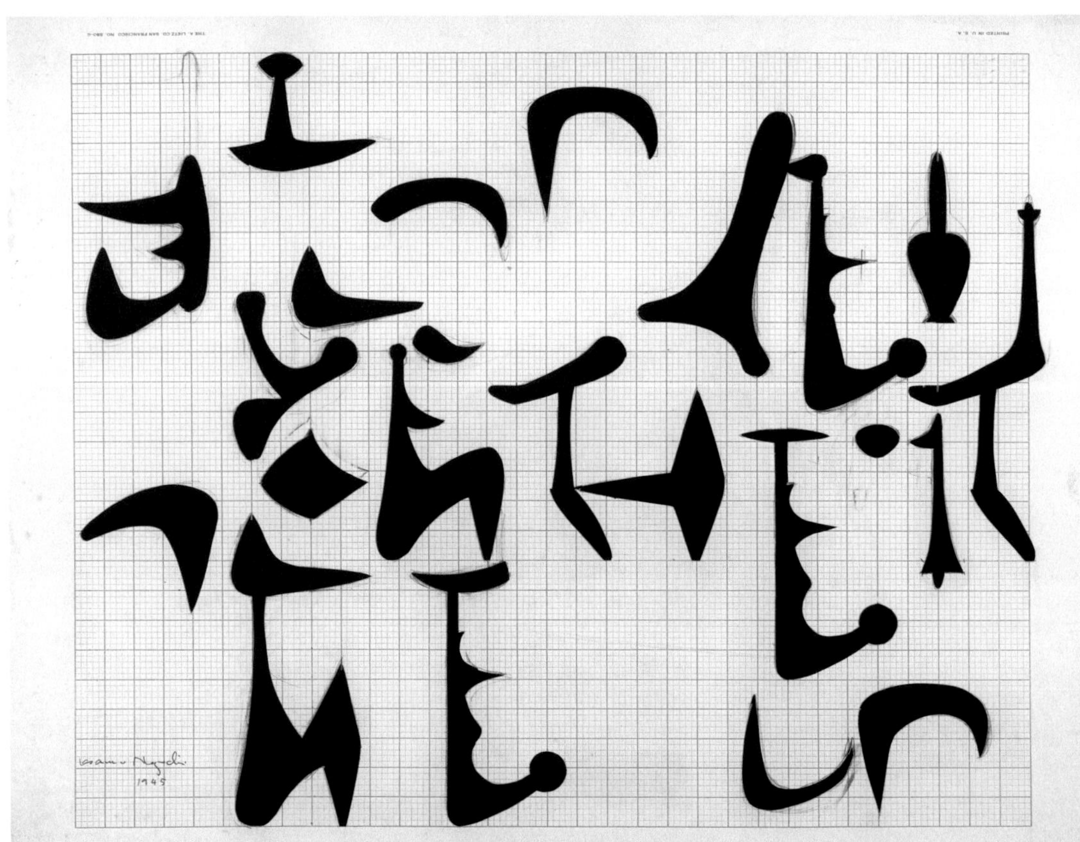

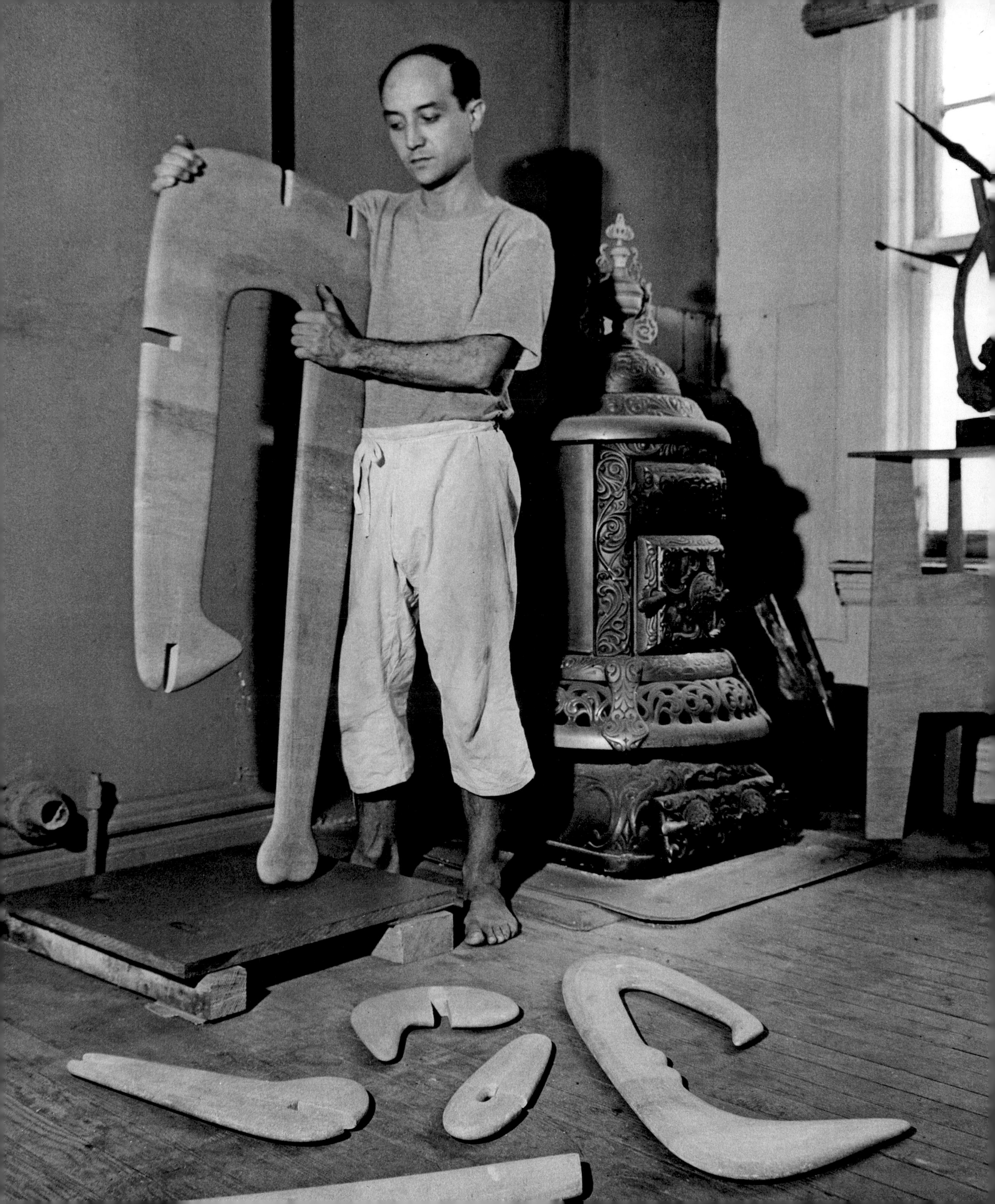

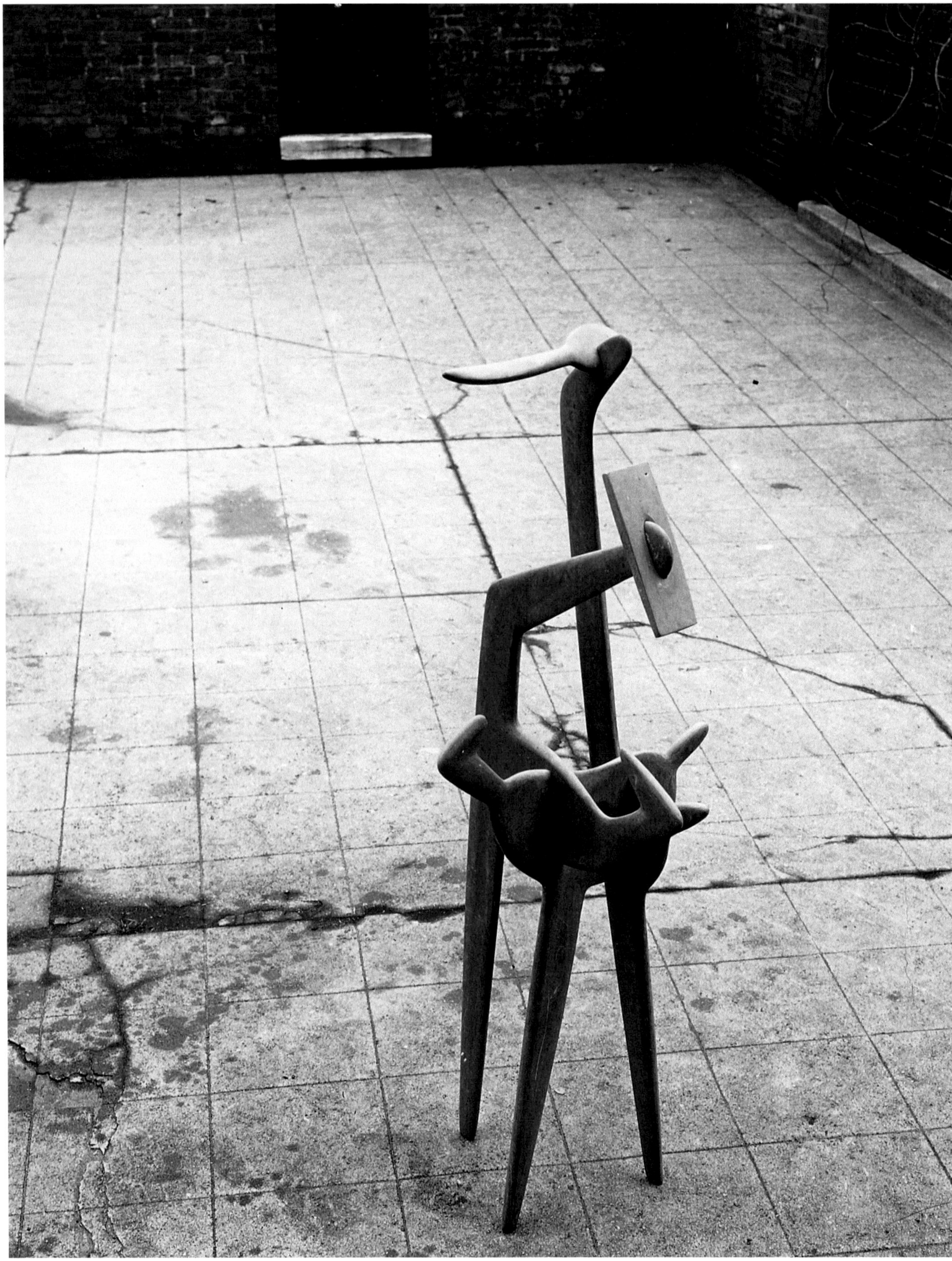

Strange Bird (To the Sunflower, Unknown Bird), 1945
Green slate
143.8 × 55.6 × 50.8 cm

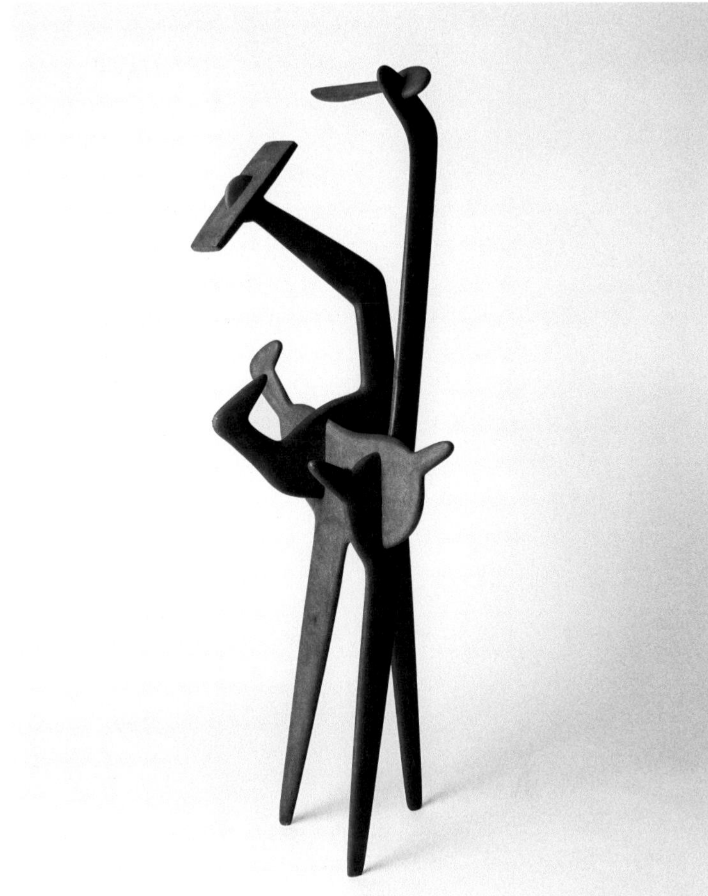

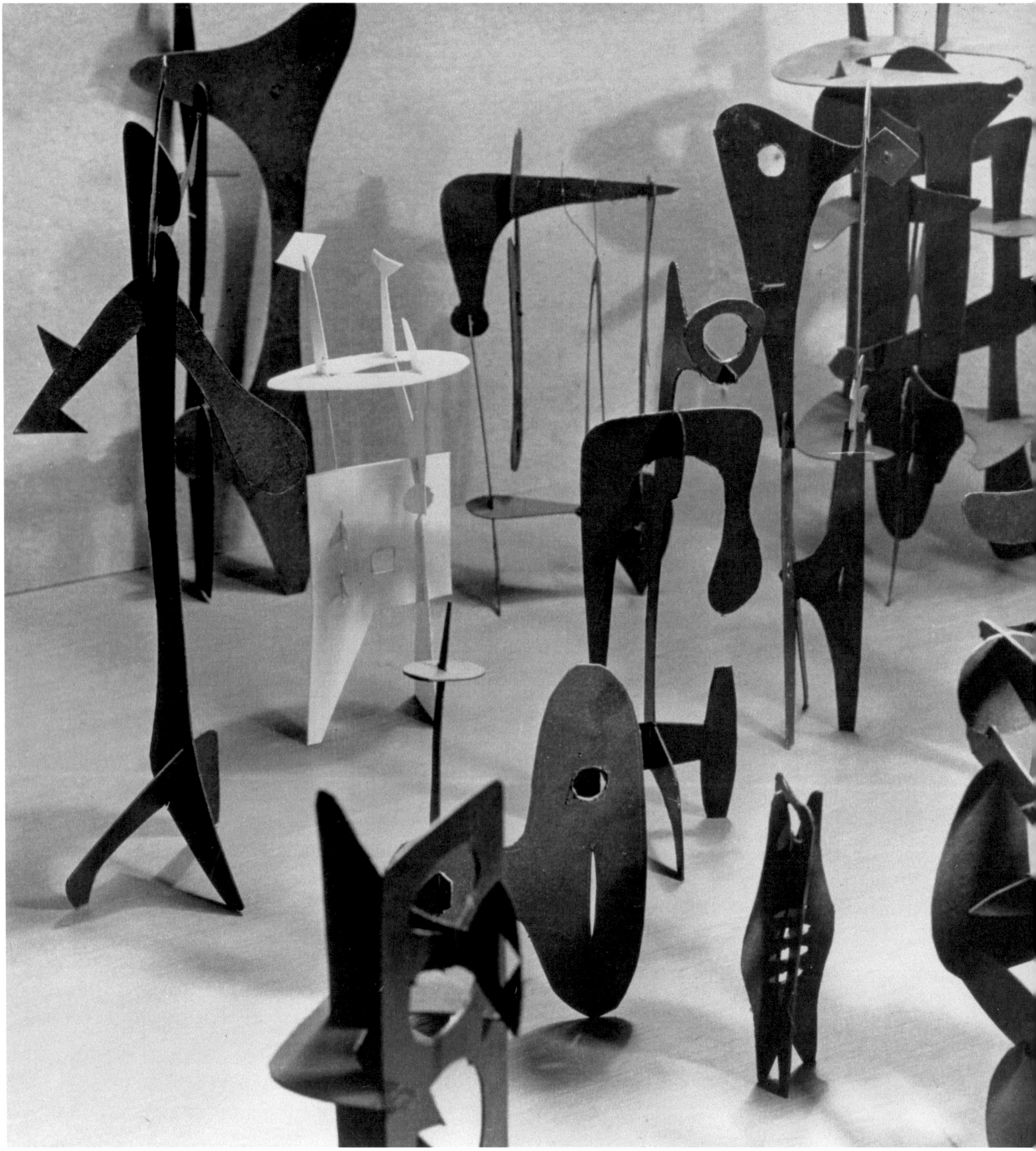

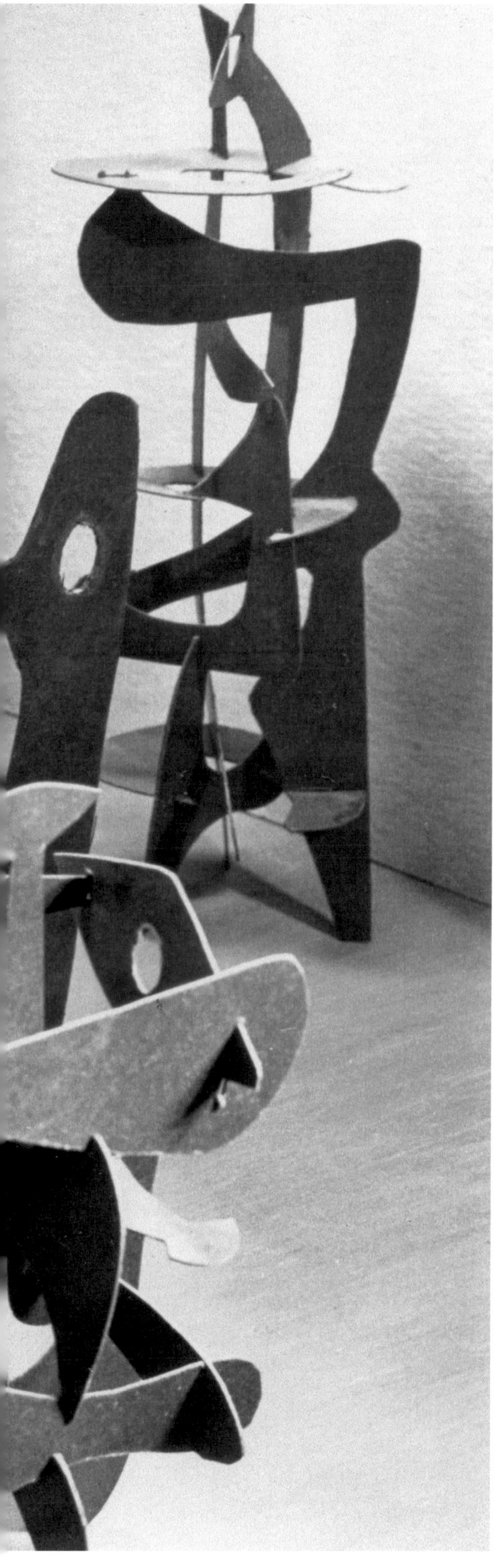

Models for sculptures in Noguchi's studio on MacDougal Alley, c. 1945

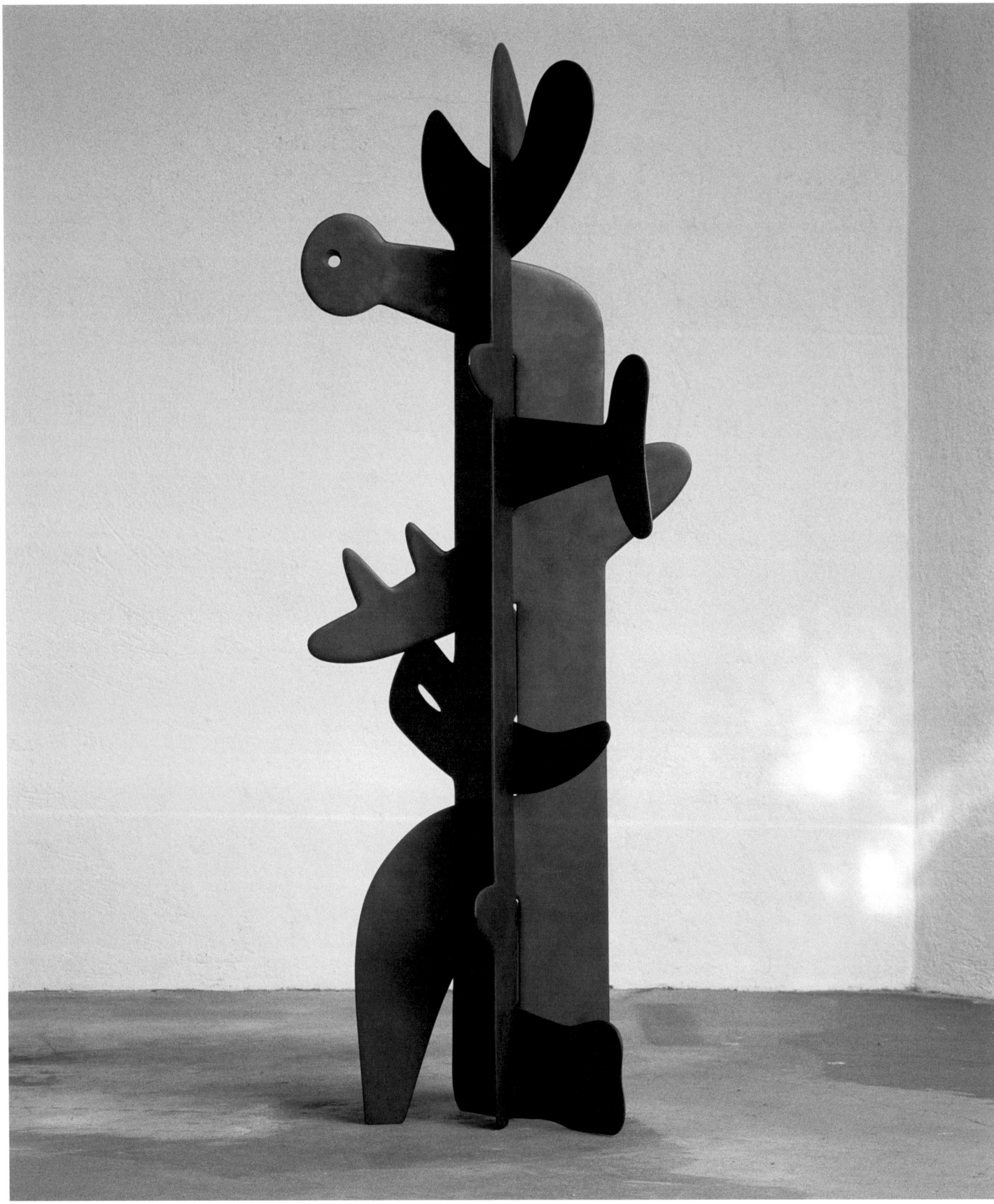

Trinity (Triple), 1945
Slate
141.9 × 55.9 × 50.8 cm

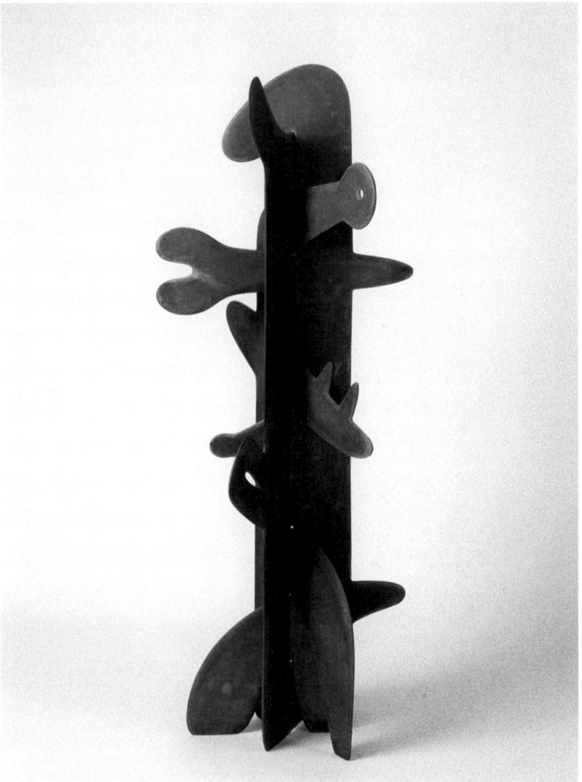

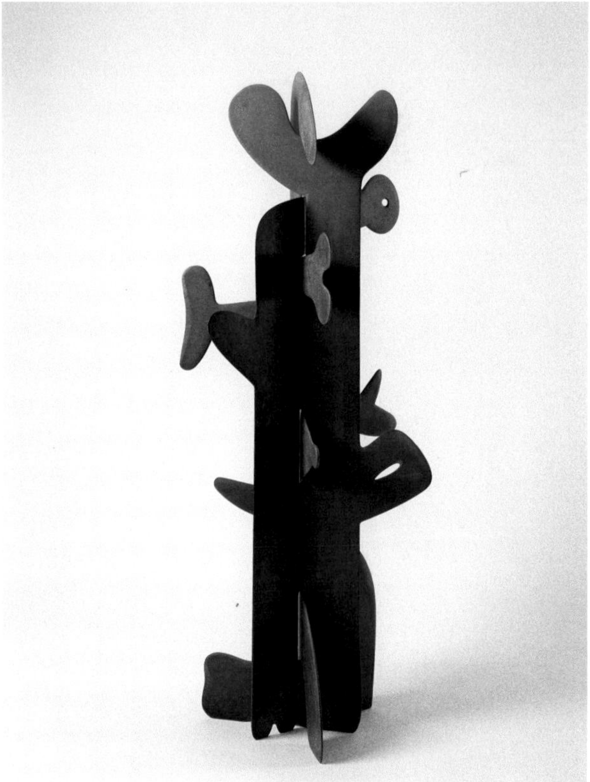

Exhibition view of *Bloodflames*,
Hugo Gallery, New York,
March–April 1947

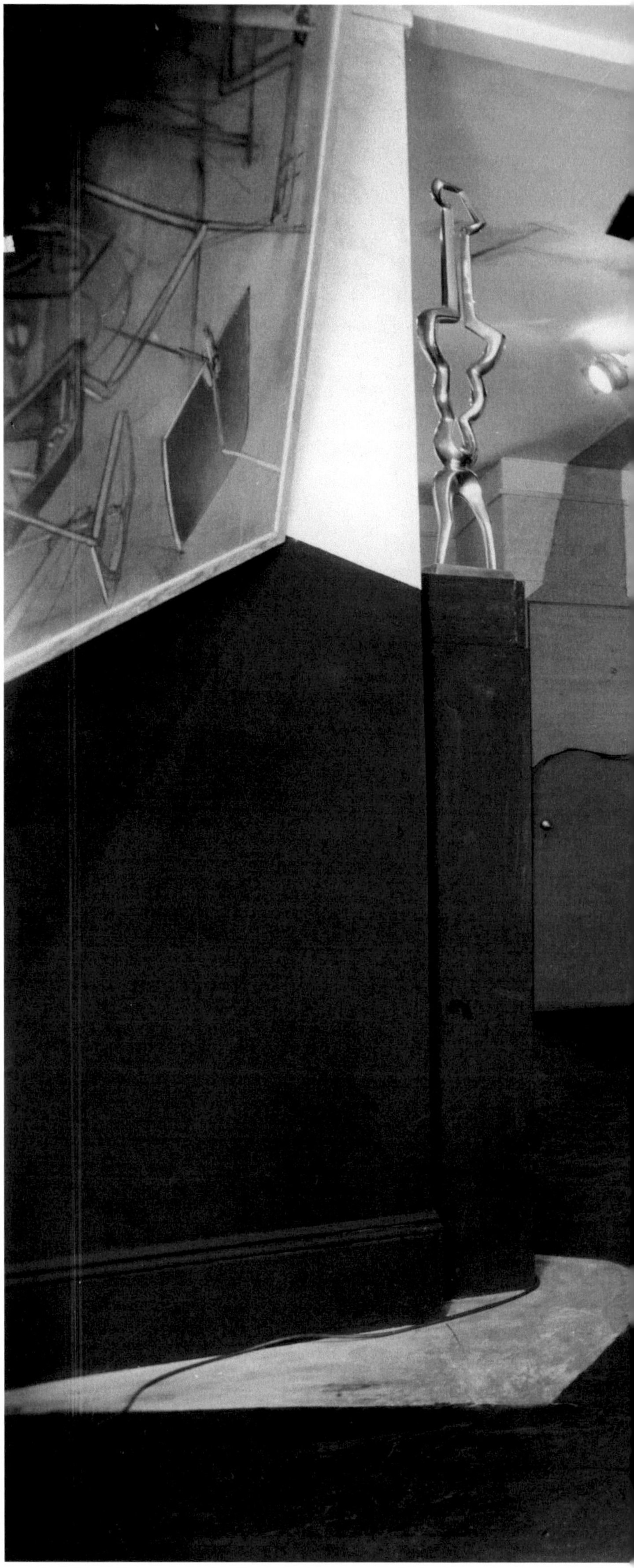

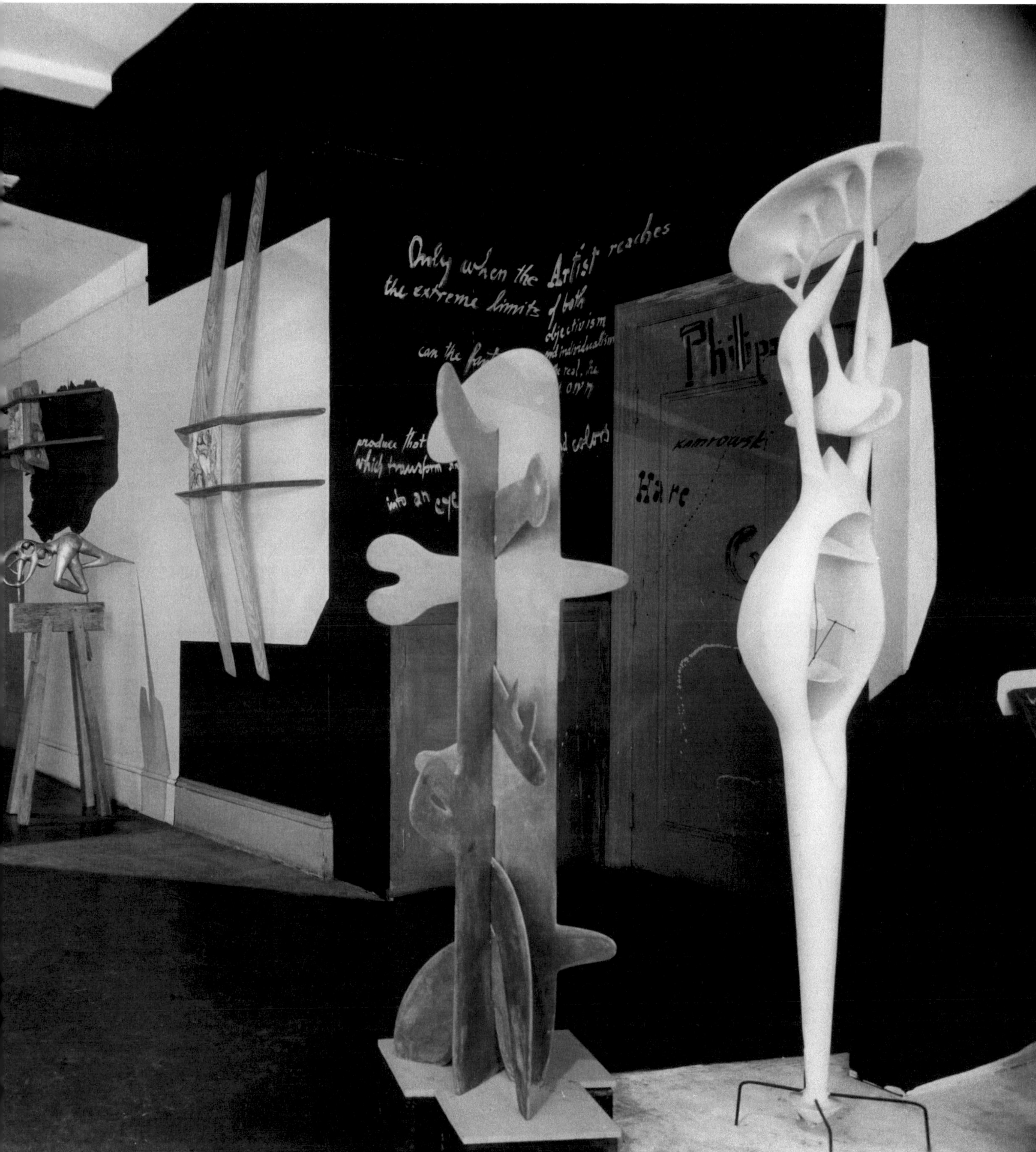
Only when the Artist reaches
the extreme limits of both
objectivism
and individualism
can the
produce that
colors
which transform
into an eye
Phillips
Kamrowski
Hare

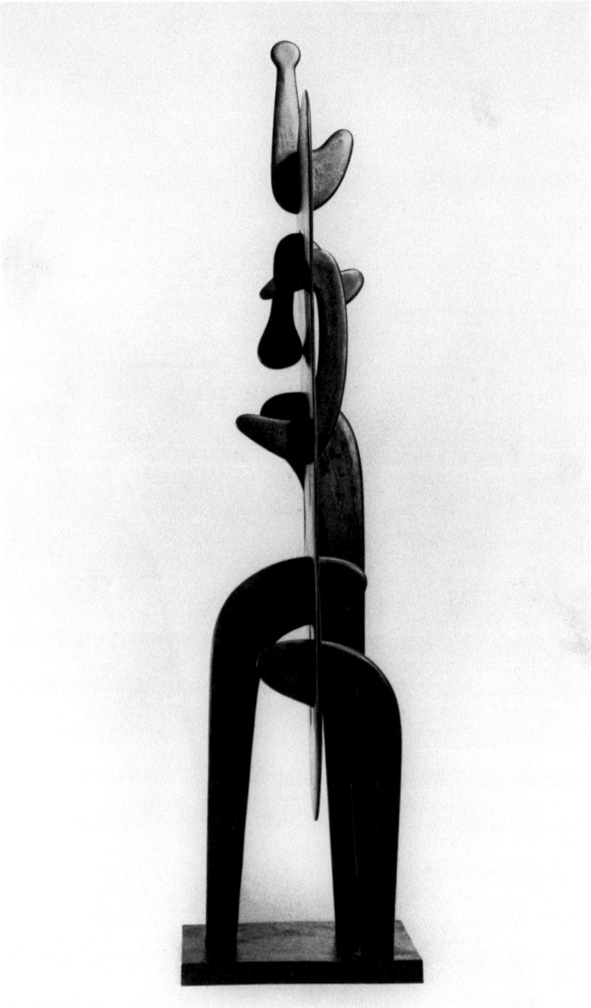

Gregory (Effigy), 1945
(cast 1969)
Bronze
175.9 × 41 × 41.6 cm

Gregory (Effigy), 1945
Slate
176.8 × 35.9 × 41.9 cm

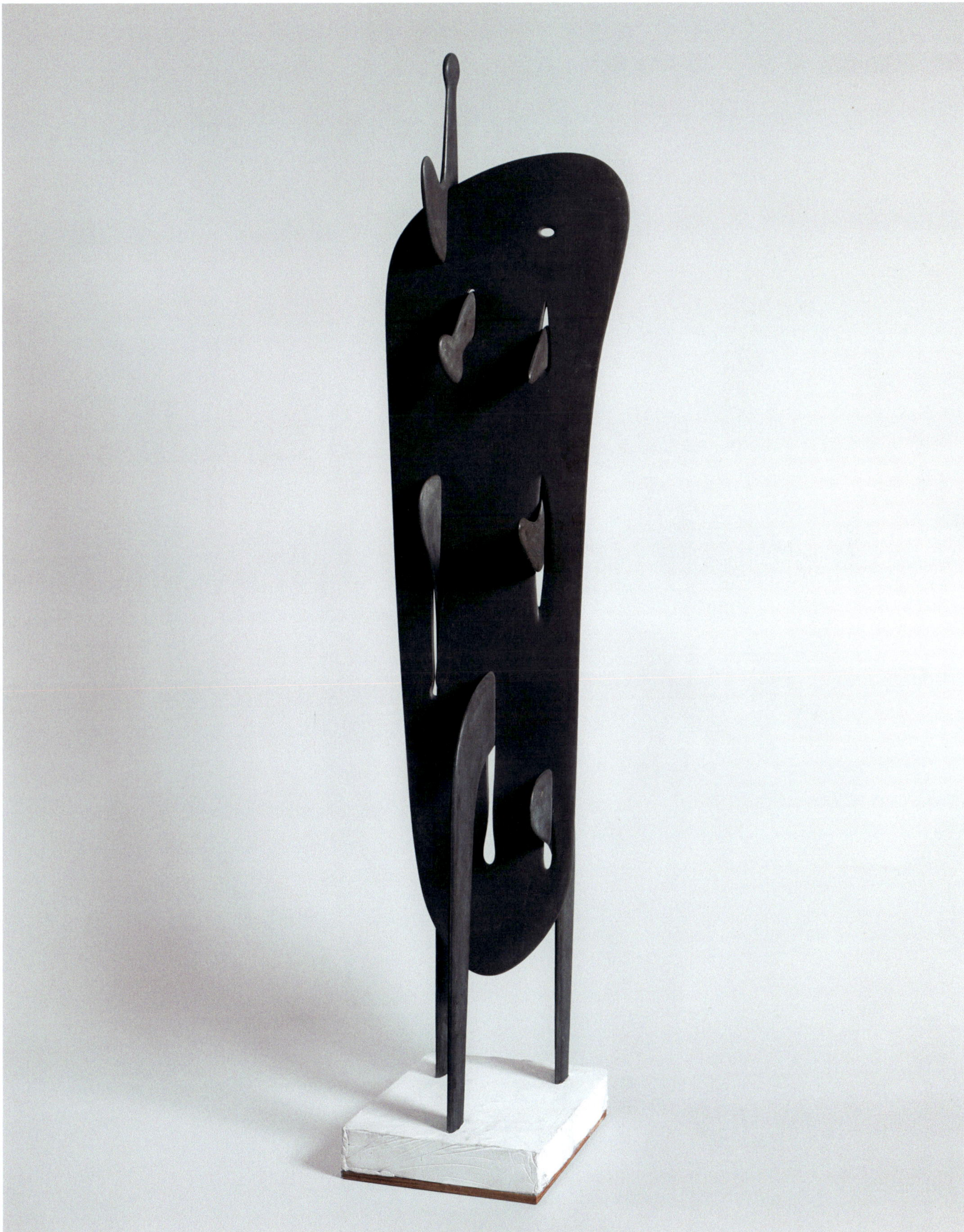

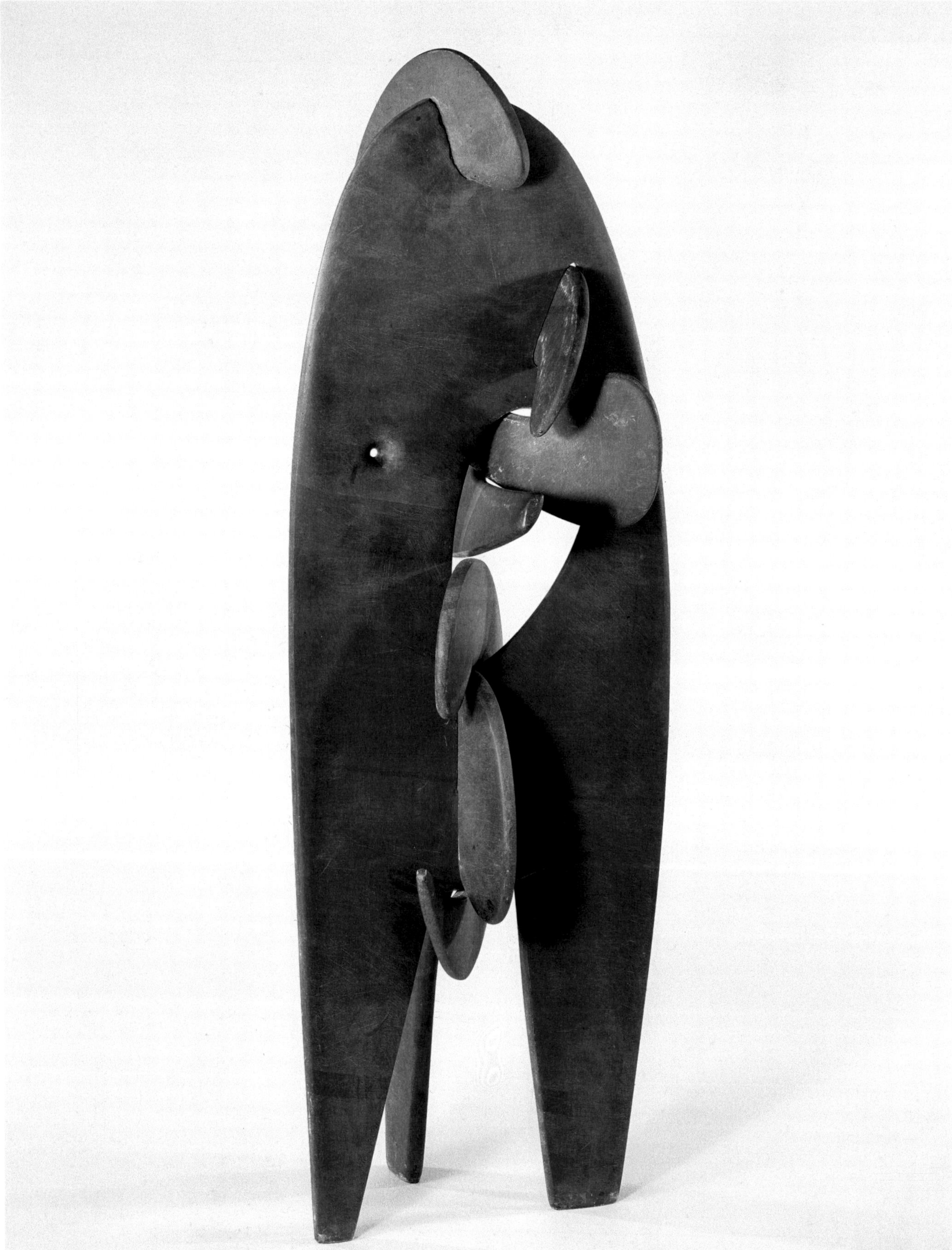

Humpty Dumpty, 1946
Ribbon slate
149.9 × 52.7 × 44.5 cm

The reason why I no longer wanted to use metal came I think from my more rigorous concept of structure. I had become entranced also with the awareness of weight and of gravity as a necessary and desirable part of composition – of verticality and balance as the resolution of gravity – and of precariousness itself as an exquisite quality of sculpture. The very fragility of such thin slabs of stone appealed to me. Transient they seemed, like nature precariously balanced in time.

c. 1979

Avatar, 1947
Georgia marble
195 × 70 × 77 cm

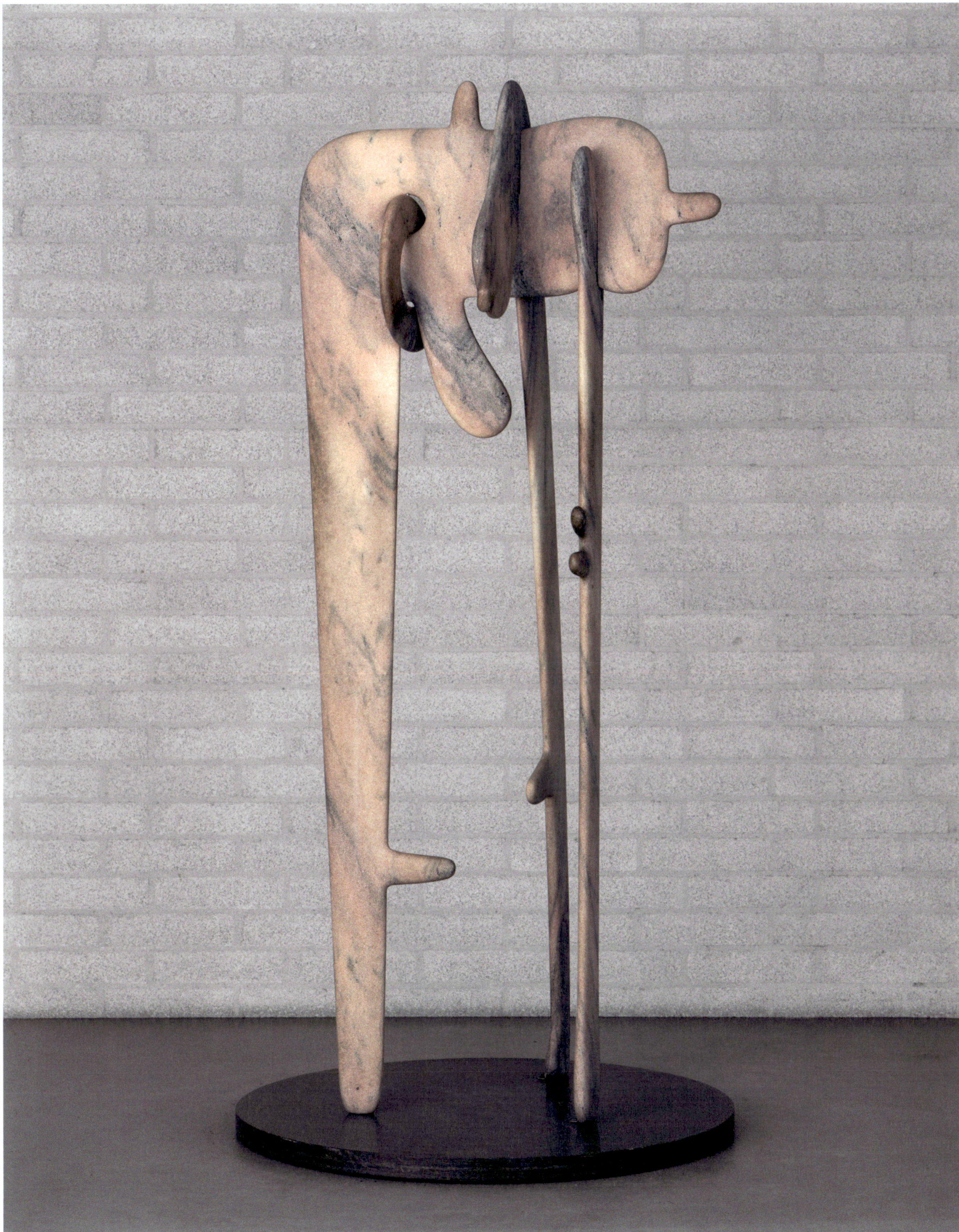

Exhibition view of *Isamu Noguchi*, Charles Egan Gallery, New York,
1–26 March 1949

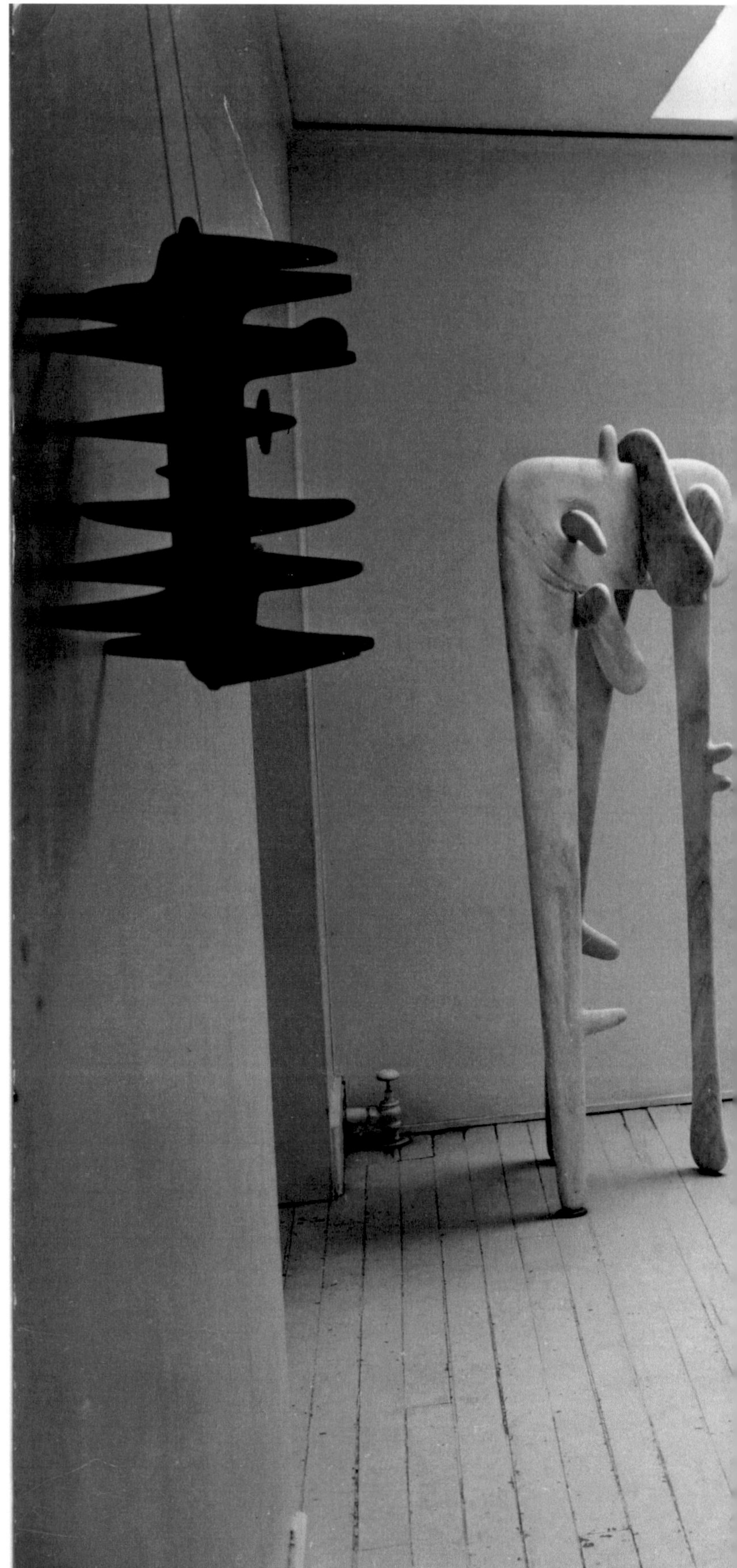

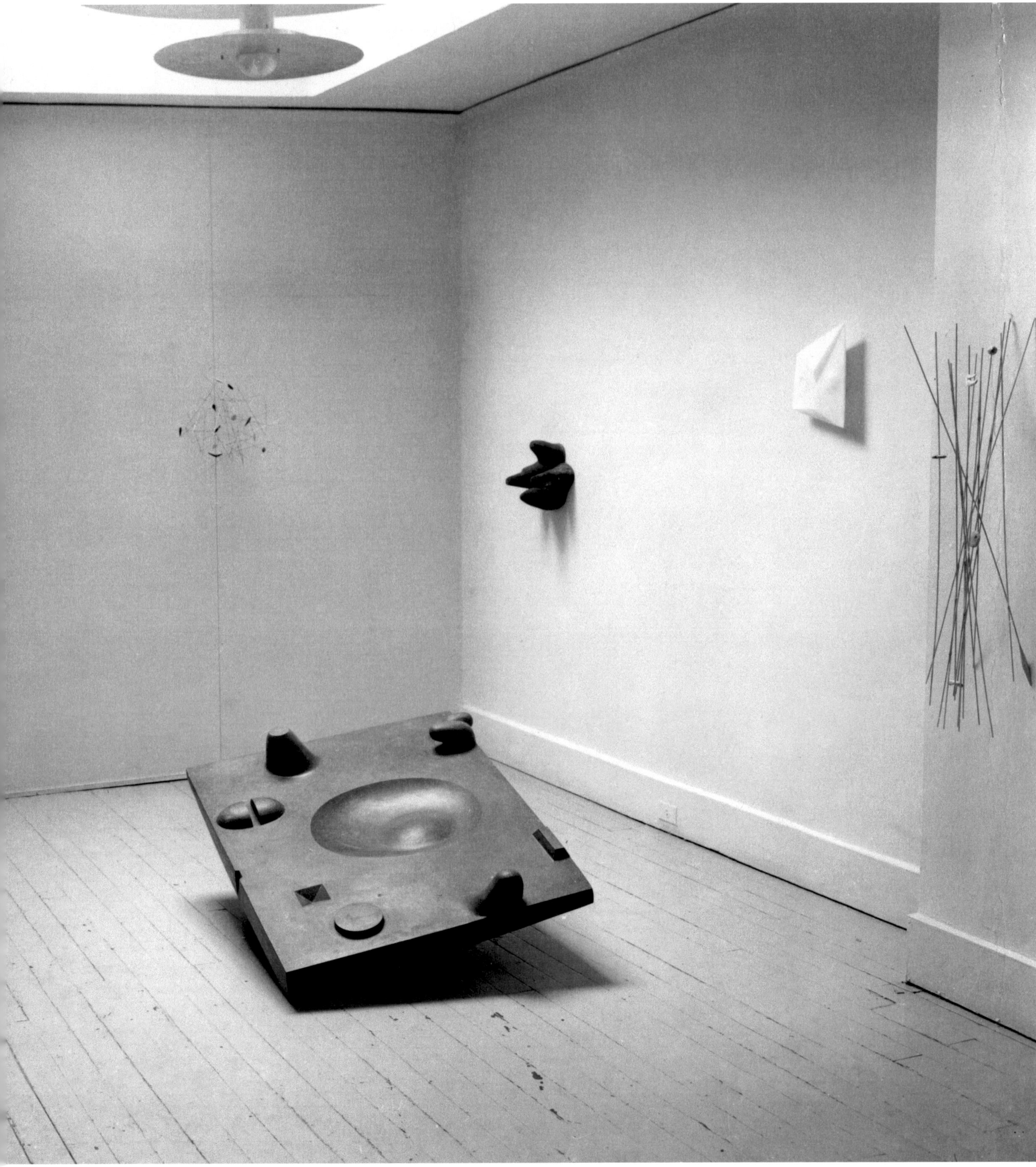

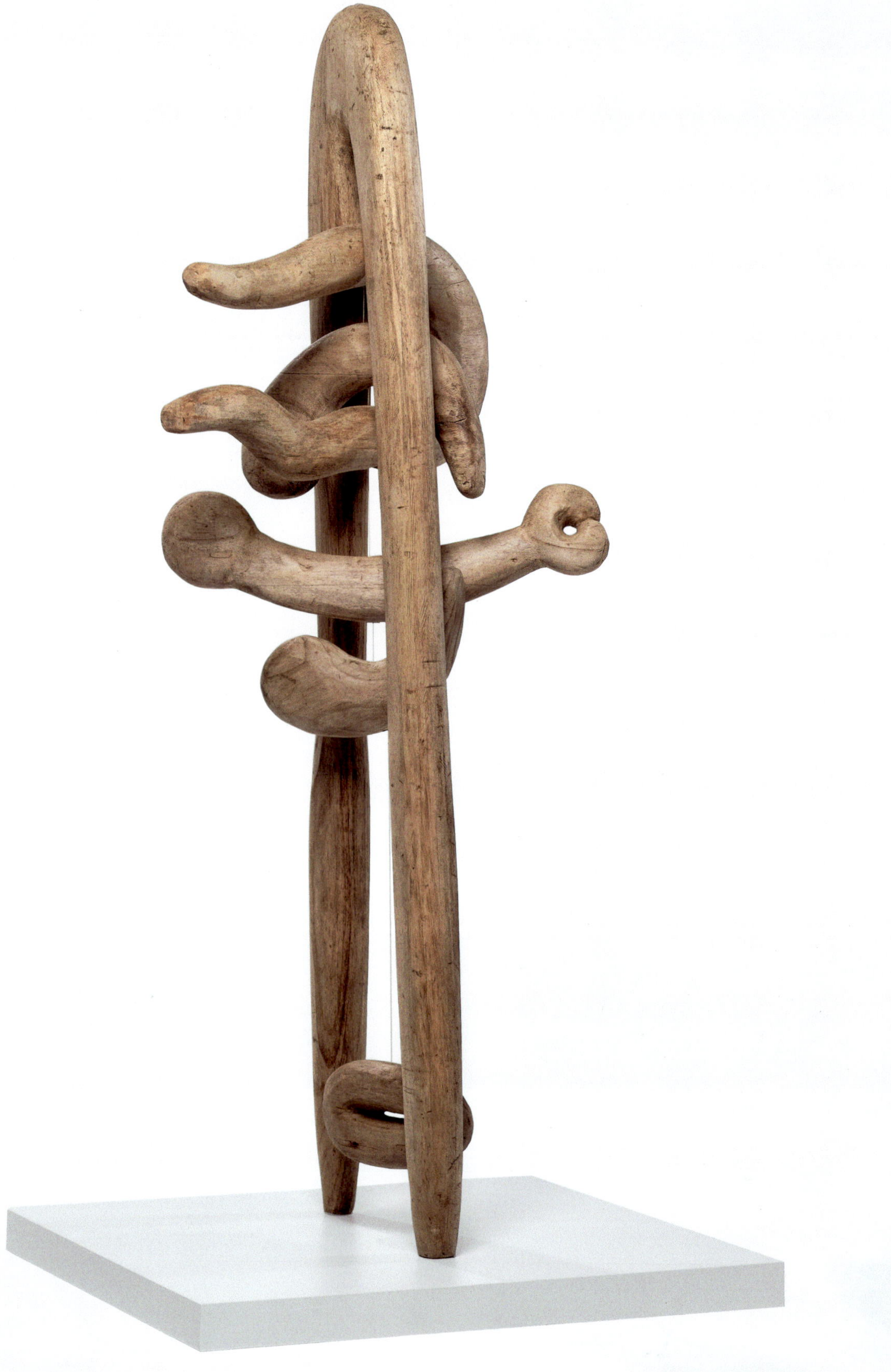

Cronos, 1947
Balsa wood
219.1 × 55.9 × 78.7 cm

Drawing after 'Cronos', 1949
Ink on paper
19.4 × 7 cm

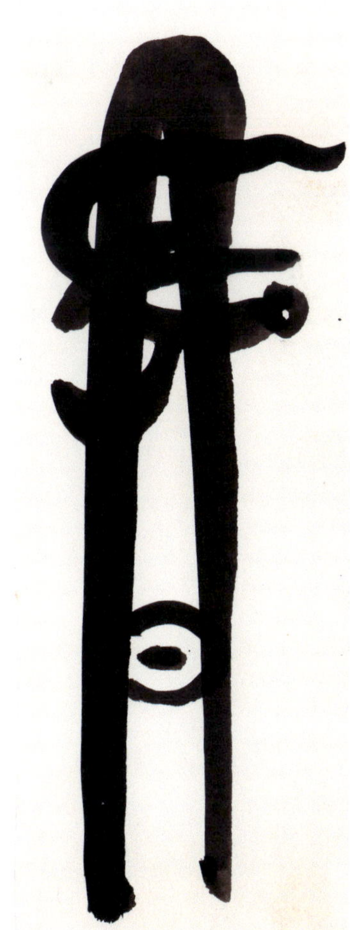

This Tortured Earth, 1942–43
(cast 1977)
Bronze
73.7 × 71.4 × 7.6 cm

Model for *Sculpture to be Seen from Mars*, 1947
(unrealised)
Sand
Dimensions unknown

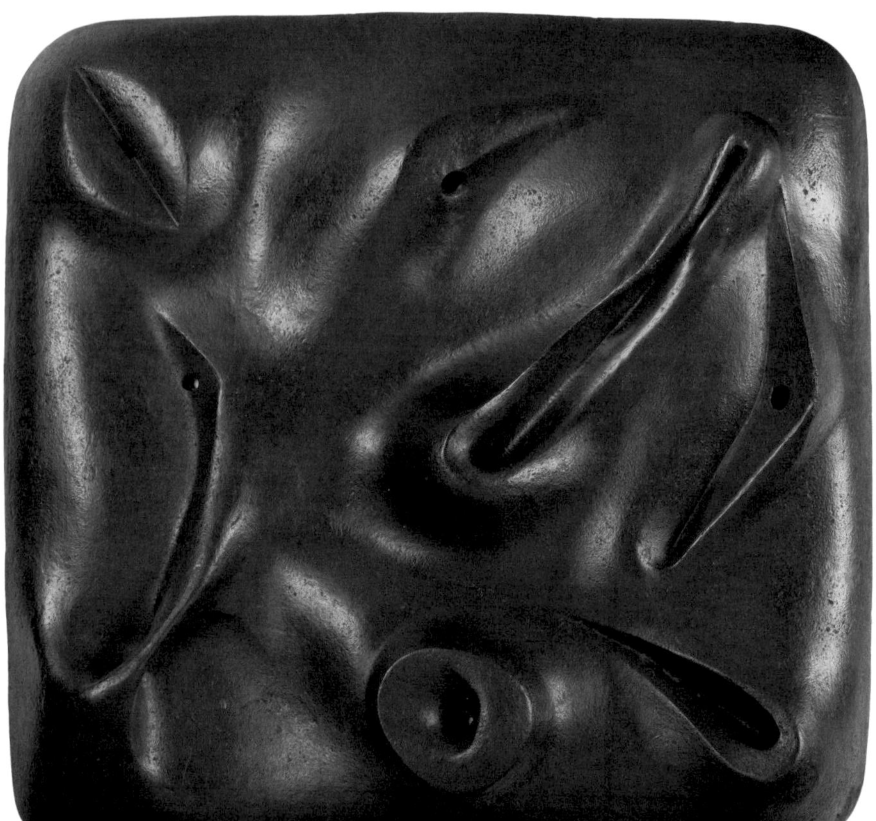

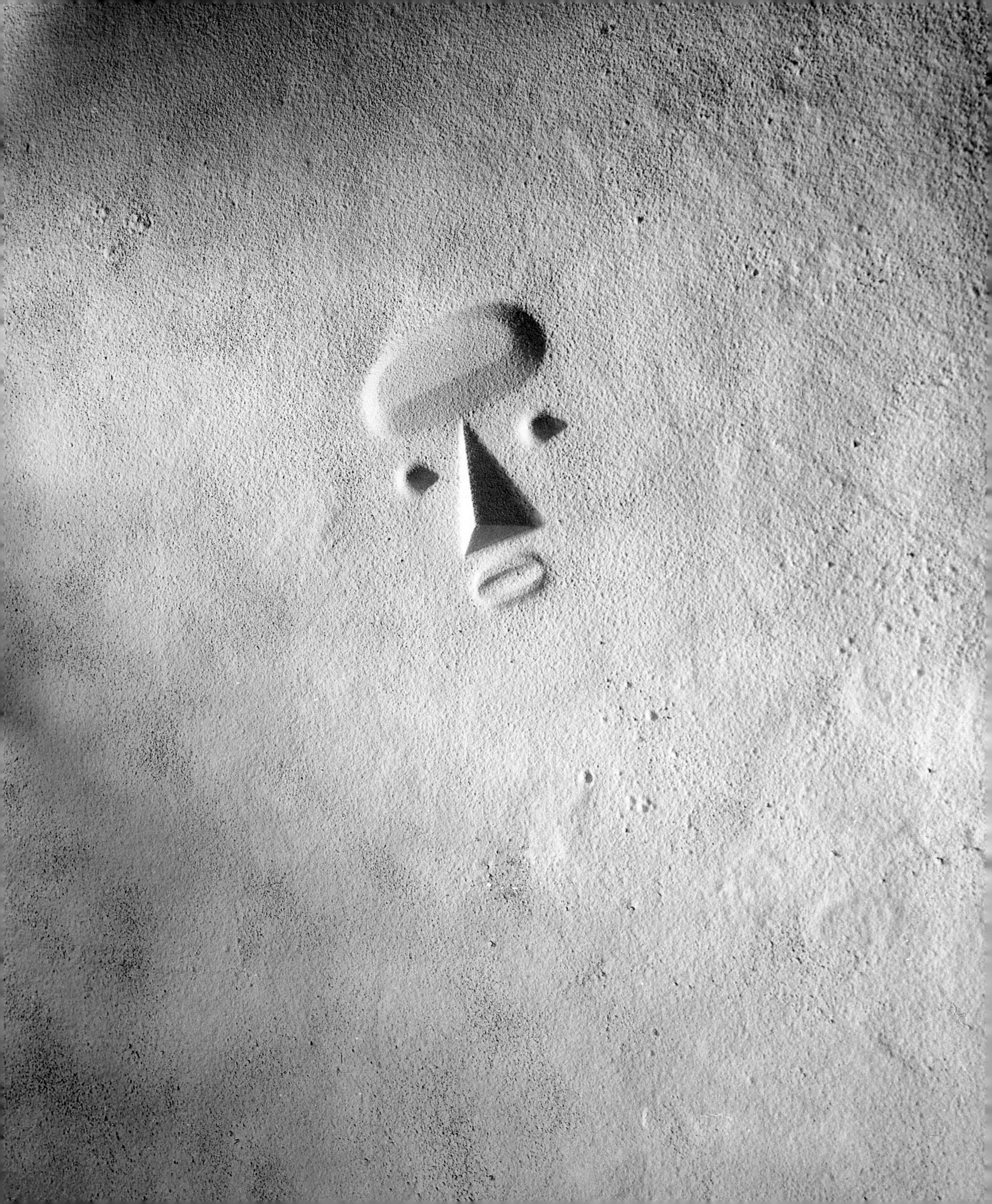

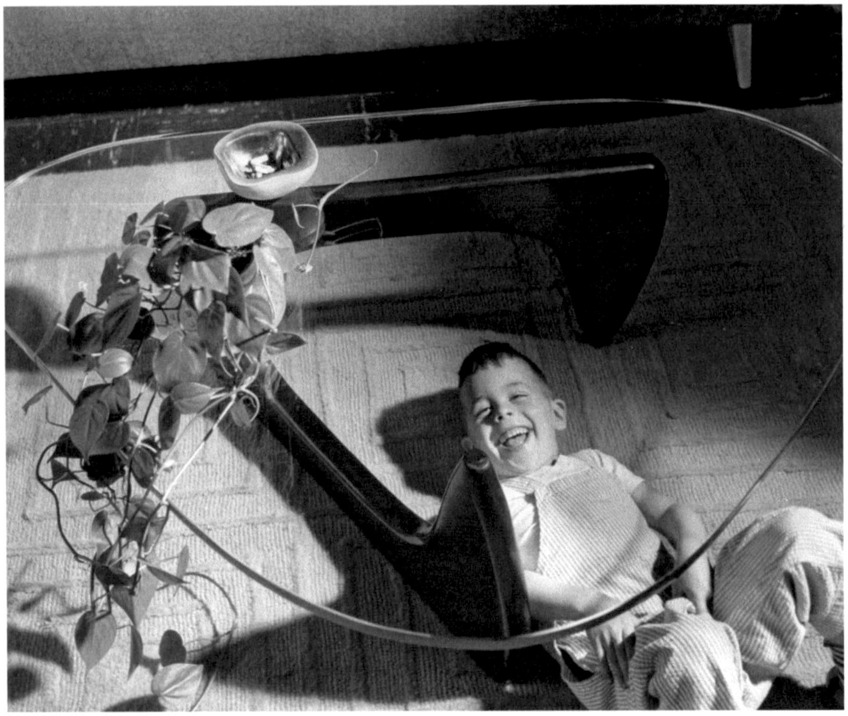

Child with *Coffee Table*, 1948

***Coffee Table*, 1944**
Manufactured by Herman Miller, 1947–73, 1984–present
Wood and plate glass
40 × 127 × 91 cm

I am not a designer. The word design implies catering to the quixotic fashion of the time. All my work, tables as well as sculptures, are conceived as fundamental problems of form that would best express human and aesthetic activity involved with these objects.

I have done some work for mass production technique. Here the problem was approached entirely freely and without compromises so far as I was concerned. Art is an act. The act of creating a fundamental form, though it may be disciplined by the fundamental nature of the object desired, is not designing in the accepted sense.

1949

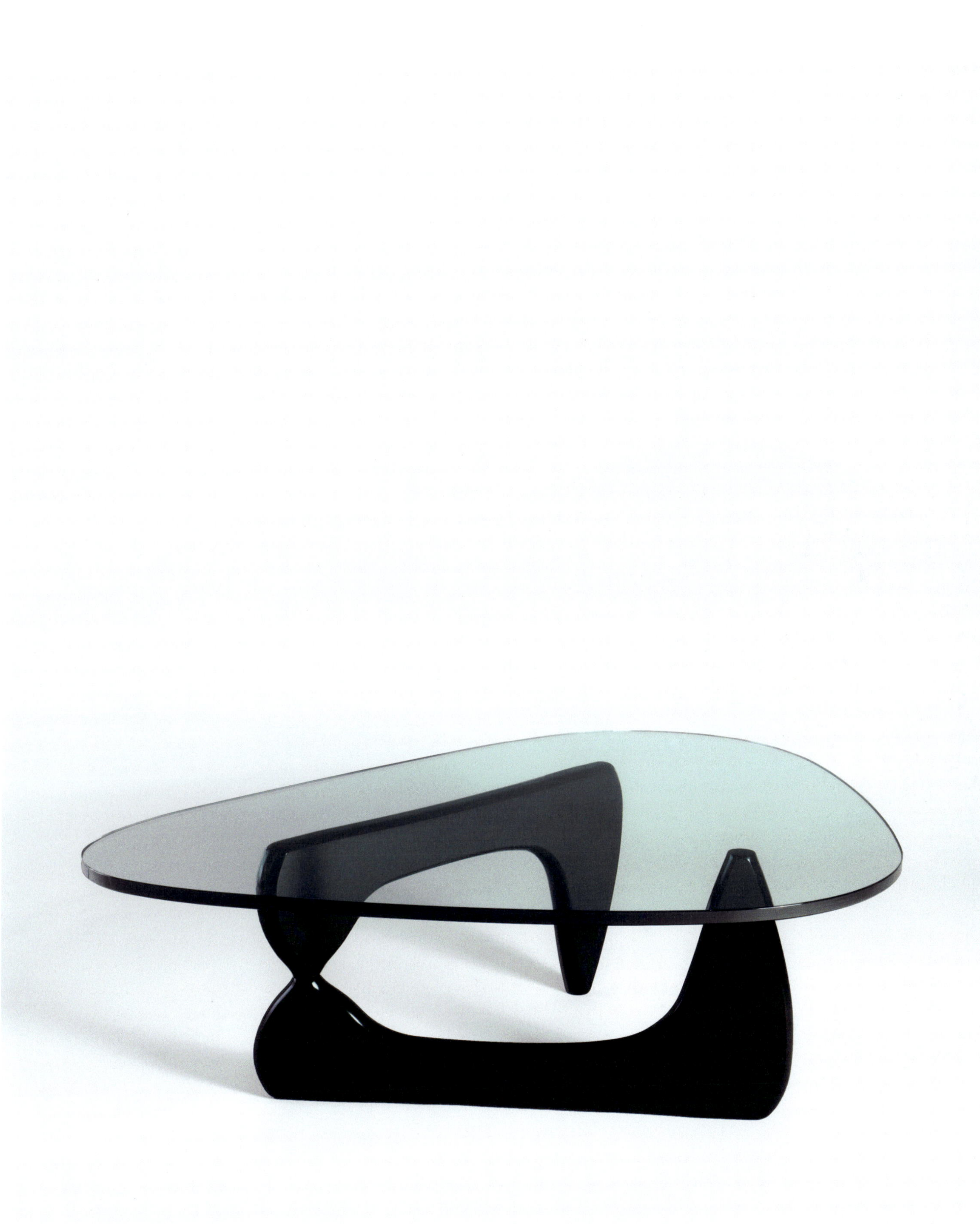

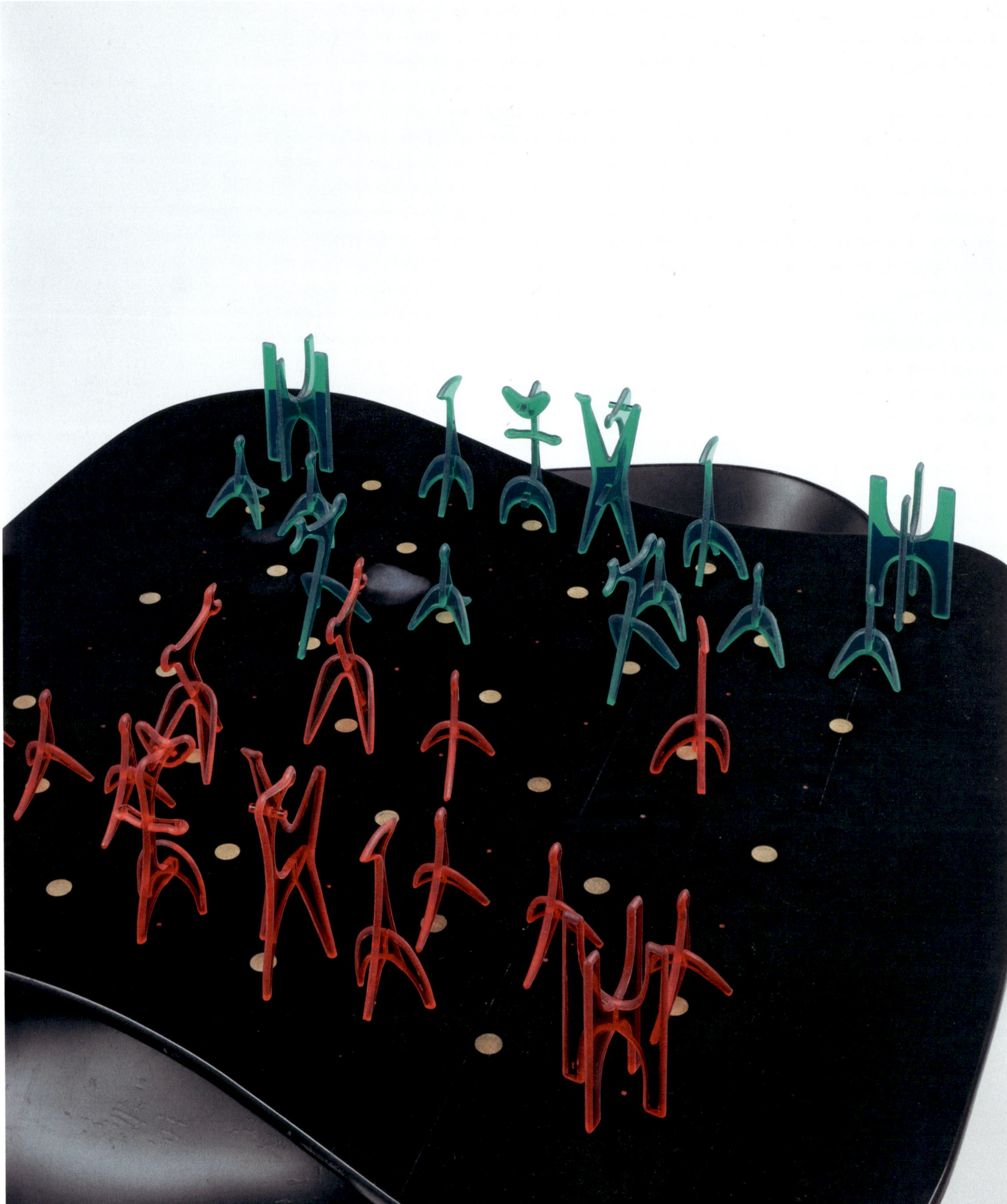

Chess Table and Chess Pieces, 1944
Ebonised plywood, cast aluminium with plastic insets and (reconstructed, 2003) plexiglass pieces
48.9 × 64.8 × 66.7 cm

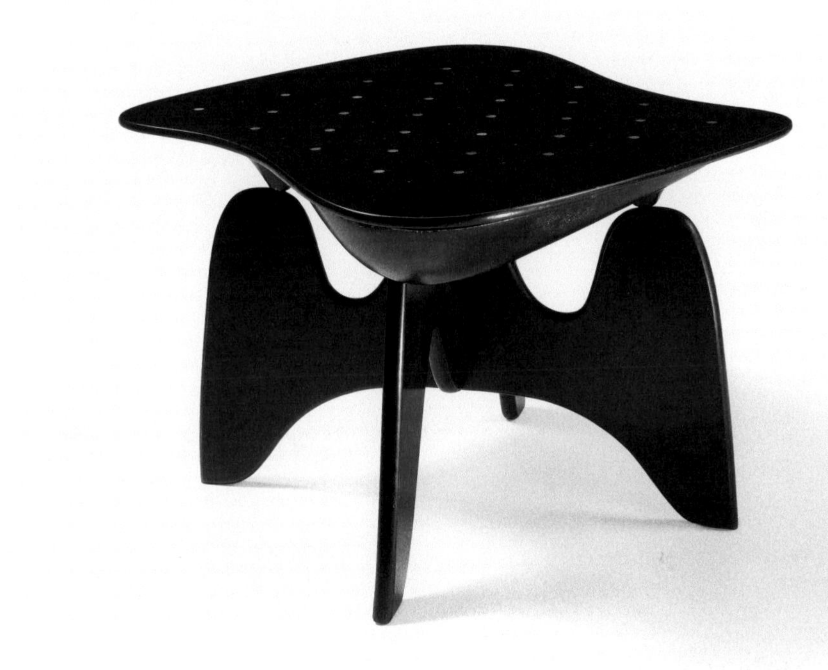

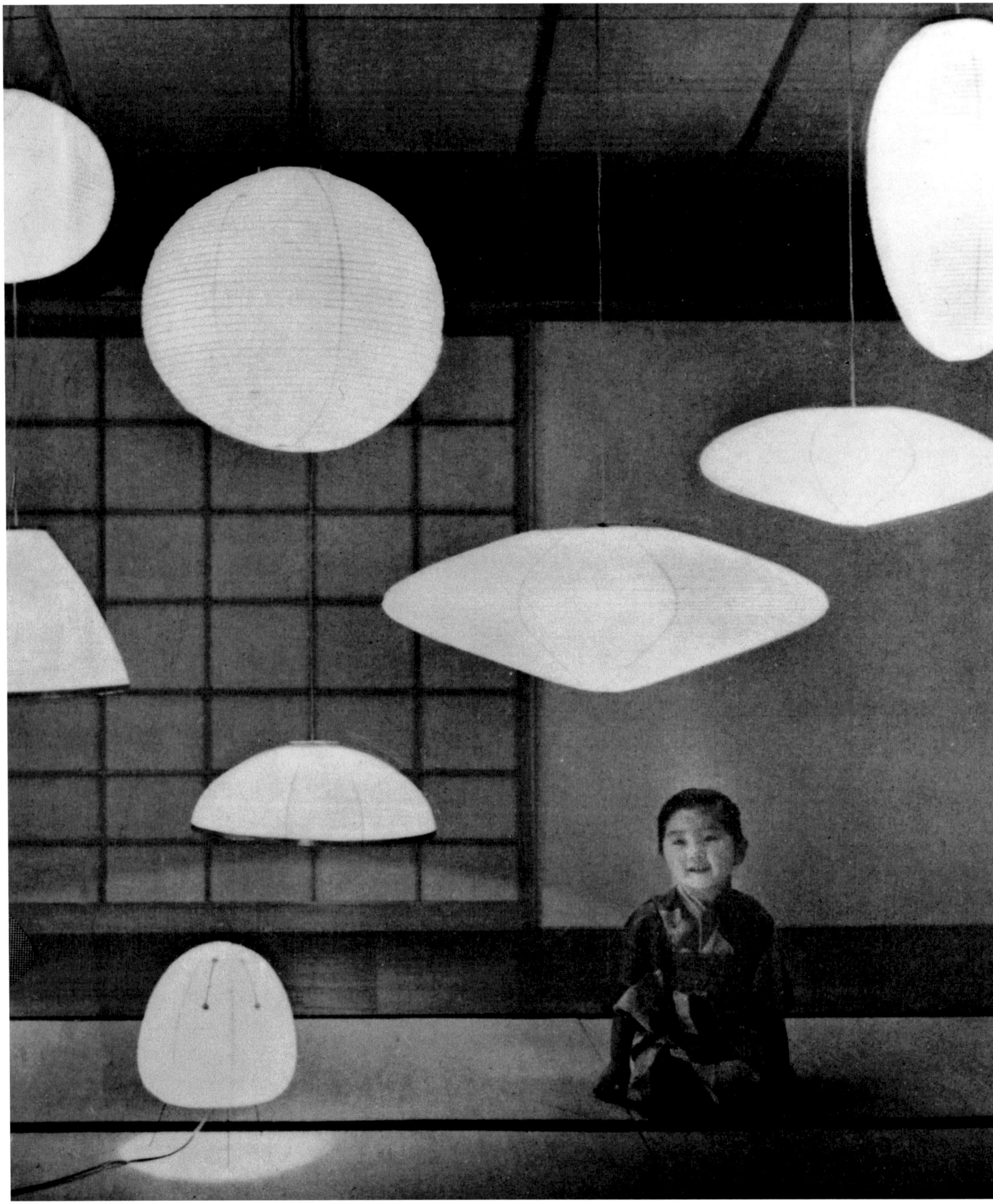

Michiko Tange with *Akari* at the Tange House, Tokyo, 1953

Exhibition view of *Akari: Lamps by Isamu Noguchi*, Chūō Kōron Gallery, Tokyo, 2–7 August 1954

What I did was to bring an ancient art into our modern art by integrating it with electricity (as I had done with lunars). I coined for them the name AKARI, which in Japanese means light as illumination, just as our word light does. It also suggests lightness as opposed to weight. The ideograph combines that of the sun and moon. The ideal of akari is therein exemplified with lightness (as essence) and light (for awareness). The quality is poetic, ephemeral, and tentative.

c. 1952

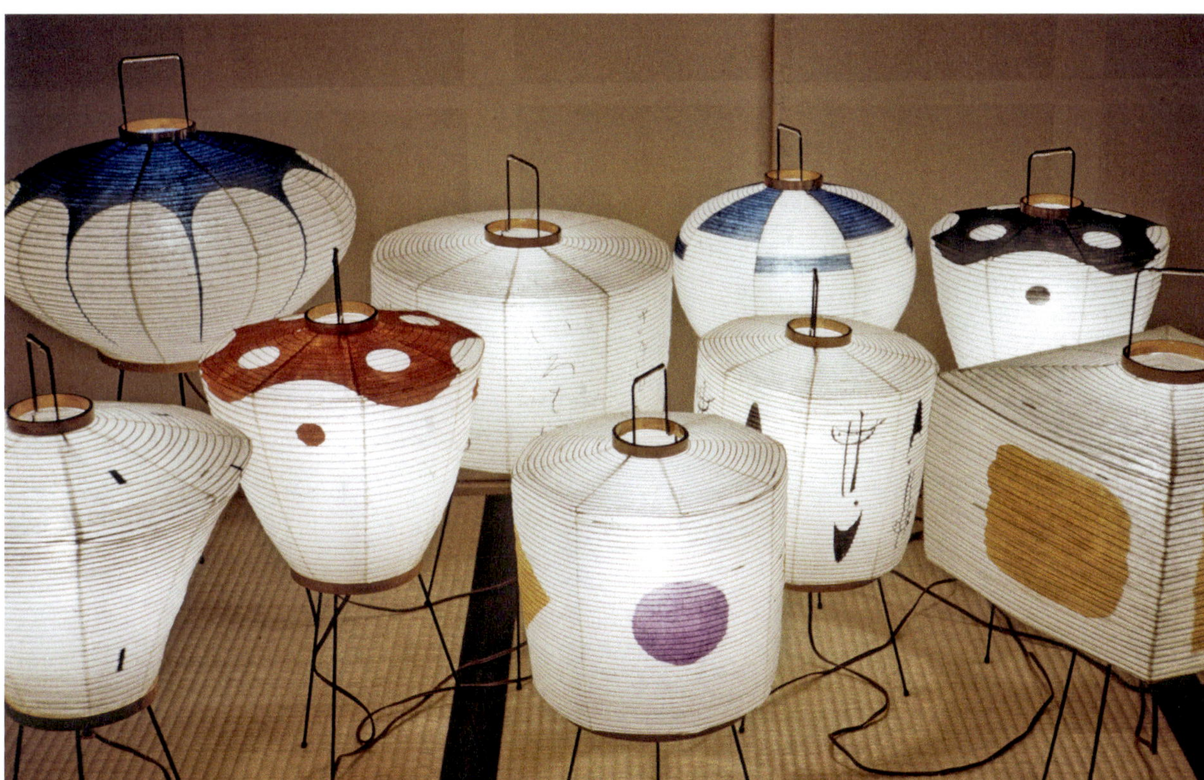

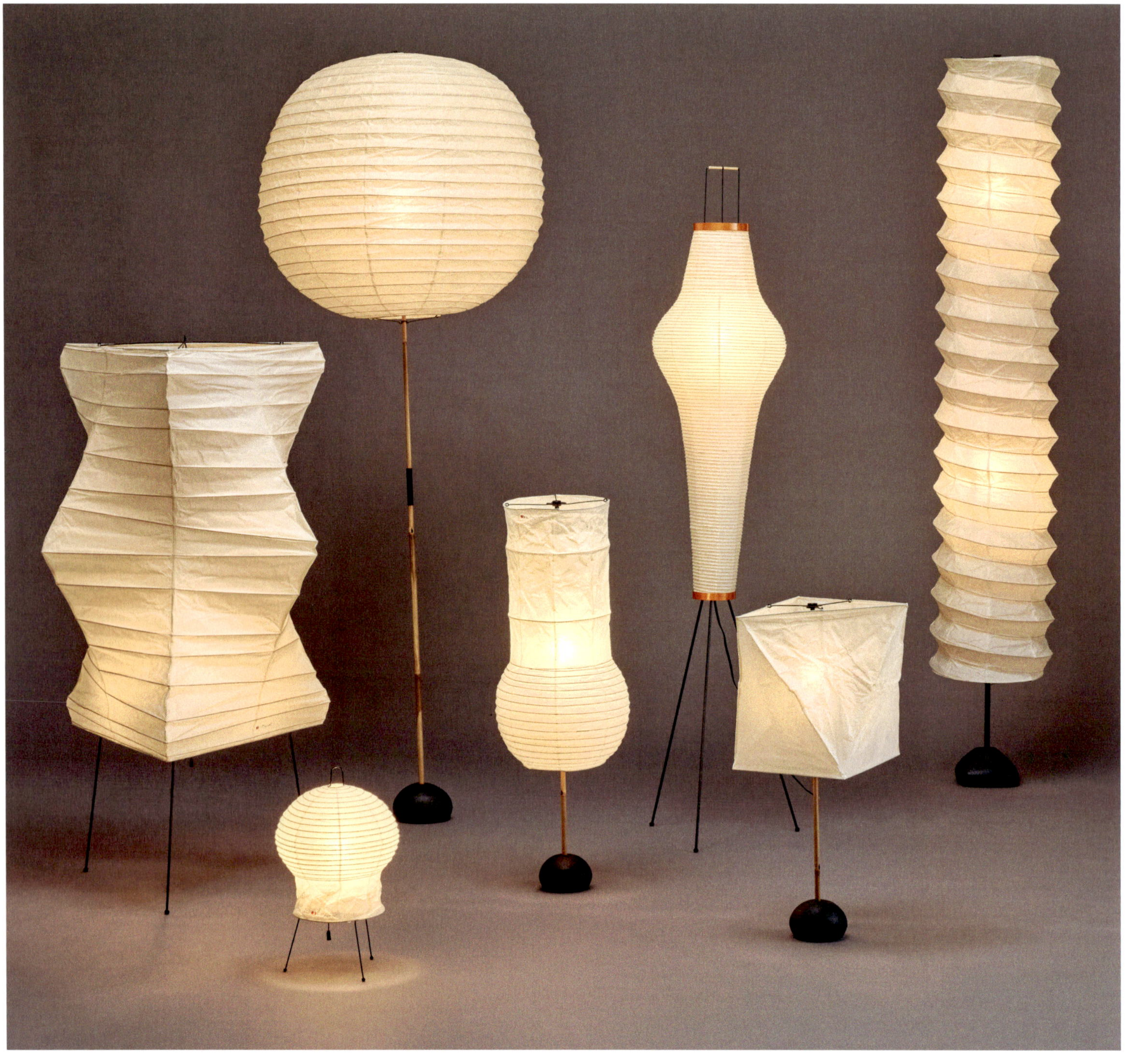

Group of *Akari* in the Kagawa Museum, Takamatsu, Japan

'Akari Lamps by Isamu Noguchi', dimensions and assembly brochure, c. 1955

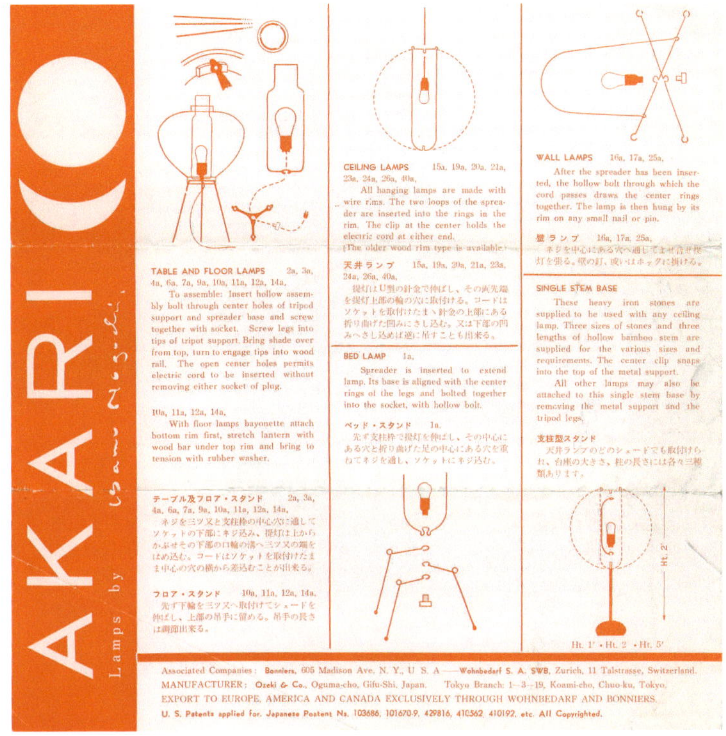

AKARI

Lamps by Isamu Noguchi

TABLE AND FLOOR LAMPS 2a, 3a, 4a, 6a, 7a, 9a, 10a, 11a, 12a, 14a,

To assemble: Insert hollow assembly bolt through center holes of tripod support and spreader base and screw together with socket. Screw legs into tips of tripot support. Bring shade over from top, turn to engage tips into wood rail. The open center holes permits electric cord to be inserted without removing either socket of plug.

10a, 11a, 12a, 14a,

With floor lamps bayonette attach bottom rim first, stretch lantern with wood bar under top rim and bring to tension with rubber washer.

テーブル及フロア・スタンド 2a, 3a, 4a, 6a, 7a, 9a, 10a, 11a, 12a, 14a,

ネジを三ツ又と支柱枠の中心穴に通してソケットの下部にネジ込み、提灯は上からかぶせその下部の口輪の溝へ三ツ又の端をはめ込む。コードはソケットを取付けたまま中心の穴の横から差込むことが出来る。

フロア・スタンド 10a, 11a, 12a, 14a,

先ず下輪を三ツ又へ取付けてシェードを伸ばし、上部の吊手に留める。吊手の長さは調節出来る。

CEILING LAMPS 15a, 19a, 20a, 21a, 23a, 24a, 26a, 40a,

All hanging lamps are made with wire rims. The two loops of the spreader are inserted into the rings in the rim. The clip at the center holds the electric cord at either end.
(The older wood rim type is available.)

天井ランプ 15a, 19a, 20a, 21a, 23a, 24a, 26a, 40a,

提灯はU型の針金で伸ばし、その両先端を提灯上部の輪の穴に取付ける。コードはソケットを取付けたまゝ針金の上部にある折り曲げた凹みにさし込む。又は下部の凹みへさし込めば逆に吊すことも出来る。

BED LAMP 1a,

Spreader is inserted to extend lamp. Its base is aligned with the center rings of the legs and bolted together into the socket, with hollow bolt.

ベッド・スタンド 1a,

先ず支柱枠で提灯を伸ばし、その中心にある穴と折り曲げた足の中心にある穴を重ねてネジを通し、ソケットにネジ込む。

WALL LAMPS 16a, 17a, 25a,

After the spreader has been inserted, the hollow bolt through which the cord passes draws the center rings together. The lamp is then hung by its rim on any small nail or pin.

壁ランプ 16a, 17a, 25a,

ネジを中心にある穴へ通して[illegible]提灯を張る。壁の釘、或いはホックに掛ける。

SINGLE STEM BASE

These heavy iron stones are supplied to be used with any ceiling lamp. Three sizes of stones and three lengths of hollow bamboo stem are supplied for the various sizes and requirements. The center clip snaps into the top of the metal support.

All other lamps may also be attached to this single stem base by removing the metal support and the tripod legs.

支柱型スタンド

天井ランプのどのシェードでも取付けられ、台座の大きさ、柱の長さには各々三種類あります。

Associated Companies: Bonniers, 605 Madison Ave, N. Y., U. S. A ——Wohnbedarf S. A. SWB, Zurich, 11 Talstrasse, Switzerland.
MANUFACTURER: Ozeki & Co., Oguma-cho, Gifu-Shi, Japan. Tokyo Branch: 1-3-19, Koami-cho, Chuo-ku, Tokyo.
EXPORT TO EUROPE, AMERICA AND CANADA EXCLUSIVELY THROUGH WOHNBEDARF AND BONNIERS.
U. S. Patents applied for. Japanese Postent Ns. 103686, 101670-9, 429816, 410562, 410192, etc. All Copyrighted.

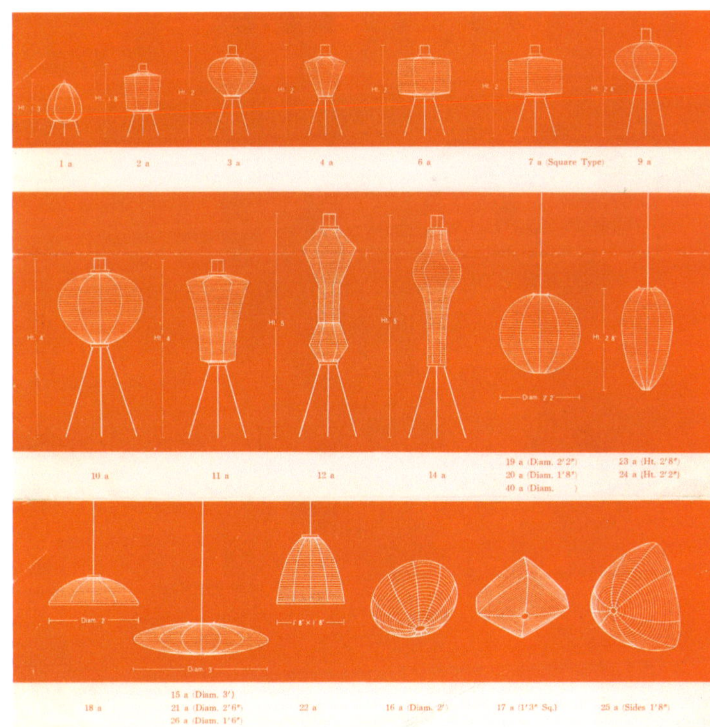

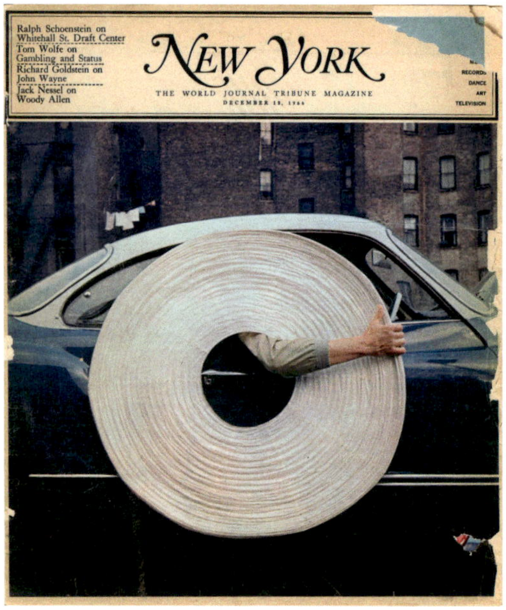

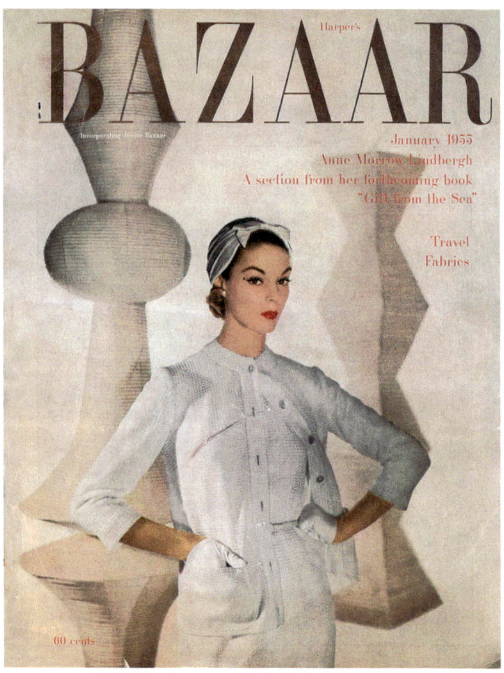

Cover of *New York: The World Journal Tribune Magazine*, 18 December 1966

Cover of *Harper's Bazaar*, January 1955

Exhibition view of *Space of Akari and Stone*, Seibu Museum of Art, Tokyo, 9–20 February 1985

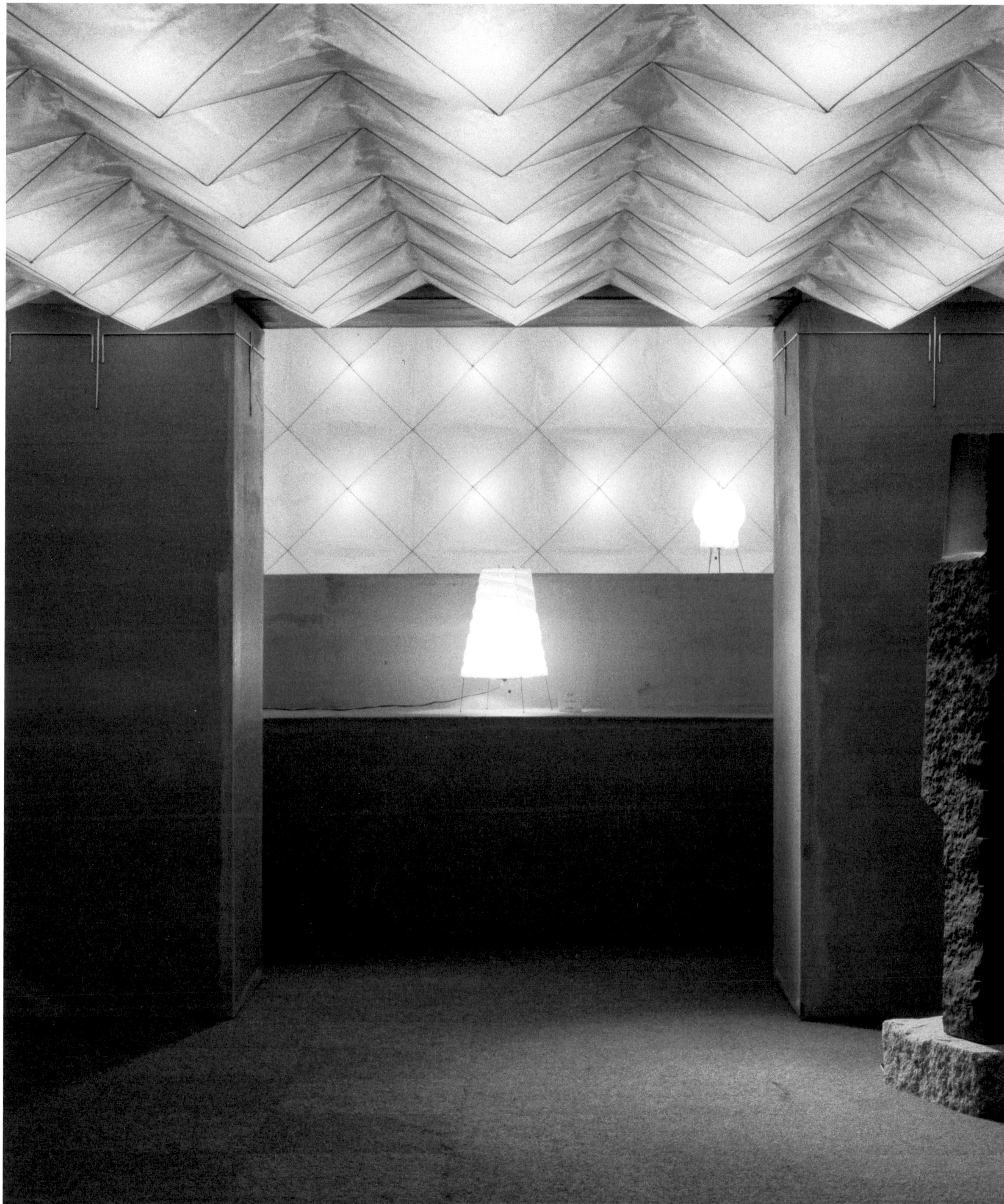

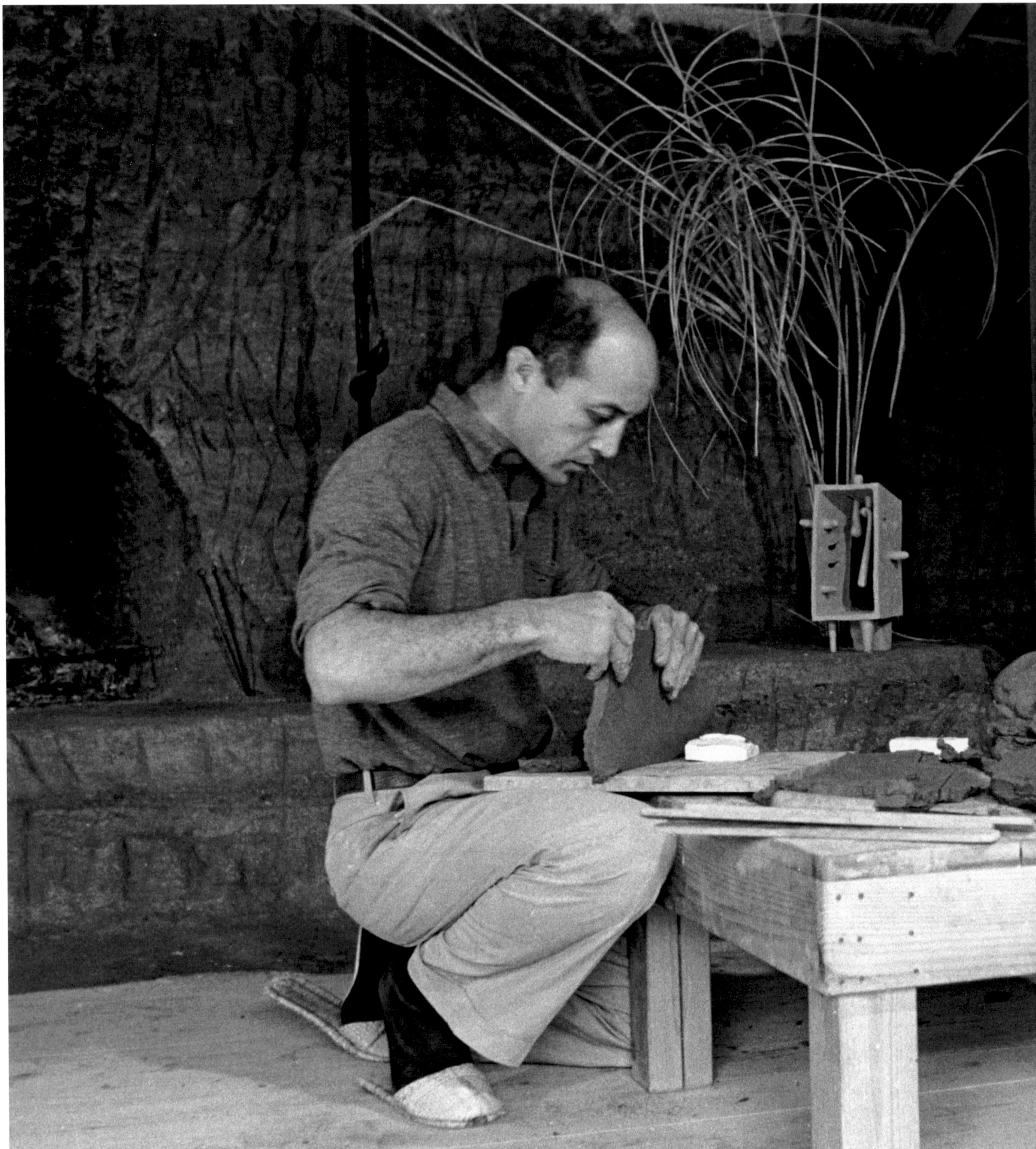

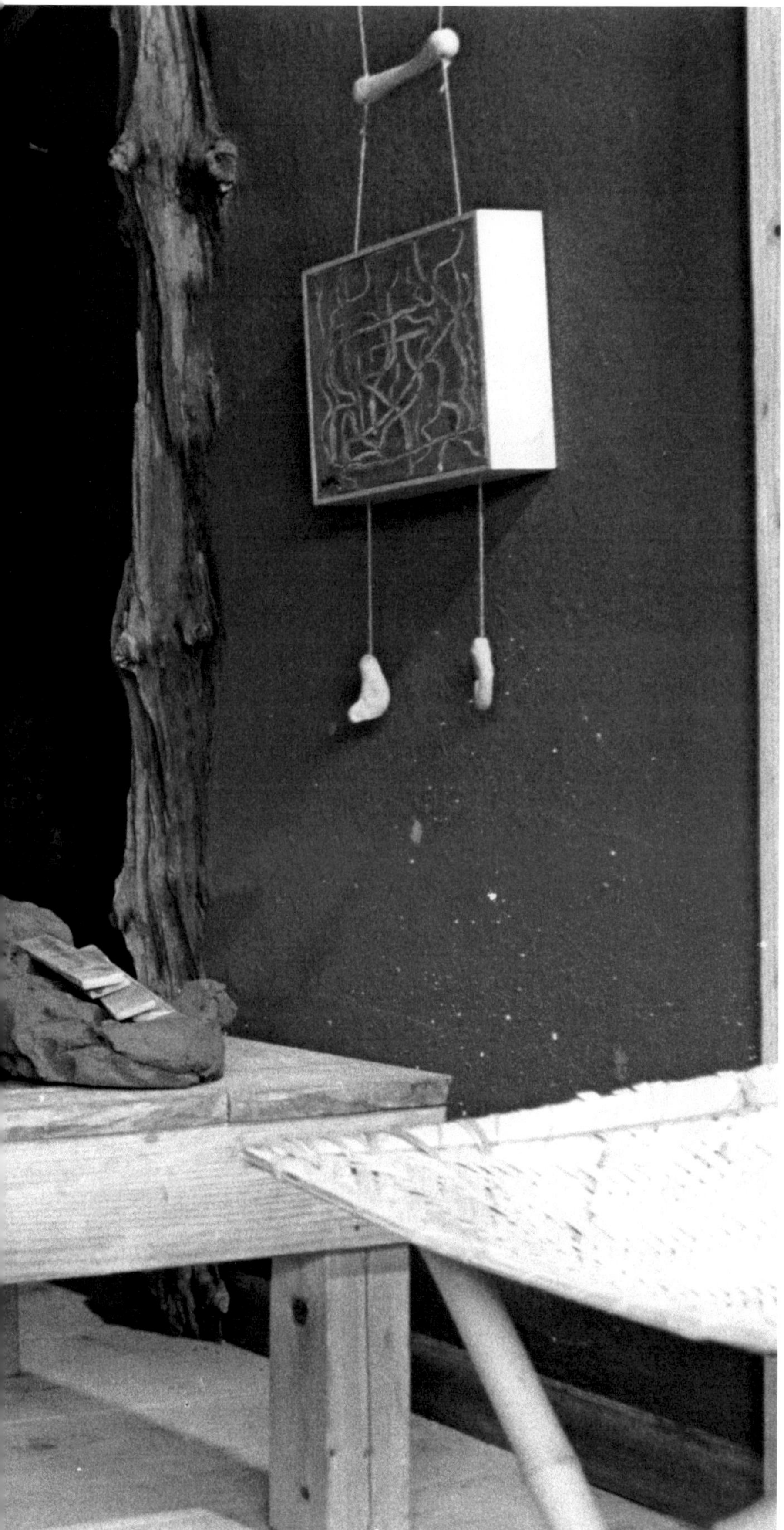

Noguchi in his Kita Kamakura studio, Japan, c. 1952

The attractions of ceramics lie partly in its contradictions. It is both difficult and easy, with an element beyond our control. It is both extremely fragile and durable. Like 'Sumi' ink painting, it does not lend itself to erasures and indecision. The best is that which is most spontaneous – or seemingly so. I have found it a natural medium to work with in Japan, but not so in America. I associate it with the closeness of earth and wood which is for me Japan and not America today.

1967

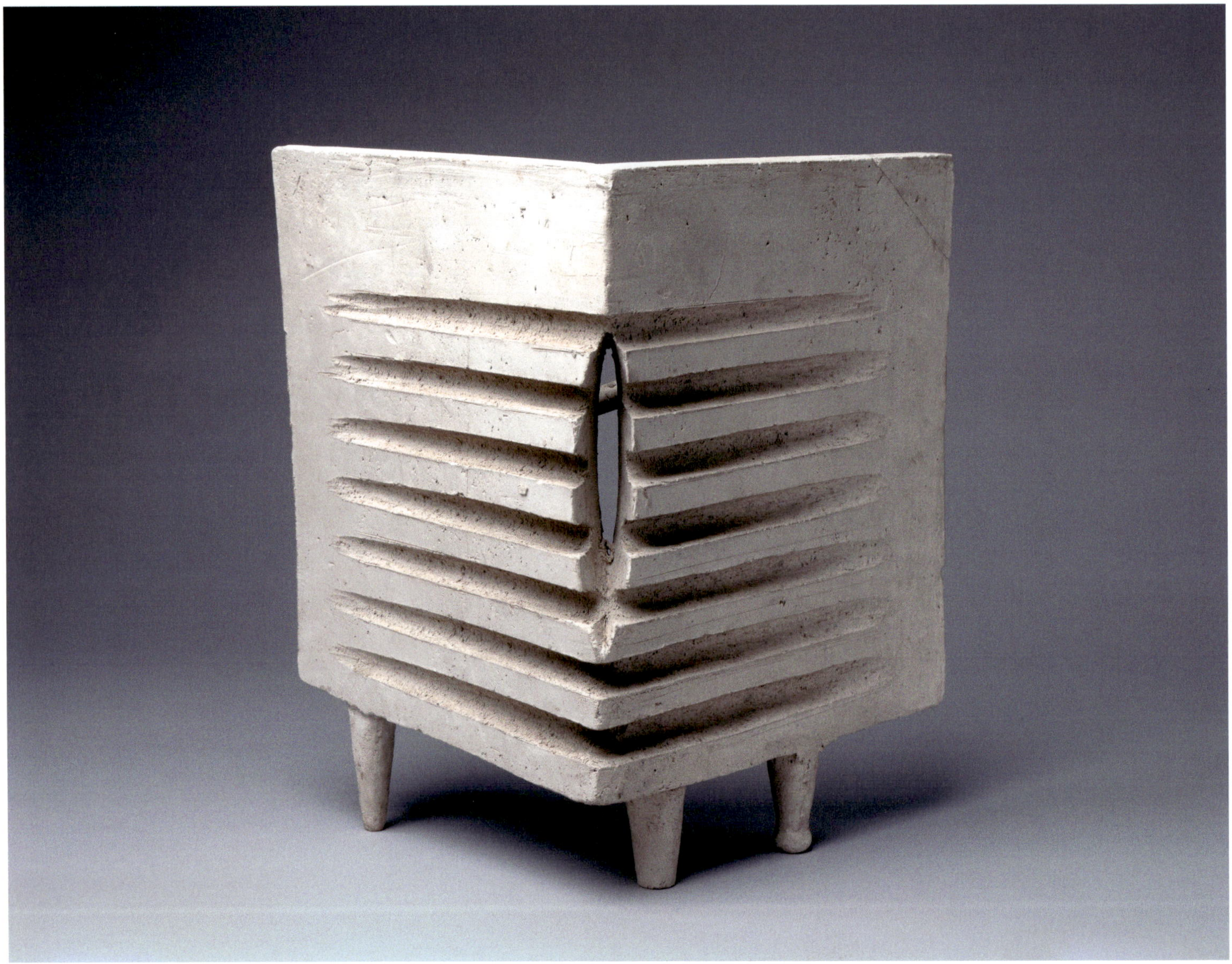

Love of Two Boards, 1950
Seto stoneware
25.7 × 25.7 × 14 cm

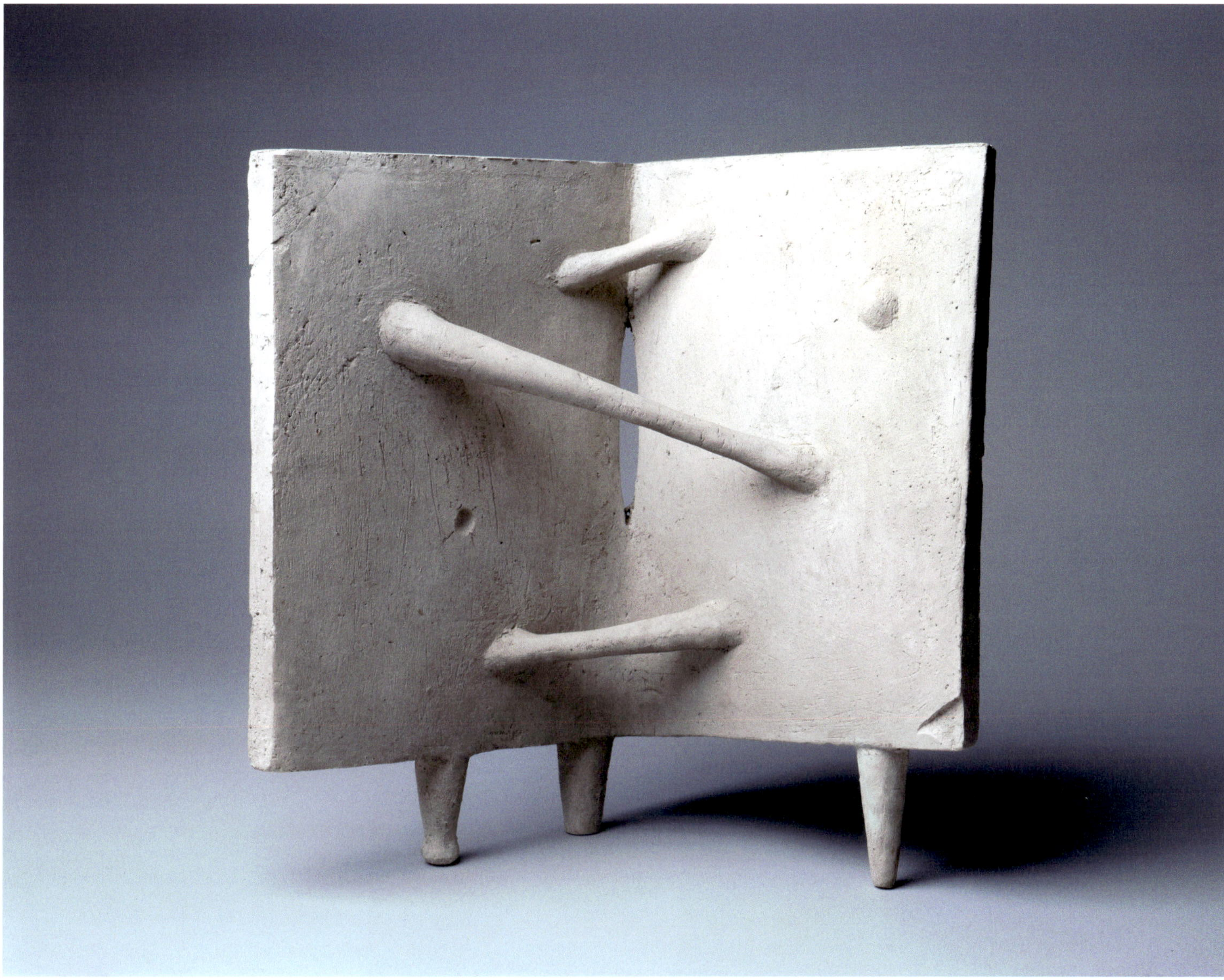

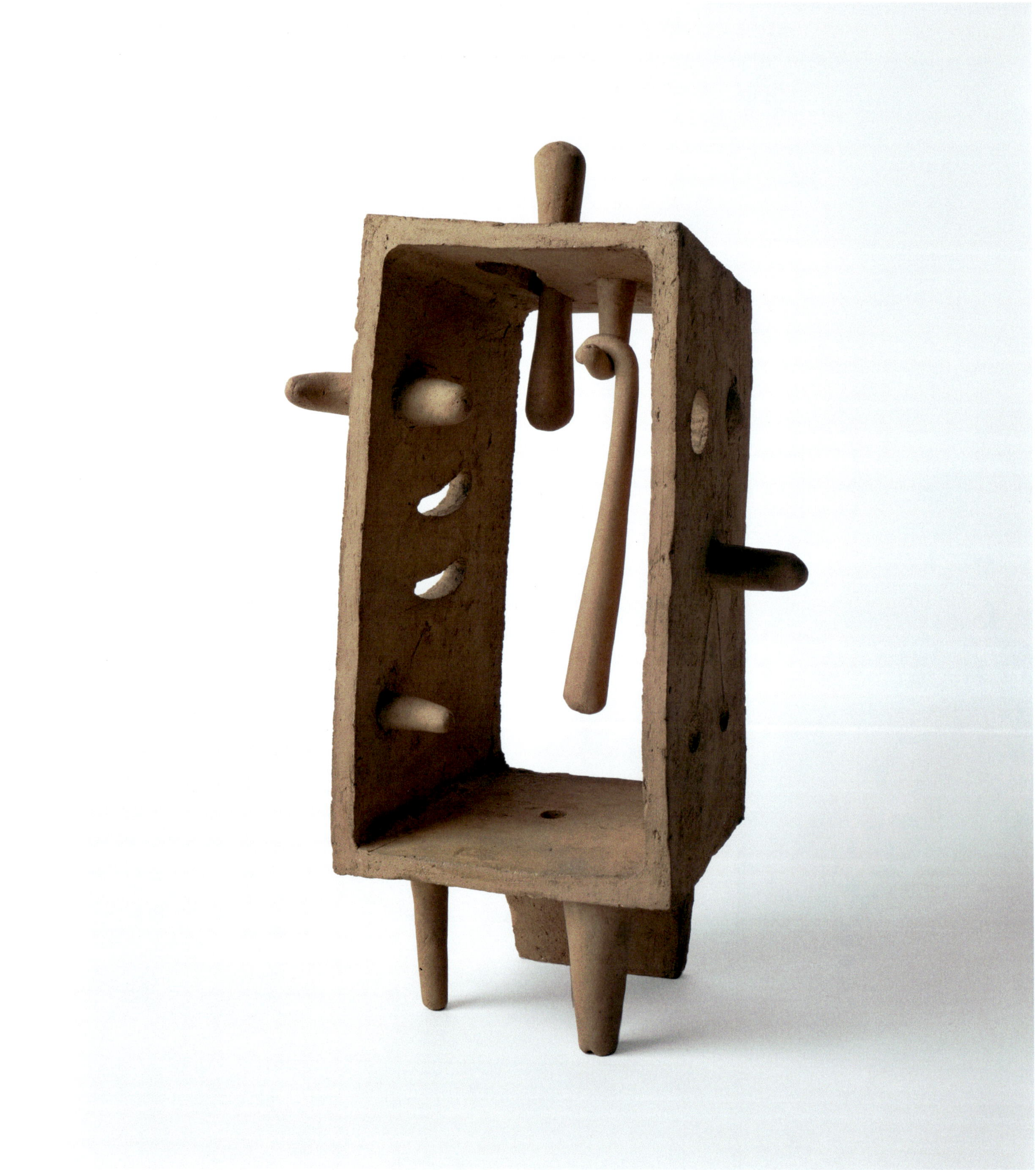

The Policeman (Junsa), 1950
Seto stoneware
34 × 22.2 × 13 cm

Skin and Bones (Bone and Skin), 1950
Seto stoneware, wood and hemp
42.9 × 30.2 × 9.2 cm

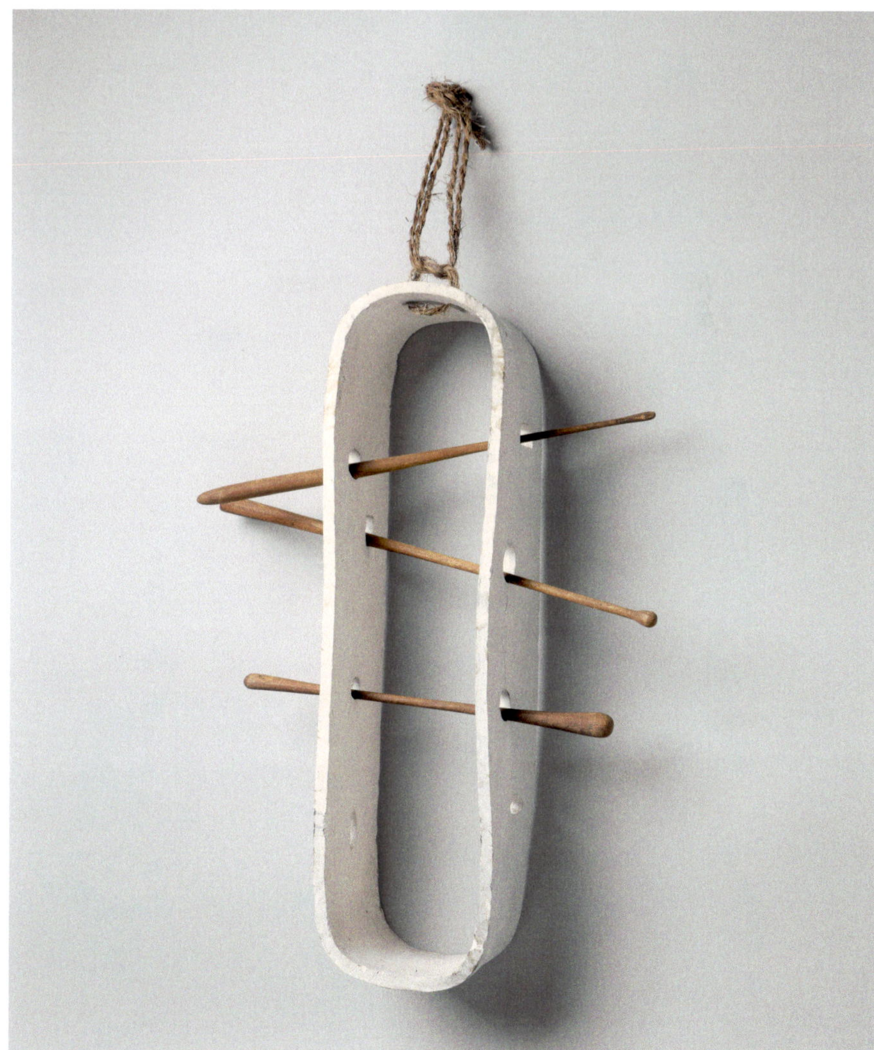

Marriage (Senbei Buton) (Worn Out Futon), 1952
Karatsu stoneware
5.4 × 32.7 × 14 cm

Buson, 1952
Karatsu stoneware
21 × 16.5 × 8.9 cm

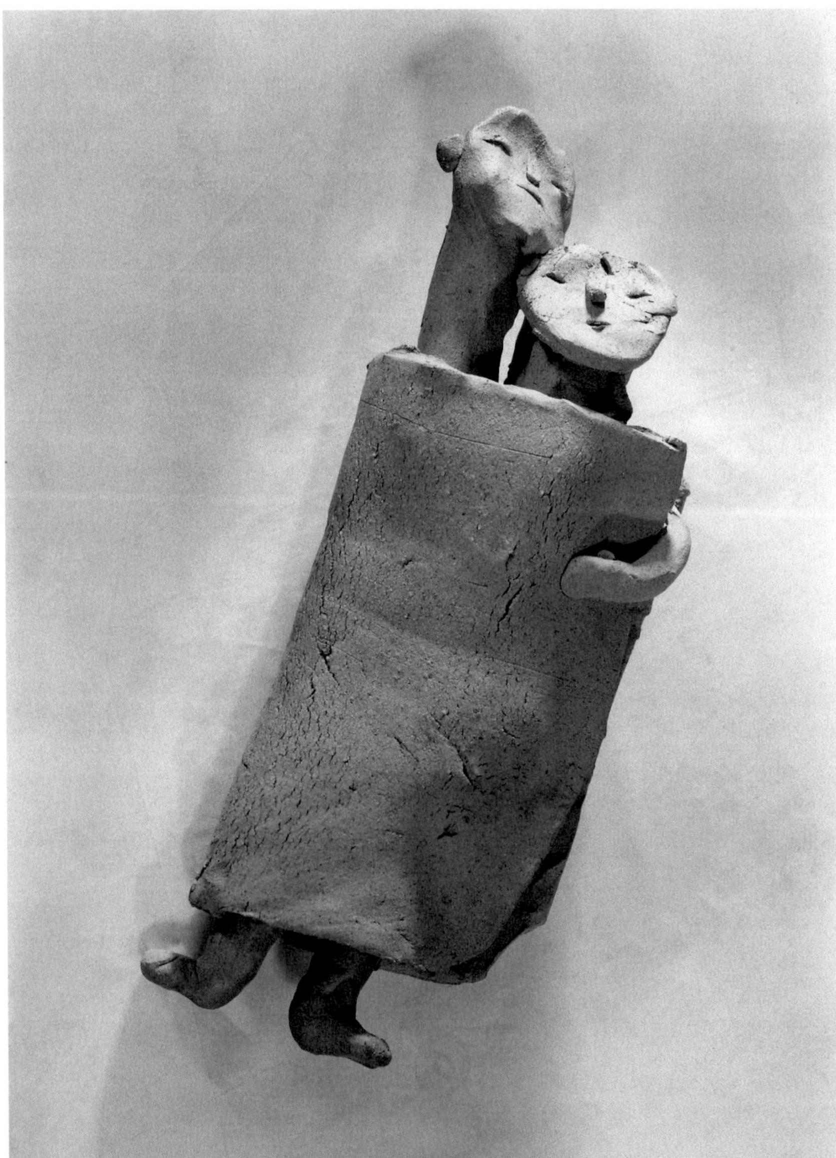

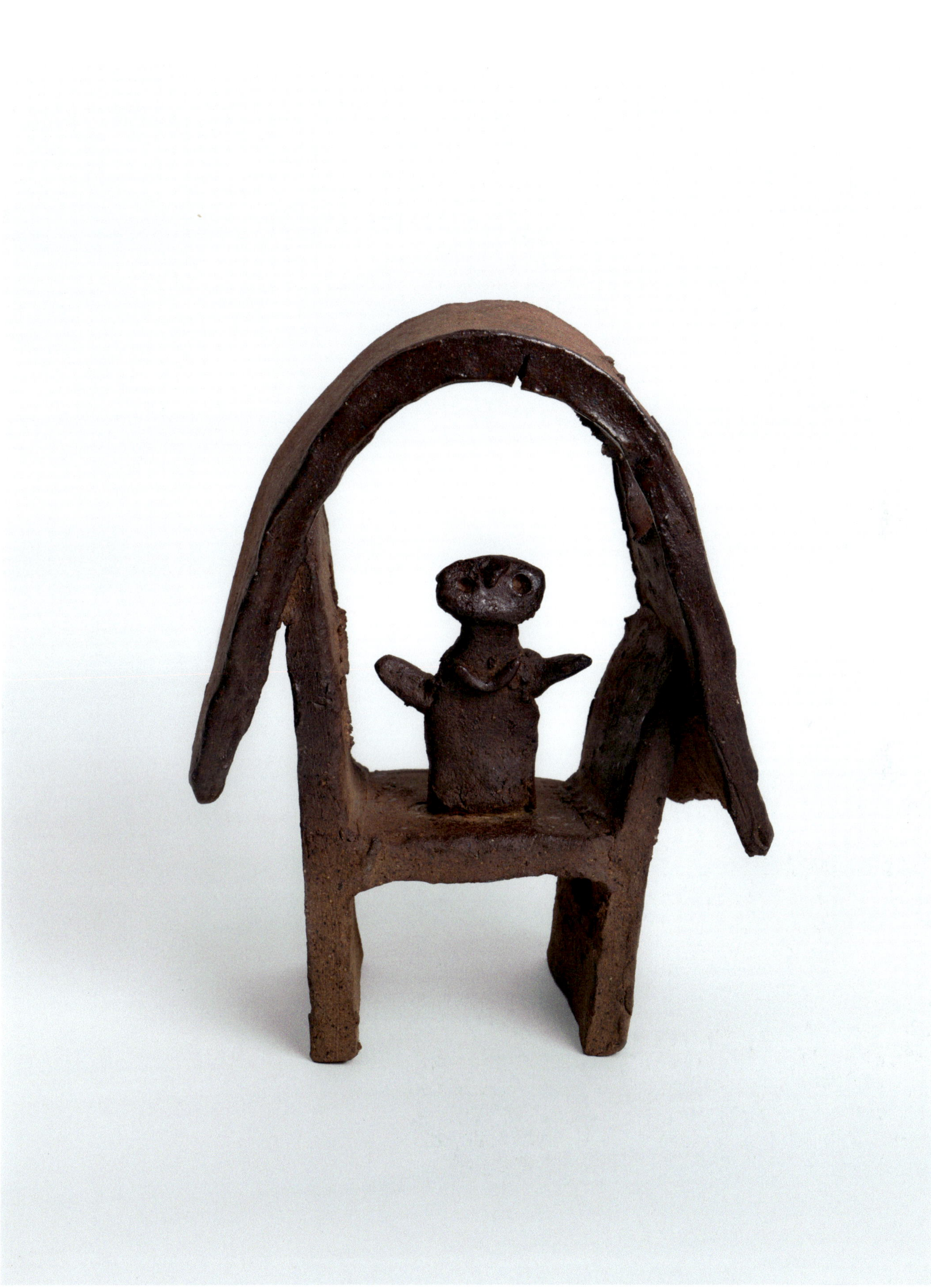

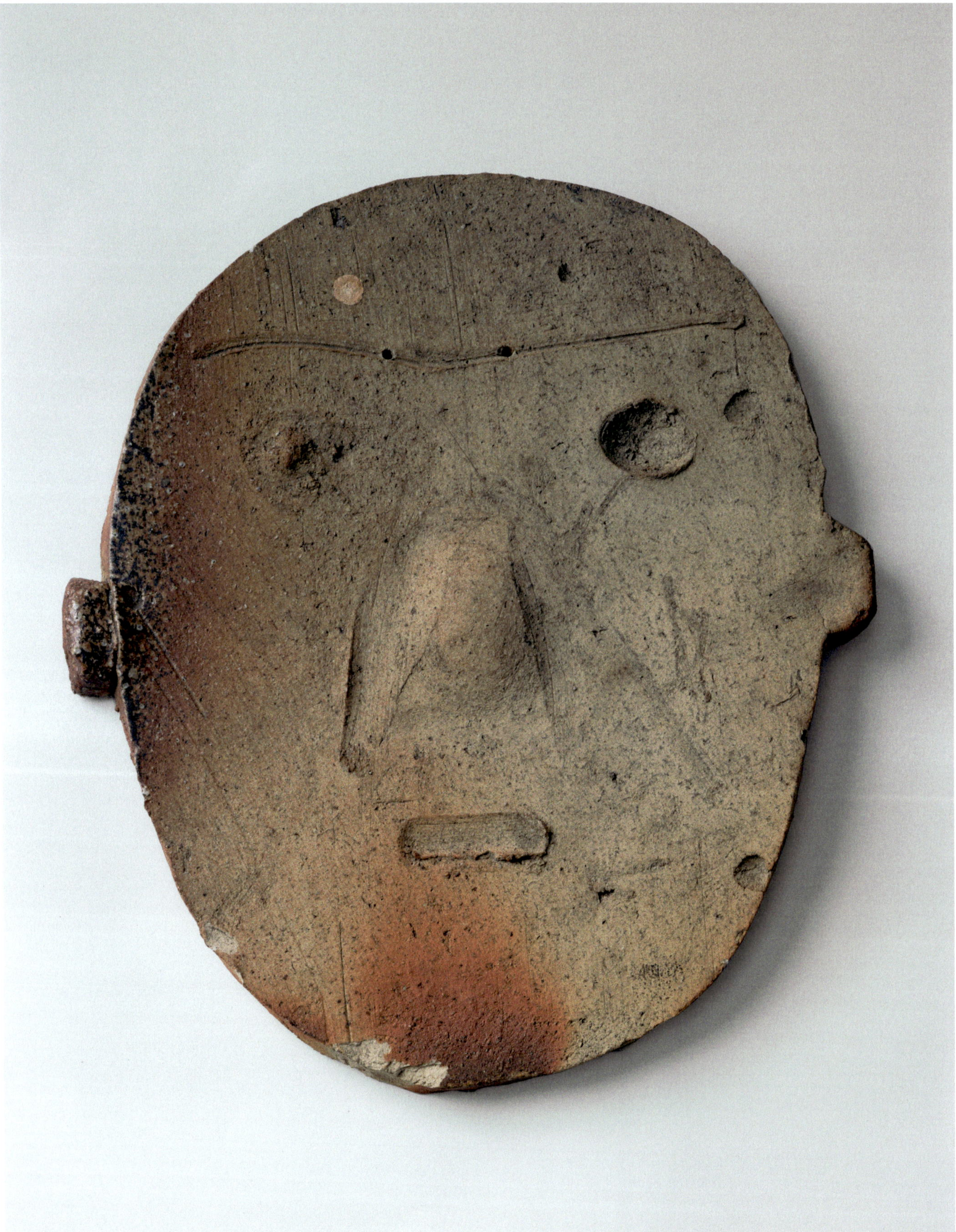

Face Dish (Boku) (Myself), 1952
Shigaraki stoneware
30.8 × 27.3 × 2.9 cm

Small Centipede (Mukade No. 2) (Centipede No. 2), 1952
Glazed Kasama stoneware
6.7 × 37.5 × 4.1 cm

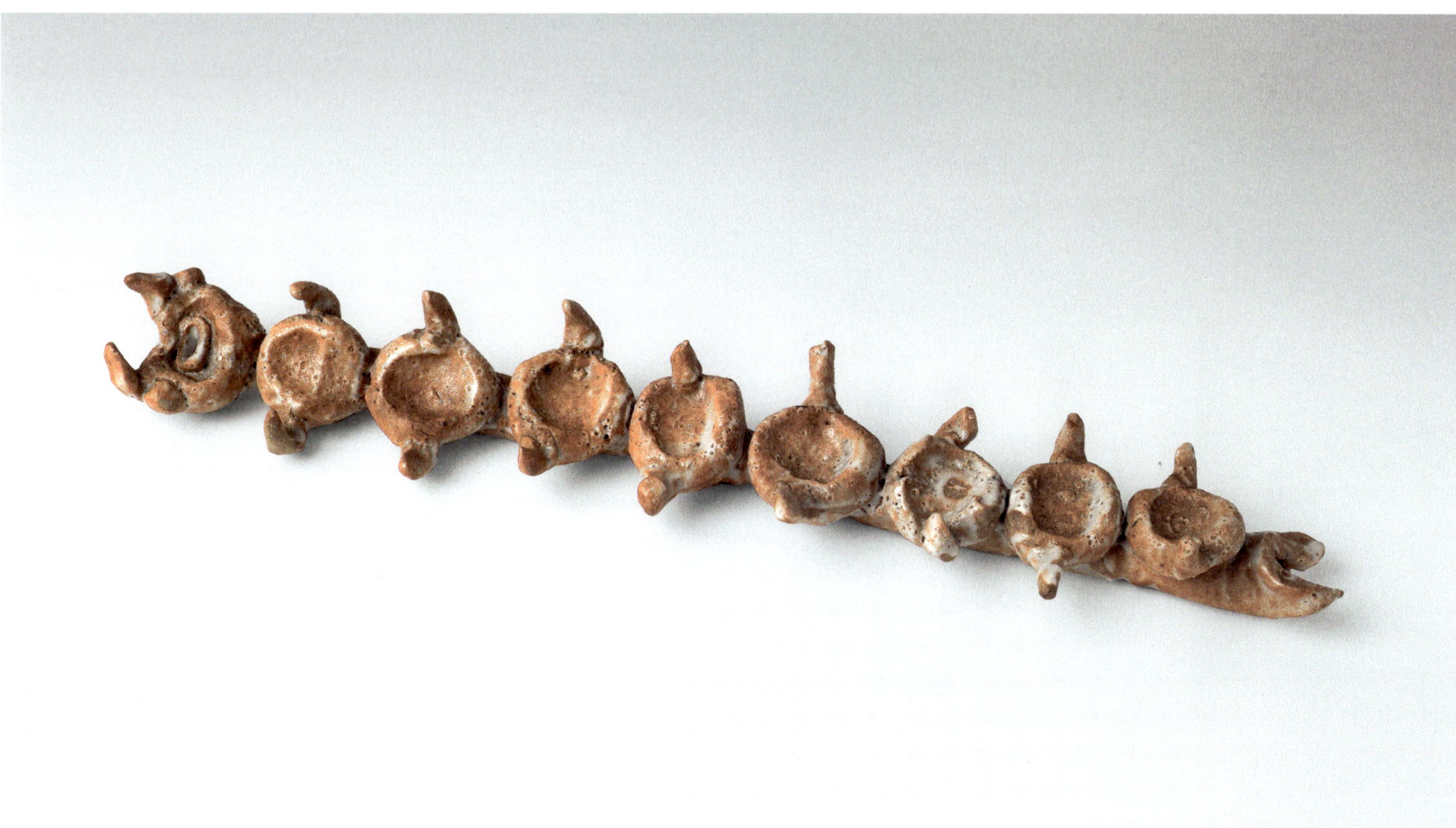

My Mu, 1950
Seto stoneware
34.3 × 24.1 × 16.8 cm

Exhibition view of *Isamu Noguchi*, Mitsukoshi department store, Nihombashi branch, Tokyo,
18–27 August 1950

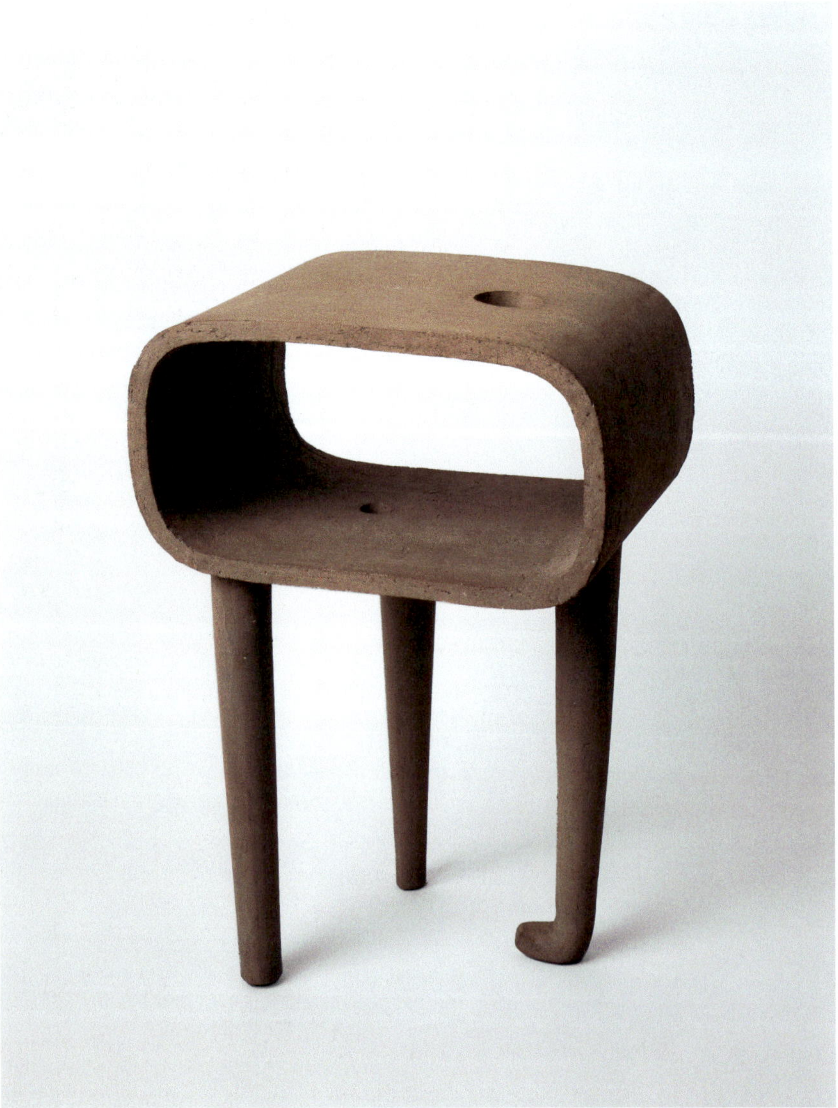

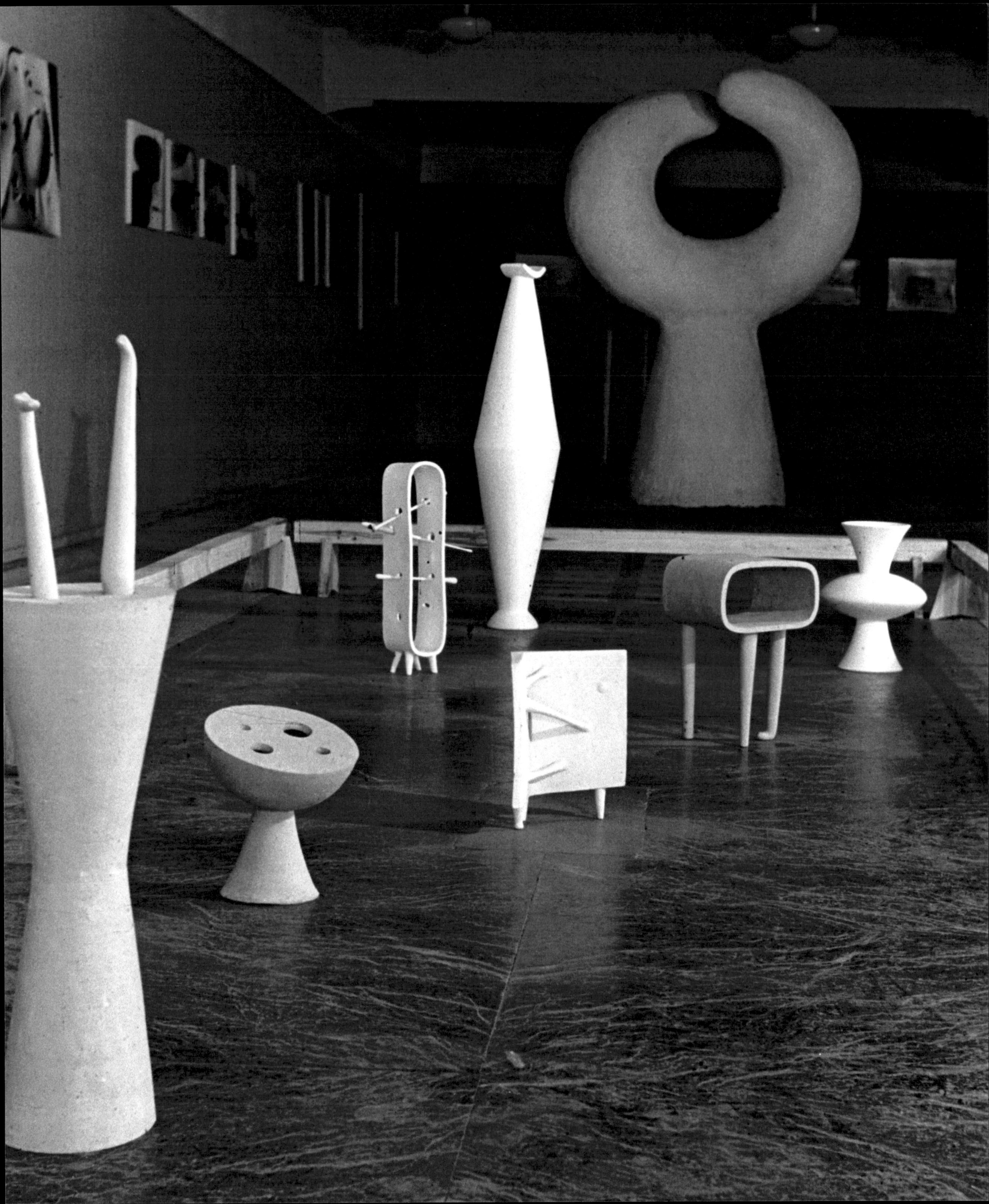

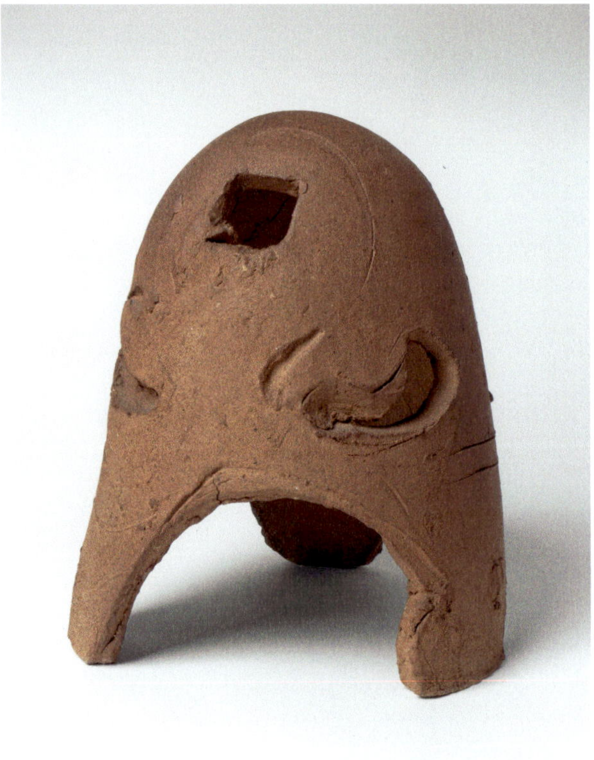

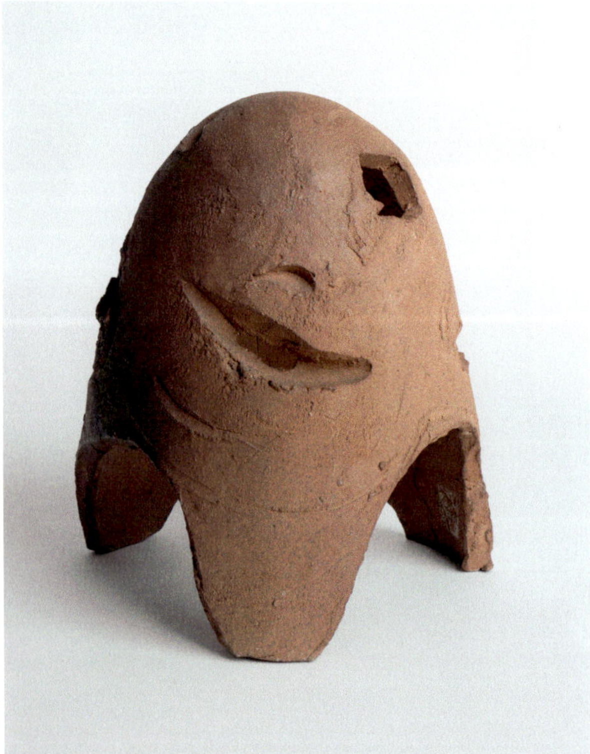

Daruma, 1952
Karatsu stoneware
26.4 × 22.9 × 21.3 cm

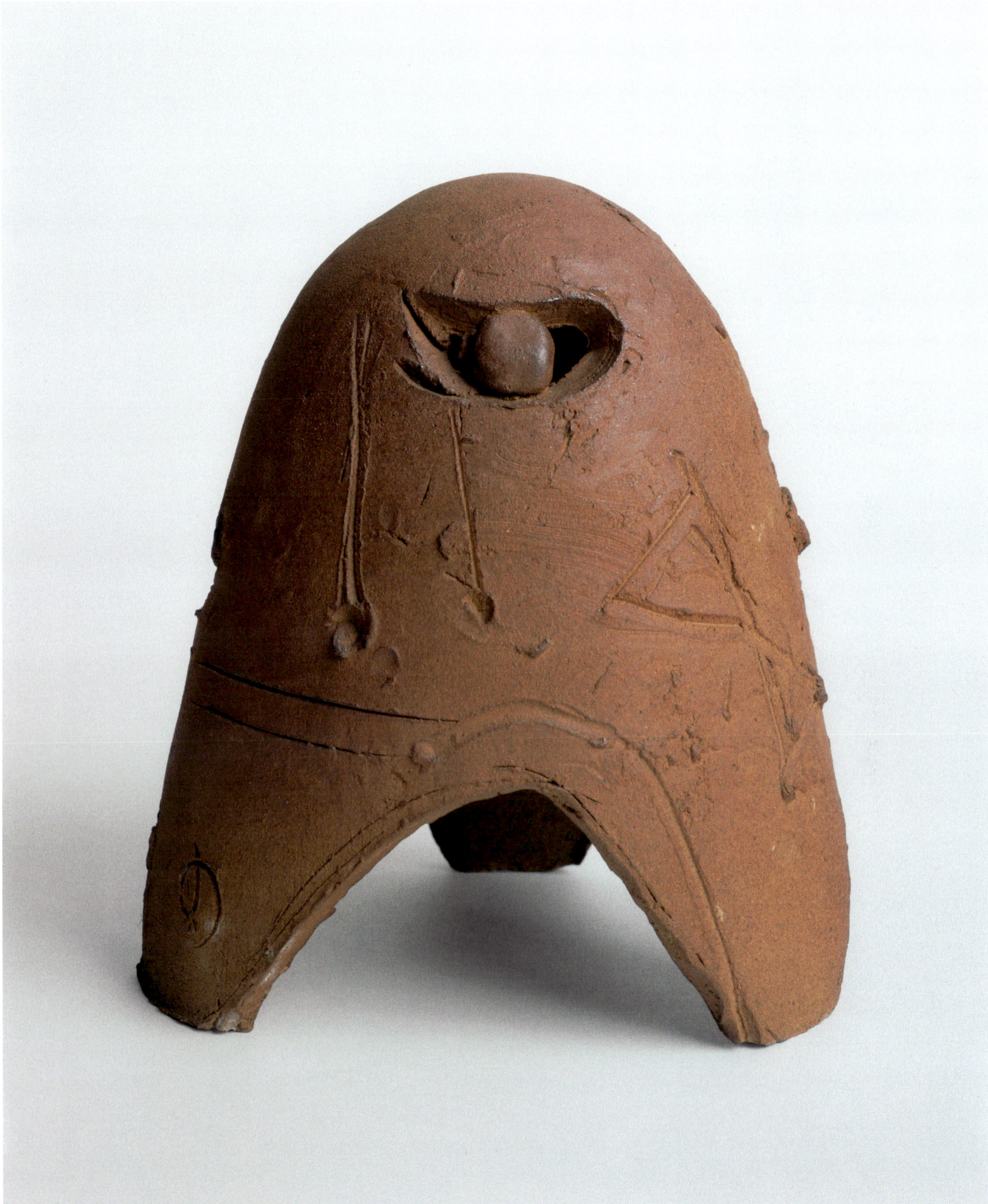

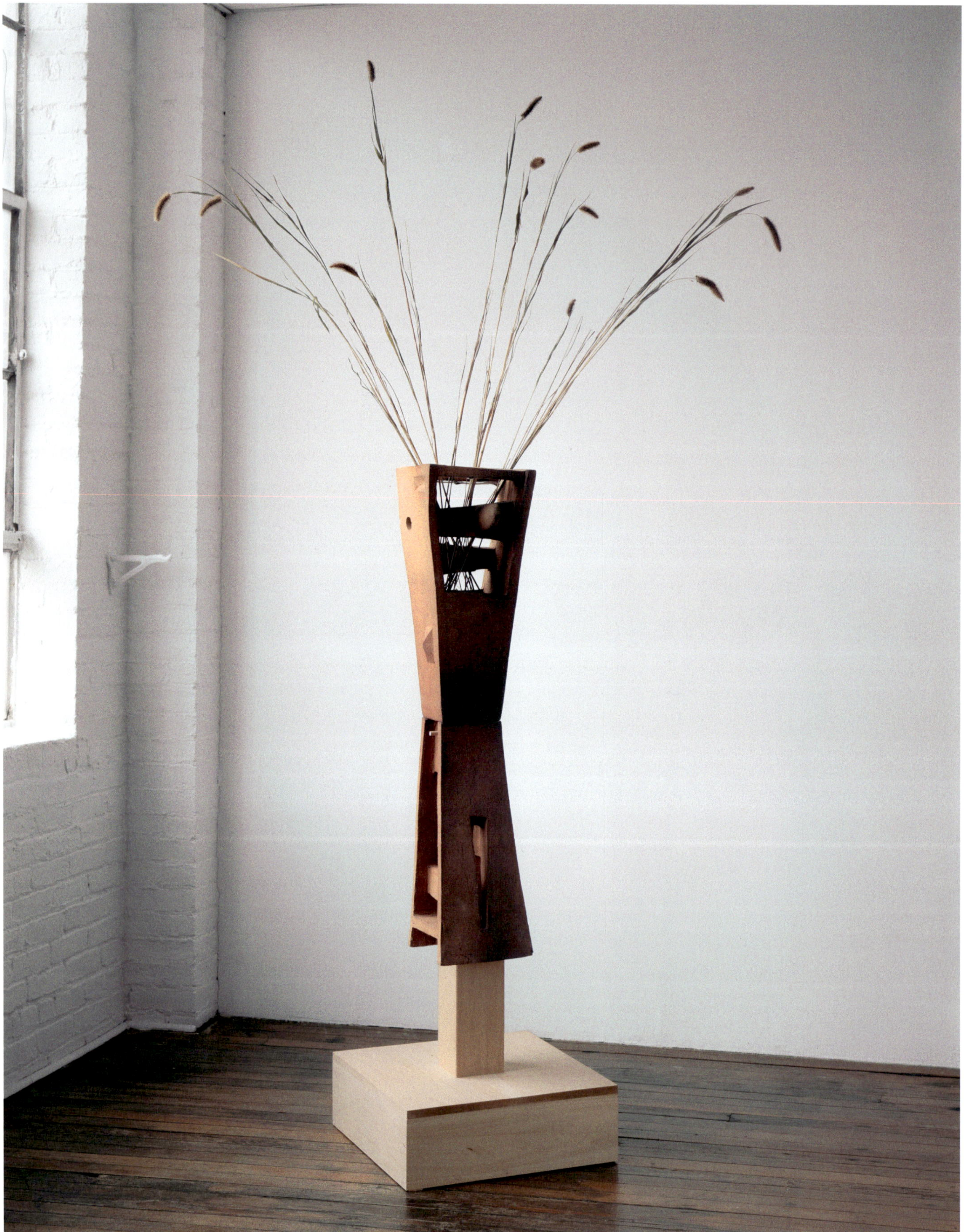

Large Square Vase
(Karatsu Kakutsubo), 1952
Karatsu stoneware
112.4 × 29.8 × 30.2 cm

The Lonely Tower
(Wabishii Toh), 1952
Shigaraki stoneware, ash glaze
63.5 × 15.6 × 17.8 cm

Cage Vase Kago (Basket), 1952
Shigaraki stoneware
47.6 × 28.6 × 28.3 cm

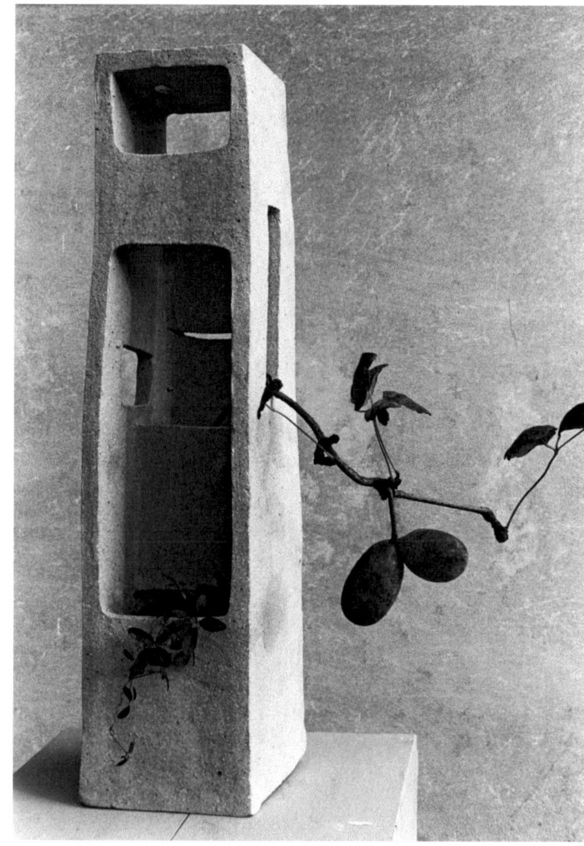

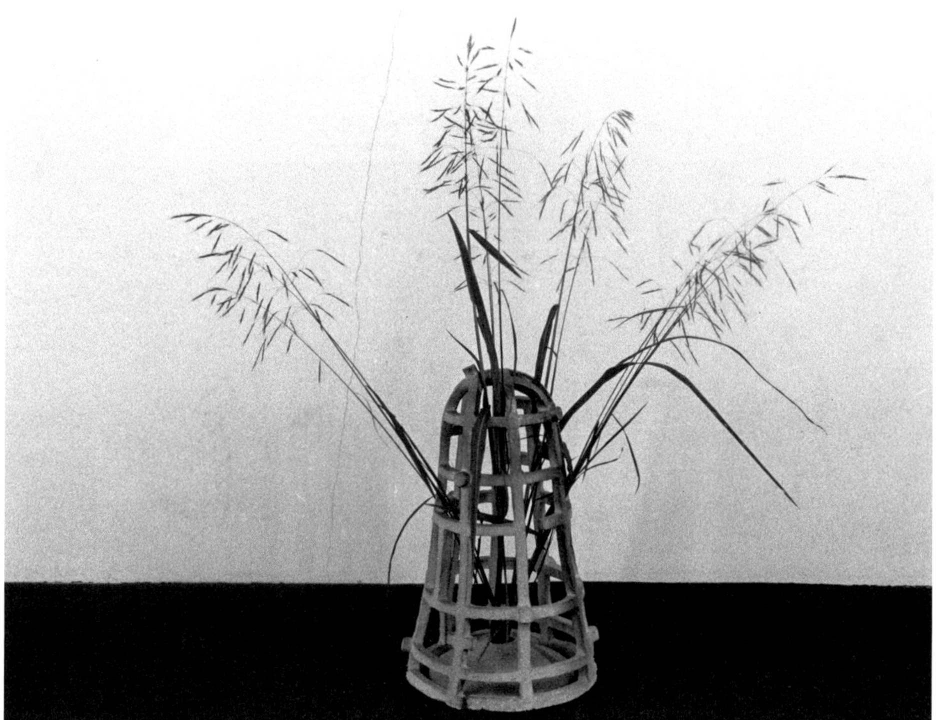

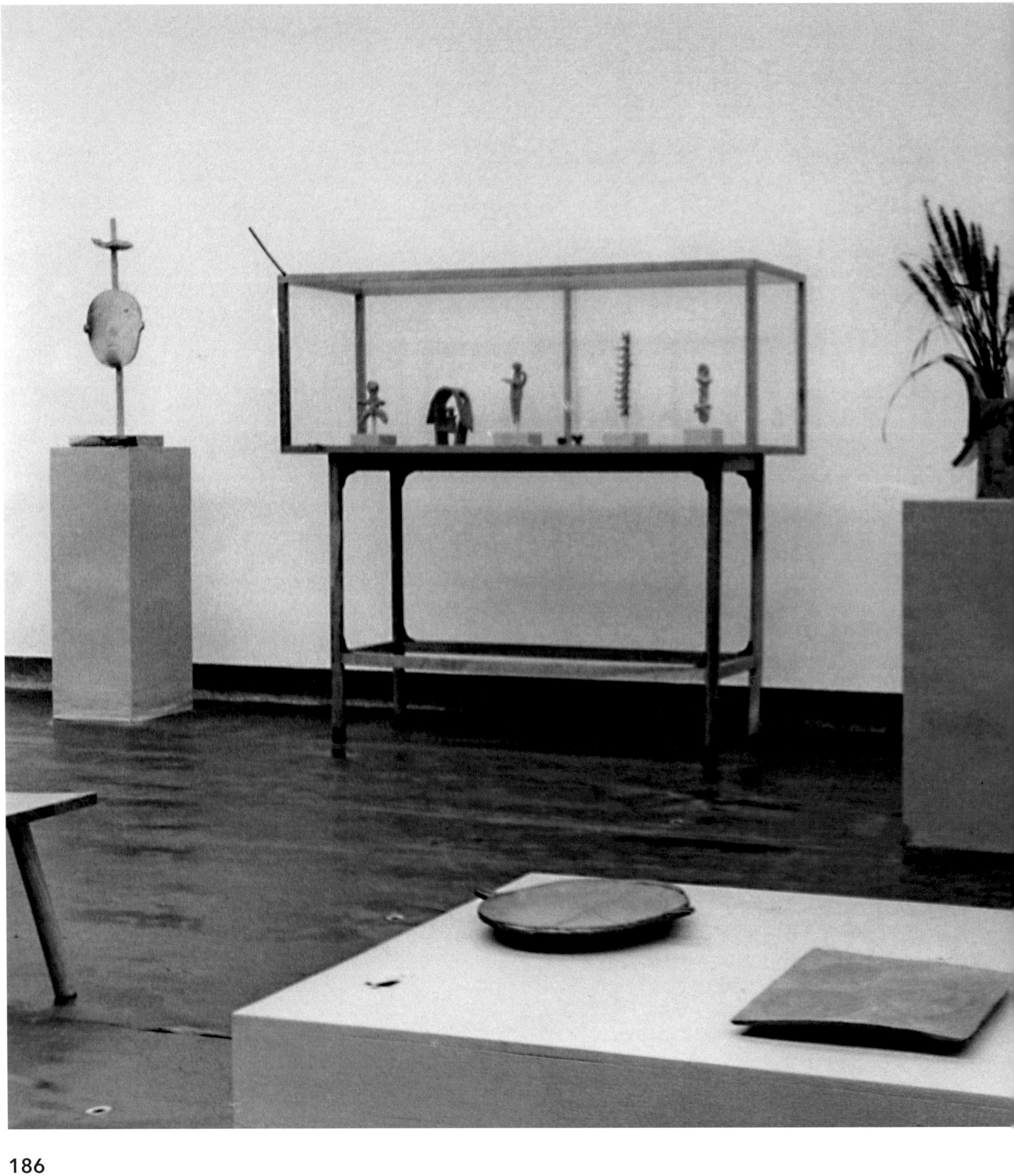

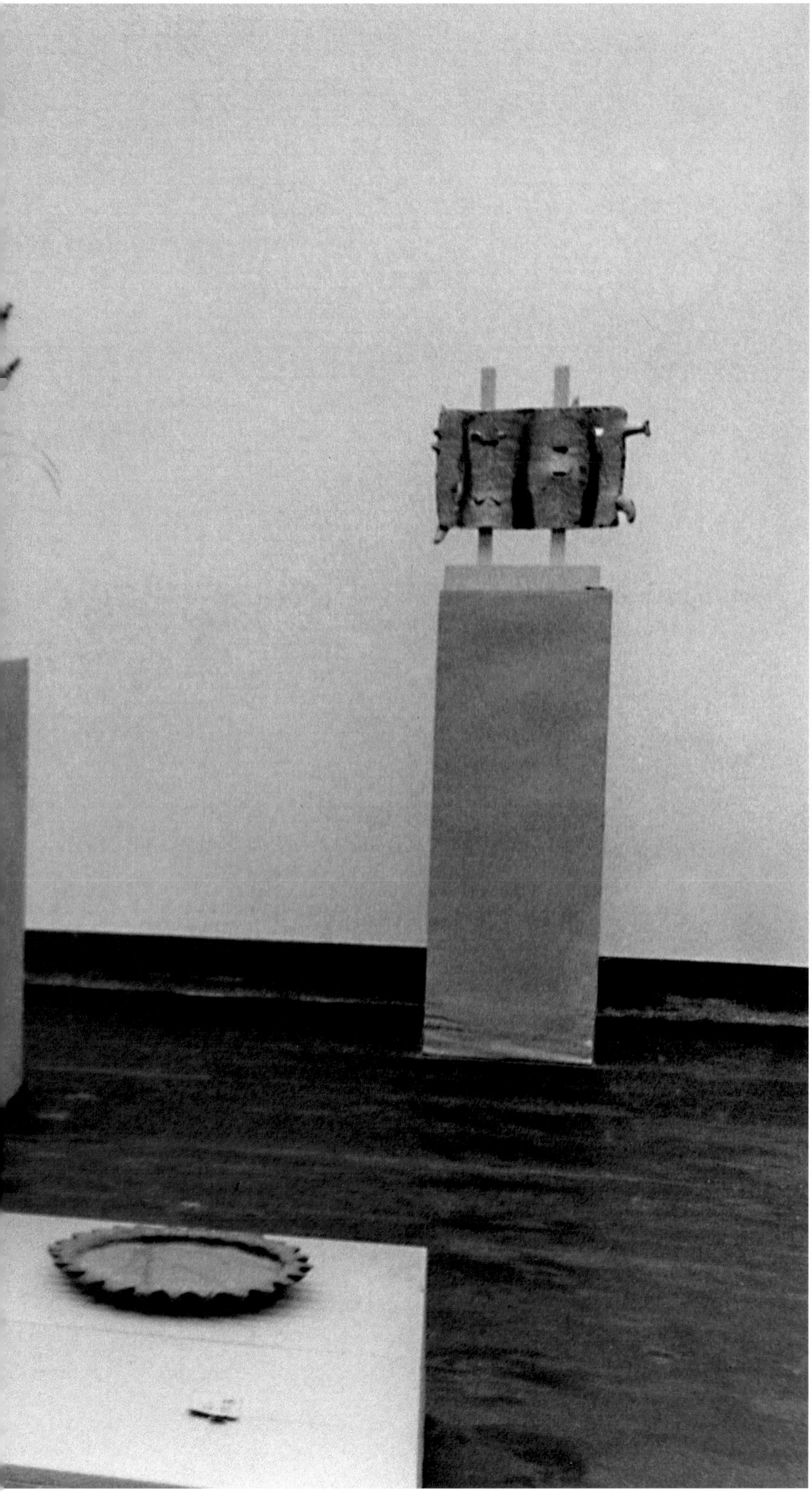

Exhibition view of *Isamu Noguchi Exhibition*, Museum of Modern Art, Kamakura, Japan, 23 September–19 October 1952

Mrs White (Shiro Fujin)
(Lady in White), 1952
Shigaraki stoneware
82.2 × 17.5 × 17.1 cm

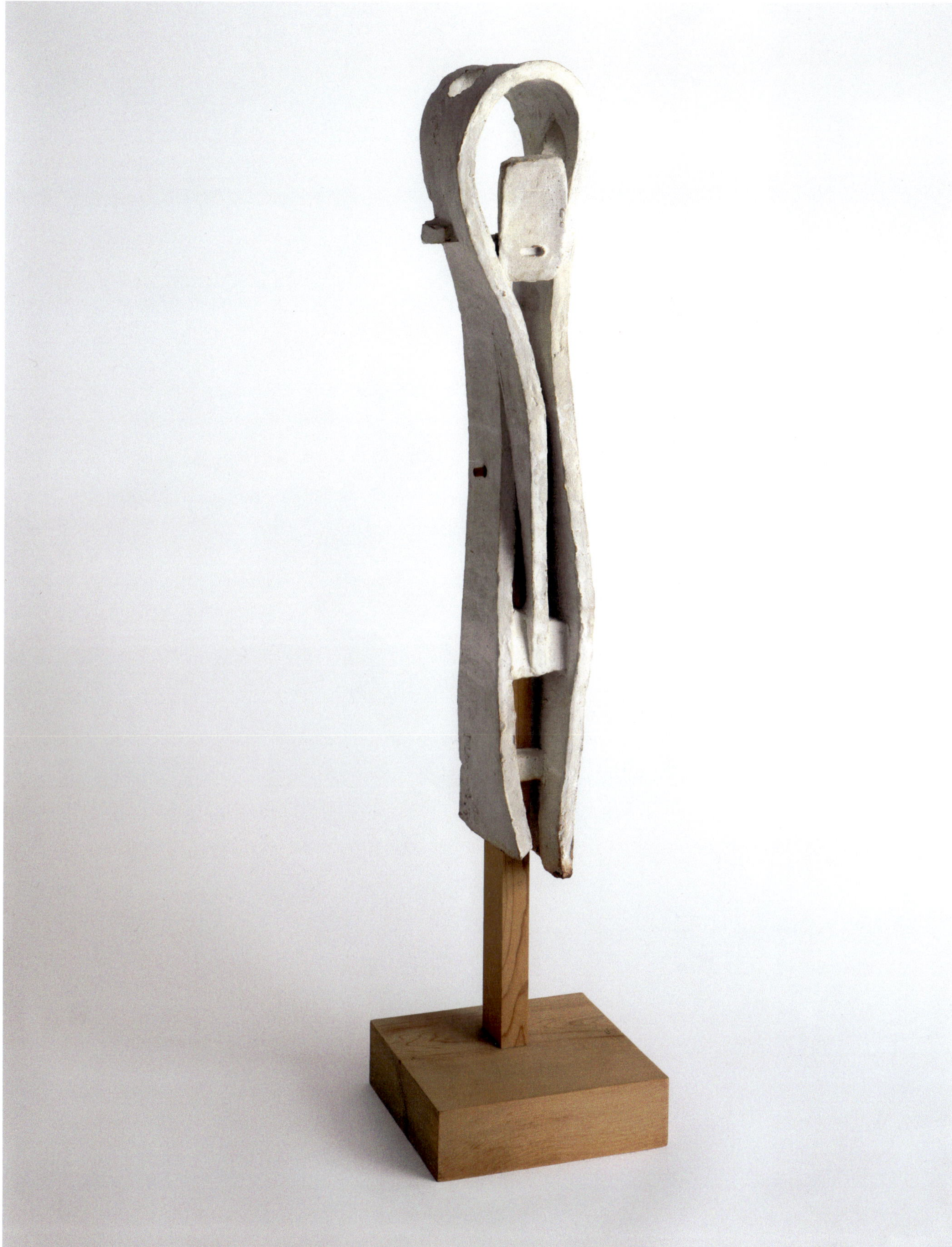

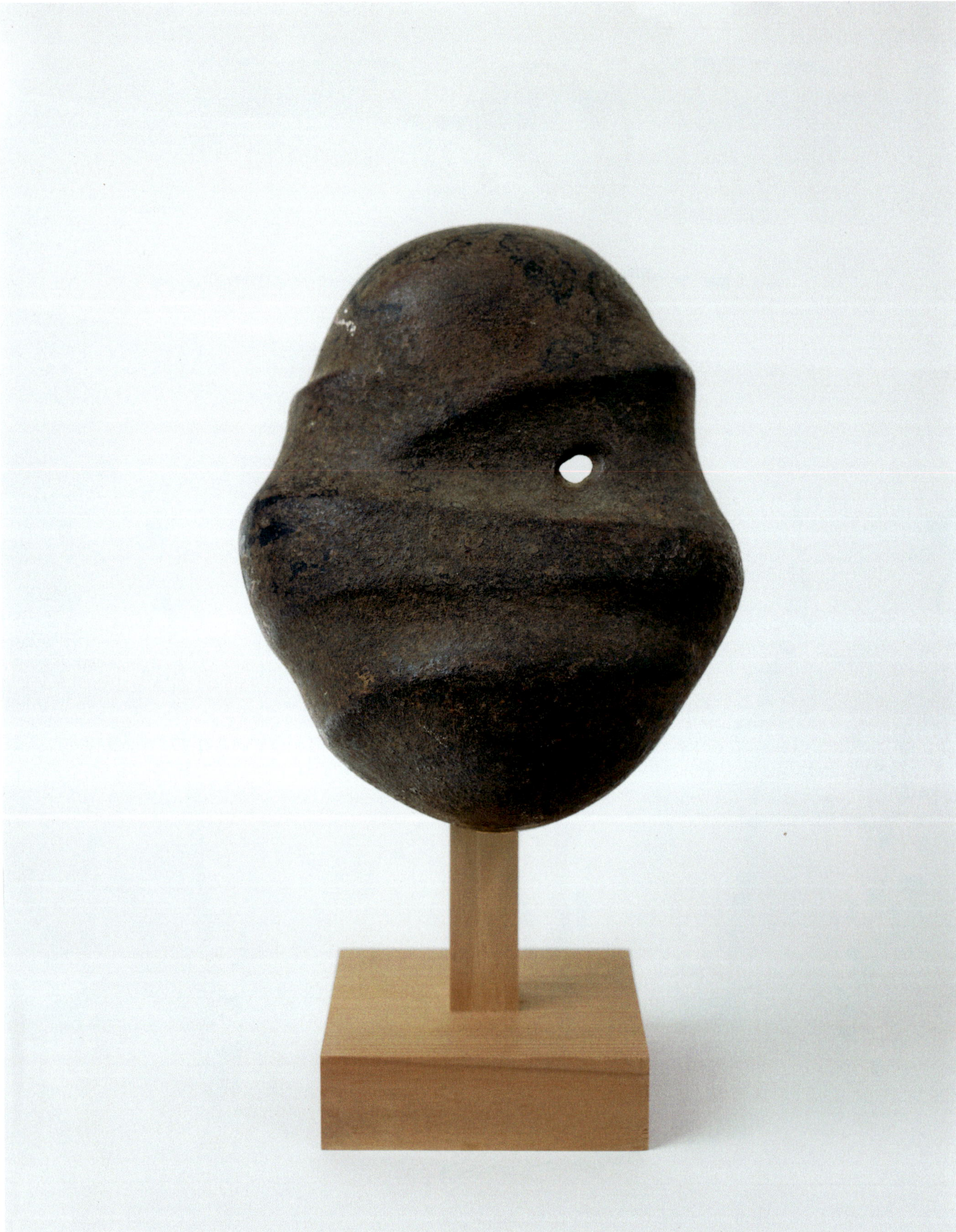

Okame (Atomic Head) (Hiroshima Mask), 1954
Iron
23.5 × 19.4 × 11.1 cm

Bell Tower for Hiroshima Replica, 1950
(partially reconstructed 1986)
Terracotta and wood
128.6 × 78.7 × 78.7 cm

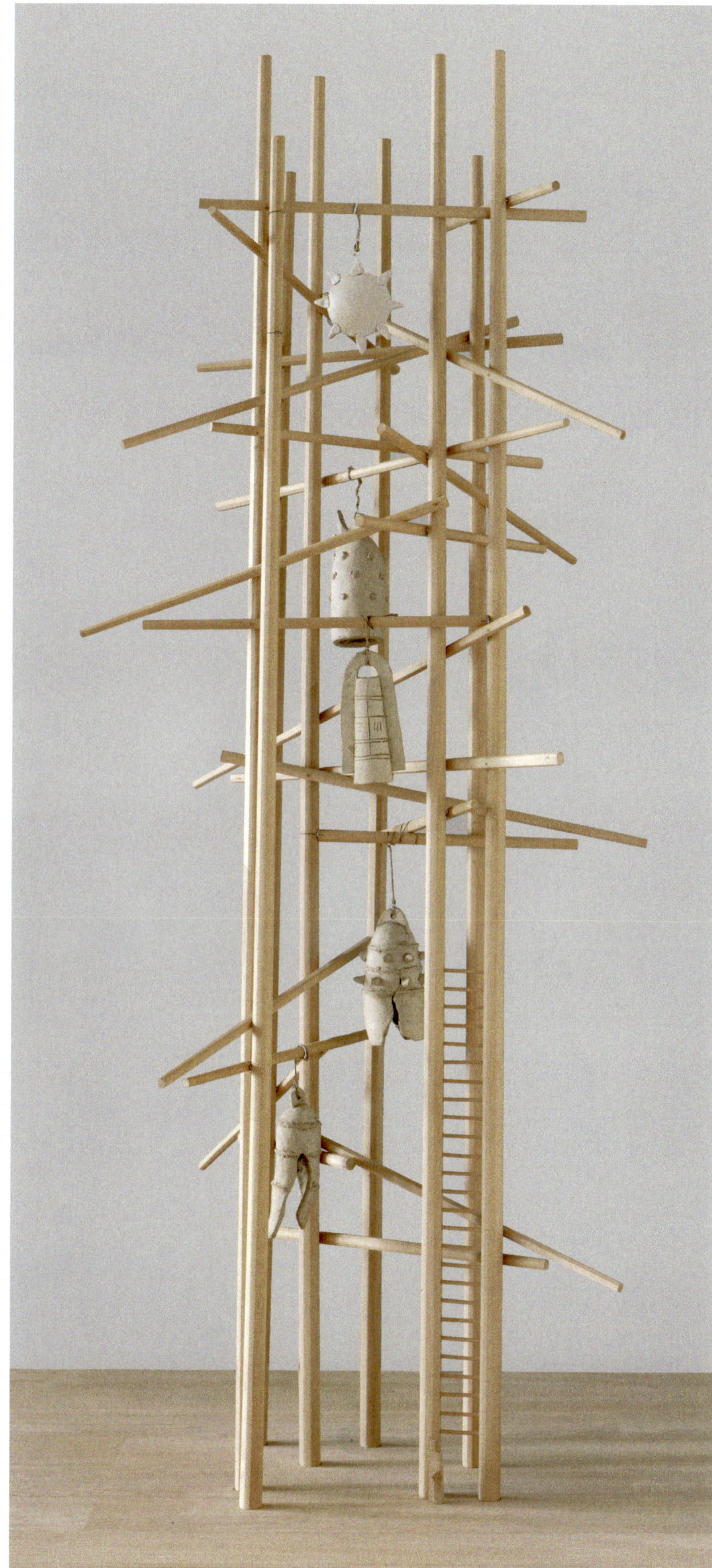

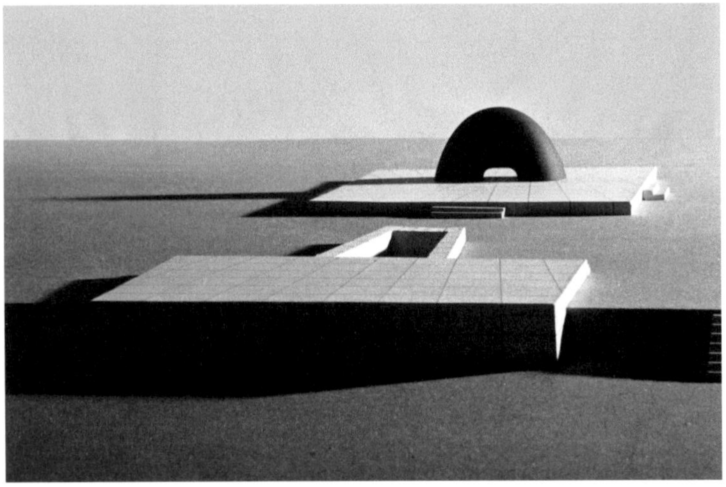

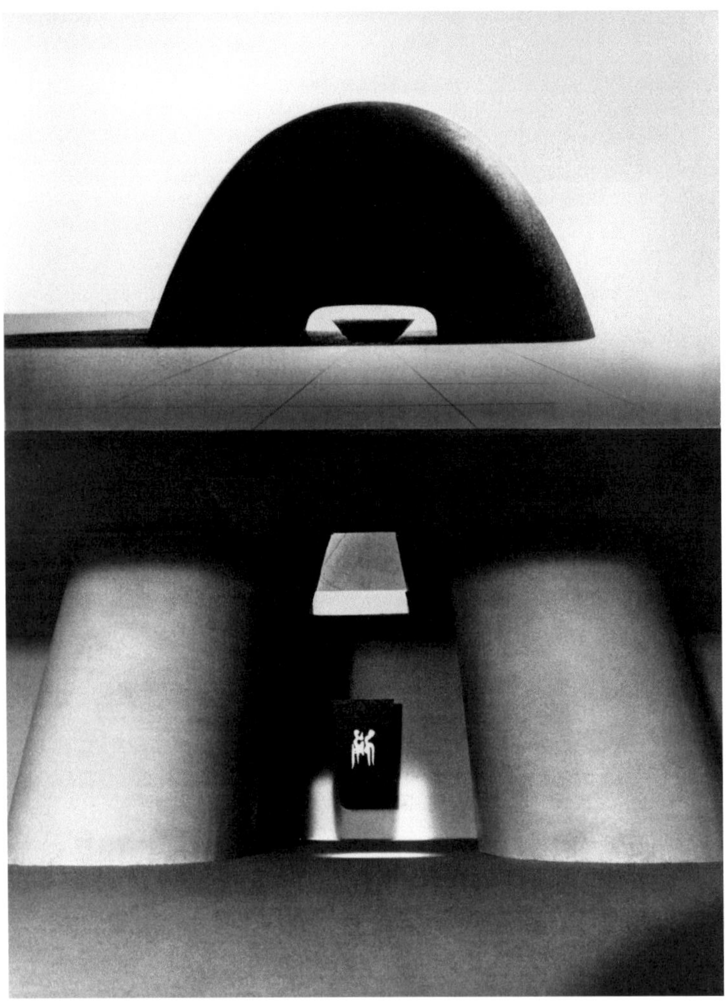

Model for *Memorial to the Dead, Hiroshima*, 1952
(unrealised)
Plaster
Dimensions unknown

Model for *Memorial to the Dead, Hiroshima*, c. 1982
(unrealised)
Brazilian granite, stainless steel and wood
81.3 × 151.4 × 51.8 cm

My symbolism derived from the prehistoric roofs of 'Haniwa' [Japanese funerary objects] like the protective abode of infancy, or even equating this with birth and death, the arch of peace with the dome of destruction.

It was to be a mass of black granite, glowing at the base from a light beyond and below. The feet of this ominous weight descended underground in concrete through the box which formed its anchorage. To be seen between heavy pillars was a granite box cantilevered out from the wall, in which were to be placed the names of the world's first atomic dead.

1967

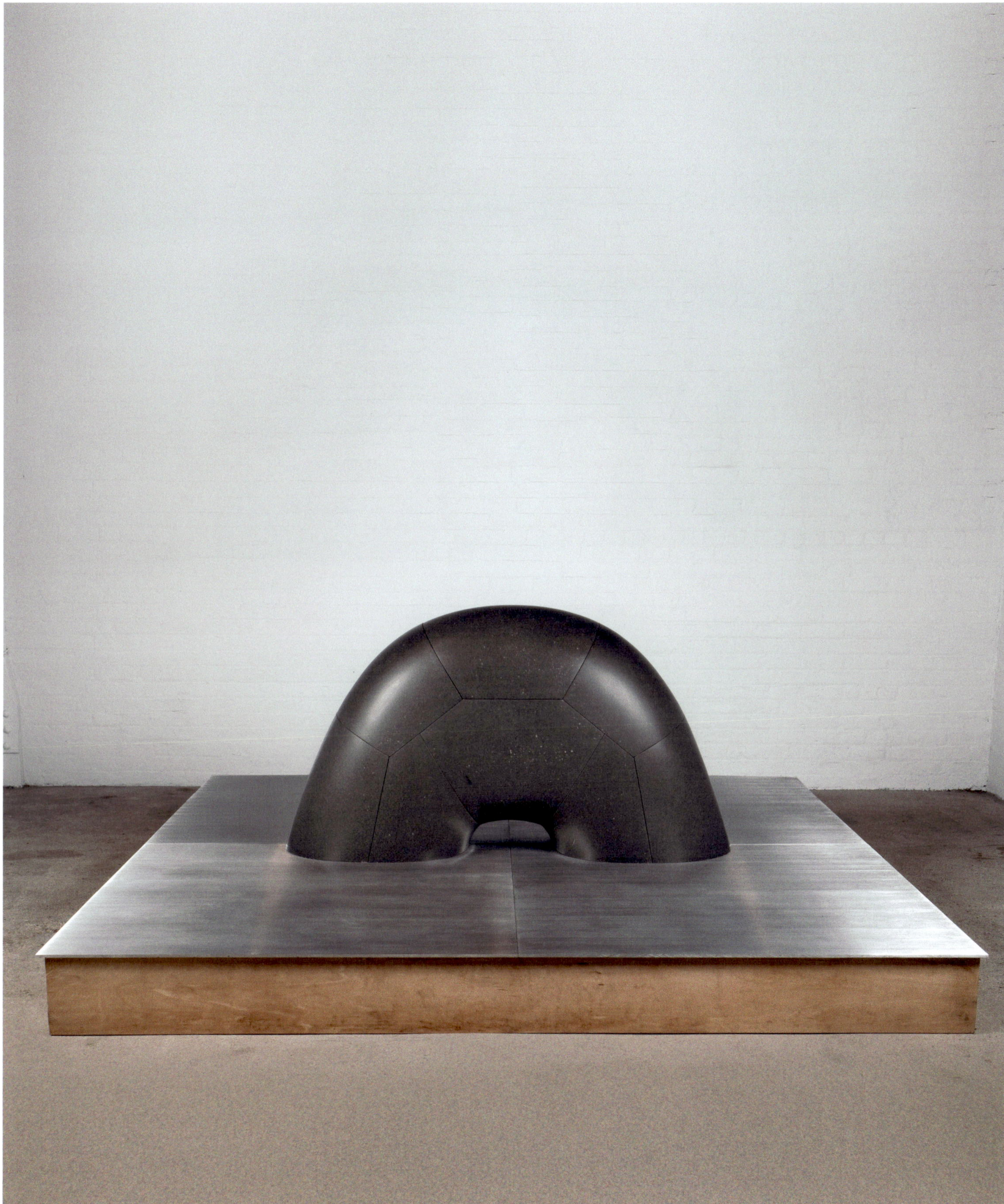

Calligraphics, 1957
Iron, wood, rope and metal
178.8 × 43.5 × 40.6 cm

Endless Coupling, 1957
Iron
148.6 × 34.6 × 34.6 cm

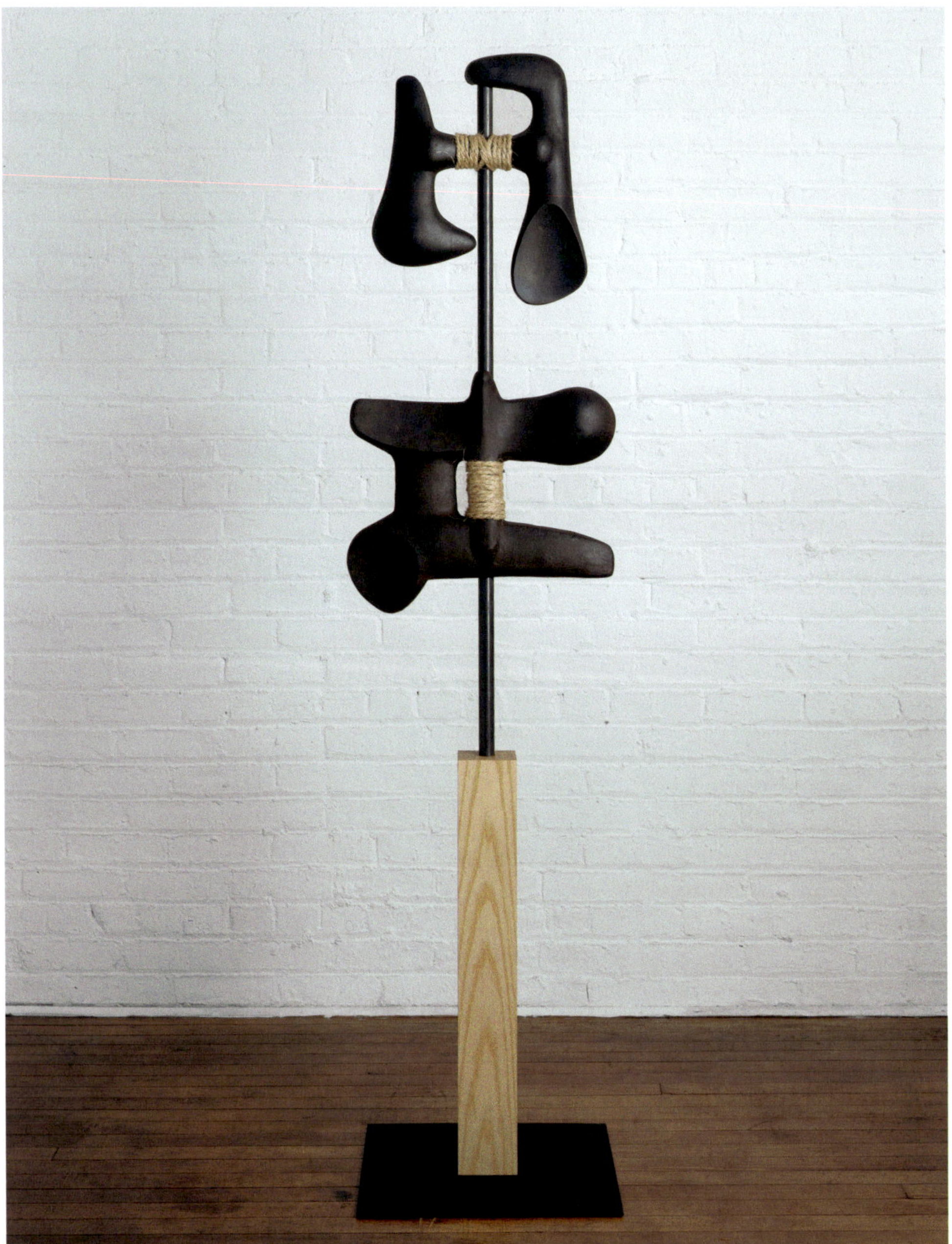

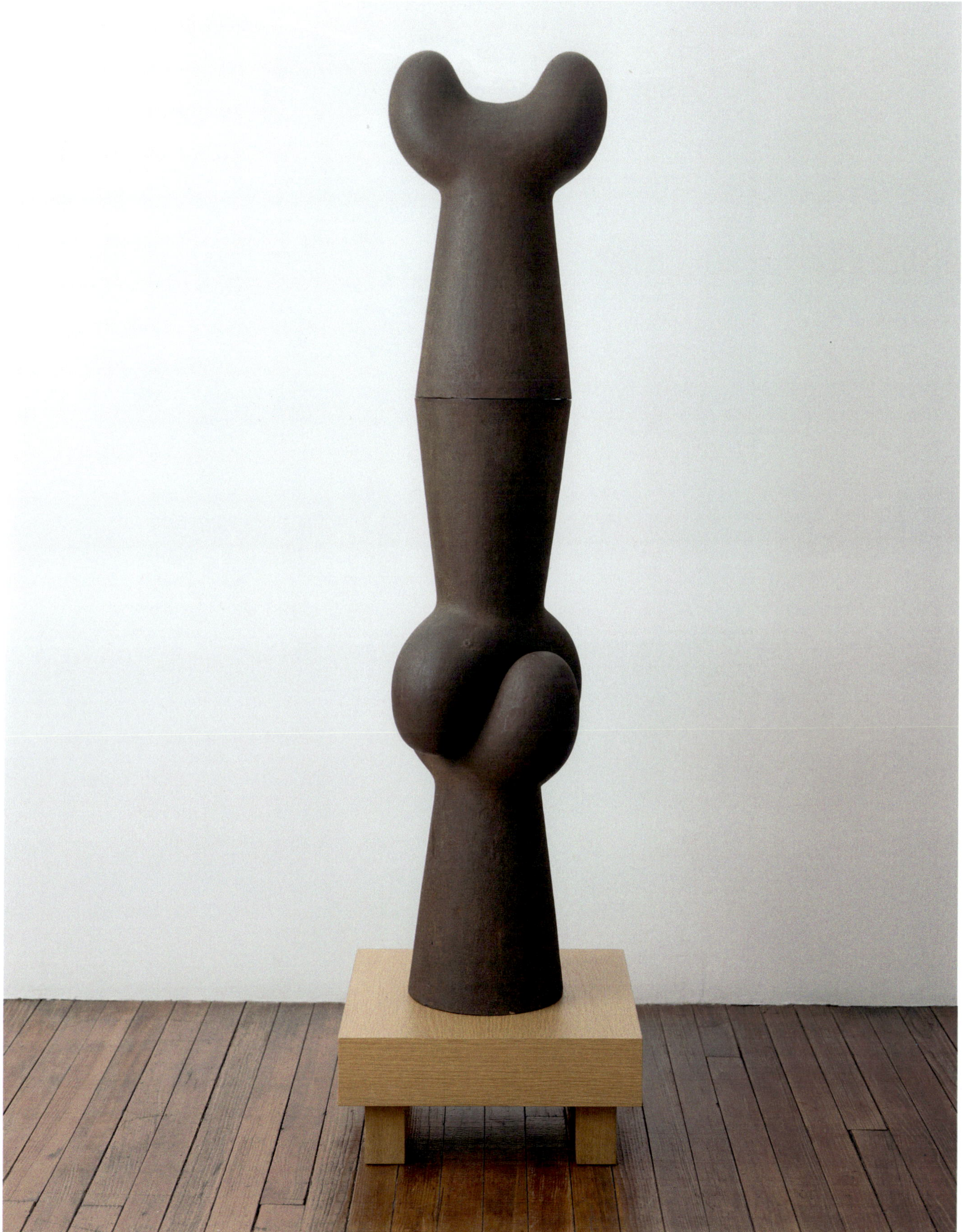

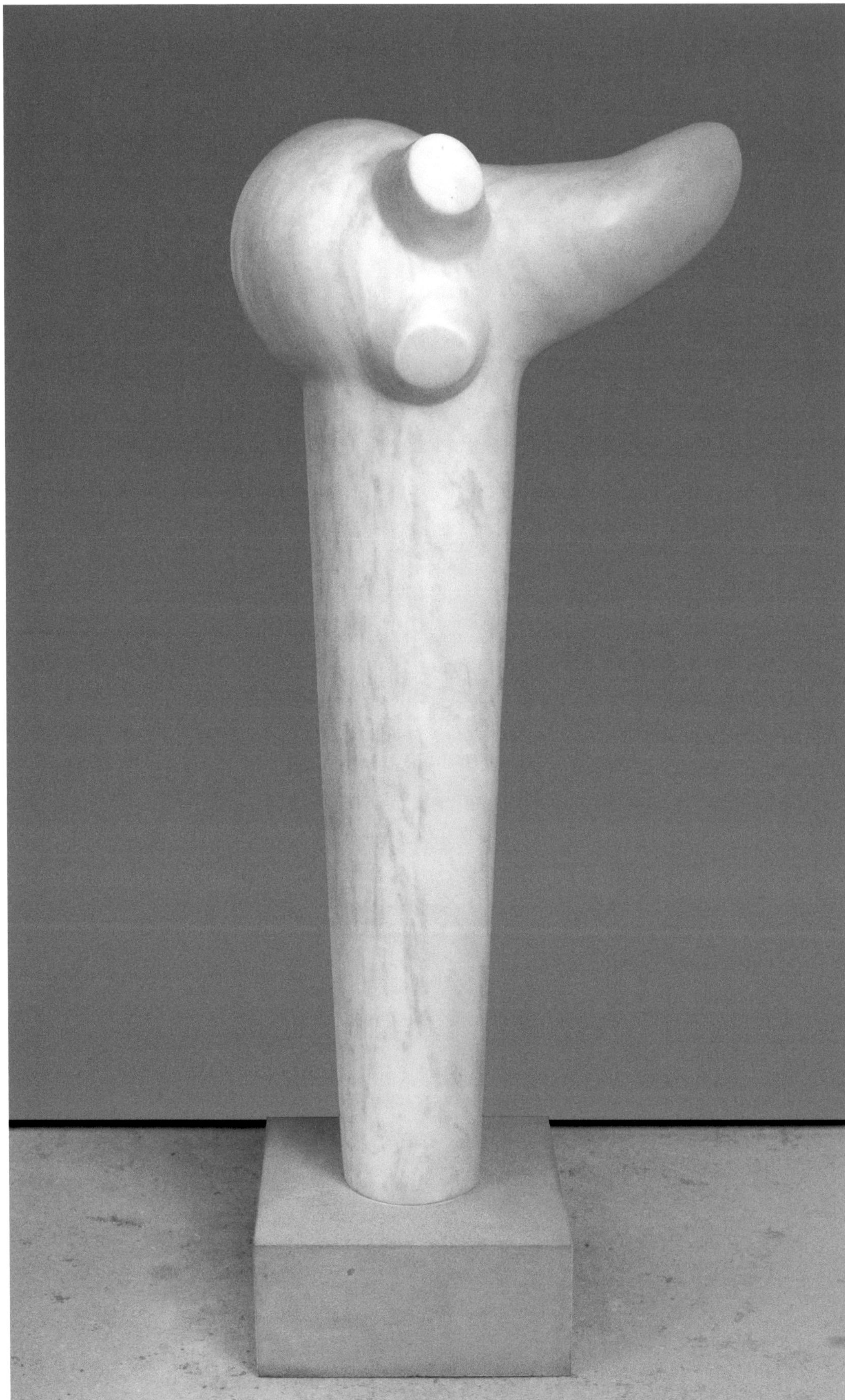

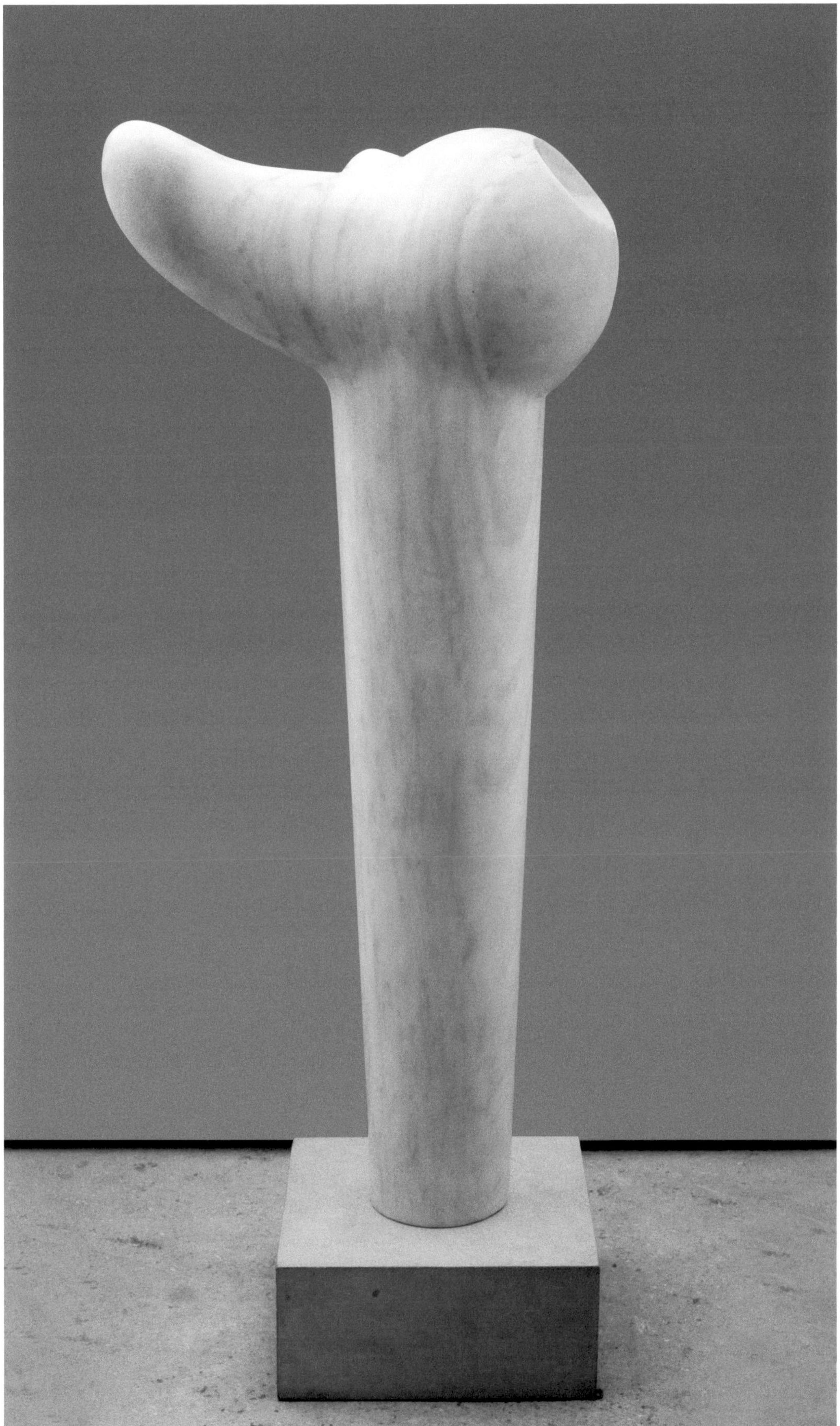

Bird B, 1958
Greek marble
130.8 × 57.8 × 33.7 cm

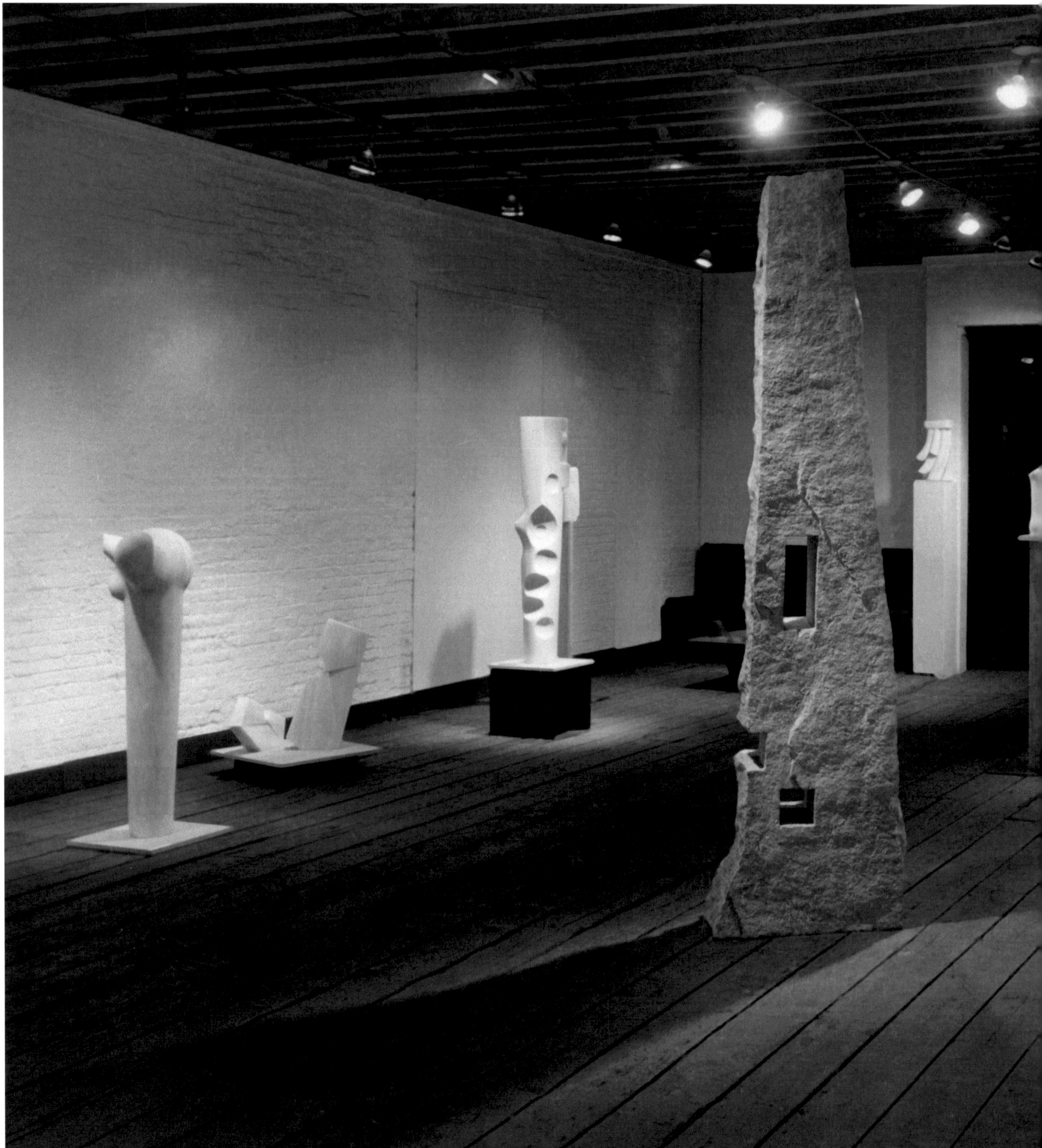

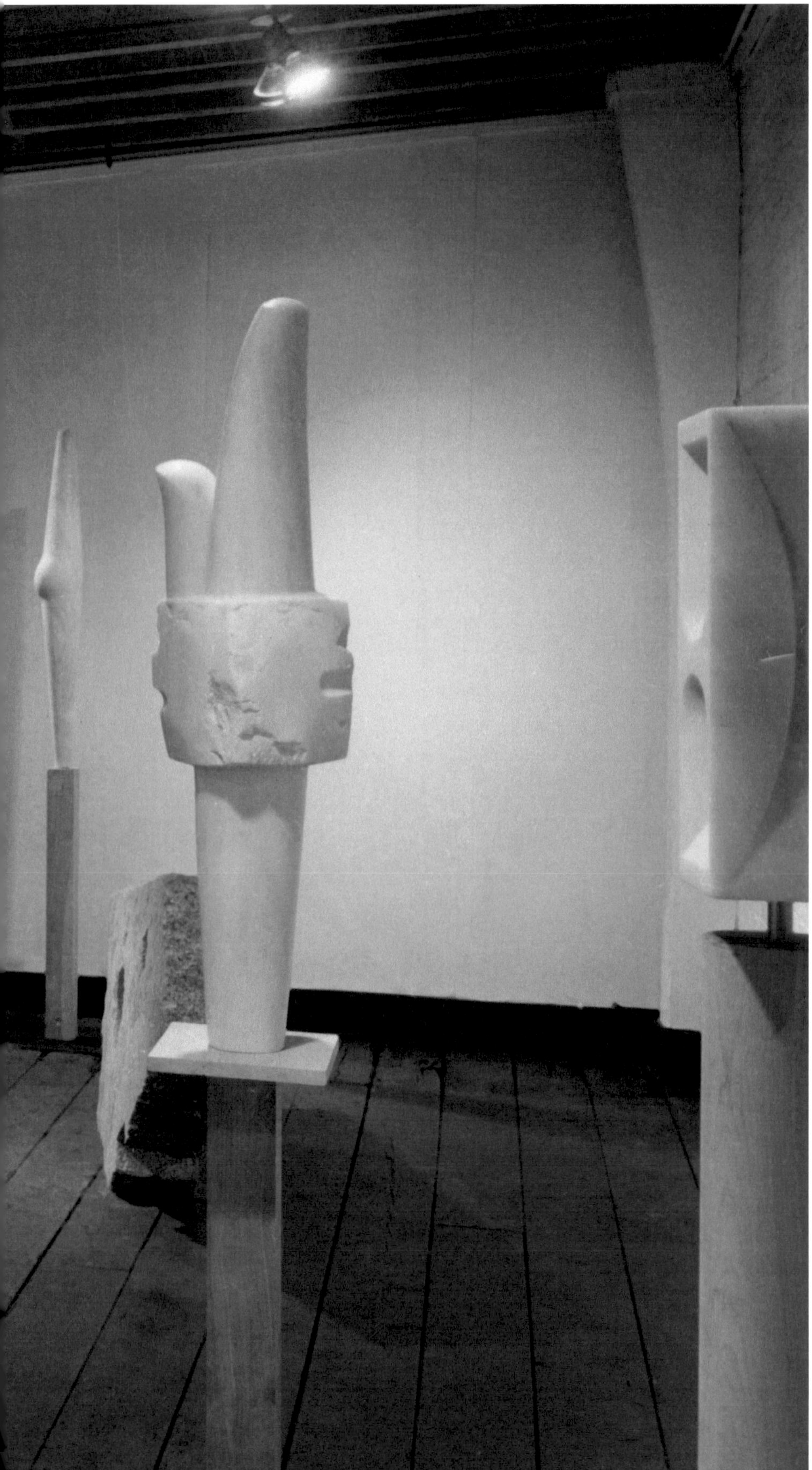

Exhibition view of *Isamu Noguchi*, Stable Gallery, New York, 29 April–30 May 1959

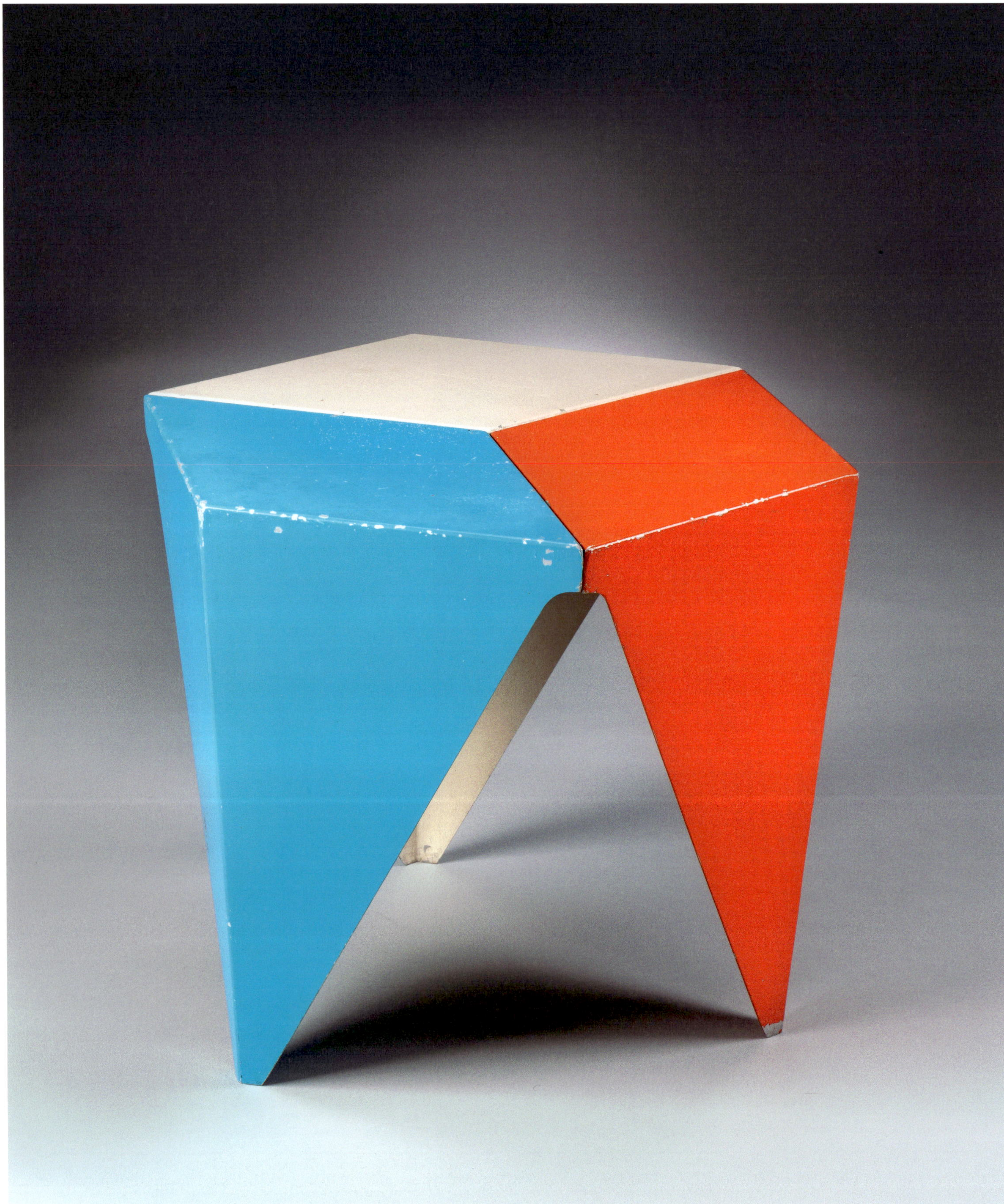

Prismatic Table, 1957
Designed for the Alcoa Forecast Program
Painted aluminium
37.5 × 47 × 40.6 cm

***Prismatic Table* graphics**, c. 1957

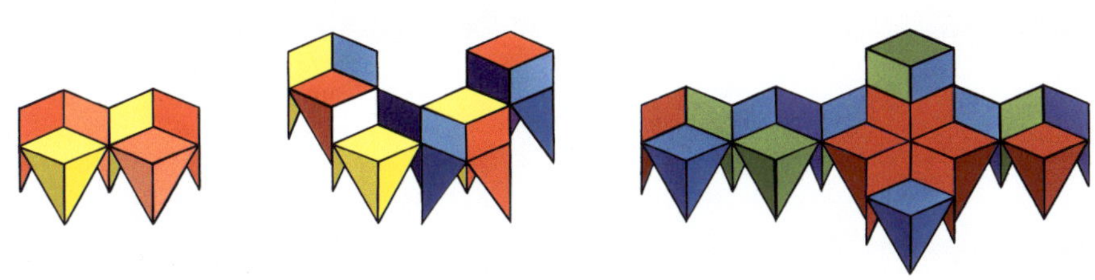

Orpheus, 1958
Aluminium
210.8 × 112.4 × 16.8 cm

It seemed absurd to me to be working with rocks and stones in New York, where walls of glass and steel are our horizon, and our landscape is that of boxes piled high in the air … In this perplexed frame of mind I visited Edison Price, my friend who manufactures lighting equipment, and looking at his machine tools for the handling of light metals, considered the use of such means for sculpture. This would bring me in contact with that industrial apparatus which is the real America … What I wanted was a timely and weightless way of expression. With Edison's help we devised a way to bend the thin metal so that the corners came out sharp to give an appearance of solidity.

1967

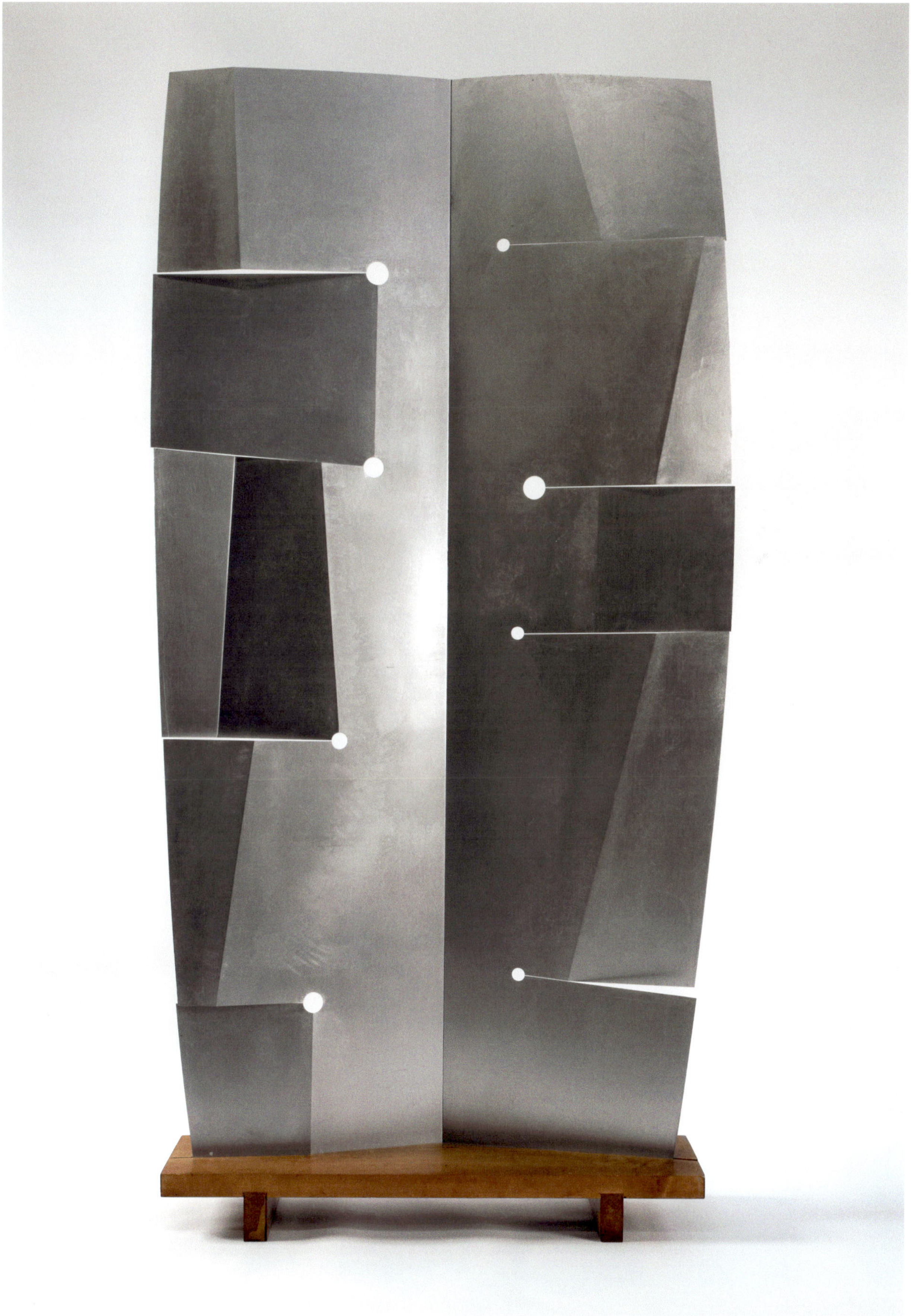

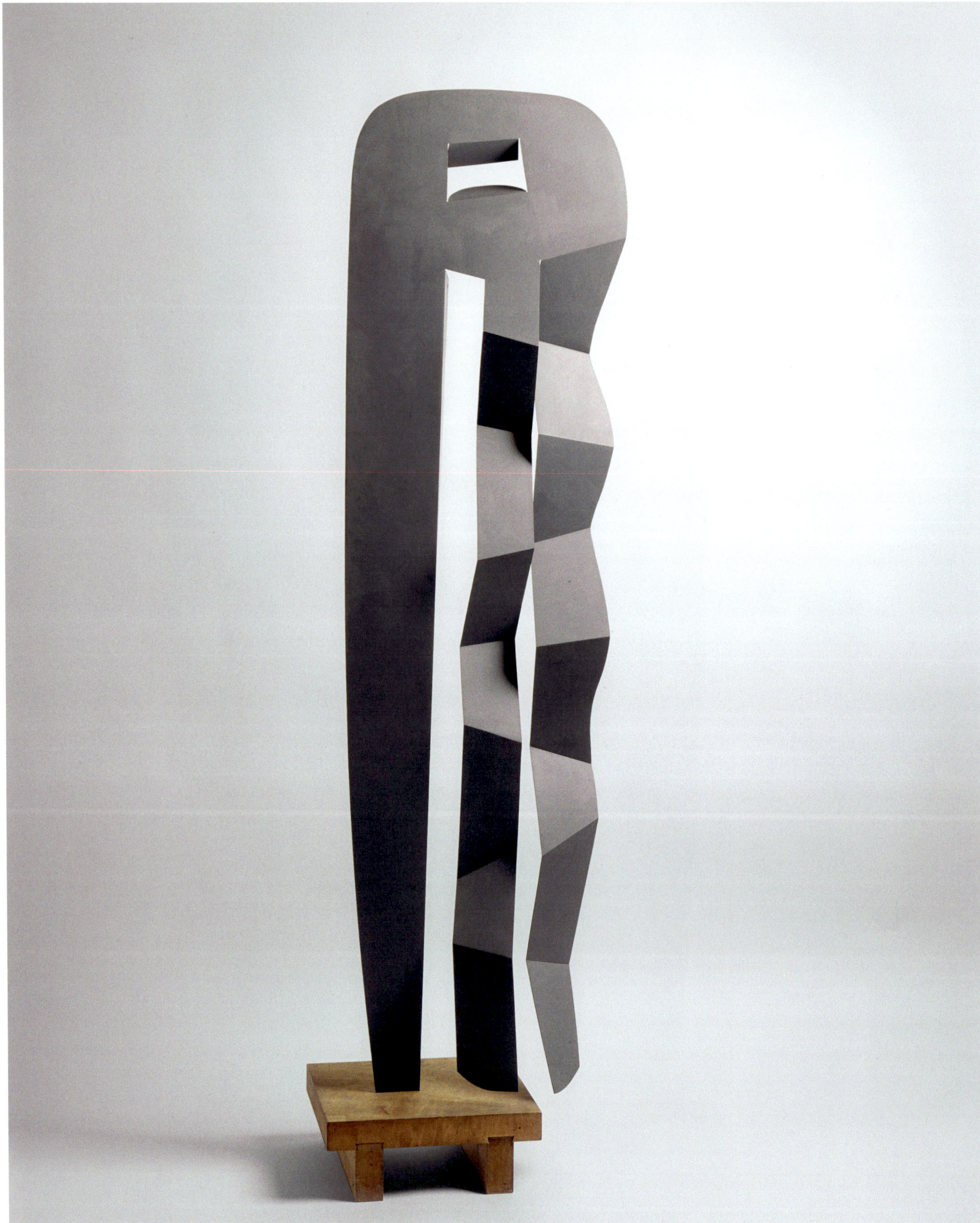

The Kite, 1959
Anodised aluminium
158.1 × 44.8 × 14 cm

Left to right:
The Kite, 1959
Anodised aluminium
158.1 × 44.8 × 14 cm

Man Walking, 1959
Anodised aluminium
220.7 × 95.9 × 87 cm

The Mirror, 1958
Anodised aluminium
161.1 × 72.2 × 9.5 cm

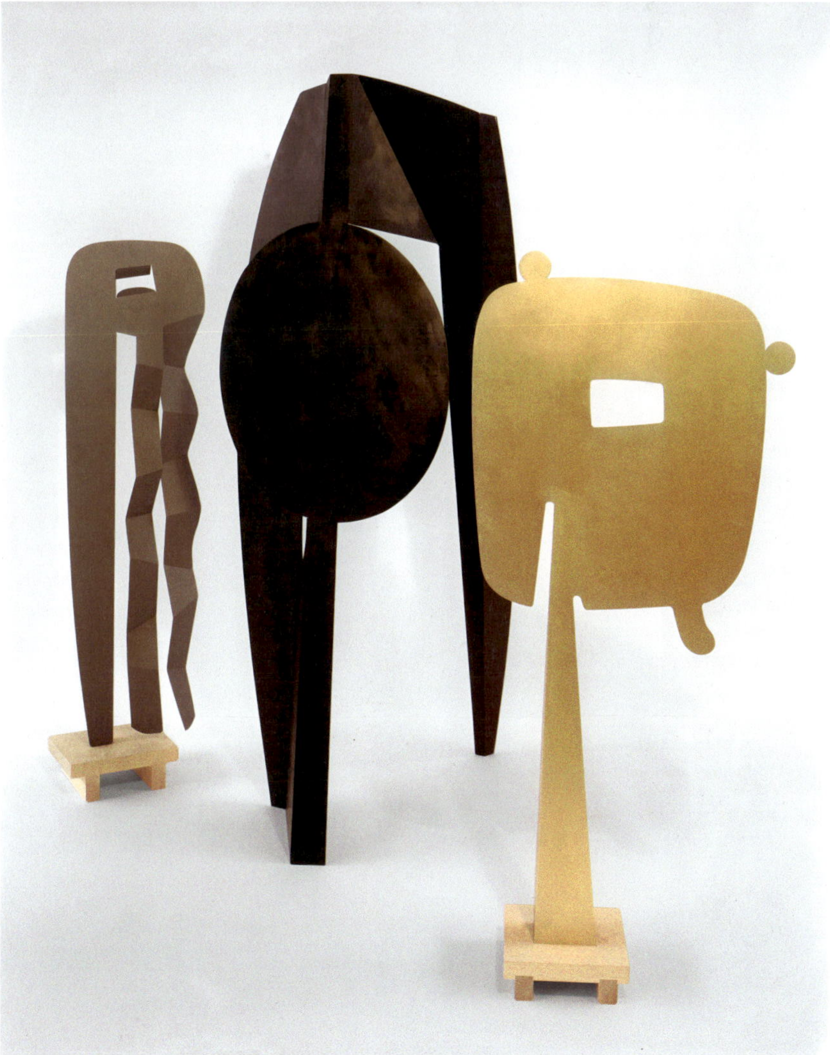

Mortality, 1959
Balsa wood
195.6 × 41 × 36.2 cm

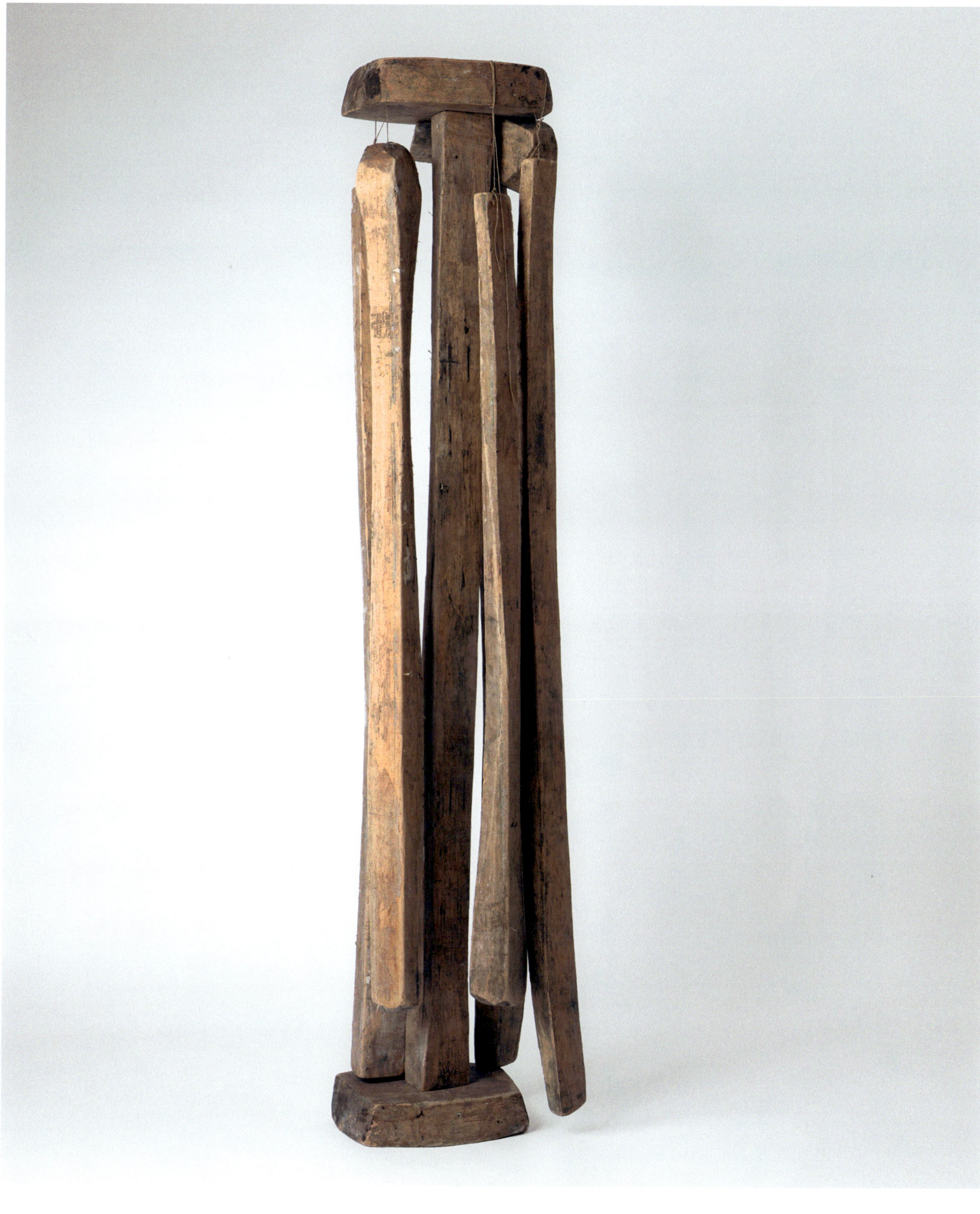

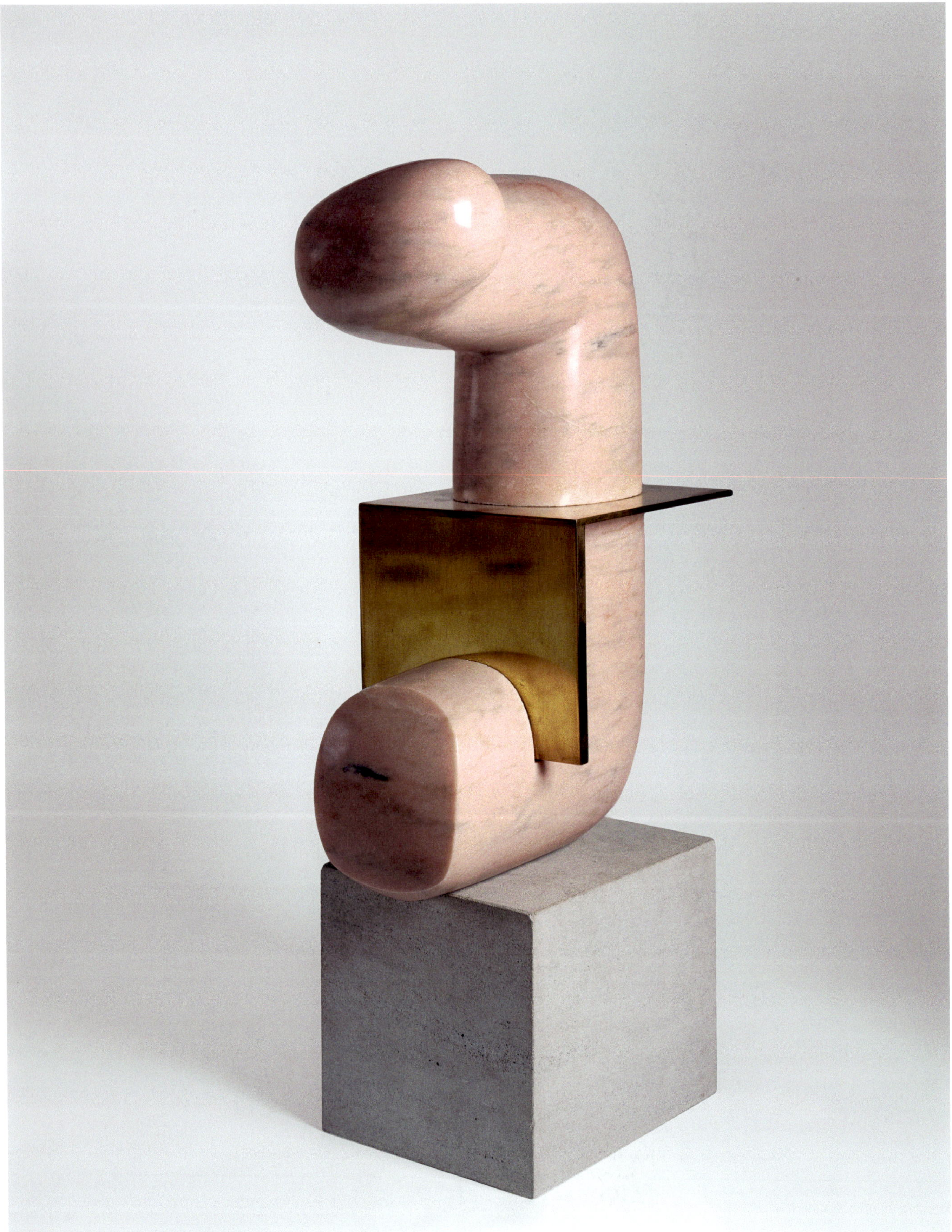

Pink Jizō, 1960
Portuguese marble,
brass and limestone
59.7 × 25.1 × 45.1 cm

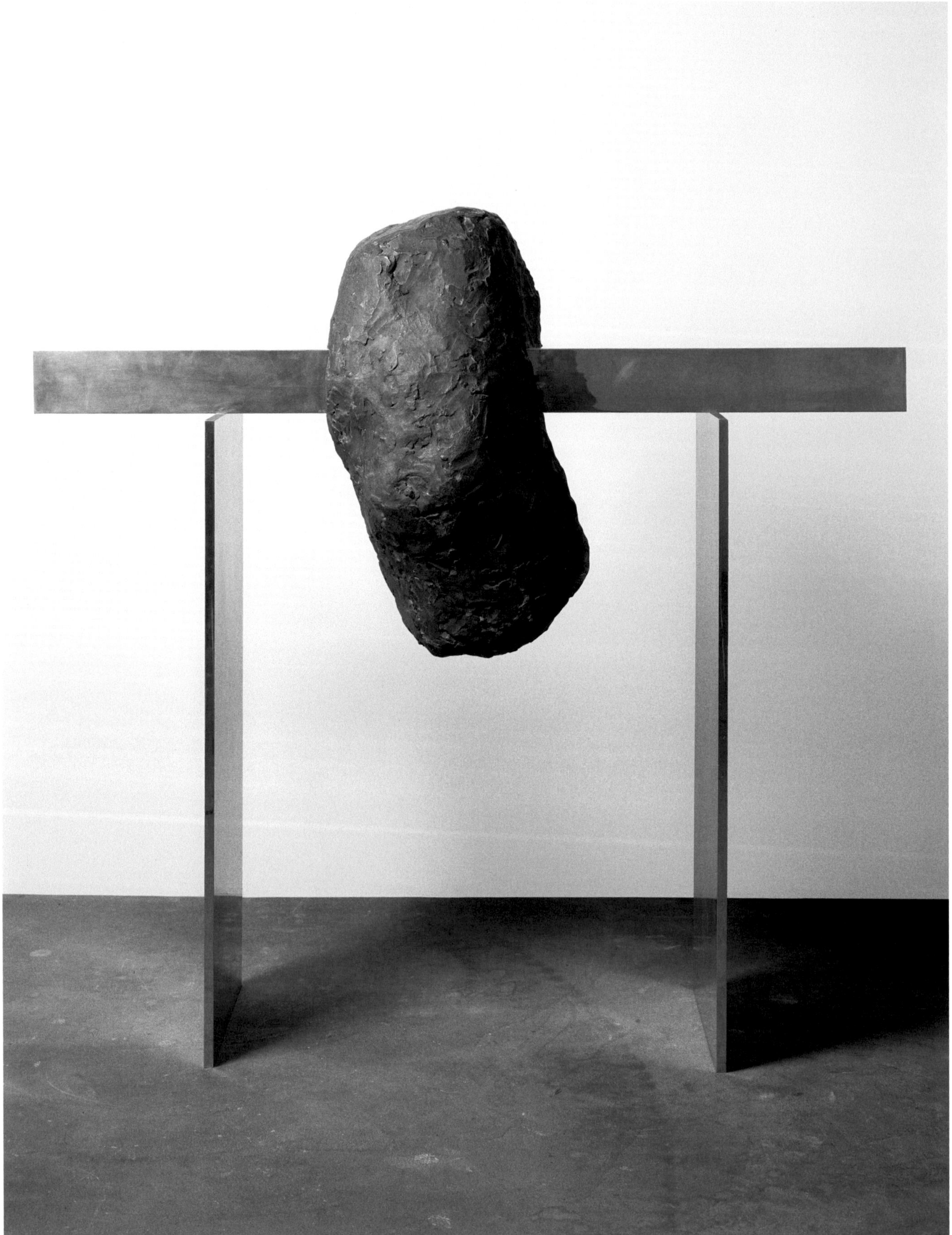

Stone of Spiritual Understanding,
1962 (cast 1963)
Bronze and aluminium
131.4 × 137.2 × 39.4 cm

This Earth, This Passage, 1962
(cast 1963)
Bronze
11.7 × 112.4 × 104.1 cm

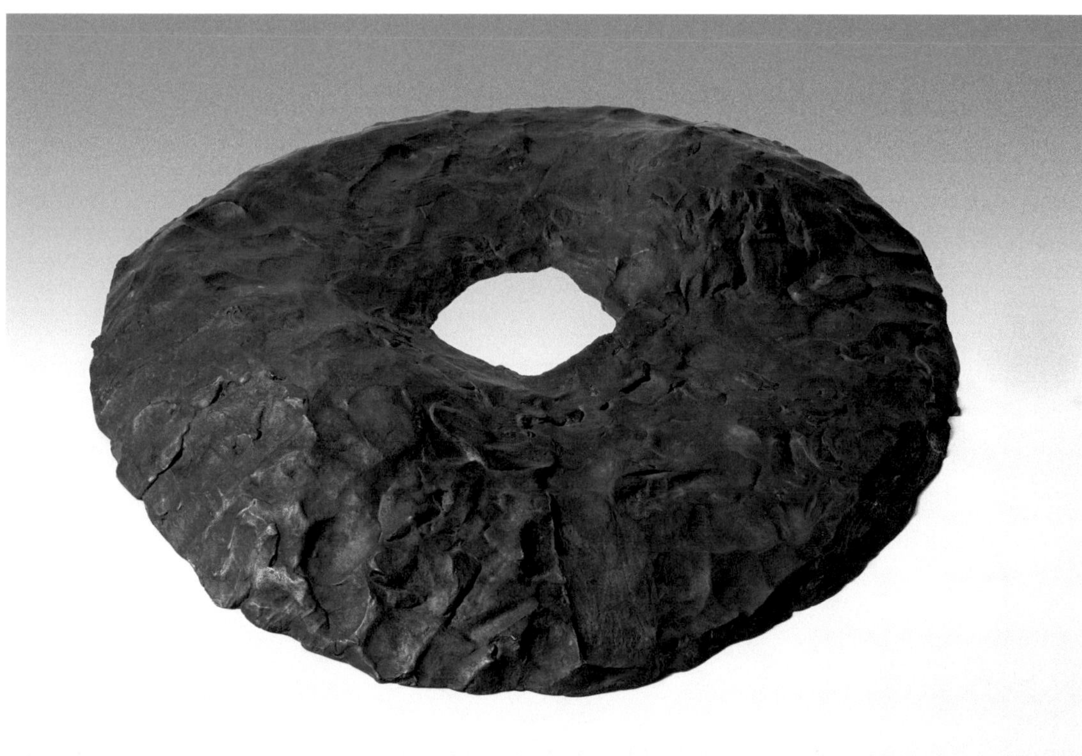

Floor Frame, 1962
(cast 1987)
Bronze with gold patina
36.8 × 103.8 × 61.9 cm;
17.1 × 34.3 × 17.1 cm

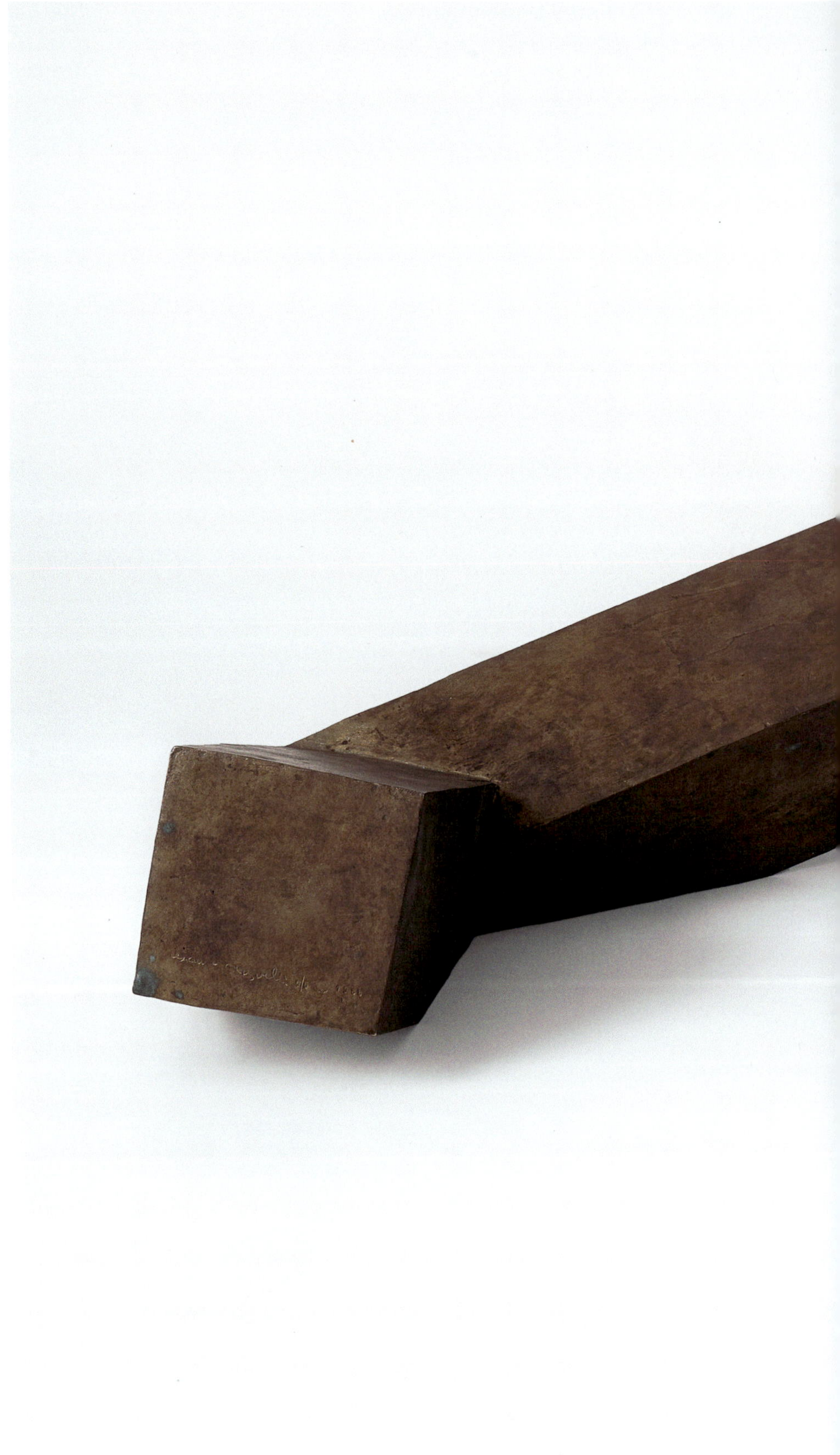

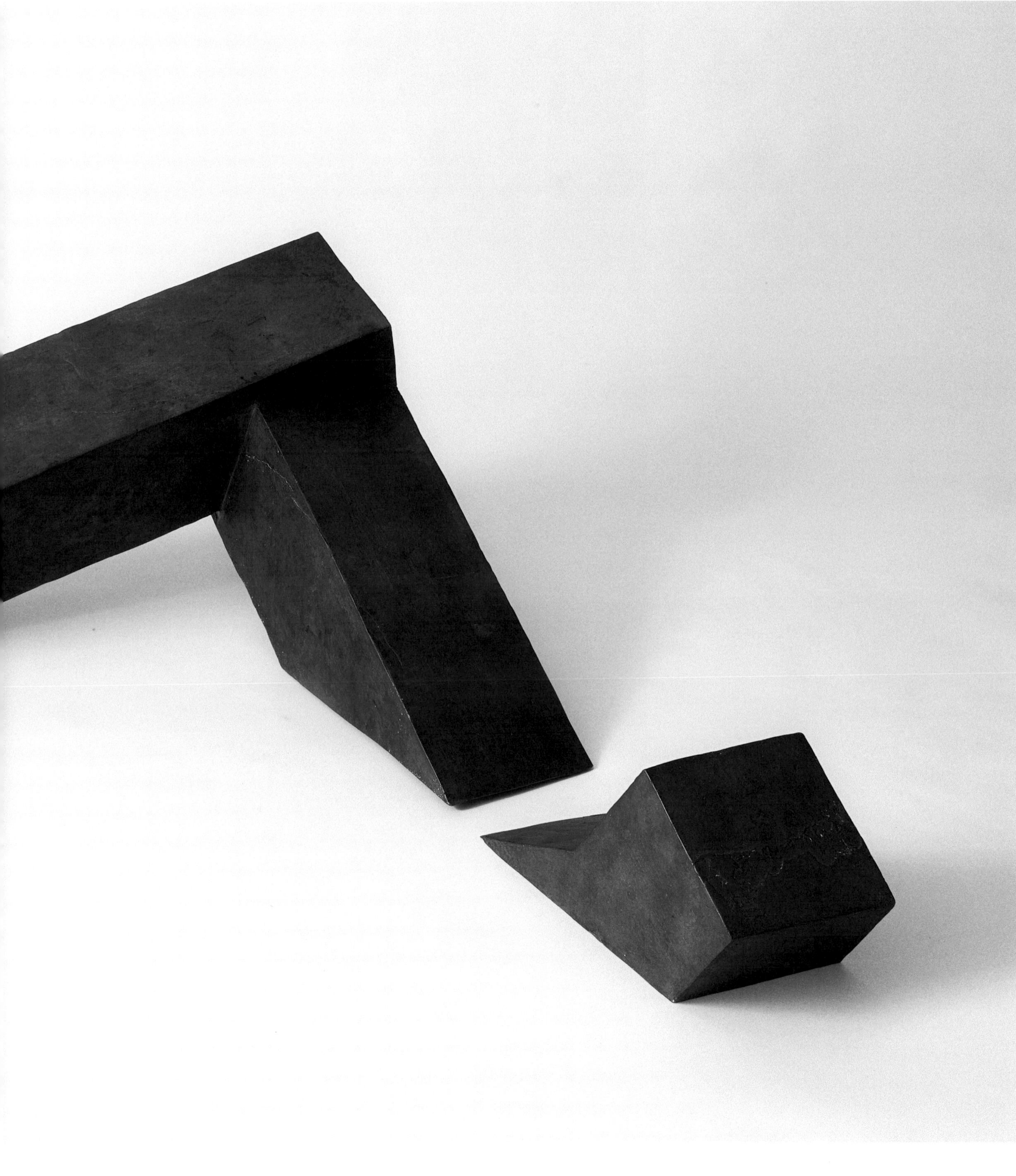

Noguchi working on *Mitosis* in Rome, 1962

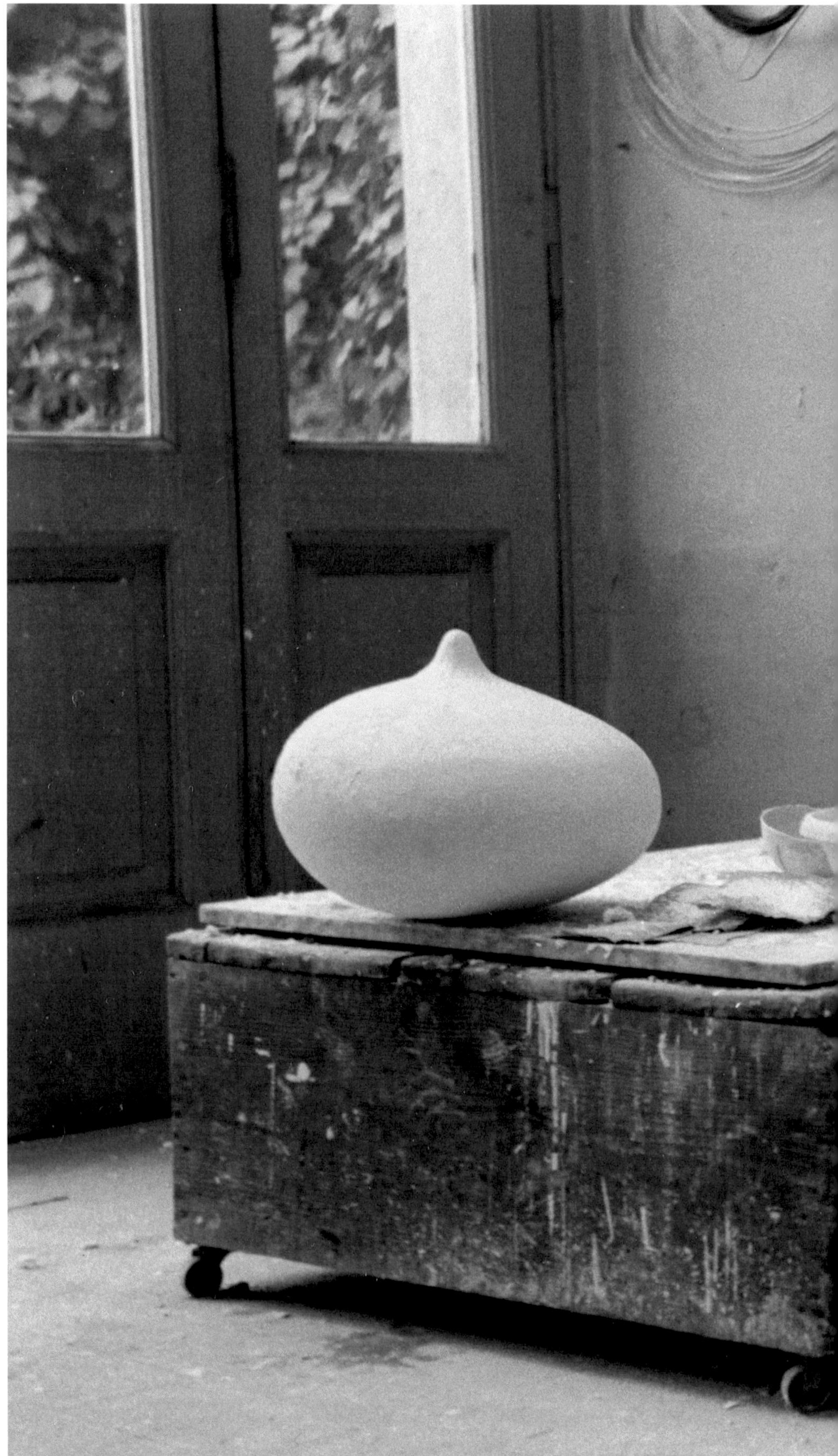

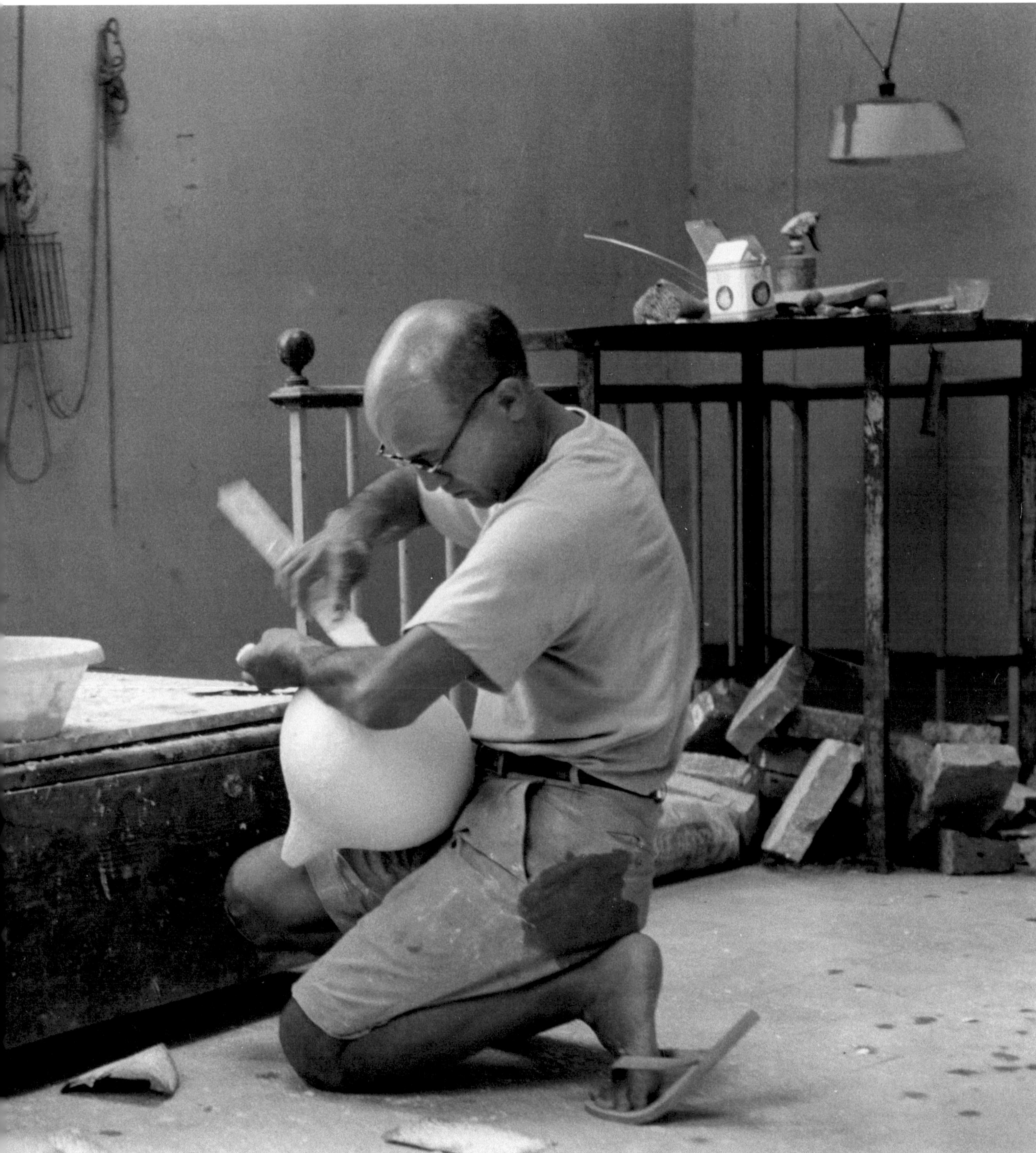

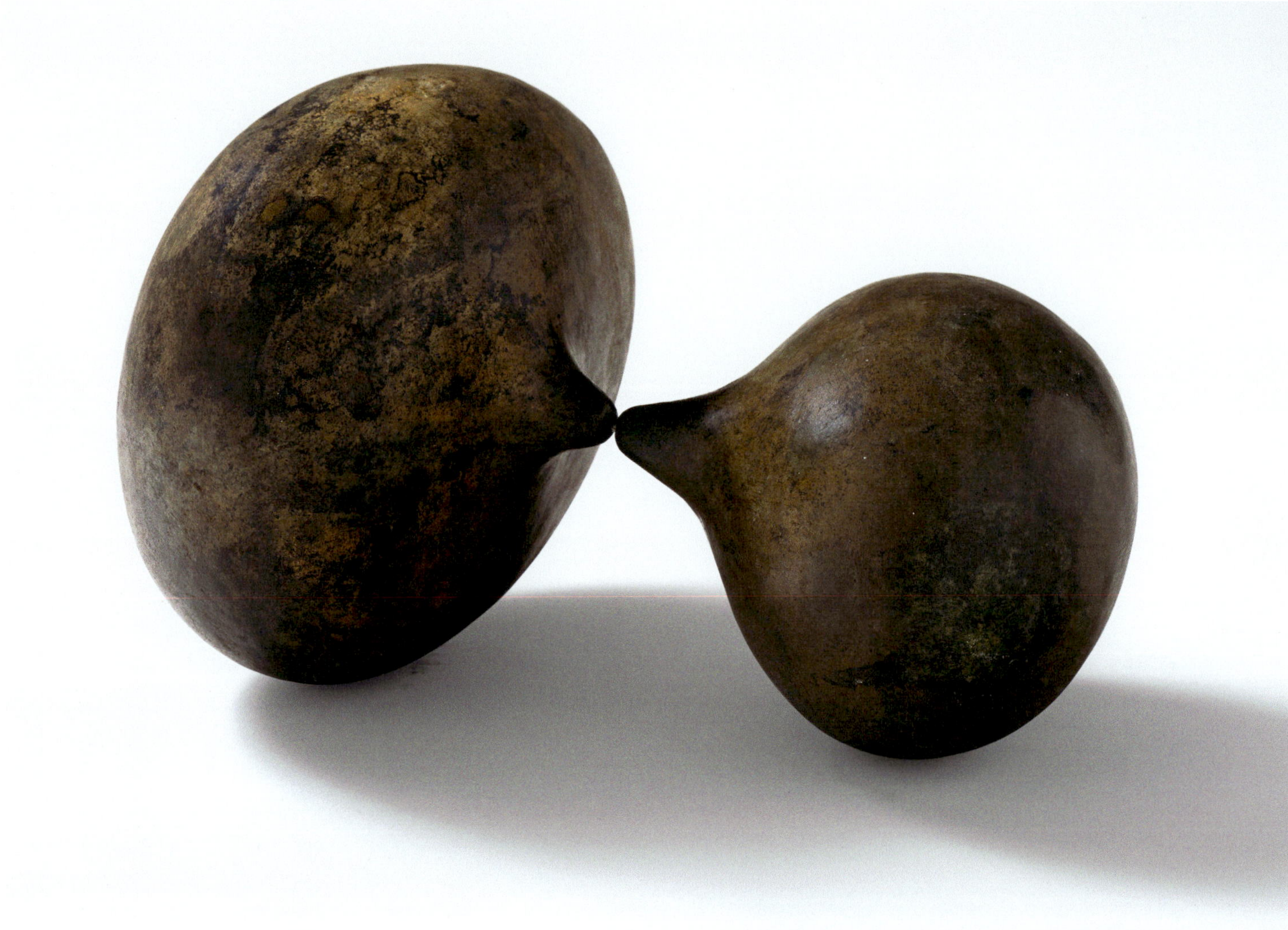

Mitosis, 1962
Bronze with gold patina
36.2 × 61.3 × 41.3 cm

Lunar Table, 1961–65
Granite
33.3 × 82.6 × 62.2 cm

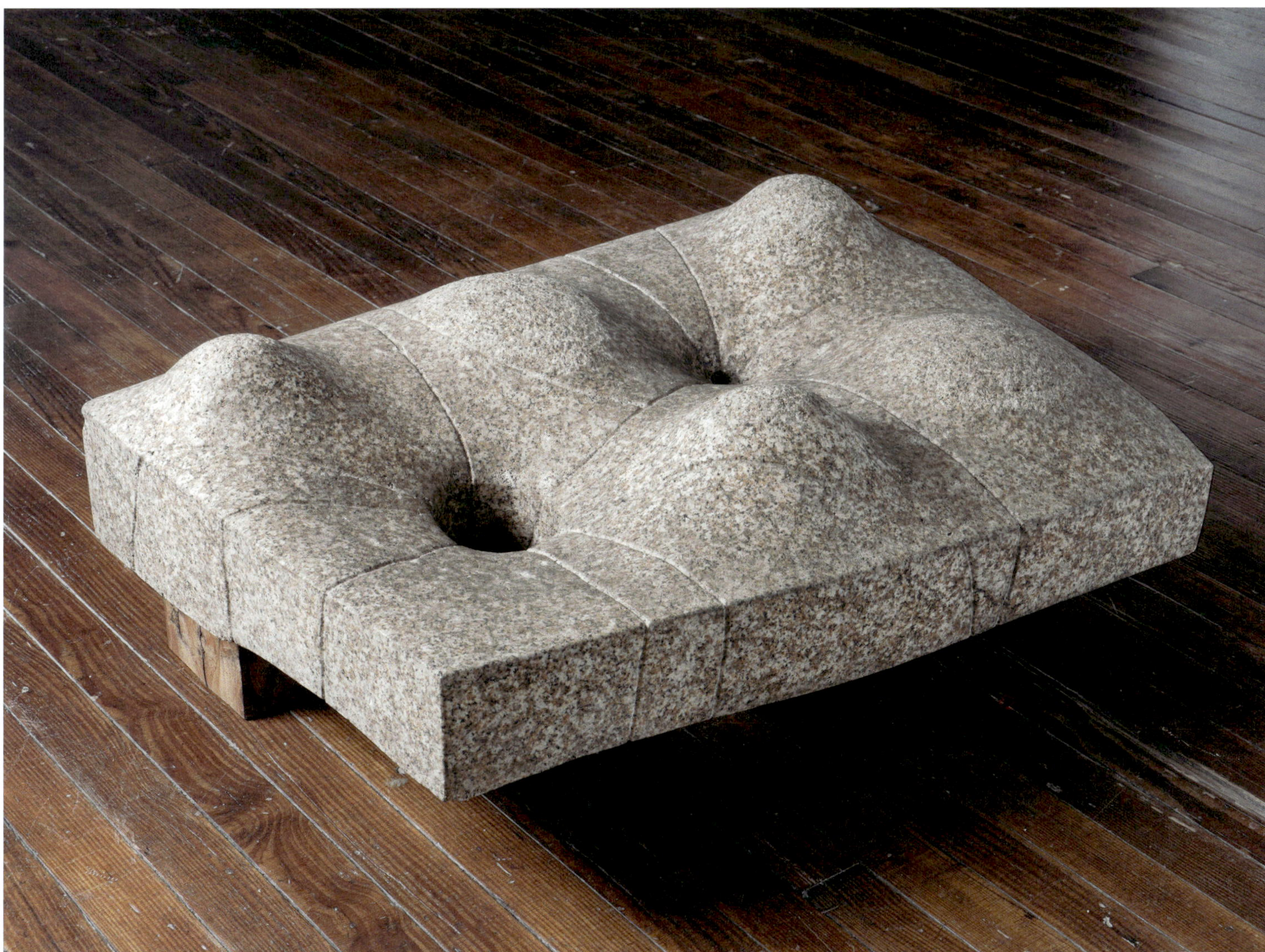

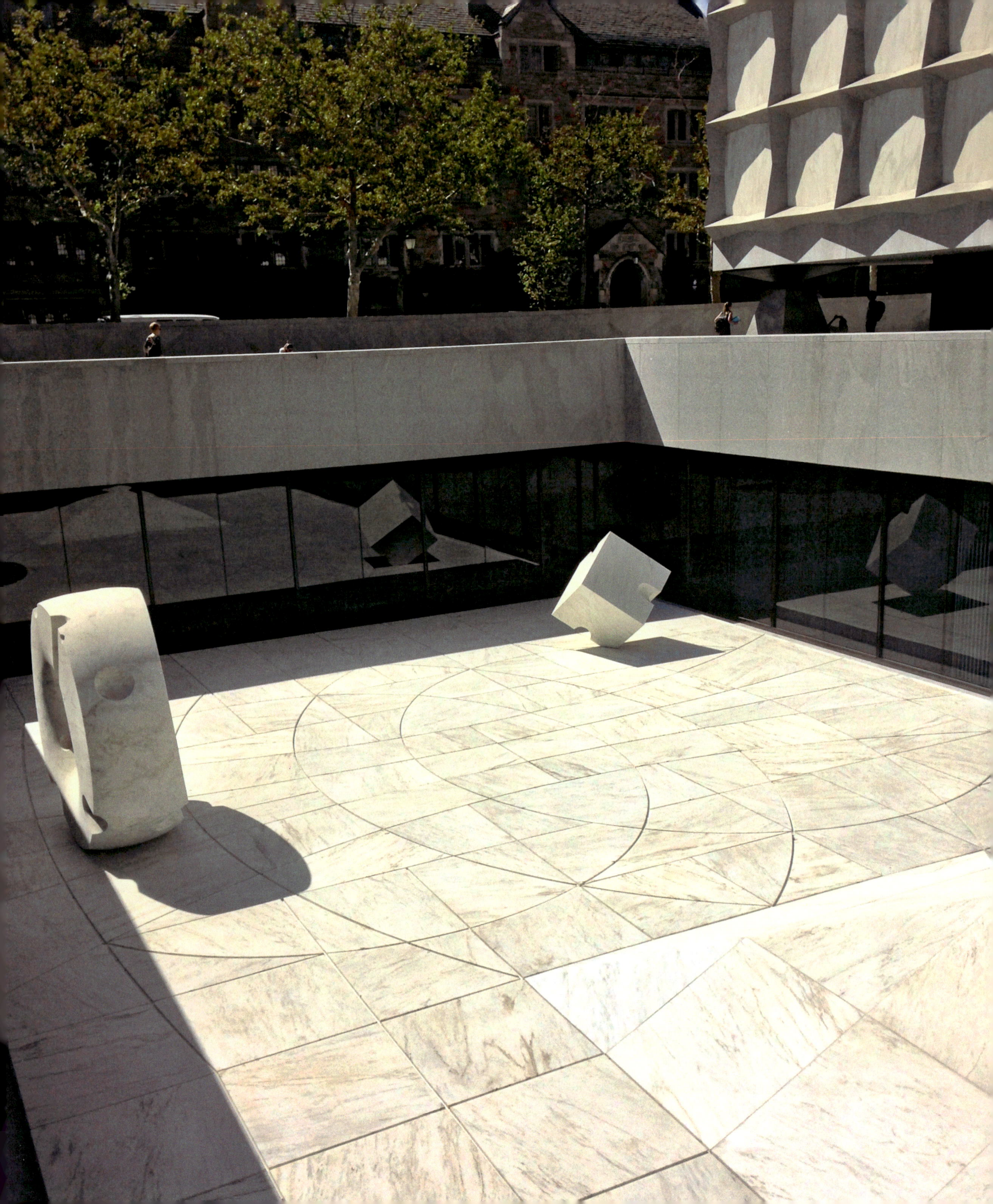

Sunken Garden for Beinecke Rare Book and Manuscript Library,
1960–64
Imperial Danby marble
3 × 24.5 × 15.3 m

Model for *Sunken Garden for Beinecke Rare Book and Manuscript Library*, c. 1963
Plaster, wood and paint
15.2 × 92.7 × 59.7 cm

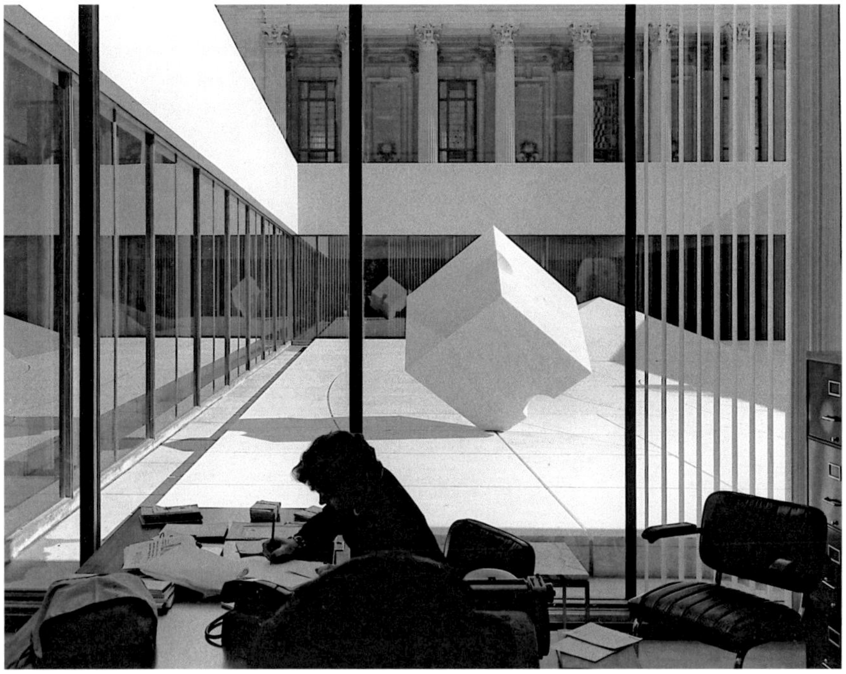

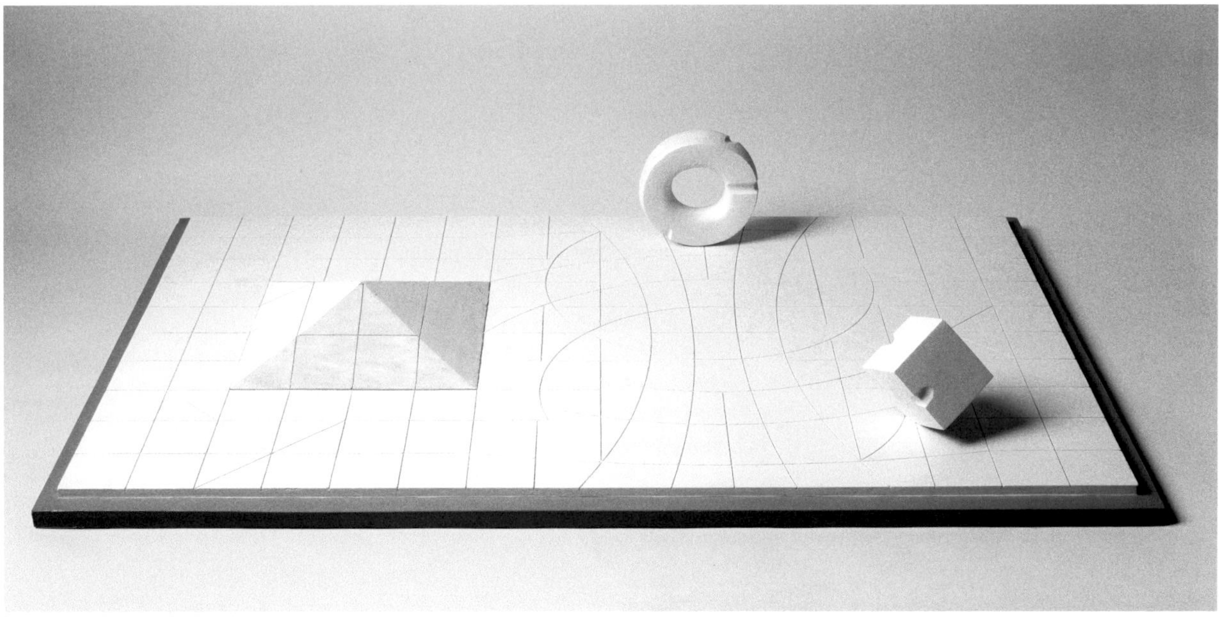

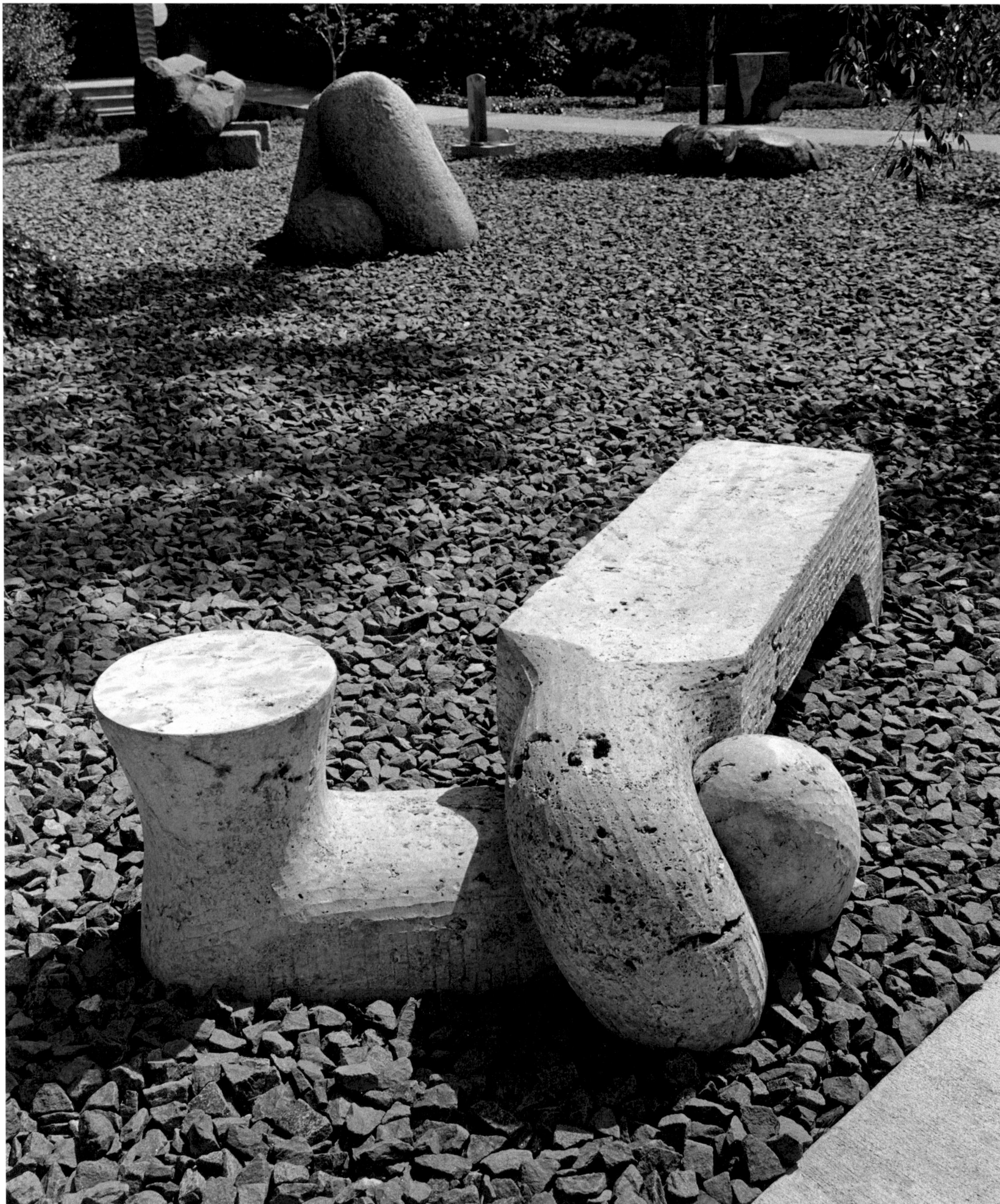

Garden, The Noguchi Museum, New York

Tsukubai (Chōzubachi), 1964
Mannari granite and water
29.2 × 51.4 × 56.8 cm

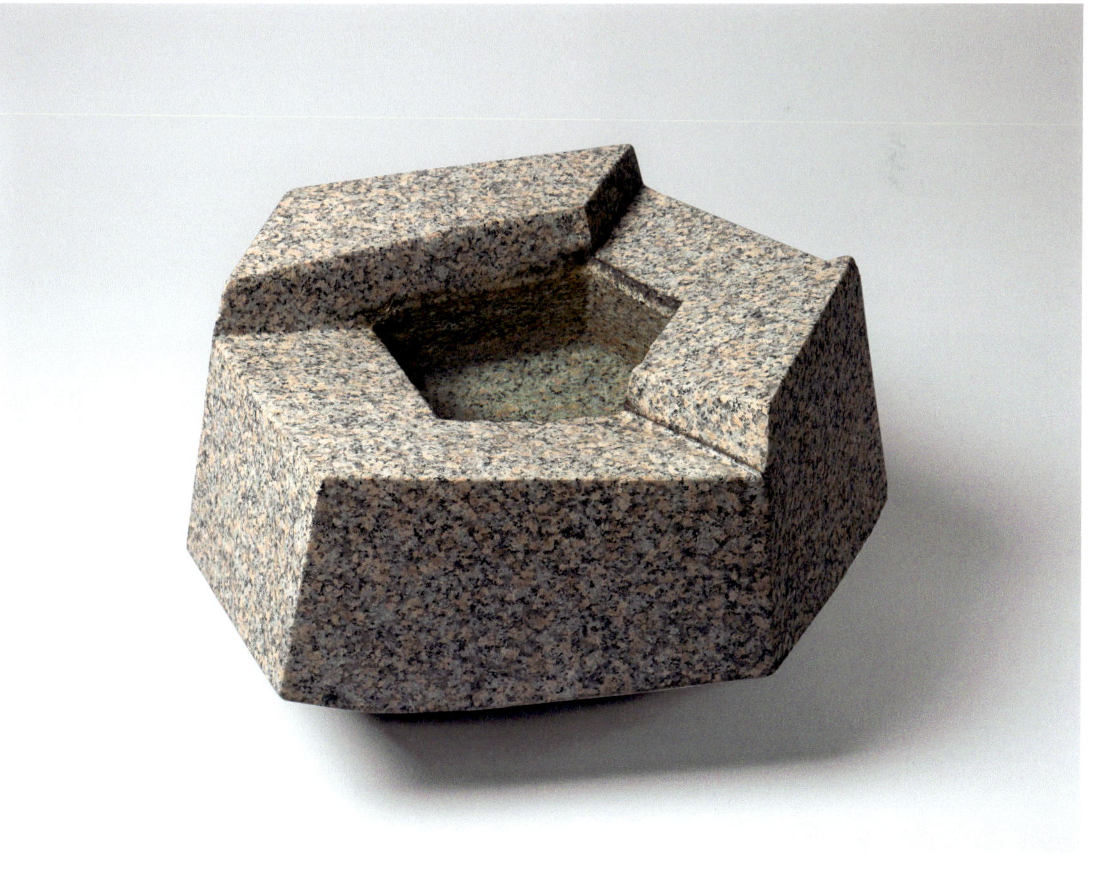

Model for *Ding Dong Bat*, 1968–74
Plaster
Approx. 5.7 × 25.4 × 7.6 cm

***Ding Dong Bat*,** 1968
White statuary marble and pink Portuguese marble
59.1 × 235.3 × 41.3 cm

The tensile strength given to the compressive strength of stone is well exemplified in this horizontal use of post-tensioning. A stainless-steel rod runs through a loose hole with the ends tightened to give continuous pressure.

1987

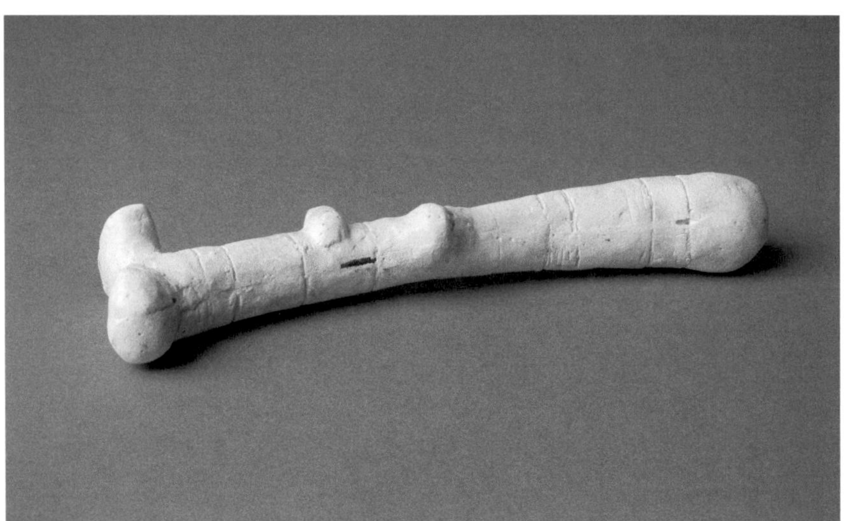

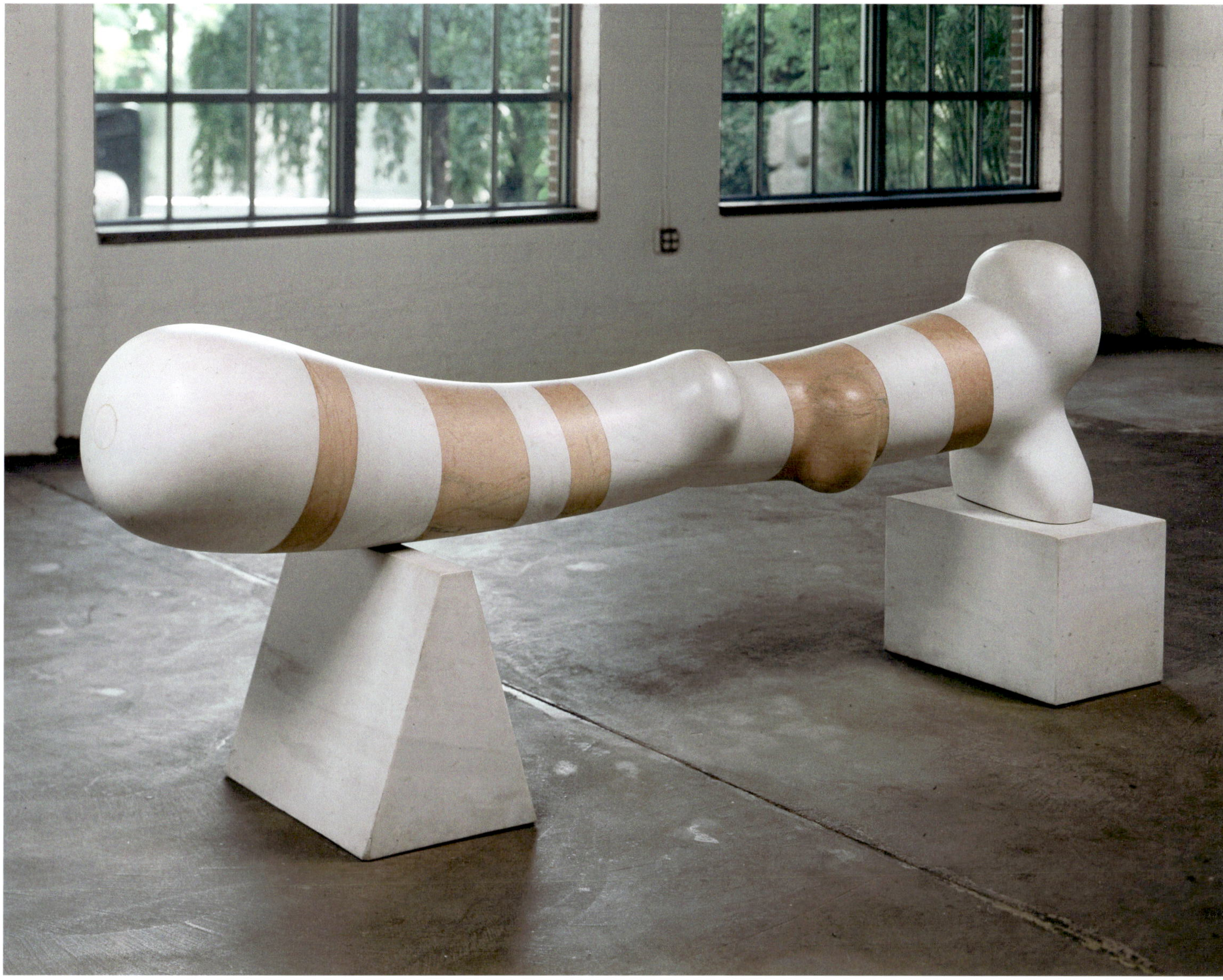

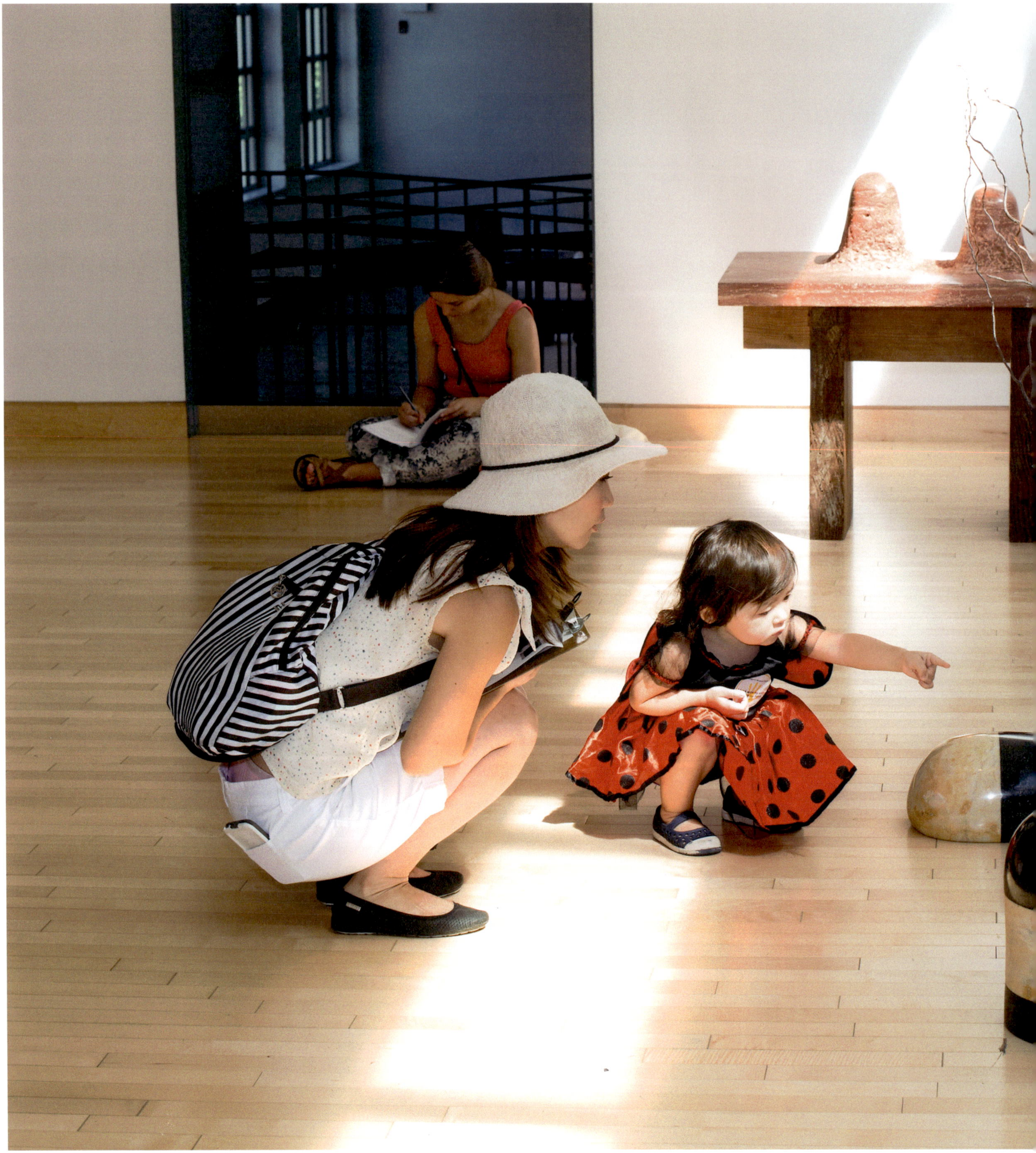

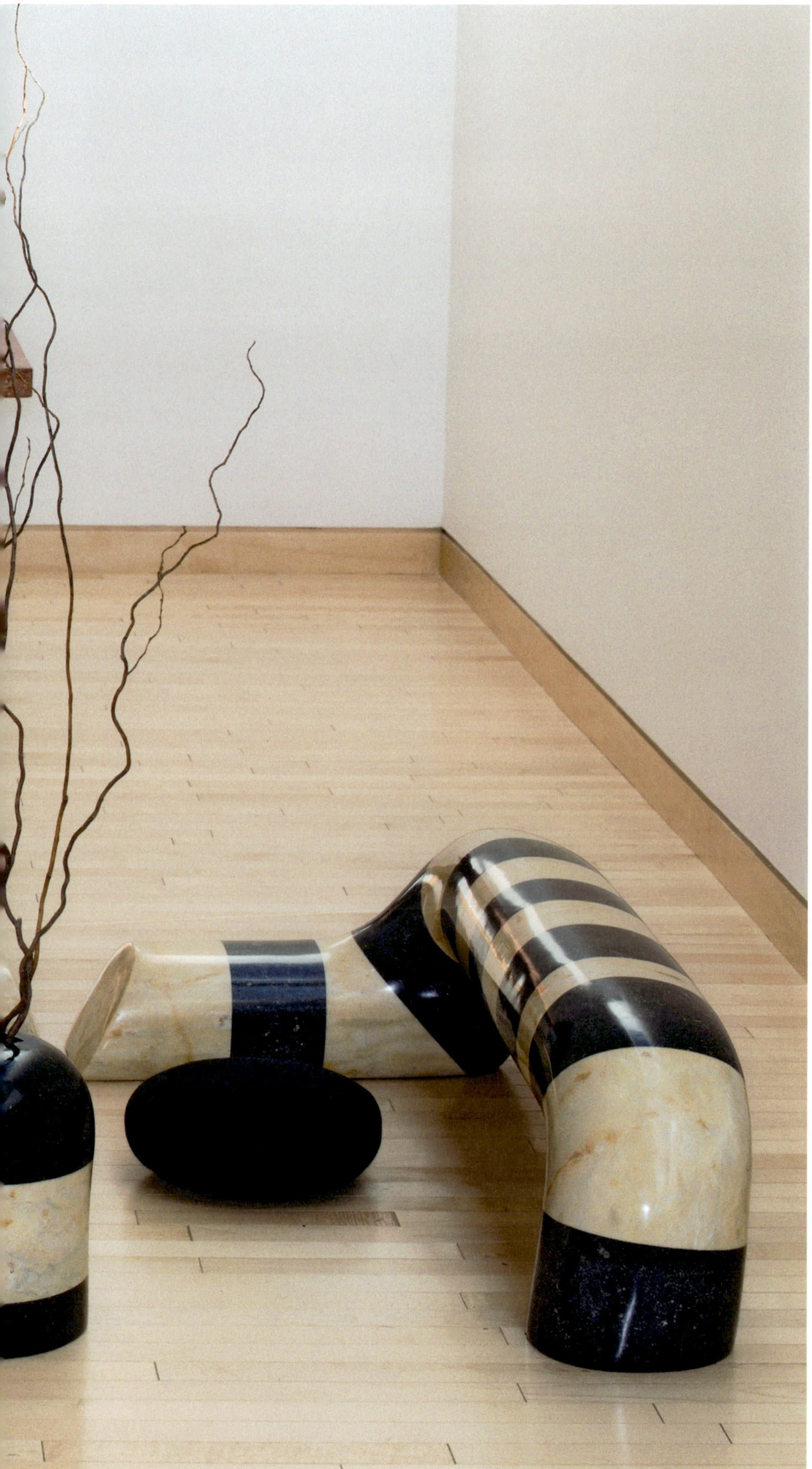

Floor Frame (Remembering India) (foreground), 1970, and *Double Red Mountain* (background), 1969, at The Noguchi Museum, New York

Planet in Transit #1, 1968–72
Swedish granite
18.1 × 122.2 × 90.2 cm

Double Red Mountain, 1969
Persian travertine
29.2 × 101.6 × 76.8 cm

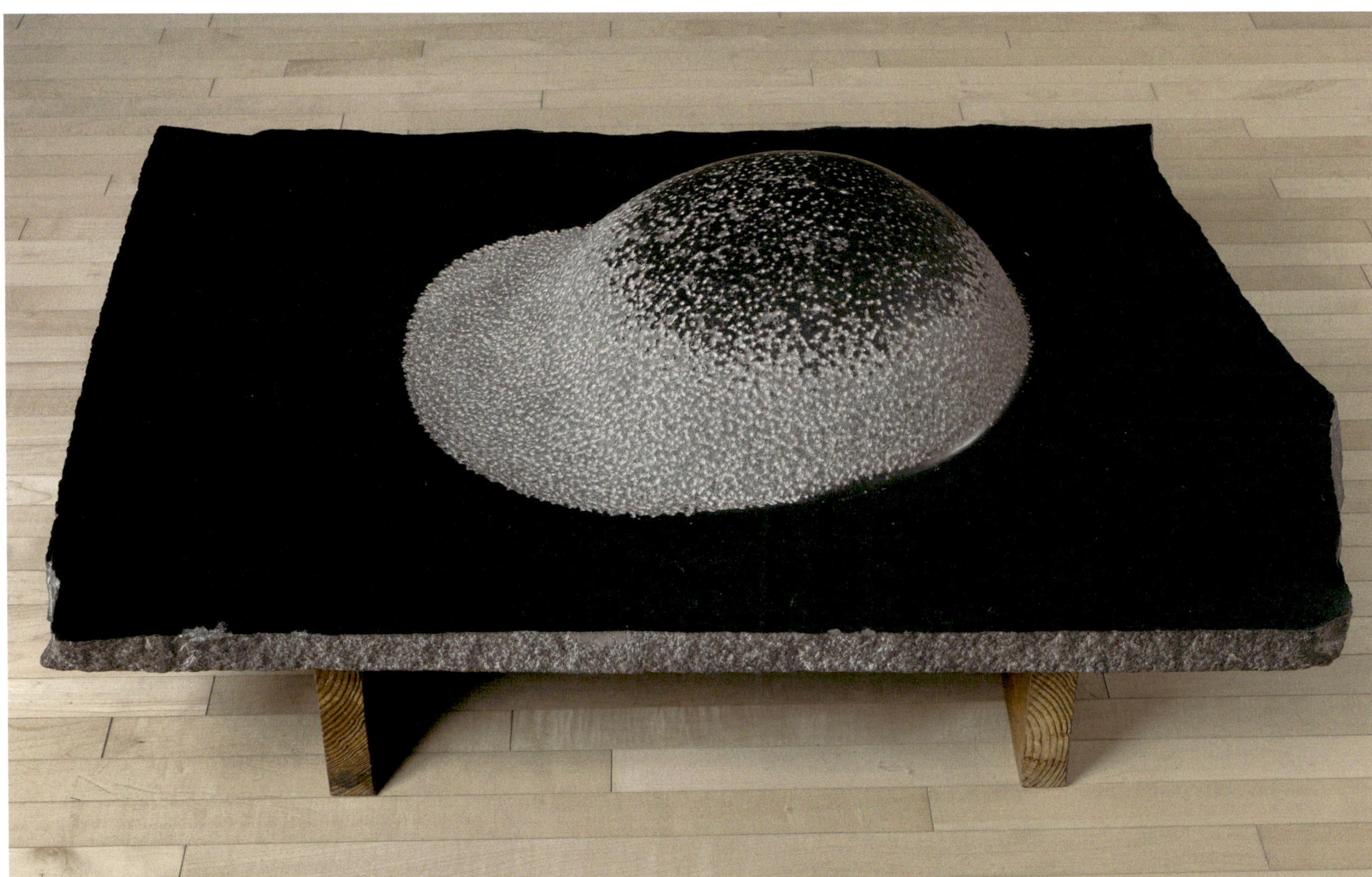

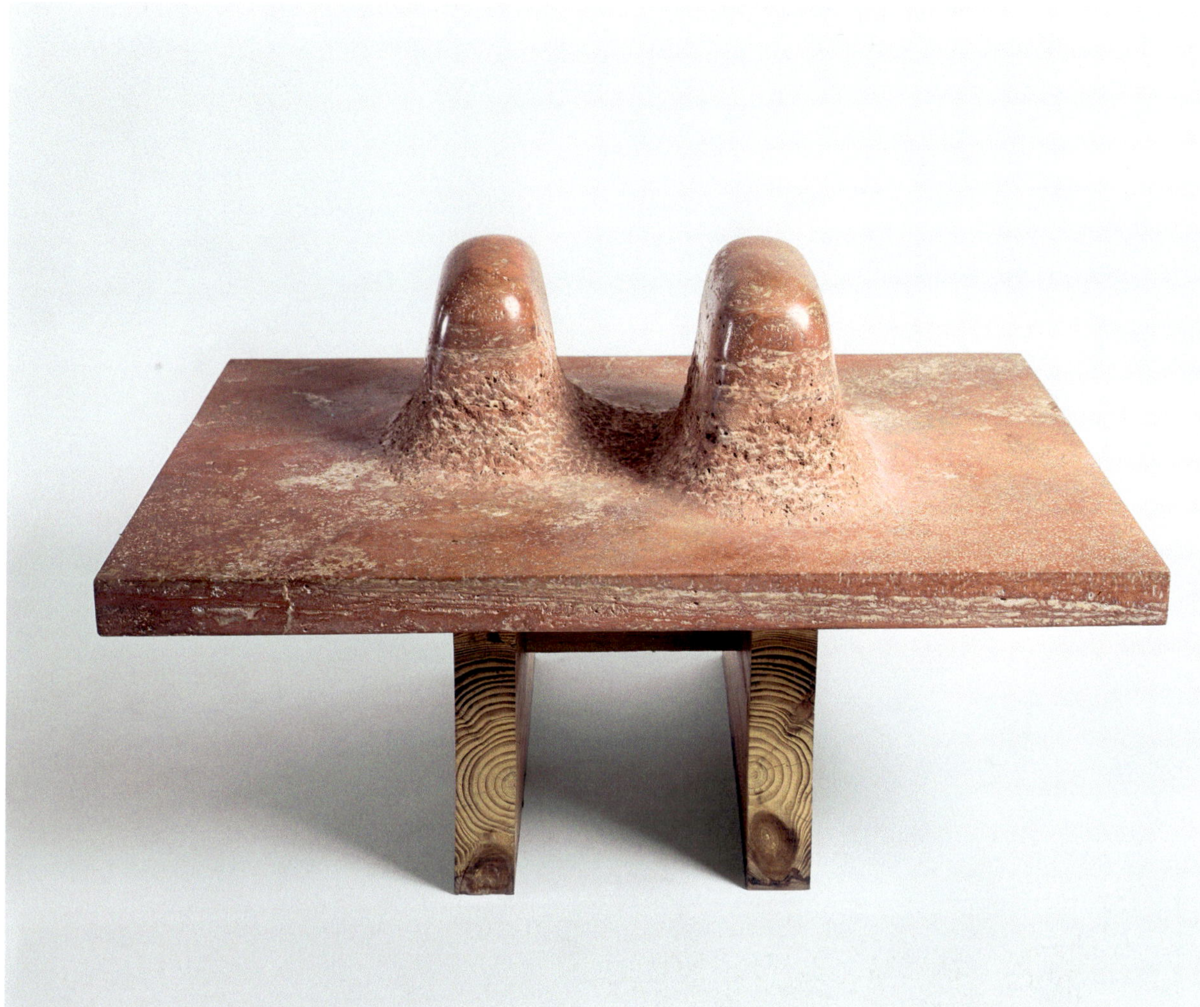

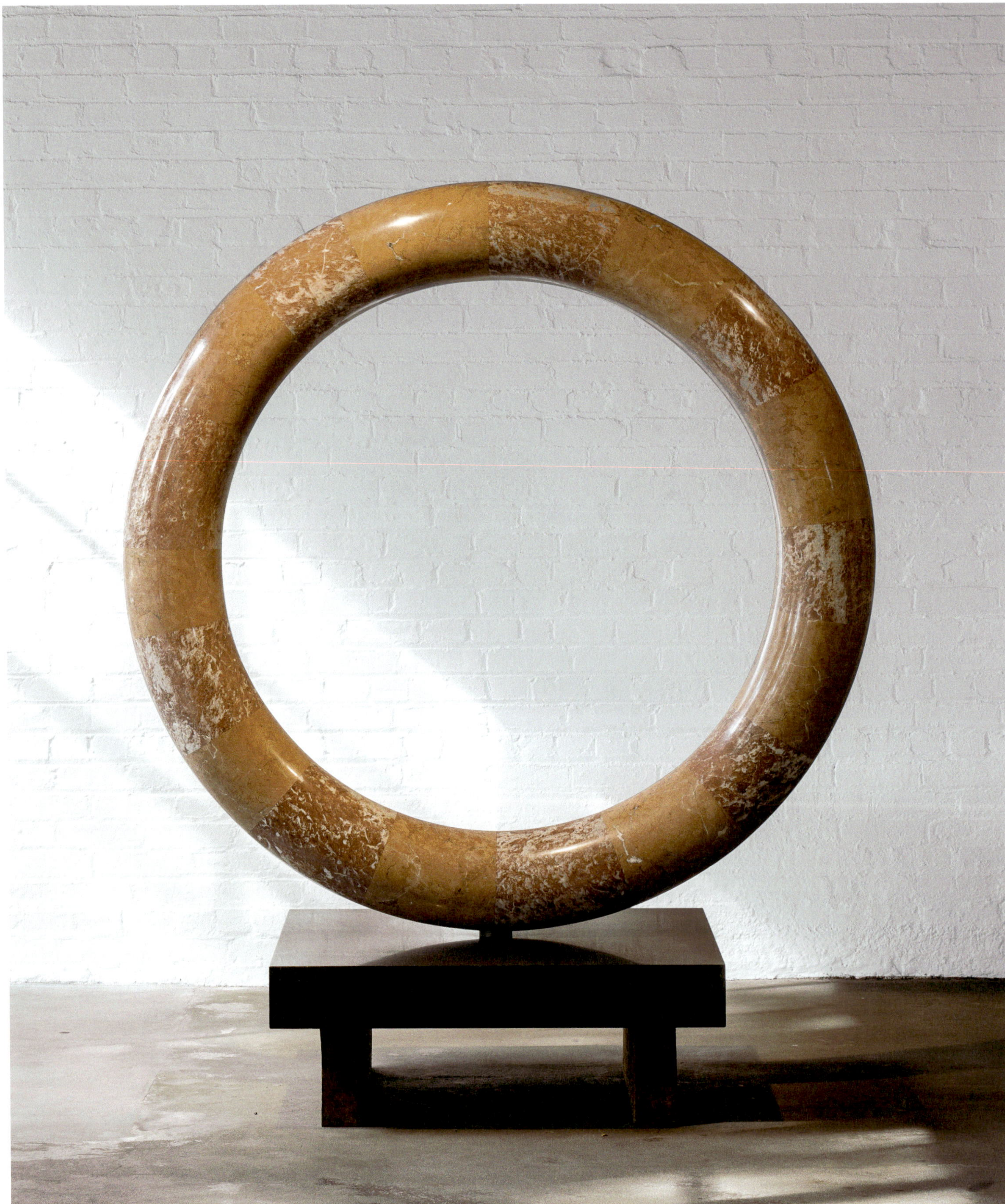

Sun at Noon, 1969
French red marble and Spanish
Alicante marble
54.9 × 154.9 × 21 cm

The Spirit's Flight, 1969
Serpentine
241 × 18.7 × 18.7 cm

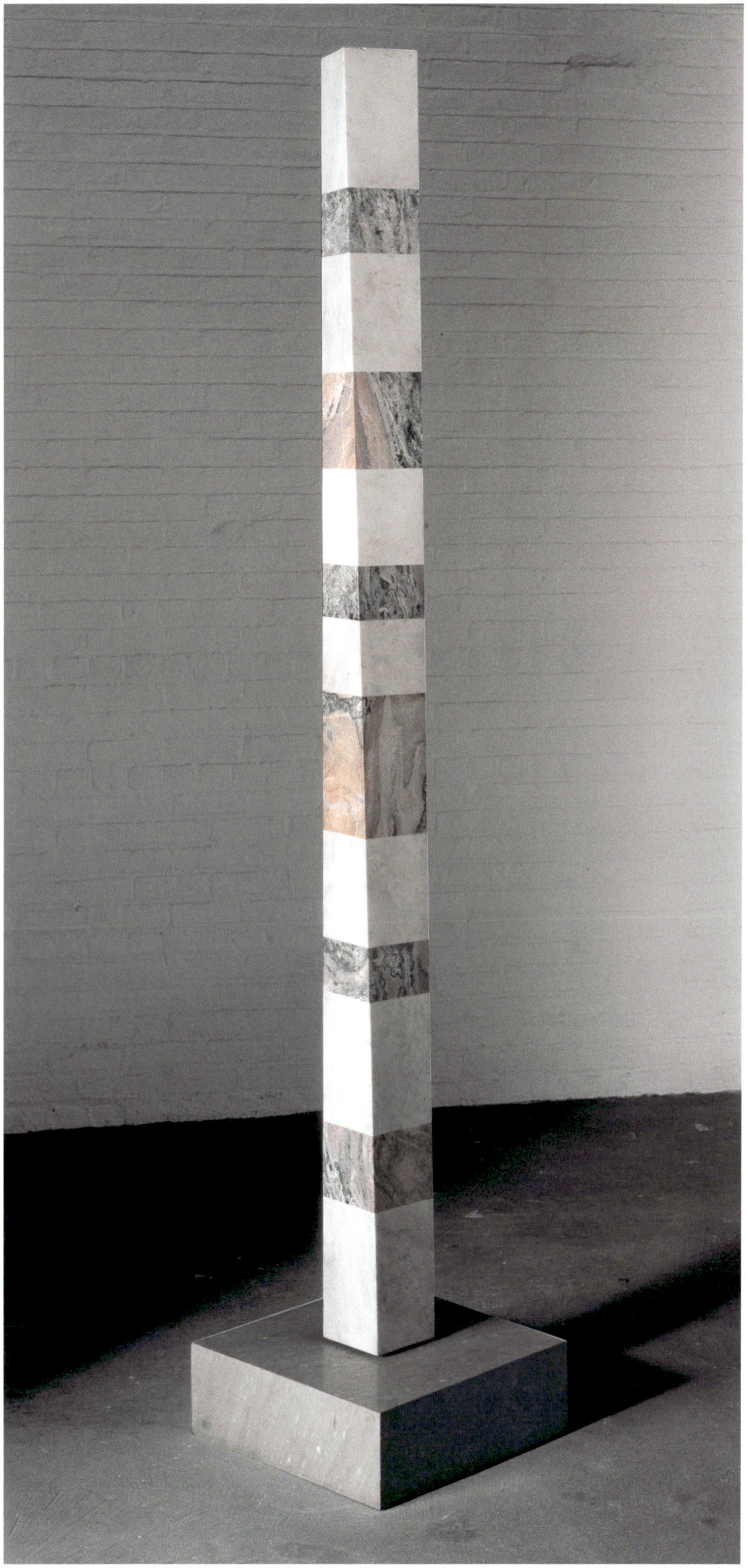

Walking Void #2, 1970
Swedish granite
172.7 × 72.2 × 84.1 cm

Walking Void #2, 1974
Swedish granite
172.4 × 71.8 × 84.5 cm

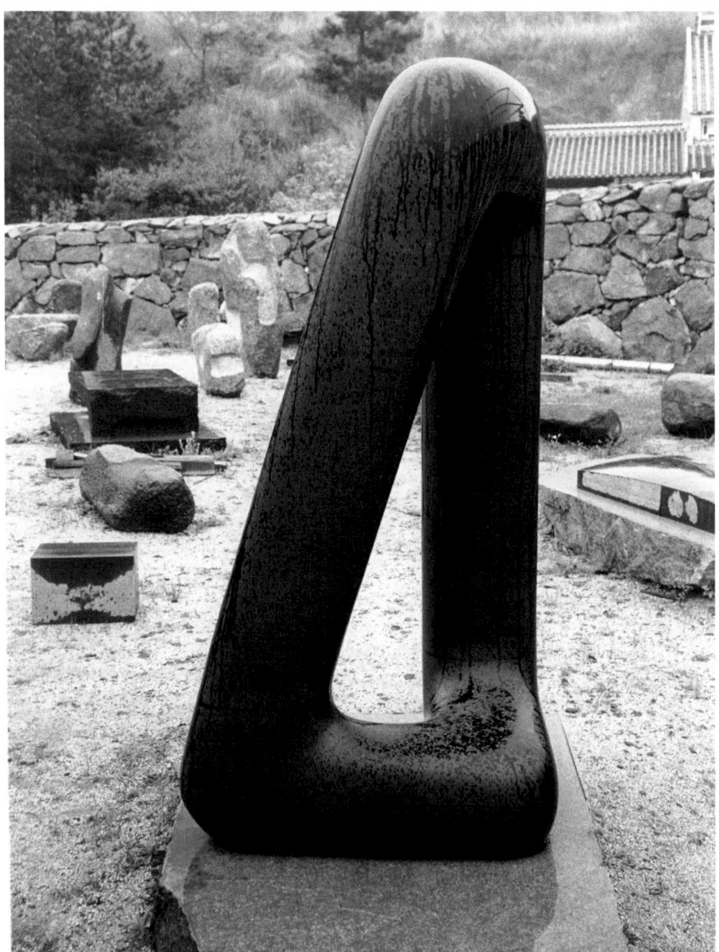

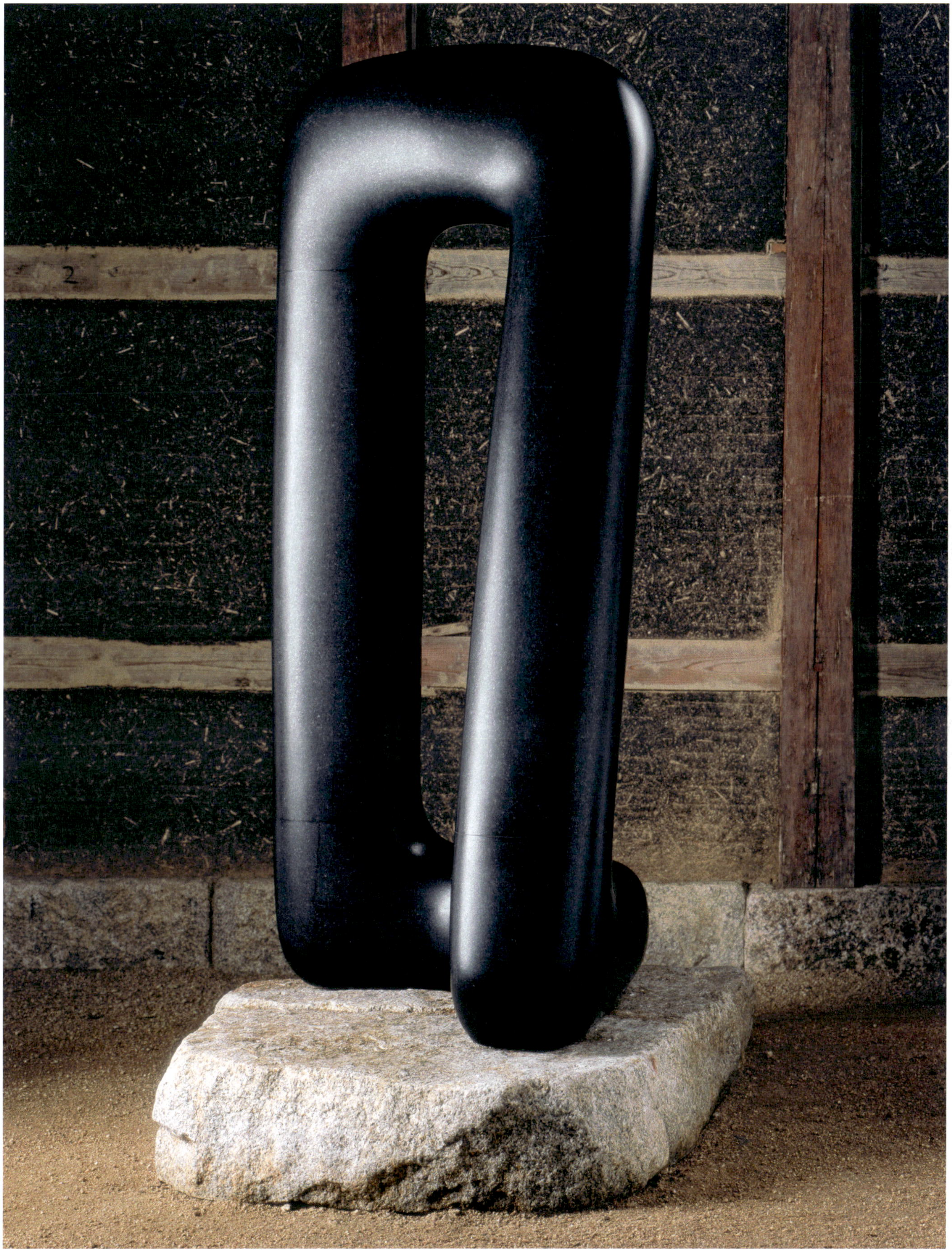

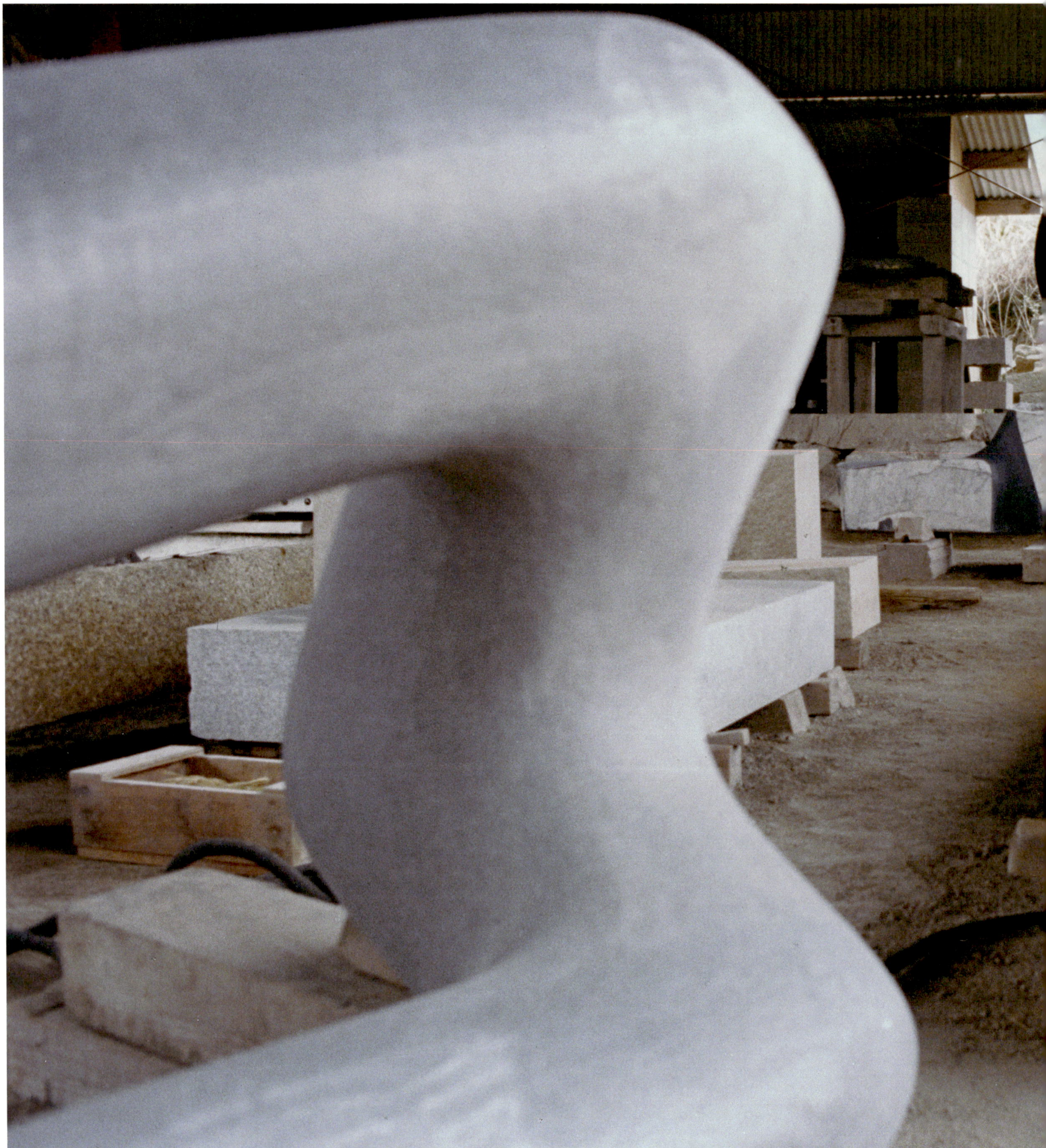

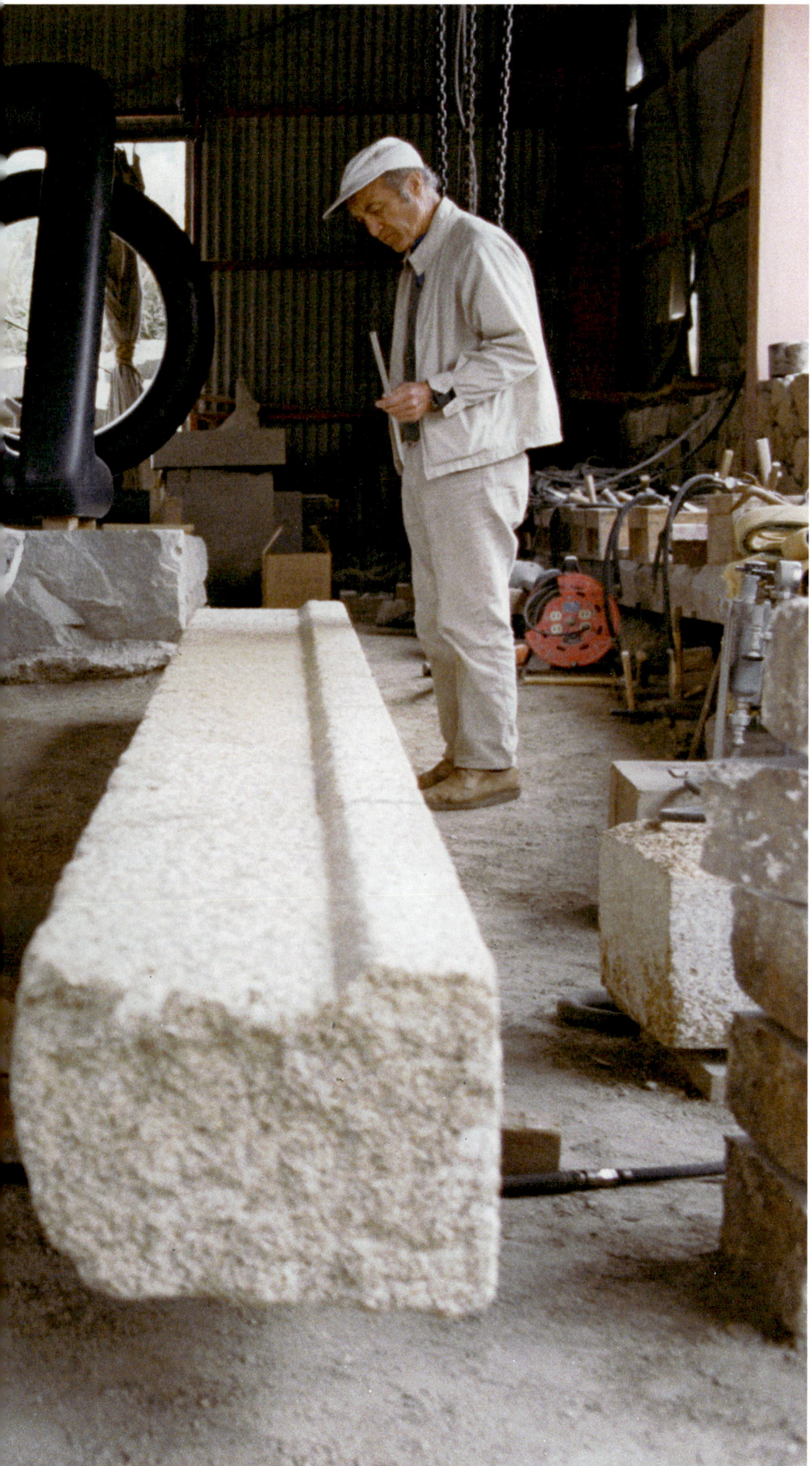

Noguchi working in Masatoshi Izumi's studio in Mure, Japan, 1978

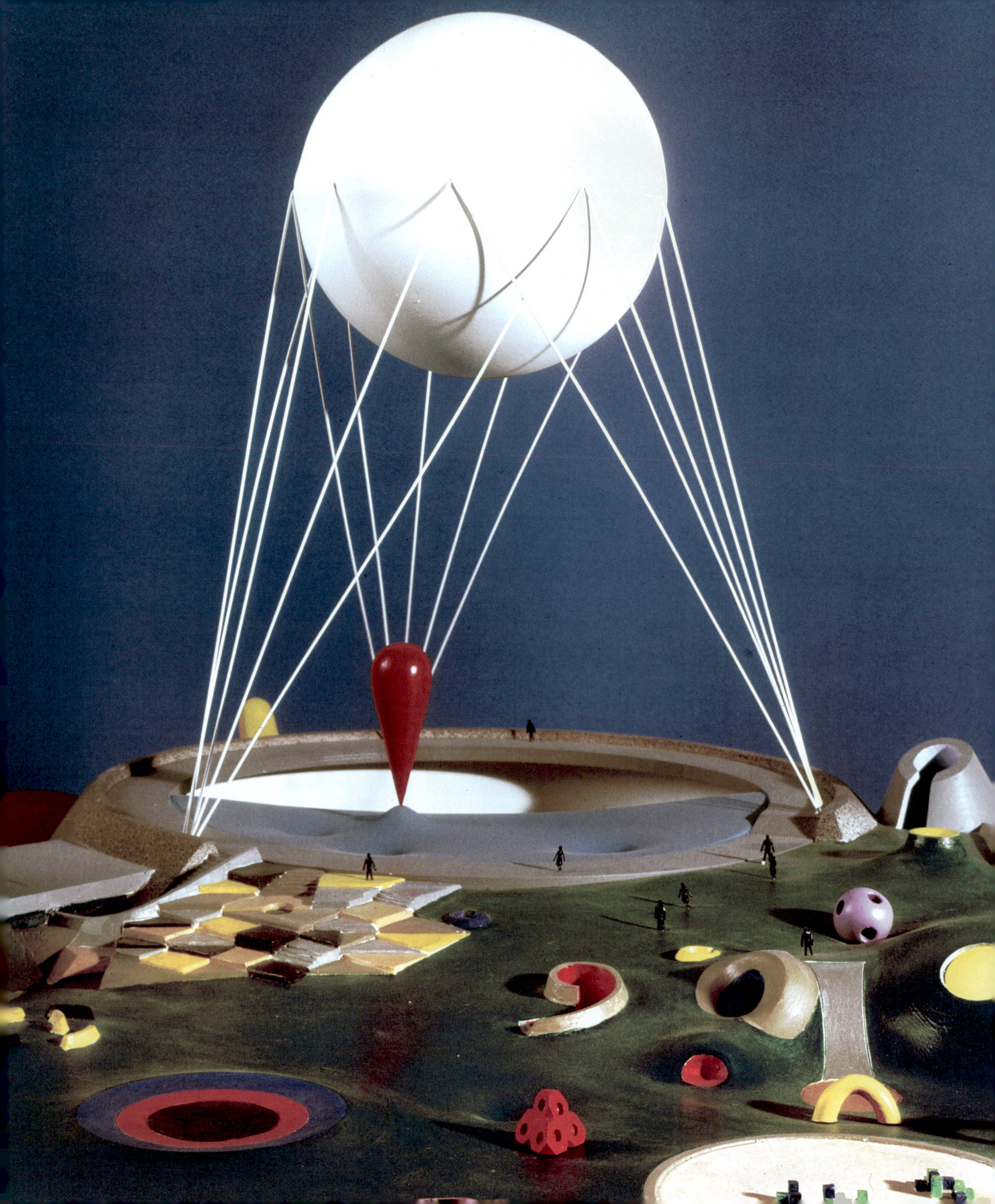

Model for *US Pavilion Expo '70 (Garden of the Moon)*, 1968
(for Expo '70, Osaka, Japan; unrealised)
Plaster, wire and paint
40.3 × 58.4 × 83.8 cm

Play Sculpture at Moerenuma Park, Sapporo, Japan, 1988–2004

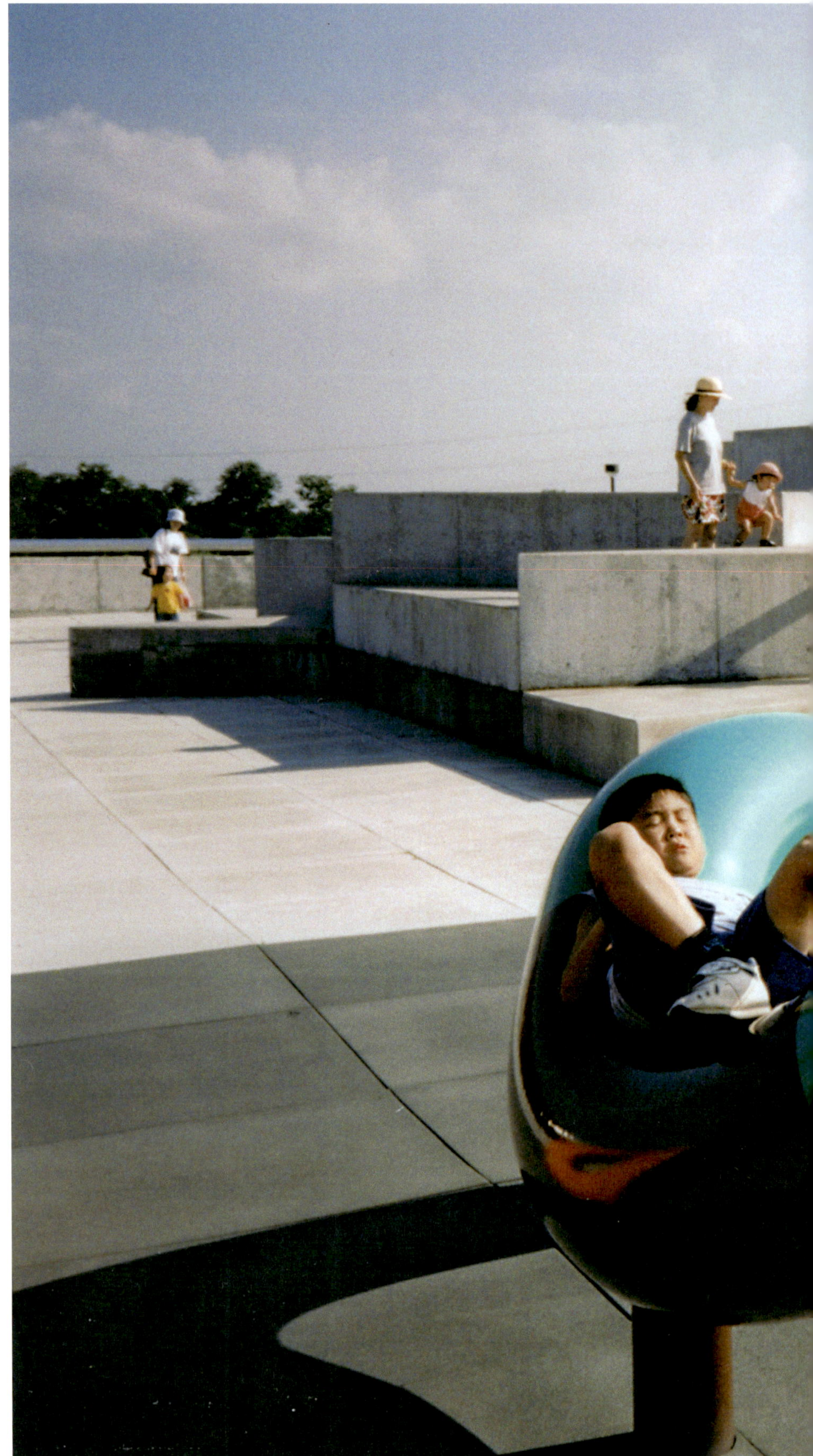

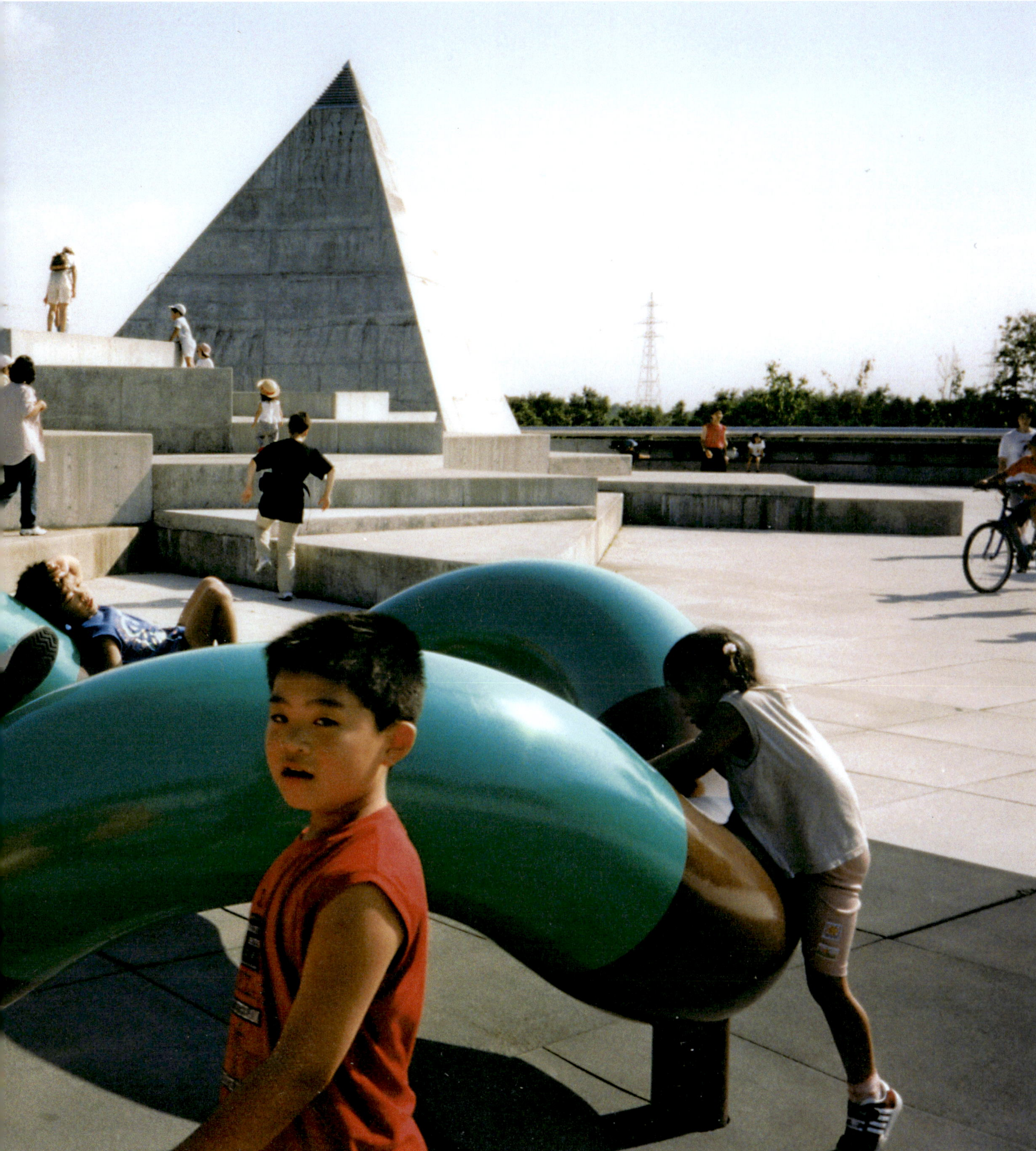

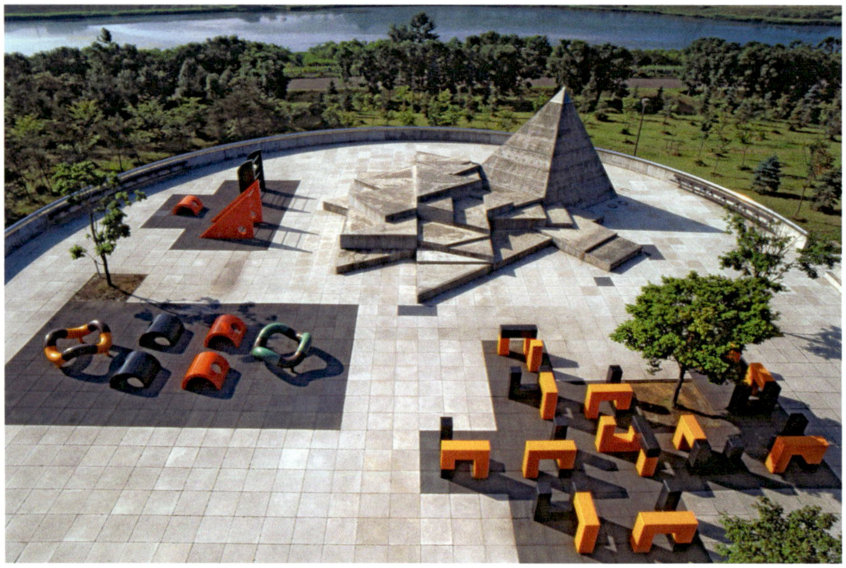

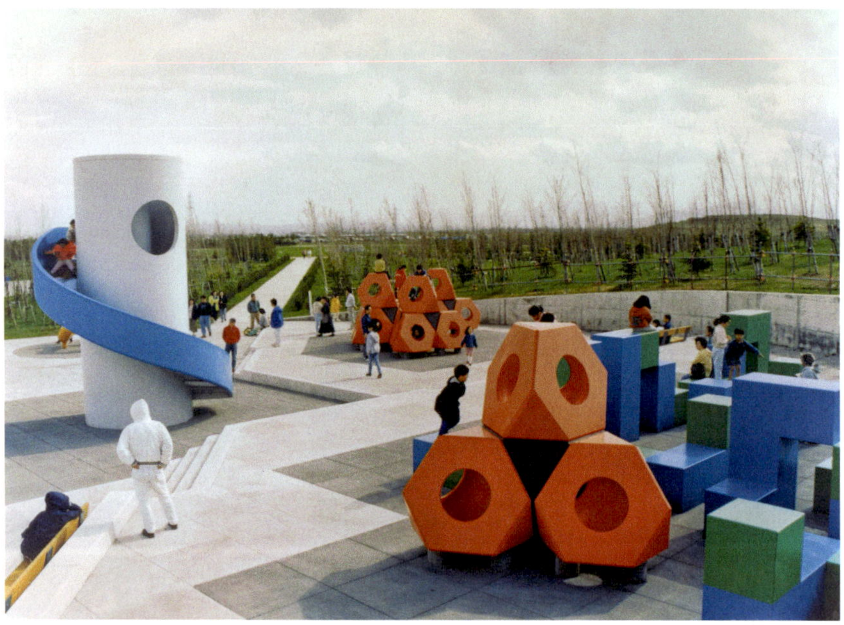

Moerenuma Park, Sapporo, Japan,
1988–2004

Play Sculpture, c. 1965/c. 1980
(fabricated 2017)
Steel and paint
112.7 × 261.6 × 261.6 cm

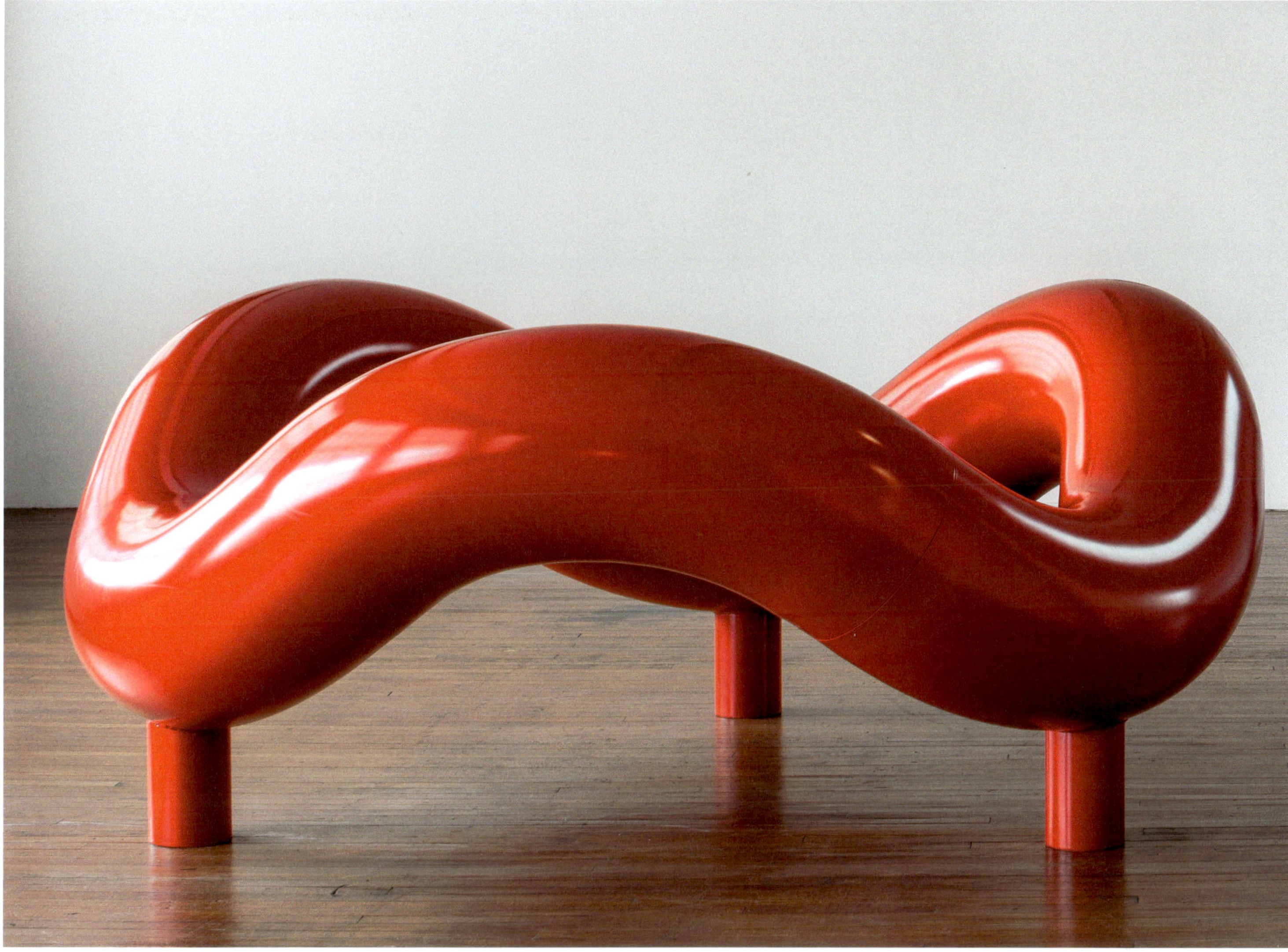

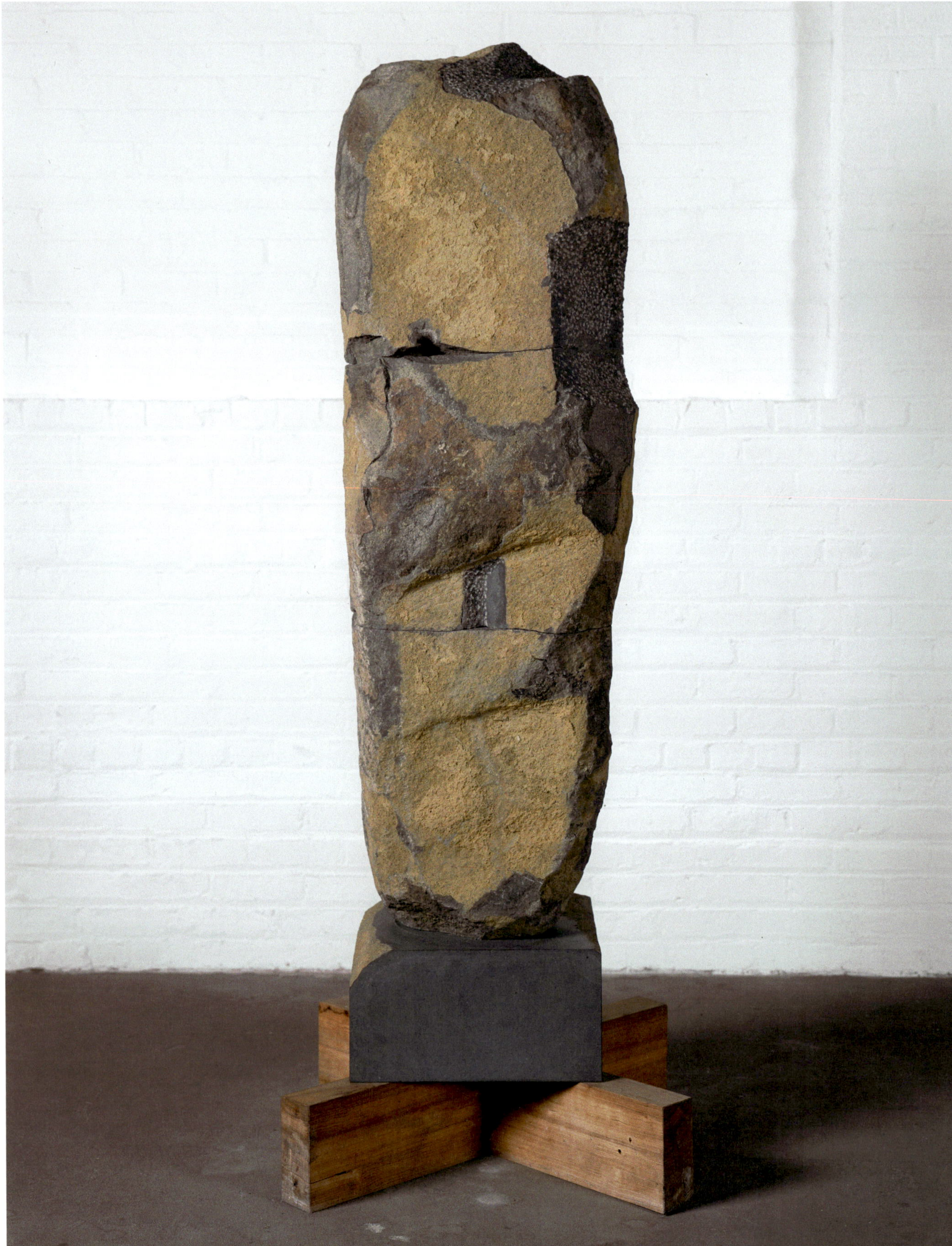

To Intrude on Nature's Way, 1971
Basalt
168.9 × 48.9 × 45.1 cm

The Inner Stone, 1973
Basalt
82.2 × 87.3 × 42.9 cm

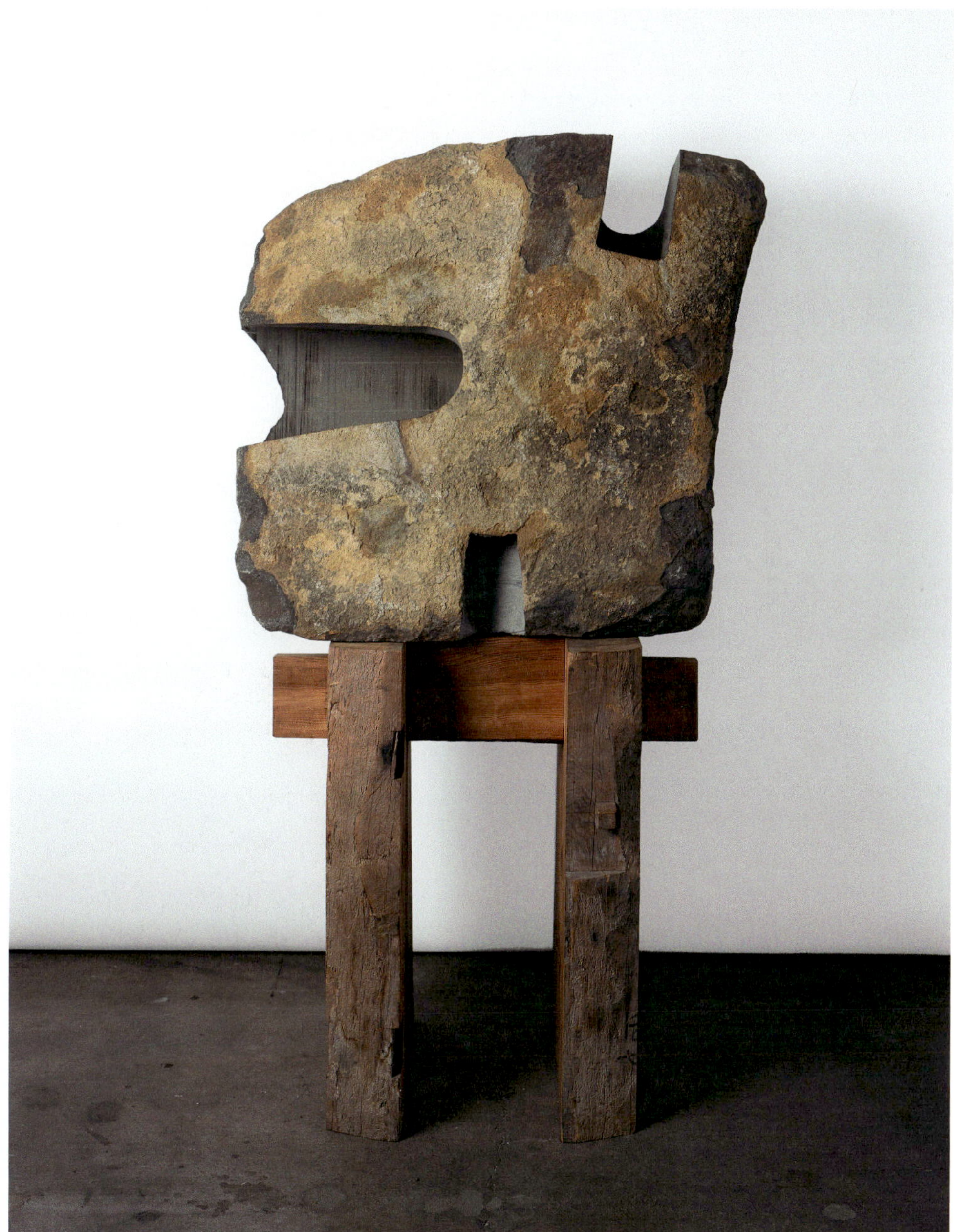

Age, 1981
Basalt
99.1 × 62.2 × 54 cm

In our times we think to control nature, only to find that in the end it escapes us. I for one return recurrently to the earth in my search for the meaning of sculpture – to escape fragmentation with a new synthesis, within the sculpture and related spaces.
I believe in the activity of stone, actual or illusory, and in gravity as a vital element.

1967

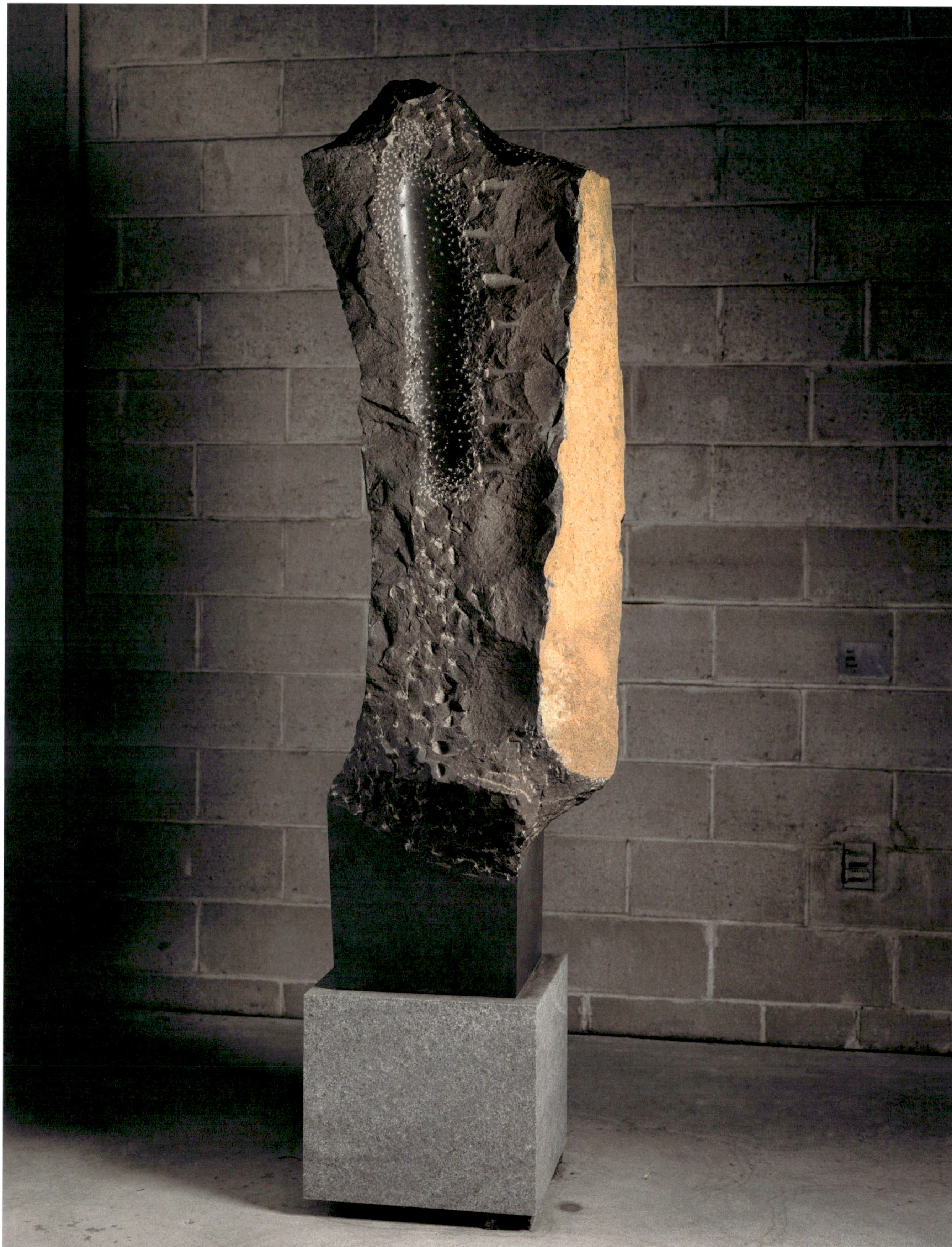

Exhibition view of *Isamu Noguchi*, Storm King Art Center, New Windsor, New York, 15 May–15 October 1984

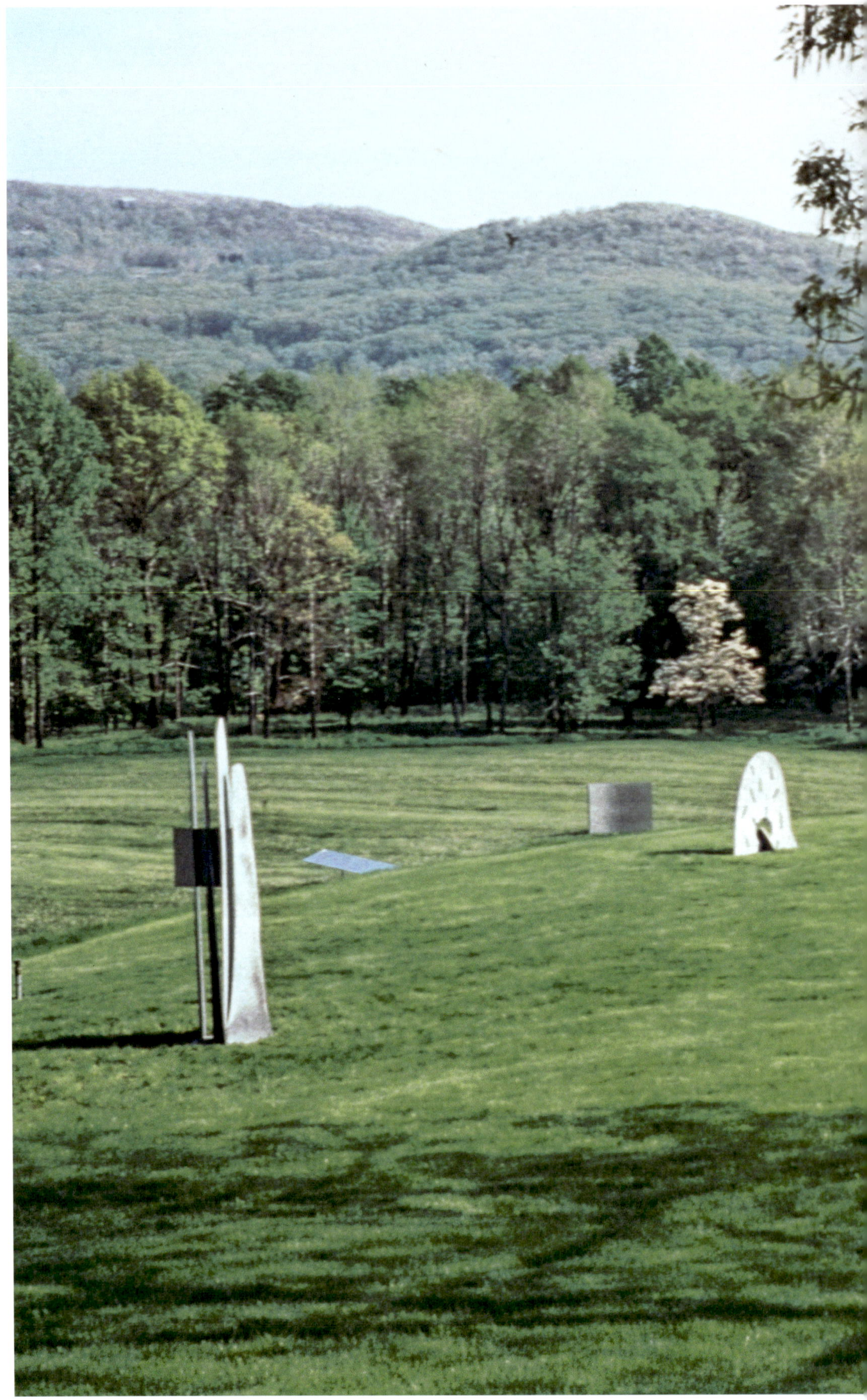

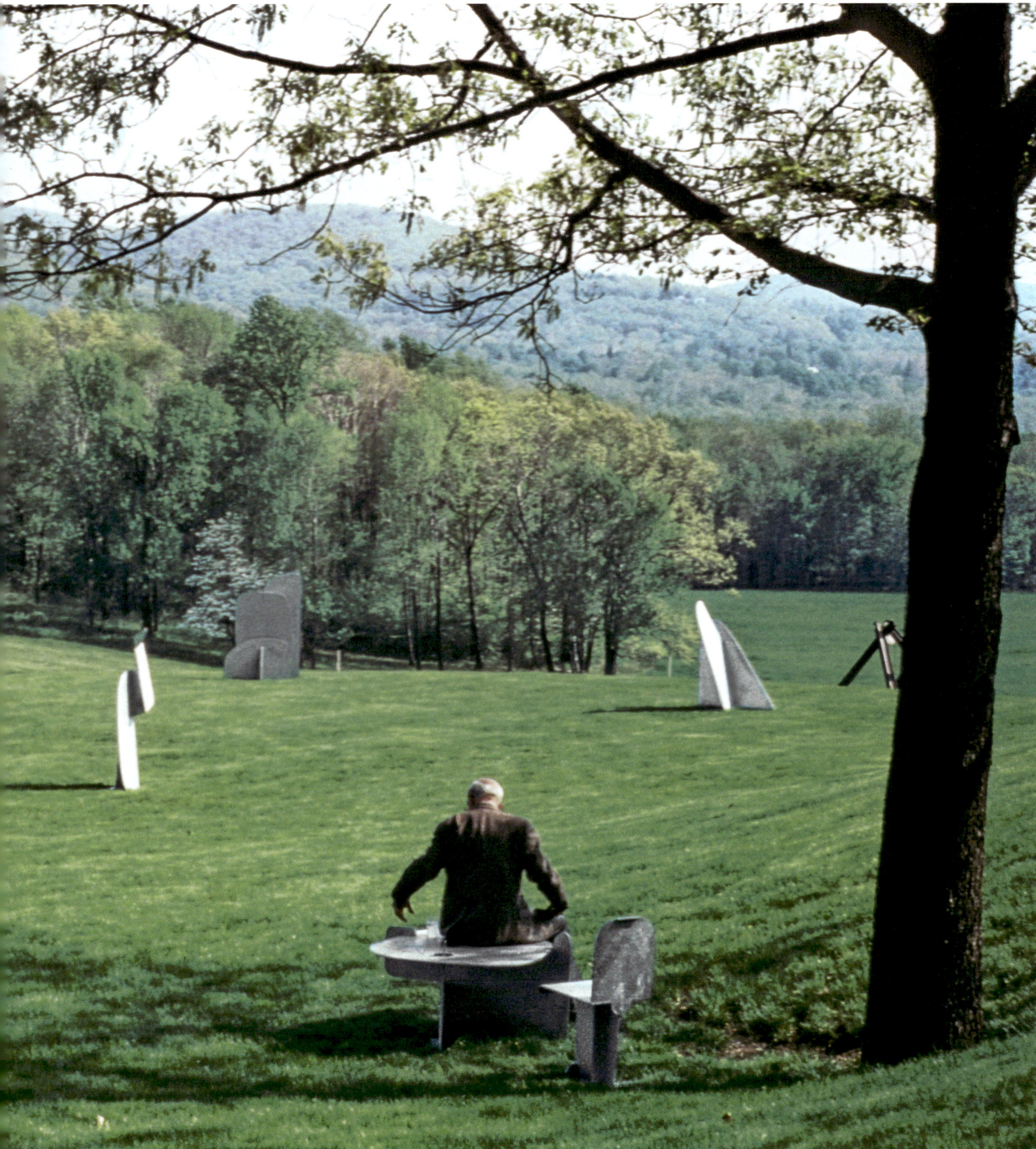

Mountains Forming, 1982–83
(fabricated 2020)
Galvanised steel
154.3 × 119.4 × 116.8 cm

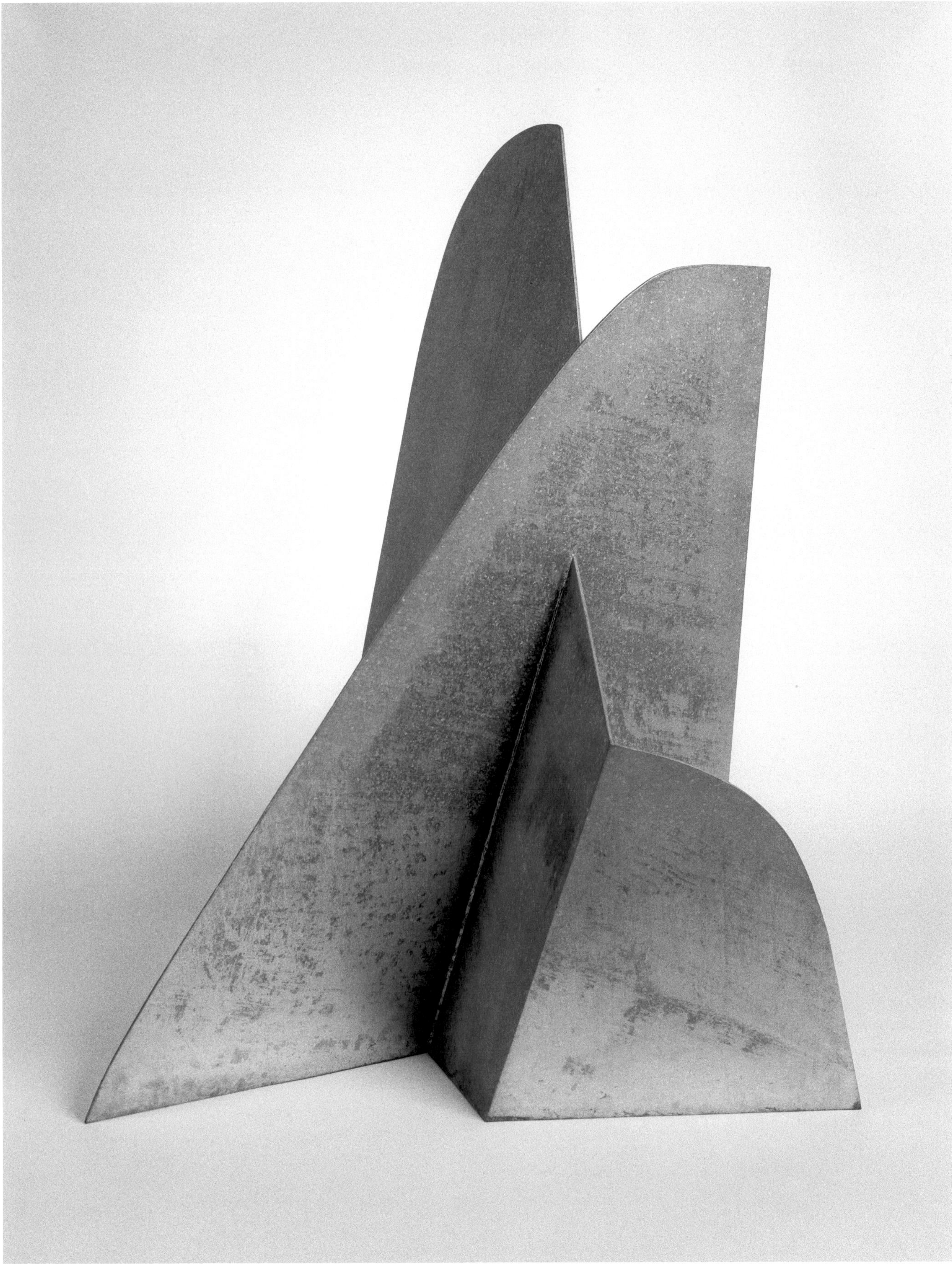

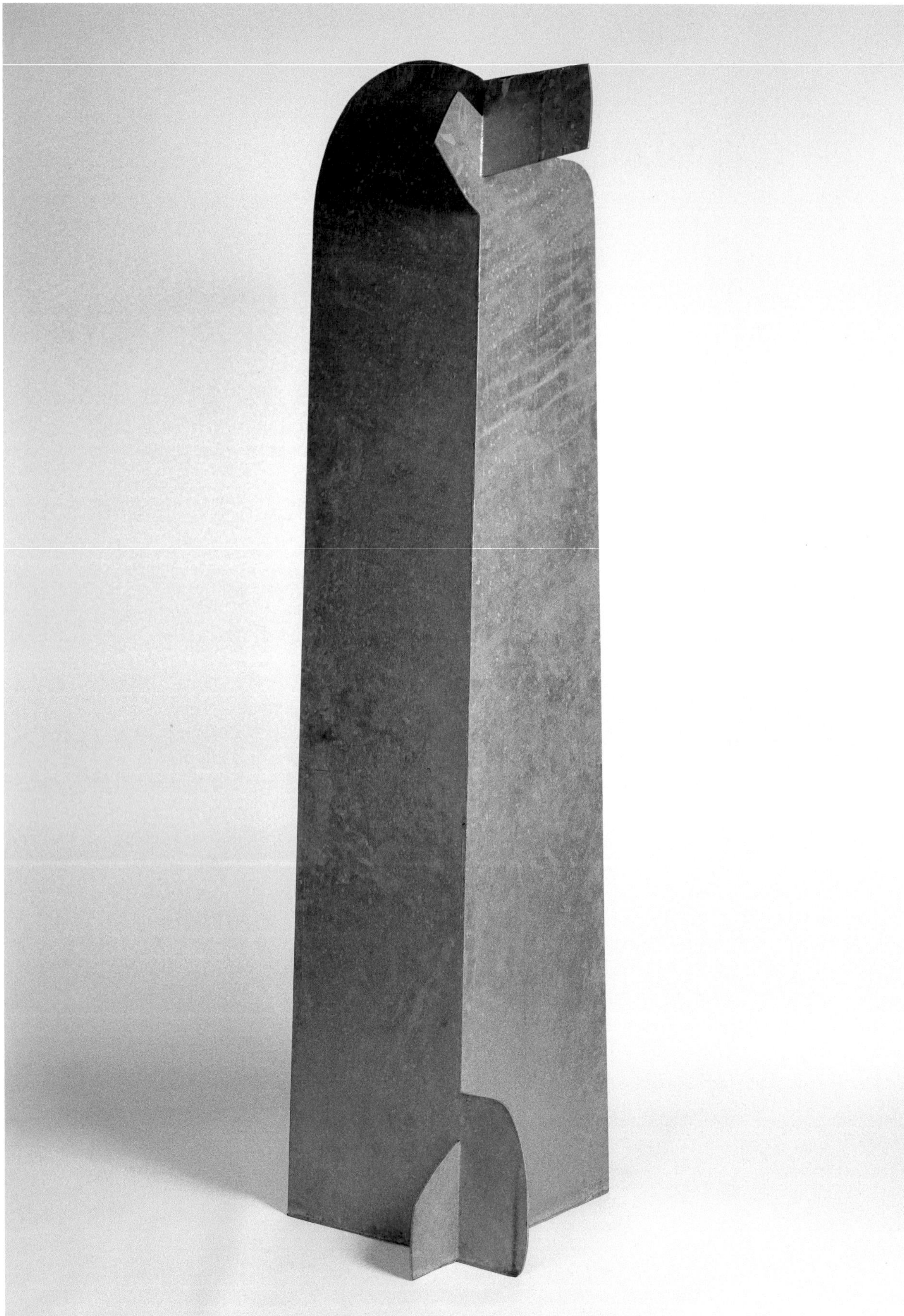

Duo, 1982–83
(fabricated 2020)
Galvanised steel
222.3 × 67.3 × 61 cm

Kyōko-san, 1984
Andesite
162.6 × 53.3 × 30.5 cm

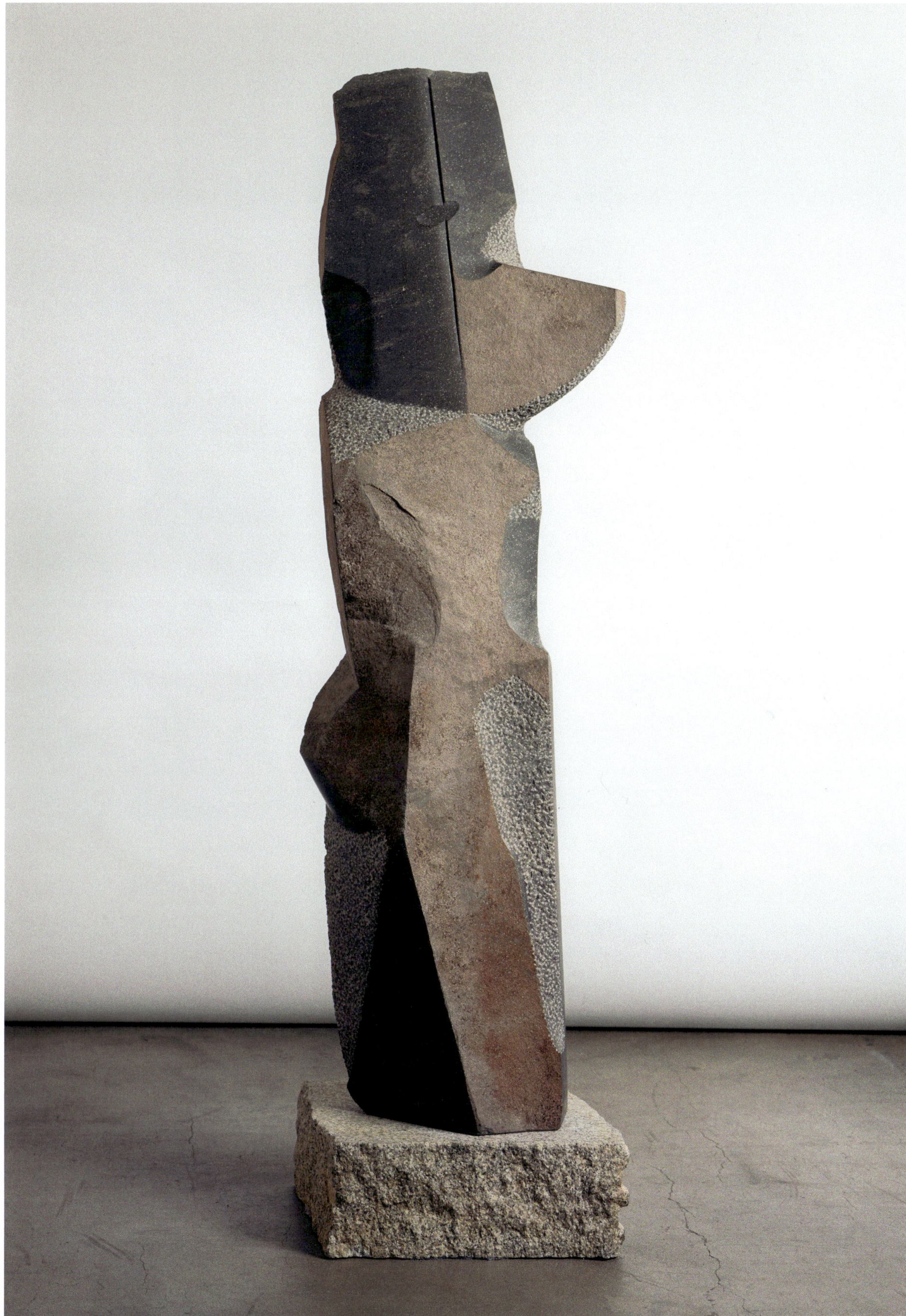

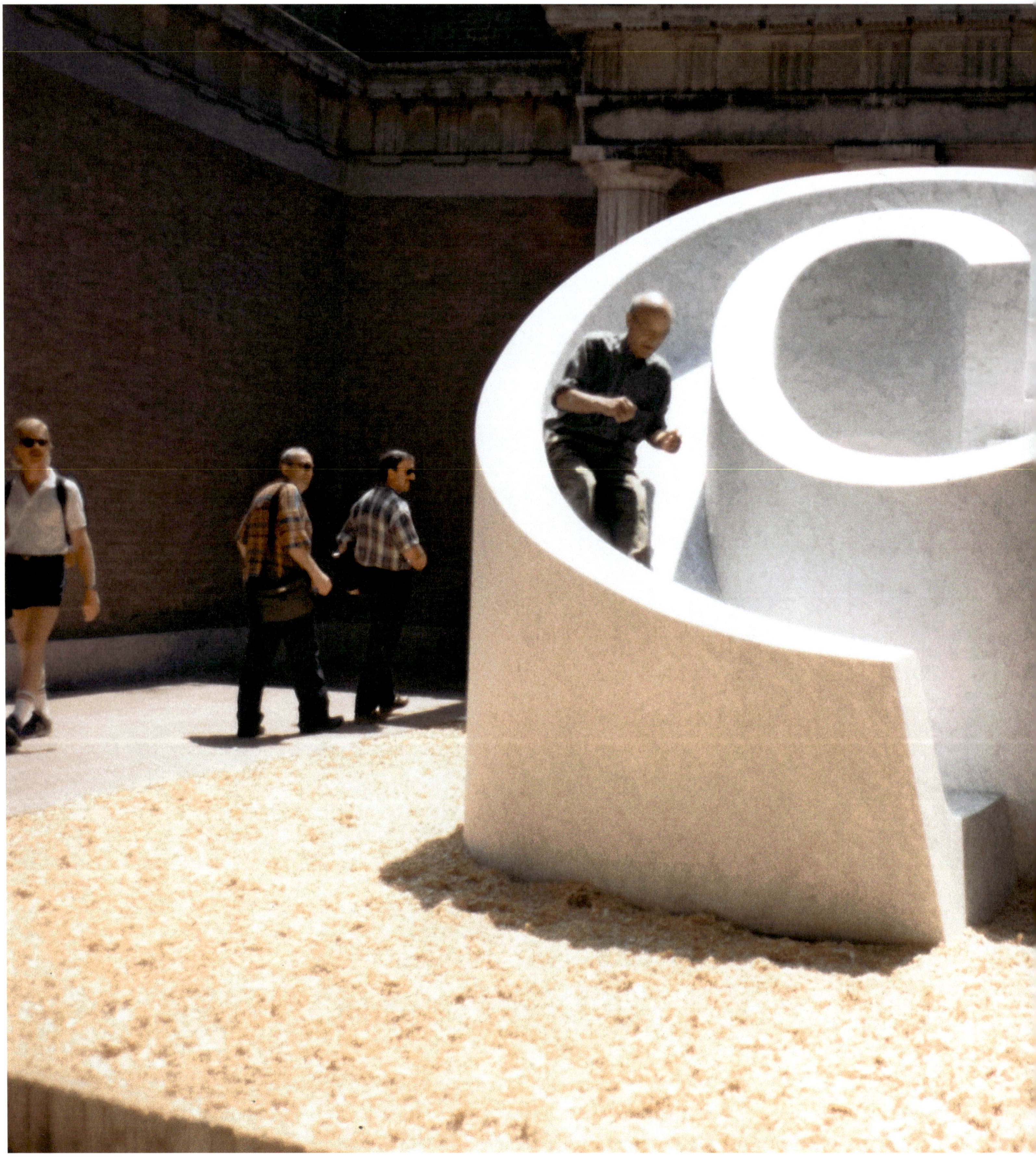

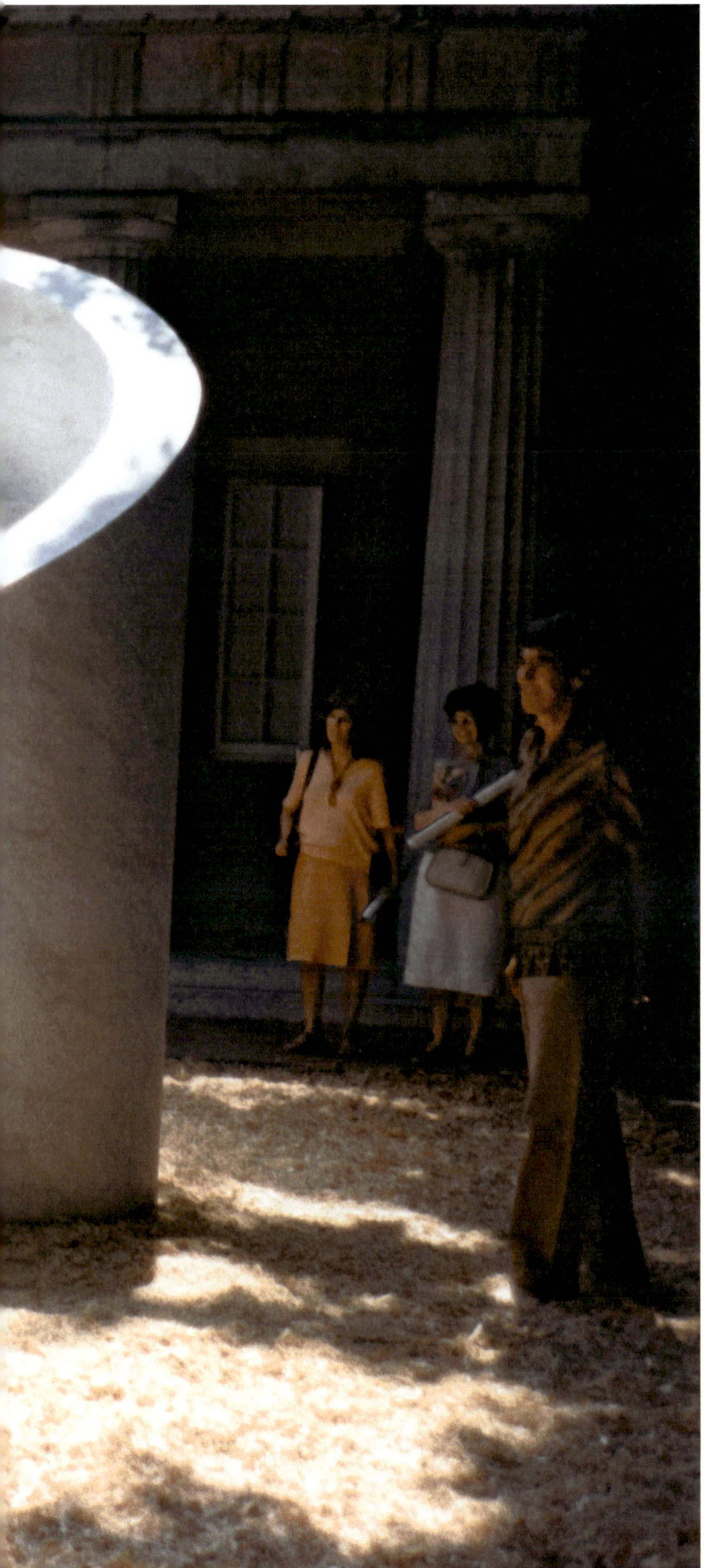

Noguchi tests *Slide Mantra* at *Isamu Noguchi: What is Sculpture?*, US Pavilion, Venice Biennale, 1986

TRANSNATIONALISM AND THE WORK OF NOGUCHI

A conversation between Karen L. Ishizuka, Katy Siegel, Danh Vo and Devika Singh (chair)

Devika Singh: I'd like to begin by asking how you believe Noguchi fits into a transnational history of American art.

Karen L. Ishizuka: As a Japanese American, Noguchi has been, I think, undervalued not only within American art but also Japanese American and Asian American art and culture. From this perspective, he is particularly significant for being one of the few people who voluntarily went into one of the American incarceration camps set up during the Second World War by the government for the forced incarceration of Japanese Americans, and also for the fact that that he never thought of himself as a Japanese American, as a Nisei [second-generation Japanese American], until that time. I think that there's a tendency for cultural groups – especially minoritised groups in the US – to be lumped together as homogeneous. Certainly, Noguchi is an artist who exemplifies the rich diversity of Japanese America.

I think of Noguchi as a-national, in terms of his identity. He had dual nationality – he was Japanese and American – but in his personhood he said he never felt comfortable in either one.

Katy Siegel: Because Noguchi spoke and wrote so much, there's an opportunity to understand him as a specific individual, rather than as representational of an identity. And because he exhibited from the very beginning in the US and then in Japan, there's also a long history of recognition of his work – even if it's troubled in many ways – that provides almost a historiography of the understanding of transnational art. There's a stress, often a racist one, on an East–West duality in his identity and work, which then shifts towards a notion of hybrid identity in the writings of Tom Hess and Dore Ashton.[1] We can follow that line through the biographies of Noguchi, the work of Bert Winther-Tamaki and Amy Lyford, and more recent scholarship: it's almost an arc tracing the understanding and the refiguration of transnationalism and its tensions, as Margo Machida and others have written about, between Asian American art history, American art history, modernist art history, and a cosmopolitan or transnational history.[2] Noguchi provides the perfect lens to reveal all these complexities.

DS: Karen, you've said that you believe Noguchi was a-national and added that he didn't quite understand himself to be a Nisei until his voluntary internment in 1942. At the same time, later on in his life Noguchi also benefited – like all recognised American artists – from how unequally structured the art world remained and the advantages that being American afforded. He represented the United States at the Venice Biennale in 1986, though he seems to have first declined the invitation on the basis of having been interned during the Second World War. So there was this ambivalence, but one articulated from within American citizenship. How should we address the experience of nationality and how it may have shaped artists' lives and reception?

Danh Vo: As the son of immigrants and as an artist, I of course relate to some of these questions about belonging and identification, which are so important to understanding Noguchi and his work. National identity shaped, even created, certain ways for Noguchi to work and to think. But the mechanisms of that are beyond him in that he could not change basic biographical factors. For me it's what he did with this information about himself that matters. When I look at artists, it's the kinship of certain ideas that I seek. These ideas have to be able to transgress artistic and national categories – not pretending they don't exist, but using them to create something new and surprising. Where I feel the closest affiliation with Noguchi is in the intense person we find behind and beyond all these labels. He had no choice but to understand his categorisation as Japanese and American. Japanese internment branded him forever as not fully belonging to a US context. At the same time, when he went to Japan and was asked by Kenzō Tange and the mayor of Hiroshima to do a project for the Hiroshima Peace Memorial Park, his *Memorial to the Dead, Hiroshima* (1949–55) was rejected by the committee, possibly because they found out he was American.

What attracts me in the way that Noguchi worked is that he used these constraints in an interesting way: he dealt with them, he confronted them. Noguchi would take a situation and make something really fantastic out of it. That's something I'm very inspired by.

DS: Following from this, what are the pitfalls of addressing artists through their nationality or a purely biographical lens? I'm thinking, Katy, of the exhibition *Postwar: Art between the Pacific and the Atlantic, 1945–1965*, which you co-curated with Okwui Enwezor and Ulrich Wilmes at Haus der Kunst in Munich (2016–17). You focused on artists who, for various reasons, were long underrepresented. At the same time, you suggested new formal and thematic affinities and dialogues among artists. These moved away from personal trajectories and emphasised the aesthetic and historical forces that motivated their art.

1 See Thomas B. Hess, 'Isamu Noguchi '46: An Art News Contemporary Contour', *Art News*, vol. 45, no. 7 (September 1946), pp. 34–38, 47–51; Dore Ashton, *Noguchi: East and West* (Berkeley and Los Angeles, CA: University of California Press, 1992).

2 For biographies of Noguchi, see Masayo Duus, *The Life of Isamu Noguchi: Life Without Borders*, trans. Peter Duus (Princeton, NJ: Princeton University Press, 2006), and Hayden Herrera, *Listening to Stone: The Art and Life of Isamu Noguchi* (New York: Farrar, Straus & Giroux, 2015). Bert Winther-Tamaki, 'Isamu Noguchi: Places of Affiliation and Disaffiliation', in *Art in the Encounter of Nations: Japanese and American Artists in the Early Postwar Years* (Honolulu, HI: University of Hawai'i Press, 2001), pp. 110–72; Amy Lyford, *Isamu Noguchi's Modernism: Negotiating Race, Labor, and Nation, 1930–1950* (Berkeley, Los Angeles and New York: University of California Press, 2013). For refiguration of transnationalism and its tensions, see for example Margo Machida, 'New Critical Directions: Transnationalism and Diaspora in Asian American Art', *Source: Notes in the History of Art*, vol. 31, no. 3 (Spring 2012), pp. 23–28, and 'Shifting Terrain: Mapping a Transnational American Art History', conference, Smithsonian American Art Museum, Washington, DC, 16–17 October 2015, and published papers in *American Art*, vol. 31, no. 2 (Summer 2017), pp. 62–117.

KS: We need to examine the way that art historians decide what's of value and what matters when we write art history. People have emphasised the US and western Europe, and then later eastern Europe, in post-war histories. Even when art historians have attempted to address the global, it's usually understood through governments and state actors, rather than artists. They tend to centre on what the Museum of Modern Art in New York was sending around the world in the 1950s, and not on the artists who were grappling with and living through experiences of mobility, containment or internment.

Noguchi was exemplary for the *Postwar* exhibition because it was about the world united - not in terms of universalism, but in a new geopolitical order based on mobility, continuous conflict among political and economic interests, the apocalyptic nature of new technology, and also new art forms. Noguchi felt pulled between multiple places; he travelled so much and was always in a shifting relation to nationality - as we've said, his Americanness was sometimes a privilege and at other times something he couldn't fully access. He was always on uneven ground. For all of these reasons, Noguchi really belongs at the centre - if there is one - not only of US art or Japanese art, but of a global post-war understanding.

DV: The way I think of it is that if you realise, at some point, that you don't belong to a certain category - that you're always pushed out, maybe because you are Asian and living in a different country - then you have to define yourself. It can be liberating, because as a human being you're now invited to question structures that seek to define what should or shouldn't be expressed. I always turn back to Noguchi because he dealt with this and used it in the best possible way - he didn't accept these exclusions; he defined his own reality. It's Noguchi's curiosity in the face of all this that's fascinating.

KI: I very much believe in the power of biography. As Noguchi stated, 'to be hybrid anticipates the future'.[3] He was not only biracial, he was also abandoned by his Japanese father, who now could arguably be considered bisexual.[4] He was taken by his white American mother to Japan at the age of three and lived there with her until he was thirteen, at which time she sent him back to the US by himself - to a boarding school in Indiana, of all places. His biography really shaped him. But at the same time, when you see someone's art primarily through a biographical lens, it preconceives and limits the art. For example, one of Noguchi's pieces, *Floor Frame* (1962), was inducted into the White House collection in 2020. The president of the White House Historical Association wrote that it was a symbol of the 'enduring relationship between the US and Japan',[5] thereby highlighting his biography, not his art. Then, on top of that, because Noguchi was the first Asian American artist to be included in the White House collection, he went on to minoritise Noguchi further by stating - or, rather, assuming - that it was a 'milestone for the Asian American community'. Since Noguchi was foremost an artist, I think he would have been aggrieved at this characterisation of his work.

DS: Do you think that the notion of craft, and the outdated and often culturally encoded distinction between art and craft or design, have further reduced and simplified the reading of Noguchi's multifaceted work?

3 Isamu Noguchi, 'I Become a Nisei', October 1942, p. 1, The Noguchi Museum Archives, MS_BIO_028_002.

4 See Amy Sueyoshi, *Queer Compulsions: Race, Nation, and Sexuality in the Affairs of Yone Noguchi* (Honolulu, HI: University of Hawai'i Press, 2012).

5 Stewart D. McLaurin, 'Isamu Noguchi's American Story: How a Small Sculpture Made a Big Impact at the White House', www.artnews.com, 24 November 2020.

KI: I think the division between craft, design and fine art is being broken down, and Noguchi definitely stands as a paean to that. It reminds me of the artist Shinkichi Tajiri (1923–2009) – who, by the way, worked with Noguchi in Poston. Tajiri fought in Europe as part of the 442nd Regimental Combat Team [made up almost entirely of Nisei soldiers] during the war. Despite that, when he returned to the US, he was still called a 'Jap'. So he left again and lived out his life in the Netherlands. Like Noguchi, everything Tajiri touched turned to art – he made no distinction between craft and fine art. This feeds into what Danh was saying about the ability of artists to use whatever comes up in their life in a fashion that other people wouldn't think of. That really is the artist's genius and their contribution to the understanding of humans in society.

DV: Precisely. This is my attraction to Noguchi. When we talk about transnational definitions and categories and how they constrain and also inspire art making, the same problem lies within any art production. There are always definitions and categories – social, material, aesthetic – to engage with, sidestep or even just play with. When I saw the exhibition of Noguchi's playgrounds, *Noguchi's Playscapes* (2017), at Museo Tamayo in Mexico City, I understood that play was the cradle of his inspiration. Play was how he transgressed categories; it was, for example, how he was able to find a way to redefine the lamp. Some have tried to separate what they call his 'design' from his sculpture. I think that's wrong, because Noguchi's thinking transgressed whatever he touched.

KS: This refusal of artistic categories can also be seen in other artists in the United States, like Toshiko Takaezu (1922–2011), and also in someone like Demas Nwoko (b. 1935) in Nigeria, who studied ancient Nok terracotta and traditional firing techniques. These experiences with different media and traditions provide an artist with more possibilities, more things she sees and wants to access.

Noguchi was in so many shows in US museums in the 1930s, 1940s and early 1950s – before the idea of what is 'American' gets reduced, not only in terms of gender, sexual orientation, ethnicity and race but in terms of practice. In 1936, he showed *Miss Expanding Universe* (1932) in *Fantastic Art, Dada, Surrealism* [organised by MoMA], in which many kinds of art were visible and appreciated, from folk art to art from the sixteenth century. But by 1958, the exhibition *The New American Painting as Shown in Eight European Countries* [organised by MoMA and which toured Europe in 1958–59] reduced the idea of contemporary American art to abstract painting – not even sculpture – by a small group of primarily white men and one woman, and Noguchi's vision was excised from the narrative. It's important to remember how much more diverse and expansive art was, even just in New York, before it got marketed and packaged by the State Department and by the art market.

DV: And even with all this Noguchi was a survivor. How do we look at this artist whose production lasted so many decades? There's the range of things he went through, which one has to take into consideration; the many phases in his career. He managed to leave behind this beautiful production in this myriad of possibilities. Perhaps the main problem, in my opinion, in looking at Noguchi's work is that it leads to stone sculpture, which is something he felt he needed to do – but why did he need his work to lead there? That being said, I believe in it. He spoke of stone as a soft material, and of water as the strength behind it. It was Félix Gonzáles-Torres who taught me that culture exists when it's needed. One can't force it. That's the brilliance of art production.

KI: Following from what has been said about historiography, and about how what is considered art has changed, do you think there's a wider understanding and appreciation worldwide of Noguchi's work today?

KS: I certainly think so. Partly because of the increasing interest in a wider range of materials and media, and also because of the expansive practices of artists like Danh, which are so much more in tune with what Noguchi was doing. Devika, maybe this is something you should also answer.

DS: In Europe, this exhibition is likely to play a major role. Audiences may not have a holistic understanding of his work, given that Noguchi hasn't had a major exhibition in Europe for many years, though they may have a few works in mind in addition to the famed *Coffee Table* and the *Akari* light sculptures. How artists relate to one another today, and who inspires them, is also something Noguchi's legacy is currently benefiting from.

This brings me to the transhistorical dimension of Noguchi's influences. When Noguchi worked in stone he was engaging, through this material, with classical Rome and overlapping a variety of references. In India, he projected Roman and Greek influences onto the eighteenth-century astronomical observatories of Delhi and Jaipur, known as the Jantar Mantar. This reveals misunderstandings, but it also pertains to artists' imagination and creative process. This phenomenon has led to the making of hybrid artworks, by Noguchi and others, that draw from a variety of sources across geographies and time periods.

DV: As I get older, when I look at stone, it becomes more and more about history, and a history that goes way beyond our own. It took me a long time to really get into Noguchi's stone sculptures. Noguchi talked about how it didn't matter if he did something wrong – if he curved something and it didn't really work. It's the expansion of his thinking that one should look for in his sculptures.

KS: One of the most important things about Noguchi is that he took a narrow, provincial concept of formalism and reframed it as materiality. Instead of fixating on a tiny point in the history of modernism, he engages with a big history: he visits the pyramids of Egypt, he goes to the Acropolis, and he has very specific relationships to place and material – ceramics, bronze, stone and plaster, and the sort of 'space age' materials like aluminium. At a time when many artists in New York were competing to see who could make the flattest painting, Noguchi's work was so much more capacious.

DV: Noguchi was almost a Pop artist in that sense: whatever material he came across, he made use of, engaging with it and updating or modifying his own approach. It comes down to curiosity. And just as he was curious about materials, he was curious about himself and what he could and should seek to achieve.

KI: We have a Noguchi plaza here in Los Angeles, at the Japanese American Cultural and Community Center in Little Tokyo. In the middle is a large stepped brick mound that people can sit and climb on. At the top is a stone sculpture that he titled *To the Issei* (1980–83). In addition to being, I think, the only one of his works that directly acknowledges his Japanese American heritage, the sculpture is remarkable in light of his fraught relationship with his Issei [first-generation] father, and how Noguchi tried to become a Nisei, as he put it, during the war but was not accepted as such.[6]

6 See Noguchi, 'I Become a Nisei'.

So it's poignant to think of him coming home – to his birthplace – to erect this plaza and sculpture within a contemporary Japanese American space. You might even say that it's the playground he wanted to make at the Poston camp but never did. And because the plaza is so embraced by the community – being used for festivals, performances, protests – in a way it feels like a homecoming: that Noguchi has finally become a Japanese American, finally becoming the Nisei he wanted to be.

DV: Noguchi's work also has a kind of elusive quality. A lot of his projects were destroyed during his lifetime. There's a certain beauty in, on the one hand, being an artist and being the author of something, and on the other hand knowing that things aren't going to last. That makes Noguchi different from a lot of artists of his generation, and from my generation too. You think your work means so much, but in the long term, and when you look at granite that has existed for millions of years, it doesn't matter that much.

KS: When he conceived the earthwork *Sculpture to be Seen from Mars* (1947), he means it is to be seen not only as if from a great distance, but also from thousands of years in the future, with the artist himself long gone. Also, Noguchi never develops a signature style – a bounded, categorisable and recognisable style – which is part of his struggle with recognition. He didn't have a self-concept that was heavy and unchanging.

DV: At the difficult time of the creation of American art history, there was Noguchi, quietly resisting.

Karen L. Ishizuka is Chief Curator of the Japanese American National Museum, Los Angeles
Katy Siegel is the Thaw Endowed Chair in Modern American Art at Stony Brook University, New York, and a Senior Research Curator at Baltimore Museum of Art
Danh Vo is an artist based in Berlin and Mexico City
Conversation chaired by Devika Singh, Curator, International Art at Tate Modern, London

EXPLORATIONS

Photographs by Isamu Noguchi

Isamu travelled on and on, not as a tourist, not as a dilettante escapist, not as a routine airline pilot, nor as sailor, soldier or gypsy, but as the intuitive artist precursor of the evoluting, kinetic one-town world man. As the unselfconscious prototype artist of the new cosmos, Isamu has always been inherently at home – everywhere. He has to-and-froed in his great back and front yards whose eastward and westward extensions finally merged to encircle the earth … it proved biologically and intellectually impossible for him to escape his fate of being a founding member of an omni-crossbred world society.

R. Buckminster Fuller, 1967

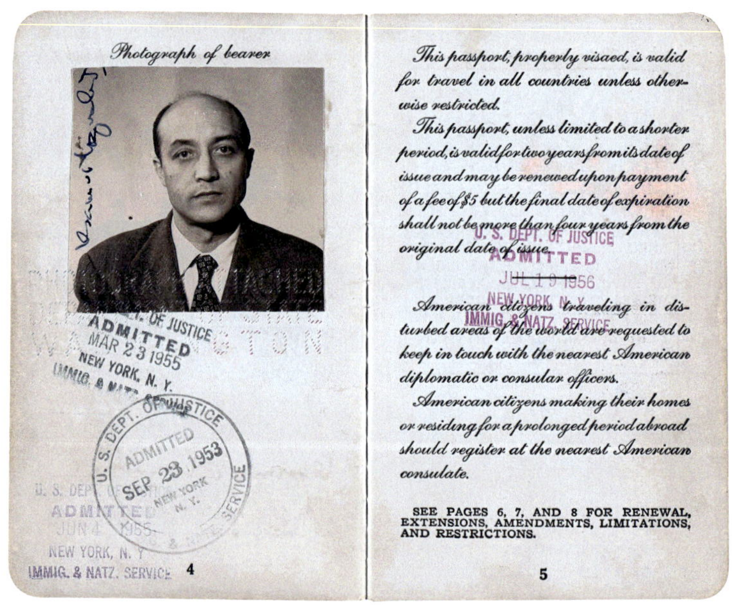
Photograph of bearer

4

This passport, properly visaed, is valid for travel in all countries unless otherwise restricted.

This passport, unless limited to a shorter period, is valid for two years from its date of issue and may be renewed upon payment of a fee of $5 but the final date of expiration shall not be more than four years from the original date of issue.

American citizens traveling in disturbed areas of the world are requested to keep in touch with the nearest American diplomatic or consular officers.

American citizens making their homes or residing for a prolonged period abroad should register at the nearest American consulate.

SEE PAGES 6, 7, AND 8 FOR RENEWAL, EXTENSIONS, AMENDMENTS, LIMITATIONS, AND RESTRICTIONS.

5

Isamu Noguchi's US passport, 27 April 1953

Noguchi in Machu Picchu, Peru, 1983

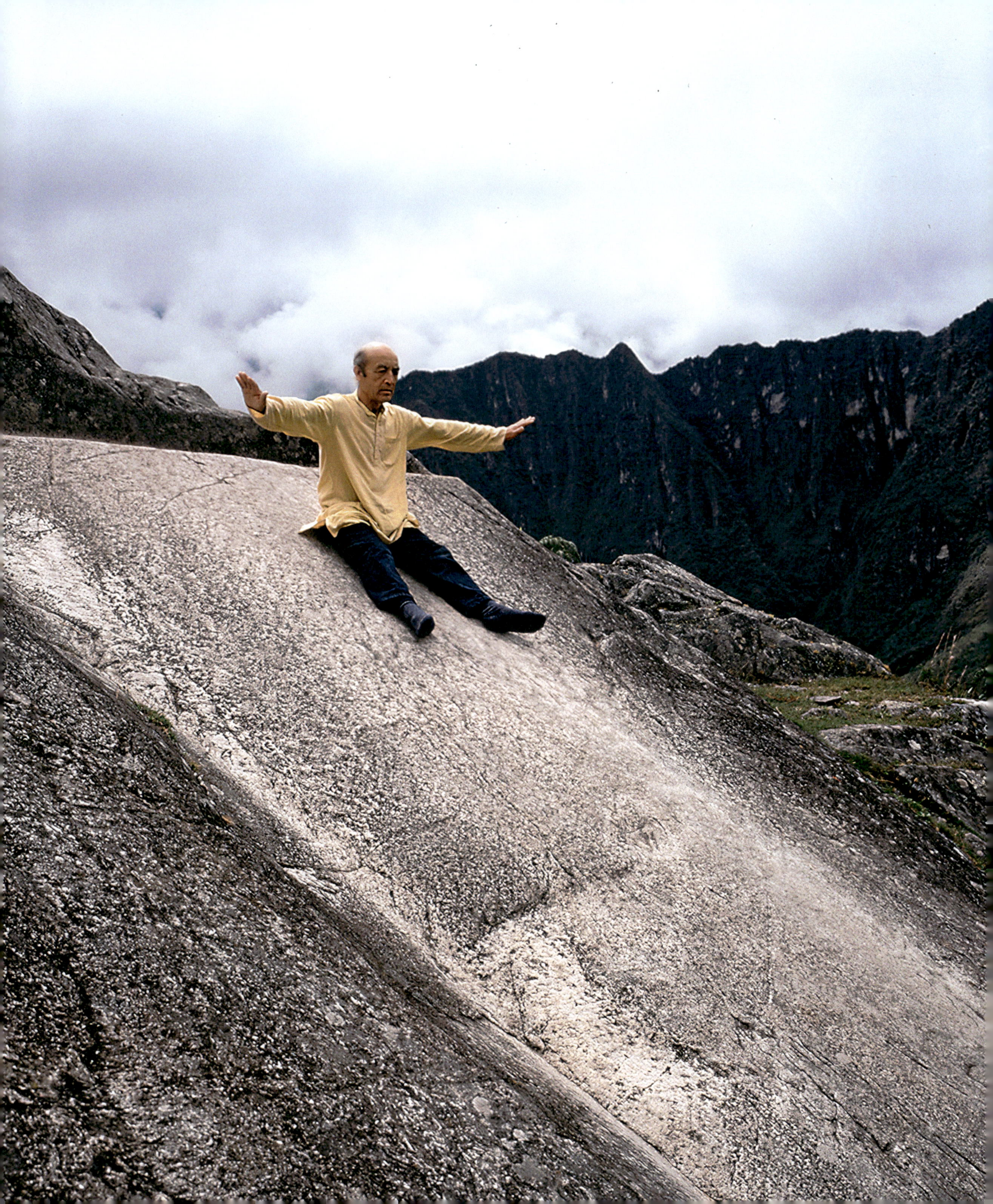

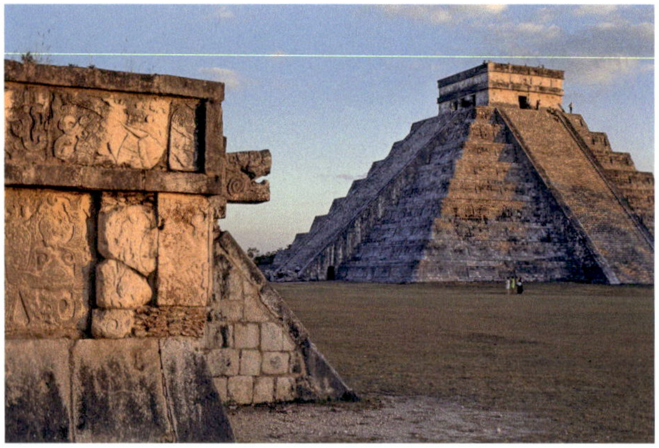

Chichen Itza, Yucatán, Mexico, 1970s

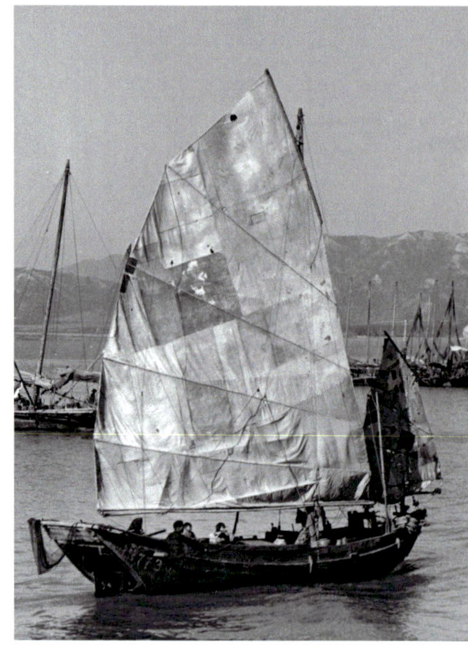

Junk in Victoria Harbour, Hong Kong, 1953–54

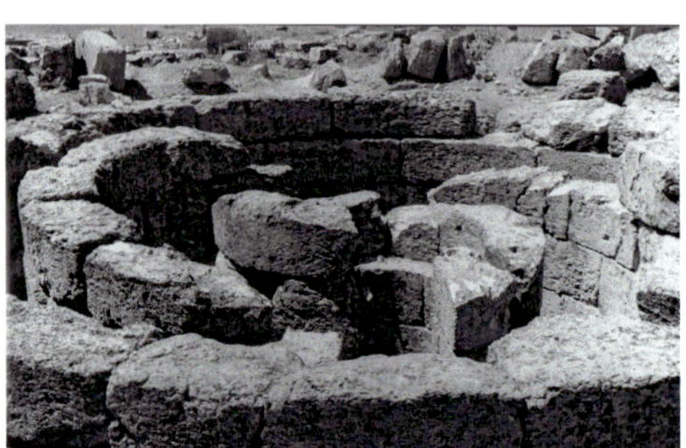

The Tholos at Epidaurus, Greece, 1949

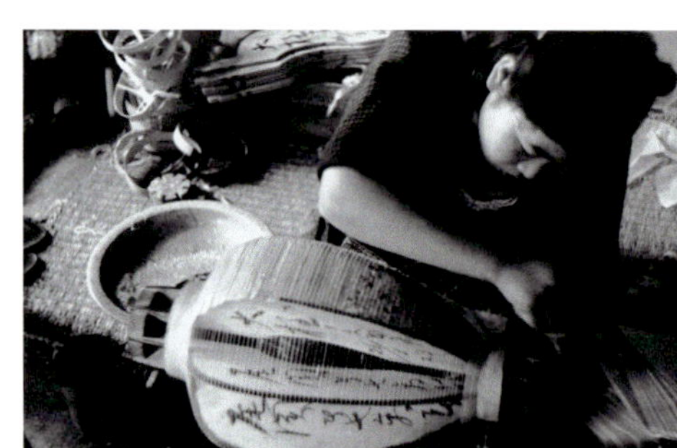

Lantern maker, Gifu, Japan, 1951

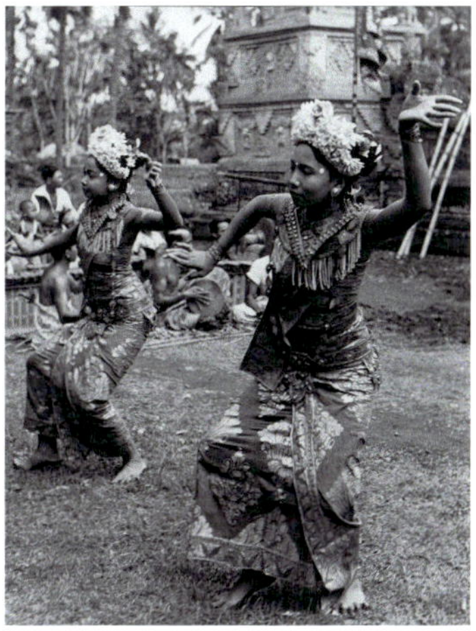

Dancers, Bali, Indonesia, c. 1950–54

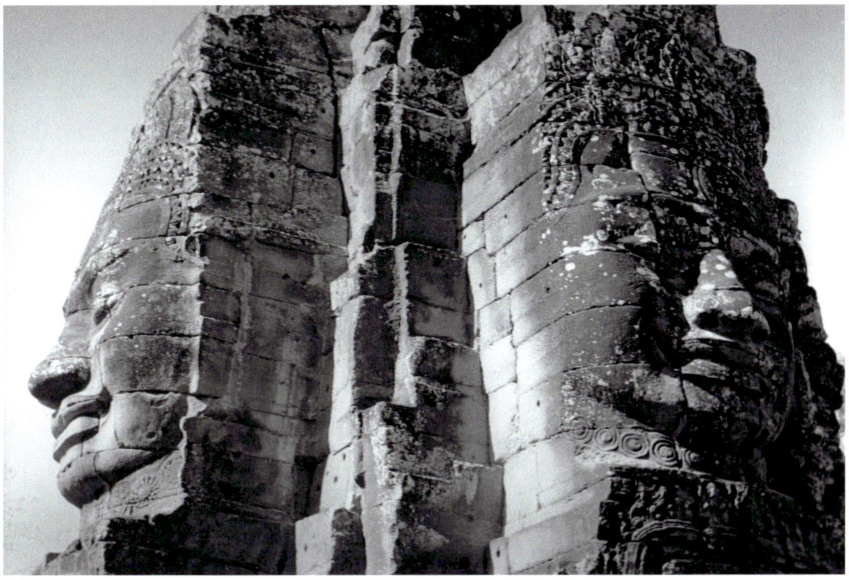

Bayon temple, Angkor Thom, Cambodia, 1950

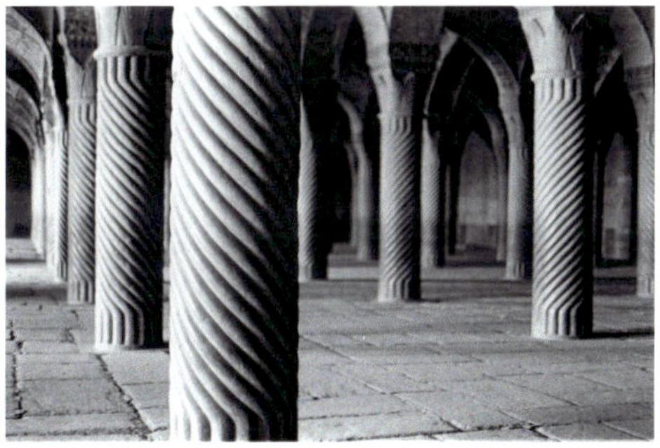

Shabestan (prayer hall) at Vakil Mosque, Shiraz, Iran, 1966

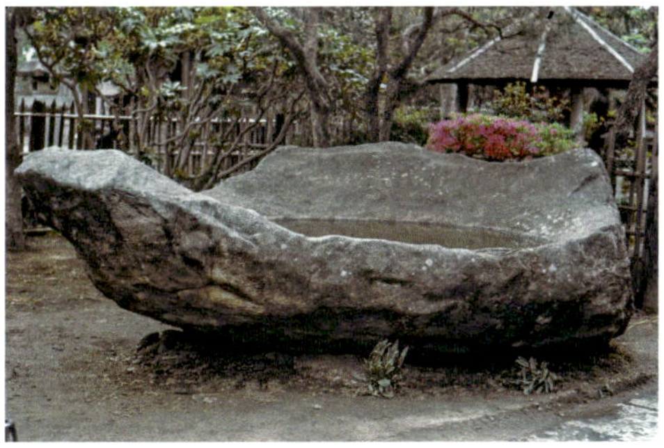

River stone used as a basin, Japan, 1960s

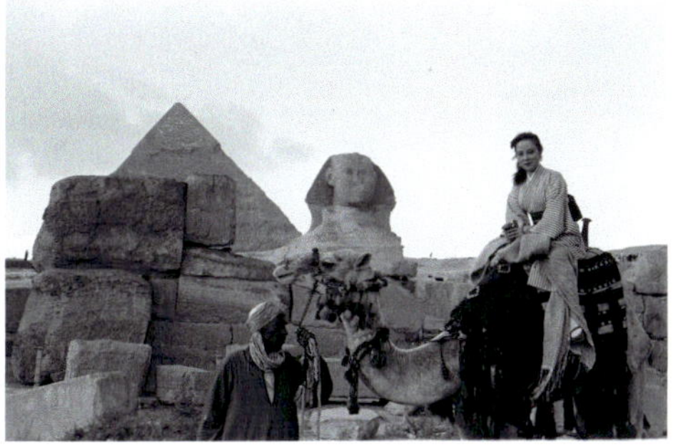

Yoshiko 'Shirley' Yamaguchi in Giza, Egypt, 1953

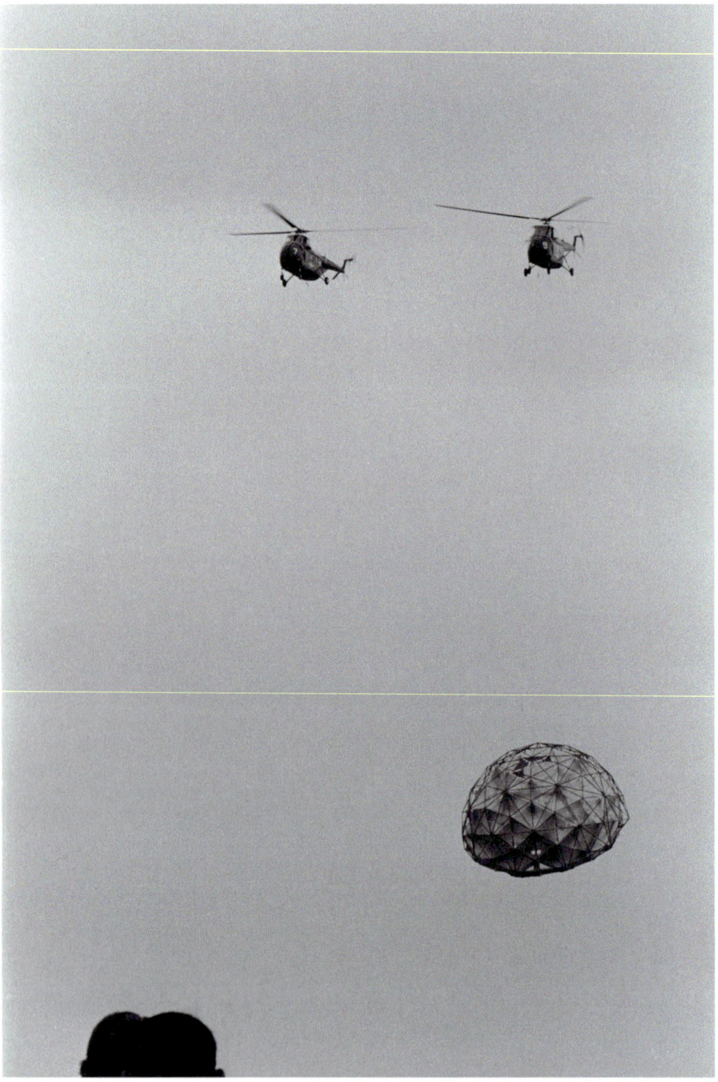

One of R. Buckminster Fuller's geodesic domes being airlifted by Marine Corps helicopters at the National Aircraft Show, Philadelphia, on Labor Day, 1955

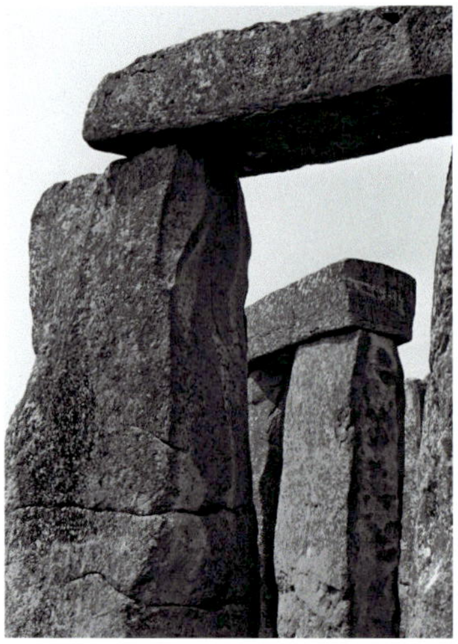

Stonehenge, Wiltshire, England, c. 1955

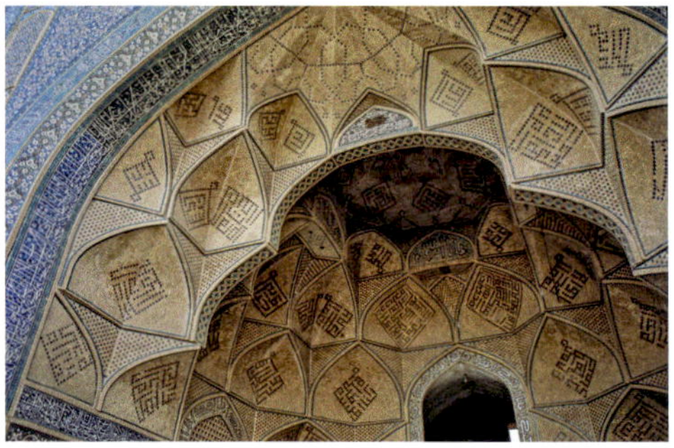

The Jameh Mosque of Isfahan, Iran, 1966

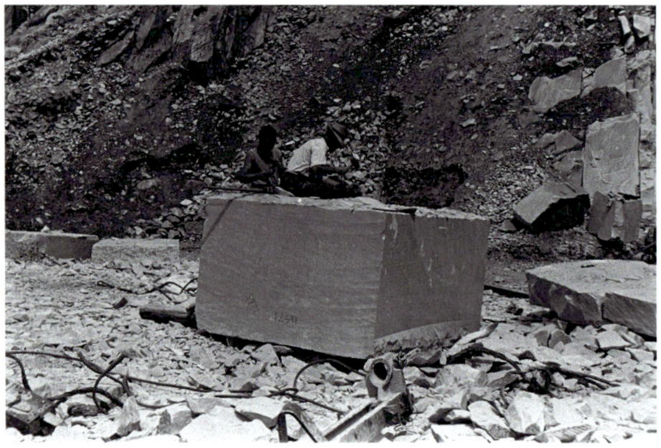

Marble quarry, Carrara, Italy, 1953

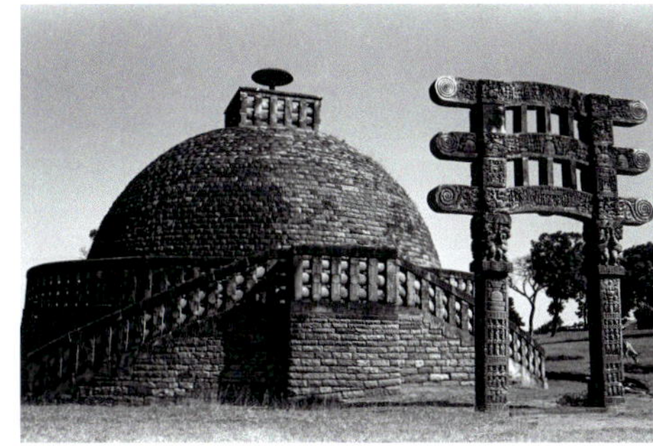

The Great Stupa at Sanchi, Madhya Pradesh, India, 1949

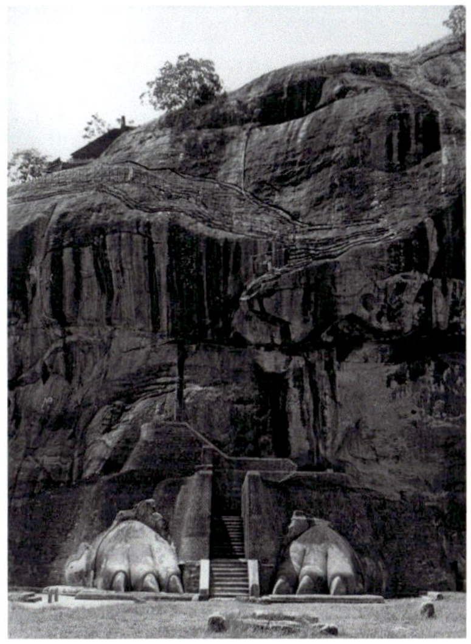

Sigiriya, Sri Lanka, 1949

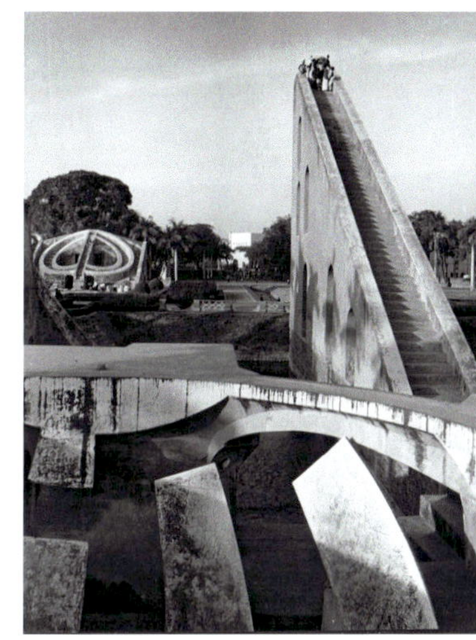

Jantar Mantar observatory, Delhi, India, 1960

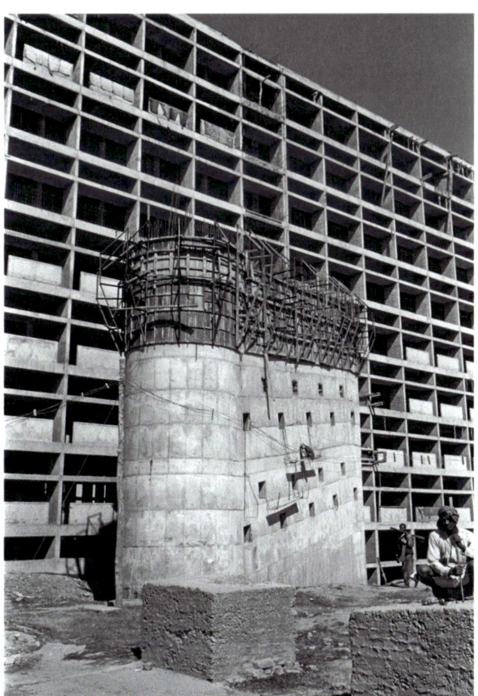

The Secretariat building, designed by Le Corbusier, under construction in Chandigarh, India, 1951

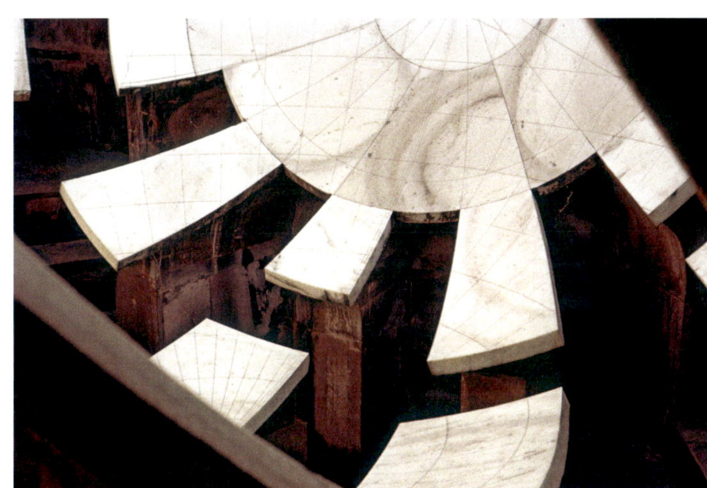

The Jai Prakash astronomical instrument, Jantar Mantar observatory, Delhi, India, 1960

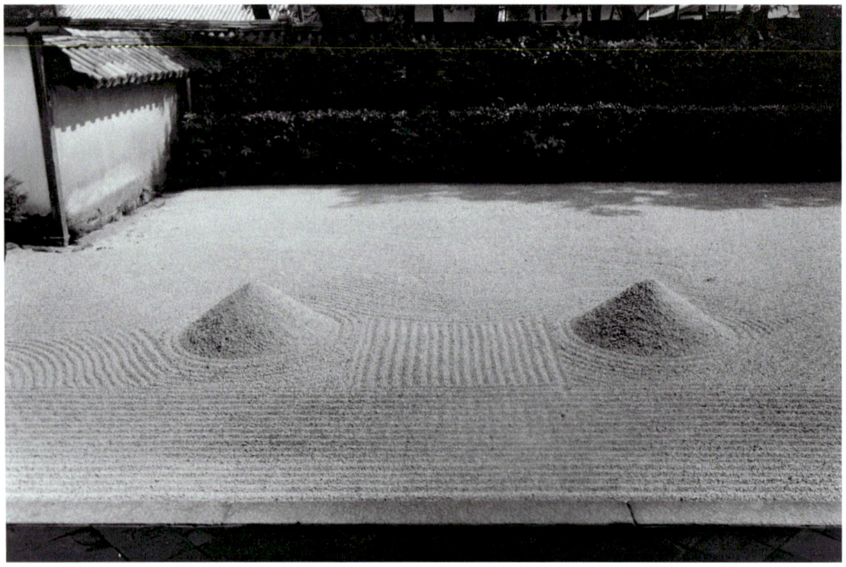

Zen garden at Daisen-in temple, Daitoku-ji, Kyoto, Japan, c. 1950

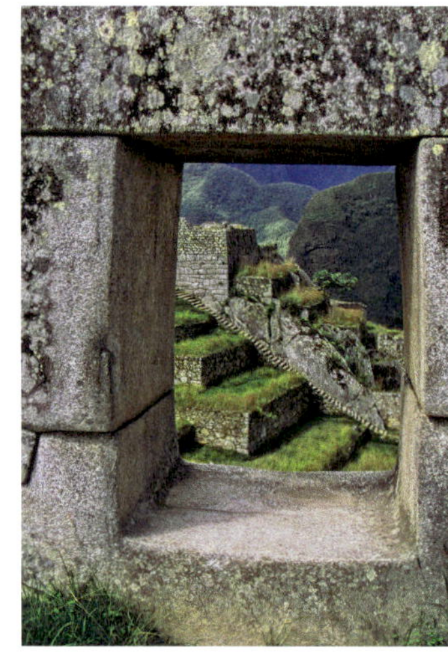

Temple of the Three Windows, Machu Picchu, Peru, 1983

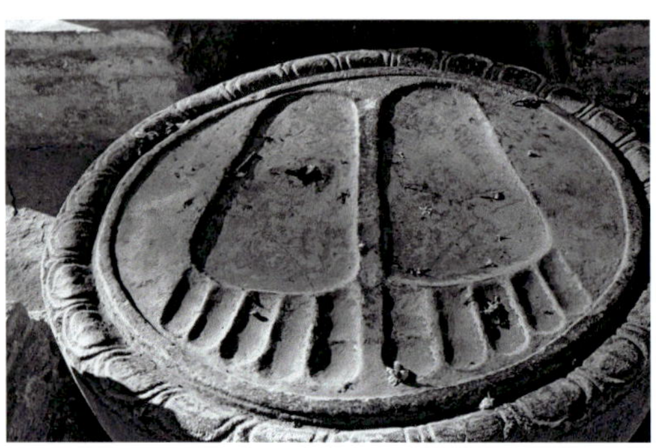

Mahabodhi Temple complex, Bodh Gaya, Bihar, India, 1949

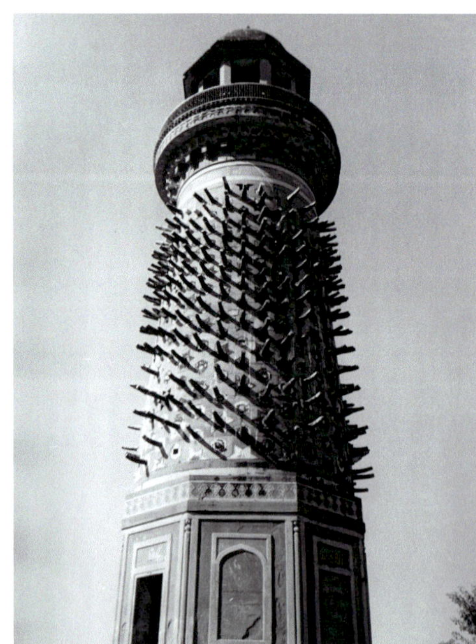

The Hiran Minar ('Elephant Tower'), Fatehpur Sikri, Uttar Pradesh, India, 1950s

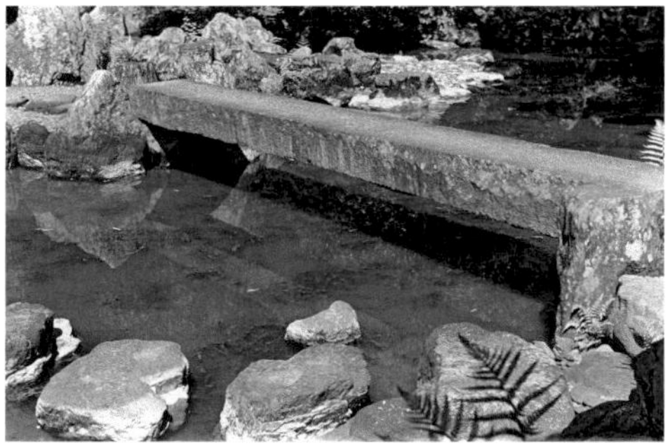

Katsura Imperial Villa, Kyoto, Japan, 1950s

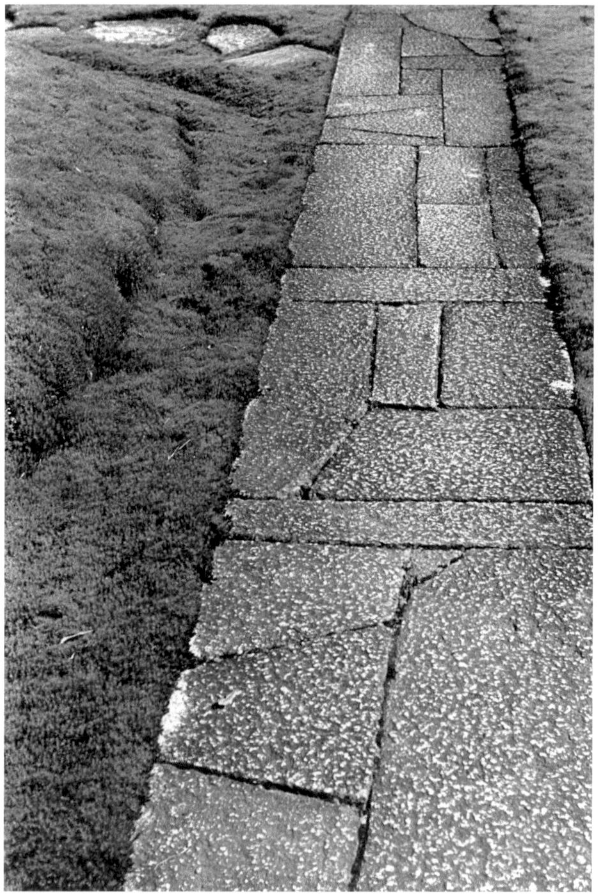

Katsura Imperial Villa, Kyoto, Japan, 1950s

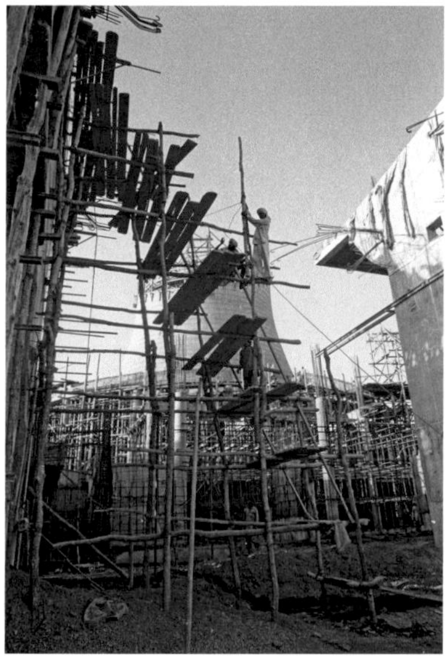

Construction at Chandigarh, India, 1960

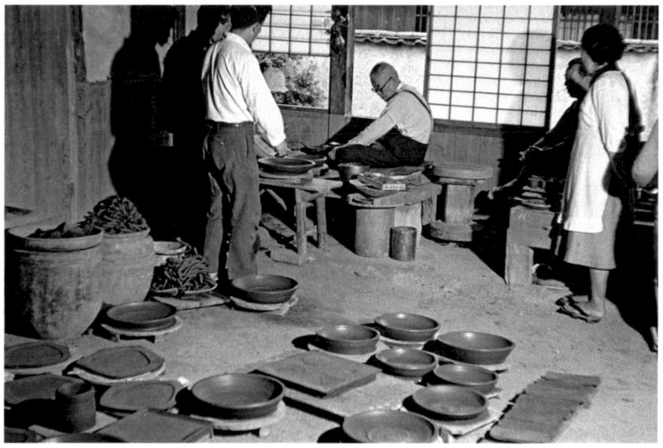

Kitaōji Rosanjin at work in the potter Tōyō Kaneshige's studio, Imbe, Okayama prefecture, Japan, May 1952

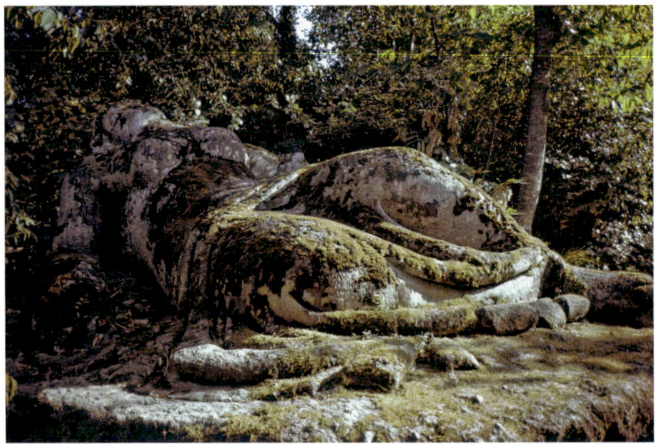

Parco dei Mostri, Bomarzo, Italy, 1962

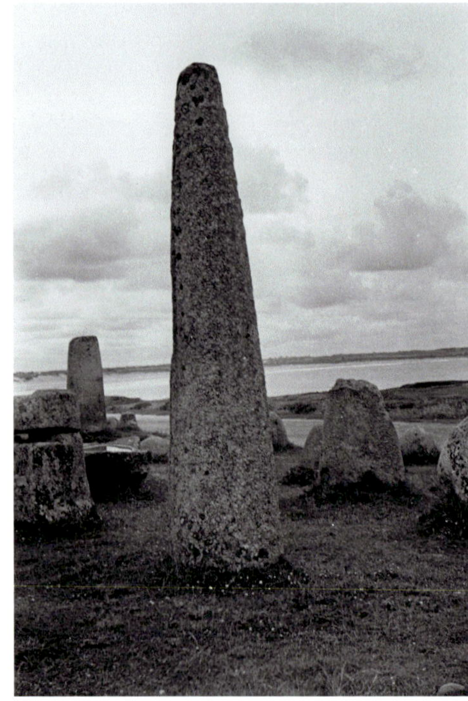

Standing stone at Carnac, Brittany, France, 1949

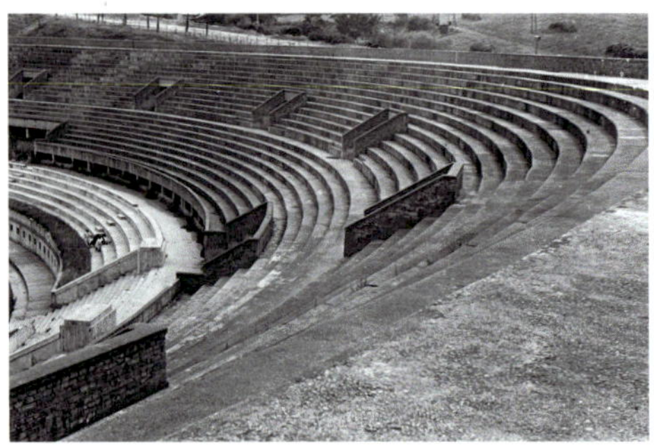

Stadio dei Marmi, Foro Italico, Rome, Italy, 1949

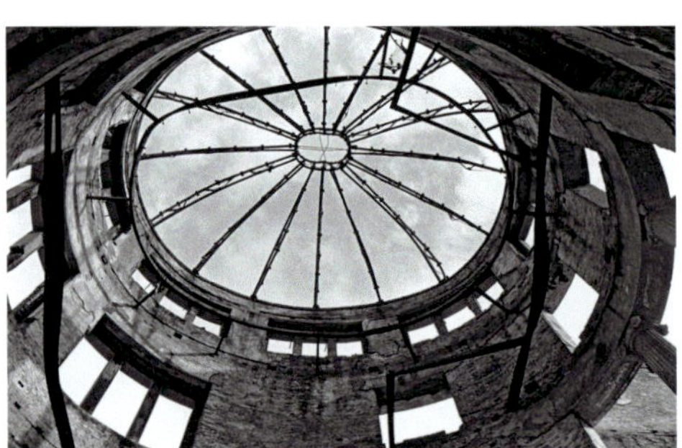

Interior of the Genbaku Dome (Hiroshima Peace Memorial), Hiroshima, Japan, 1951

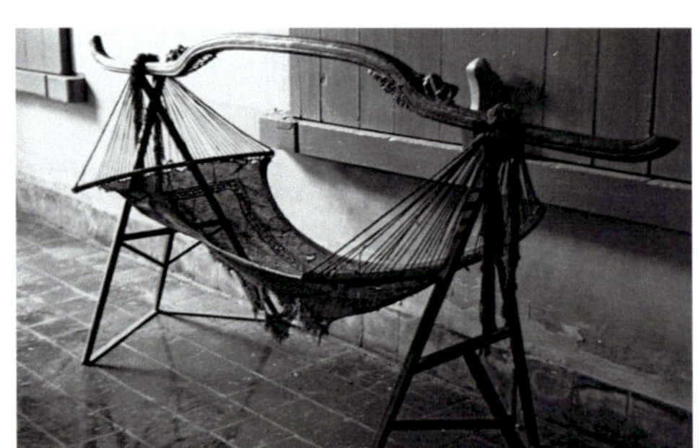

Museum in Cambodia, c. 1950s

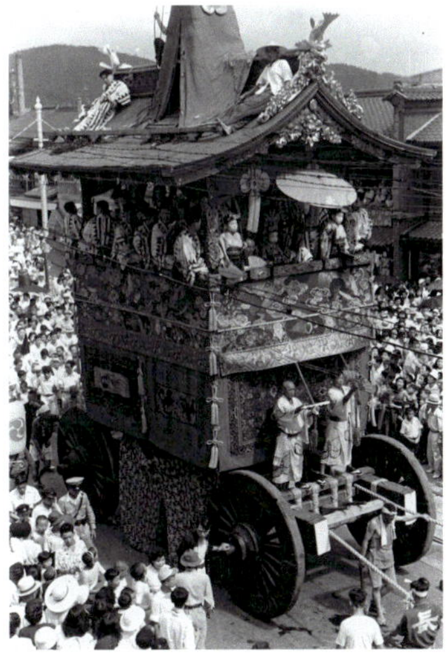

Danjiri Matsuri (cart-pulling festival), Japan, 1950s

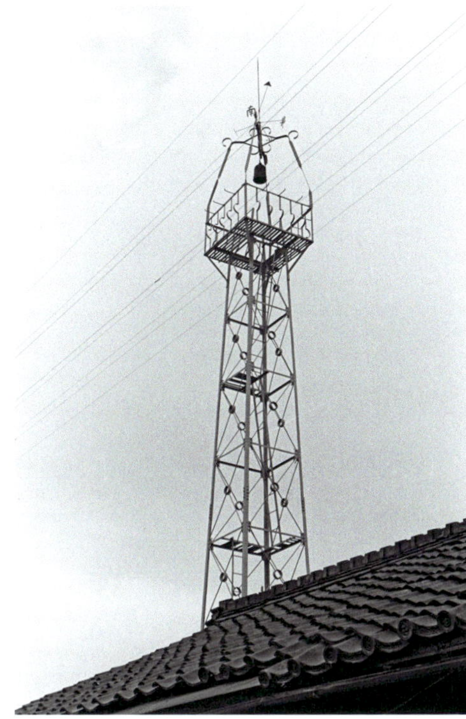

Fire lookout tower, Hiroshima, Japan, 1950s

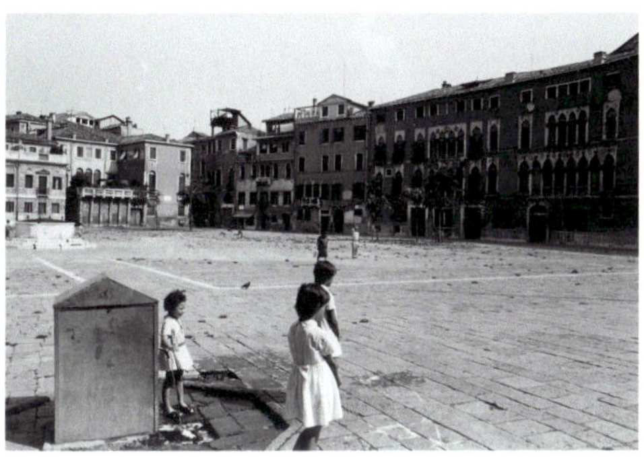

Piazza in Tuscany, Italy, 1970s

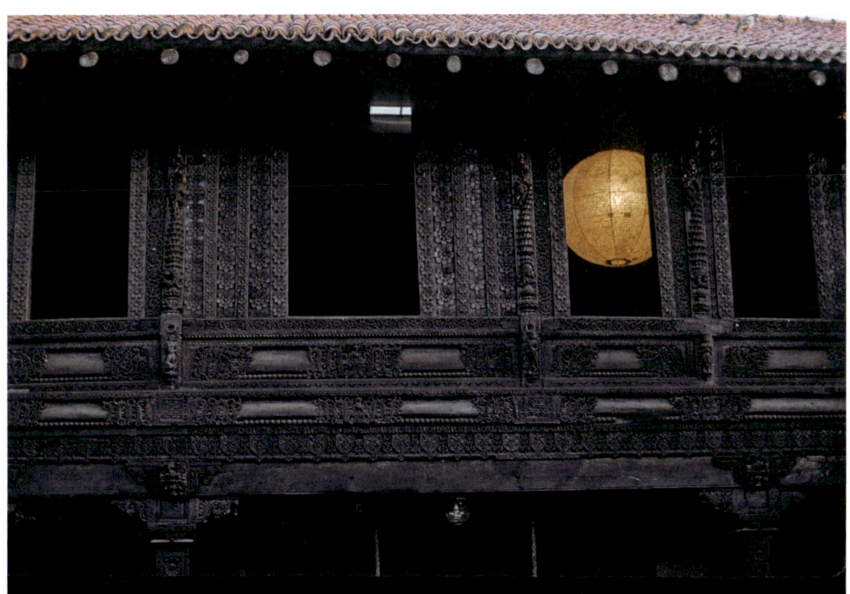

Akari 120A in the Villa Sarabhai, Ahmedabad, India, 1971

SELECTED TRAVELS AND STUDIOS

1904: Los Angeles, California, USA
1907: Japan
1918: Rolling Prairie and La Porte, Indiana, USA
1922: Connecticut and New York City, USA
1924–27: New York City studios, USA
1927: Paris and Gentilly, France
1928–30: Gentilly studios, France
1928: London, UK
1930: Chicago, Illinois, and Cambridge, Massachusetts, USA / Paris, France / Moscow, Russia / Beijing, China
1931: Kobe, Tokyo and Kyoto, Japan / Chicago, Illinois, and Hawaii, USA
1933: Haiti / Paris, France / London, UK
1934: Woodstock, New York, USA
1935: Havana, Cuba / Los Angeles, California, USA / Mexico City, Mexico
1939: Boston, Massachusetts, USA
1940: Hawaii, USA
1941: California, USA
1942: Poston War Relocation Center, Arizona, USA
1942–50: MacDougal Alley studio, Greenwich Village, New York City, USA
1945: Ohio, USA
1949: Paris, Brittany and Marseille, France / Switzerland / Rome, Florence, Naples, Pompeii, Lucca and Bergamo, Italy / Barcelona, Spain / Greece / Cairo and Luxor, Egypt / Ahmedabad, Jaipur, Delhi, Chennai, Varanasi, Bombay (Mumbai), Santiniketan and Orissa, India
1950: Colombo, Ceylon (Sri Lanka) / Java and Bali, Indonesia / Bangkok, Thailand / Angkor Wat, Cambodia / Hong Kong / Tokyo, Kyoto, Nara and Ise, Japan
1951: Tokyo, Gifu and Hiroshima, Japan / Los Angeles, California, USA / Europe / India
1952: Kamakura and Imbe, Japan
1952–54: Kita Kamakura studio, Japan
1953: Paris and Versailles, France / Carrara, Italy / Athens, Greece / Cairo and Luxor, Egypt / Burma (Myanmar) / Bangkok, Thailand / Hong Kong / Macau / Cambodia
1954: Indonesia / Singapore / Tokyo, Japan
1955: London, UK
1956: London, UK / Paris, France / Zurich, Switzerland / Karachi, Pakistan / Kathmandu, Nepal / Patna and Calcutta (Kolkata), India / Hong Kong / Kyoto, Japan
1957: Osaka, Shikoku and Okayama, Japan / Paris, France
1958: Japan / Greece / Paris, France
1959: Paris, France / London, UK / Rome, Italy
1960: Jerusalem / Japan / Chandigarh, New Delhi and Jaipur, India
1961–88: Long Island City studio, Queens, New York City, USA
1962: Israel / Rome and Tuscany, Italy
1964–88: Tuscany studio, Italy
1966: Iran / Venice, Italy
1967: New York City, USA / Mure, Japan / Tuscany, Italy
1967–88: Mure studio, Japan
1969: Bellingham, Washington, USA
1971: Munich, Germany / Israel
1972: London, UK / Zurich, Switzerland
1976: Honolulu, Hawaii, USA
1977: Honolulu, Hawaii, USA
1981: Romania
1983: Peru
1985: Mexico City, Mexico
1988: Greece

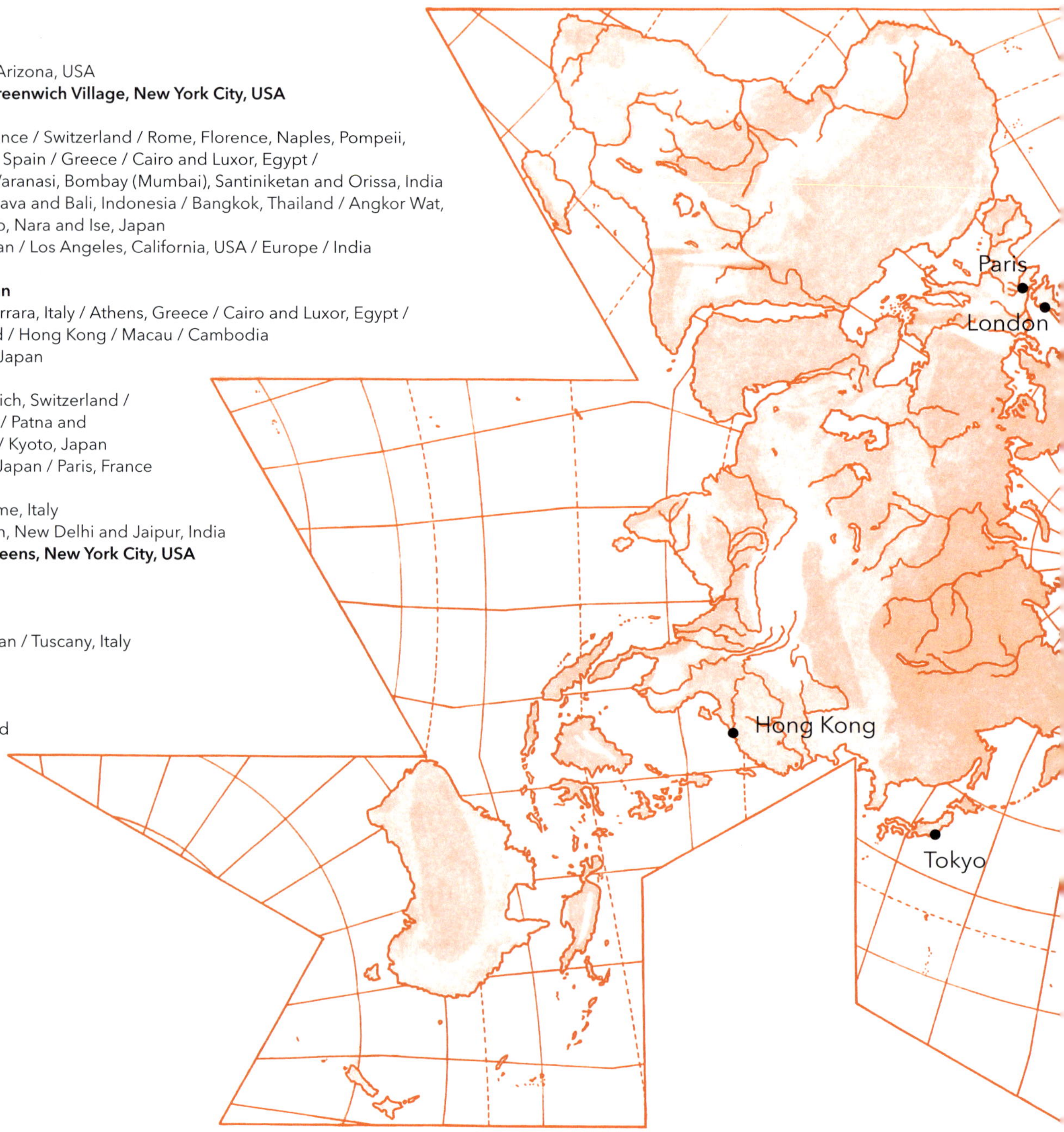

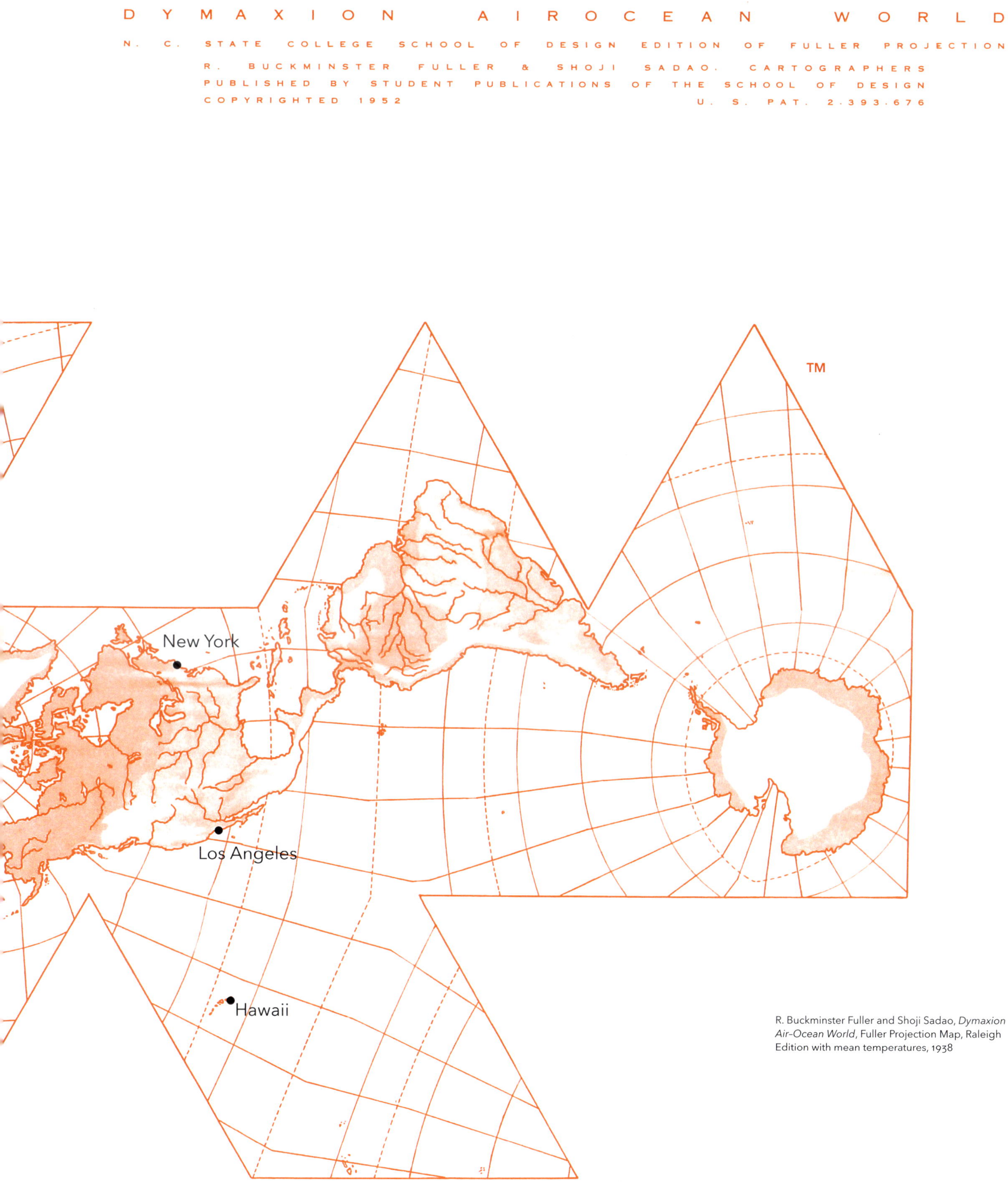

R. Buckminster Fuller and Shoji Sadao, *Dymaxion Air-Ocean World*, Fuller Projection Map, Raleigh Edition with mean temperatures, 1938

CHRONOLOGY

Noguchi in his studio in Long Island City, Queens, 1964

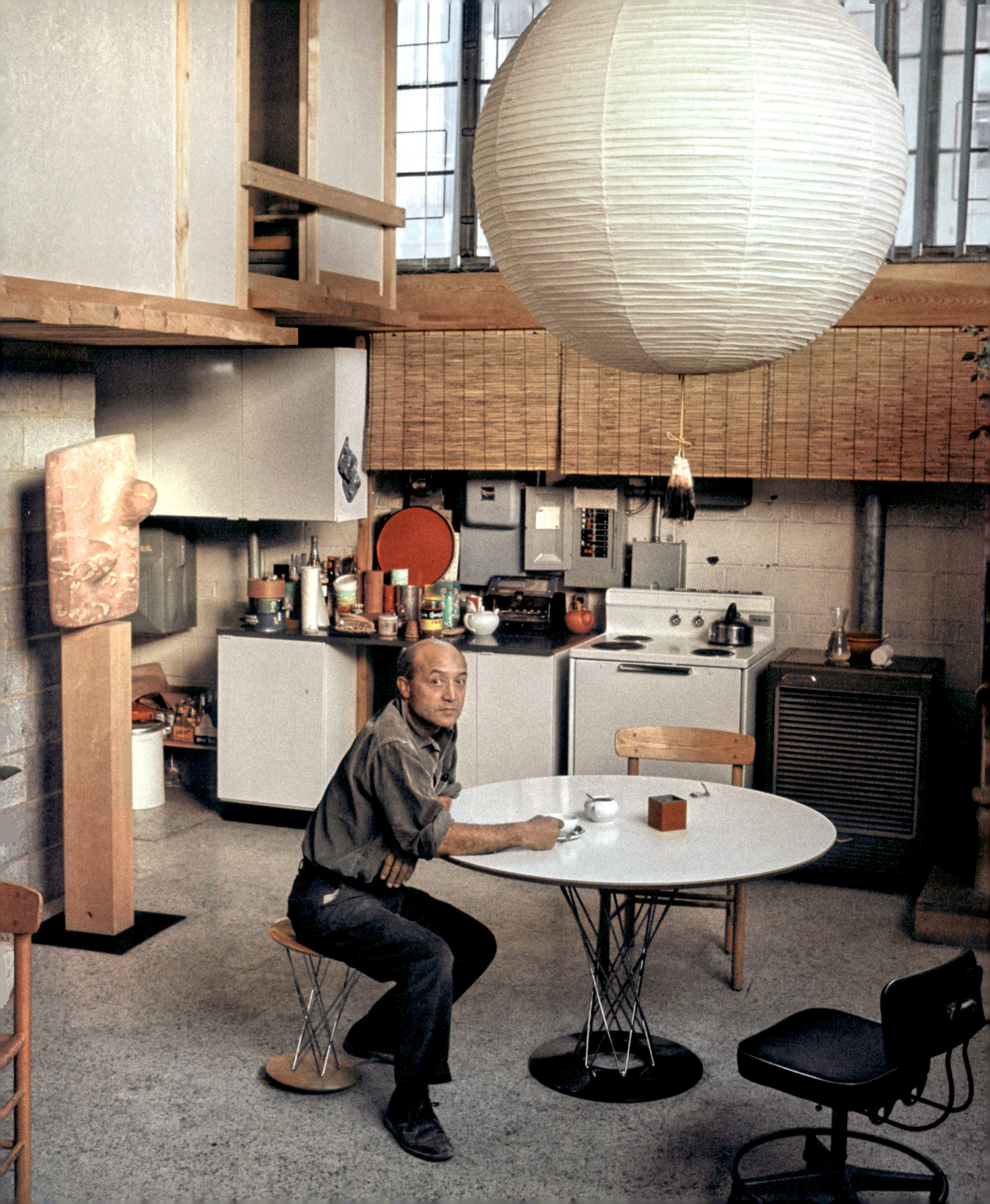

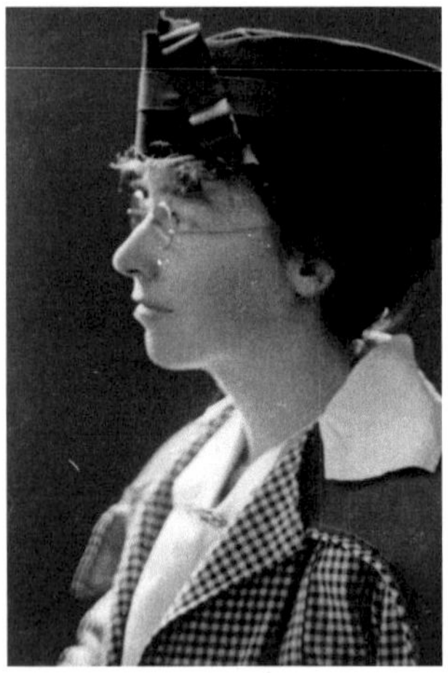

Portrait of Léonie Gilmour, 1904

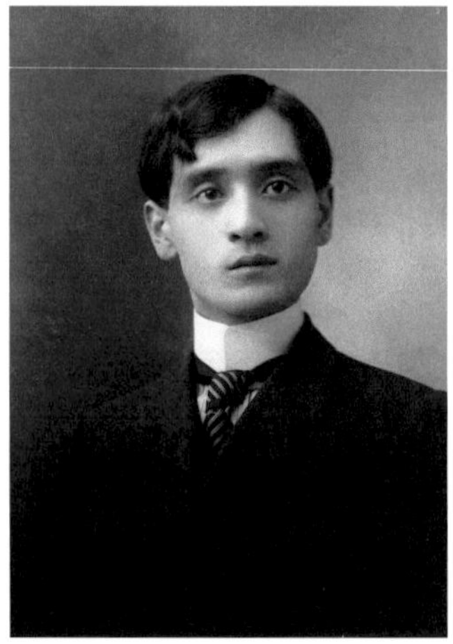

Portrait of Yonejirō Noguchi, 1904

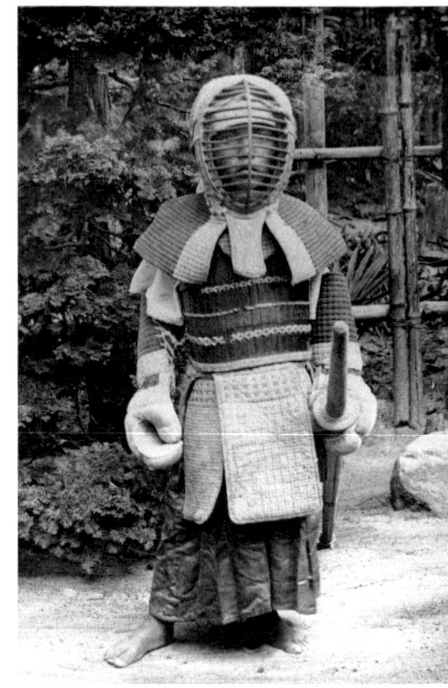

Noguchi as a child in Japan wearing kendo armour, 1911

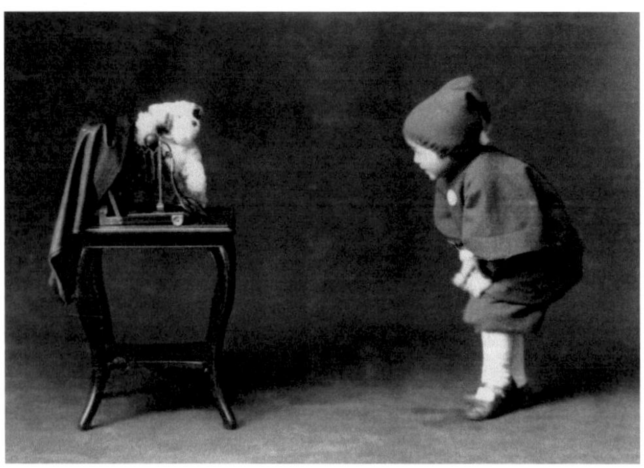

Portrait of Noguchi as a child in Japan, 1909

1904

Isamu Noguchi is born in Los Angeles on 17 November to Léonie Gilmour (1873–1933), an Irish American writer and educator, and the Japanese poet Yonejirō (Yone) Noguchi (1875–1947), who is living in Tokyo. For the first years of his life he has no given name, though his mother calls him Yosemite.

1907

Léonie moves with her son to Tokyo, where they are met by his father, who has since become involved in a relationship with a woman named Matsuko Takeda. Yone names his son Isamu, meaning 'courage'.

1911–12

Noguchi and his mother move to Chigasaki, a city 60 kilometres south-west of Tokyo, where he attends a Japanese school.

1912: Ailes Gilmour (1912–1993), Noguchi's half-sister, is born. She later becomes a dancer with the Martha Graham Company.

1913

Starts attending an English-language international school at Saint Joseph College in Yokohama. Helps his mother with the building of their new home in Chigasaki, assisting the carpenter and learning Japanese woodworking techniques.

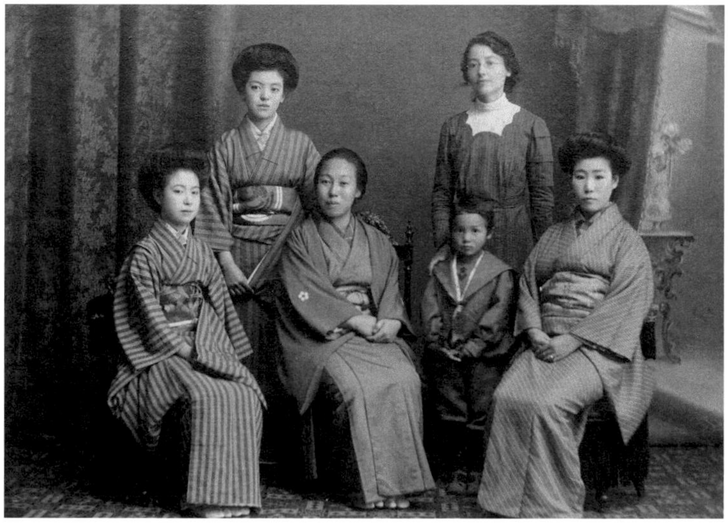

Noguchi with his mother and her pupils, Japan, 1910

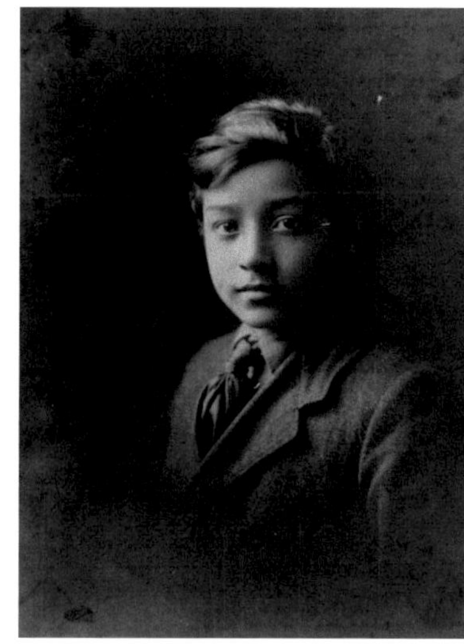

Passport photo of a young Noguchi, 1917–18

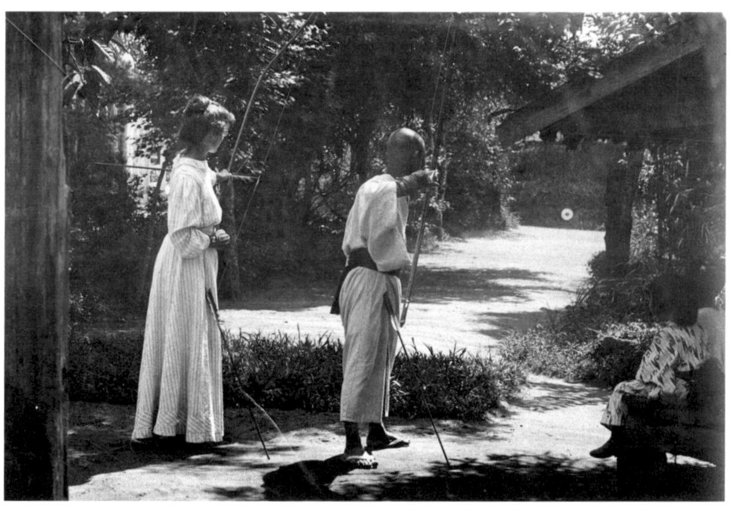

Léonie Gilmour practising archery with an instructor as Ailes and Isamu watch, 1916

1918

Under the name Sam Gilmour, travels alone to Rolling Prairie, near La Porte, Indiana, to attend the Interlaken School, a progressive boarding school. Arrives there in July, but it closes for the war effort in August. Enters a local public school in December.

1919–20

Dr Edward Rumely (1882–1964), founder of the Interlaken School, befriends Noguchi and arranges for him to stay with a family in La Porte, where he attends the local high school.

1920: Léonie and Ailes return to the US, arriving in San Francisco.

1922

Graduates from high school. Rumely arranges a summer apprenticeship for him in Connecticut with sculptor Gutzon Borglum (1867–1941) as well as funding to study on the premedical programme at Columbia University, New York. Lives with the Rumely family there.

1923

Lives with Léonie and Ailes after they move to New York.

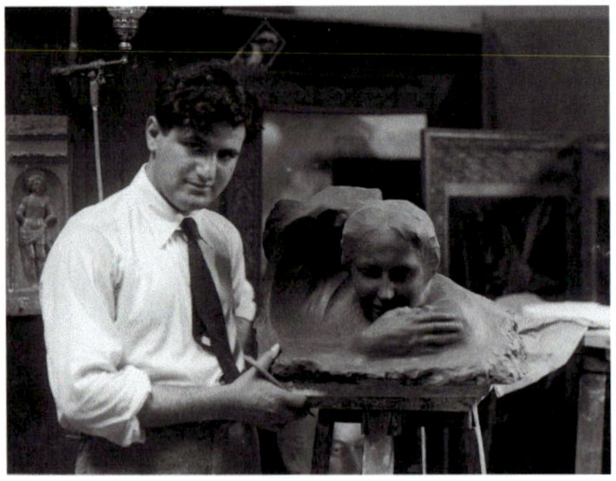

Onorio Ruotolo in his studio, c. 1922

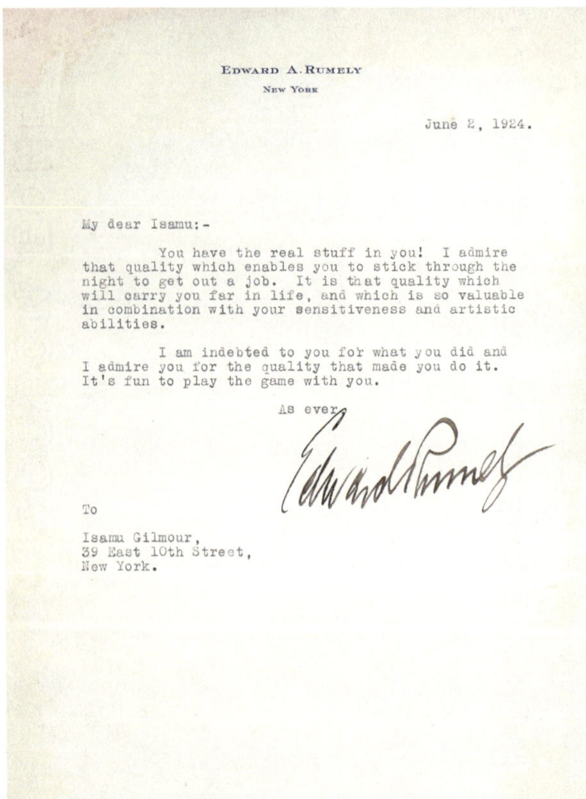

EDWARD A. RUMELY
NEW YORK

June 2, 1924.

My dear Isamu:-

You have the real stuff in you! I admire that quality which enables you to stick through the night to get out a job. It is that quality which will carry you far in life, and which is so valuable in combination with your sensitiveness and artistic abilities.

I am indebted to you for what you did and I admire you for the quality that made you do it. It's fun to play the game with you.

As ever,

To

Isamu Gilmour,
39 East 10th Street,
New York.

Letter to Noguchi from Edward Rumely, 2 June 1924

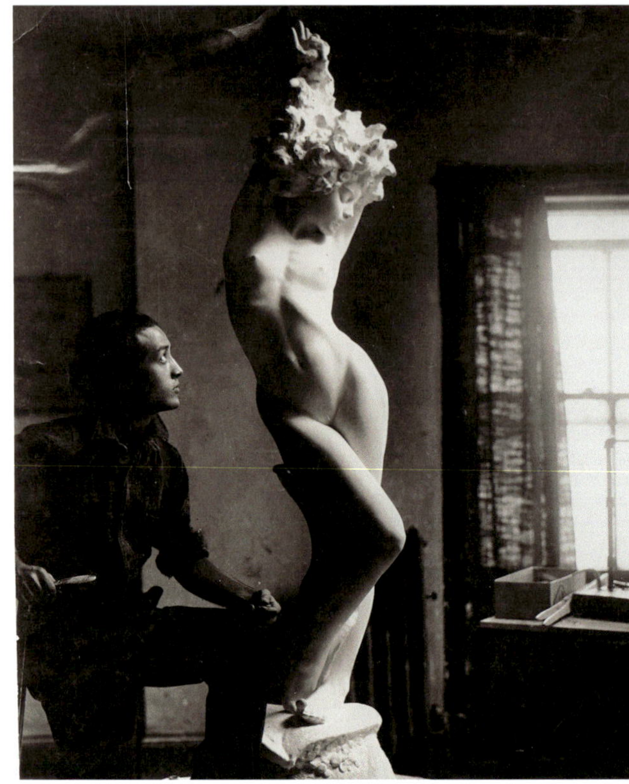

Noguchi with *Undine (Nadja)*, 1926

1924

Begins taking sculpture classes at the Leonardo da Vinci Art School, where he studies with Onorio Ruotolo (1888–1966), the 'Rodin of Little Italy'. The first exhibition of his work takes place in July at the school. Ruotolo gives him a studio space and recommends him as a member of the National Sculpture Society.

Decides to devote himself solely to sculpture and starts referring to himself as Isamu Noguchi, having previously used the surname Gilmour. Moves into a new studio with Rumely's assistance. Begins creating portraits of the Rumely family; portrait commissions will serve as an important source of income over the next two decades.

1926

Designs masks for the Japanese dancer Michio Itō's performance of *At the Hawk's Well* by W. B. Yeats.

Frequents New York galleries showing avant-garde art, such as Alfred Stieglitz's An American Place and J. B. Neumann's New Art Circle.

January: The first group exhibition to include works by Noguchi is held, the 121st Annual Exhibition at Pennsylvania Academy of Fine Arts.

May: Exhibits in the Grand Prix de Rome competition at Grand Central Art Galleries, New York, where he receives honourable mention.

November: Visits an exhibition of the work of Constantin Brâncuși (1876–1957) at the Brummer Gallery, New York.

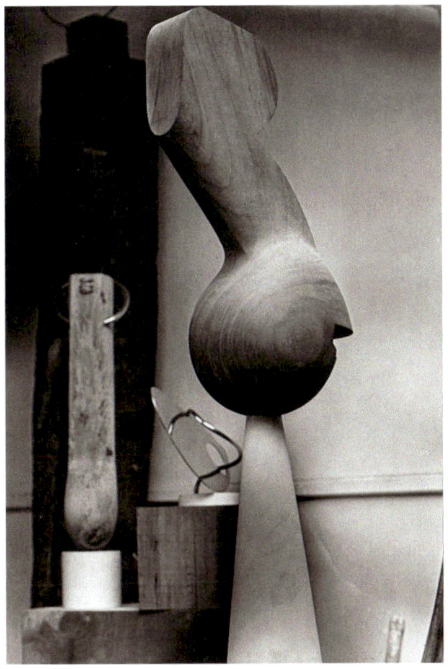

Bird Cry, 1928, wood, h. 60 cm

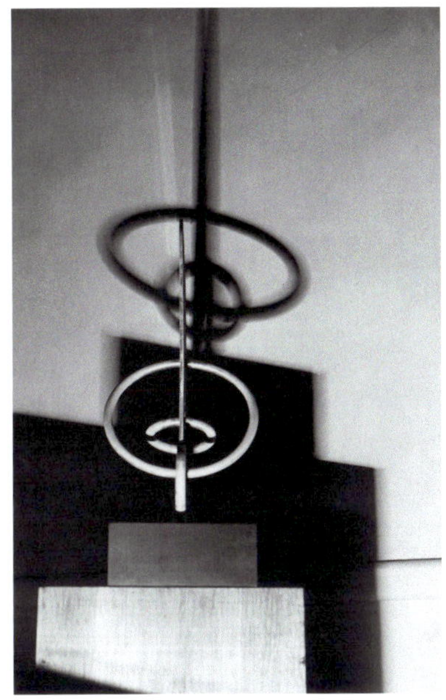

Abstraction, 1928, metal, dimensions unknown

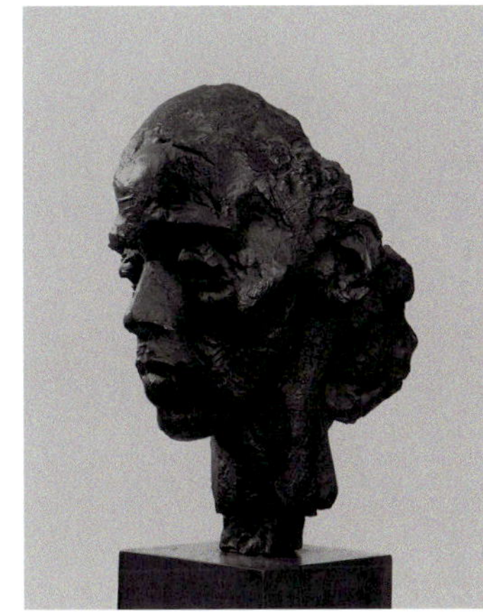

Martha Graham, 1929, bronze, 34.9 × 20 × 26 cm

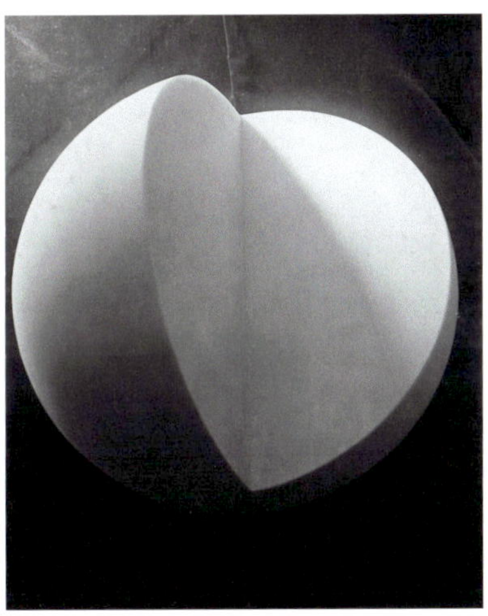

Sphere Section, 1927, marble, dia. 40.6 cm

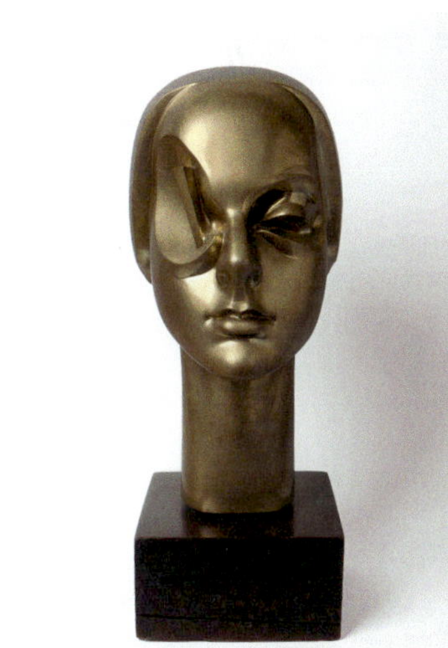

Edla Frankau (Mrs Peter Cusick), c. 1929, bronze, 39.4 × 19.1 × 25.7 cm

1927

March: Noguchi is awarded a John Simon Guggenheim Fellowship to travel to Paris and East Asia.

April: Arrives in Paris and starts to work as an assistant in Brâncuşi's studio. Attends life drawing classes at the Académie de la Grande Chaumière and Académie Colarossi. Meets other American artists in the city, such as Alexander Calder (1898–1976), Stuart Davis (1892–1964) and Marion Greenwood (1909–1970).

Autumn: Leaves Brâncuşi and establishes his own studio in Gentilly, on the southern outskirts of Paris. Begins experimenting with abstraction and kinetic and neon sculptures. Creates works in bent metal, wood and stone.

1928

January: Travels to London to study East Asian art at the British Museum.

March: His Guggenheim Fellowship is renewed for a year. Returns to Paris, where he develops his abstract sculptures and creates gouache drawings.

1929

March: Returns to New York, where he establishes a studio. Meets R. Buckminster Fuller (1895–1983), an architect, engineer and inventor, at Romany Marie's tavern in Greenwich Village, and Martha Graham (1894–1991), a dancer and choreographer. He will develop long-lasting friendships with both and collaborate with them on various projects.

April: Has his first solo exhibition, at the Eugene Schoen Gallery, New York.

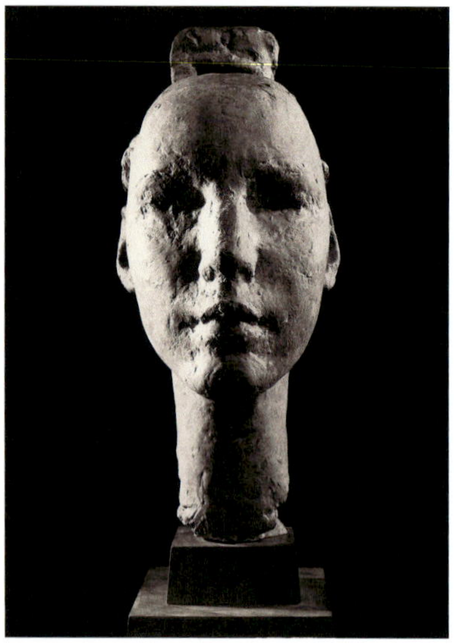

Ruth Parks, 1929, bronze, 41.9 × 18.1 × 26.4 cm

Noguchi with *Glad Day*, c. 1930

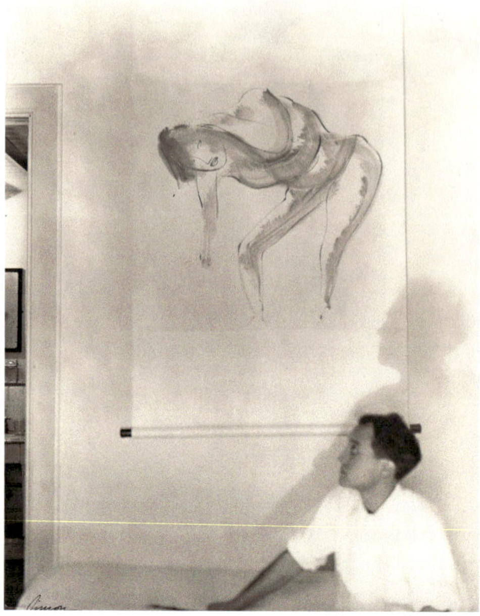

Noguchi at the 1932 exhibition of his *Peking Brush Drawings* at Demotte Gallery, New York

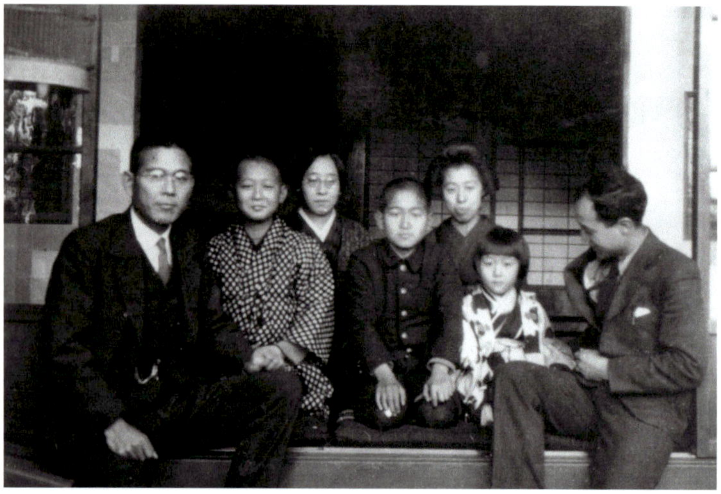

Noguchi (right) with his uncle Tōtarō Takagi (left) and his children and grandchildren, Japan, 1931

1930

February: *Fifteen Heads*, a solo show, is held at Marie Sterner Gallery, New York.

March: Has as a solo show at The Arts Club of Chicago.

April: With the money earned from portrait commissions, he travels to Paris, then on to Moscow, Russia and China. Studies traditional brush drawing techniques in Beijing with the master painter Qi Baishi (1863–1957).

1931

January: Sails to Japan.

February: In Tokyo, Noguchi meets his father for the first time in more than fourteen years.

March–May: Stays with his uncle Tōtarō Takagi, a Buddhist priest, in Tokyo and sets up a studio in the Kodenmachō district. Creates a terracotta figure of a famous sumo champion.

May–August: Travels to Kyoto and establishes a studio in the Higashiyama district. Develops an interest in ancient Japanese culture, including gardens, temples and *haniwa*, figurines used in funerary rituals. Studies with the potter Jinmatsu Uno.

September: Takes part in his first group exhibition in Japan, at the Ueno Art Gallery, Tokyo.

September–October: Returns via Hawaii to New York, where he sets up a studio at 58 West 57th Street.

November: The bronze head of *Ruth Parks* (1929), a dancer, is purchased by the Whitney Museum of American Art, New York – his first museum acquisition.

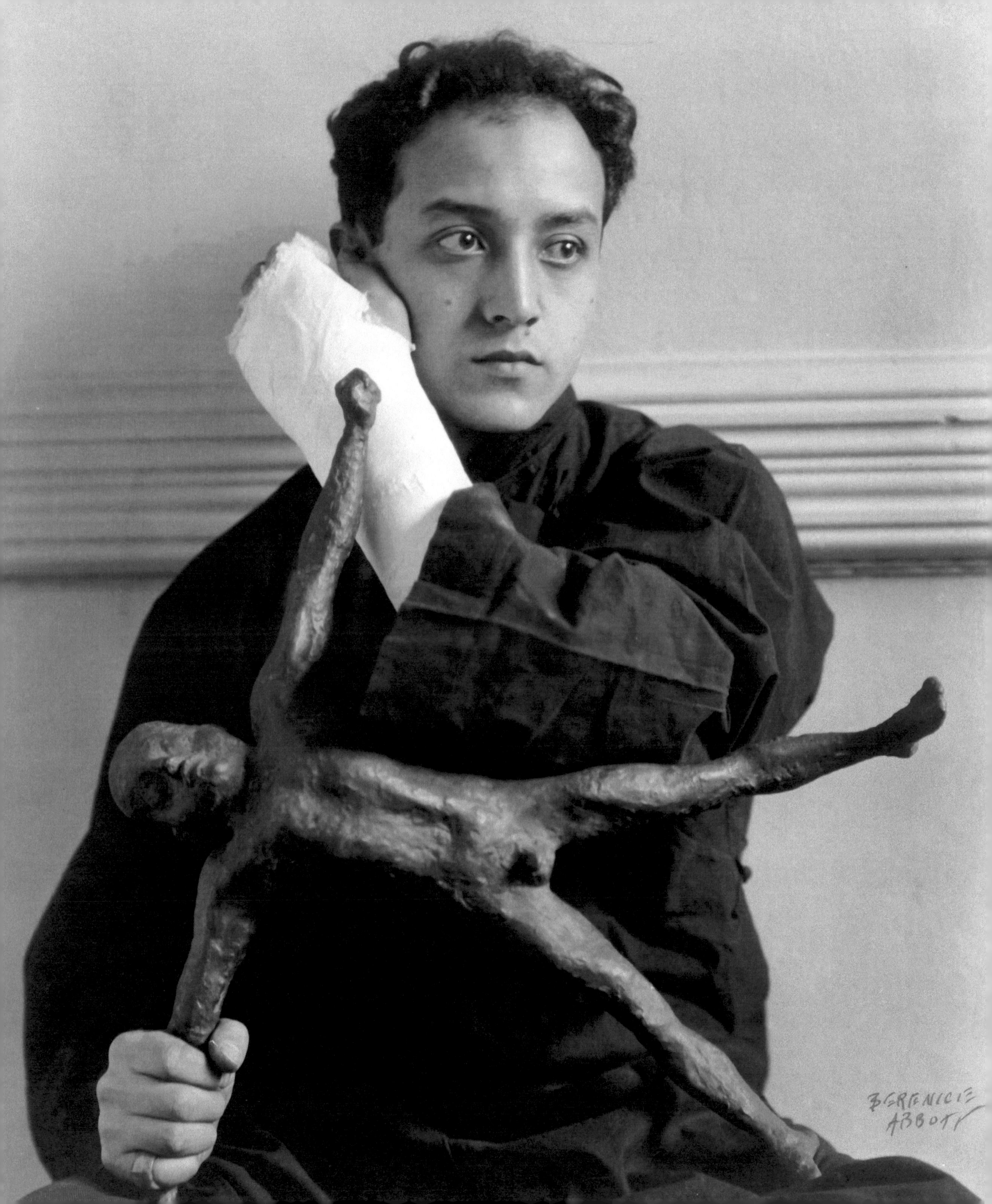
BERENICE
ABBOTT

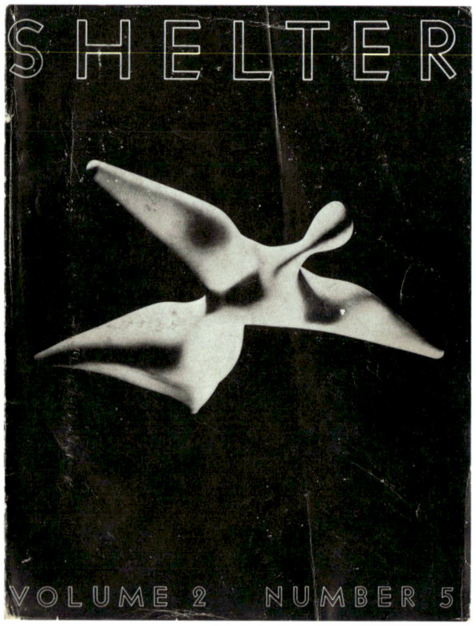

Cast of *Miss Expanding Universe* on the cover of *Shelter*, November 1932

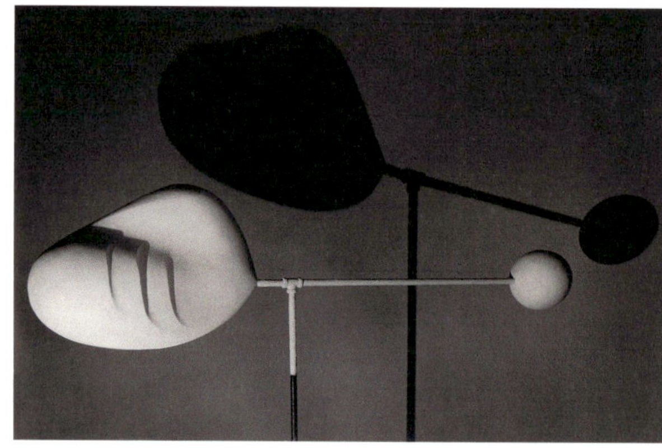

Musical Weathervane (Lunar Weathervane), 1933, plaster and electrical components, dimensions unknown

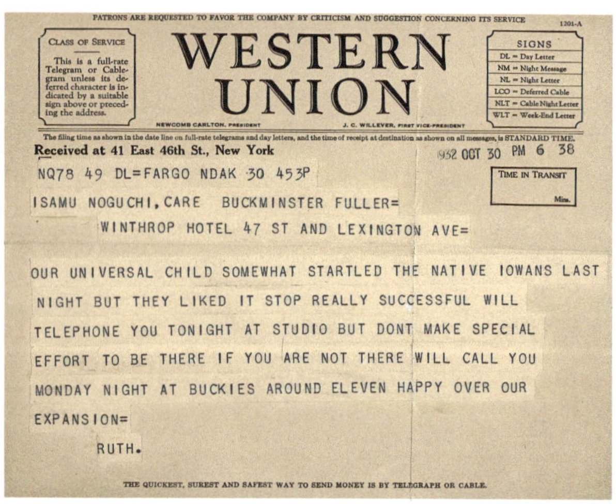

PATRONS ARE REQUESTED TO FAVOR THE COMPANY BY CRITICISM AND SUGGESTION CONCERNING ITS SERVICE

1201-A

CLASS OF SERVICE

This is a full-rate Telegram or Cablegram unless its deferred character is indicated by a suitable sign above or preceding the address.

WESTERN UNION

NEWCOMB CARLTON, PRESIDENT — J. C. WILLEVER, FIRST VICE-PRESIDENT

SIGNS
DL = Day Letter
NM = Night Message
NL = Night Letter
LCO = Deferred Cable
NLT = Cable Night Letter
WLT = Week-End Letter

The filing time as shown in the date line on full-rate telegrams and day letters, and the time of receipt at destination as shown on all messages, is STANDARD TIME.

Received at 41 East 46th St., New York — 1932 OCT 30 PM 6 38

TIME IN TRANSIT Mins.

NQ78 49 DL=FARGO NDAK 30 453P

ISAMU NOGUCHI, CARE BUCKMINSTER FULLER=
WINTHROP HOTEL 47 ST AND LEXINGTON AVE=

OUR UNIVERSAL CHILD SOMEWHAT STARTLED THE NATIVE IOWANS LAST NIGHT BUT THEY LIKED IT STOP REALLY SUCCESSFUL WILL TELEPHONE YOU TONIGHT AT STUDIO BUT DONT MAKE SPECIAL EFFORT TO BE THERE IF YOU ARE NOT THERE WILL CALL YOU MONDAY NIGHT AT BUCKIES AROUND ELEVEN HAPPY OVER OUR EXPANSION=
RUTH.

THE QUICKEST, SUREST AND SAFEST WAY TO SEND MONEY IS BY TELEGRAPH OR CABLE.

Telegram to Noguchi from Ruth Page, 30 October 1932

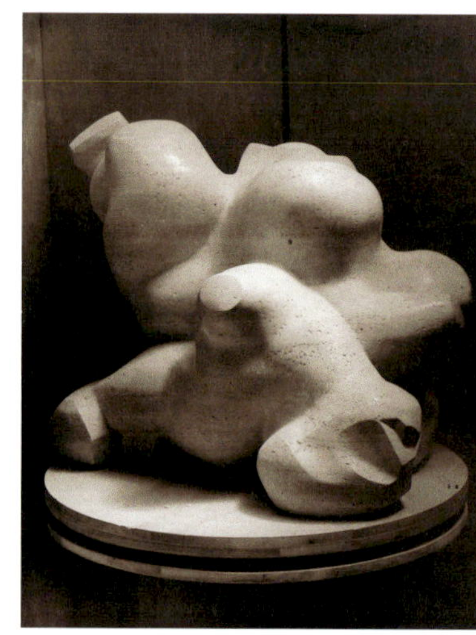

Birth, 1934, travertine

1932

Designs the Bakelite casing for a kitchen timer, *Measured Time*, for a company of the same name owned by Rumely – his first mass-produced industrial design.

Works with Buckminster Fuller on the design of the Dymaxion Car.

Meets the painter Arshile Gorky (c. 1902–1948), with whom he will visit many exhibitions.

March: Meets the dancer and choreographer Ruth Page (1899–1991) through Alexander Calder.

April–May: Moves his studio to 446 East 76th Street.

November: Premiere of Ruth Page's dance *Expanding Universe*, inspired by Noguchi's sculpture *Miss Expanding Universe* (1932). Page wears a jersey sack costume designed by Noguchi in collaboration with his half-sister, Ailes, also a dancer. *Miss Expanding Universe* and *Glad Day* (1930) are featured on the covers of the November issue of *Shelter* magazine, published by Fuller. The same issue contains Noguchi's text 'Shelters of the Orient', on the subject of Japanese architecture.

Solo shows this year at the John Becker Gallery, Reinhardt Gallery and Demotte Gallery in New York, and the San Diego Museum of Art, The Arts Club of Chicago, and California Palace of the Legion of Honor, San Francisco.

1933

Noguchi designs large-scale landscape works and memorials, including *Monument to the Plow* and *Play Mountain* (both unrealised) and *Monument to Ben Franklin*.

January: The first essay on Noguchi's work, written by the art dealer Julien Levy, is published in *Creative Art*.

February: Auctions pencil and ink drawings in New York due to rent arrears.

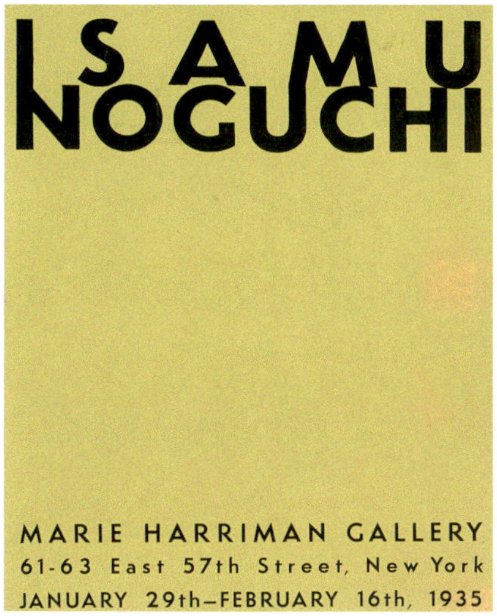

Brochure from *Isamu Noguchi* at Marie Harriman Gallery, New York, 1935

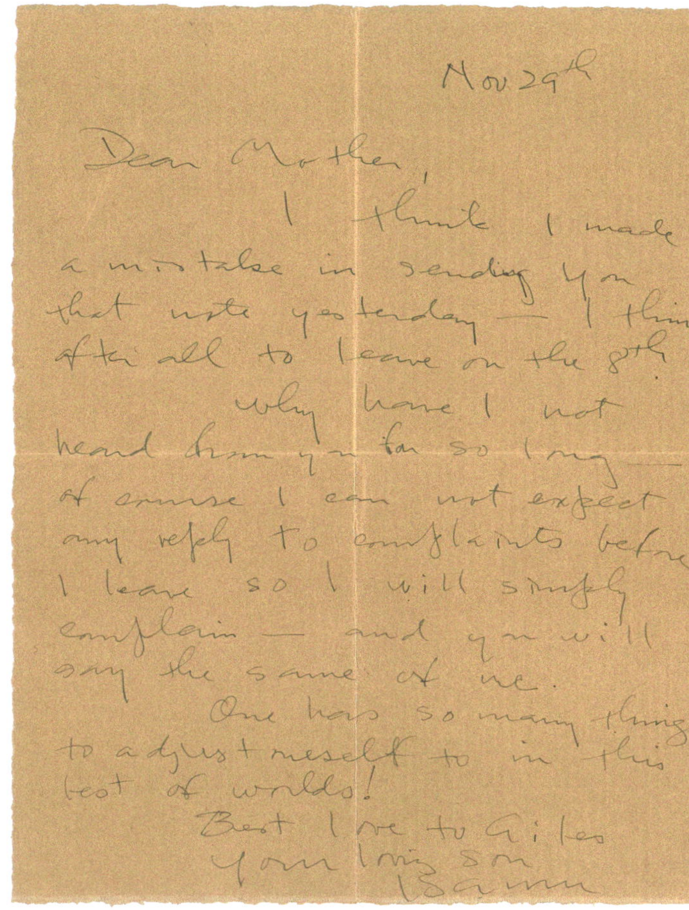

Nov 29th

Dear Mother,
I think I made a mistake in sending you that note yesterday — I think after all to leave on the 8th.
Why have I not heard from you for so long — of course I can not expect any reply to complaints before I leave so I will simply complain — and you will say the same of me.
One has so many things to adjust myself to in this best of worlds!
Best love to Giles
Your loving son
Isamu

Letter from Noguchi to his mother, 29 November 1933

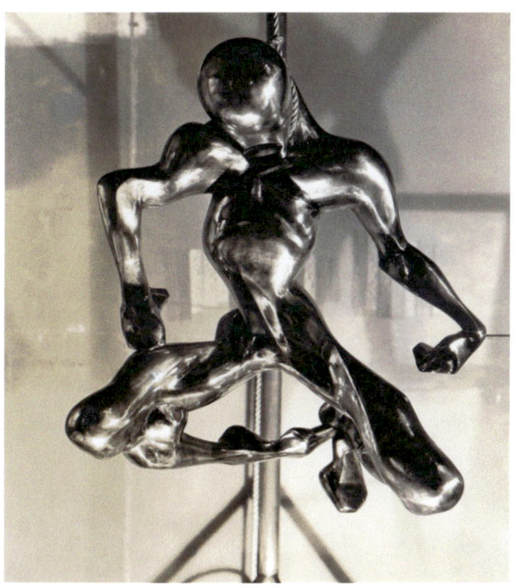

Death (Lynched Figure), 1934, Monel metal, steel, wood and rope, 231.1 × 94 × 94 cm

March: Travels to Haiti with his lover Dorothy Hale and A. Conger Goodyear, president of the Museum of Modern Art (MoMA), New York.

Summer: Travels to Paris and London, where he keeps a studio in Chiswick for two months.

December: Returns to New York. On 31 December, his mother dies.

Solo shows this year at the Honolulu Museum of Art, the Mellon Galleries in Philadelphia, the Art Institute of Pasadena and Faulkner Memorial Art Gallery in Santa Barbara.

1934

Noguchi's proposal for *Play Mountain*, a sculptural playground for New York, is rejected by the city's parks commissioner, Robert Moses. Proposals made to the government's Public Works of Art Project (PWAP) are also rejected.

Rents a studio at the Woodstock artists' colony in upstate New York for six months in the summer.

Joins the Artists' Union, established in New York the previous year.

1935

January: Solo exhibition of sculptures and models for public projects at Marie Harriman Gallery, New York. Noguchi presents *Death (Lynched Figure)* (1934) for the first time, a metal figure representing George Hughes, an African American man who was lynched in 1930. The work may have been based on a photograph in the communist magazine *Labor Defender*. Art critic Henry McBride describes Noguchi's 'gruesome study of a

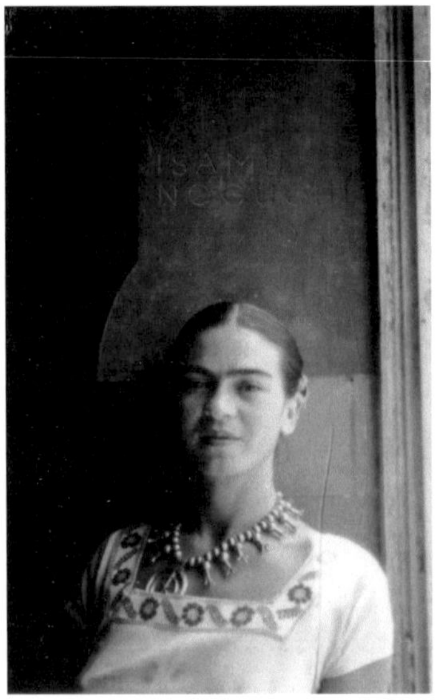

Portrait of Frida Kahlo at Noguchi's mural *History Mexico*, Mexico City, 1930s

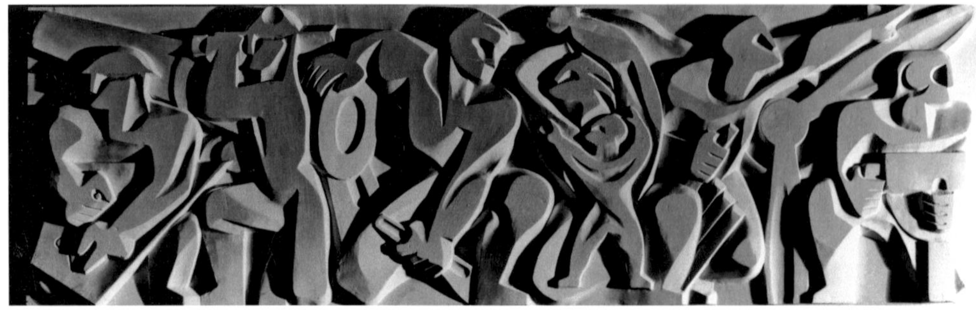

Fight for Freedom, study for a mural, c. 1937, plaster, dimensions unknown

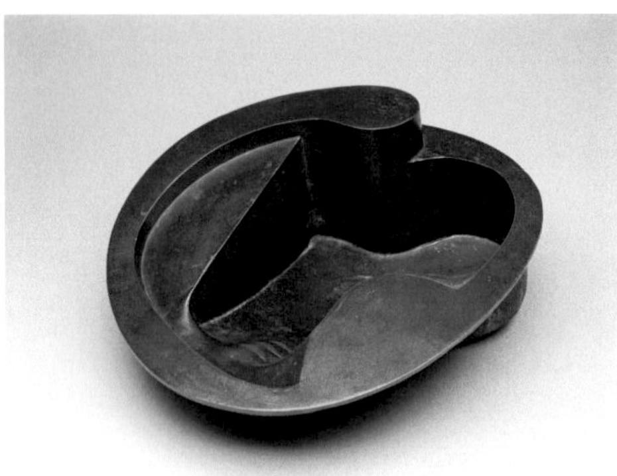

Model for *Swimming Pool for Josef von Sternberg*, 1935 (cast 1977; unrealised), bronze, 16.5 × 38.1 × 36.8 cm

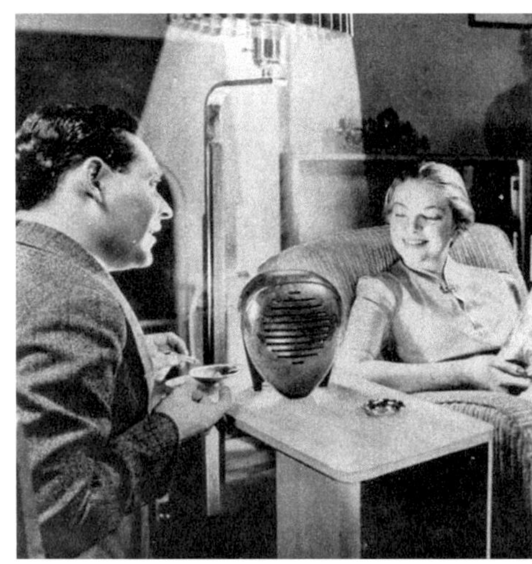

'"Radio Nurse" Watches Child', illustration from *Mechanix Illustrated*, July 1938

lynching' as 'just a little Japanese mistake' and continues his racist attack on the artist with the remark: 'Once an Oriental, always an Oriental, it appears.' The work goes on to be shown in anti-lynching art exhibitions, such as *An Art Commentary on Lynching*, organised by the NAACP at the Arthur U. Newton Galleries, and *The Struggle for Negro Rights* at the ACA Gallery, both in New York.

April: Designs his first stage set, for Martha Graham's dance *Frontier*. Exhibits in *Working Class Sculpture* at the John Reed Club, an organisation of the Communist Party USA.

Summer: Travels to California and works in Hollywood. Creates models for a pool for Richard Neutra's Von Sternberg House in Northridge, Los Angeles, his first domestic design commission.

Autumn: Travels to Mexico City. Marion and Grace Greenwood offer him space to create a mural in the Mercado Abelardo L. Rodríguez, where they are working under the direction of Diego Rivera. Begins construction of the sculptural mural *History Mexico*. Befriends Frida Kahlo.

1936

July: Returns to New York.

September: Publishes the essay 'What's the Matter with Sculpture' in *Art Front*.

December: *Miss Expanding Universe* is included in Alfred H. Barr's exhibition *Fantastic Art, Dada, Surrealism* at MoMA. Martha Graham's *Chronicle* opens, with set design by Noguchi.

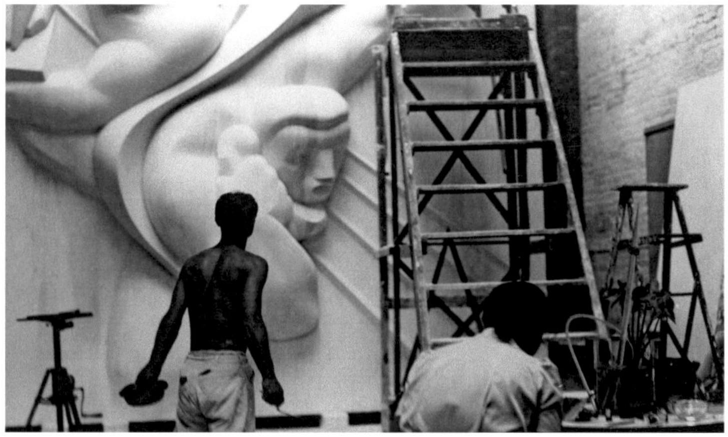

Noguchi working on *News (Associated Press Building Plaque)*, 1939

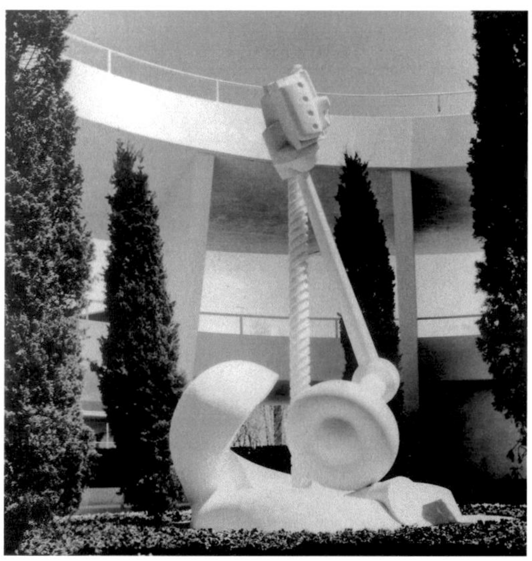

Ford Fountain (Chassis Fountain), 1938, for the 1939 New York World's Fair

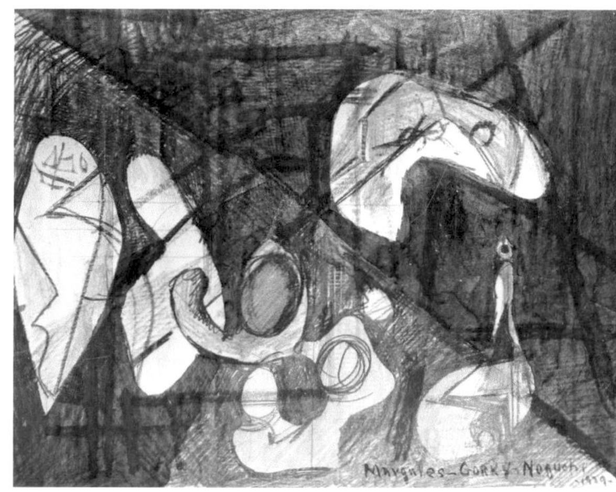

Isamu Noguchi, Arshile Gorky and De Hirsch Margules, *Collaborative Drawing*, 1939, dimensions unknown

1937

Creates *Radio Nurse*, a baby monitor design for the Zenith Radio Company.

December: Donates one of his *Peking Brush Drawings* to be sold at an auction in support of China's defence against the Japanese invasion.

1938

October: Receives his first major commission in the United States, a sculpture for the Associated Press Building in New York.

November: Designs *Ford Fountain*, in magnesite, for the Ford pavilion at the 1939 New York World's Fair.

1939

Travels between New York and Boston to work at the General Alloys Company foundry until completion of *News* in 1940.

Designs his first table, a commission for A. Conger Goodyear.

January: *Radio Nurse* is exhibited as sculpture at the Whitney Annual. *Time* magazine describes it as 'the most exotic' work on display, 'prettier as a radio than as a nurse'.

September: Creates collaborative drawings with Arshile Gorky and De Hirsh Margules (1899–1965) in reaction to the Nazi invasion of Poland.

Participates in group shows at the Whitney Museum and in *Art in Our Time*, celebrating the tenth anniversary of MoMA and the opening of its new building.

Noguchi working in the courtyard of his MacDougal Alley studio, New York, 1940s

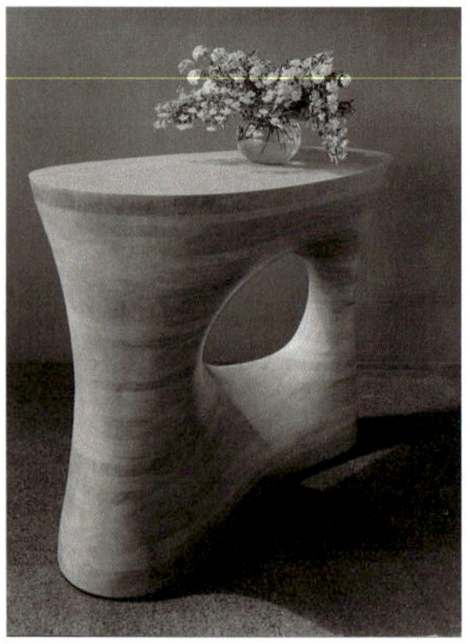

Table for Philip Goodwin, 1940–41, laminated primavera wood, 76.2 × 104.5 × 42.5 cm

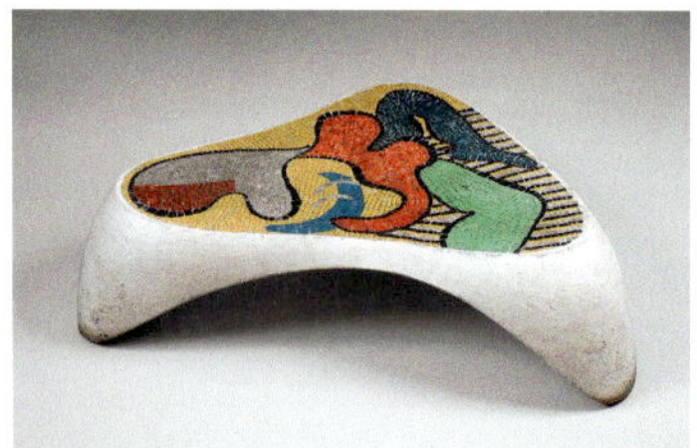

Table for Mosaic by Jeanne Reynal, 1942, magnesite, paint and mosaic tiles, 33.7 × 121.9 × 90.8 cm

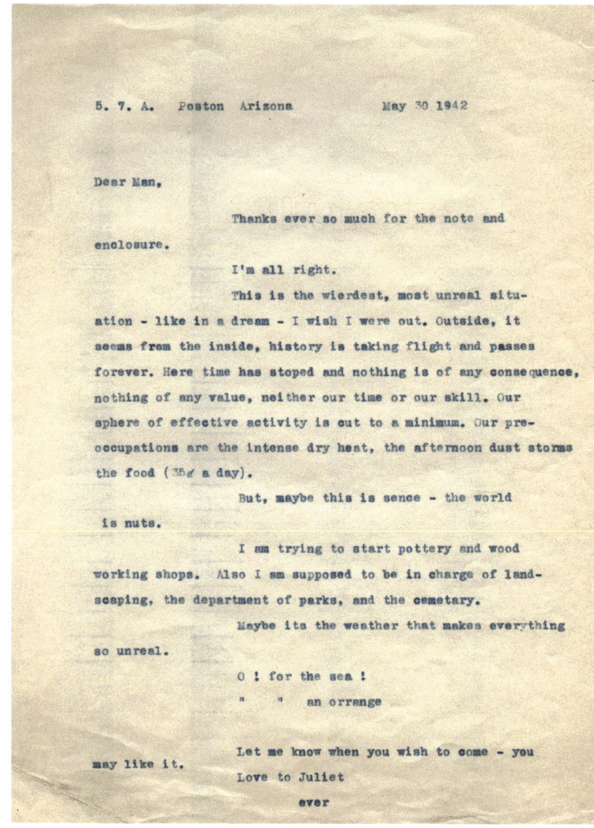

5. 7. A. Poston Arizona May 30 1942

Dear Man,

Thanks ever so much for the note and enclosure.

I'm all right.

This is the wierdest, most unreal situation - like in a dream - I wish I were out. Outside, it seems from the inside, history is taking flight and passes forever. Here time has stoped and nothing is of any consequence, nothing of any value, neither our time or our skill. Our sphere of effective activity is cut to a minimum. Our preoccupations are the intense dry heat, the afternoon dust storms the food (35¢ a day).

But, maybe this is sence - the world is nuts.

I am trying to start pottery and wood working shops. Also I am supposed to be in charge of landscaping, the department of parks, and the cemetary.

Maybe its the weather that makes everything so unreal.

O ! for the sea !

" " an orrange

Let me know when you wish to come - you may like it.

Love to Juliet

ever

Letter from Noguchi to Man Ray, 30 May 1942

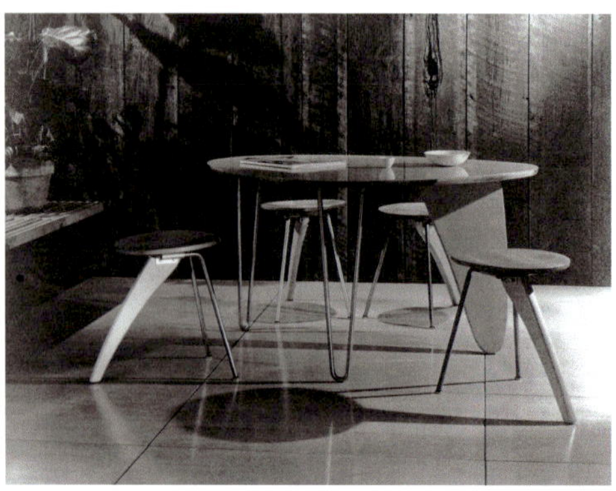

Three-Legged Dinette Table and Chairs (Rudder Table and Chairs), 1944, 66 × 127 × 90.2 cm; 45 × 35.5 × 46 cm

1940

May: Travels to Hawaii for the opening of a solo show at the Honolulu Museum of Art. Begins a proposal for playground equipment at Ala Moana Park, which will be rejected.

1941

MoMA acquires *Capital* (1939).

Proposes *Contoured Playground* and *Playground Equipment for Ala Moana Park* to the New York City Parks Department, but both are rejected.

July–December: Drives to San Francisco with Gorky and his fiancée, Agnes Magruder, and the painter Urban Neininger. Noguchi is living in Hollywood at the time of the attack on Pearl Harbor.

1942

January: Participates in founding the Nisei Writers and Artists Mobilization for Democracy group.

February–March: On 19 February, Franklin D. Roosevelt signs Executive Order 9066, authorising the internment of Japanese-born citizens and American citizens of Japanese heritage living in the western United States. Noguchi travels to New York and Washington, DC, to raise awareness of the relocation of Japanese Americans from the West Coast.

May: Although exempt as a New York resident, Noguchi voluntarily enters the Poston War Relocation Center in Arizona, hoping to improve conditions there. During his time there he creates proposals for recreational facilities and a large park project and writes the essay 'I Become a Nisei'.

November: Returns to New York after being granted temporary leave from Poston and soon sets up a studio at 33 MacDougal Alley in Greenwich Village.

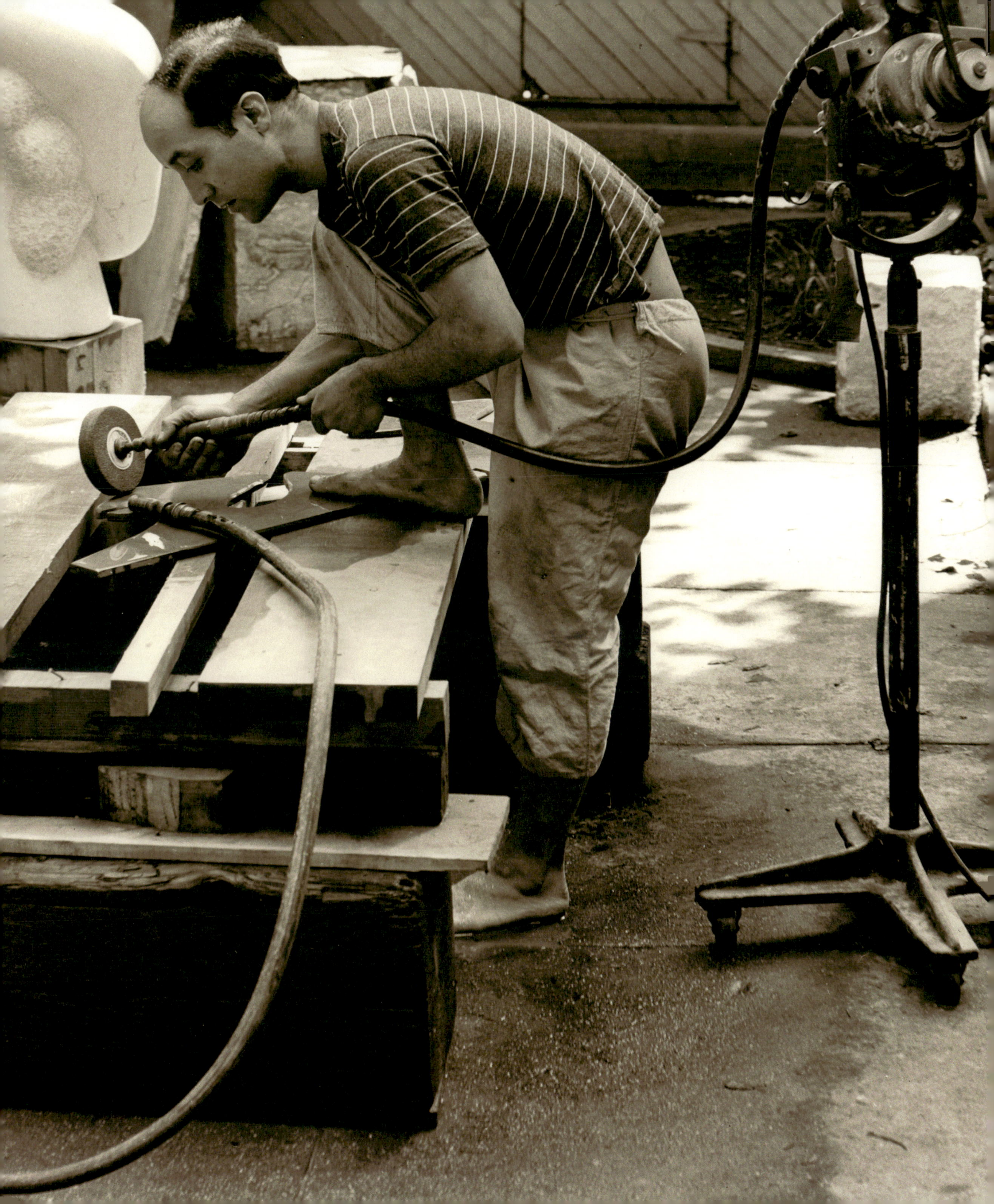

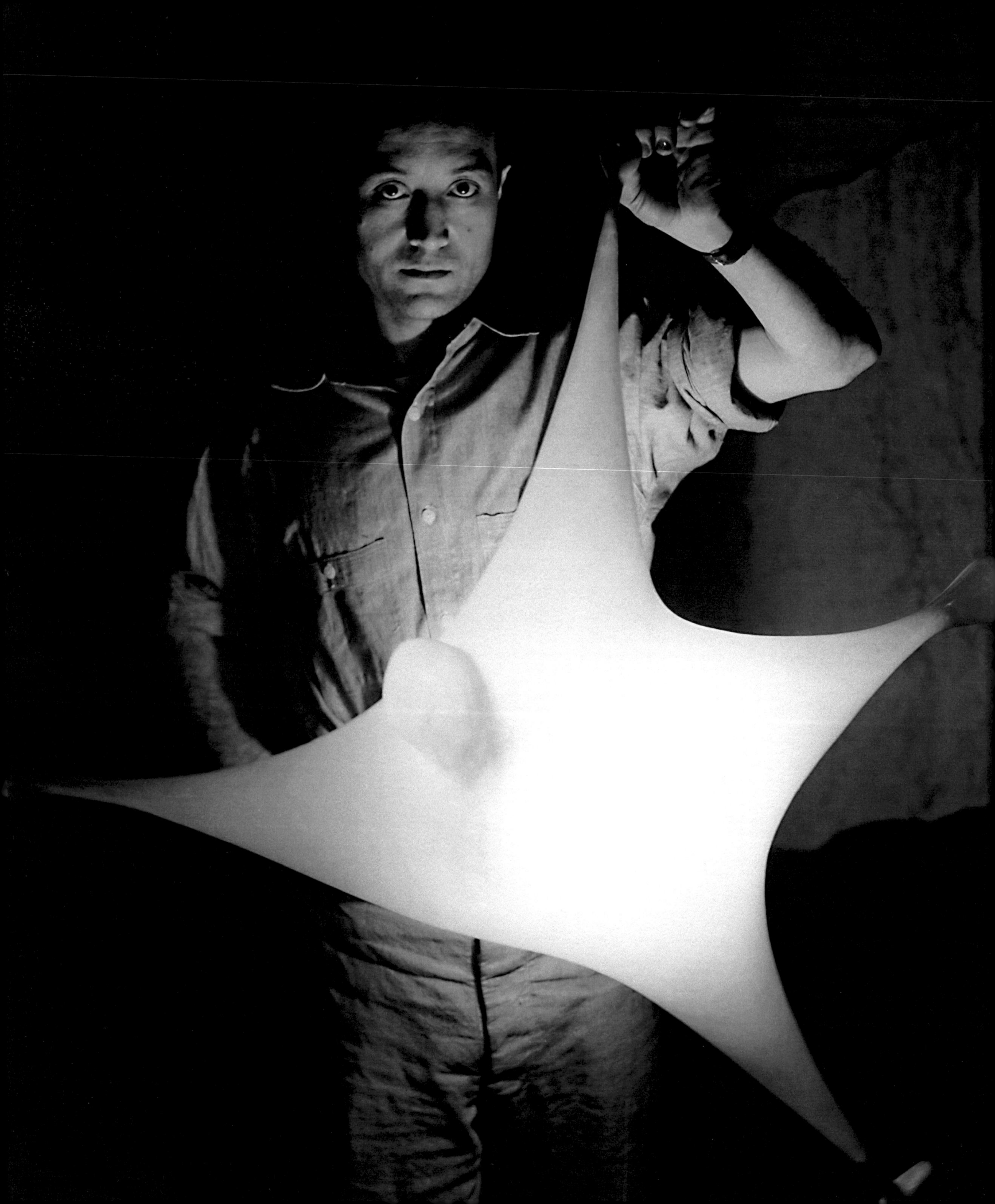

Noguchi with *Study for Luminous Plastic Sculpture*, 1943

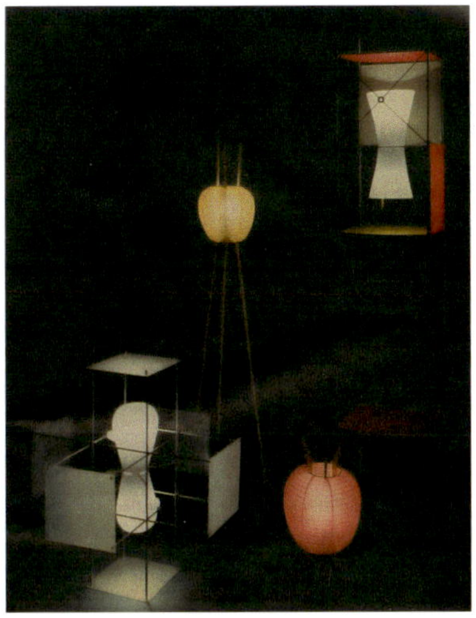

Prototype 'lunar' lamps, 1944

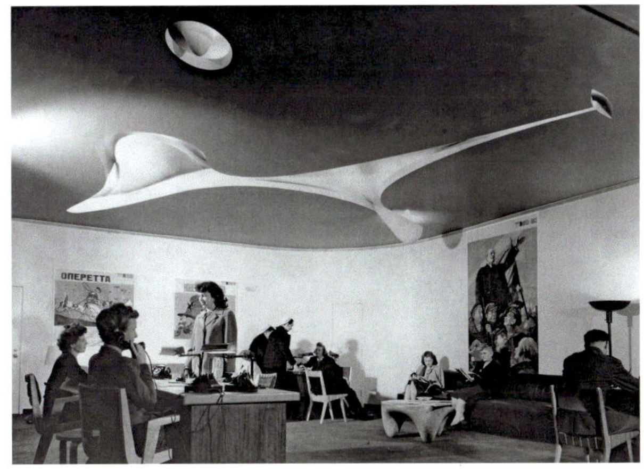

Waiting Room and Reception Area for the Time and Life Building, Rockefeller Plaza, New York, 1944

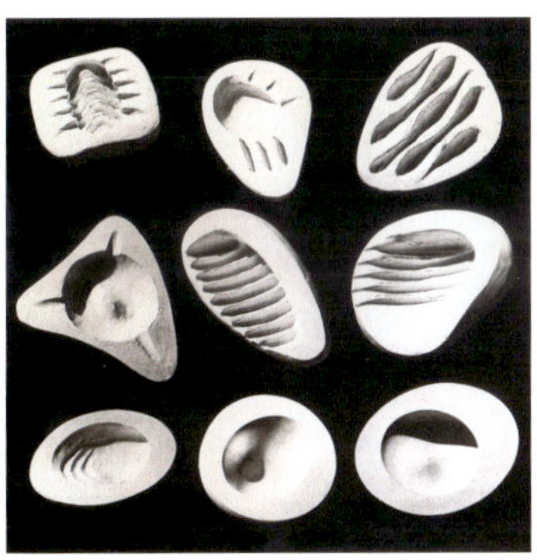

Photocollage of plaster ashtray designs, c. 1944

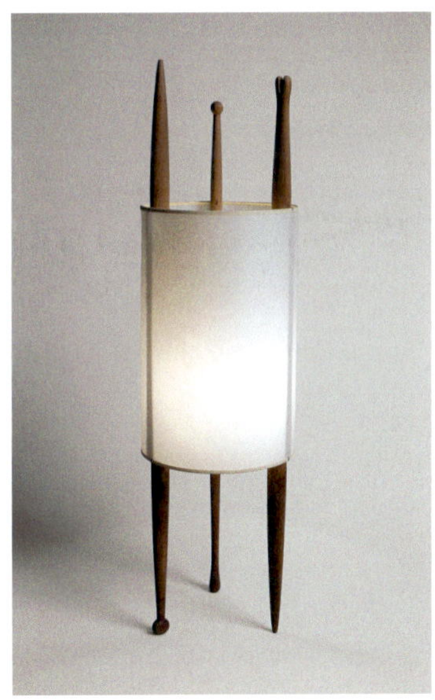

Three-Legged Cylinder Lamp, c. 1944, mahogany and PVC, 93.3 × 26 × 26 cm

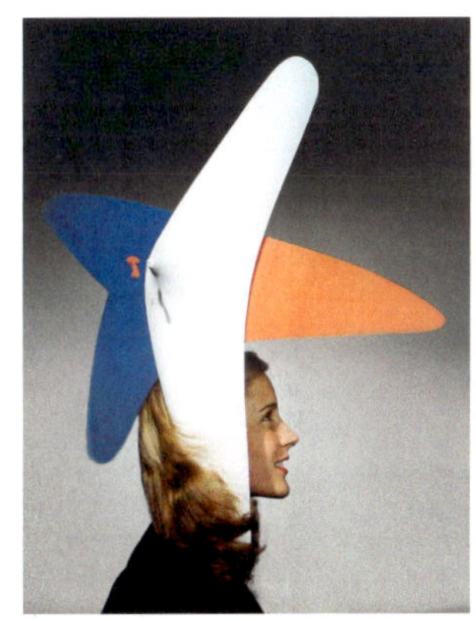

Cover photograph for *Junior Bazaar*, October 1944, with object by Noguchi

1943

Makes his first illuminated sculptures, the 'Lunars'; experiments with materials including ironwood, driftwood and plastic.

Attends meetings of the India League of America.

1944

Organises the Arts Council of Japanese Americans for Democracy with painter Yasuo Kuniyoshi and architect Minoru Yamasaki.

Designs the *Three-Legged Dinette Table* (*Rudder Table*, model IN-20), *Three-Legged Dinette Chair* (*Rudder Stool*) and *Coffee Table* (model IN-50).

May: Martha Graham's *El Penitente* (1940) reopens in New York with redesigned set by Noguchi.

October: In Washington, DC, three productions by Martha Graham premiere with set designs by Noguchi: *Appalachian Spring*, *Hérodiade* and *Imagined Wing*.

December: The new Information Center opens in the Time & Life Building, Rockefeller Center, with lighting and ceiling reliefs by Noguchi. He participates in *The Imagery of Chess* at Julien Levy Gallery with his *Chess Table and Pieces*, which will be manufactured by Herman Miller later in the decade. Begins the 'interlocking sculptures'.

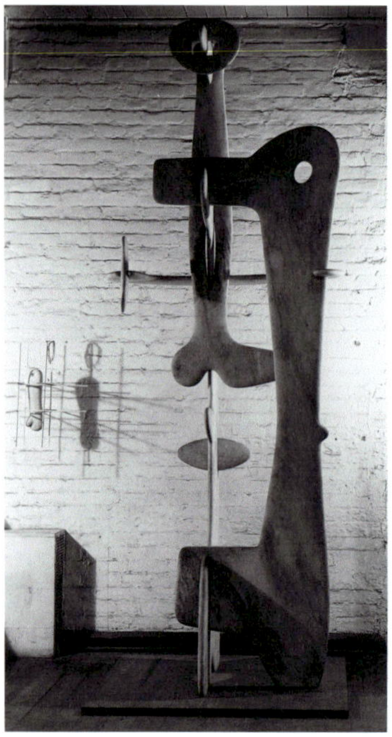

Kouros, 1945, Georgia marble, 297.2 × 107 × 86.7 cm

Exhibition view of *Fourteen Americans*, Museum of Modern Art, New York, 10 September–8 December 1946

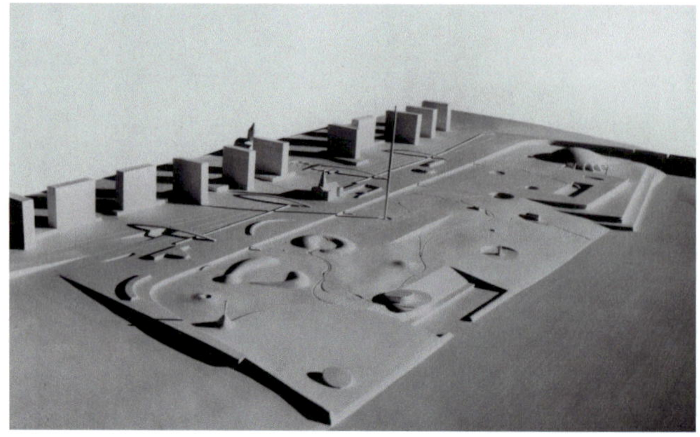

Model for *Jefferson Memorial Park*, 1945 (unrealised), plaster, dimensions unknown

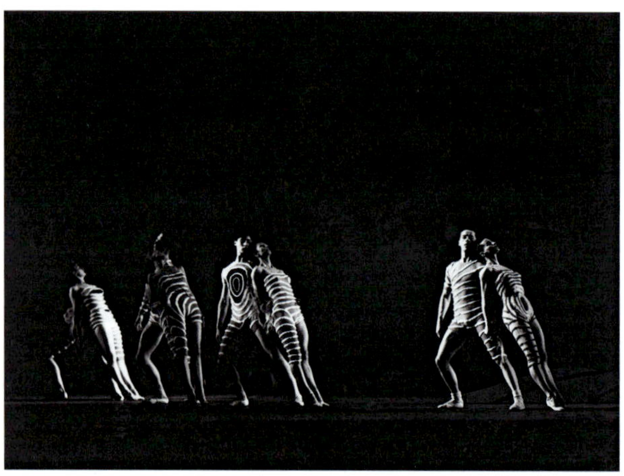

Stage set and costumes for *The Seasons*, ballet by Merce Cunningham with music by John Cage, 1947

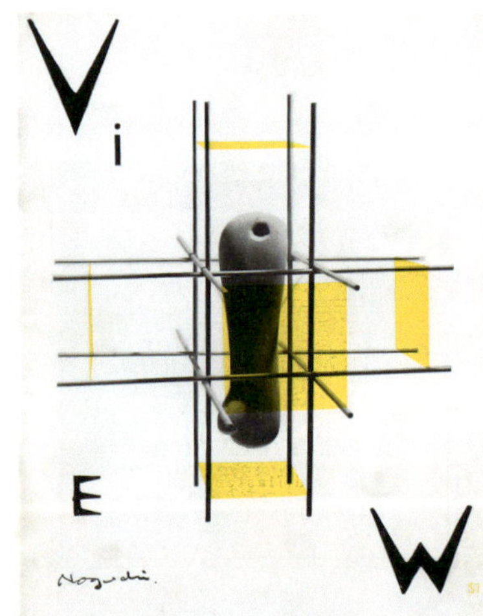

Cover by Noguchi for *View* magazine (Fall 1946), edited by Charles Henri Ford

1945

Travels to Ohio to visit the Great Serpent Mound. Collaborates with architect Edward Durell Stone on a plan for Jefferson Memorial Park (now Gateway Arch National Park) in St Louis, Missouri (unrealised).

May: Premiere in New York of Erick Hawkins's (1909–1994) dance piece *John Brown*, with set design by Noguchi.

1946

Set designs by Noguchi feature in Martha Graham's *Dark Meadow* and *Serpent Heart* (later *The Cave of the Heart*), Yuriko's *Shut Not Your Doors* and Ruth Page's *The Bells*, for which he also creates costumes.

Autumn: Exhibits in *Fourteen Americans* at MoMA. Noguchi states in the catalogue: 'The essence of sculpture is for me the perception of space, the continuum of our existence.'

1947

February–May: Designs sets for Martha Graham's *Errand into the Maze* and *Night Journey*, as well as for Erick Hawkins's *Stephen Acrobat* and Merce Cunningham and John Cage's *The Seasons* (including costumes).

March: Participates in the Surrealist exhibition *Bloodflames*, designed by Frederick Kiesler at the Hugo Gallery in New York and including Roberto Matta, Arshile Gorky and Wifredo Lam.

July–August: Noguchi is chosen to represent Japan in the Exposition Internationale du Surréalisme (*Le Surréalisme en 1947*) at Galerie Maeght, Paris, organised by Marcel Duchamp and again designed by Kiesler. His *Lunar Landscape (Woman)* (1944) and *Contoured Playground* (1941) are reproduced in Duchamp's *Prière de toucher* (Please Touch) exhibition catalogue for the show.

On 13 July, Noguchi's father dies in Tokyo.

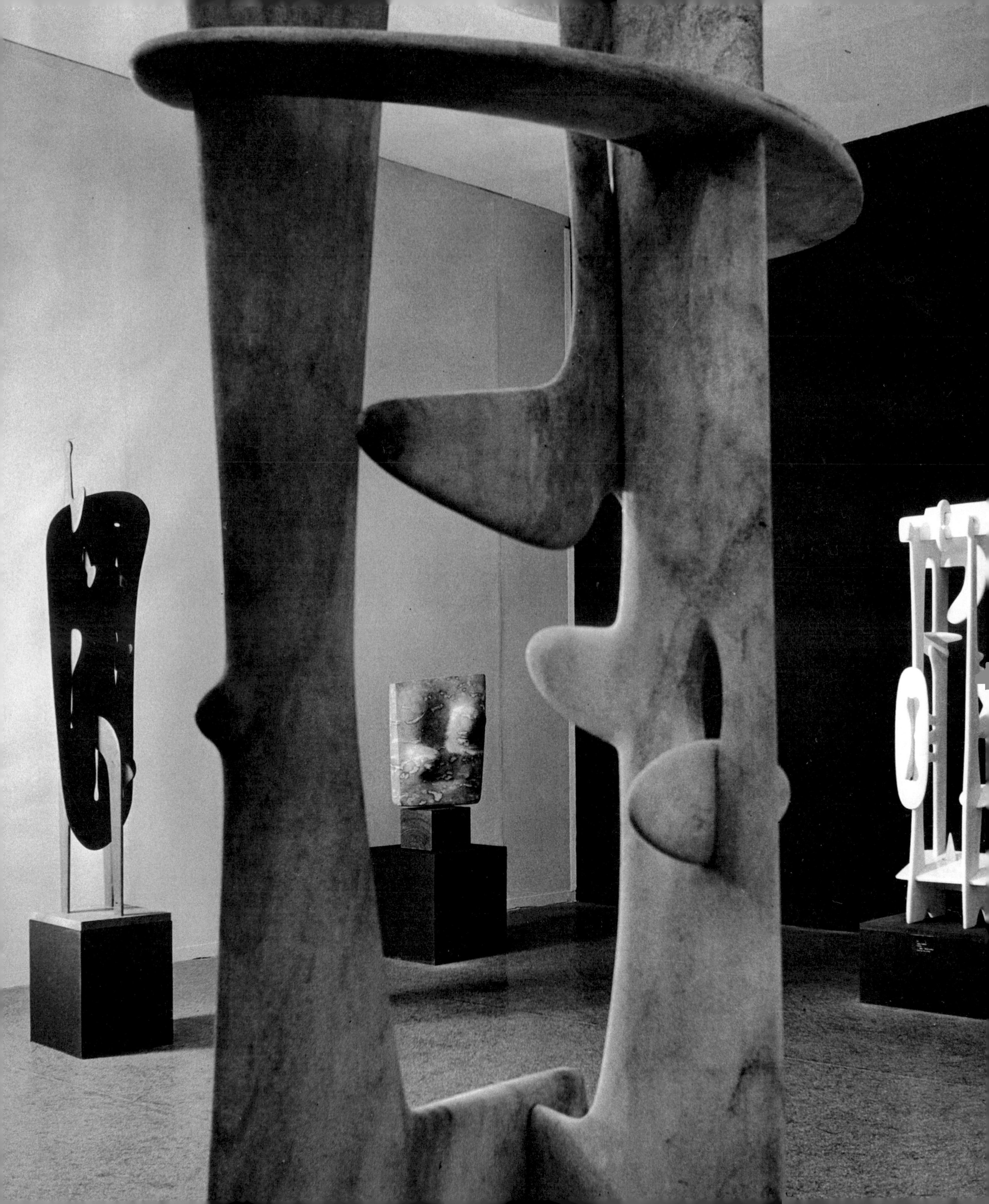

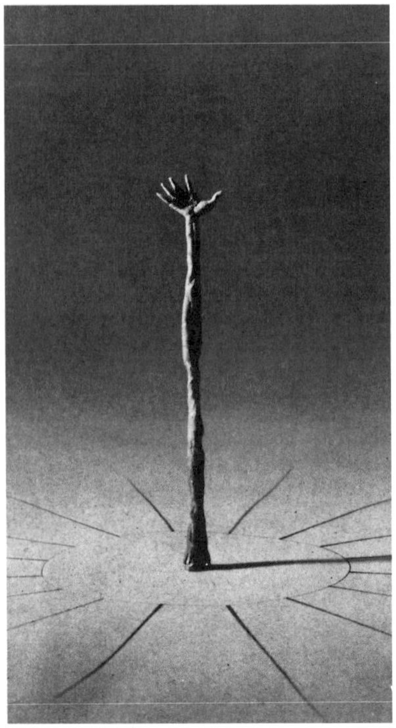

Model for *Memorial to Gandhi*, 1948 (unrealised), bronze, dimensions unknown

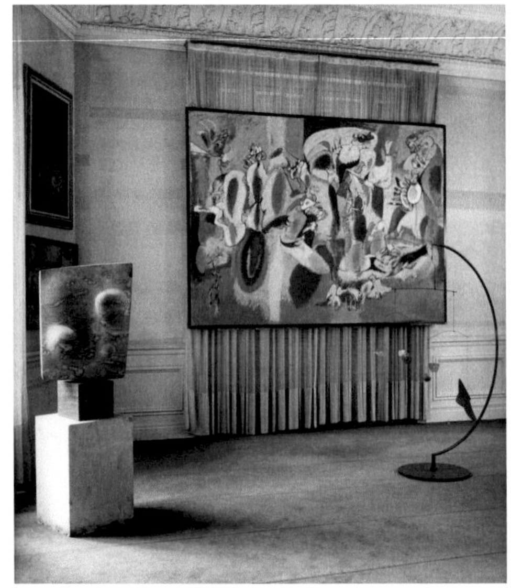

View of the Exposition Internationale du Surréalisme, Galerie Maeght, Paris, 1947

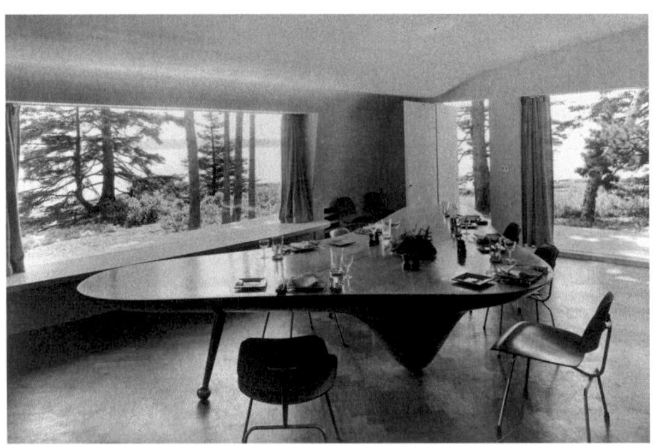

Interior and furniture for the William A. M. Burden House, Maine, 1947–48

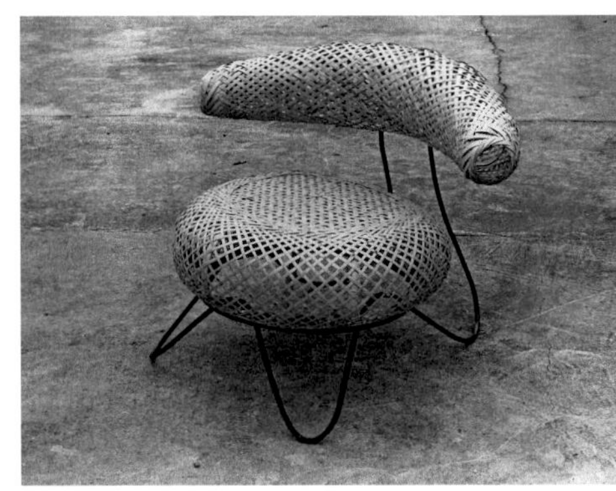

Isamu Noguchi and Isamu Kenmochi, *Basket Chair*, 1950, bamboo and iron, 71.8 × 85.1 × 76.2 cm

1948

Submits the funding proposal 'A Proposed Study of The Environment of Leisure' to the Bollingen Foundation. Designs furniture for private clients including William A. M. Burden.

April: George Balanchine's ballet *Orpheus*, with set and costumes by Noguchi, premieres in New York.

July: Arshile Gorky dies by suicide.

August: Designs the set for Martha Graham's *Diversion of Angels*.

1949

The *Three-legged Dinette Table and Chairs* and *Free-form Couch and Ottoman* are put into production by Herman Miller.

March: A solo show of Noguchi's work is held at the Charles Egan Gallery, New York.

May–August: Travels to Europe on a travel grant awarded by the Bollingen Foundation for his 'Proposed Study of The Environment of Leisure'; visits France, Switzerland, Italy, Spain and Greece. Visits André Breton, Brâncuşi and Alberto Giacometti in Paris and the construction site of Le Corbusier's Unité d'Habitation in Marseille. Stays at the American Academy in Rome while in Italy. Travels to Egypt, visiting Luxor, Abydos, Saqqara and Cairo, where he meets the architect Hassan Fathy.

September–December: Travels to India and tours the country. Receives a portrait commission from India's first prime minister, Jawaharlal Nehru, and meets and photographs the Indian artist Ramkinkar Baij and his sculptures at the Kala Bhavana in Santiniketan, West Bengal.

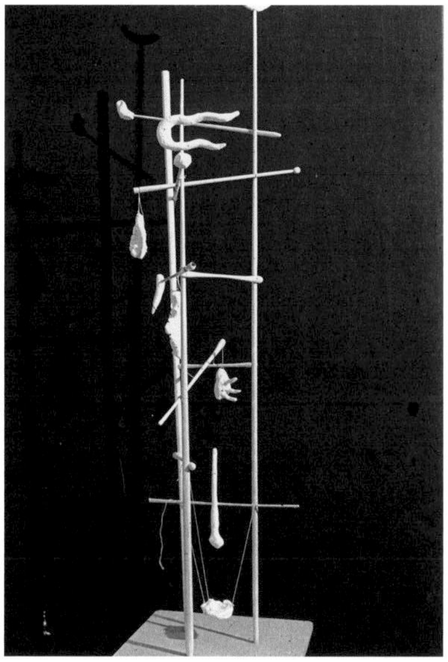

Bell Tower for Hiroshima, 1950, exhibited in *Isamu Noguchi* at Mitsukoshi department store, Nihombashi, Tokyo, 18–27 August 1950

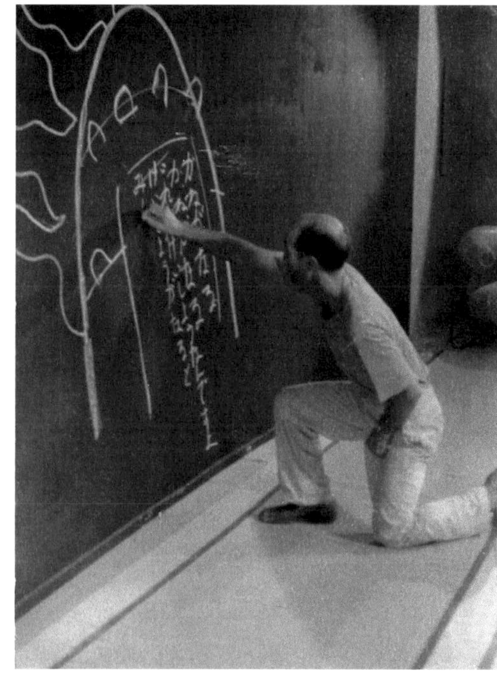

Noguchi writing his father's poem 'Kane ga naru' (A Bell Rings) at his exhibition at Mitsukoshi department store, Tokyo, August 1950

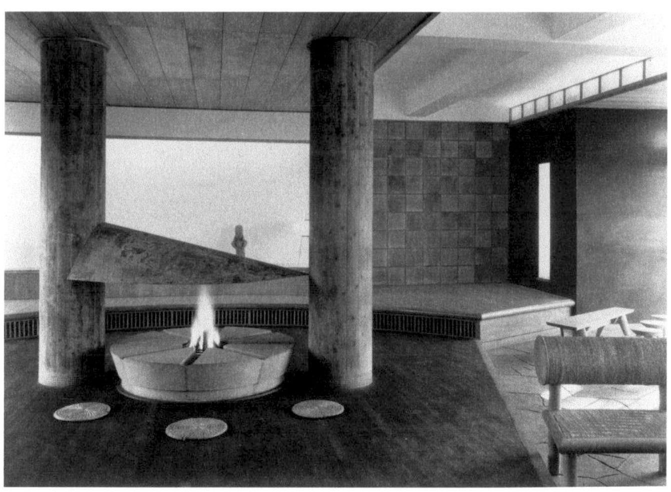

Shin Banraisha Faculty Room, Keio University, Tokyo, 1950–51

1950

January: Martha Graham's *Judith* premieres in Louisville, Kentucky, with set design by Noguchi.

January–April: Travels to Sri Lanka, Indonesia, Thailand, Cambodia and Hong Kong.

May: Travels to Japan, his first return since 1931. Meets the architect Kenzō Tange (1913–2005) and members of the Japan Abstract Art Club. After meeting his half-brother Michio Noguchi (1931–1999), who will assist him on his visit and on other occasions over the following decades, Noguchi visits his father's family in Tokyo.

June: Visits temples and gardens in Ise, Nara and Kyoto with artist and writer Saburo Hasegawa (1906–1957).

July–August: The designer Isamu Kenmochi arranges a studio residency for Noguchi at the Industrial Arts Research Institute (IARI), Tokyo. Meets the mayor of Hiroshima to discuss a collaboration with Kenzō Tange on his Peace Memorial Park and designs a memorial garden and faculty room in honour of his father at Keio University, Tokyo, in collaboration with architect Yoshirō Taniguchi (1904–1979).

August: Has a solo show at the Mitsukoshi department store in Tokyo, featuring ceramics made in Seto that summer.

September: Returns to New York.

November: Meets Yoshiko 'Shirley' Yamaguchi (1920–2014), a Japanese actor who was born in China, whom he will marry in 1951.

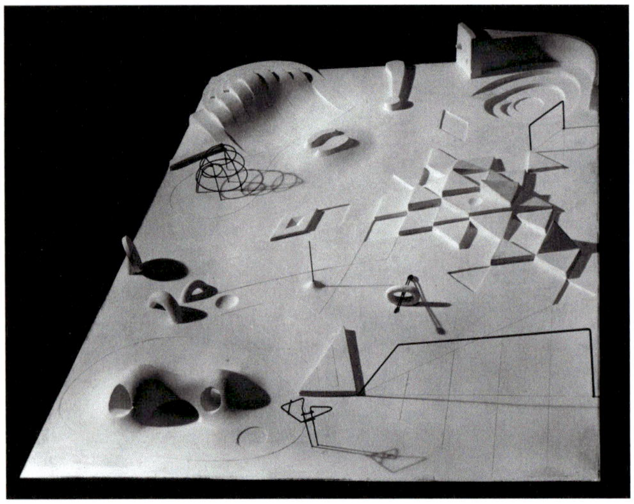

Model for *United Nations Playground*, 1952–63 (unrealised), plaster, dimensions unknown

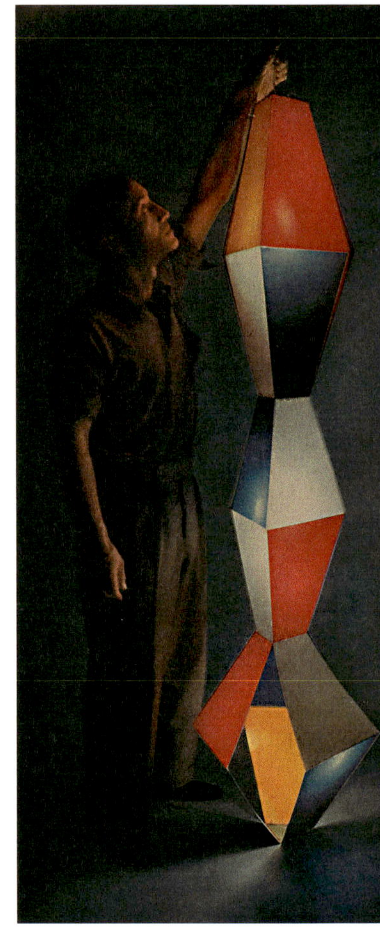

Noguchi with *Column of Light* in *Life* magazine, March 1952

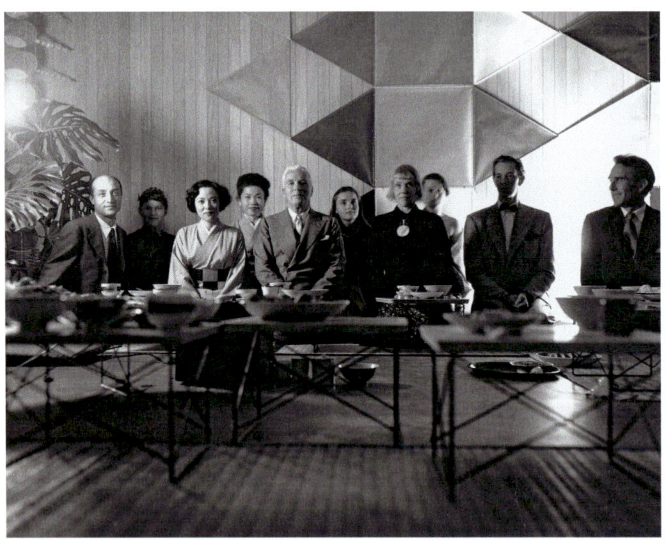

A tea ceremony at Charles and Ray Eames' house, Pacific Palisades, California, 1951. From left: Noguchi, Ray Eames, Shirley Yamaguchi, unknown tea master, Charlie Chaplin; fourth from right: Iris Tree; far right: Charles Eames

1951

Designs a playground for the United Nations Headquarters in New York (unrealised).

March: Returns to Japan. Designs a garden for the new Reader's Digest Building in Tokyo, his first realised garden project.

June–July: Visits the Ozeki lantern factory in Gifu, where he produces his first *Akari* lamp prototypes. Visits Hiroshima with Kenzō Tange to discuss a commission for bridge railings at the Peace Park.

September: Exhibits in the first São Paulo biennial.

Autumn: Travels to Hollywood with Yamaguchi, where he meets the designers Ray and Charles Eames, then on to sites in India and Europe.

November: Returns to Japan, where he is asked to design a cenotaph for Tange's Hiroshima Peace Park.

5 December: Marries Yoshiko Yamaguchi in Tokyo.

Winter: Receives a commission for a lobby courtyard at the Lever Brothers building on Park Avenue, New York, his first from Gordon Bunshaft of Skidmore, Owings & Merrill.

1952

The *Akari* light sculptures are put into commercial production and are sold at Takashimaya department stores in Tokyo and Osaka.

February: Noguchi's design for a *Memorial to the Dead, Hiroshima* at Tange's Peace Park is rejected.

Spring: Meets the potter Rosanjin Kitaōji (1883–1959) and lives with Yamaguchi in a house on his property in Kita Kamakura, Kanagawa

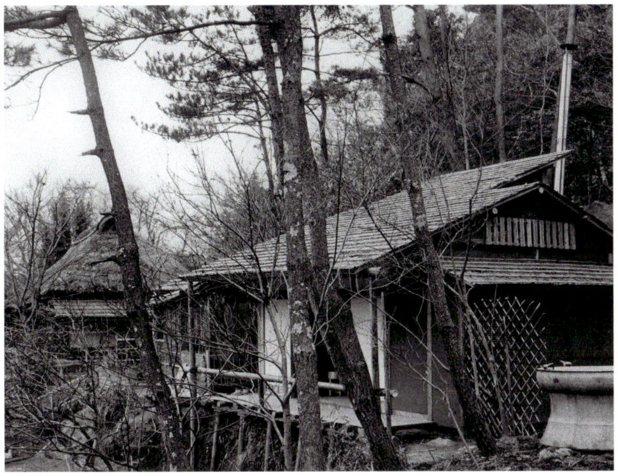

Noguchi's studio and home in Kita Kamakura, Japan, 1950s

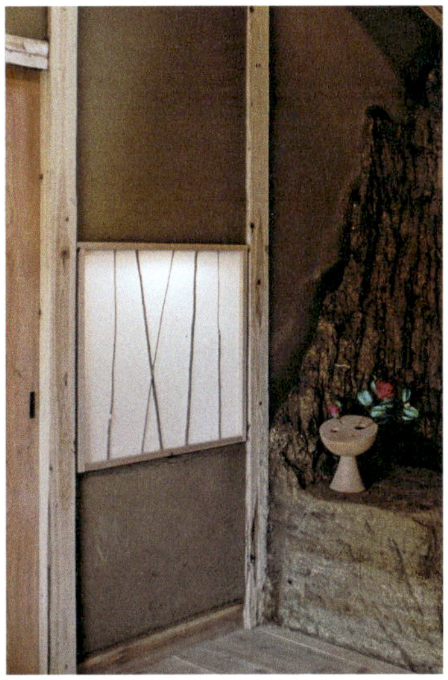

Interior of Noguchi's studio in Kita Kamakura, Japan, 1952

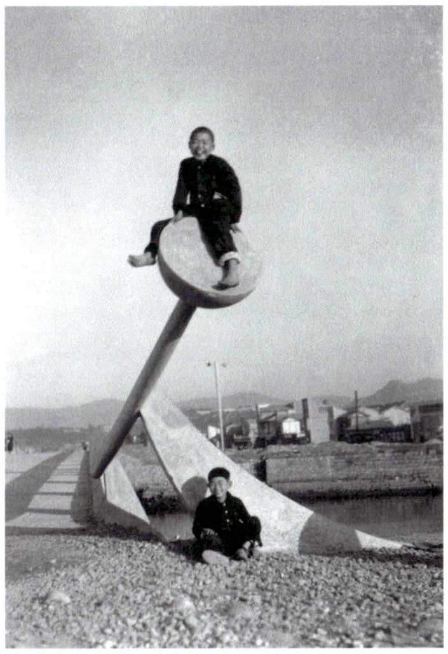

Tsukuru (To Build), bridge railings, Hiroshima, 1950s

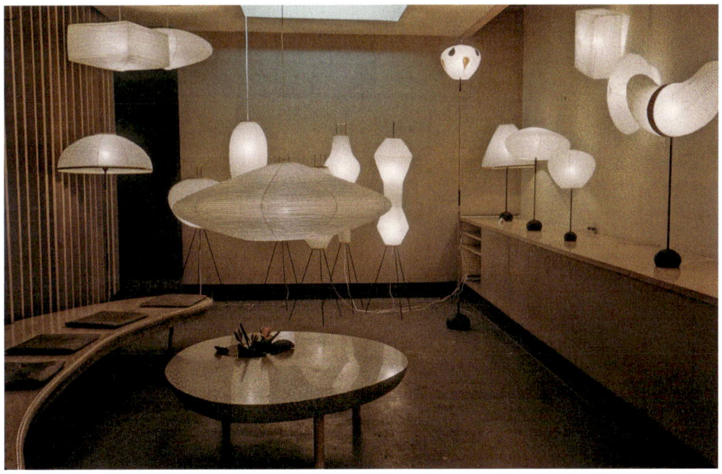

Exhibition of *Akari* at Chūō Kōron Gallery, Tokyo, 2–7 August 1954

prefecture. Creates a studio and uses Rosanjin's kilns to create new ceramic works.

August–September: Visits Imbe in Okayama, famous for its Bizen pottery.

September: A solo exhibition of Noguchi's ceramics is held at the Museum of Modern Art in Kamakura.

1953

Kouros (1945) is acquired by the Metropolitan Museum of Art, New York.

January: The couple return to New York, but Yamaguchi's visa is denied due to suspected past associations with communists in Hollywood.

March: Noguchi submits patent applications for the *Akari*.

May: Enters into a commercial agreement with the Bonniers store in New York to sell the *Akari*. Martha Graham's *Voyage*, with set design by Noguchi, premieres in New York.

July–August: Visits Yamaguchi in Paris and they travel together around France. Visits marble quarries in Carrara, Italy.

November: Returns to Paris from New York. Travels with Yamaguchi for several months around Greece, Egypt, Burma, Thailand, Hong Kong, Macau, Cambodia, Indonesia and Singapore. Visits marble quarries while in Greece.

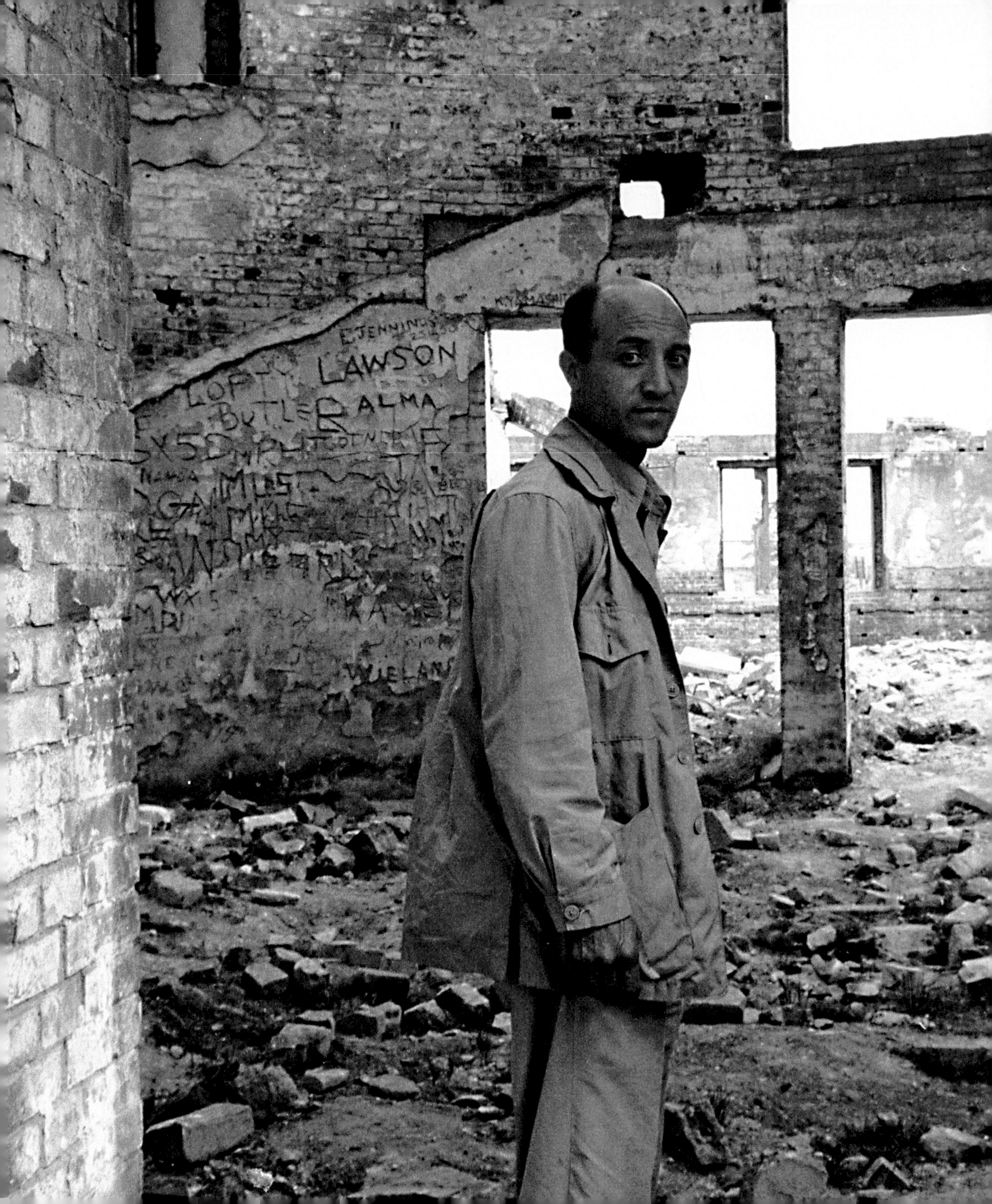
E JENNINGS
LAWSON
LOFTY
BUTLER
ALMA

Noguchi in Hiroshima, Japan, 1951

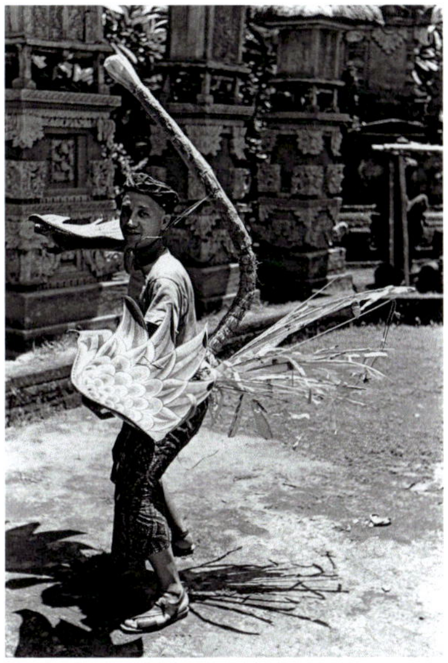

Noguchi in Bali, Indonesia, dressed as Garuda, a mythical bird-like figure, 1950–53

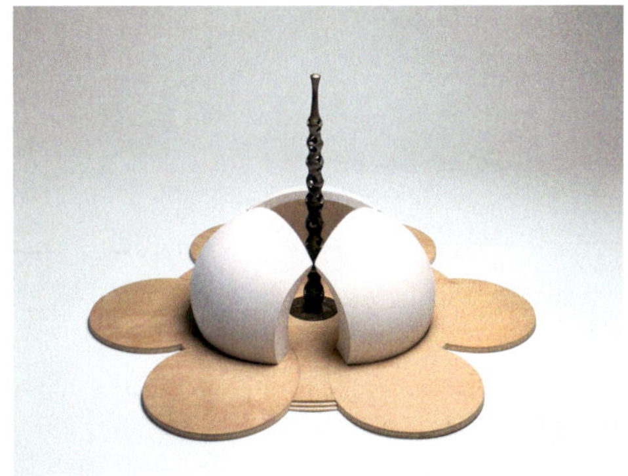

Model for *Memorial to Buddha*, 1957 (unrealised), bronze, plaster and wood, 47.6 × 84.5 × 84.5 cm

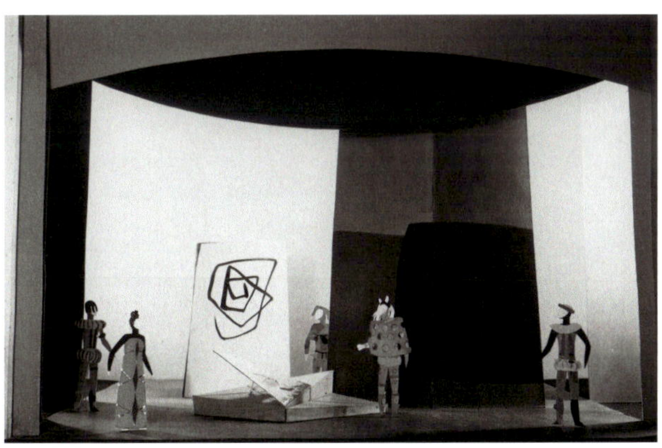

Model stage set for *King Lear*, Royal Shakespeare Company, 1955

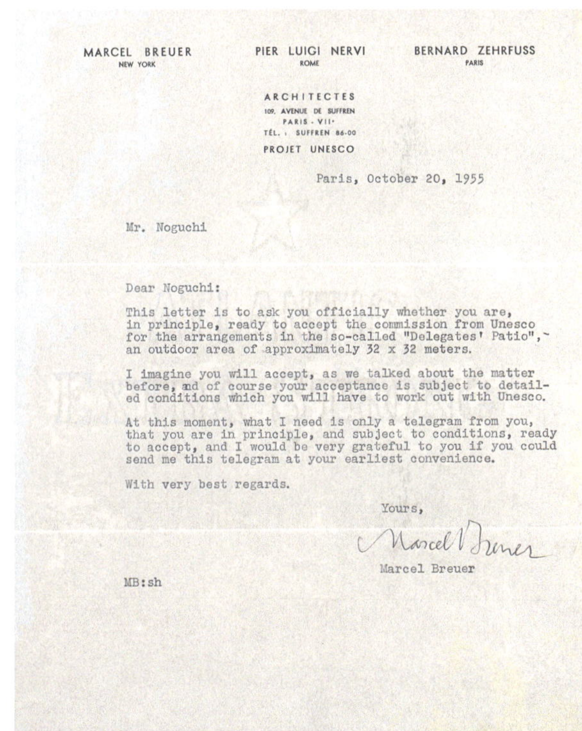

MARCEL BREUER NEW YORK — PIER LUIGI NERVI ROME — BERNARD ZEHRFUSS PARIS

ARCHITECTES
109, AVENUE DE SUFFREN
PARIS - VIIe
TÉL. : SUFFREN 86-00
PROJET UNESCO

Paris, October 20, 1955

Mr. Noguchi

Dear Noguchi:

This letter is to ask you officially whether you are, in principle, ready to accept the commission from Unesco for the arrangements in the so-called "Delegates' Patio",- an outdoor area of approximately 32 x 32 meters.

I imagine you will accept, as we talked about the matter before, and of course your acceptance is subject to detailed conditions which you will have to work out with Unesco.

At this moment, what I need is only a telegram from you, that you are in principle, and subject to conditions, ready to accept, and I would be very grateful to you if you could send me this telegram at your earliest convenience.

With very best regards.

Yours,

Marcel Breuer

MB:sh

Letter to Noguchi from Marcel Breuer, 20 October 1955

1954

February: Travels from Hong Kong to Indonesia.

May: Noguchi's Bollingen grant is extended for a further year. Returns to Japan, where he moves from Kamakura to Tokyo.

August: An exhibition of the *Akari* is held at Chūō Kōron Gallery, Tokyo. Noguchi also designs the gallery's interior, including a table and bench.

November: Noguchi's first exhibition at Stable Gallery, New York, opens, featuring terracotta works.

1955

February–March: Stays in London and Paris with Yamaguchi. Designs costumes and sets for a London production of *King Lear* by the Royal Shakespeare Company.

May: Set designs by Noguchi feature in Martha Graham's *Theatre of a Voyage* and *Seraphic Dialogue*.

Summer: Returns to New York. Enters into an agreement with Knoll Associates, Inc. to manufacture his furniture designs and with Wohnbedarf AG in Switzerland for distribution of the *Akari*. Submits a proposal for a monument to the Buddha for the 2,500th Buddha Jayanti celebration in Kathmandu, Nepal.

September: Meets the architect Shoji Sadao (1927–2019), who will work with Noguchi on the realisation of many projects.

UNESCO Gardens, Paris, 1956–58

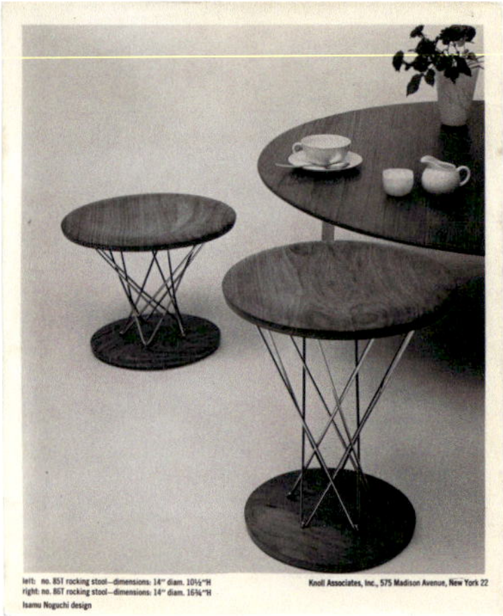

Advertisement for the *Rocking Stool* (Knoll 85-T and 86-T), 1954–60

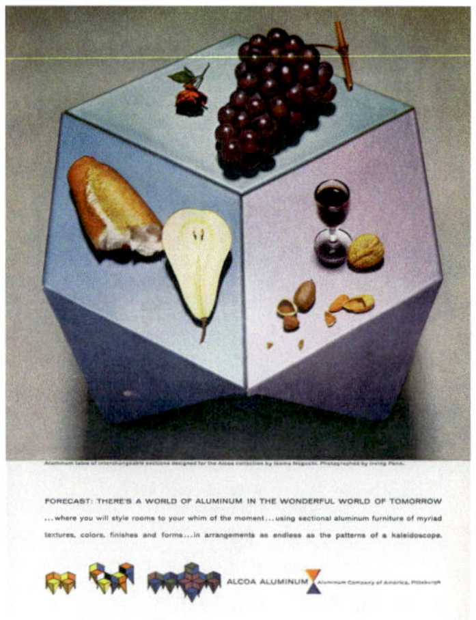

Advertisement for Alcoa Aluminum showing the *Prismatic Table*, photographed by Irving Penn, *Industrial Design*, July 1957

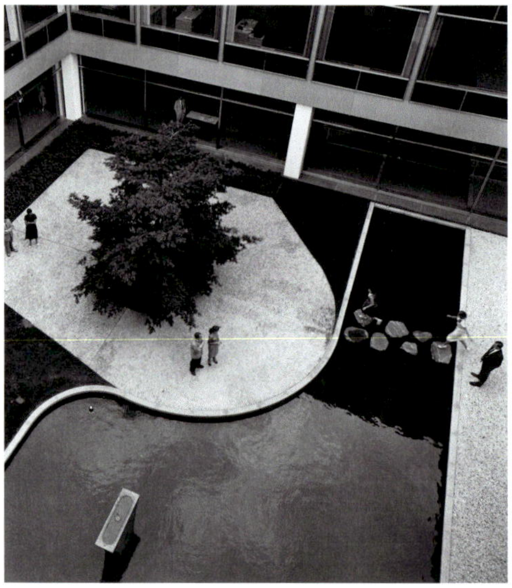

Gardens for Connecticut General Life Insurance Company, Bloomfield, Connecticut, 1956–57

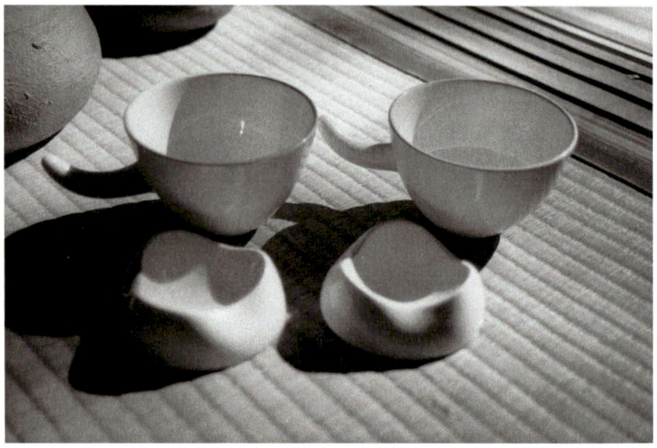

Cup and saucer prototypes, 1956, glazed porcelain, 6.4 × 14.3 × 10.2 cm; 3.2 × 8.3 × 8.3 cm

Autumn: Receives important commissions: the gardens at the UNESCO Headquarters in Paris; an interior design for 666 Fifth Avenue, New York; and a landscape design project at the Connecticut General Life Insurance headquarters in Bloomfield, Connecticut, designed by Skidmore, Owings & Merrill.

1956

US patents (applied for in 1953) are granted for the stretchers and supports for the *Akari* lamps.

January–June: Travels to London, Paris, Zurich, Karachi, Kathmandu, Patna, Calcutta, Hong Kong and Japan.

March: Noguchi and Yamaguchi file for divorce.

Summer: Creates iron sand-castings in Gifu and bell-bronze castings in Kyoto.

1957

April: Meets Mirei Shigemori (1896–1975), author of *Nihon teien-shi zukan*, a landmark 26-volume history of Japanese gardens, who helps with the search for stones for Noguchi's *UNESCO Gardens*, sourcing them in Shikoku and Okayama.

June: In Tokushima, Noguchi and Shigemori work on arrangements of the stones for the UNESCO project; Sadao assists.

September: Noguchi returns to Paris and rents a studio. Designs a *Prismatic Table* for Alcoa (Aluminum Company of America); prototypes are made but it never goes into production.

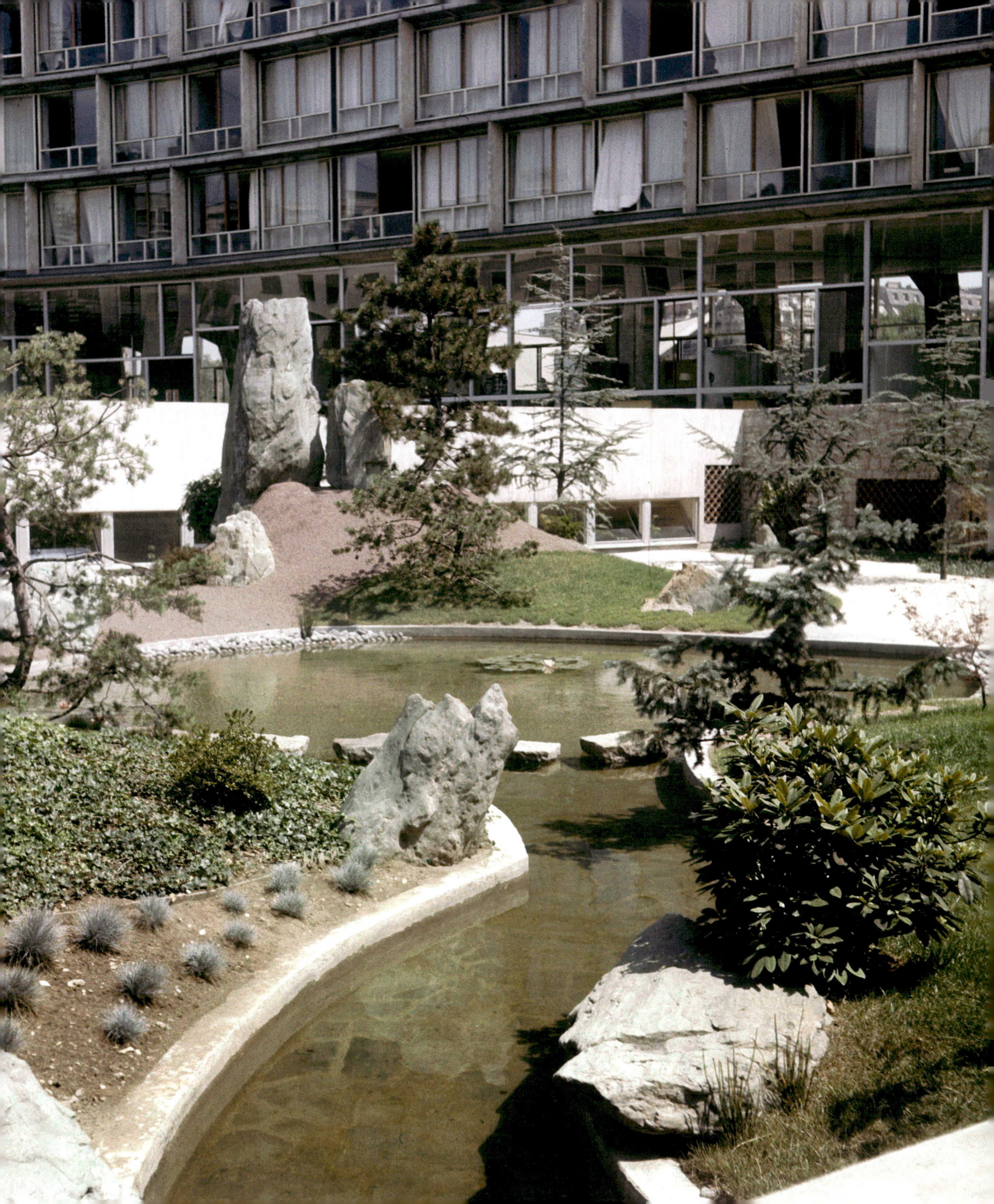

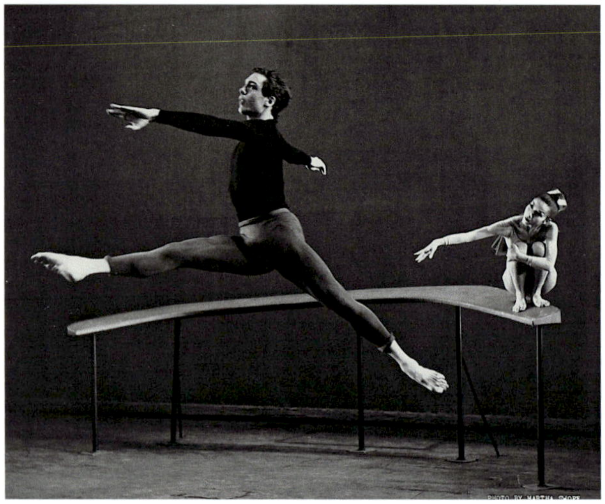

Stage set for Martha Graham, *Acrobats of God*, 1960

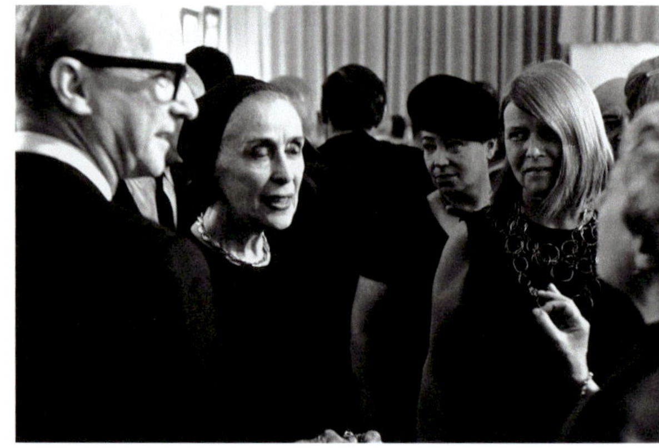

Martha Graham and Priscilla Morgan at the opening of Noguchi's retrospective at the Whitney Museum, April 1968

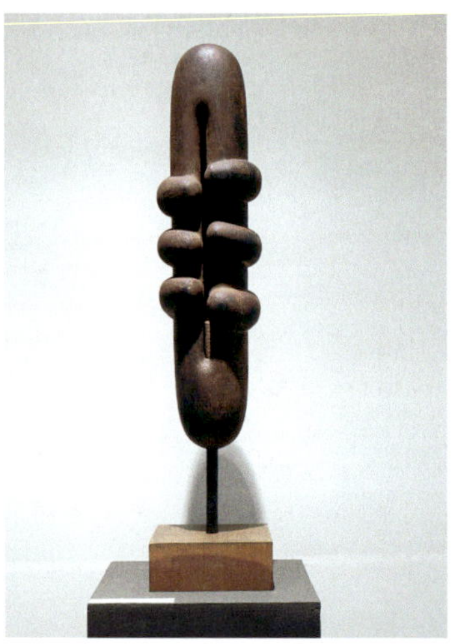

The Self, 1956, iron, 87.3 × 24.4 × 23.5 cm

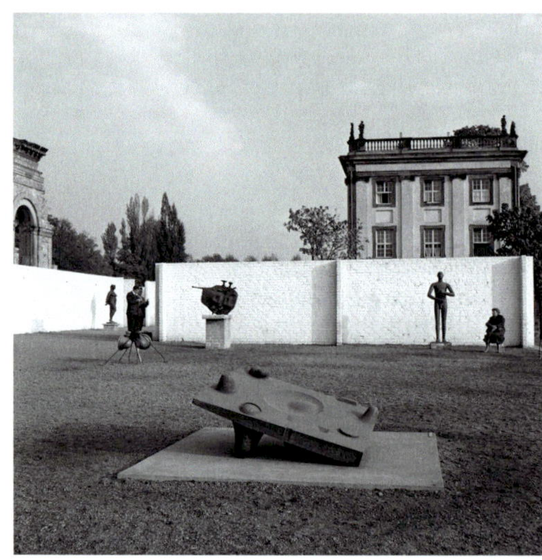

Night Land (Night Voyage) at documenta II, Kassel, Germany, 1959

1958

February: Travels to Greece to obtain marble for sculptural works.

April: Martha Graham's *Clytemnestra* and *Embattled Garden* premiere in New York with Noguchi's set designs. A stainless steel sculpture by Noguchi is included in the US Pavilion at Expo 58, Brussels.

November: Completes work on the *UNESCO Gardens* in Paris and returns to New York.

December: Starts to work with sheet aluminium at the workshop of lighting designer Edison Price, assisted by Sadao.

1959

April: Noguchi's second solo show at Stable Gallery.

July: Participates in documenta II in Kassel, Germany.

Summer: Travels to Paris, London and Rome.

1960

The Self (1956) is acquired by the Tate Gallery, London.

January–February: Travels to Jerusalem on the invitation of Billy Rose to consult on the design of a sculpture garden for the planned Israel Museum.

April: Martha Graham's *Acrobats of God* and *Alcestis* premiere in New York with stage designs by Noguchi.

Spring–Summer: Travels to Japan to search for granite and stone for

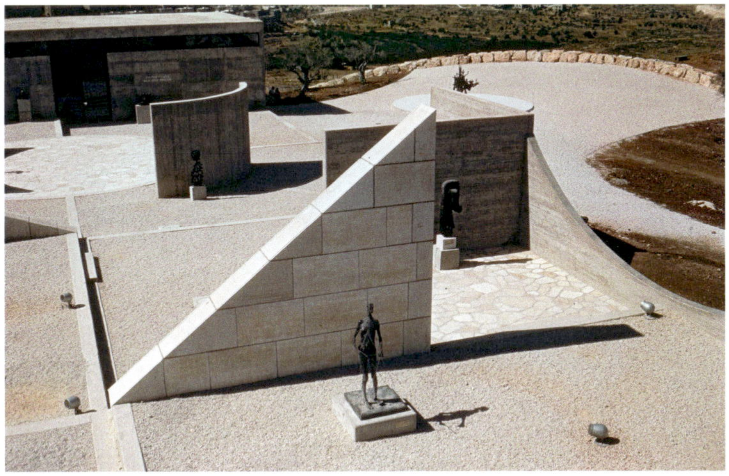

The Billy Rose Art Garden, Israel Museum, Jerusalem, 1960–65

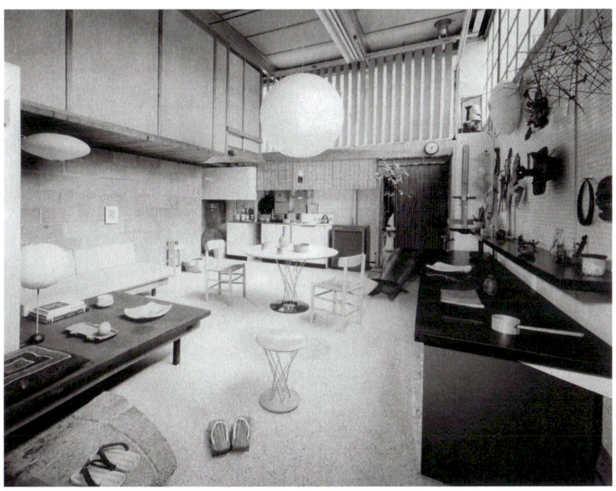

Noguchi's studio on 10th Street, Long Island City, Queens

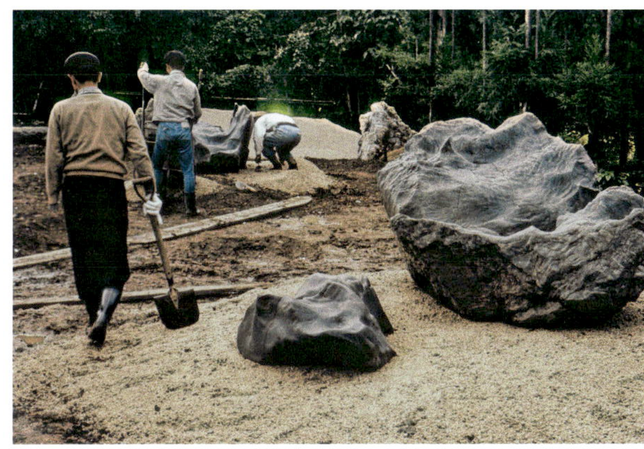

Test positioning of stones from the Uji river in Japan for *Sunken Garden for Chase Manhattan Bank Plaza*, early 1960s

a commission at the First National Bank building in Fort Worth, Texas (completed 1961), and for stones that will later be used in his *Sunken Garden* at Chase Manhattan Plaza, New York.

October–November: Travels to Kyoto and then India with Gordon and Nina Bunshaft. Goes to Chandigarh to see Le Corbusier and Pierre Jeanneret and returns to the Jantar Mantar astronomical observatory in Jaipur.

1961

Establishes a studio and home in Long Island City, Queens, close to stone suppliers and metal fabricators (and across the street from the future site of The Isamu Noguchi Foundation and Garden Museum).

Begins a collaboration with architect Louis I. Kahn on the Adele Rosenwald Levy Memorial Playground for Riverside Park, New York.

Solo exhibitions at Fort Worth Art Center and at Daniel Cordier & Michael Warren, Inc. in New York.

1962

January: The *Sunken Garden* design for Chase Manhattan Plaza is approved.

March: Premiere of Martha Graham's *Phaedra* in New York, with set design by Noguchi.

March–April: Returns to Israel to start work on the Billy Rose Art Garden (completed in 1965).

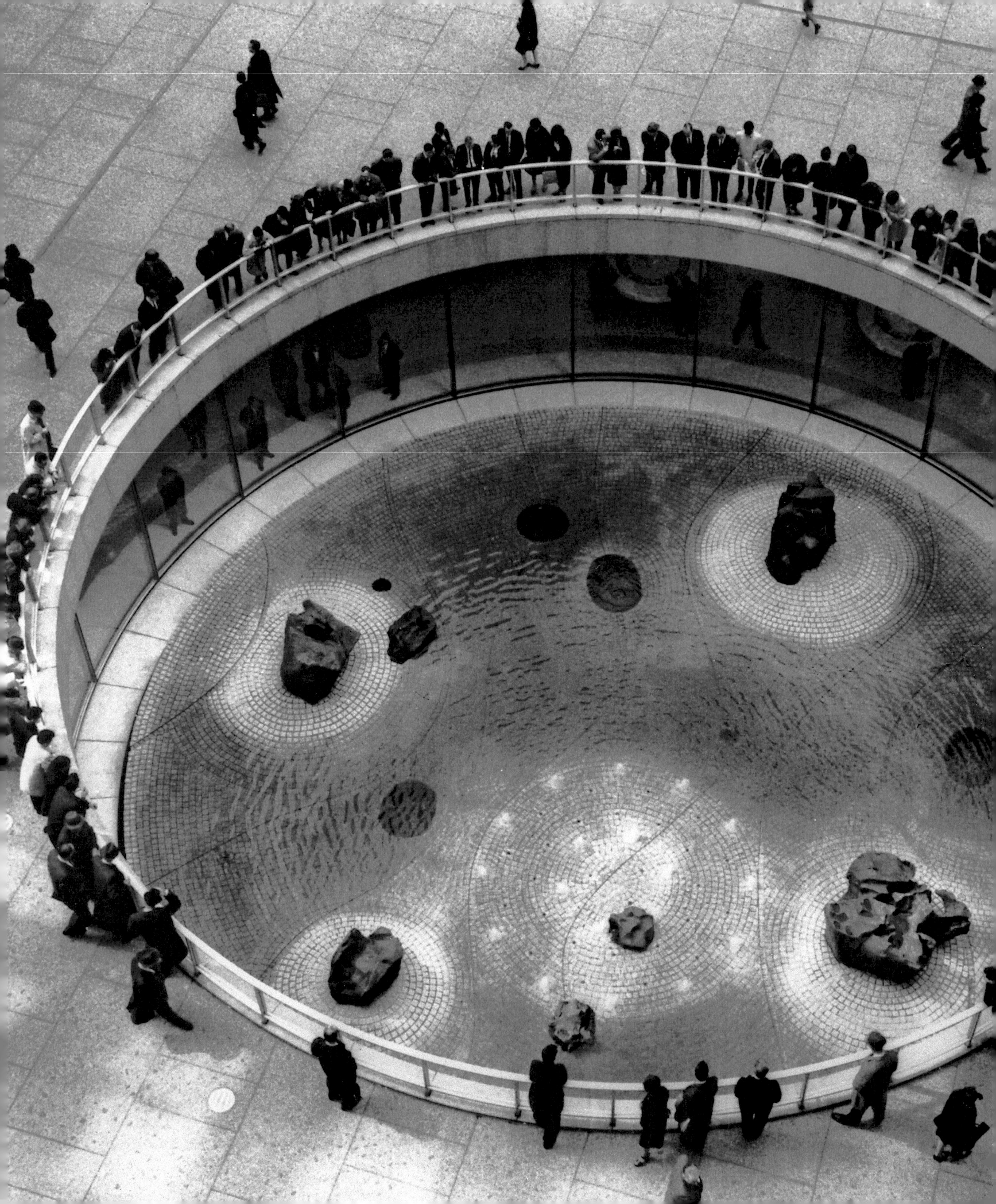

Sunken Garden for Chase Manhattan Bank Plaza, New York, 1961–64

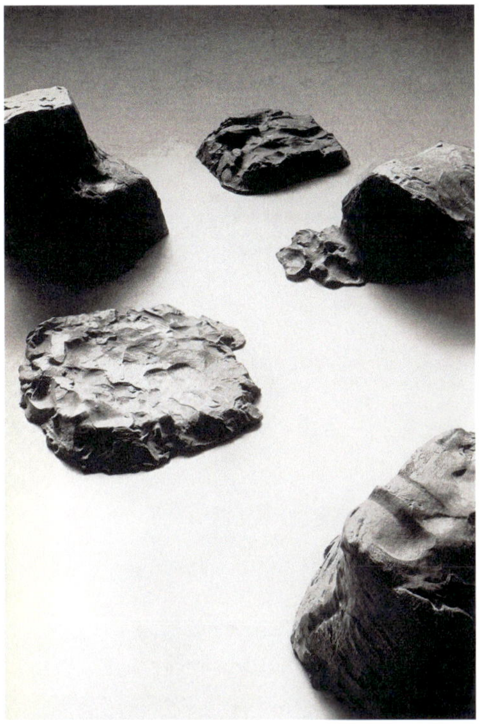

Lessons of Musokokushi, 1962, photographed for the catalogue of an exhibition at Galerie Claude Bernard, Paris, 1964

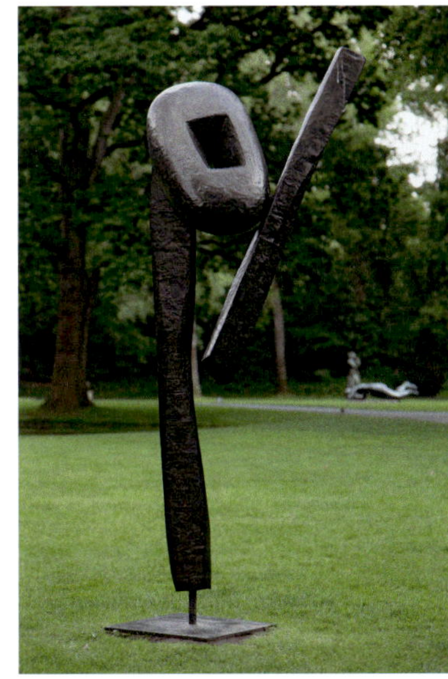

The Cry, 1959–61/62, bronze, 217.5 × 77 × 63 cm, Kröller-Müller Museum sculpture garden, Otterlo

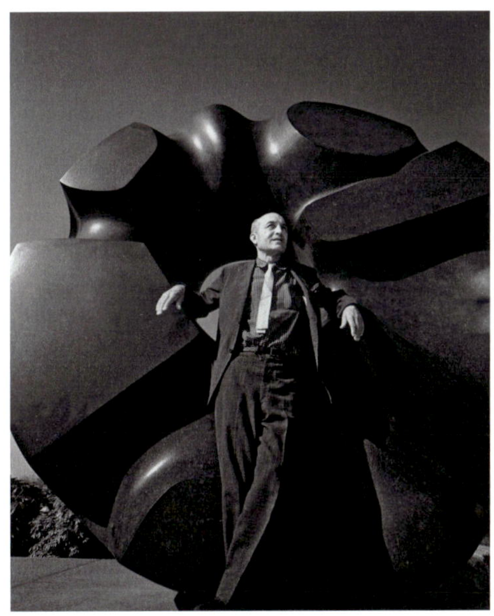

Noguchi with *Black Sun*, Volunteer Park, Seattle, 1969

Summer: Travels to Rome, where he is given a studio at the American Academy. Creates sculptures in balsa wood and clay, to be cast in bronze. Works in Erminio Cidonio's marble studios, close to the marble quarries in Pietrasanta, Tuscany. Establishes the Baraka Corporation to manage his bronze editions.

September: Returns to New York.

1964

February: Completes the *Sunken Garden for Chase Manhattan Bank Plaza*. Creates gardens for the IBM Headquarters in Armonk, New York. Designs a tomb for John F. Kennedy (unrealised).

June: Noguchi's first solo show in Europe is held at Galerie Claude Bernard, Paris. Participates in documenta III in Kassel, Germany.

1966

Two Noguchi works are shown in the Sonsbeek sculpture exhibition in the Netherlands; two other works, *The Cry* (1959–61/62) and *Avatar* (1947), are acquired for the collection of the Kröller-Müller Museum, Otterlo.

October: Noguchi and Kahn's proposed Adele Rosenwald Levy Memorial Playground project is abandoned.

1967

February: Premiere of the last collaboration with Martha Graham, *Cortege of Eagles*.

Summer: Receives an invitation from the United States Information Agency to create an exhibition design for the US Pavilion at Expo '70 in Osaka, Japan (unrealised). Begins working with the Japanese stone carver Masatoshi Izumi (b. 1938) at his studios in Mure (now Takamatsu) on *Black Sun*, a commission for the Seattle Art Museum (completed 1969).

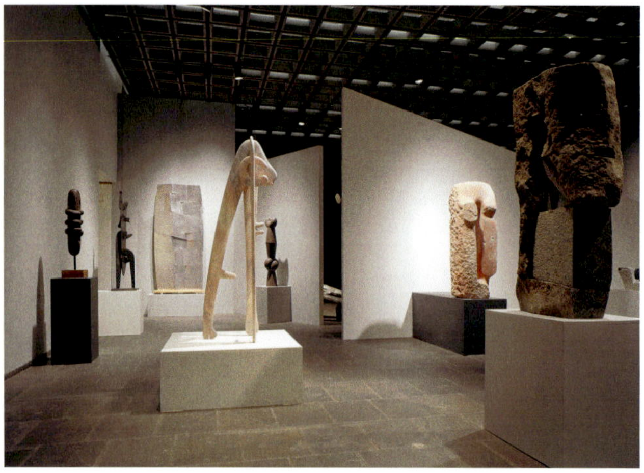

Exhibition view of *Isamu Noguchi*, Whitney Museum of American Art, New York, 17 April–16 June 1968

Octetra in the Piazza del Duomo, Spoleto, Italy, 1968

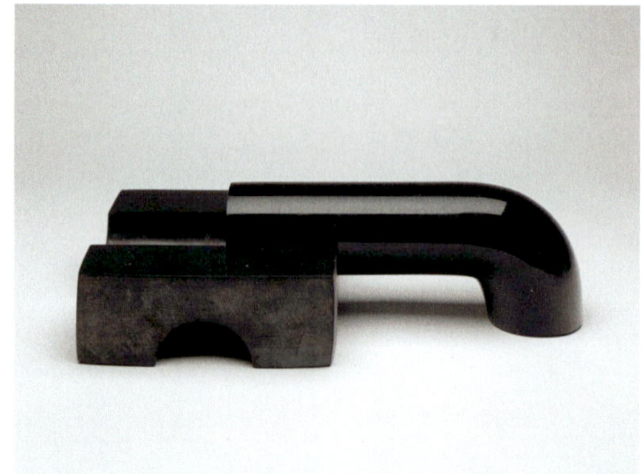

Sharpshooter, 1966–67 (renamed *Squareshooter / Homage to Martin Luther King* in 1968), granite, 11.4 × 38.7 × 20 cm

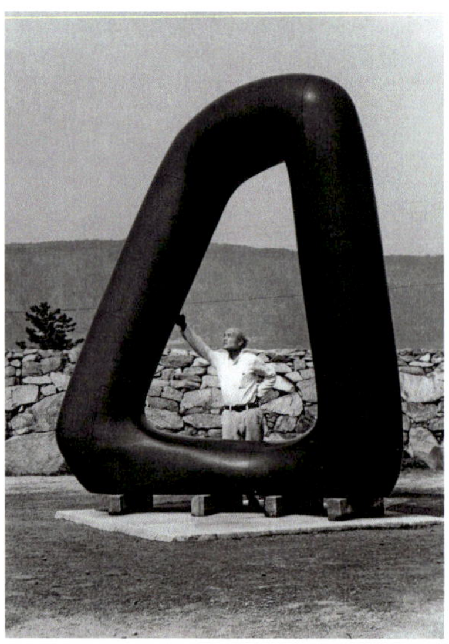

Noguchi with *Energy Void* in Mure, Japan, 1971

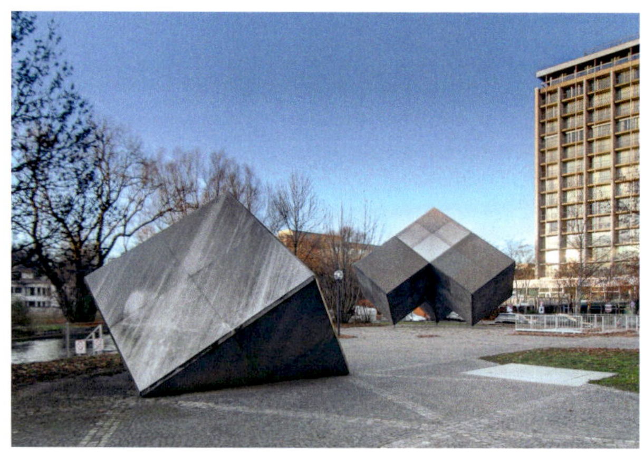

Twin Sculpture, Bayerische Vereinsbank, Munich, Germany, 1970–72

1968

April: Noguchi's first retrospective exhibition is presented at the Whitney Museum.

Summer: Invited by Kenzō Tange to design fountains for the central lake of the Expo '70 village in Osaka. Solo shows take place at Gimpel Fils, London, and Gimpel & Hannover, Zurich. Harper & Row publish Noguchi's autobiography, *A Sculptor's World*.

1969

Sets up a studio in Mure, Japan, aided by Masatoshi Izumi, where he works on large stone sculptures.

Forms Akari Associates in New York to manage worldwide distribution of the light sculptures.

1971

Summer: Participates in the Middelheim sculpture biennial in Belgium.

1972

May: The film *Isamu Noguchi: A Sculptor's World*, produced by Arnold Eagle, is released.

May–June: Solo exhibition *Strange Birds* at Cordier & Ekstrom Gallery, New York. The *Twin Sculpture* (1970–72) is erected in the Tucherpark district of Munich.

June: Participates in the Venice Biennale.

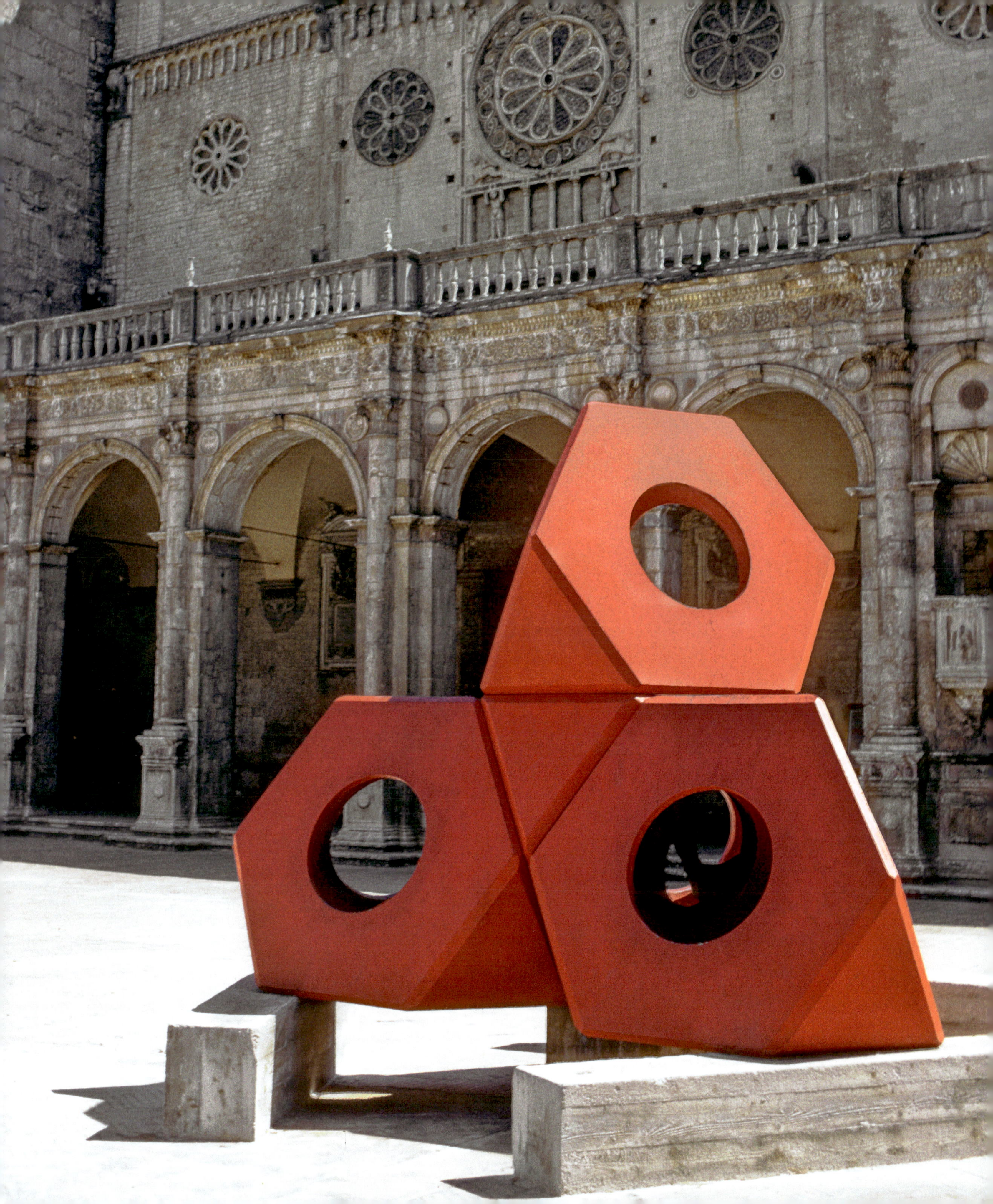

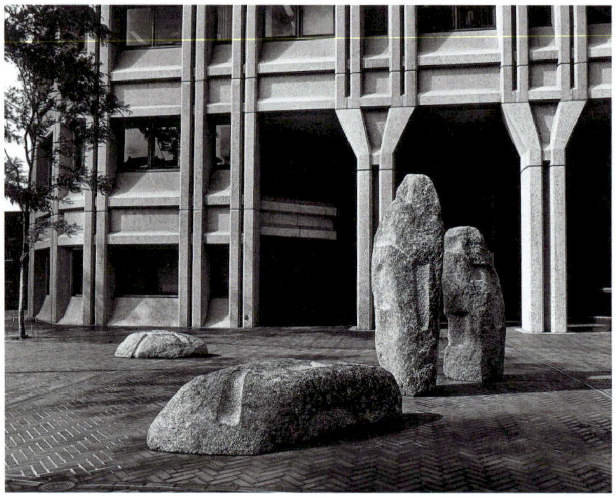

Landscape of Time, Henry M. Jackson Federal Building Plaza, Seattle, 1975

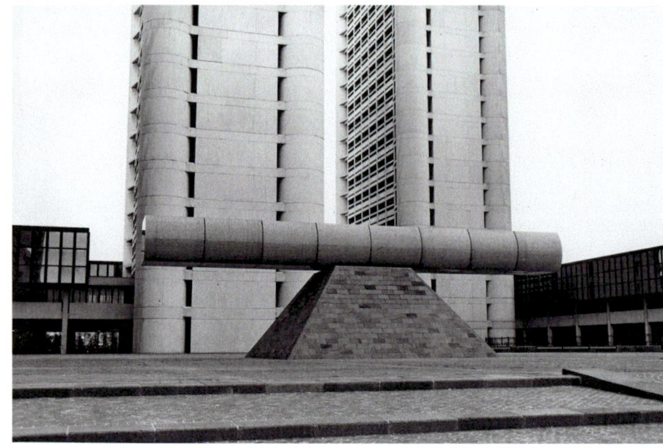

Noguchi and Kenzō Tange, piazza for the Fiere di Bologna, Italy, 1979

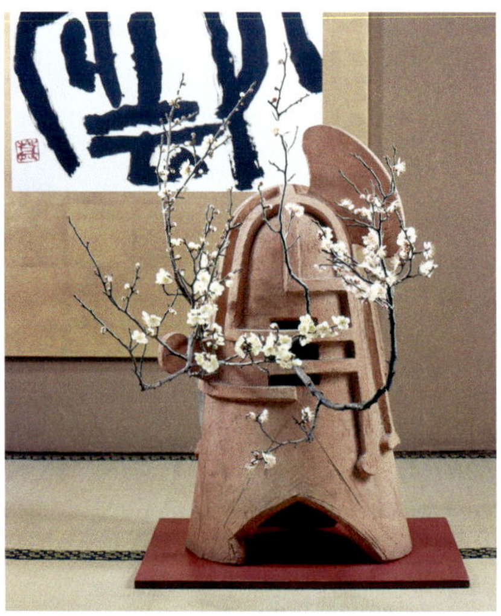

War/Senso (Helmet/Kabuto), 1952, with *ikebana* arrangement by Sōfū Teshigahara, 1973

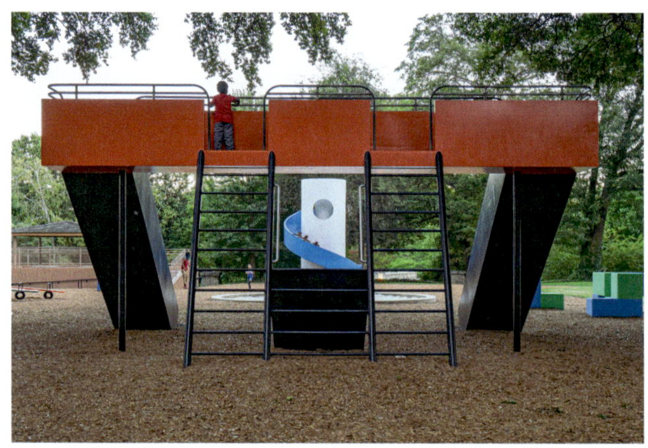

Playscapes, Piedmont Park, Atlanta, Georgia, 1975–76

1974

Participates in *Japan: Tradition und Gegenwart* (Japan: Tradition and the Present) at the Kunsthalle Düsseldorf and Louisiana Museum of Modern Art, Denmark.

Acquires the building at 33rd Street and Vernon Boulevard, across the street from his Long Island City studio.

1975

Landscape of Time is installed at the Jackson Federal Building in Seattle, Washington.

Playscapes, made with Shoji Sadao, opens in Piedmont Park in Atlanta, Georgia.

1977

Works on *Momo Taro*, a stone sculpture for the Storm King Art Center in Mountainville, New York.

Designs *Heaven*, an interior plaza for the Sōgetsu Kaikan, Tokyo (headquarters of the Sōgetsu school of *ikebana*, with architecture by Kenzō Tange).

Is awarded a gold medal from the American Academy of Arts and Letters.

November: *Noguchi: Sculptor as Designer*, a solo show, is held at MoMA.

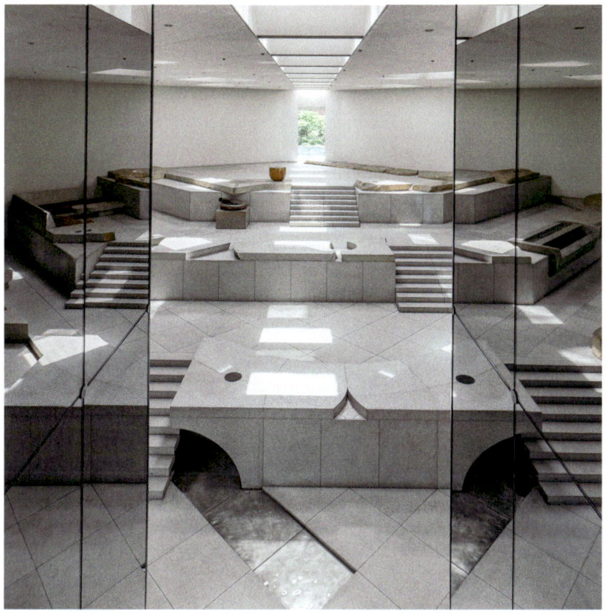

Heaven (Tengoku), interior garden for the Sōgetsu school of *ikebana*, Tokyo, 1977–78

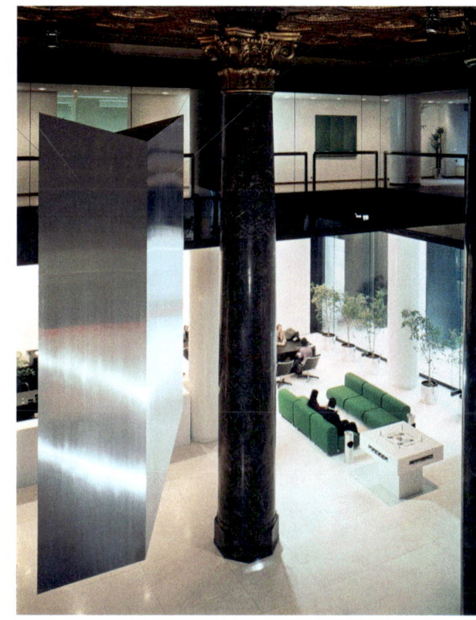

Shinto, Bank of Tokyo Building, New York, 1974–75 (destroyed 1980)

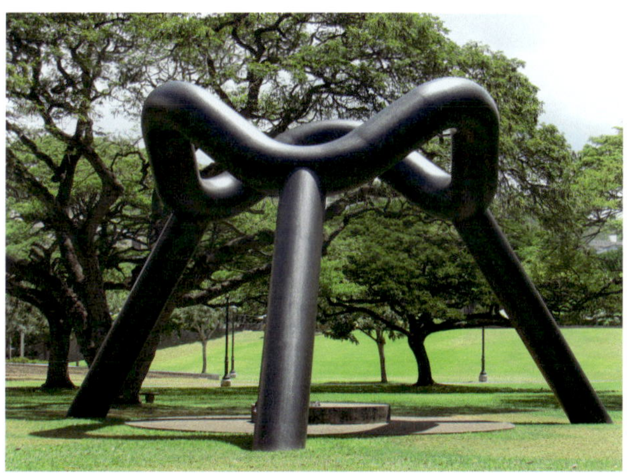

Sky Gate, Honolulu, Hawaii, 1976–77

1978

The first monograph on Noguchi, written by Sam Hunter, is published by Abeville Books.

April: The solo exhibition *Noguchi's Imaginary Landscapes* opens at Walker Art Center, Minneapolis. It will travel to the Denver Art Museum, Cleveland Museum of Art, Detroit Institute of Arts and San Francisco Museum of Modern Art before concluding in January 1980 at the Philadelphia Museum of Art.

1979

Meets the fashion designer Issey Miyake at the International Design Conference in Aspen, Colorado.

Begins work on *Bolt of Lightning*, a memorial to Benjamin Franklin, initially designed in 1933. Installation is completed in 1985 in Philadelphia.

1980

The Akari Foundation is renamed the Isamu Noguchi Foundation.

Works on *California Scenario* (Costa Mesa, California, completed 1982) and on *Fountain for Bayfront Park* (Miami, Florida, completed 1996 by Shoji Sadao).

February: The solo exhibition *Isamu Noguchi: The Sculpture of Spaces* opens at the Whitney Museum.

April: *Shinto* (1974–75), an earlier commission for the Bank of Tokyo in New York, is removed and dismantled without Noguchi's consent, with the incident widely covered in the press. Begins the large outdoor sculpture *To the Issei* (1980–83) for the Japanese American Cultural and Community Center in the Little Tokyo area of Los Angeles.

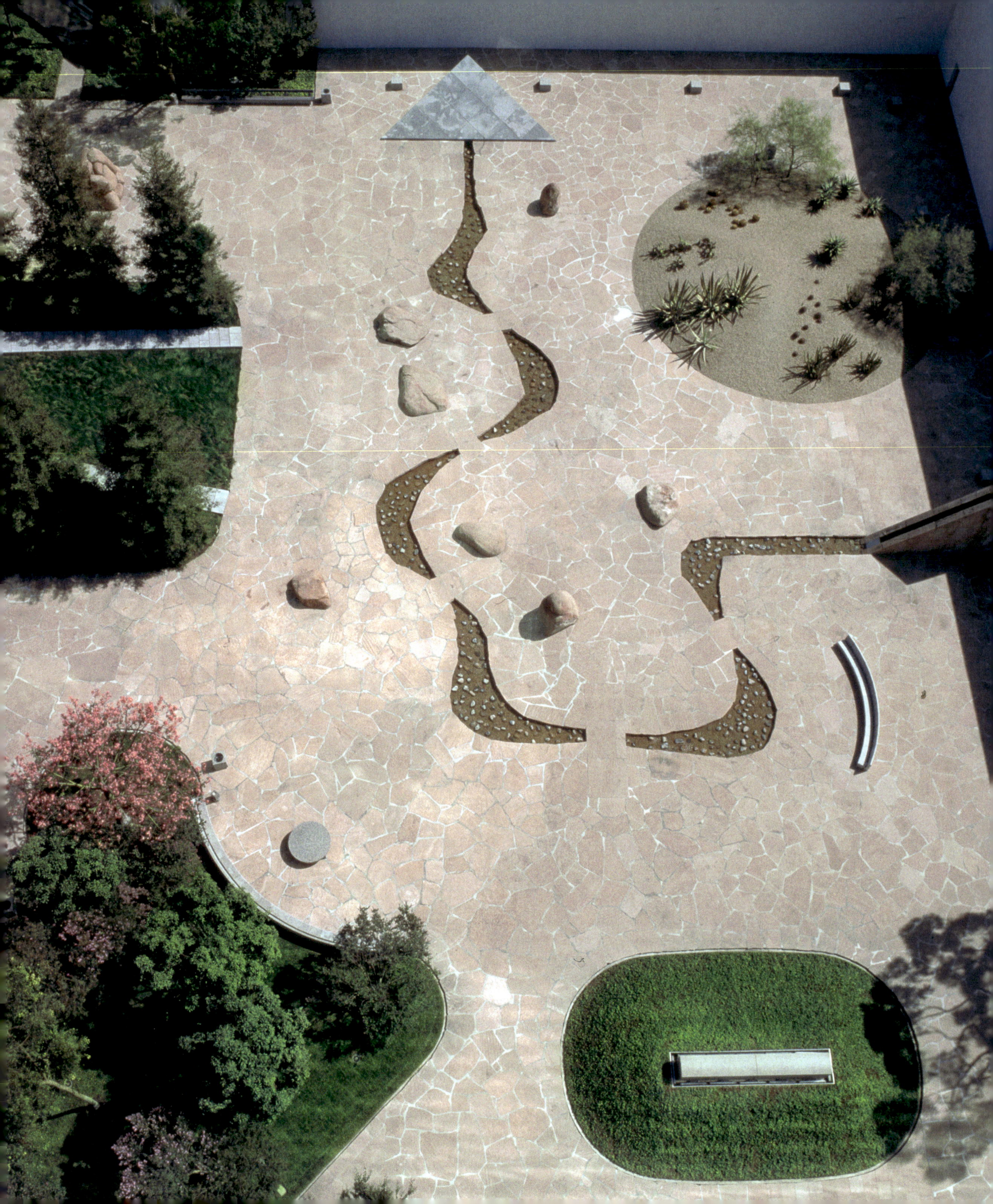

California Scenario, 1980–82, Costa Mesa, California

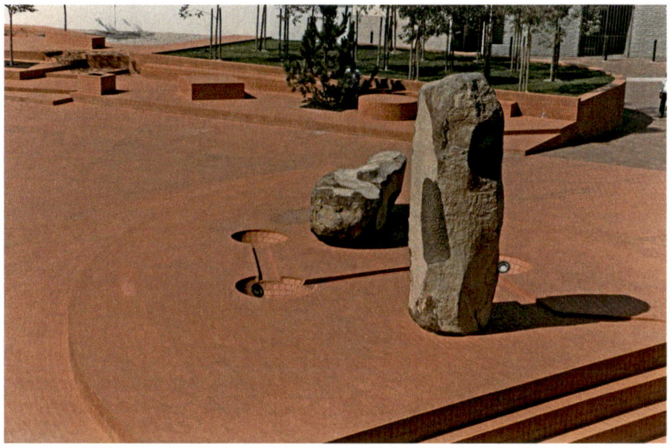

To the Issei, 1980–83, Japanese American Cultural and Community Center, Los Angeles

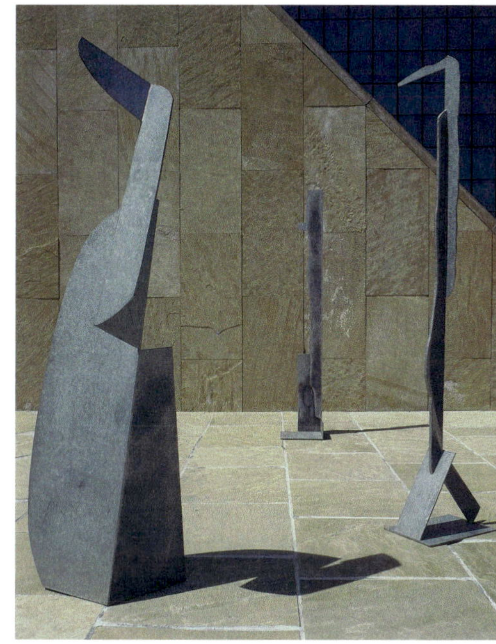

Left to right: *Figure Emerging*, 1982–83; *Root and Stem*, 1982–83; *Giacometti's Shadow*, 1982–83, galvanised steel

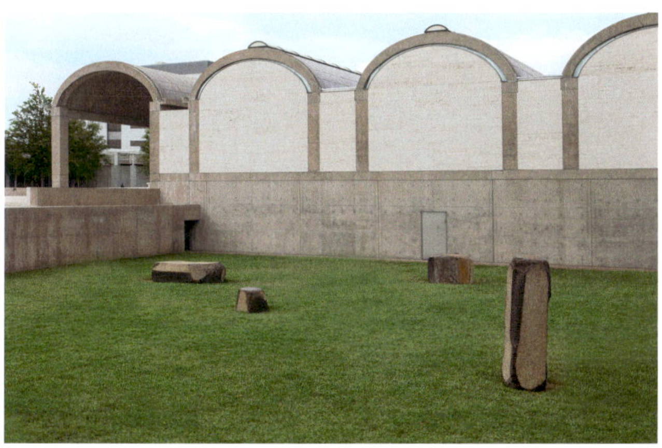

Constellation (for Louis Kahn), 1982, basalt, Kimbell Art Museum, Fort Worth, Texas

1981

June: Visits Brâncuși's public artworks in Târgu Jiu, Romania. Begins design and building of The Isamu Noguchi Garden Museum in Long Island City with Shoji Sadao.

1982

Works on a series of galvanised steel sculptures with the printing workshop Gemini G.E.L. in Los Angeles.

1983

March: Visits Peru, including Machu Picchu, accompanied by his half-brother Michio and Masatoshi Izumi.

April: Works on a garden at his studio in Mure, Japan, with Izumi. The Isamu Noguchi Garden Museum opens by appointment in Long Island.

July: The Japanese American Cultural and Community Center Plaza, designed by Noguchi and featuring two granite forms entitled *To the Issei*, opens in Los Angeles.

Numerous solo shows this year: Pace Gallery, New York; Gemini G.E.L., Los Angeles; Richard Gray Gallery, Chicago; George J. Doizaki Gallery, Los Angeles; TLK Gallery, Costa Mesa; Janet Fleischer Gallery, Philadelphia; Gallery Kasahara and Gallery Yamaguchi, both in Osaka; and the Newport Harbor Art Museum, Newport Beach, California.

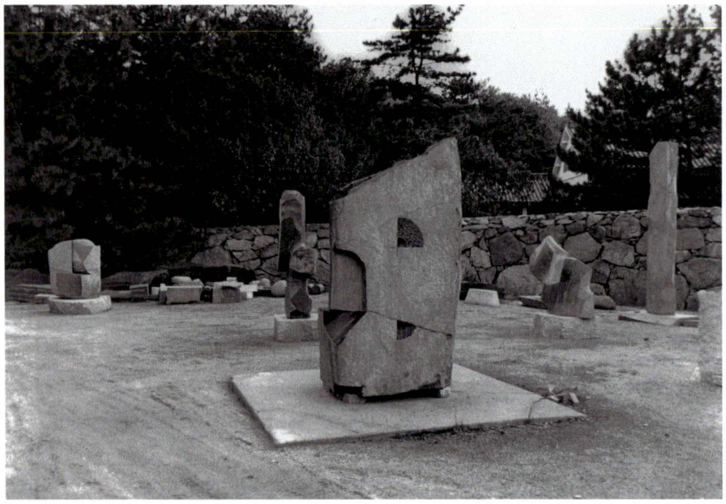

Sculptures in the courtyard outside Noguchi's studio in Mure, Japan, 1986

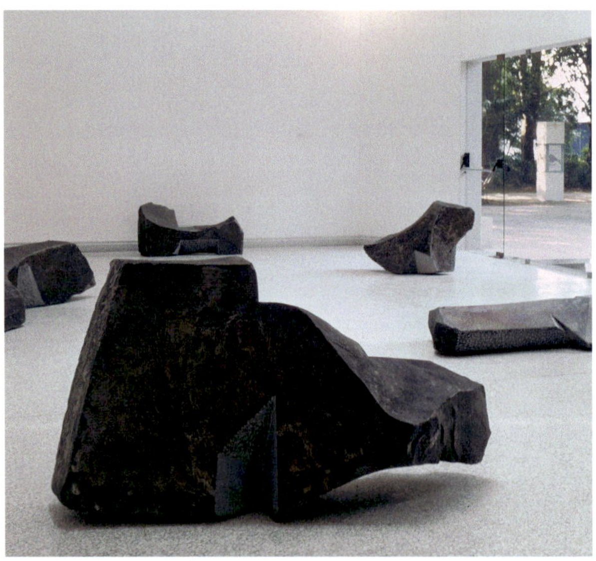

Beginnings, 1985, installed at *Isamu Noguchi: What is Sculpture?*, Venice Biennale, 1986

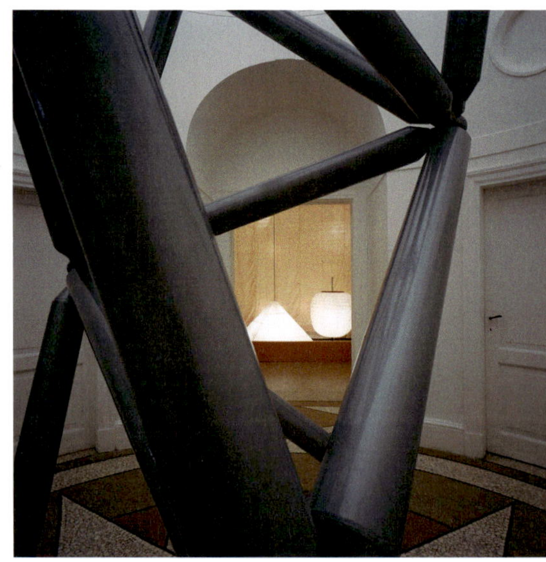

View of *Isamu Noguchi: What is Sculpture?*, Venice Biennale, 1986

1984

Works on the *Water Garden* and sculpture for Ken Domon Museum of Photography, Yamagata, Japan.

Celebrates his 80th birthday at the Sōgetsu Kaikan in Tokyo, where new stone works are exhibited alongside the *Akari*.

The IN-50 *Coffee Table* is put back into commercial production by Herman Miller.

Numerous solo shows this year: Gallery Suzukawa, Hiroshima; Sōgetsu Foundation Plaza, Tokyo; Max Protetch Gallery, New York; Carl Solway Gallery, Cincinnati; Fort Wayne Museum of Art; Storm King Art Center, New Windsor, New York; Basket Park Base, Oita; and Sōgetsu Art Gallery, Tokyo.

1985

The Isamu Noguchi Garden Museum opens to the public.

1986

June: Represents the US at the 42nd Venice Biennale, selected by Henry Geldzahler. The exhibition is titled *Isamu Noguchi: What is Sculpture?* and includes *Slide Mantra* and *Akari* light sculptures.

Works on the *Challenger Memorial*, commemorating the space shuttle accident earlier that year, for Bayfront Park, Miami (completed posthumously in 1989).

Receives the Kyoto Prize in Arts in Japan.

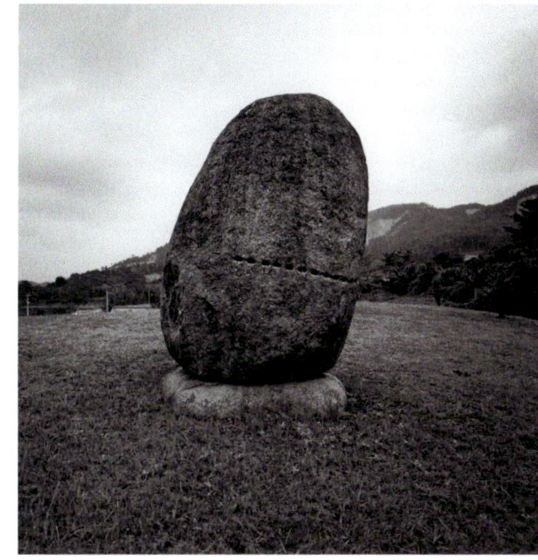

Noguchi's grave in Mure, Japan, 1989

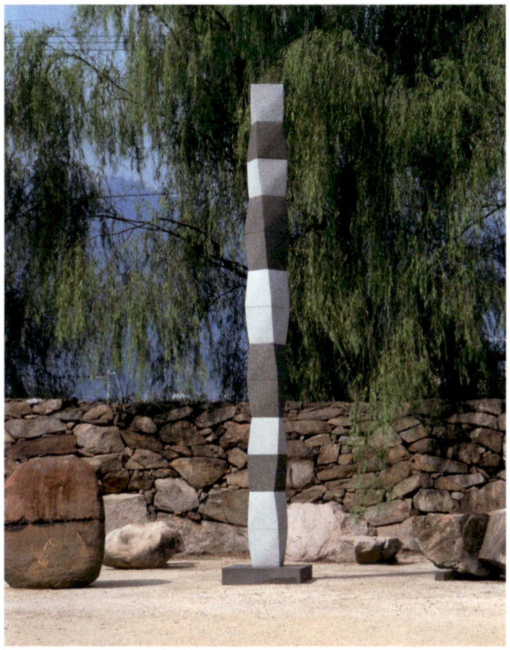

Helix of the Endless #2, 1987, Aji granite and Brazilian granite, 472.1 × 43.2 × 43.2 cm

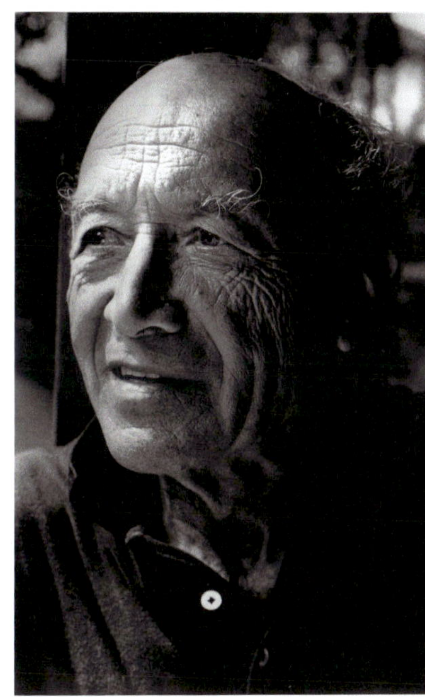

Noguchi photographed by Jun Miki, 1987

1987

Noguchi is awarded the National Medal of Arts by President Ronald Reagan in Washington, DC.

1988

Begins the ambitious outdoor sculpture *Time and Space* (1988–91), comprising hundreds of basalt boulders, for Takamatsu Airport in Kagawa, Japan.

Begins planning Moerenuma Park, a 200-ha park in Sapporo, Japan (posthumously completed in 2005 by Shoji Sadao).

November: Travels to Querceta in Tuscany, Italy, to work on marble sculptures.

30 December: Noguchi dies of heart failure in New York. He is buried in Mure, Japan.

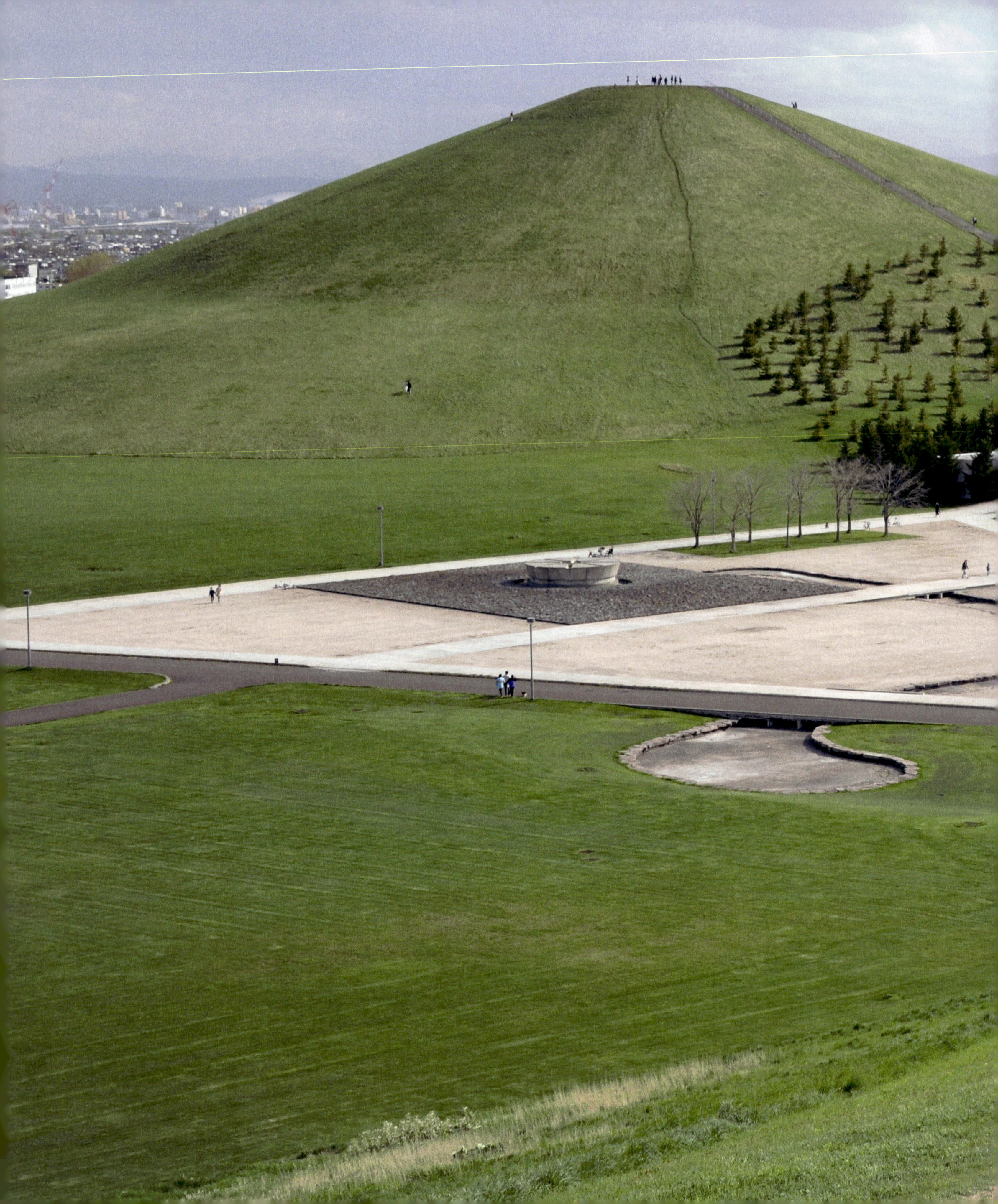

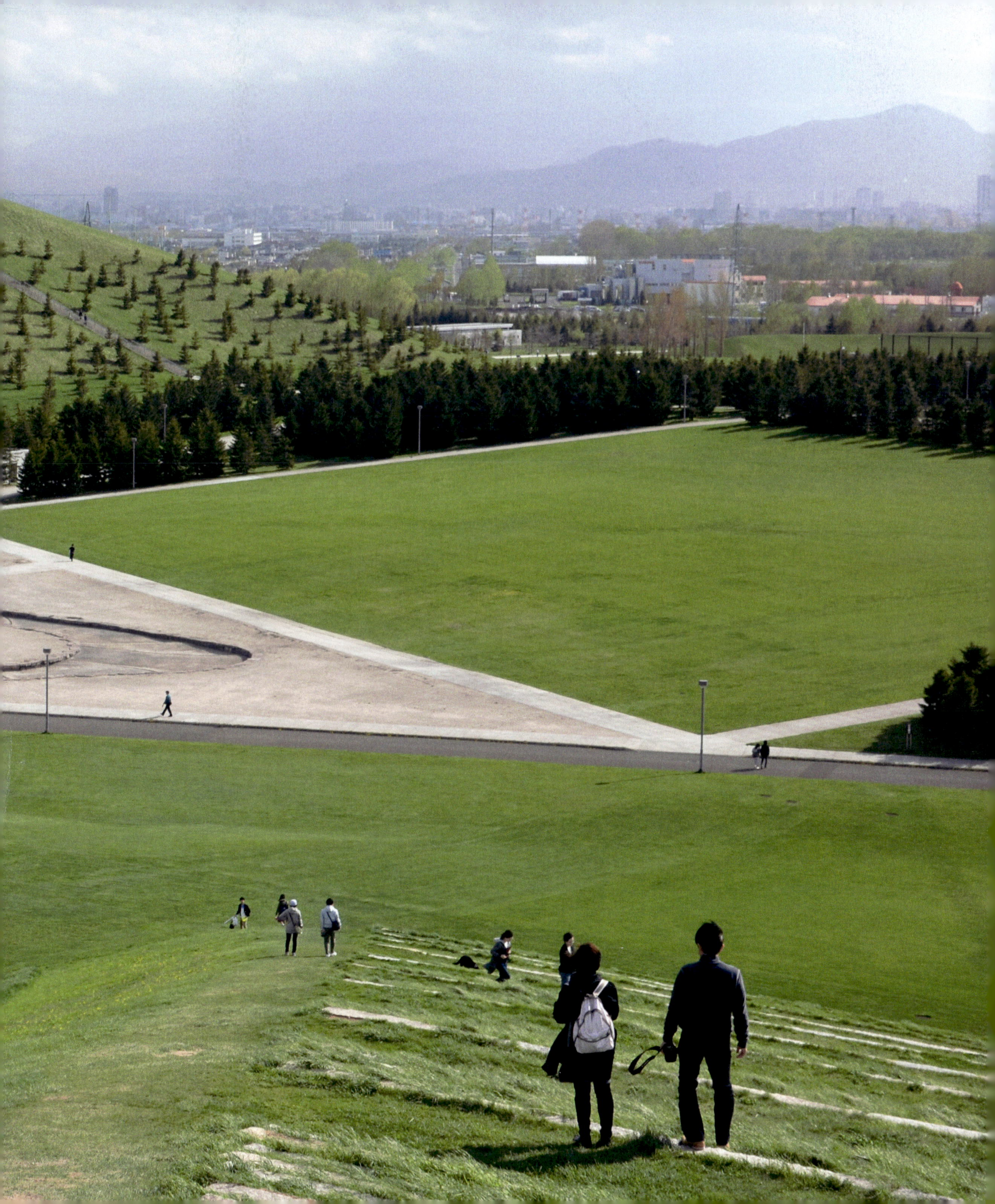

Sources of Quotations

p. 21: Isamu Noguchi, *A Sculptor's World* (London: Thames & Hudson, 1967), p. 18.
p. 24: Ibid., p. 16.
p. 51: Isamu Noguchi, Kyoto Prize 'Commemorative Lecture', 13 November 1986, p. 3, The Noguchi Museum Archives, MS_WRI_077_001.
p. 75: Isamu Noguchi, *The Isamu Noguchi Garden Museum* (New York: Harry N. Abrams, 1987), p. 236.
p. 83: Noguchi, *A Sculptor's World*, p. 23.
p. 86: Ibid., p. 161.
p. 89: Ibid., p. 176.
p. 100: Isamu Noguchi, *I Become a Nisei* [1942] (Holyoke, MA: The Brother in Elysium, 2020), n.p.
p. 118: Noguchi, *A Sculptor's World*, p. 125.
p. 120: Ibid., p. 123.
p. 151: Isamu Noguchi, 'Rough Draft of "A Sense of Place" or "1949"', c. 1979, p. 131, The Noguchi Museum Archives, MS_BOL_017_001.
p. 160: 'From an Interview with Isamu Noguchi', *The League Quarterly*, vol. 20, no. 3 (Spring 1949), p. 8.
p. 165: Isamu Noguchi, 'Sculpture as Invention', c. 1952, pp. 4–5, The Noguchi Museum Archives, MS_WRI_017_001.
p. 171: Noguchi, *A Sculptor's World*, p. 34.
p. 192: Ibid., p. 164.
p. 202: Ibid., pp. 35–36.
p. 222: Noguchi, *The Isamu Noguchi Garden Museum*, p. 100.
p. 242: Noguchi, *A Sculptor's World*, p. 39.
p. 260: R. Buckminster Fuller, 'Foreword', in Noguchi, *A Sculptor's World*, p. 7.
Back cover: Noguchi, *A Sculptor's World*, p. 26.

Images pp. 1–7

View of *Slide Mantra* in *Isamu Noguchi: What is Sculpture?*, Venice Biennale, 1986

Playscapes, 1967
Piedmont Park, Atlanta, Georgia

Octetra, Forest of Cherry Trees, 1982–95
Moerenuma Park, Sapporo, Japan

Red Cube, 1968
140 Broadway, Manhattan, New York City

Tetra Mound, 1988–2000
Moerenuma Park, Sapporo, Japan

California Scenario, 1980–82
Costa Mesa, California

Sky Gate, 1976–77
Honolulu, Hawaii

Image pp. 310–11

Moerenuma Park, 1988–2000,
Sapporo, Japan

The Isamu Noguchi Foundation and Garden Museum, New York, Gifts and Purchases:

pp. 22 (top left, bottom left, bottom right), 23 (top and bottom): *Paris Abstractions*, 1928
Gift of Mrs Gertrude Dennis, 1998

p. 38 (top): *Peking Brush Drawing (Baby with String)*, 1930
Gift of the Estate of Charles Lieb, 2000

p. 45: *Tsuneko-san (Head of a Japanese Girl)*, 1931 (cast c. 1933)
Gift of the Estate of Charles Lieb, 2000

p. 70: *Boy Looking through Legs (Morning Exercises)*, 1933
Museum purchase, 2018

p. 86: Models for playground equipment for Ala Moana Park, Hawaii, 1940
Gift of Linda Tatti Beck and Steven Beck, from the collection of the Alexander Tatti Family, 2006

p. 123: *Tree with Noose*, *Fence with Branches*, *Gravestones*, 1945
Gift of Erick Hawkins, 1992

p. 125: *Jungle Gym*, *Hanging Tree*, 1947
Gift of Erick Hawkins, 1992

pp. 162–63: *Chess Table and Chess Pieces*, 1944
Museum purchase, 2006

pp. 172–73: *Love of Two Boards*, 1950
Gift of Tsutomu Hiroi, 2013

p. 175: *Skin and Bones (Bone and Skin)*, 1950
Gift of Tsutomu Hiroi, 2013

p. 179: *Small Centipede (Mukade No. 2) (Centipede No. 2)*, 1952
Museum purchase, 2012

All illustrated works are held in the collection of The Isamu Noguchi Foundation and Garden Museum, New York, with the exception of:

p. 41: *The Queen*, 1931/c. 1943
Whitney Museum of American Art, New York, Gift of the artist 69.107a-c

p. 50: *R. Buckminster Fuller*, 1929
Alexandra Snyder May

p. 52: R. Buckminster Fuller and Isamu Noguchi, model for the Dymaxion Car, 1932–33
Private Collection

p. 104: *Lunar Landscape*, 1944
Hirshhorn Museum and Sculpture Garden, Smithsonian Institution, Washington, DC, Gift of Joseph H. Hirshhorn, 1966

p. 106: *Lunar Landscape (Woman)*, 1944
The Fralin Museum of Art, University of Virginia

p. 151: *Humpty Dumpty*, 1946
Whitney Museum of American Art, New York, Purchase 47.7a-e

p. 156: *Cronos*, 1947
Walker Art Center, Minneapolis; Gift of the artist, 1979

p. 176: *Marriage (Senbei Buton) (Worn Out Futon)*, 1952
Lucy Lamphere

p. 185: *Cage Vase (Kago) (Basket)*, 1952
Private Collection

p. 200: *Prismatic Table*, 1957
Designed for the Alcoa Forecast Program
Carnegie Museum of Art, Pittsburgh: Gift of Torrence M. Hunt, Sr, 2004.9.2

p. 216: *Mitosis*, 1962
The Museum of Modern Art, New York, James Thrall Soby Bequest 1241.1979

p. 231: *Walking Void #2*, 1974
Masatoshi Izumi, on long-term loan to The Isamu Noguchi Garden Museum, Japan

p. 277 (top right): *Martha Graham*, 1929
Collection of the Honolulu Academy of Arts

p. 277 (bottom right): *Edla Frankau (Mrs Peter Cusick)*, c. 1929
Private Collection

p. 287 (bottom middle): *Three-Legged Cylinder Lamp*, c. 1944
Private Collection

p. 288 (top left): *Kouros*, 1945
The Metropolitan Museum of Art, New York (Fletcher Fund, 1953)

p. 298 (bottom left): *The Self*, 1956
Tate, London

p. 298 (bottom right): *Night Land (Night Voyage)*, 1947
The Nelson-Atkins Museum of Art, Kansas City (F99-33/67)

p. 301 (top right): *The Cry*, 1959–61/62
Kröller-Müller Museum, Otterlo, Netherlands, KM 125.070

Image Credits

**t = top, b = bottom, l = left, m = middle, r = right; cw = clockwise;
INFGM = Isamu Noguchi Foundation and Garden Museum, New York.
Numbers in brackets denote cataloguing numbers in the Noguchi Museum Archives**

© Austrian Frederick and Lillian Kiesler Private Foundation, Vienna, photograph by Willy Maywald: p.290tr. © Austrian Frederick and Lillian Kiesler Private Foundation, Vienna/ ARS – DACS/ProLitteris, Zurich/VG Bild-Kunst, Bonn, photograph by Bernice Kaufmann: pp.146–47. © Tina Barney/© INFGM/ARS – DACS/ProLitteris, Zurich/VG Bild-Kunst, Bonn, photograph by Tina Barney: pp.224–25. © Mark Alden Branch/Yale Alumni Magazine: p.218. © The Buckminster Fuller Institute; The Fuller Projection Map design is a trademark of the Buckminster Fuller Institute, © 1938, 1967, 1992. All rights reserved, www.bfi.org: pp.270–71. © documenta archiv / photograph by Günther Becker/INFGM/ARS – DACS/ ProLitteris, Zurich/VG Bild-Kunst, Bonn: p.298br. © Fay S. Lincoln photograph collection, HCLA 1628, Special Collections Library, Pennsylvania State University, photograph by F. S. Lincoln: p.53. © Getty/ARS – DACS/ProLitteris, Zurich/VG Bild-Kunst, Bonn, photograph by Joseph Scherschel: p.160. © Hirshhorn Museum and Sculpture Garden / © INFGM / ARS – DACS/ProLitteris, Zurich/VG Bild-Kunst, Bonn, photograph by Cathy Carver: p.104. © INFGM/ARS – DACS/ProLitteris, Zurich/VG Bild-Kunst, Bonn, photographer unknown: p.1 (05859), p.6, p.19 (01382), p.26, p.27 (01395), p.67 (151562), p.71 (01476), pp.72–73 (03739), p.79 (01538), p.80 (01531), p.82t (01518), p.83t (12675), pp.88–89 (03775), p.120 (01615), p.122b (01589), p.148 (12802), p.156, p.161 (10179), p.165 (07137), p.167 (MS_AKA_008_041, MS_AKA_008_041), p.169 (02897), pp.170–71 (09165.2), p.201 (12434), p.205 (07007), p.220 (142570), p.229 (00686), p.231 (00759), pp.236–37, pp.244–45 (07201), p.260 (MS_BIO_010_002), p. 274tl (06000), p.274bl (06031), p.274r (06034), p.275tl (06036), p.275bl (06001), p.275r (06035), p.276bl (MS_COR_316_007), p.276r (04320), p.277tl (01387), p.277tr (01419), p.278bl (06055), p.278r (03722), p.280tl (BM_JOU_0403.1_1932), p.280tr (01490), p.280bl (MS_COR_305_004), p.280br (01503), p.281tl (MS_EXH_014_001), p.281r (MS_COR_373_004), p.282br (BM_AD_1000_1938), p.283t (03756), p.283bl (01528), p.283br (06851), p.284tm, p.284tr (MS_BIO_022_002), p.284b (02234), p.287tl (03591), p.287tr (01644), p.287bm, p.288br (BM_JOU_0485_1946), p.290tl (151778), p.290bl (01685), p.291r (03791), p.293tl (03256), p.293tr (BM_JOU_0660_1960), p.293br (07132), p.294 (08846.1), p.295tr (08721.2), p.295bl (152133), p.295br (MS_PROJ_078_001), p.296tl (02245), p.296tm (B_CLI_2000_1957), p.296br (152005), p.297 (00389), p.298bl (00371), p.299t (00484), p.299bl (03274), p.301tl (MS_EXH_066_005), p.302tl (02872), p.304tr (02250), p.307tl (02284), p.308bl (01067), p.309tl (01063); photograph by Cris Alexander: p.121 (01619); photograph by Atelier Stone: p.24 (01392), pp.28–29 (03716), p.277m (01381), p.277bl (01379); photograph by BartPhotography: p.4; photograph by M. I. Boris: pp.14–15 (03710); photograph by Martha Clifford: p.2, p.304br; photograph by Kyoko Dame: p.7, p.305b; photograph by Frank B. Denman: p.301b (03987); photograph by Arnold Eagle: p.118 (01578); photograph by Eliot Elisofon: p.286 (03766), p.289 (05468); photograph by Nobuo Fujiwara, courtesy of Akio Nishikiori: p.293bl; photograph by Rafael Gamo: pp.82b–83b (152293); photograph by Good! Hokkaido!: pp.310–11; photograph by Chuji Hirayama: p.291b (12903); photograph by Peter A. Juley & Son: pp.48–49 (05467); photograph by Nicholas Knight: p.228, p.239; photograph by Daniel Kramer: p.122t (01584); photograph by Arthur Lavine: p.300 (01935); photograph by Tom Little: p.200; photograph by Jun Miki: pp.164 (03577), p.309b (04268); photograph by Peter Moore: p.234 (147228), p.238b (12149); photograph by Grant Mudford: p.307r (MS_EXH_279_002); photograph by Kevin Noble: p.16 (00001), p.18 (9823), p.20 (00004), p.21 (00006), pp.22–23 (10381, 147306, 10378, 02635, 01204, 10377), p.25, p.38t (10370), p.38b (151109), p.39 (01230), p.40, p.41 (00011), p.44 (00022), p.45, p.46 (00196), p.47 (9907), p.66 (00024), p.70 (147079, 147080), p.86 (147122), pp.98–99 (00056), p.101 (00071), p.102 (00060), p.103 (00078), p.107 (00076), p.108 (150799), p.109 (9864), p.112 (9859), p.113 (00163), p.115 (9858), p.123t–b, p.125l (147136), p.125r (00189), p.134 (00087), p.136 (00084), p.138t (01286), p.138b (7563), p.141 (00113), p.144 (00123), p.145 (00118, 00120), p.149 (00127), p.150 (9899), p.157 (10593), p.158 (9860), p.162 (00857), p.172 (00211), p.173 (00210), p.174 (00213), p.175 (00214), p.177 (00238), p.178 (00256), p.179, p.180 (00212), p.182 (9916, 00244), p.183 (00243), p.184 (00312), p.189 (00322), p.190 (00358), p.193, p.194 (00405), p.195 (00408), p.196 (147148), p.197 (147147), p.203 (9996), p.204 (00453), p.207 (00464), p.208 (00486), p.210 (00545), p.211 (10048), pp.212–13 (10036), p.217 (10022), p.219b (10012), p.221 (00566), p.223 (147223), p.226 (147226), p.227 (00677), p.240 (00767), p.241 (00777), p.243 (00935), p.247 (01007), p.248 (01016), p.251 (01042), p.277br, p.282bl (00034), p.295tr (00412), p.302tr (00632); photograph by Isamu Noguchi: p.181 (08819.6), p.185t (09228.3), p.185b (09226.3), pp.186–87 (05493), p.192 (08834.5, 142920), p.222 (150836), p.262 (cw: 07994, 09084.2, 09583.3, 04393), p.263 (cw: 05098, 04838, 08307.4, 08299.3, 07563), p.264 (cw: 09434.2, 08274.6, 07755, 08264.5), p.265 (cw: 04512, 08323.2, 04973, 08018, 08479.5), p.266 (cw: 05460, 07724, 04403, 05362), p.267 (cw: 09536.2, 09588.5, 09395.1, 08472.6), p.268 (cw: 07802, 05397, 08977.2, 08846.2, 08238.6), p.269 (cw: 09654.2, 08826.2, 07959, 143368), p.282tl (06064), p.290br (02244), p.291tl (08818.3), p.298tr (09426.3), p.299br (07535), p.303 (07076), p.308t (03297); photograph by Michio Noguchi: p.230 (12222), pp.232–33 (04140), pp.252–53 (144398), p.261 (06974), p.302br (04072), p.306 (00928); photograph by Otto Sarony Co.: p.274tr (06010); photograph by Mary Randlett: p.304tl (02160); photograph by Stable Gallery: p.135 (142942), p.176 (01750); photograph by Soichi Sunami: p.106 (01570), p.159 (01646); photograph by Bill Taylor: p.64 (00023); photograph by Heinz Theuerkauf: p.302br; photograph by Charles Uht: p.292tl (01783); photograph by Patty Wallace: p.191 (00217). © INFGM/ARS – DACS/ProLitteris, Zurich/ VG Bild-Kunst, Bonn, photograph by Toshishige Mizoguchi, courtesy of The Isamu Noguchi Foundation of Japan: p.3. © INFGM/ARS – DACS/ProLitteris, Zurich/VG Bild-Kunst, Bonn, Courtesy of the Kagawa Museum: p.166. © INFGM/ARS – DACS/ProLitteris, Zurich/ VG Bild-Kunst, Bonn, Courtesy of Moerenuma Park: p.5, p.238t. © INFGM/ARS – DACS/ ProLitteris, Zurich/VG Bild-Kunst, Bonn, Courtesy of Sogetsu Foundation, photograph by Yoshiki Nakano: p.305tl. © INFGM/ARS – DACS/ProLitteris, Zurich/VG Bild-Kunst, Bonn/Shigeo Anzai, photograph by Shigeo Anzai: pp. 42–43 (142938), p.74 (142937), p.308br (02913), p.309tr (06647). © INFGM/ARS – DACS/ProLitteris, Zurich/VG Bild-Kunst, Bonn/ARTRES/Scala: p.307bl (02310). © INFGM/ARS – DACS/ProLitteris, Zurich/VG Bild-Kunst, Bonn/2021 The Estate of Dan Budnik, All Rights Reserved, photograph by Dan Budnik: p.273 (07281). © INFGM/ARS – DACS/ProLitteris, Zurich/VG Bild-Kunst, Bonn/ Estate of Rudolph Burckhardt, photograph by Rudolph Burckhardt: p.105 (01628), p.114 (151637), pp.116–17 (03201), p.139 (03765), p.140 (12791), pp.154–55 (05472), pp.198–99 (05530), p.288tl (12736). © INFGM/ARS – DACS/ProLitteris, Zurich/VG Bild-Kunst, Bonn/ Eames Office, photograph by Charles Eames: p.292b (06935). © INFGM/ARS – DACS/ ProLitteris, Zurich/VG Bild-Kunst, Bonn/Getty, photograph by Berenice Abbott: p.65 (01488), p.279 (03719), p.281bl (06796). © INFGM/ARS – DACS/ProLitteris, Zurich/ VG Bild-Kunst, Bonn/Halsman, photograph by Philippe Halsman: p.124 (01659). © INFGM/ ARS – DACS/ProLitteris, Zurich/VG Bild-Kunst, Bonn/Harper's Bazaar: p.168 (BM_AD_1000_1955), p.287b (244.01). © INFGM/ARS – DACS/ProLitteris, Zurich/VG Bild-Kunst, Bonn/© Estate of André Kertész/Higher Pictures: pp.110–11 (03205), pp.142–43 (143204), p.285 (03210). © INFGM/ARS – DACS/ProLitteris, Zurich/VG Bild-Kunst, Bonn/Kröller-Müller Museum, Otterlo, photograph by Kevin Noble: p.153. © INFGM/ARS – DACS/ ProLitteris, Zurich/VG Bild-Kunst, Bonn/Barbara and Willard Morgan photographs and papers, Library Special Collections, Charles E. Young Research Library, UCLA, photograph by Barbara Morgan: pp.76–77 (01508). © INFGM/ARS – DACS/ProLitteris, Zurich/VG Bild-Kunst, Bonn/Penn State University Libraries, photograph by F. S. Lincoln: p.50 (01411), p.68 (01451), p.69 (01455, 01457), p.84 (01530), p.87 (01552), p.278tl (01427), p.284tl (12704). © INFGM/ARS – DACS/ProLitteris, Zurich/VG Bild-Kunst, Bonn/Courtesy of Rago/Wright: p. 85, p.163. © INFGM/ARS – DACS/ProLitteris, Zurich/VG Bild-Kunst, Bonn/Smithsonian American Art Museum, photograph by Peter A. Juley & Son: p.276t (143454). © INFGM/ARS – DACS/ProLitteris, Zurich/VG Bild-Kunst, Bonn/Ezra Stoller/ Esto, photograph by Ezra Stoller/Esto: p.219t (01898), p.282tr, p.288tr (00126), p.296bl (12942), p.305tr (00790). © INFGM/ARS – DACS/ProLitteris, Zurich/VG Bild-Kunst, Bonn/TIME LIFE: p.292tr (BM_OS_0545_1952). © Joseph Bellows Gallery, La Jolla, CA / ARS – DACS/ProLitteris, Zurich/VG Bild-Kunst, Bonn, photograph by Larry Colwell: p.288bl (01652). © Martha Graham Dance Company/ARS – DACS/ProLitteris, Zurich/ VG Bild-Kunst, Bonn, photograph by Melissa Sherwood: p.119. © Museum of Fine Arts, Boston/ARS – DACS/ProLitteris, Zurich/VG Bild-Kunst, Bonn, photograph by Dimitri Hadzi: pp.214–15. © Digital image, The Museum of Modern Art, New York/Scala, Florence: p.216. © National Archives, Washington, DC, photograph by Fred Clark: p.98b. © New York Magazine: p.168 (BM_MTN_1000_1966). © The New York Public Library for the Performing Arts, photograph by Martha Swope: p.298tl (01886). © Property of a Private Collection, photo courtesy of Sotheby's: p.52. © PvE/Alamy Stock Photo, INFGM/ARS – DACS/ ProLitteris, Zurich/VG Bild-Kunst, Bonn: p.301tr. © Sōfū Teshigahara/INFGM/ARS – DACS/ ProLitteris, Zurich/VG Bild-Kunst, Bonn, Courtesy of Sogetsu Foundation, photograph by Takeshi Fujimori: p.304bl. © Courtesy of the Western Regional Archives, State Archives of North Carolina, photograph by Masato Nakagawa: p.51. © Whitney Museum of American Art, New York, purchase, with funds from the Photography Committee/Tōyō Miyatake Studio, photograph by Tōyō Miyatake: p.17.

Acknowledgements

With thanks to The Isamu Noguchi Foundation and Garden Museum, New York, for their trust and expertise and for generously lending to the exhibition.

With thanks to the lenders:

The Isamu Noguchi Foundation and Garden Museum, New York; The Fralin Museum of Art, University of Virginia; Kröller-Müller Museum, Otterlo, Netherlands; Lucy Lamphere, New York; Museum für Angewandte Kunst, Cologne; Museum of Modern Art, New York; Alexandra Snyder May; Walker Art Center, Minneapolis; Whitney Museum of American Art, New York; and those lenders who wish to remain anonymous.

We would like to extend our thanks to the following individuals for their invaluable support and guidance with the research, development and realisation of this ambitious exhibition and catalogue:

LaRue Allen, Imogen Ayres, Ann Berni, Janine Biunno, Eddie Bruce-Jones, Carla Caputo, Maria Carroll, Anna Casey, Mary Ceruti, Kate Coyne, Katrina Crookall, Janet Dees, Sébastien Delot, Josie Dick, Katherine Duke, Gwen Ellis, Harald Gaspers, Lily Goldberg, Paul Goodwin, Rebecca Gould, Andrew Hardman, Barbara Haskell, Petra Hesse, Wobke Hooites, Sharon Kent, Dienke van der Kuijl, Annie Jael Kwan, David Lally, Louise Lamphere, Camilla Lawson, Margaret Liley, Glenn Lowry, Matthew McLendon, Janice Mitchell, Shannon Murphy, Andreas Niegl, Kayla Nordlund, Jean Pagano, Lisette Pelsers, Grégoire Prangé, Melanie Pyne, Romana Rebbelmund, Daisy Robinson-Smyth, Angus Sanders-Dunnachie, Bruce Stracy, Alina Tiits, Laure Rolland, Eve Scott, Christopher Senger, Melissa Sherwood, Ly Soulemane, Oliver Tobin, Matthew Turner, Mark Wainwright, Kova Walker-Lečić, Adam D. Weinberg, James Yang.

This exhibition and publication would not have been possible without the collaboration of The Isamu Noguchi Foundation and Garden Museum, New York.

The exhibition has been generously supported by the Terra Foundation for American Art.

TERRA
FOUNDATION FOR AMERICAN ART

Barbican
Silk Street
London EC2Y 8DS
United Kingdom
barbican.org.uk

Curator: Florence Ostende
Curatorial Assistant: Andrew de Brún
Exhibition Organisers: Kate Fanning, Ross Head
Exhibition Managers: Alice Lobb, Miranda Stacey
Production Manager: Peter Sutton
Exhibition Designer: Cut-Out / Lucy Styles
Exhibition Graphics: Kellenberger-White
Assistant Curator for Public Programme: Jon Astbury
Digital Residency Curator: Annie Jael Kwan
Research Assistants: Catherine Howe, Coralie Malissard
Art Gallery Placement: Angelica Jopling

This exhibition has been made possible as a result of the Government Indemnity Scheme. Barbican would like to thank HM Government for providing Government Indemnity and the Department for Digital, Culture, Media and Sport and Arts Council England for arranging the indemnity.

The exhibition at the Barbican has also been made possible through support from the Great Britain Sasakawa Foundation, White Cube and U.S. Embassy London.

CITY OF LONDON

The City of London Corporation is the founder and principal funder of the Barbican Centre

Museum Ludwig
Heinrich-Böll-Platz
50667 Köln
Germany
www.museum-ludwig.de

Curator: Rita Kersting
Curatorial Assistant: Nana Tazuke-Steiniger
Registrars: Stephanie Decker, Anna Höfinghoff, Luis Müller Philipp-Sohn
Exhibition Management: Iris Maczollek, Helen Meßler
Exhibition Design: Tino Graß
Conservation: Kristof Efferenn, Sophia Elze, Yvonne Garborini, Katrin Keßler, Petra Mandt, Astrid Schubert
Carpentry: Michael Bangert, Nathalie Hansmeyer, Philipp Hawlitschek, Leif Lenzner, Milan Scharf, Katrin Schwarz
Press and Public Relations: Seher Anilgan, Kirsten te Brake, Sonja Hempel, Anne Niermann, Donata Rahnenführer, Judith Specht
Fundraising: Lisa Schade, Julia Maximidou

The exhibition at the Museum Ludwig has also been made possible through support from:

Stadt Köln

International Society Museum Ludwig Cologne

Gesellschaft für Moderne Kunst am Museum Ludwig Köln

REWE GROUP

Stiftung Der bewohnte Garten

Beatrix Lichtken Stiftung

Zentrum Paul Klee
Monument im Fruchtland 3
3001 Bern
Switzerland
www.zpk.org

Curator: Fabienne Eggelhöfer
Curatorial Assistant: Myriam Dössegger
Registrar: Svenja Eckell
Design: Lea Rey
Conservator: Myriam Weber
Art Handling: Hansruedi Pauli
Art Education: Dominik Imhof
Social Media: Maria Horst
Marketing: Lorena Montanarini
Press: Martina Witschi, Aleksandra Zdravkovic
Fundraising: Birgit Achatz

The exhibition at the Zentrum Paul Klee has also been made possible through support from:

Kanton Bern
Canton de Berne

Burgergemeinde Bern

SWISSLOS
Amt für Kultur Kanton Bern

ART MENTOR FOUNDATION LUCERNE

PHILLIPS

Exhibition organised and curated by the Barbican, London, Museum Ludwig, Cologne, and Zentrum Paul Klee, Bern, in partnership with LaM – Lille Métropole Musée d'art moderne, d'art contemporain et d'art brut.

Barbican, London
30 September 2021 – 23 January 2022
Curated by Florence Ostende

Museum Ludwig, Cologne
26 March – 31 July 2022
Curated by Rita Kersting

Zentrum Paul Klee, Bern
23 September 2022 – 8 January 2023
Curated by Fabienne Eggelhöfer

LaM – Lille Métropole Musée d'art moderne, d'art contemporain et d'art brut
17 March – 16 July 2023
Curated by Sébastien Delot

barbican

MUSEUM LUDWIG

Zentrum Paul Klee
Bern

First published in 2021 by Prestel in association with Barbican, Museum Ludwig, Zentrum Paul Klee on the occasion of the touring exhibition

ISAMU NOGUCHI

Fourth edition 2025

produktsicherheit@penguinrandomhouse.de
(The above information is mandatory information according to GPSR and should be used for all queries relating to the safety of our books)

Editors: Fabienne Eggelhöfer, Rita Kersting, Florence Ostende
Editorial Coordination: Anna Godfrey, Katrin Sauerländer
Editorial Assistants: Andrew de Brún, Myriam Dössegger, Nana Tazuke-Steiniger
Copy-editing: Frauke Berchtig, Aimee Selby
Translation: Norma Keßler, Rebecca van Dyck
Design: Tino Graß
Production Management: Corinna Pickart
Origination and Separations: Reproline Mediateam, Unterföhring
Printing and Binding: Grafisches Centrum Cuno, Calbe
Paper: Magno Matt

Printed in Germany

Prestel Verlag, Munich · London · New York, a member of Penguin Random House Verlagsgruppe, Neumarkter Straße 28, 81673 Munich

A CIP catalogue record for this book is available from the British Library.

MIX
Paper from responsible sources
FSC® C043106

Penguin Random House Verlagsgruppe FSC® N001967

ISBN 978-3-7913-7979-1

www.prestel.com

Cover image: Isamu Noguchi, *My Arizona*, 1943. Photograph by Kevin Noble © INFGM